Communicating

A Social, Career and Cultural Focus

Twelfth Edition

ROY M. BERKO
Communic-aid Consulting
Cleveland, Ohio

ANDREW D. WOLVIN
University of Maryland
College Park, Maryland

DARLYN R. WOLVIN
Prince George's Community College
Largo, Maryland

JOAN E. AITKEN
Park University
Parkville, Missouri

PEARSON

Boston Columbus Indianapolis New York San Francisco Upper Saddle River
Amsterdam Cape Town Dubai London Madrid Milan Munich Paris Montréal Toronto
Delhi Mexico City São Paulo Sydney Hong Kong Seoul Singapore Taipei Tokyo

Editor-in-Chief, Communication: *Karon Bowers*
Senior Editor: *Melissa Mashburn*
Editorial Assistant: *Megan Sweeney*
Director of Development: *Eileen Calabro*
Development Editor: *Hilary Jackson*
Marketing Manager: *Blair Tuckman*
Associate Development Editor: *Angela Mallowes*
Senior Digital Editor: *Paul DeLuca*
Digital Editor: *Lisa Dotson*
Production/Project Manager: *Barbara Mack*
Project Coordination, Text Design, and Electronic Page Makeup: *Integra*
Senior Cover Design Manager/Designer: *Nancy Danahy*
Cover Photos: *iStock*
Manufacturing Manager: *Mary Fischer*
Procurement Specialist: *Mary Ann Gloriande*
Printer/Binder: *Von Hoffmann dba RRD/Jefferson City*
Cover Printer: *Lehigh-Phoenix/Hagerstown*

Credits and acknowledgments borrowed from other sources and reproduced, with permission, in this textbook appear on the appropriate page within text or on page 464.

Library of Congress Cataloging-in-Publication Data
Berko, Roy M.
Communicating : a social, career and cultural focus / Roy M. Berko . . . [et al.]. — 12th ed.
p. cm.
ISBN-13: 978-0-205-02941-9
ISBN-10: 0-205-02941-8
1. Communication. I. Title.
P90.B416 2012
302.2—dc23

2011032483

10 9 8 7 6 5 4 3 2 1—RRD—14 13 12 11

www.pearsonhighered.com

ISBN 10: 0-205-02941-8
ISBN 13: 978-0-205-02941-9

BRIEF CONTENTS

CONTENTS

PREFACE

Welcome to this, the twelfth edition of *Communicating: A Social, Career and Cultural Focus.* Little did we expect in the Fall of 1977, when our experimental text was published, that more than thirty years later the book would not only still be in print, but would be one of the best-selling texts in the field. *Communicating* has been a forerunner. It was ahead of its time, being one of the first speech texts to combine the areas of public speaking and intrapersonal and interpersonal communication in a single volume, laying the foundation for what has become known as the "hybrid" communication course. Even before the academic world was sensitized to cultural awareness, we insisted on using gender-neutral language, photos, and illustrations that portrayed many cultures and persons of differences.

What's New in this Edition?

- The major new addition to this edition is Dr. Joan E. Aitken, as our co-author. A Professor of Communication at Park University, Joan has authored eight textbooks, five instructor's manuals, has done Web development for four publishers, and has developed more than 50 book chapters, articles, and reports. As a former editor of the National Communication Association's *The Communication Teacher* and editorial board member of NCA's *Communication Education*, Joan's ongoing focus has been communication education, including work with students with exceptionalities and students who are English language learners. For 30 years, Joan has studied communication technology, and her scholarly research was recently recognized when she received Park University's "Distinguished Faculty Scholar" of the year. Joan has taught internationally in Jamaica and the People's Republic of China.
- **New emphasis on electronically mediated communication (EMC).** EMC not only has its own section in Chapter 6 (and is now part of the chapter title), but it has been incorporated into all chapters. There are also numerous new boxes which discuss the impact of EMC on our daily communication and interactions with others, including exploring the influence of Facebook and social networking, using electronic interviewing techniques, and incorporating new software programs into public speaking presentations.

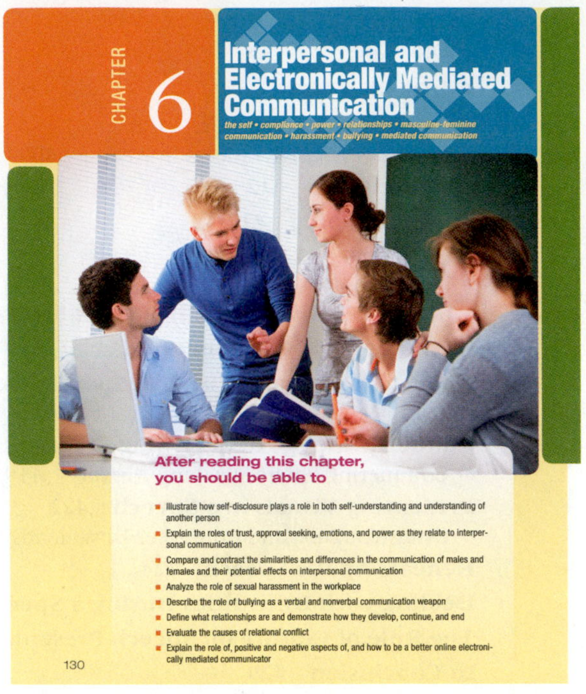

Socially COMMUNICATING

Facebook May Help Shy People Open Up

Josh Chiles is shy. In a gathering of unfamiliar people, he often waits for someone, anyone, to ask him a question or make small talk. At a party, bar or restaurant, "I just sit there, hoping someone will talk to me," he said.

But on Facebook, he is Mr. Personality. He constantly refreshes his status; comments on others' updates, posts pictures, makes jokes and registers his likes. He states, "There is no doubt Facebook has changed my life."

A study published in the journal *CyberPsychology, Behavior and Social Networking*, showed that the Internet and social networks helped the lonely fill "critical needs of social interactions, self-disclosure, and identity exploration." As a result, another study shows, "shy people are spending more time on Facebook than more socially confident people."

Source: "Facebook May Help Shy People Open Up, New Studies Suggest" by M. Rosenwald, from *Cleveland Plain Dealer,* February 14, 2011. Copyright © 2011 by The Plain Dealer. Used with permission.

REFLECT ON THIS: Though Facebook and other social media sites may help the shy, some experts consider these sources a crutch to avoid human contact. Do you agree with the findings noted about the positive effects, or side with those who think social media sources are a crutch?

- **Reexamination and expansion of key topic areas.** There is an added emphasis on and expanded discussions of topics such as perception, conflict management, leadership principles, and digital communication. New boxes explore these topic areas as well.
- **Significantly expanded and updated research base.** More than a hundred NEW scholarly journal article and conference paper citations have been added, thus expanding the contemporary research base in communication studies and related fields. American Psychological Association (APA) reference style is used throughout, thus modeling that format for students. Research-based sources have been added in the footnotes so students can further investigate updated text content.

- **Digital communication has been integrated into each chapter.** We have included theoretical information about digital communication, as well as specific guidelines on how to communicate more effectively using electronic communication. Digital public speaking presentation applications and software references have been updated, and the overall digital database has been expanded and updated.
- **Reorganization of public speaking chapters.** In response to reviewers' requests, the public speaking chapters have been reorganized to separate preparation techniques from presentation techniques, with discussion of delivery and presentation skills now concluding the public speaking section.
- **Streamlined coverage.** While continuing to capture the ever-changing field of communication, the text has nonetheless been streamlined throughout to eliminate outdated or redundant information and to make the text more concise without losing the readability, research, and engaging examples and anecdotes.
- **Numerous new examples,** boxes, figures, and cartoons throughout. New material reflects current events that have lasting significance such as media influence on the 2011 uprisings in the Middle East and offers fresh and sometimes provocative perspectives such as how Facebook helps shy people to open up or whether we are becoming "an uncivil society."

Culturally COMMUNICATING

The Haka Race of Taipei, Taiwan's View of Listening

When you listen, you use your ears, eyes, and heart to determine *the* meaning. The eyes are actually more important than the ears. You have to learn to listen to the content, but you have to know what people mean.

Source: "The Haka Race of Taipei, Taiwan's View of Listening" from *Intercultural communication: A text with readings*, 1st Edition by Pamela J. Cooper, Carolyn Calloway-Thomas, Cheri J. Simonds. Copyright © 2007 by Pamela J. Cooper, Carolyn Calloway-Thomas, Cheri J. Simonds. Printed and electronically reproduced by permission of Pearson Education, Inc., Upper Saddle River, New Jersey.

REFLECT ON THIS:

1. What do you think the authors mean by "listen with your heart" as it relates to the meaning of messages you receive?
2. What do you think is meant by "but you have to know what people mean"?

Socially COMMUNICATING

The Power of the Internet

Bill Clinton wandered into the University of South Carolina Student Center around midnight and found a single student on a computer. The student said, "give me a minute," and within 10 minutes, a flash crowd of 300 students had arrived to hear the former president give an impromptu speech.

Source: From S. Schifferes, *Internet, key to Obama victories*, BBC News, November 10, 2008, http://news.bbc.co.uk/l/hi/technology/7412045.stm

REFLECT ON THIS:

1. In 2011, the social media was credited with getting flash crowds in Egypt to take a stand for Democracy and overthrow the govern-

Distinctive Features of Our Book

We are not resting on our laurels. Long-time users will note changes in this new edition, yet will feel comfortable that we have continued to produce a book that is well-researched, interesting to read, pragmatic, and continues to showcase features that have come to be recognized as hallmarks of our book such as the numerous examples and anecdotes, the concern about skills and application of the material, the inclusion of self-assessments and questionnaires, and the custom-drawn cartoons, done by a former communication student. In addition:

- **Longstanding emphasis on diversity and intercultural communication.** The eleventh edition brought forth a new subtitle for the book which included "cultural." Although we added this to the title, the concept was not new. We have always included references to inclusiveness, gender, ethnicity, sexual orientation, age, and nationality. Through the editions, the emphasis on diversity and intercultural communication has increased.

Multiculturalism

When people from various cultures live in the same place, unique multicultural situations can emerge. The term *multiculture* refers to a society consisting of varied cultural groups. The United States is a multicultural country. It is ethnically composed of African Americans, Hispanic Americans, Irish Americans, and many other cultures. It is also multicultural as it relates to the broader definition of culture because it is made up of such differences as women and men, homosexuals and heterosexuals, and religious belie

Ethnocentrism

Jon, a Christian Euro American male, is introduced to Aaron and thinks it is ridiculous that he wears a skullcap (a *yarmulke*) all the time. He is invited to Partha's home and is repulsed when he is told that the meat being served at dinner is snake. He is disturbed when he hears that in many Arabic countries women have to cover their entire bodies when they are in public. Jon's reactions reflect ethnocentrism.

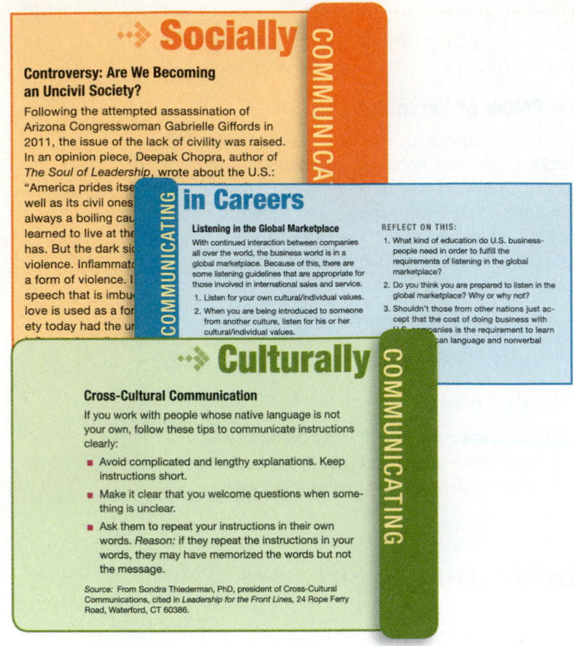

Socially
COMMUNICATING
Controversy: Are We Becoming an Uncivil Society?
in Careers
Listening in the Global Marketplace
With continued interaction between companies all over the world, the business world is in a global marketplace. Because of this, there are some listening guidelines that are appropriate for those involved in international sales and service.
1. Listen for your own cultural/individual values.
2. When you are being introduced to someone from another culture, listen for his or her cultural/individual values.
REFLECT ON THIS:
1. What kind of education do U.S. business-people need in order to fulfill the requirements of listening in the global marketplace?
2. Do you think you are prepared to listen in the global marketplace? Why or why not?
Culturally
COMMUNICATING
Cross-Cultural Communication
If you work with people whose native language is not your own, follow these tips to communicate instructions clearly:
Avoid complicated and lengthy explanations. Keep instructions short.
Make it clear that you welcome questions when something is unclear.
Ask them to repeat your instructions in their own words. Reason: if they repeat the instructions in your words, they may have memorized the words but not the message.
Source: From Sondra Thiederman, PhD, president of Cross-Cultural Communications, cited in Leadership for the Front Lines, 24 Rope Ferry Road, Waterford, CT 60386.

- In keeping with our three-pronged approach, "A Social, Career and Cultural Focus," the book includes **three types of thematic boxes** to highlight the social, career, and cultural aspects of communication.

  "Socially Communicating" boxes offer guidelines and skills for communicating in relationships and other interpersonal contexts.

  "Communicating in Careers" boxes provide insight into workplace communication with tips on how to communicate more effectively at work and in your career.

  "Culturally Communicating" boxes focus on different cultural communication norms and expectations and how to adapt one's communication in an increasingly diverse world.
- **Self-Assessment Questionnaires,** a valued feature of past editions, allow the reader to find and assess a variety of skills or issues, from listening ability to communication apprehension.

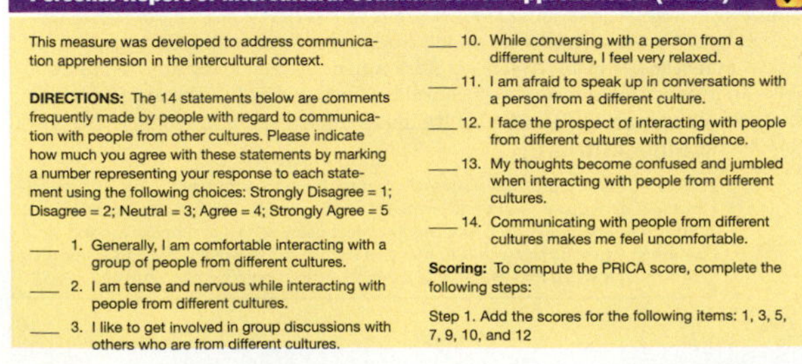

Personal Report of Intercultural Communication Apprehension (PRICA)

This measure was developed to address communication apprehension in the intercultural context.

DIRECTIONS: The 14 statements below are comments frequently made by people with regard to communication with people from other cultures. Please indicate how much you agree with these statements by marking a number representing your response to each statement using the following choices: Strongly Disagree = 1; Disagree = 2; Neutral = 3; Agree = 4; Strongly Agree = 5

____ 1. Generally, I am comfortable interacting with a group of people from different cultures.

____ 2. I am tense and nervous while interacting with people from different cultures.

____ 3. I like to get involved in group discussions with others who are from different cultures.

____ 10. While conversing with a person from a different culture, I feel very relaxed.

____ 11. I am afraid to speak up in conversations with a person from a different culture.

____ 12. I face the prospect of interacting with people from different cultures with confidence.

____ 13. My thoughts become confused and jumbled when interacting with people from different cultures.

____ 14. Communicating with people from different cultures makes me feel uncomfortable.

Scoring: To compute the PRICA score, complete the following steps:

Step 1. Add the scores for the following items: 1, 3, 5, 7, 9, 10, and 12

LEARN BY DOING

1. Identify an experience in which your attempt to communicate was a failure. Use the classification of sources of noise given in the text to label the type of interference you encountered. Why did this happen? What, if anything, could you have done to correct the interference problem?
2. Describe a context in which you find it difficult to communicate. Describe a context in which you find it easy to communicate. Why did you select each one? What implications for communication are involved in your choices?
3. Describe the system of communication by which your family operates (or operated) by investigating the patterns of communication and the rules

a. You are taking a public speaking course. The instructor requires three quoted references in the speech that you are to present in five minutes. You had a week to get ready but did not do the necessary research. Would you make up three references, not give the speech and get a failing grade, give the speech without the references and hope for the best, or take some other action? If you would take another action, what would it be?

b. You have just finished eating in a restaurant. You check the bill and realize that the waiter has made a $10 error in your favor. The waiter sees your reaction and asks if anything is wrong. How do you respond?

- **Numerous pedagogical aids** include chapter objectives and summaries, valuable "Learn by Doing" skill-building activities, boldfaced key terms, sample speeches and outlines, and extensive examples, many of which have been updated.
- **A comprehensive Glossary,** expanded and updated in this edition, defines key terms which are boldfaced throughout the text, as well as words which are italicized in the text which we think are important for the reader to acknowledge.
- **A new design** for this edition continues the tradition of making the book accessible and attractive for students.

A Message to Students

As you undertake the study of communication, you might be asking yourself, "Why do I need to study this? I've been talking and listening all of my life." Research indicates that although you may have been participating in the act of communication your whole life, if you are fairly typical, your skills may not be extremely good.

One of the most important skills you need in your career, in your social life, or in relating to people of various cultures is to be an effective communicator. Research shows:

- "All students, including those at the graduate level, need to learn to communicate orally, interpersonally, in small groups and teams, and in public. Interestingly, students also need to learn to communicate effectively outside the classroom with other students and with teachers."[1]
- Communication competency is indispensable for successful participation in careers. Interested in getting a job? The number-one requirement for job attainment and accomplishment is communication skills.

[1]Morreale, S. & Pearson, J. (2008) Why communication education is important: The centrality of the discipline in the 21st century. *Communication Education, 57*(2), 224–240.

- The ability to communicate is central to a person's self-development and contribution to society, as well as to one's educational and career success.[2]
- Relationships with friends and family depend on your listening and responding to each other.
- As the world becomes "flatter," where communication takes place globally, the ability to understand not only your own culture but that of others becomes imperative.
- The purpose of this text is to give you the opportunities to attain communication competency and not only to gain an understanding of the communication process but also to improve the skills that you will possess for the rest of your life.

A Message to Instructors

This text is developed centering on the 3 Cs: *Conciseness, Comprehensiveness, and Creativity.*

Conciseness: Communication is an ever-expanding field. As new editions of basic course texts are published, the trend has been for books to get longer and longer, making it difficult for instructors to cover all the material in the time allotted for a course. With this in mind, we have concentrated on stemming this tide. This edition, although it continues to include up-to-date research and approaches to contemporary and emerging communication issues, reinforces the conciseness established in previous editions.

Comprehensiveness: We continue to cover the full range of basic communication principles and relevant theory and research. We have updated examples, discussions, and the research base.

Creativity: Historically, students and faculty alike have praised the writing style of the book. As has been the case with previous editions, we have again given special attention to making this book readable, student centered, and practical. We have provided examples of enlightened and entertaining value and have also included custom-drawn cartoons. The cartoonist, a former communication student, not only is creative but also knows the field of communication.

[2]Morreale, S. & Pearson, J. (2008) Why communication education is important: The centrality of the discipline in the 21st century. *Communication Education,* 57(2), 224–240.

Acknowledgments

As he has done in previous editions, Tony Zupancic of Notre Dame College, South Euclid, Ohio, added insight and information to the public speaking chapters and made himself continuously available as a resource person.

We are indebted to those professors who have been loyal users of this book through its first eleven editions. We hope that you will continue to use the text and to provide us with insightful and helpful comments for future editions.

Appreciation to our professional colleagues who read and critiqued the manuscript through its development: Kathleen Czech, *Point Loma Nazarene University;* Dr. Terry Trafton, *Coastal Carolina Community College;* Dr. Nadia Ramoutar, *Art Institute of Jacksonville;* Stephen Yungbluth, *Northern Kentucky University;* Isabel Del Pino-Allen, *Miami Dade College;* Jennifer Lehtinen, *SUNY Orange;* Nancy Petersen, *Los Medanos College;* and Jeffrey S. Hillard, *College of Mount St. Joseph.*

Kudos to Hilary Jackson, Developmental Editor, for her editorial assistance and advice, and to Karon Bowers of Pearson, our Editor-in-Chief, for her patience and unwavering support.

A Special Thanks

For the last six editions of *COMMUNICATING* a special feature has been the creative and relevant cartoons of Bob Vojtko, which he created specifically for our book. Bob, a nationally known cartoonist, is a former communication student of one of your authors. He was a special student in class, and he has a great understanding of the field. We appreciate Bob's efforts and hope our long and pleasant collaboration continues for many more editions!

In Conclusion

COMMUNICATE COMPETENTLY!

Roy, Andy, Darlyn, and Joan

Resources in Print and Online

Name of Supplement	Availability	Instructor or Student Supplement	Description
Instructor's Resource Manual (ISBN: 0205238807)	Print & Online	Instructor Supplement	The **Instructor's Resource Manual,** prepared by text author Joan E. Aitken, Park University, is comprehensive, rigorous, and easy to use. The manual includes a sample syllabus, course outlines, more than 125 chapter-by-chapter class activities, and over 20 oral and written assignments with matched assessment instruments. Available in print or online at www.pearsonhighered.com/irc (access code required).
Test Bank (ISBN: 0205237436)	Print & Online	Instructor Supplement	The **Test Bank,** prepared by Christopher Ames, University of Maryland University College, contains multiple-choice, true/ false, and essay questions for each chapter. Questions are referenced by text chapter and page number. Available in print or online at www.pearsonhighered.com/irc (access code required).
MyTest (ISBN: 0205856888)	Online	Instructor Supplement	This flexible, online test generating software includes all questions found in the Test Bank, allowing instructors to create their own personalized exams. Instructors can also edit any of the existing test questions and even add new questions. Other special features of this program include random generation of test questions, creation of alternate versions of the same test, scrambling of question sequence, and test preview before printing. Available at www.pearsonmytest.com (access code required).
PowerPoint™ Presentation Package (ISBN: 0205243894)	Online	Instructor Supplement	Prepared by text author Joan E. Aitken, Park University, this text-specific package provides a basis for your lectures with PowerPoint™ slides for each chapter of the book. Available at www.pearsonhighered.com/irc (access code required).
Pearson's Introduction to Communication Video Library	VHS/DVD	Instructor Supplement	Pearson's Introduction to Communication Video Library contains a range of videos from which adopters can choose. The videos feature a variety of topics and scenarios for communication foundations, interpersonal communication, small group communication, and public speaking. Please contact your Pearson representative for details and a complete list of videos and their contents to choose which would be most useful to your course. Some restrictions apply.
Lecture Questions for Clickers for Introduction to Communication (ISBN: 0205547230)	Online	Instructor Supplement	Prepared by Keri Moe, El Paso Community College, this is an assortment of questions and activities covering culture, listening, interviewing, public speaking, interpersonal conflict, and more, presented in PowerPoint™. These slides will help liven up your lectures and can be used along with the Personal Response System to get students more involved in the material. Available at www.pearsonhighered.com/irc (access code required).
A Guide for New Teachers of Introduction to Communication, 4th Edition (ISBN: 0205750001)	Print & Online	Instructor Supplement	Prepared by Susanna G. Porter, Kennesaw State University, with a new chapter on using MyCommunicationLab by Heather Dillon, Urbana, Illinois, this guide is designed to help new teachers effectively teach the introductory communication course. It is full of first day of class tips, great teaching ideas, a guide to Pearson resources, and sample activities and assignments. Available at www.pearsonhighered.com/irc (access code required).
Pearson's ClassPrep	Online	Instructor Supplement	Pearson's ClassPrep makes lecture preparation simpler and less time-consuming. It collects the very best class presentation resources—art and figures from our texts, videos, lecture activities, audio clips, classroom activities, demonstrations, and

Name of Supplement	Availability	Instructor or Student Supplement	Description
			much more—in one convenient online destination. You may search through ClassPrep's extensive database of tools by content topic (arranged by standard topics within the communication curriculum), content type (video, audio, activities, etc.), or key word. You will find ClassPrep in the Instructor's section of MyCommunicationLab for *Communicating: A Social, Career and Cultural Focus.*
Preparing Visual Aids for Presentations, Fifth Edition (ISBN:020561115X)	Print	Student Supplement	Prepared by Dan Cavanaugh, this 32-page visual booklet provides a host of ideas for using today's multimedia tools to improve presentations, including suggestions for planning a presentation, guidelines for designing visual aids and storyboarding, and a walkthrough that shows how to prepare a visual display using PowerPoint™ (available for purchase).
Pearson's Introduction to Communication Study Site (open access)	Online	Student Supplement	This open-access student resource features practice tests, learning objectives, and Web links organized around the major topics typically covered in the Introduction to Communication course. Available at www.pearsonintrocommunication.com.
Public Speaking in the Multicultural Environment, Second Edition (ISBN:0205265111)	Print	Student Supplement	Prepared by Devorah A. Lieberman, Portland State University, this booklet helps students learn to analyze cultural diversity within their audiences and adapt their presentations accordingly (available for purchase).
The Speech Outline (ISBN:032108702X)	Print	Student Supplement	Prepared by Reeze L. Hanson and Sharon Condon of Haskell Indian Nations University, this workbook includes activities, exercises, and answers to help students develop and master the critical skill of outlining (available for purchase).
Multicultural Activities Workbook (ISBN:0205546528)	Print	Student Supplement	By Marlene C. Cohen and Susan L. Richardson of Prince George's Community College, Maryland, this workbook is filled with hands-on activities that help broaden the content of speech classes to reflect the diverse cultural backgrounds. The checklists, surveys, and writing assignments all help students succeed in speech communication by offering experiences that address a variety of learning styles (available for purchase).
Speech Preparation Workbook (ISBN: 013559569X)	Print	Student Supplement	Prepared by Jennifer Dreyer and Gregory H. Patton of San Diego State University, this workbook takes students through the stages of speech creation–from audience analysis to writing the speech–and includes guidelines, tips, and easy to fill-in pages (available for purchase).
Study Card for Introduction to Speech Communication (ISBN: 0205474381)	Print	Student Supplement	Colorful, affordable, and packed with useful information, the Pearson Study Cards make studying easier, more efficient, and more enjoyable. Course information is distilled down to the basics, helping students quickly master the fundamentals, review a subject for understanding, or prepare for an exam. Because they're laminated for durability, they can be kept for years to come and pulled out whenever students need a quick review (available for purchase).
MyCommunicationLab	Online	Instructor & Student Supplement	MyCommunicationLab is a state-of-the-art, interactive and instructive solution for communication courses. Designed to be used as a supplement to a traditional lecture course or to completely administer an online course, MyCommunicationLab combines a Pearson eText, MySearchLab®, MediaShare, multimedia, video clips, activities, research support, tests, and quizzes to completely engage students. See next page for more details.

MyCommunicationLab®

The moment you know.

Educators know it. Students know it. It's that inspired moment when something that was difficult to understand suddenly makes perfect sense. Our MyLab products have been designed and refined with a single purpose in mind–to help educators create that moment of understanding with their students.

The new MyCommunicationLab delivers proven results in helping individual students succeed. It provides engaging experiences that personalize, stimulate, and measure learning for each student. And, it comes from a trusted partner with educational expertise and a deep commitment to helping students, instructors, and departments achieve their goals.

MyCommunicationLab can be used by itself or linked to any learning management system. To learn more about how the new MyCommunicationLab combines proven learning applications with powerful assessment, read on!

MyCommunicationLab delivers proven results in helping individual students succeed.

Pearson MyLabs are currently in use by millions of students each year across a variety of disciplines.

MyCommunicationLab works–but don't take our word for it. Visit our MyLab/Mastering site www.pearsonhighered.com/mylabmastering to read white papers, case studies, and testimonials from instructors and students that consistently demonstrate the success of our MyLabs.

MyCommunicationLab provides engaging experiences that personalize, stimulate, and measure learning for each student. MyCommunicationLab is available for Introduction to Communication, Interpersonal Communication, Mass Communication, and Public Relations courses.

Pearson eText: Identical in content and design to the printed text, the Pearson eText lets students access their textbook anytime, anywhere, and any way they want—including downloading to an iPad. Students can take notes and highlight, just like a traditional book.

Assessments: Pre- and Post-Tests for each chapter enable students and instructors to track progress and get immediate feedback. Results from the Pre and Post-Tests generate a personalized study plan that helps students master course content. Chapter Exams allow instructors to easily assign exams online. Results feed into the MyLab gradebook.

MediaShare: A cutting-edge video upload tool that allows students and instructors to upload speeches, video assignments, role plays, or group projects for viewing, commenting, and grading (whether face-to-face or online). Structured much like a social networking site, MediaShare can help promote a sense of community among students.

Videos and Video Quizzes: Interactive videos provide students with the opportunity to watch and evaluate multimedia pertaining to chapter content. Many videos are annotated with critical thinking questions or include short, assignable quizzes that report to the instructor's gradebook.

ClassPrep: Collects the very best class presentation resources in one convenient online destination, so instructors can keep students engaged throughout every class.

MyOutline: This valuable tool provides step-by-step guidance and structure for writing an effective outline, along with a detailed help section to assist students in understanding the elements of an outline and how all the pieces fit together. Students can download and email completed outlines to instructors, save for future editing, or print—even print as notecards. Instructors can choose from our templates or create their own structure for use. (Available with Introduction to Communication course only.)

Topic Selector: This interactive tool helps students get started generating ideas and then narrowing down topics. Our Topic Selector is question based, rather than drill-down or simply a list of ideas, in order to help students really learn the process of selecting their topic. Once they have determined their topic, students are directed to credible online sources for guidance with the research process.

MyPersonalityProfile: Online resources that provide students with opportunities to learn about the various communication styles of themselves and others are housed in MyPersonalityProfile, Pearson's online library for self-assessment and analysis. Instructors can use these tools to show learning and growth over the duration of the course. (Available with Introduction to Communication and Interpersonal Communication courses only.)

MySearchLab: Pearson's MySearchLab® is the easiest way for students to start a research assignment or paper. Complete with extensive help on the research process and four databases of credible and reliable source material, MySearchLab® helps students quickly and efficiently make the most of their research time.

Audio Chapter Summaries: Every chapter includes an audio chapter summary, formatted as an MP3 file, perfect for students reviewing material before a test or instructors reviewing material before class.

MyCommunicationLab comes from a trusted partner with educational expertise and a deep commitment to helping students, instructors, and departments achieve their goals. Pearson supports instructors with workshops, training, and assistance from Pearson Faculty Advisors–so you get the help you need to make MyCommunicationLab work for your course. Pearson gathers feedback from instructors and students during the development of content and the feature enhancement of each release to ensure that our products meet your needs.

No matter what course management system you use—or if you do not use one at all, but still wish to easily capture your students' grades and track their performance—Pearson has a MyCommunicationLab option to suit your needs.

A MyCommunicationLab access code is no additional cost when packaged with print versions of select Pearson Communication texts. To get started, contact your local Pearson Publisher's Representative at www.pearsonhighered.com/replocator.

The Human Communication Process

the communication process • cultural and communication • first amendment speech • ethical communication

CHAPTER 1

After reading this chapter, you should be able to

- List and explain the components of human communication
- Explain the effects of perceptions on the human communication process
- Identify, define, and give examples of the noise factors that affect the human communication process
- Illustrate, define, and give examples of the linear, interactional, and transactional models of communication
- Describe the concept of communication as a system
- Explain the role of the media as a communicator
- Give evidence of the relationship between communication and culture
- Define and explain ethnocentrism
- Give an example of the role of First Amendment speech as a rhetorical tool
- Explain the role of the ethical value system in communication
- Analyze the basis for ethical communication

When confronted with the requirement of taking a communication course, students sometimes ask, "Why do I need that? I know how to talk." Communication, though, is more than talking. When you answer a question in class, receive a compliment, challenge another person's ideas, interact with a family member, touch someone, participate in a job interview, take part in a group meeting, listen to a classroom lecture, do a victorious high-five, select clothing to wear, or go through the process of buying a car, you are involved in acts of communicating! Significant friendships, successful family relationships, academic and occupational success, and understanding others from various cultures depend on communication abilities. Communication encompasses not only face-to-face and public communication, but also the ability to navigate Twitter, MySpace, and Facebook.[1]

"Communication skills are essential to personal, academic, and professional success."[2] A recent study indicated that employers want colleges to produce graduates with these learning outcomes: the ability to communicate effectively, critical thinking and analytical reasoning skills, ability to connect choices and actions to ethical decisions, teamwork skills and ability to collaborate with others in diverse group settings, and understand the role of cultural diversity in the United States and other countries. The study went on to state that employers want employees to "possess knowledge of and facility with navigating the world of social media and to know how to create polished communicative messages that have an impact in cyberspace."[3] Also important is "intercultural awareness and facility in communicating successfully in a richly diverse world and workplace."[4]

Communication skills are essential to personal, academic, and professional success.

Another study also stressed that "communication instruction is critical to students' future personal and professional success."[5] This was further stressed in a recruitment and talent management study which revealed that there were "soft" skills that could land a recruit a job. Included were: leadership/team building and being an excellent communicator.[6]

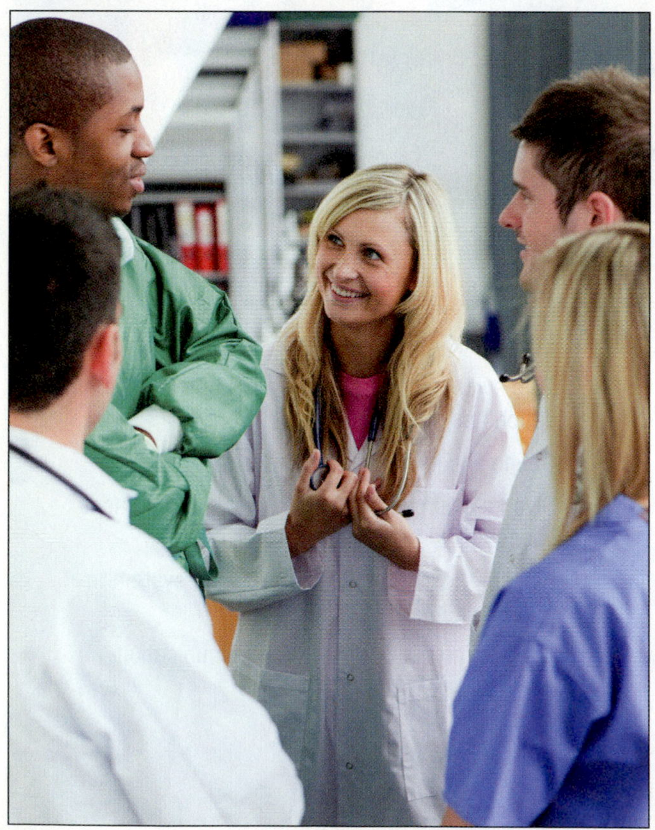

Scholars outside the communication discipline recognize the importance of oral communication training. For example, the American Institute of Certified Public Accountants stated, "Individuals entering the accounting profession should have the skills necessary to exchange information with a meaningful context and with appropriate delivery."[7]

"When the Harvard Medical School surveyed more than 2000 patients about their office visits, poor communication emerged as the most important factor affecting patients' trust in their doctors."[8] "Communication skills are as essential to the legal profession as they are to the medical profession."[9]

Communication competency is crucial to more than the workplace and the classroom. We also need speaking and listening skills to function at the personal level. Relationships depend on listening and responding to each other. The business of life is a communication interaction—whether it is with the doctor, the college registrar, the repairperson, your best friend, or the 911 operator.

COMMUNICATING in Careers

Why Good Communication Is Good Business

Flatter organizations, a more diverse employee base and greater use of teams have all made communication essential to organizational success. Flatter organizations mean managers must communicate with many people over whom they may have no formal control. Even with their own employees, the days when a manager can just order people around are finished. The autocratic management model of past generations is increasingly being replaced by participatory management in which communication is the key to build trust, promote understanding and empower and motivate others.

Because the domestic workforce is growing more diverse, an organization can no longer assume its employee constituencies are homogenous. Employees reflect difference in age, ethnic heritage, race, physical abilities, gender and sexual orientation. Diversity is not just a matter of social responsibility; it is also an economic issue. Companies are realizing the advantage of making full use of the creativity, talents, experiences and perspectives of a diverse employee base.

Teams are the modus operandi in the 21st century workplace. In a recent survey of Fortune 1000 companies, 83 percent reported that their firms use teams; teams are all about communication. The collaboration that allows organizations to capitalize on the creative potential of a diverse workforce depends on communication.

Source: "Why Good Communication Is Good Business" by Marty Blalock, from *Wisconsin Business Alumni Update*. Reprinted with permission of Update and the University of Wisconsin School of Business.

REFLECT ON THIS:

1. Do you think all college students who are majoring in business should be required to take a course in communication?
2. Do you think diversity makes for a more complicated work environment?
3. How does working in a team differ from working individually?

"Direct contact with culturally different people in our neighborhoods, community, schools and workplaces is an inescapable part of life."[10] As the world becomes flatter, where communication takes place internationally, the ability to understand not only your own culture, but that of others, becomes imperative. As the method of communicating with others transfers from one-on-one communication to a *flat world platform* where there is a convergence of the personal computer, fiber-optic cable, and work flow software (which enables individuals all over the world to collaborate regardless of the distance between them), the knowledge of world cultures and their communication patterns is critical.[11]

As you read through this text and study the field of communication, hopefully you will gain both an understanding and gain the skills to be a competent communicator.

Communication Defined

Communication is a conscious or unconscious, intentional or unintentional process in which feelings and ideas are expressed as verbal and/or nonverbal messages that are sent, received, and comprehended. This process can be *accidental* (having no intent), *expressive* (resulting from the emotional state of the person), or *rhetorical* (resulting from specific goals of the communicator).

Human communication occurs on intrapersonal, interpersonal, and public levels. **Intrapersonal communication**, also referred to as *personal communication,* is communicating with yourself. It encompasses such activities as thought processing, personal

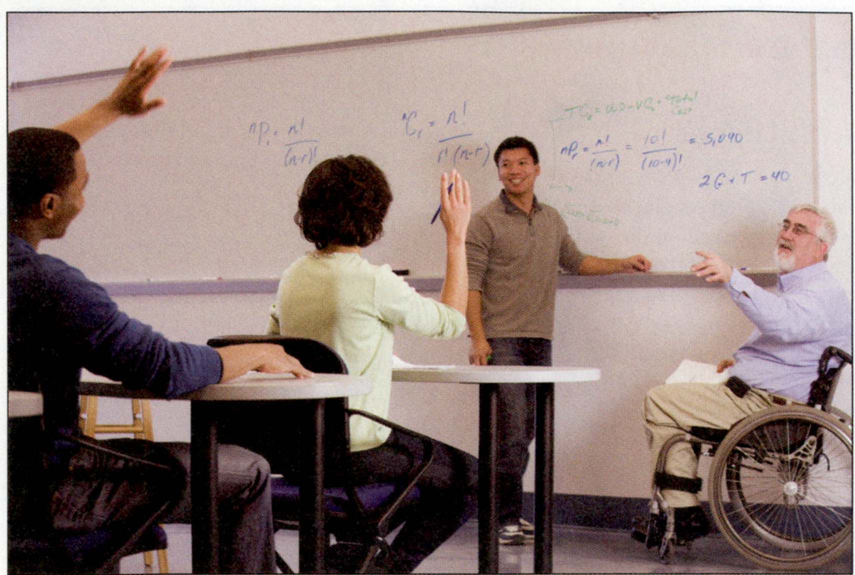

Communication is dynamic because as the attitudes, expectations, feelings, and emotions of persons change the nature of their communication changes as well.

decision making, listening, and determining self-concept. **Interpersonal communication** refers to communication that takes place between two or more persons who establish a communicative relationship. Forms of interpersonal communication include face-to-face or mediated conversations, interviews, and small-group discussions. **Public communication** is characterized by a speaker sending a message to an audience. It may be direct, such as a face-to-face message delivered by a speaker to an audience, or indirect, such as a message relayed over radio or television.

Communication is dynamic, continuous, irreversible, interactive, and contextual.[12]

Communication is *dynamic* because the process is constantly in a state of change. As the attitudes, expectations, feelings, and emotions of persons who are communicating change, the nature of their communication changes as well.

Communication is *continuous* because it never stops. Whether asleep or awake, we are always processing ideas and information through our dreams, thoughts, and expressions. Our brains remain active; we are communicating.

Communication is *irreversible.* Once we send a message, we cannot undo it. Once we make a slip of the tongue, give a meaningful glance, send an angry e-mail, or generate an emotional outburst, we cannot erase it. Our apologies or denials cannot completely eradicate what has taken place.

We sometimes find ourselves in situations where stress causes us to send messages ineffectively

Communication is *interactive.* We react to our own speech and actions, and then we react to those reactions, and others react to our speech and actions. Thus, a cycle of action and reaction becomes the basis for our communication.

Communication is *contextual.* The complexity of communication dictates that we develop the awareness and the skills to function effectively as communicators and to adapt to the setting (both where it is taking place and the attitudes of those who are in the environment), the people who are present, and the purpose of the communication. A word-processing advertisement summarized this well: "You don't talk to your mother the same way you talk to your buddies. (Better not, for your sake.) That nice polite talk is perfect for Sunday dinners. Or when you're asking for money. That's why you've got Street talk. Small talk. Back talk. Coffee talk. Baby talk. And—even when you're not saying a word—Body talk, which has absolutely no regard for syntax and grammar. Custom languages made to order."[13]

To be an effective communicator, you need to understand how the communication process operates as a system, how you send and process information, how you reason your way to conclusions and evaluate the ideas that others send, and the relationship between communication and culture. In addition, good communicators know what ethical standards they use in making their decisions.

The Components of Human Communication

As human beings, we are capable of **selective communication**. That is, from the wide repertory available to us, we can choose the symbol we believe best represents the idea or concept we wish to express. We can think in abstractions, plan events in the future, and store and recall information. Selective communication allows us to combine sounds into complicated sentences and therefore describe feelings, thoughts, events, and objects. This ability to selectively communicate also allows us to decide how to send intentional messages to others.

Figure 1.1 illustrates how the components of the communication process work. The circles representing the **source** (the originator of the message) and the **receiver** (the recipient of the message) overlap as each person sends **messages** (communication) and **feedback** (response to a message) to the other through a **frame of reference** (a perceptual screen) *communication noise* (the potential for communication disruption). The overlapping circles suggest that communication is possible only when each communicator understands the other's message. The variables that affect the frame of reference make up the perceptual screen through which verbal and nonverbal messages are communicated.

Communicator Perceptions

Your **perceptions**—the way you view the world—affect your interpretation of a communication stimulus. Many factors make up your perceptual filter. These factors, listed in Figure 1.1, include your *culture* (the background worldview you hold), *communication skills* (developed from experience and training), *physical and emotional states* (how you feel at this particular time), *experiences* (your cultural background), *attitudes* (negative and positive predispositions to respond to any particular stimulus), *memory* (ability to store and recall information), and *expectations* (what you anticipate will occur). Because of perceptual differences, two people reporting on an incident they have both seen may report their observations differently.

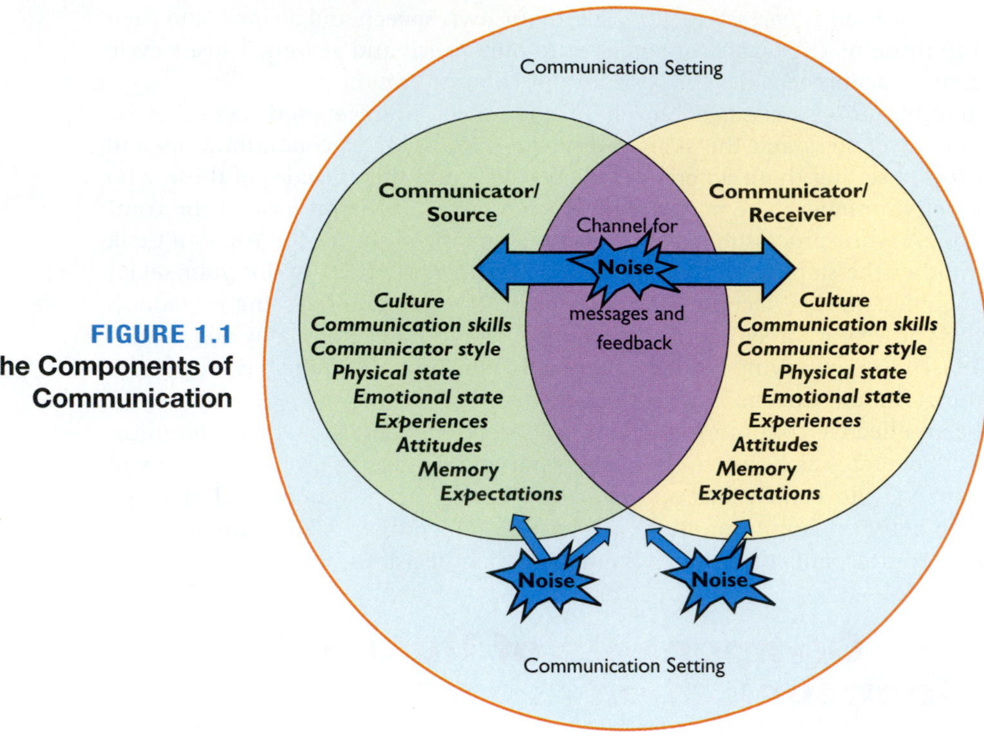

FIGURE 1.1
The Components of Communication

Source

1. Senses aroused by idea or need to communicate
2. Chooses to communicate the message using language symbols (the code)
3. Uses memory and past experiences to find language symbols to communicate the message (encoding)

Receiver

1. Senses aroused by stimuli or need to communicate
2. Receives symbols (the code) in distorted form
3. Uses memory and past experiences to attach meaning to symbols (decoding)
4. Stores information
5. Sends feedback

You encode and decode messages through your perceptual filters. These perceptual filters establish expectations for the outcome of the communication, and expectations guide your interpretation of the communicator's message. A person who expects to hear bad news, for instance, probably will interpret what the boss says in a performance review as negative even if the focus of the review highlights many of the positive aspects of the individual's work.

The Communication Process

When we communicate, we **encode** (take ideas and put them into message form), send the ideas through a channel composed of our **primary signal system** (the senses: seeing, hearing, tasting, smelling, and touching) to someone who receives them via her or his primary signal system, and **decodes** (translates) the received messages. We express our reactions to what we have sensed by both verbal and nonverbal signs. You might say, "I heard the bell" or, "It feels soft." These are examples of verbal communication that are responses to what your senses have received. You also can respond on a nonverbal level. You frown, feel your body tighten up, and wiggle in your chair as you listen

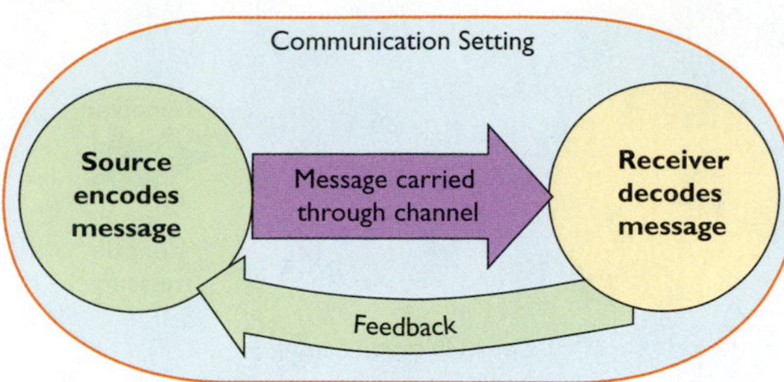

FIGURE 1.2
Effective Encoding and Decoding without Noise

to your psychology instructor detail all the homework you have to finish before you can leave for spring vacation. Your frowning, tensing, and wiggling are nonverbal responses of stress that your body is sending to you and to anyone else who is observing you.

In any communication process, the degree to which the communication is effective depends on the communicators' mutual understanding of the signals being used. Suppose you are about to take an examination and suddenly realize you forgot to bring a pencil to class. You ask one of your friends, "May I please borrow a pencil?" She says, "Yes" and gives you a pencil. You have just participated in an effective communication transaction. You (communicator A) *encoded* a message ("May I please borrow a pencil?") and sent it out over a *channel* (vocal tones carried on sound waves) to your friend (communicator B). Your friend *received* the message (by using sensory agents, ears) and *decoded* it (understood that you wanted a pencil). Your friend's *feedback* (the word *yes* and handing the pencil to you) indicated that the message was successfully *received* and *decoded*. (This is illustrated in Figure 1.2.)

Now suppose that the person sitting next to you is from France and speaks no English. The symbol that he uses for pencil is *crayon*. Unless both of you communicate in French, he will be unable to decode your message, so no successful communication takes place. (See Figure 1.3.)

Remember that *the act of speech is not itself communication*. Speech is a biological act: the utterance of sounds, possibly of vocal symbols of language. Communication is vastly more complex. It involves the development of a relationship among people in which there is shared meaning among the participants. That is, the intent of the message received is basically the same as the intent of the message sent.

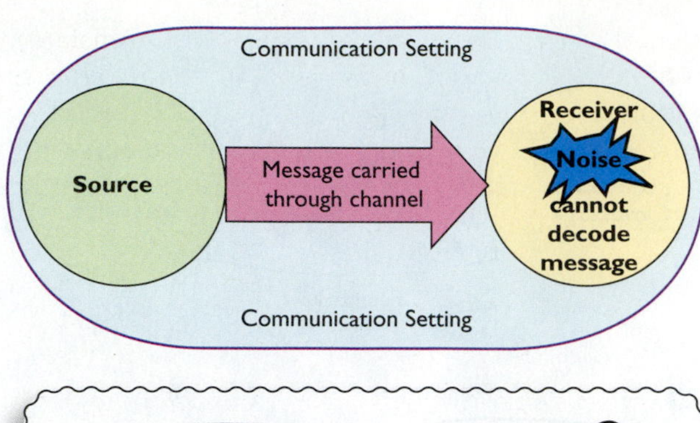

FIGURE 1.3
Encoding with Inappropriate Semantics Can Cause Decoding Problems

The Source and the Message

The communication process begins when the source is consciously or unconsciously stimulated by some event, object, or idea. This need to send a message is then followed by a memory search to find the appropriate language (verbal or nonverbal or both) in which to encode the message.

The Channel

During a communicative act, the encoded message is carried through a **channel** or channels. If the communication occurs face-to-face, these channels may be some or all of the five senses. Typically, we rely on sight and sound as channels in speaking and listening. Instead of communicating face-to-face, however, we may choose an electronic channel that uses sound (e.g., the telephone) or seeing and hearing (e.g., television). In some instances, we may elect to send a message to someone by means of physical contact, such as by tapping the person on the shoulder. In this case, we use the touch channel.

The Receiver and the Message

After receiving verbal and nonverbal signals through the senses, the receiver must decode the message before communication can be accomplished. When gaining verbal and nonverbal signals, the receiver processes them through a memory search so that the signals are translated into the receiver's language system. This decoded message is not identical to the one encoded by the source because each person's symbol system is shaped by a unique set of perceptions. A Euro American professor who says, "Assignments should be turned in on time," might be surprised when a student from a culture that has a flexible time system, such as Mexico, attempts to turn in his homework the day after the assignment was due.

Feedback

Once the receiver assigns meaning to the received message, he is in a position to respond. This response, *feedback*, can be a verbal or a nonverbal reaction to the message, or both. Feedback indicates whether the receiver understands (e.g., by nodding), misunderstands (e.g., by shrugging the shoulders and saying, "I don't understand"), encourages the source to continue (e.g., by leaning forward and saying, "Yes"), or disagrees (e.g., by pulling back and saying, "No way!"). The act of responding, by which the receiver sends feedback to the source, actually shifts the role of the receiver to that of the source.

Communication Noise

Messages are influenced not only by the interpretations of each communicator but also by **communication noise**, which is any internal or external interference in the communication process.[14] Noise can be caused by environmental obstacles, physiological impairment, semantic problems, syntactic problems, organizational confusion, cultural influences, and/or psychological problems. The communication breakdown can be caused by one or a combination of the noise factors.

Environmental Noise *Environmental noise* is outside interference that prevents the receiver from gaining the message. This can happen when you are in the kitchen running water and the sound muffles your friend's voice when she asks you a question from the adjoining room.

Physiological-Impairment Noise A physical problem can block the effective sending or receiving of a message, thus creating *physiological-impairment noise*. For example, people who are deaf or blind do not have the specific sensory capabilities to receive a message in the same way as do people who can hear or see.

Semantic Noise Problems may arise regarding the meaning of words—*semantics*—creating *semantic noise*. For example, semantic noise may result when people use language that is common only to one specific group, a particular part of a country, another nation, or a particular field, profession, or organization.

Travelers frequently encounter semantic problems. The U.S. Midwesterner who goes into a store in many parts of the country's East Coast and asks for a *soda* will probably get a soft drink (*pop* in some regions in the Midwest) rather than a mixture of ice cream, fruit flavoring, and soda water (a *soda* in some parts of the country).

Experts—professors, doctors, mechanics—sometimes forget that those who do not have as much knowledge of their field may not be familiar with its vocabulary. For example, clients often complain that lawyers fail to communicate clearly because they use legal jargon, which is confusing to non-lawyers.

Those who instant message or text message frequently forget that not everyone has learned the texting acronyms and abbreviations. Although phrases like "LMK"

A physical problem can block the effective receiving of a message, thus creating physiological-impairment noise, thus requiring adaptive communication techniques.

and "AFAIK" may make sense to you, as the texter, are you sure the person to whom you are sending the message is aware that those letters mean, "Let me know," and, "As far as I know"?

General Motors discovered the necessity of being sure that the language of the country in which they are selling products is compatible with their product names. Years ago when they tried to sell their Nova product line in Mexico, the reaction was very negative and the cars did not sell well. The reason? In Spanish, *nova* means "doesn't go." Obviously that was not a good message to send to prospective car buyers.

Syntactical Noise Each language has a *syntax*, a customary way of putting words together in a grammatical form. *Syntactical noise*, inappropriate grammatical usage, can interfere with clear communication. For example, receivers may become confused if someone changes tenses in the middle of a story ("She *went* down the street and *says* to him...").

The usual sequence of a grammatically correct English sentence is noun-verb-object ("I give him the book"). But other languages—Spanish, for example—do not follow this pattern. In Spanish, the same sentence reads *Le doy el libro* ("To him I give the book"). Thus, someone who is learning a new language must master not only its vocabulary but also an entirely different system of grammar. Until this new system becomes natural, the language may be quite difficult both to encode and decode.

Organizational Noise When the source fails to realize that certain ideas are best grasped when presented in a structured order, *organizational noise* may result. A geography instructor presents ideas in a random fashion: first he talks about India, then China, then Greece, then India, and then China. After a while, his students become so confused they have absolutely no idea which country he is discussing.

Using a method of organization can provide a clear structure. In giving directions, a person may set a pattern by starting at the departure point and proceeding in geographical order (e.g., "Go to the first street, turn right, proceed three blocks, and turn left"). If material is presented in a specific pattern, the receiver is likely to grasp the meaning. In addition to a clear pattern, you will want to use specific language that indicates spatial relationships ("Place piece B two inches to the right of ...").[15]

Cultural Noise *Cultural noise* results from preconceived, unyielding attitudes derived from a group or society about how members of that culture should act or in what they should or should not believe. Individuals in a culture who believe in a set pattern of rules and regulations might say, "Nice people don't do things like that" and, "We do it this way."

An instance of cultural noise is the attitude that any action by a representative of one's own group is always right, whereas the actions by a member of another group are wrong. Thus, those who live in the United States who are part of the English-only movement believe "If you are an American, you have to speak American English!" Thus, those people who don't speak American English, according to this group, aren't "Americans."

Cultural noise may be present when members of two religious or nationality groups interact. Most Jews, Buddhists, and Muslims do not believe in the divinity of Christ as the Messiah. They do not celebrate Christmas, nor do they usually put up Christmas decorations. Although wishing someone "Merry Christmas" may be the tradition among Christians, the phrase may be unnerving to a Jewish, Buddhist, or Muslim acquaintance.

Psychological Noise We sometimes find ourselves in situations where *psychological noise*—stress, frustration, or irritation—causes us to send or receive messages ineffectively. Think of what happens when you are so angry that you "can't think straight." For example, as you sit in class, upset over the argument you had with your suitemate before leaving for class, you may be so distracted that you can't concentrate on the professor's lecture.

The Effect of Communication Noise Communication noise factors can interfere with effective communication in varying stages of the linear, interactional, or transactional models. For example, semantic noise may stop the sender from encoding a message if she does not have the vocabulary to create the message. The message may not get into the channel if there is physiological-impairment noise because the sender has laryngitis. The receiver may not be able to receive the message if she is deaf and can't hear the intended message. The message may not get clearly out of the channel if there is environmental noise that creates static on the telephone line carrying the signal. (See Figure 1.4.) The receiver may be experiencing psychological noise. Although she receives the message, she may be so disoriented that she doesn't really grasp the intent of the information. Or, due to semantic and syntactic noise, she may not be able to decode the message because she doesn't speak the same language as the sender.

Dealing with Communication Noise Communication noise interferes with communication, but because it is commonly present, we must learn to adapt to and compensate for it. For example, a source should offer opportunities for feedback to make sure that a message has been received and understood. Rather than assuming that someone in another room has heard your message, you might word the statement so that it requires an answer: "The phone is for you; are you going to answer it?" Another way to compensate for noise is to define terms that might be misunderstood. Rather than repeating the same words in a message that has been misunderstood, you can change the terms or the sentence structure to aid the receiver in decoding the message. In the same way, a receiver should ask questions or repeat the message's general ideas to be sure that distractions have not interfered with comprehension.

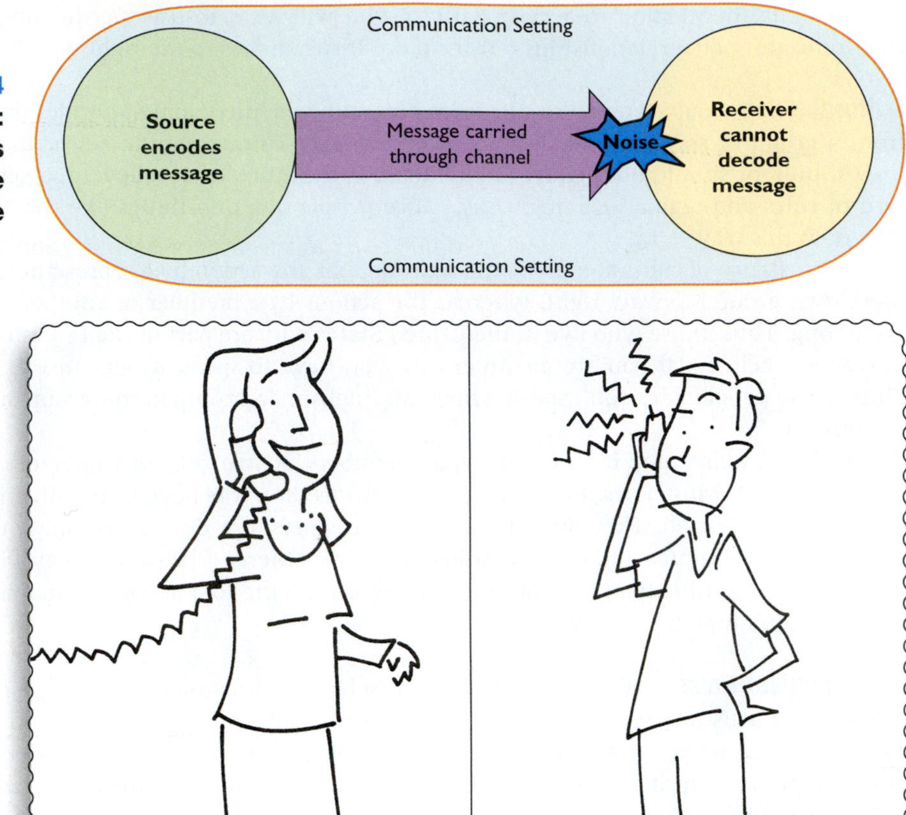

FIGURE 1.4
Environmentel Noise: The Coded Message Is Not Received Because of Channel Interference

The way a person does or does not respond may give you some clues as to how to compensate for a noise problem. For instance, consider what happens if you request a sheet of paper, and the other person does not do anything. Environmental noise may have stopped the message from being received. The person may not have been paying attention because of psychological or cultural noise. Or, for instance, the person may say, "I have difficulty hearing. Could you repeat what you said, and speak up a little?" In this case, you must increase the volume level when you repeat the message. A response of "No comprende!" to the question "Where is the Grande Hotel?" likely indicates that the person of whom you asked the question does not speak English. You may then want to switch to Spanish, if you know the language, or show the person a brochure from the hotel.

The Context

Communication does not occur in a vacuum. It always relates to the *context:* where the communication is taking place, and the general attitude of those assembled. Such factors as the size of the room, the color of the walls, and the type and placement of the furniture can all affect how we feel, the way we communicate, and the type of communicating we engage in. For example, placing a large number of people in a small work area, as is often the case with direct-phone salespeople, may bring about emotional stress that can be reflected by erratic communication.

Communication as a System

Think of your daily sending and receiving of messages. There is a *system,* a pattern, to the way you communicate with others. The pattern centers on who speaks, what the speaker says or is allowed to say, the way in which the message is sent, and where the speaker and receiver are. The *participants,* the *setting,* the *purpose,* and how they interact form the basis of the *communication system.*

The flow of communication in a consistent pattern allows communication to be regular and predictable, not random, and gives everyone who participates a sense of assurance and security. Identify a communication system with which you are familiar (e.g., your family or work unit). You can probably anticipate what is going to happen and how your actions will affect others before you actually act. Your awareness of how well your ideas will be accepted or of how much encouragement or discouragement you will receive may dictate what you do and do not say.

The type of communication system used affects who speaks. In a strongly parent-dominated home, for example, a parent may place restrictions on the type of language children may use and the topics they can discuss. Any attempt by the children to challenge the system may be met with strongly negative reactions and may result in verbal or even physical punishment.

A communication system can be shaped by the communicators' age, status, gender, attraction for each other, and cultural heritage. For example, in a family system, the rules for male members may be different from those for female members, regulations may alter as the children get older, and favored children may be allowed more freedom than the others.

A particular setting may encourage or discourage communication. In some settings, people may feel free to disagree, whereas in others they may feel restricted. Some instructors, for example, encourage differences of opinion in their classrooms; others demand adherence to their philosophy and discourage interpretations. Students quickly learn the rules in classrooms and conform accordingly; if they do not, they may be faced with lowered grades or verbal reprimands.

The purpose of the communicative act also may result in limits to the system. Trying to tell someone what you believe is a different task and experience from attempting to persuade that person to take some action you desire. An employee may not like a particular regulation, for instance, but if it has been made clear that the supervisor is not interested in input regarding company policies, and that she has the power to fire an employee, it is probably unwise for an employee who wants to retain his job to present his thoughts about perceived changes.

An artistic mobile is a good analogy for visualizing a system. It swings around until, by addition, subtraction, and other alterations, it attains balance. It remains that way until something disturbs the balance. In human communication, once a system is set up and operating, any attempt to alter that system and its pattern of rules can impair the system or cause it to stop functioning. This does not mean that all systems that are working are good ones. It merely suggests that when a system is functioning, regardless of whether the participants are happy with the pattern, at least there is a basis for understanding how the communication of the people within that system will take place. For instance, if you are aware that your supervisor is not going to accept anyone else's ideas, you learn to live with the system or find another job. A relationship in which there is abuse may function well because of a clear pattern of action–reaction. The abuser says, "You do what I say or I will punish you." The recipient of the abuse accepts and operates under those rules. Thus, a functional system is established. This does not mean the system is healthy, but it is functional.

Interestingly, positive results can emerge from a system that is not working well because awareness of a problem may halt a negative system. For example, if a family unit has been operating under a reign of physical and verbal abuse, something that happens to stop the abuse could result in a much-needed change or could bring the system to an end.

Once the rules become nonexistent or fuzzy, chaos may result. When a step parent comes into a home which previously was made up of child(ren) and a single parent, there may be a disintegration of the previously developed system. The newcomer causes the entire system to go out of sync as the household adjusts to that person's mode of operation.

In the complex process of human communication, it is not enough simply to be able to identify the component parts and realize that communication is systematized. We must also understand how these components fit together. A useful way of doing this is to look at models of the communication process that illustrates how the various elements relate to each other.

Models of Human Communication

Any model is a simplification that may leave out steps or omit details. Despite this limitation, communication models can help us see the components of the system from a perspective that will be useful in analyzing and understanding the process.

Although there are many models that can be used to illustrate the act of communication, three are used here to illustrate the process: the linear, the interactional, and the transactional.

Linear Model of Communication

Early theoretical work concerning verbal communication evolved from ancient Greek and Roman rhetoricians who were concerned with the proper training of orators. For this reason, early theories of communication stressed the role of the orator, the public speaker. The theories reflected what might be called a one-directional view of communication, in which a person performs specific actions in a specific sequence during a speech and elicits specific desired responses from listeners. This view is called the linear model of communication. (See Figure 1.5.)

In the **linear model of communication**,[16] a source encodes a message and sends it to a receiver through one or more sensory channels. The receiver then receives and decodes the message. For example, after you buy a computer, you view and listen to the message on a CD provided by the manufacturer. The CD explains how to download the operating system. When you follow the directions and the computer boots up and operates, the communication has been successful.

When using one-directional communication, unless there is careful analysis by the speaker of the intended audience, the setting, and the purpose, noise factors may be present. To illustrate this, let us consider an example. José (the speaker/source) says, "Please put the book on the table when you are done with it." He then turns and walks from the room. Brooke (the listener/receiver) has a stack of books in front of her; she is not certain which one to place on the table. In this example, José is assuming that this sending of a message is all there is to communicating.

Does this mean that a sender should not use the linear model? No. Sometimes senders have no choice about whether they should use the linear model. Advertisers, public speakers appearing on television, people leaving messages on answering machines, and

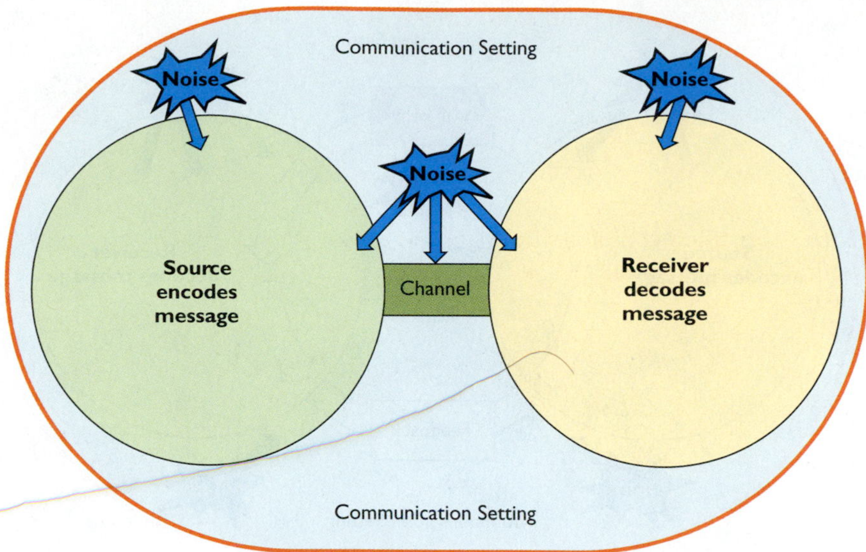

FIGURE 1.5
The Linear Model of Communication (One-Directional Communication)

producers of documentaries have no choice but to use the linear model. Therefore, they must give careful consideration to figuring out the most appropriate language, clarifying examples, and determining what structure should be used to assist in avoiding listener or viewer communication noise. In the book example José should have indicated specifically which book and what table.

Interactional Model of Communication

The linear model of communication does not take into account all of the variables in the communication process. For this reason, some early behavioral scientists, influenced by research in psychology, expanded the notion of the process to encompass greater interaction and to demonstrate the dynamic, ongoing nature of communication. Communication scholars point to David Berlo's *The Process of Communication*[17] as the influential work that introduced this perspective. The interactional model of communication is displayed in Figure 1.6.

FIGURE 1.6
The Interactional Model of Commuincation (Two-Directional Communication)

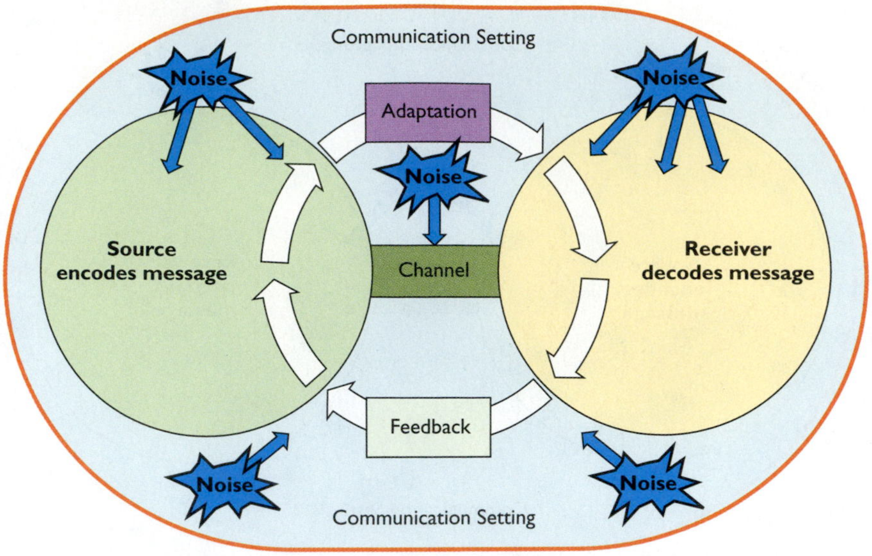

In the **interactional model of communication**, a source encodes and sends a message to a receiver (through one or more of the sensory channels). The receiver receives and decodes the message, as in linear communication, but then encodes *feedback* and sends it back to the source, thus making the process two-directional. The source then decodes the feedback message. Based on the original message sent and the feedback received, the source encodes a new message that adjusts to the feedback *(adaptation)*. For example, José says to Brooke, "Please hand me the book." Brooke looks at the pile of books in front of her and says, "Which one?" (feedback). José responds, "The red one on the top of the pile" (adaptation).

This view of communication accounts for the influence of the receiver's responses. It suggests a process that is somewhat circular: sending and receiving, receiving and sending, and so on.

Whenever possible, communicators should attempt to interact so that they can find out how effective their communication actually is. For example, José's analysis of the number of books available might have led him to the conclusion that he needed to be more specific, and he therefore could have said, "Please hand me the red book on the top of the pile." Or he might have wanted to ask, "Do you know which book I want?," after saying "Hand me the book." Or he might have waited to see which volume Brooke put on the table to see whether she understood him. If she did not, he could have corrected his error by being more specific in his directions.

Managers in organizations, parents, and professors should make use of this communication model in order to ensure that their employees, customers, children, and students have received and can react appropriately to their messages.

Transactional Model of Communication

Theorists have suggested that communication may not be as simple a process of stimulus and response as the linear and interactional models suggest. This view supports the idea that communication is a transaction in which source and receiver play interchangeable roles throughout the act of communication.[18] Because of the complexity of this process, a clear-cut model of the process is not easy to construct. Figure 1.7 is designed to illustrate the **transactional model of communication**. In this model, the communicators simultaneously process messages. Communicator A encodes a message and sends it. Communicator B then encodes feedback and sends it to A, who decodes it. But these steps are not mutually exclusive; encoding and decoding may occur simultaneously. Speakers may send a verbal message and at the same time receive and decode a nonverbal feedback message from listeners. Because messages can be sent and received at the same time, this model is multidirectional and the message overlaps. Think of the instances when you were speaking to someone and he simultaneously nodded as you were speaking, said, "Yes," and then, "and?," which gave you his message while you were simultaneously giving yours.

Notice that one person is not labeled the source and the other the receiver. Instead, both communicators assume the roles of encoder and decoder in the transaction, thus simultaneously communicating—for example:

Miguele says, "I love you," *while*

Miguele sees Latica walk away as he is speaking, *while*

Latica walks away from Miguele, *while*

Latica says, "I love you," *while*

Miguele stops, turns, frowns, and says, "I'm not sure you mean that," *while*

Latica sees Miguele nod his head and walk toward her as she speaks, *while*

Miguele hears her words, *while*

Miguele smiles and nods his head and walks toward Latica as she speaks.

Throughout the encounter, both Miguele and Latica are simultaneously sending and receiving (encoding and decoding) verbal and nonverbal messages.

Although use of the transactional model may result in the most effective communication, applying this model will be successful only if the communicators are continually aware of adapting the communication by being alert to feedback, anticipating

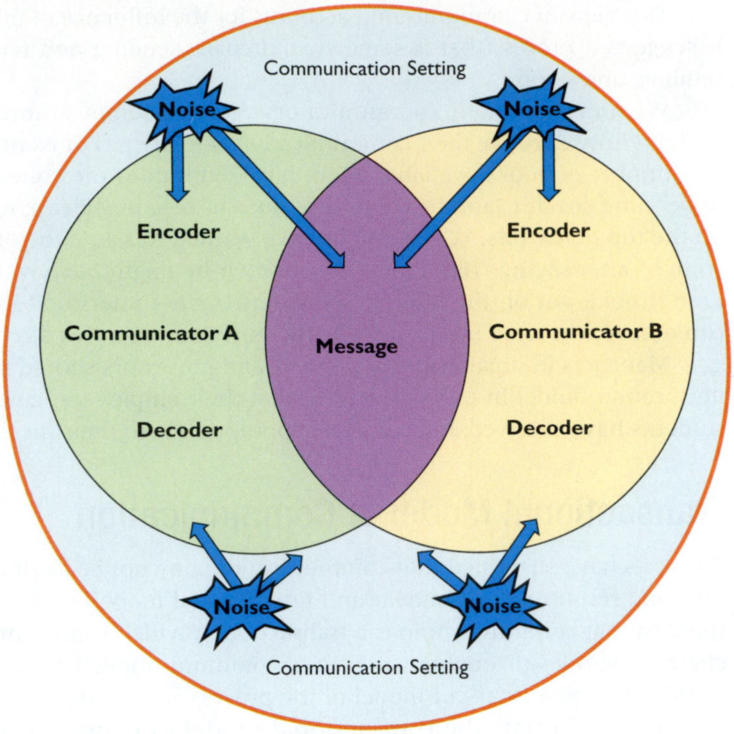

FIGURE 1.7
The Transactional Model of Communication (Multidirectional Communication)

potential noise factors, and considering the participants, setting, and purpose of the communication act.

The Models Compared

Comparing the three models in an example may enhance your understanding of how each differs from the others.

The director of public relations of a major corporation presents a speech over closed-circuit television from the headquarters' media studio to the marketing personnel at district offices located throughout the country. This is an example of the *linear model of communication* (one-directional, no chance for feedback, no opportunity to evaluate noise).

Next, the director gives the same presentation in the corporation's boardroom. She sticks to the manuscript she prepared, making no effort to seek feedback or detect noise. Following the speech, she asks if there are any questions. A member of the board asks a question, which she answers. The question-and-answer session demonstrates the *interactional model of communication:* The sender encoded and sent a message, it was received and decoded, feedback was given (the question), and adaptation was made (the answer).

Then the sales staff enters the room. The public relations director starts to speak. As she does, a salesperson asks a question. While the question is being asked, the speaker nods her head. She then verbally agrees with the salesperson. While this is happening, the salesperson also nods his head, indicating that he understood what was just explained, and says, "I get it." This is an example of the *transactional model of communication.*

Besides understanding what the communication process is, it also is important to understand how we are affected not only by communication that is face-to-face but also by communication that is media derived.

The Media as Communicators

We are influenced by **media**—radio, television, the Internet, magazines, newspapers, and film. "There is a long history (or tradition) of sociological theories of mass communication and critical studies of culture that attempt to understand these many effects."[19] When you consider that the typical U.S. American spends more than half of his or her leisure time watching television, you can appreciate the potential influence the media can have.[20] Add to this, in 2010, 77.3 percent of the people in the United States were using the Internet;[21] it is easy to understand why electronic media is considered by many to be the major communication tool in the twenty-first century.

Some lives are shaped by the media. People develop role models based on seeing sports and entertainment celebrities on television, listening to them being interviewed on radio, or reading what is being said about them on the Internet. The images that the media project tell us how to dress, how to spend our time, and how to be a consumer. As political, business, and social attitudes are relayed, we form our beliefs on war, what stocks to buy or sell, or whom to vote for in an upcoming election.

The result of this media exposure can be positive. Children learn the alphabet and numbers through *Sesame Street.* They learn values from *Barney. National Geographic* specials and print sources provide information about people, animals, and places. We attend symphonies and dance performances without leaving our homes. Dr. Phil (McGraw) informs us about how to cope with trauma and Dr. Oz alerts us to medical issues.

But there can be a downside to media exposure. As people spend time in front of television sets or texting, they have less time to engage in direct conversations with others and participate in other activities.

There is also the question of whether exposing people to information about violence can result in further violence. The number of copycat crimes after the Columbine shootings was perceived to have resulted from exposure to the coverage of the murders on television. For example, a sixteen-year-old Red Lake (Minnesota) High School student killed a security guard, teacher, and five fellow students and then shot himself. The crime had direct echoes of the Columbine massacre: the

Radio and television have profound effects on our everyday lives, including creating iconic figures like Dr. Oz, whose views on medical related issues have a strong influence on his viewers.

killer's adoration of Hitler, his social isolation, his frightening Web postings, his Goth clothing and trench coat, and his being a loner.[22]

Radio and television have profound effects on our everyday lives. The products you buy, the attitudes you hold, and the political candidates you choose to vote for or against may well be influenced by the media you listen to and watch. History, too, has been influenced by media events. For example, it is perceived that major media presentations have been influential in changing history. Dr. Martin Luther King's "I Have a Dream" speech (August 28, 1963) is credited as being a pivotal force in advancing the civil rights movement.[23] The Nixon–Kennedy television debate (September 26, 1960), which is considered to be the pivotal factor in John F. Kennedy's election, illustrated the necessity of being aware of the visual effects of television. Richard Nixon, the Republican candidate, was recovering from the flu and did not look very well. Kennedy, on the other hand, appeared tan and relaxed. Barack Obama gained national attention when, on December 12, 2010, as he signed the repeal of the US military's "Don't Ask, Don't Tell" Policy, he stated, "No longer will tens of thousands of Americans in uniform be asked to live a lie, or look over their shoulder in order to serve the country that they love."[24]

The rapid advances in technology have enabled us to watch films online, do banking, be in constant contact with friends, and shop online with our computers, iPhones, and personal digital assistants.[25]

Some critics fear that the glut of technology will turn users into social isolates who interact less with each other face-to-face and more with our computer screens or smart phones.[26] Others point out, however, that the Internet brings friends and families together in meaningful ways as people maintain ongoing e-conversations, as well as allowing them to conduct personal and professional business without leaving their homes or businesses.[27]

A media critic maintains that we have to be trained to understand technology in order to use it positively. He argues, "Only when we recover a critical distance from the technology which seduces us with its amusing appeal, can we recover the appropriate balance of mediums that will make us an intelligent culture."[28] An

Socially COMMUNICATING

Facebook May Help Shy People Open Up

Josh Chiles is shy. In a gathering of unfamiliar people, he often waits for someone, anyone, to ask him a question or make small talk. At a party, bar or restaurant, "I just sit there, hoping someone will talk to me," he said.

But on Facebook, he is Mr. Personality. He constantly refreshes his status; comments on others' updates, posts pictures, makes jokes and registers his likes. He states, "There is no doubt Facebook has changed my life."

A study published in the journal *CyberPsychology, Behavior and Social Networking*, showed that the Internet and social networks helped the lonely fill "critical needs of social interactions, self-disclosure, and identity exploration." As a result, another study shows, "shy people are spending more time on Facebook than more socially confident people."

Source: "Facebook May Help Shy People Open Up, New Studies Suggest" by M. Rosenwald, from *Cleveland Plain Dealer,* February 14, 2011.

REFLECT ON THIS: Though Facebook and other social media sites may help the shy, some experts consider these sources a crutch to avoid human contact. Do you agree with the findings noted about the positive effects, or side with those who think social media sources are a crutch?

intelligent culture is one in which the inhabitants are competent communicators. Understanding how culture affects communication is another important concept to investigate in order to understand the world of communication.

Communication and Culture

What phrases or terms immediately come to mind when you are asked, "What is your culture?" How do your cultural affiliations affect you? How does culture affect your communication?

Intercultural and Intracultural Communication

Usually when one speaks of culture, nationality comes to mind. In reality, *nationality* refers to the nation in which one was born, now resides, or has lived or studied for enough time to become familiar with the customs of the area. Some nationality identifiers are Irish and Korean. Nationality is only one factor of culture, however. Other cultural group identifiers are the region of a country (e.g., the southern part of the United States), religious affiliation or orientation (e.g., Muslim), political orientation (e.g., Democrat), socioeconomic status (e.g., upper middle class), gender (e.g., female), sexual orientation (e.g., gay male), age or generation (e.g., senior citizen), vocation (e.g., executive), avocation (e.g., stamp collector), family background (e.g., Italian Catholic from a large family), marital status (e.g., married), and parental status (e.g., single father).

We are each culture-filled, a combination of many cultures. You may not have thought about it, but you are the sum total of your environmental influences—the influences of your family, your community, your religious or lack of religious upbringing, your education, and the media with which you have come in contact. Because you have so many cultural influences, you are a multicultural being.

It is culture that gives us our language, ethics, morals, and social and political ideals. It is culture that gives us our art forms, our way of relating to others, and our value system. In other words, in many ways, it is culture that makes us human. The words you utter and think, the actions you take, and your ability to interact with others have all been laid out for you by your cultural influences. You are human because

Culture is a communication phenomenon because it is passed from generation to generation through interactions.

you have the ability to selectively use language to think about what has happened, use those experiences to perceive in the present tense, and project into the future.

Communication and culture have a direct link. A *culture* consists of all those individuals who have a shared system of interpretation. Culture is a communication phenomenon because it is passed among its adherents by communication: written, oral, verbal and nonverbal. You might think of it this way: Culture is the software that allows the hardware (the person) to operate. Your parents, the schools you have attended, and the media were all influential in aiding you to develop your belief system through communication. You were spoken to and listened to, and you saw and read about the rules, customs, and habits of those with whom you lived in your home, region of the country, and nation. This process is ongoing; it was and is done through communication. Your culture has been passed on to you through proverbs, family stories, fairytales, songs, poetry, and literature.

A great deal of your daily communication centers on your cultural identifications. As a student, for example, how many times do you refer to student-oriented topics, including the institution you attend, your classes, and how your education will help you in the future? You probably compare and contrast your "studentness" with qualities of other students and nonstudents.

When you interact with those with whom you have a cultural bond, you are participating in **intracultural communication**. Sometimes a cultural connection enhances the interaction because people feel a special connection. For example, two college students in the U.S. who come from Morocco may feel that their communication is intracultural. An international student from Morocco speaking to an international student from Algeria may feel a cultural bond too. Because they are attending a U.S. college, they may feel a cultural bond because they are international students or because they are both from Africa.

When you speak to those with whom you have little or no cultural bond, you are engaging in **intercultural communication**. An Indian citizen with little knowledge of New Zealand and a New Zealander with little knowledge of India or its customs who are speaking with each other are involved on an intercultural level.

Have you ever wondered how comfortable you are in speaking to people from cultures other than your own? If so, fill out the Personal Report of Intercultural Communication Apprehension questionnaire.

Multiculturalism

When people from various cultures live in the same place, unique multicultural situations can emerge. The term *multiculture* refers to a society consisting of varied cultural groups. The United States is a multicultural country. It is ethnically composed of African Americans, Hispanic Americans, Irish Americans, and many other cultures. It is also multicultural as it relates to the broader definition of culture because it is made up of such differences as women and men, homosexuals and heterosexuals, and religious believers and atheists.

Historically, the term *melting pot* was used to describe the United States, indicating it was desirable for everyone to lose their individual identities and blend into a one-dimensional society. This is still the view of many social conservatives, who

Personal Report of Intercultural Communication Apprehension (PRICA)

This measure was developed to address communication apprehension in the intercultural context.

DIRECTIONS: The 14 statements below are comments frequently made by people with regard to communication with people from other cultures. Please indicate how much you agree with these statements by marking a number representing your response to each statement using the following choices: Strongly Disagree = 1; Disagree = 2; Neutral = 3; Agree = 4; Strongly Agree = 5

____ 1. Generally, I am comfortable interacting with a group of people from different cultures.

____ 2. I am tense and nervous while interacting with people from different cultures.

____ 3. I like to get involved in group discussions with others who are from different cultures.

____ 4. Engaging in a group discussion with people from different cultures makes me nervous.

___ 5. I am calm and relaxed when interacting with a group of people who are from different cultures.

____ 6. While participating in a conversation with a person from a different culture, I get nervous.

____ 7. I have no fear of speaking up in a conversation with a person from a different culture.

____ 8. Ordinarily I am very tense and nervous in a conversation with person from a different culture.

____ 9. Ordinarily I am very calm and relaxed in conversations with a person from a different culture.

____ 10. While conversing with a person from a different culture, I feel very relaxed.

____ 11. I am afraid to speak up in conversations with a person from a different culture.

____ 12. I face the prospect of interacting with people from different cultures with confidence.

____ 13. My thoughts become confused and jumbled when interacting with people from different cultures.

____ 14. Communicating with people from different cultures makes me feel uncomfortable.

Scoring: To compute the PRICA score, complete the following steps:

Step 1. Add the scores for the following items: 1, 3, 5, 7, 9, 10, and 12

Step 2. Add the scores for the following items: 2, 4, 6, 8,11,13, and 14

Step 3. Complete the following formula:
PRICA score = 42 – Total from Step 1 + Total from Step 2.

Scores can range from 14 to 70. Scores below 32 indicate low intercultural communication apprehension (CA). Scores above 52 indicate high intercultural CA. Scores ranging between 32 and 52 indicate a moderate level of intercultural CA.

Source: Neuliep, J. W., & McCroskey, J. C. (1997). The development of intercultural and interethnic communication apprehension scales. *Communication Research Reports*, 14, 385–398.

believe that "foreigners," those who speak languages other than English and have food, religious, and clothing styles that are different than the Euro American norm, are not "real" Americans.

More liberal believers have embraced *pluralism,*[29] in which individuals are encouraged to maintain their individual identities and still be part of the larger group. Also referred to as *multiculturalism,* the movement evolved because "a lot of people are ignorant about people of color, gays and lesbians, or whatever [e.g., Hispanics, Spanish Americans, Asian]. These minority groups often feel like they are marginalized."[30]

Non-Hispanic whites now make up two-thirds of the total U.S. population, but that proportion is predicted to dip to one-half by 2042.[31] And, white children are predicted to become a minority in 2023."[32]

Many people who are long-time residents of the United States have verbal and nonverbal patterns quite different from those of Euro Americans because of their cultural background—in this case, their ethnic or racial group. The multicultural approach, instead of using the *melting pot analogy,* views the U.S. more as a *tossed salad,* where each person has a cultural flavor, but we are touched and enhanced by those around us. Immigrant group members, who desire to do so, retain some or all of their past histories, including language, customary foods, and religious beliefs. For example, Mexican Americans may speak English when mixing with the general society,

Communicating Socially

Hate Speech Has Its Consequences

"Might be a racist joke but it's still funny."

—Subject line of a mass e-mail sent by Burke Country (N.C.) School Board member Rob Hairfield, that contained an epithet-laden racist joke and racist photo illustrations, resulted in the board censuring Hairfield.

"The U.S. Hispanic Chamber of Commerce is effectively an organization that is interested in ... Mexico's export of drugs and illegal aliens to the United States."

—Lou Dobbs, on an edition of CNN's "Lou Dobbs Tonight," for which he later offered a rare apology.

"Poor, without skills, without language, not shar[ing] our culture, not shar[ing] our hygiene. It's millions of leeches form a primitive country, come here to leech off you and, with it, they are ruining the schools, the hospitals, and a lot of life in America."

—Jay Severin, during an edition of his talk radio show on Boston's WTKK-FM, characterizing Mexican immigrants in a tirade that resulted in his indefinite suspension.

"There goes the neighborhood."

—Subject line of a mass e-mail depicting a watermelon patch outside the White House, shortly after the election of Barack Obama as president, forwarded by North Carolina Alcoholic Beverage Commission Chairman Douglas A. Fox. He was forced to resign.

Source: "Hate Speech Has Its Consequences," from *Intelligence Report*, 135, fall 2009, page 4. Copyright © 2009 by Southern Poverty Law Center. Reprinted with permission.

REFLECT ON THIS:

1. Do you think that quotes like these and similar ones are leading to the lack of civility in the United States?
2. These speakers received varying degrees of penalties for their statements. Do you think the penalties were fair? Just? Too severe? Severe enough?

but speak Spanish within their household or at social events attended by Mexicans. They may eat pizza outside of their homes, but the food of choice within the Mexican American community tends to include tortillas, chiles rellenos, and frijoles.

People from ethnic and racial minority groups face a different and sometimes hostile and alien culture, value system, and communication system when entering school, corporate, social service, and governmental environments. As a result, some minority students might perform poorly in school classes because they lack competence in the majority culture's language and rules of communication.

The ethnic majority often doesn't understand or has biases against those who are in the minority, and the culturally different may not understand the motives and patterns of the mainstream.

Accepting that you are a cultural being, understanding the process you use to discuss cultural affiliations as well as other aspects of yourself, is an important part of learning to be a competent communicator. Ask yourself, "What is my cultural composite (e.g., gender, ethnicity, race, and sexual orientation)? How do these factors affect my communication?"

Ethnocentrism

Jon, a Christian Euro American male, is introduced to Aaron and thinks it is ridiculous that he wears a skullcap (a *yarmulke*) all the time. He is invited to Partha's home and is repulsed when he is told that the meat being served at dinner is snake. He is disturbed when he hears that in many Arabic countries women have to cover their entire bodies when they are in public. Jon's reactions reflect ethnocentrism.

Ethnocentrism means that we consider the views and standards of our own in-group as much more important than any out-groups.[33] The founder of the sociology movement in the United States explained the concept of ethnocentrism as the result of people's perceptions that they belong to an *in-group*, defined as a collectivity with which an individual identifies. An *out-group* is a collectivity with which an individual does not identify. The in-group's beliefs are perceived to be right, the out-group's wrong. As a result of ethnocentrism, out-groups are often at a disadvantage because we constantly make judgments about them based on our standards and values and reject the other group's standards and values. When Jon encountered Aaron, Partha, and the notion of an Arabic woman enclosed in a *burka,* he put into effect his concept system of what he is used to, what his culture's rules are, what he believes to be the "right" way.

Generally, we view life in terms of our own group being the center of everything, and all others being scaled and rated with reference to it. Think of the clothing worn on your campus by the majority of students. That's the "in" clothing. On many campuses in the early 2010s, that consisted of jeans or shorts and T-shirts. A student showing up for class in an African *dashiki* or an Indian *sari* may be met with strange looks. That's ethnocentrism in action. The in-group's style is considered the only right one.

National conflicts often center on the perception that what is in our national interest is right. What is in the national interest of another country is not acceptable. In reality, no one can claim that only certain groups have a cultural perspective or identity that is superior to another's perspective or identity. Although we might like to think so, the "U.S. American way" is not superior to the "Chinese way" or the "Egyptian way." Some Polish people eat duck blood soup and pierogies; many people from Thailand eat kaeng hang and kai; many U.S. Americans eat hamburgers and French fries. Which of these foods is best? None, per se. What a person eats is based on cultural patterns, availability, and sometimes necessity.

Communicating Culturally

You Are a Citizen of a Very Diverse World

If we shrank the earth's population to a "global village" of only 100 people and kept all the existing human ratios, there'd be:

61	from Asia
21	from China
17	from India
13	from Africa
12	from Europe
5	from the U.S.
1	from Australia and New Zealand
22	who speak a Chinese dialect,
18	of whom speak Mandarin
9	who speak English
8	who speak Hindi
50	females
50	males
32	Christians
68	non-Christians,
15	of whom are nonreligious
19	Muslims
6	Buddhists
1	Jew
30	who have enough to eat
88	old enough to read,
17	of whom cannot read at all
1	teacher

and you are one person traveling that world.

Source: "You Are a Citizen of a Very Diverse World," from *World Citizens Guide*, www.worldcitizensguide.org. Reprinted with permission.

The United States is a multicultural country as it relates to ethnic derivation.

Culturally COMMUNICATING

Cross-Cultural Communication

If you work with people whose native language is not your own, follow these tips to communicate instructions clearly:

- Avoid complicated and lengthy explanations. Keep instructions short.
- Make it clear that you welcome questions when something is unclear.
- Ask them to repeat your instructions in their own words. *Reason:* if they repeat the instructions in your words, they may have memorized the words but not the message.

Source: From Sondra Thiederman, PhD, president of Cross-Cultural Communications, cited in *Leadership for the Front Lines*, 24 Rope Ferry Road, Waterford, CT 60386.

Ethnocentrism is not a new concept. It was expressed, and reinforced in many ways, by the European colonizers. White-skinned colonists considered themselves more advanced than the natives, who were people of color. They subjugated the native peoples of the Americas, Africa, and Asia, whom they considered inferior. Often, if they would not convert to these cultural values, the natives were killed or enslaved. Entire cultures were wiped out or nearly destroyed because of ethnocentrism.

The definition of what it means to be an "American" is under constant redefinition. Nationality diversity is part of the present national perspective. Among some in the Euro American community this means that "our" country is no longer ours. It is this fear of losing control of their country that motivates some to attack any immigration into the United States. As part of this paranoia, in 2010 Arizona enacted a stringent law on illegal immigration with the aim "to identify, prosecute and deport illegal immigrants."[34] "The move unleashed immediate protests and reignited the divisive battle over immigration reform nationally."[35]

In its highest forms, extreme ethnocentrism leads to a rejection of the richness and knowledge of other cultures. It impedes communication and blocks the exchange of ideas and skills among peoples. Because it excludes other points of view, an ethnocentric orientation is restrictive and limiting. It can lead and has led to racism, sexism, and even war.

Can ethnocentrism be decreased or eliminated? Two major actions might help change the perspective: direct, personal (one-on-one) contact with an unalike other and intercultural communication training that is experiential. These actions can be implemented by increasing contact between unalike individuals. In this way, through travel and interactions, people can become aware of others' patterns and learn to accept them as being as valid as their own patterns. And through training, individuals can understand the nature of their ethnocentric beliefs and increase their empathy by experiencing the unalike culture.

Some communication experts believe that ethnocentrism must be replaced by *cultural relativism* through a concentrated effort to educate students about the dangers of being self-absorbed. "*Cultural relativism* is a worldview and standpoint that no culture as such is superior to any other one, and that any culture deserves to be described, understood, and judged on its own premises."[36]

They further contend that to counter ethnocentrism, students must be taught and given the opportunity to recognize individual differences and the uniqueness of each person and culture. The Semester at Sea[37] program has college students traveling to ten to fifteen countries during a semester. Students are instructed about the unique features of each nation, including its language, treatment of the sexes, nonverbal patterns, and religions. A student in the program who took an Intercultural Communication class expressed the point in a letter to one of your authors who was his instructor: "When people ask me about the voyage and what it taught me about cultures, I often respond with the statement, 'It's not good. It's not bad. It's just different.' Those words of yours brought home a new-found awareness that I can use every day as I continue to encounter people and cultures different from my own. I truly learned the meaning of differences."[38]

First Amendment Speech

In the United States, one of our cultural cornerstones is freedom of speech. As a competent communicator, you should know your privileges and responsibilities concerning your constitutional rights. Your communication liberties are soundly influenced by the First Amendment to the U.S. Constitution, which bans Congress from passing laws "abridging the freedom of speech." Therefore, when we are confronted with the question of the meaning of **first amendment speech** the answer tends to be that it is the protected right to speak without restrictions—to be free to say what we want. In reality, however, the language of the First Amendment leaves much to interpretation. Because of this, courts have been called on to establish standards and guidelines to resolve free-speech disputes.

The 2010–2011 session of the Supreme Court was topped with First Amendment cases. Included were provocative anti-gay protests at military funerals, a California law banning the sale of violent video games to children, and whether Arizona's income tax credit scholarship program for religious schools is in violation of the constitutional separation of church and state.[39]

Communicating Socially

Controversy: Are We Becoming an Uncivil Society?

Following the attempted assassination of Arizona Congresswoman Gabrielle Giffords in 2011, the issue of the lack of civility was raised. In an opinion piece, Deepak Chopra, author of *The Soul of Leadership*, wrote about the U.S.: "America prides itself on its uncivil liberties as well as its civil ones. The fabled melting pot was always a boiling cauldron of differences. We've learned to live at the boil as no other society has. But the dark side of our uncivil liberty is violence. Inflammatory and vitriolic words are a form of violence. In many wisdom traditions, speech that is imbued with compassion and love is used as a form of healing. Our society today had the unmistakable symptoms of inflammatory disease, with violence and hostility at home and abroad. How long can we live with this sickness?. . . Can we start our healing process with civil speech while maintaining our civil liberties?"

Source: From "The Tucson tragedy, are we becoming an uncivil society?" *Time*, January 12, 2011.

REFLECT ON THIS: Do you believe that we can start our healing process through civil speech while maintaining our civil liberties?

An investigation of court cases shows the complexity of the issue of freedom of speech:

- A student at Los Angeles City College sued the instructor of his public speaking course because the teacher called him a "fascist bastard" and told him to "ask God what your grade is." This followed the student's speech on his religious views about marriage. The question was whether the informative speech was "polemical, not informative" and was "hateful propaganda" since it "opposed same sex marriage" and "is inappropriate in a public school."[40]
- A group of student organizations, known collectively as the Free Speech Coalition of West Virginia University, sued the university over the school's free-speech zone policy. In *Free Speech Coalition of West Virginia University v. Hardesty*, the student groups allege that the policy, which now allows for seven campus free-speech zones, violates the students' First Amendment rights.[41]

The question of free speech also invades the world of electronic media, such as Twitter. "One man thought he was just bantering with his pals when he joked about blowing an airport sky high. Another was reacting to a radio phone-in when he mused about stoning a journalist to death."[42] The writer of the first tweet lost his job and faces several thousand dollars in fines. The other tweet resulted in an arrest on suspicion of sending an offensive or indecent message.

Facebook is not immune from the question of free speech. An example of the ramifications of posting on someone's wall were brought out when a Connecticut-based ambulance service fired an emergency medical technician after she criticized her supervisor on Facebook. The question is whether offensive statements are protected by federal law.[43]

Is there justification for limitations placed on freedom of speech, or are such restrictions unacceptable?

One of the justifications offered for limitations on freedom of speech is that *words are deeds*. It contends that some symbolic behavior may be so harmful that we are justified in restraining it. A verbal threat in public may be considered so serious that it warrants an arrest. A presidential assassin might plead that he or she acted for the purpose of sending a political message to the public. To regard such a claim as legitimate may blur the line that must be maintained between speech and action.[44]

A further contention against limitations on freedom of speech proposes that "more often than not, *the free-speech issue becomes a weapon to fight some other cause* ... flag burning, blocking access to abortion clinics, pornography."[45] This assertion suggests that it is not freedom of speech or the First Amendment that is being dealt with in these cases, but rather the causes themselves.

Also questioned is: If one speaker is banned, must every speaker be banned?

A leading civil libertarian wonders where the founding fathers, those who wrote the Constitution of the United States, would draw the line. He concludes "that we ought not to censor the speech of even the most violent leaders."[46] Echoing Jefferson, he adds that any censorship would not prevent either violence or incitement.[47]

In her U.S. Supreme Court nomination hearings, Ruth Bader Ginsburg stated, "We are a society that has given, beyond any other, maximum protection for the speech that we hate, and on the other hand, are concerned for the quality and dignity of individuals. Those two principles collide in this area [hate speech]."[48] Hate speech challenges effective communicators in both face-to-face and online contexts.[49] Following the September 11, 2001, terrorist attacks, much controversy arose concerning how many and what kind of restrictions could or should be placed on an individual's rights. Six weeks after the terrorist attacks, Congress, over vigorous objections from civil liberties organizations, approved the USA PATRIOT Act.[50] The act has allowed surveillance of U.S. citizens even when there was no probable cause and minimal judicial involvement, roving wiretaps, eavesdropping on inmates' attorney–client conversations, and the questioning of 5,000 people, who appear to have been selected according to their ethnicity or religion.[51]

While some people perceive the narrowing of freedoms, other people believe that because of the Internet, freedom of speech is more pervasive than ever. In many ways, a wider range of people have more direct communication through the Internet. Social networking, blogs, and websites, for example, give people an opportunity to communicate what they think.

How might this conflict about freedom of speech affect you on a personal level? Should your communication instructor limit what topics you may speak about in a speech? Should Internet providers be allowed to censor what you send or receive? Should your collegiate organization be allowed to bring a speaker to campus who attacks others' religious or ethnic heritage? Should an instructor lower your grade because you speak out in class in opposition to her view?

Not only is what you are allowed to and not allowed to communicate an issue, but also important is knowing what your ethical standards are as you act as a speaker and as a listener.

Ethics and Comunication

Ethics is the systematic study of what should be the grounds and principles for acceptable and unacceptable behavior.[52] Ethics are not just something that individuals practice; instead, they are the perceived values shared by a society. The importance of conducting our human affairs in ethical, responsible ways has recently been highlighted by corporate financial scandals, political campaigns that used lies and innuendoes to coerce voters and perhaps even to take this country to war in Iraq, the role of pharmaceutical and health-care companies in influencing government decisions regarding their industries, and the role of advertising in persuading people to buy products and services that are often unnecessary and sometimes dangerous. These situations have prompted a renewed emphasis on ethics.

Your *personal ethical value system* is the basis for your decision making and your understanding of why you will or will not take a particular stand or action. It is the basis for your communication ethics.

Communication Ethics

Over the decades, speech communication instructors and theorists have stressed that competent speakers should, by definition, be ethical speakers. "Potential ethical issues are inherent in any instance of communication between humans to the degree that the communication can be judged on a right–wrong dimension, involves possible significant influence on other humans, and to the degree that the communicator consciously chooses specific ends sought and communicative means to achieve those ends."[53] Therefore, it is contended that speakers should give the audience assistance in making wise decisions and that speakers' decisions about what to say should be based on moral principles.

Questions arise when speakers, whether verbally or in print, spread information which is questionable or untrue. For example, blogger Ben Domenech asserted in a CBS column that then Supreme Court nominee Elena Kagan was gay.[54] The White House demanded a retraction for "false charges" because of the lack of proof. The acquisition was picked up by blogger Andrew Sullivan. When Sullivan was accused of spreading false information in an e-mail interview he said, "one needs to have no evidence" and "we have been told by many that she is gay" (he failed to clarify who the "they" were). A journalism professor who specializes in ethics indicated that "Sullivan's explanation of his role as a blogger is problematic."[55]

Representative Keith Ellison, a Minnesota Democratic, had to pen a response to an attack by Judson Phillips, founder of the Tea Party Nation, who urged that Ellison be voted out of Congress for being a Muslim who supports terrorists. When Phillips was accused of being unethical, he offered no definitive proof other than to say, "I am not going to apologize because I'm bothered by a religion that says kill the infidel, especially when I am the infidel. I learned everything I needed to know about tolerance on September 11th."[56] Ellison stated, "I issue a call to civility, and urge Americans to reject the divisive rhetoric of Judson Phillips, including calls for my defeat solely because of my religion."[57]

Ethical Communicators

Ethical communicators are those who "respect the integrity of ideas and concerns from the listeners."[58] They are generally defined as those who conform to the moral standards a society establishes for its communicators. Although this definition seems

Questions of right and wrong arise whenever people communicate. Ethical communication is fundamental to responsible thinking, decision making, and the development of relationships and communities within and across contexts, cultures, channels, and media. Moreover, ethical communication enhances human worth and dignity by fostering truthfulness, fairness, responsibility, personal integrity, and respect for self and others. We believe that unethical communication threatens the quality of all communication and consequently the well-being of individuals and the society in which we live. Therefore we, the members of the National Communication Association, endorse and are committed to practicing the following principles of ethical communication:

- We advocate truthfulness, accuracy, honesty, and reason as essential to the integrity of communication.
- We endorse freedom of expression, diversity of perspective, and tolerance of dissent to achieve the informed and responsible decision making fundamental to a civil society.
- We strive to understand and respect other communicators before evaluating and responding to their messages.
- We promote access to communication resources and opportunities as necessary to fulfill human potential and contribute to the well-being of families, communities, and society.
- We promote communication climates of caring and mutual understanding that respect the unique needs and characteristics of individual communicators.
- We condemn communication that degrades individuals and humanity through distortion, intimidation, coercion, and violence, and through the expression of intolerance and hatred.
- We are committed to the courageous expression of personal convictions in pursuit of fairness and justice.
- We advocate sharing information, opinions, and feelings when facing significant choices while also respecting privacy and confidentiality.
- We accept responsibility for the short- and long-term consequences for our own communication and expect the same of others.

FIGURE 1.8 NCA Credo for Ethical Communication

Source: "NCA Credo for Ethical Communication" by NCA Legislative Council, 1999. Copyright © 1999 by National Communication Association. Reprinted with permission. www.natcom.org

plausible, it contains a major flaw: The words ring hollow because it is impossible either to list or to gain acceptance for *universal* moral standards. Although some people claim they have the true answer, in reality there is no universal agreement on what exactly it means to be moral.

The National Communication Association, the major voice of communication educators, has approved a *Code of Ethics for Speakers*. (See Figure 1.8.) It isolates specific traits that define an ethical speaker in the Euro American culture. It also may have some implications for global communication as the organization has international members.

Because most readers of this book live in a society that stresses Western philosophy, the discussion of what it means to be an ethical communicator centers on this viewpoint. Nevertheless, this perspective may not be appropriate or acceptable to you, based on your ethnic, racial, and other cultural influences.

As a student of communication, the credo stresses that you should realize you:

- Should not knowingly expose an audience to lies
- Should not alter the truth
- Should tell the truth as you understand it

The question of free speech invades the world of electronic media. One man thought he was just bantering with his pals when he joked about blowing up an airport. He lost his job and faces several thousand dollars in fines.

- Should supply the necessary facts, definitions, descriptions, and substantiating information to lead the speaker to a reasonable conclusion
- Should not invent or fabricate statistics or other information intended to serve as a basis for proof of a contention or belief
- Should give credit to the source of information

Not only speakers but also listeners need to operate within an ethical framework. From the standpoint of the receiver, in most public and private communication, a fundamental implied and unspoken assumption is that words can be trusted and people will be truthful. This does not mean that you should accept everything that is said; doing so would be naive. To be an ethical receiver, you should listen carefully to the information presented and ask yourself whether the conclusions reached are reasonable and expected.

Be aware that there are urban legends, myths consisting of stories thought to be factual by those circulating them. They are not necessarily untrue, but they are often distorted, exaggerated, or sensationalized. These stories are often spread on the Internet. Before accepting accounts that may seem questionable, check them on www.snopes.com, which is a site that specializes in tracking down the facts concerning urban legends.

In Conclusion

IN CONCLUSION

Communication is a conscious or unconscious, intentional or unintentional process in which feelings and ideas are expressed as verbal and/or nonverbal messages sent, received, and comprehended. It can take the form of intrapersonal, interpersonal, or public messages. Three factors are present in any communicative event: the communicators, the purpose, and the setting. We communicate through our senses. The process of communication can be understood by investigating the linear, the interactional, and the transactional communication models and the components that make up the process. As a system, communication is directly influenced by culture. Media is an important source of communication. In the United States, multiculturalism is an important aspect of communication, as are freedom of speech and an understanding of what is meant by ethical communication.

LEARN BY DOING

1. Identify an experience in which your attempt to communicate was a failure. Use the classification of sources of noise given in the text to label the type of interference you encountered. Why did this happen? What, if anything, could you have done to correct the interference problem?
2. Describe a context in which you find it difficult to communicate. Describe a context in which you find it easy to communicate. Why did you select each one? What implications for communication are involved in your choices?
3. Describe the system of communication by which your family operates (or operated) by investigating the patterns of communication and the rules of operation. What were the advantages and disadvantages of that system?
4. Write one phrase or expression that is unique to your family or group of friends. It should be an expression that has meaning only for that group, not one commonly used in society as a whole. It may be an ethnic expression, an in-group reference, or some other special phrase. The other students will read the expression and try to figure out what it means. Draw inferences about semantic noise from this activity.
5. Individually, each student decides what he or she would do in each of the following situations. You will then be divided into small groups to discuss your answers and report back to the class as a whole on the choices made by each group.
   a. You are taking a public speaking course. The instructor requires three quoted references in the speech that you are to present in five minutes. You had a week to get ready but did not do the necessary research. Would you make up three references, not give the speech and get a failing grade, give the speech without the references and hope for the best, or take some other action? If you would take another action, what would it be?
   b. You have just finished eating in a restaurant. You check the bill and realize that the waiter has made a $10 error in your favor. The waiter sees your reaction and asks if anything is wrong. How do you respond?
   c. You look up during a test and see that your best friend, who needs a passing grade in this class to get off academic probation, is using cheat notes. You think the instructor also saw the action. As you hand in your paper, the instructor says to you, "Remember, this class operates on the honor system. Is there anything you want to say to me?" How do you respond?
6. Your class will discuss or debate the following resolution: "Resolved: A higher educational institution must be a platform for the debate of social issues. Therefore, it is resolved that [name of your college/university] allow, encourage, and invite *all* speakers to present their views in public forums on this campus."

7. Write a list of words or phrases that answer the question, "What factors or identities constitute my culture?" Your answers will be used by your instructor as the basis for a discussion of "What is culture?"

8. Answer this question. A class discussion will follow in which you need to state and defend your answer. A colleague and friend knocks on the door of your home one evening. "I've got great news," he says. "I'm buying the house of my dreams." You know that your friend will lose his job in the next few weeks as your company reorganizes. Your company has sworn you to secrecy until the announcement is made. What do you do?

KEY TERMS

communication 3
intrapersonal communication 3
interpersonal communication 4
public communication 4
selective communication 5
source 5
receiver 5
messages 5
feedback 5
frame of reference 5
perceptions 5
encode 6
primary signal system 6
decodes 6
channel 8
communication noise 9
linear model of communication 14
interactional model of communication 16
transactional model of communication 17
media 19
intracultural communication 22
intercultural communication 22
first amendment speech 27
ethical communicators 29

CHAPTER 2

Foundations of Verbal Language

origins of human language • symbols and functions of language • standard and nonstandard language

After reading this chapter, you should be able to

- Name and describe several theories of the origins of human language
- Analyze how thought is shaped by language
- Explain and illustrate how people select, process, use, and learn symbols
- Identify the features common to all languages
- Define and illustrate the emotive, phatic, cognitive, rhetorical, and identifying functions of language
- Explain the roles of ambiguity, vagueness, inference, and message adjustment in relation to language distortion
- Define and contrast standard versus nonstandard dialects, and relate the effects of speaking a nonstandard dialect
- Analyze slang as it relates to standard dialects
- Explain Standard American English
- Relate the effects of speaking a dialect or nonstandard language
- Describe the effects of using verbal language

Each culture conveys a value system to its children. These assumptions are reflected and reinforced in language, and language thus creates or recreates the culture's social reality.[1] "Language shapes thought. The effect is powerful enough that the private mental lives of speakers of different languages may differ dramatically, not only when they think in order to speak, but in all manner of cognitive tasks, including basic sensory perception."[2] "Language even shapes what we see. People have a better memory for colors if different shades have distinct names [e.g., dark blue or light blue, rather than blue]."[3]

There is a connection between the language we use, our self-perception, and our behavior. Language reflects our attitudes. Words can create categories and expectations so deep-seated that only such devices as affirmative action and anti-hate laws can force individuals to act differently than their language seems to allow. For example, the Supreme Court's decision in 1954 regarding *Brown v. Board of Education* caused widespread concerns in southern states and brought up not only changes in attitudes but also changes in the language used to describe white–black relations. Another vivid example took place when in 2010 there was a proposal for a mosque to be built in the vicinity of Ground Zero, the former site of the Twin Towers which were destroyed on 9/11. Glenn Beck and Newt Gingrich, both then Fox news employees, labeled those pushing the effort and their backers to be terrorists, "part of the stealth jihad."[4] The language creates an illusion, people believe the illusion, and the well is poisoned against the "enemy."

What is **language**? It is a system of arbitrary signals, such as sounds, gestures, or symbols, used by a nation, people, or distinct community to communicate thoughts and feelings. The system includes rules for combining its components, which is referred to as *grammar*.[5]

The study of language involves the study of meaning. The meaning is based on words, the way the words are placed together, and the backgrounds and experiences of the communicators. The channels by which the words are conveyed help create their meanings. When they appear on a printed page, words are linear, one-dimensional; their meaning is based on what the reader thinks the words mean, with no other clues for interpretation. But the words pick up additional dimensions when they are spoken because the rate, pitch, pause, and volume of the spoken words help us figure out the meaning of the words and the intent of the sender. Even more dimensions are available when the receiver can see the speaker and note facial expressions, gesture patterns, and body positions.

Origins of Human Language

The origin of language remains one of human evolution's enduring puzzles. Some anthropologists believe that two critical mutations in our human ancestors 200,000 years ago provided for a degree of control over mouth and throat muscles. They maintain that this control gave our ancestors the ability to create sounds that served as the foundation of language.[6]

Another researcher has proposed that language has its roots in gestures, not vocalics.[7] The theory suggests that speech evolved from grunts and vocal cries that were involuntary, emotional responses to human movements of the hands and face, gestures that people used to communicate with each other.[8]

A computer neuroscientist believes that speech is based on mental reflexes.[9]

However it started, "once speech caught on, it gave Homo sapiens a decisive advantage over less verbal rivals, including Homo erectus and the Neanderthals, whose lines eventually died out."[10] As one researcher puts it, "We talked them out of existence."[11]

Once verbal language was developed, an additional way to convey messages was needed, which resulted in the creation of written codes.

Language does not remain static; it is constantly changing. Changes in technology, lifestyles, and social attitudes lead to new words and phrases. For example, in the English language, each year, Merriam-Webster adds about 100 words to its dictionary.[12] Words recently added include "*locavore* (one who eats foods grown locally), *frenemy* (someone who acts like a friend but is really an enemy), *vlogs* (a blog that contains video material) and *webisode* (a TV show that can be viewed at a website)."[13] Other added words are *reggeaeton* (music of Puerto Rican origin that combines rap and Caribbean rhythms) and *flash mob* (a group of people summoned electronically to a designated spot at a specified time to perform an indicated action). The words are added because, "we've made the judgment that these [chosen words] are not just words used by specialists. These really are words that are so common that they regularly pop up in conversations."[14] The same publication crowned *austerity* (enforced or extreme economy) as the Word of the Year (2010),[15] while *The New Oxford American Dictionary* awarded the honor to *refudiate*, a verb Sarah Palin apparently invented."[16]

Sometimes when words are added due to usage, there is a protest regarding the word. McDonald's Corporation started a campaign to "ditch the dictionary definition of *McJob*,"[17] defined in *The Oxford English Dictionary* as "an unstimulating, low-paid job with few prospects."[18] McDonald's contended that "the definition is demeaning to its workers."[19] Both *The Oxford English Dictionary* and *Merriam-Webster Dictionary* declined to remove or change their definition, declaring that the definition was "accurate and appropriate."

There are 6,910 documented languages in the world."[20] "The ten most influential languages in the world are English, French, Spanish, Russian, Arabic, Chinese, German, Japanese, Portuguese and Hindi/Urda."[21]

"New York [City] is home to as many as 800 languages."[22] "It is the capital of language density in the world."[23]

Some languages are disappearing. As one linguist states, "We are surrounded by languages that are not going to be around even in 20 or 30 years."[24] Included in the disappearing languages are: Pennsylvania Dutch, Yiddish, Irish Gaelic, and Aramaic[25] (the original language of large sections of the biblical books of *Daniel* and *Ezra*, and the language spoken by Jesus).[26]

You might be surprised to know that several of the disappearing languages are spoken in the United States. Included are Siletz Dee-ni, the last of twenty-seven languages once spoken on the Siletz reservation in Oregon and Yuchi, a language once spoken by the Yuchi tribe.[27]

People in the United States speak English, right? In spite of the belief by some that English is the official language of the United States, there is

Culturally COMMUNICATING

Language Mirrors Life

Within each speech community, the language spoken mirrors human life—the personalities of the speakers, their attitudes and beliefs, their styles of thought and expression, their interactions with one another. Language so interpenetrates the experience of being human that neither language nor behavior can be understood without knowledge of both.

Source: From P. Farb, *Word play: What happens when people talk* (New York: Knopf, 1974), pp. 366–367.

REFLECT ON THIS:

1. Your family and friends influence your language. Name several phrases or words you use that are unique to your family or friends.
2. Name several attitudes you hold, which you express verbally or nonverbally, that display who you are.

nothing in the Constitution and no law that declares English the country's official or legal language.[28] It is interesting to note that the census indicates "nearly 1 in 5 people living in the United States speak a language at home other than English."[29]

Selecting and Processing Symbols

How are we able to select the symbols we want to use at the split second when the need arises to use them? Our senses bombard us with signals that beg to be interpreted and stored in our information bank. In response, the cortex, an area of the human brain that stores, computes, and eventually processes some of these incoming signals, puts forth the necessary information. This operation, the **cybernetic process**, functions much like a computer. For example, if a person in one of your classes holds up a cylindrical piece of graphite about one-eighth of an inch in diameter, covered with wood, painted yellow, with an eraser on one end and a sharpened point on the other, and asks you what the object is, if you speak English, you will probably respond, "A pencil."

By investigating the process you used to identify the pencil, you can gain an understanding of the operation of the *cybernetic process* (Figure 2.1). You have been taught the word *pencil (input)*, and it has been placed *(stored)* in your cortex along with the image of a pencil. Thus, when you see an object made of graphite, wood, and an eraser, the sight of the object *(stimulus)* activates your storage system to sort through its stored visual signals *(search)*, find the symbol that represents the image *(recall)*, and allows you to identify the combination of the stored term and the object, and you say, "Pencil" *(output)*. You have just experienced the cybernetic process in action.

A mathematician/logician who played an important role in the development of high-speed computers coined the term *cybernetics*.[30] It comes from the Greek word for "steersman." The term is significant in that the means for internal control and communication in an animal—its nervous system—are similar to those of self-regulating machines, such as furnaces with thermostats. In human beings, the input comes in the form of a sense image *(taste, smell, sight, sound, touch)* that is tested against stored material *(symbols, images)*; the output *(feedback)* represents the symbol or image. Because humans can't be flawlessly programmed, there is always the possibility of human communication being less than perfect. This error factor accounts for some of our language problems, such as why you sometimes can't remember the information when you take a test, even though you studied. Sometimes the stored information is incorrect. Sometimes not enough information has been stored. Sometimes an overload occurs. Just as machines trip circuit breakers because the demand placed on their circuitry is too great, so too can you trip psychological breakers from too much pressure. It is possible to become so upset that you block messages from coming forth. But when the emotional pressure is removed, the normal flow returns. That is why experts advise people taking a test or under other stress to "turn off" every so often—look out the window, put their head down, walk around, sing a song to themselves to break the tension—and then return to their work.

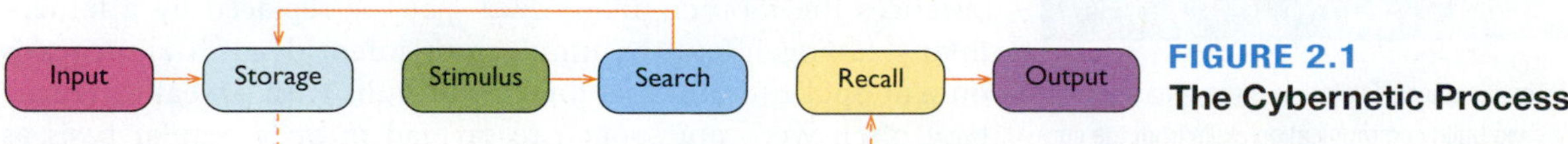

FIGURE 2.1
The Cybernetic Process

Cybernetic processing starts to develop in humans at about the third month after birth. It does not become fully operative, however, until a child is capable of processing the image–symbol relationship, selecting symbols, and articulating the symbols.

Look around you and focus on one object, then identify it. Did you respond quickly with a word for the object? Now think back to the experience. Did you (as you did with *pencil*) think of all the parts that describe the object you just named? Probably not. Instead, you looked at the object, recognized it, assigned the symbol to it if you could, and then spoke or thought the relevant word. All of this happened below your level of awareness.

Try another experiment. Picture these objects: a pen, an apple, and a glass of milk. You probably had little trouble "seeing" these objects. This visualization means that you have been exposed to the objects and can identify their symbols. Try the experiment again and picture these objects: a finger, a book, and a jerboa. The first two words in the series were probably familiar, but what about the third? *Jerboa?* A jerboa is a mouse-like rodent found in North Africa and Asia that has long hind legs for jumping and looks a little like a miniature kangaroo with the head of a mouse. You had no trouble with the words *finger* and *book* because you have been told what to call them. But few U.S. Americans have had any exposure to the word *jerboa.*

Consider your symbol selection in this way. As you acquire language, you do so by hooking ideas together. When you pictured the "pencil," you saw the form of what you have been taught was identified with the word *pencil.* You saw the image and searched for the word identification you have been taught, *the symbol*. It is easy to do this with those items in our vocabulary that we can visualize. It is more difficult with abstract words. For example, what is your image of *nice* or *good* or *bad?* These conceptual words cause us problems because they have no exact definition, no image. In these cases, we probably imagine a definition and hook the word that describes it to the concept. That explains why we can often get a universal agreement in English on what a pencil is but not on what a *good* person is.

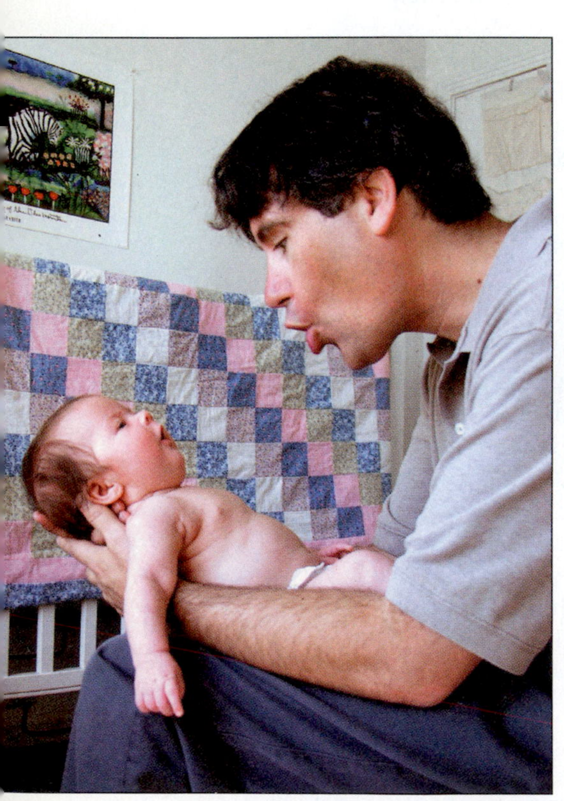

The Language-Explosion Theory proposes that we build communication skills from the core of language we develop early in life.

Learning Symbols

There are varying views of how we acquire our unique language along with our beliefs, values, and attitudes. Included are the Language-Explosion Theory and the Significant-Other Theory.[31]

Language-Explosion Theory The **Language-Explosion Theory** proposes that we build communication skills from the core of language we develop early in life. If you were asked to name the one person who had the most influence on your ability to communicate, you probably would name an immediate family member. The most common response is "my mother." In some instances the mother–infant *dyad* (pair) is replaced by a father–infant, sibling–infant, or grandparent–infant dyad. It all depends on who spoke to the child the most. Adults with a weak language base often were not spoken to or read to on a regular basis as youngsters.

Whatever the child's primary influence, his or her circles of influence quickly expand to include the communication patterns of many other people. The child's neighborhood, the area of the country in which he or she lives, and the schools attended all influence overall ability to communicate, as do religious institutions and exposure to the media.

Significant-Other Theory When we are young, all of the sources around us influence us. But at a certain stage in our lives, we start selecting specific people or groups whose language, ideals, and beliefs we allow to influence us. These people become the significant others in our lives, and their effects are great. Indeed, social psychologists contend that we have no identity whatsoever except in relationship to others. This view is called the **Significant-Other Theory**,[32] which centers on the principle that our understanding of self is built by those who react to and comment on our language, actions, ideas, beliefs, and mannerisms. Thus, if you respect someone, you are likely to adjust your behavior and your messages to derive the most encouraging evaluation from that person.

You constantly come into contact with people who have the potential to be significant others in your life. If you think about who you are today and compare your current language, beliefs, values, and attitudes with those you held five years ago, you probably will find some noticeable differences. These very likely were brought about by your acceptance of someone else's influence.

The Concept of Meaning

Understanding what language is, and how we acquire and access it, gives us an important basis for understanding how meaning results. The study of the sounds, structure, and rules of human language is **linguistics**. It tells us that certain features are common to all languages. Among these are:

- *Languages are based on a set of symbols, both verbal and nonverbal.* In English, we use the letters *s-c-i-s-s-o-r-s,* for example, to represent an instrument that is used for cutting. Or in the U.S. Euro American culture, forming a circle with the thumb and index finger and extending the other three fingers signifies that everything is "okay."
- *Languages that are alphabetically based recognize the differences between vowels and consonants.* In English, the vowel sounds are represented by the letters *a, e, i, o,* and *u,* singly or in combination. The consonants are such letters as *b, c, r,* and *m.* Not all languages use an alphabet. Some languages—for example, Chinese—are pictographical. A symbol represents a single word and is not made up of letters.
- *Languages have ordered structural categories, such as verbs, nouns, and objects.* English is symbolic; we use words to represent objects and ideas. The sentence *The car is beautiful* designates the object *(car)* and expresses an idea about the car *(is beautiful).*
- *Words in and of themselves are not inherently meaningful.* The meaning derived from our language stems from how we interpret the symbols used in that language. Because words carry no meaning as such, we derive our meaning for the symbols through our own backgrounds, experiences, and perceptions. Two generations can be divided by the same language. Examine this conversation between a father and son who are shopping for clothing for the youth.

Father: (picks up a shirt) Do you like this?

Boy: I'm down with that.

The father puts down the shirt and starts to walk away.

Boy: Where are you going? I want that shirt.

Father: You said you didn't like it.

Boy: No, I didn't.

The *Sapir-Whorf Hypothesis,* also known as the *Linguistic Relativity Hypothesis,* theorizes that a person's understanding of the world and how the person behaves in it are based on the language a person speaks.[33] The theory, which is controversial due to the lack of definitive research, indicates that different language patterns yield differing patterns of thought. For example, various cultures have differing viewpoints regarding color perception. As Figure 2.2 illustrates, those speaking English tend to perceive a rainbow as "seeing" six bands of color. The Shonas of Zimbabwe and Mozambique describe the rainbow with four bands, whereas the Bassa language, used by those in parts of Liberia and Sierra Leone, perceive two bands.[34] These descriptions create our "color reality" of the world. Doubt this? What's your visual and linguistic image or description of the colors amaranth, fuchsia, and puce? Are any of these names of colors you don't know? Those who believe in the concept of linguistic relativity would say that if you don't have those words in your vocabulary, you are incapable of having an image or description (meaning). This could account for why, when listening, since we have different *frames of reference,* our interpretation may vary from the sender's intent. Curious about amaranth, fuchsia, and puce? In English, they are all words that represent varying shades of pink.

We assign words **denotative meanings**—direct, explicit meanings—when we want to categorize them. For instance, the denotative word *dog* carries the denotative meaning of a "four-legged, furry animal; a canine." This denotation enables anyone to classify the animal and understand the literal characteristics of the term. In contrast, *connotative words* have an implied or suggested meaning. Words such as *good, pretty,* and *nice* have many **connotative meanings**. It is often difficult for people to agree on exactly what these words mean.

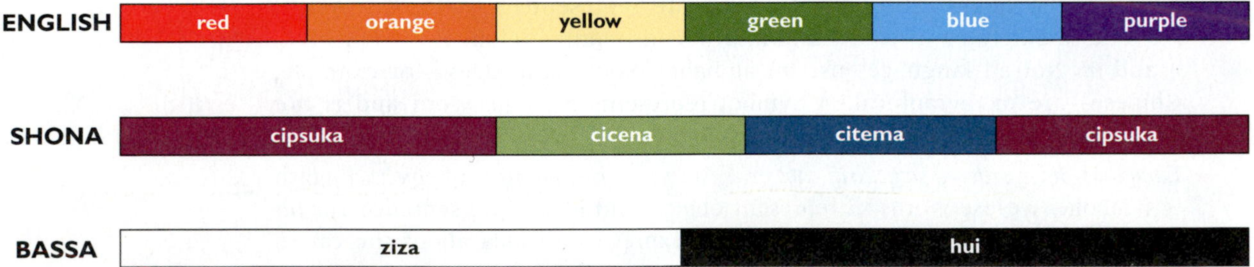

FIGURE 2.2 Colors of a Rainbow

When you look at a rainbow, how many colors do you see? Each language encourages its speakers to tell certain things and to ignore others. All human eyes see the same colors because colors have their own reality in the physical world. But when speakers in most European [and U.S.] communities look at a rainbow, they imagine they see six sharp bands of colors. People elsewhere in the world, who speak languages unrelated to European ones, have their own ways of partitioning the color spectrum.

Source: From *Word Play:* "What Happens When People Talk" by Peter Farb, p. 197. Copyright © 1973 by Peter Farb. Used by permission of Alfred A. Knopf, a division of Random House, Inc.

To make matters even more confusing, all meanings for symbols are not easily definable. Our language is filled with connotative meanings that derive from denotative words. Thus, the denotative word *dog* may carry pleasant connotations, such as *lovable, friendly,* and *warm,* if we have had pleasant associations with these animals. A child once attacked by a dog, however, may find that the word has negative connotations; to that child, *dog* may carry the connotative meaning of *a dangerous, snarling, biting animal.*

Along with making us aware of connotative problems, people who study **semantics**—the relationship of language and meaning—warn us to avoid a rigid orientation that sees everything as falling into a *two-valued orientation* that only allows for the options of good or bad, or right or wrong. This type of narrow reasoning leaves no room for "neither right nor wrong" or "could be right or could be wrong."

Have you, as a student, ever taken a true-or-false test and found that when the instructor gave back the exam, the "correct" answers differed from yours? If a question asked for a specific definition, date, or name of a person, there was no issue—your answer was clearly right or wrong. However, if a question contained connotative words that could be interpreted in various ways, then you and the instructor may have been at odds. To compensate for this either–or situation, some instructors tell students, "Read the question. If you can't clearly identify a true or false answer, pick the answer that you think is correct and explain your choice, or indicate that the answer could be either true or false and tell why."

Also, how irritated do you get when your literature instructor says, "This is what the poem means"? This manner of thinking—in which something that is not provable is put into a two-valued format ("my way or wrong")—reflects irrational thinking. There may be numerous ways of interpreting the poem.

Social issues are sometimes forced into a right or wrong/good or bad structure. For example, consider these questions: Should the United States have become involved in the war in Iraq? Is the death penalty justified? Should gay marriage be legalized? There may be political, cultural, or religious perceptions of the "correct" answers to them, but that doesn't make the conclusions two-valued. If these questions had clear "yes" or "no" answers, there would be no controversies. However, controversy is based on differences of perceptions and no clear way to prove whatever conclusion is reached. Therefore, these questions are not candidates for two-valued/either-or answers.

Are you interested in finding out if you use two-valued reasoning? If so, fill out the Two-Valued Reasoning Questionnaire.

Two-Valued Reasoning Questionnaire

DIRECTIONS: This activity is designed to ascertain your value orientation. Read each statement and indicate if it is *T* (true, proved accurate by information provided in the story); *F* (false, proved inaccurate by the information provided in the story); or *I* (inconclusive or cannot be proved accurate or inaccurate because the story does not indicate whether the information is true or false). (Check your answers on page 464.)

Dale went to a travel agency to arrange some plane reservations. When Dale arrived in St. Louis, it was only two days before the wedding. After the wedding, the bride and groom took a trip to Hawaii.

a. Dale arrived in St. Louis two days before the wedding.
b. Dale got married in St. Louis.
c. She went to a travel agency.
d. The plane reservation to get to the wedding in St. Louis was made by a travel agent.
e. Dale went to Hawaii on her honeymoon.

A sender should attempt to use language as precisely as possible to reduce misunderstanding and thus avoid semantic noise. The use of definitions, examples, synonyms, and explanations can serve to clarify terminology. Consider an example: A dentist says to an assistant, "Hand me the instrument." The assistant looks at a tray of fifteen different instruments and responds, "Which one?" Obviously, the word *instrument* was so imprecise in this situation that the assistant was unable to determine the intended meaning.

Remember that not just the source has a responsibility in the transaction; the receiver is also an active participant and must filter for potential noise factors. Following the format of the interactional model of communication (page 15)—giving feedback, such as asking questions and repeating the message—can aid in clarifying the meaning in a communication interaction.

The Functions of Language

The way in which a person uses language is affected not only by the vocabulary available but also by the functions of language.[35] These functions are generally classified into five categories: emotive, phatic, cognitive, rhetorical, and identifying.

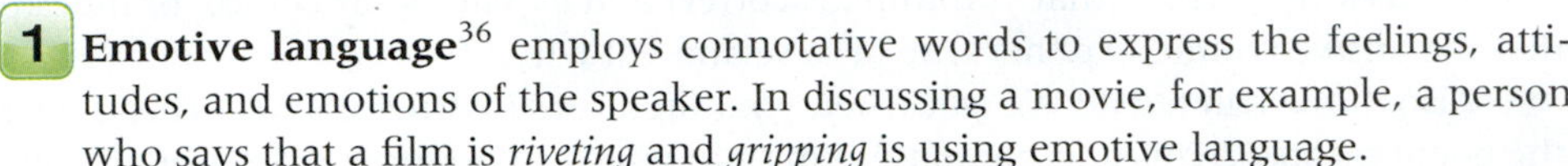

1 **Emotive language**[36] employs connotative words to express the feelings, attitudes, and emotions of the speaker. In discussing a movie, for example, a person who says that a film is *riveting* and *gripping* is using emotive language.

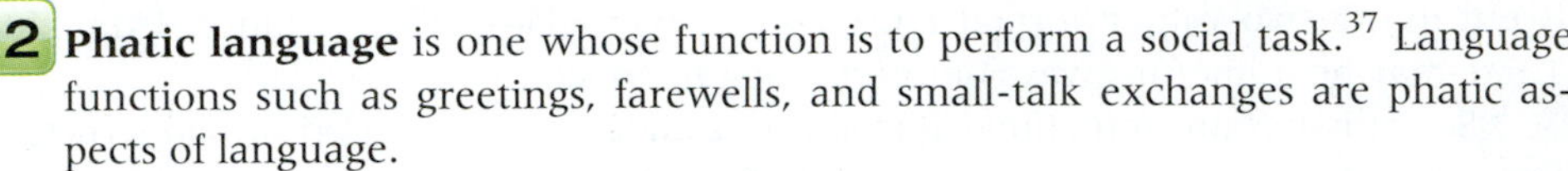

2 **Phatic language** is one whose function is to perform a social task.[37] Language functions such as greetings, farewells, and small-talk exchanges are phatic aspects of language.

COMMUNICATING in Careers

Linguistic Gobbledygook Has Taken over America's Conference Rooms

"For people bent on achieving superstar status in the business world, knowing one language is often not enough. Unfortunately the second tongue most popular to many in American corporate types isn't Spanish, German, French, Italian or Chinese. It's jargon, an amalgamation of terms with unknown origins and delivered with no explanation."

Jargon-slingers lurk everywhere.

A new crop of buzzwords usually sprouts every three to five years. Some can be useful, others are less than useful, often devious.

What do you think is meant by *delayering*? Delayering means managers are being fired. It's the latest manifestation of *rightsizing* and *downsizing*.

"People use jargon because they want to sound smart and credible when, in fact, they sound profoundly dim-witted and typically can't be understood."

Source: From "The Most Annoying Business Jargon" by Christopher Steiner, *Forbes*, January 14, 2011.

REFLECT ON THIS:

1. What do you think these gobbledygook jargon words mean: drill down, let's talk that, ducks in a row, hard stop, price point, synergize? (To find the definition go to the online source reference for this activity.)
2. What problems are caused by use of gobbledygook jargon words?

3 The function of **cognitive language** is to convey information.[38] Cognitive language tends to be denotative. This section on the functions of language is an example of cognitive language.

4 The purpose of **rhetorical language** is to influence thoughts and behaviors. The speaker employs words to be persuasive by using emotionally vivid pictures and drawing implications while developing logical appeals. A speech supporting organ donations that use examples of people who died because organs weren't available is an example of the rhetorical function of language.

5 The role of **identifying language** centers on naming persons or things specifically, thus being able to clarify exactly what we are speaking about—for example, *Ming went to Midway Mall.* Using the name *Ming,* rather than *she* or *someone,* is identifying language that clarifies who (Ming) and where she went (Midway Mall). Compare that to, *She went to the mall.* Which is more precise?

Identification also carries implications beyond just hanging a name on something. There are cultural inferences for many people, places, and things. In Sanskrit, for example, the word for *name* is derived from *gna,* meaning "to know."[39] Naming defines people and influences communication responses. In the Bible, the book of Genesis reports that Adam's dominion over animals was demonstrated by his being given the *power* to name them. And the North American Indian "regards his [her] name as a distinct part of his [her] personality, just as much as his [her] eyes or teeth."[40]

To be unnamed is to be unknown, to have no identity. Names can be positive, elevating the in-group with positive terms, or negative, stigmatizing the outgroup. The out-group is generally dehumanized, and this justifies oppression or even extermination. Hitler used the technique of dehumanization before and during World War II to attack Jews by labeling them *enemies of the country* and taking away their name identities and branding them with numbers, making them no more than cattle. Thus, it was "okay" to slaughter them. Native Americans were debased when they were given the name *savages,* implying they were less than human. For years, male terms for females included demeaning names such as *chick* (dumb fowl) and *doll* (a toy to be played with). To avoid the results of negative labels, some groups have changed their names. For example, in the 1960s, civil rights leaders rejected the terms *Negro* and *colored* as historical terms that identified a weak and controlled people, and labeled themselves *black* as a clear identifier of their individuality, their skin color. Later came the belief that a name should connect the people to their country of origin, so the name was changed to *African American.*[41] Much of what is called hate speech falls within the realm of identification. The labels become the identification that demoralizes the recipient, and a tool to be used as the reason for psychological or physical destruction. From this hate speech perspective, it becomes acceptable to bash a *faggot* or burn down the store of a *rag head.*

Language Distortion

Words stand for different meanings. People intentionally or unintentionally distort information as they process it, and people intentionally or unintentionally use language that is unclear. These factors lead to **language distortion**, which is caused by ambiguity, vagueness, inferences, or message adjustment.[42]

Ambiguity can be present when a word has more than one interpretation. For example, does the word *hog* mean "a fat pig," "someone who eats too much," "a person who controls others' attention," "a large car," or "a motorcycle"? All of these definitions are appropriate depending on the context. Fortunately, ambiguity can often be overcome if the listener refers to the *hog* word's context to determine whether it describes an overindulging dinner guest or the purchase of a Harley motorcycle.

Vagueness results when words or sentences lack clarity. Use of words such as *it, they, he,* and *things like that* are vague unless we specifically know to whom or to what the speaker is referring. For clarity, nouns are more precise than pronouns.

Many connotative words, because they have no specific definition, are vague. A form of vagueness that is deceptive, evasive, or confusing is **doublespeak**.[43] It is the intended or accidental purpose of doublespeak to mislead, distort reality, make the bad seem good, create a false verbal map of the world, or create incongruity between reality and what is said or not said. Examples of doublespeak abound.

President George W. Bush appeared to use a language of his own, which became known as *Bushism,* "peculiar words, phrases, pronunciations, malapropisms and semantic or linguistic errors and gaffes that appeared in his speeches."[44] He stated, for example, "We're going to—we'll be sending a person on the ground there pretty soon to help implement the malaria initiative, and that initiative will mean spreading nets and insecticides throughout the country so that we can see a reduction in the death of young children that—a death that we can cure."[45]

Inferences result when we interpret beyond available information or jump to conclusions without using all of the information available. If we do not have enough material, we complete an idea with what seems logical to us, what we have experienced in the past, or what we hope or fear will be the potential outcome. Read the following sentence quickly:

The cow jump over over thee noon.

Did you see *jump,* or did you read the word as *jumped?* What about the first and the second *over,* or *thee* and *noon?* Many people see the first couple of words and, based on their experience, instinctively infer the nursery rhyme statement, "The cow jumped over the moon."

The function of *cognitive language* is to convey information.

The Languages We Use

Language, like chemical compounds, has a structure. There is a limited set of elements—vowels and consonants—and these are combined to produce words, which in turn can be compounded into sentences.[46] It is the work of the **linguist**—a social scientist who studies the structures of various languages—to provide concepts that describe languages.

"Systematic and rule-governed differences exist between languages."[47] "Each language is a collection of similar **dialects** [a social or regional variation of a language]. Dialects, like languages, differ from each other in terms of pronunciation, vocabulary, grammar, and *prosody* [accent or tone]."[48] Over long periods of time, dialects may develop into separate languages. For instance, French, Italian, and Spanish were originally dialects of Latin.[49] Each speaker of a language speaks some dialect of it or a combination of dialects.

> **Socially COMMUNICATING**
>
> **The Little Word that Could**
>
> What is the world's most popular spoken and gestured word? The symbol is "okay," "o.k.," "okey dokey," "okay," or the circle formed by the thumb and pointing finger with the other three fingers extended. It was the first word spoken on the moon. "Okay, let's roll," was the command for the heroic charge against the terrorists on the 9/11 plane that was intended to crash into the White House." It is one of the most often used word in texting: k.
>
> *Source:* From Jeremy McCarter, "The Little Word That Could," *Newsweek*, November 8, 2010.

There are significant variations in languages within the United States based on region, social class, religious and ethnic group, gender, and age. The same item may carry different word identifiers according to the region of the country. Philadelphia's *hoagie* is a *bomber* in upstate New York, a *hero* in New York City, a *grinder* or *sub* in Boston, a *Cuban sandwich* in Miami, and an *Italian* in Kansas City.

In reality, the dialects of the English language have more similarities than differences. For this reason, speakers of different English dialects can communicate with relative ease, although sometimes, an **accent**—the pronunciation and intonation used by a person—may cause some difficulty in understanding. Southerners, for example, may be difficult for some northerners to understand, and the "New York–New Jersey" sound is clearly identifiable yet not easily understood by those outside that area.

A common mistake is to view one dialect as best. No single dialect of a language is *the* language. But in every language, there is a continuum of prestige dialects from the lowest to the highest. High-prestige dialects are called **standard dialects**, and low-prestige dialects are called **nonstandard dialects**. The dialects of those who are in power, have influence, and are educated become the standard dialects of a language; and the literature, science, and official records are written using the vocabulary and grammar that approximate the standard dialects.[50]

Not only do dialects and accents create some difficulties, but the choice of which to use also can create controversy.

Standard American English

To the surprise of many, the United States has no legal language. The *English-only movement,* based on the concept that the glue that holds a society together is the ability of the citizens to interact with each other, and that in the U.S. the language of interaction should be English, is attempting to change that through constitutional amendments and state and city laws.[51] About 30 states already have English-only laws requiring them to conduct official business in English.[52]

Some linguists contend that so long as no single pattern of language has been legally declared, there can be no such thing as a standard by which American English can be judged. In spite of this contention, there are generally accepted patterns of pronunciation, semantics, and syntax.

Standard American English is the language generally recognized by linguists as representative of the general population of the United States.[53] It is the oral form usually spoken by national news personalities and generally characterized by the oral sounds of the residents of the Midwest and West. Standard American English differs from the dialects spoken in the other principal regional-pronunciation areas: the Midland, New England, and the South. (See Figure 2.3.)

Although there may not be one "best" way of pronunciation, if some pronunciations are used, they become problematic. The words *pitcher* and *picture* do not have the same meaning and are not pronounced the same way. Such words as "hunderd" *(hundred),* "liberry" *(library),* "secatary" *(secretary),* and "alls" *(all)* linguistically do not exist. Words ending with *-ing,* such as *going* and *coming,* when pronounced as "goin" and "comin" can result in negative listener reaction regarding the speaker's sophistication. Saying "jeet yit?" is not a substitute for *Did you eat yet? Many* isn't "minnie," and *didn't* is not "dint," and there is no such word as "nu- uh" (often used as a negative response to "uh-huh").

The Standard American English words and grammatical forms are those of nationally published magazines (such as *Time*) and newspapers (e.g., *USA Today*).

Culturally COMMUNICATING

English Is a Crazy Language

Let's face it—English is a crazy language. There is no egg in eggplant; no apple in pineapple. English muffins weren't invented in England and French fries aren't necessarily native to France. (Belgium claims they were conceived in their country.) Boxing rings are square and a guinea pig is neither from Guinea nor is it a pig. How can a slim chance and a fat chance be the same thing, while a wise man and a wise guy are opposites? And, think of this: The farm is used to produce produce. The soldier decided to desert his dessert in the desert. Since there is no time like the present, he thought it was time to present the present. The wind was too strong to wind the sail.

You have to marvel at the unique lunacy of a language in which your house can burn up as it burns down, in which you fill in a form by filling it out and in which an alarm goes off by going on.

REFLECT ON THIS: Based on the idea presented, what are the implications for those trying to learn and/or non-native speakers who try to communicate in English?

FIGURE 2.3
Principal Regional Pronunciation Areas

Source: "Principal Regional Pronunciation Areas" from *The Cultural Geography of the United States,* A Revised Edition by Wilbur Zelinsky. Copyright © 1992 by Wilbur Zelinsky. Printed and Electronically reproduced by permission of Pearson Education, Inc., Upper Saddle River, New Jersey.

Words creep into the general American language usage, become understood, but are not officially part of the language, meaning they are not in standard dictionary. Terms such as "mama grizzly" came into usage during and following Sarah Palin's run for Vice President in 2008. She was not referring to a large brown bear, but a "conservative woman with common sense."[54] Other terms that fit into the unofficial use category are *soccer mom* (suburban mothers who are constantly driving their children to various activities) and *Joe Six-Pack* (blue collar men).[55]

Some words become hot-button terms as they insight strong reactions. When the word *sharia*, for example, which in Arabic means *way* or *path* is used by speakers to explain an idea, it insights response and "becomes a rallying cry for those critical of Islam."[56]

In addition to dialects and accents, slang plays a role in language.

Slang

The English language contains somewhere between 600,000 and 1 million words. But the average U.S. American's vocabulary consists of about 20,000 words, 2,000 of which may be slang.[57]

Slang denotes words that are related to a specific activity or incident and are immediately understood by members of a particular group. Sometimes slang terms such as *cool* start out as an in-group term and become a generally used term. *Cool*, which, early on, was used commonly to describe a smooth sound of jazz, has continued to change in meaning. Interestingly, the word *cool* remains the gold standard of slang in the twenty-first century, surviving like few expressions in our constantly evolving language."[58]

Slang comes into being because a group needs words to describe their ideas and "things." The slang forms a bond among the people of the group who use their unique terms.

Types of Slang Slang may come from anywhere. All it requires is a group of people who use and understand it. Those who text, IM, and communicate via Facebook and other internet sites *techno-babble*. Techno-babblers *interface with each other*, *debug their relationships*, write on each other's *walls* and *friend* or *defriend* each

Techno-babble describes communication via text, IM, Facebook, and other Internet sites.

other.[59] Because of the prevalence of computers and smart phone users, technobabble is becoming a permanent part of Standard American English, so it is losing its status as slang. Once slang becomes mainstream language, it is no longer slang and is included in dictionaries, the chronicles of language.

Regional slang is prevalent. In Vermont, a *flatlander* is anybody who does not live in that geographical area, whether or not the person is from a state that has a higher elevation than Vermont.

Inarticulates

Inarticulates are uttered sounds, words, or phrases that have no meaning or do not help the listener gain a clear understanding of the message, such as the phrase *stuff like that.* They constitute what is considered to be "powerless language," language usage that diminishes rather than enhances the communication effect you wish to achieve. Studies of the negative perceptions of powerless language extend to tag questions ("Put away your toys, *okay?*"), hedges ("It's *like* difficult to concentrate"), hesitations (*"um," "you know"*), and intensifiers ("It's *so awesome* of you to come"). Such inarticulates become conversational mannerisms that can distract from the substance of the message and from the speaker's credibility.[60]

Some recent thinking regarding inarticulates perceive "um" and "er" to be part of the cycle of thinking and speaking, not a display of lack of knowledge.[61] This is based on studies that indicate "the causes are the discrepancies between the planning and executing functions of the brain—between planning what we are going to say and saying it."[62] They further indicate that, in spite of the idea that people can multitask, "the old warning is true: We can't think and talk at the same time."[63]

Nonstandard English Dialects

Many people in the United States speak languages or dialects that differ from Standard American English. Some of these speakers use a recognizable alternative language form, such as Spanish, Chinese, or one of the Native American tongues. In some cases, speakers present their ideas in identifiable dialects of Standard American English, such as Spanglish.[64] It is common linguistic currency wherever concentrations of Hispanics are found. Spanglish takes a variety of forms, ranging from *hasta la bye-bye* and *lonche* (a quick lunch rather than a leisurely one), the description of a group of *los teenagers,* and the almost universally used *no problema.* "A sign in a story window warns, "No Hangear"—don't hang out on this corner.[65] Other Spanglish terms are *averjae* (average), *chopin* (going shopping), *delof* (day off) and *marqueta* (supermarket).[66] Spanglish sentences are mostly Spanish, with a quick detour for a few English words and some fractured syntax.[67]

Effects of Speaking a Dialect or Nonstandard English Recent studies have reinforced the concept that for those living in the United States, speaking a nonstandard dialect rather than Standard American English can be detrimental to a person's educational and economic health.[68] The message seems clear: "You need to speak right to go to college, to get a good job."[69]

Children entering schools with weak Standard American English skills are at a definite disadvantage.[70] Since they may not know the alphabet or have the vocabulary, learning to read and understanding class discussions become extremely difficult. They often tune out and eventually drop out. Research shows that "while 75 percent

Communicating Culturally

English By Non-English Speakers

Non-native speakers of English not only find the language's words confusing, but the grammar structure baffling. This results in some strange communication. Here are some actual signs and notices that have been seen around the world as local residents attempt to convey information to English speakers:

- In a Belgrade hotel elevator: To move cabin, push the button for wishing floor. If the cabin should enter more persons, each one should press a number of wishing floor.
- In a Japanese hotel: You are invited to take advantage of the chambermaid.
- In a Rhodes tailor shop: Order your summer suits. Because is big rush we will execute customers in strict rotation.
- In an advertisement by a Hong Kong dentist: Teeth extracted by the latest methodists.
- In a Copenhagen airline ticket office: We take you bags and sent them in all directions.
- In the office of a Roman doctor: Specialist in women and other diseases.

and

- Two signs that summarize the language problem from a Moroccan shop entrance: English well speaking. Here speeching American.

Source: http://ayersline.com/Jokes/badtrans.htm

of white students graduated from U.S. high schools, only 50 percent of all Black students, 51 percent of Native American students, and 53 percent of all Hispanic students got a high school diploma. The study also found that the drop-out problem was even worse for Black, Native American, and Hispanic young men at 43 percent, 47 percent and 48 percent, respectively."[71]

In economic terms, nonstandard speakers are given shorter interviews and fewer job offers than Standard American English speakers. When job offers are presented, nonstandard speakers are offered positions paying as much as 35 percent less than jobs offered to Standard American English speakers.[72]

In social terms, speakers of nonstandard dialects often are confronted with mistaken, negative assumptions concerning their intelligence, dependability, and creativity. Many different languages and accents make the United States a rich tapestry; however, people speaking dialects should be aware that in some instances, education and speech therapy can make alterations in their vocabulary and speaking patterns if they desire change. That desire is usually based on a person's awareness that her or his career and social goals include particular language requirements that the person does not possess.

Using Verbal Language

Because language is symbolic, it is necessary to be as clear and precise as possible when using words. You need to consider the other person's frame of reference and whether he or she will share your interpretation of the language used. If not, it is important to adjust your vocabulary level and word

Communicating Socially

Were You Taught Not To Swear?

The next time you stub your toe, don't worry about biting your tongue. British researchers found that swearing can actually help increase your pain tolerance. The study concluded that swearing may trigger a fight-or-flight response that helps reduce your body's perception of pain.

Did you know that the number of taboo or swear words spoken per day, by the average English speaker is 85?

Source: Profane brain: The world of taboo word (2010, July/August) *Psychology Today*, p.22.

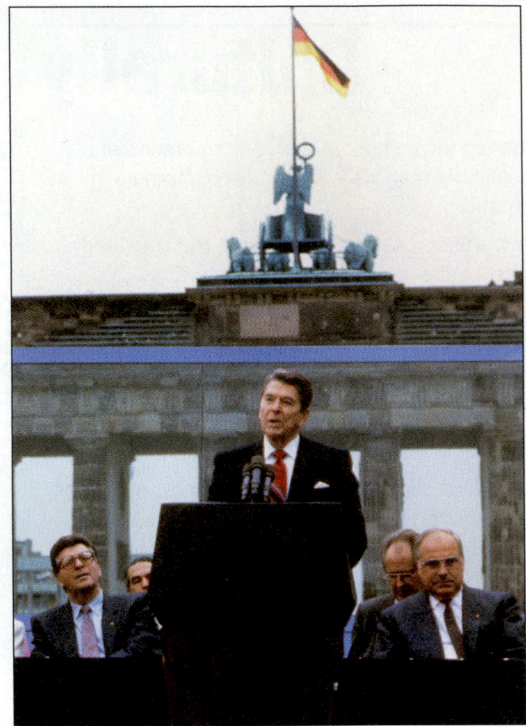

Standing by the Brandenburg Gate in West Berlin in 1983, then President Ronald Reagan, in an attempt to defuse Iron Curtain tensions, intoned "tear down this wall." The phrase became the battle cry for the destruction of communist control over Eastern Europe.

choice to fit that of the listener. For example, you must be careful not to use technical terms that are beyond your listener's experience. Have you ever found yourself confused in a classroom because the instructor was using terms you didn't understand? The problem may well have centered on the fact that as an expert in the field, the instructor was using words with which she was familiar, but you, as a neophyte to the subject area, weren't familiar with them. You can increase your clarity by defining your terms, offering synonyms, or providing examples of terms you are using. Remember that slang expressions, words unique to a culture or a region, texting abbreviations, and euphemisms work against clarity and precision.

In addition to striving to be clear, it also is necessary to consider ways to make your language memorable. To be attention getting, words and phrases should be colorful, and compelling. After listening to a speech, a listener often will remember only one phrase. In fact, some speeches are identified by a single phrase. In 1983, President Ronald Reagan, standing at the Brandenburg Gate in West Berlin, in an attempt to diffuse Iron Curtain tensions, intoned "tear down this wall." The phrase became the battle cry for the destruction of communist control over Eastern Europe.[73]

Words have an impact. "There are words whose effects are subtle and unperceived; there are words that comfort ["I'm very sorry for your loss"] and words that pain ["You are so dumb!"]; words that support ["I believe you are doing the right thing"] and that undermine ["That's a bad decision"]; words that inform ["Thank you for being such a good friend"] and that mislead ["Call me soon" (when you don't want him to call)]; that foster rationality ["Think before you speak"] and that impede it ["You'll never do it right"]; words that unite ["All for one and one for all"] and words that divide ["You are either with us or against us"]."[74]

Research shows that the adage "Sticks and stones will break my bones, but words will never hurt me" is not true. Words can, according to the findings, "cause physical harm."[75] Investigations of emotionally abused women discovered that they suffered from illnesses strikingly similar "to those affecting physically abused women."[76] As a result of these findings, health-care providers are being encouraged to regularly screen women for psychological abuse as well as for physical and sexual violence.[77]

Yes, words are powerful. For example, "I once read that a word is like a living organism, capable of growing, changing, spreading, and influencing the world in many ways, directly and indirectly through others. I never thought about a word being 'alive' but then I thought of words spoken 3,000 years ago, written down and passed through many generations, and they seem quite alive when read or spoken today, having lived 3,000 years. As I ponder the power of the word to incite and divide, to calm and connect, or to create and effect change, I am ever more cautious in what I say and how I listen to the words around me."[78]

In Conclusion

IN CONCLUSION

In this chapter, the foundations of verbal language were discussed. Although there is no one accepted theory of the origins of human language, the operation of the human brain in acquiring, retaining, and allowing for language usage can be explained by the cybernetic process. We acquire our language, beliefs, values, and attitudes from people and influences surrounding us. Languages are based on a set of symbols, both verbal and nonverbal. Successful communication takes place when the sender adapts the message to the background and knowledge of the particular person or audience being addressed. A dialect is used by people from the same geographical region, occupational group, or social or educational class.

Standard American English is the language usually recognized by linguists as being representative of the general society of the United States. Aspects of language are slang, inarticulates, and dialects.

LEARN BY DOING

1. A major controversy was ignited when the Oakland, California, school district recognized Ebonics as a language. Research the topic, and have a class discussion or debate that agrees or disagrees with this statement: "Resolved: Accepting Black English as a language is a sellout to street slang and puts the users in a position of being second-class citizens."
2. Find an example of doublespeak in a speech, a letter to the editor, or a newspaper or magazine article. Bring the material to class. Discuss what you think the speaker was trying to hide or manipulate by using doublespeak.
3. Write down one phrase or expression that has meaning only for a select group. It may be an ethnic expression or an in-group reference. You will read the expression to other students, who will try to figure out what it means.
4. Make a list of five people who have had a significant effect on your own language use. Identify which of these people was the most influential and why.
5. List five words that have different meanings depending on the people who use them or the place in which they are used. See how many different definitions you can develop for each word.

KEY TERMS

language 35
cybernetic process 37
Language-Explosion Theory 38
Significant-Other Theory 39
linguistics 39
denotative meanings 40
connotative meanings 40
semantics 41
emotive language 42
phatic language 42
cognitive language 43
rhetorical language 43
identifying language 43
language distortion 43
doublespeak 44
inferences 44
linguist 45
dialects 45
accent 45
standard dialects 45
nonstandard dialects 45
slang 47
inarticulates 48

CHAPTER 3

Nonverbal Communication

sources of nonverbal communication • categories and uses of nonverbal communication

After reading this chapter, you should be able to

- Explain the importance of nonverbal communication as a message-sending system
- Categorize and discuss the origins of nonverbal messages
- State and evaluate the relationship between verbal and nonverbal communication
- List and illustrate the categories of nonverbal communication
- Analyze the role of culture in the development and use of nonverbal communication

Good communication is the foundation of successful relationships: both personally and professionally. With this in mind, do you believe that when you communicate with another person, your *words* carry the majority of the meaning of the message? If you answered "yes," you are mistaken. As you read this chapter you will become aware of the relevance of nonverbal communication and why, in many instances it carries as much, if not more meaning, than verbal language. "Nonverbal communication is a major force in our lives."[1] Nonverbal behaviors such as smiling, crying, pointing, caressing, and staring appear to be used and understood the world over.[2]

Nonverbal communication is composed of "all those messages that people exchange beyond the words themselves."[3] Historically, people have interpreted body talk, perhaps without knowing they were doing so, but only in recent years have attempts been made to analyze and explain nonverbal communication in a scientific manner.

Are you interested in finding out how much you know about nonverbal communication? If so, fill out the Nonverbal Communication Pretest.

Research has established that nonverbal language is an important means of expression. Experts in the field have identified patterns of body language usage through the study of films and videotapes and through direct observation.

Traditionally, experts tend to agree that nonverbal communication itself carries the impact of a message. "The figure most cited to support this claim is the estimate that 93 percent of all meaning in a social situation comes from nonverbal information, while only 7 percent comes from verbal information."[4] The figure is deceiving, however.[5] It is based on two studies that compared vocal cues with facial cues.[6] It appears that the "percentage of our total communication [that] is nonverbal ranges from 60 percent to 93 percent. But the percent of emotional communication that is nonverbal exceeds 99 percent. When it comes to emotions, instead of verbalizing how we feel, our bodies do the talking."[7]

In the effort to read nonverbal communication, we must remember that no one signal carries much meaning. Instead, such factors as gestures, posture, eye contact, clothing styles, and movement must all be regarded together. This grouping of factors is called a *cluster.*

Nonverbal Communication Pretest

DIRECTIONS: Answer *true* or *false,* then check your answers.

____ 1. Females are more sensitive than males to nonverbal cues—especially facial cues—and they transmit more accurate nonverbal cues to others.

____ 2. When contradictory messages are sent through both verbal and nonverbal channels, most adults see the nonverbal message as more accurate.

____ 3. People with low self-esteem use more eye contact when receiving negative messages than when receiving positive ones, whereas while those with high self-esteem do just the opposite in each case.

____ 4. When people are conjuring up a lie, their pupils tend to become smaller. However, when they tell the lie, their pupils tend to dilate.

____ 5. The three nonverbal cues an interviewer remembers most about a job applicant are gestures, posture, and handshake.

Answers: 1. true, 2. true, 3. true, 4. true, 5. false—interviewers remember eye contact, appearance, and facial expressions.

We also must remember that, just as in verbal communication, nonverbal signs can have many different meanings. For example, crossing the arms over the chest may suggest that a person is cold. But crossed arms accompanied by erect posture, tightened body muscles, setting of the jaw, and narrowing of the eyes could indicate anger.

A person's background and past patterns of behavior also must be considered when we analyze nonverbal communication. The relationship between current and past patterns of behavior, as well as the harmony between verbal and nonverbal communication, is termed *congruency.* When you say to a friend, "You don't look well today," you are basing your statement on an evaluation of the person's appearance today compared with her appearance in the past. In other words, something has changed, and you have become aware of a difference. If you did not have experience to draw on, you would not have noticed the change.

Few of us realize how much we depend on nonverbal communication to encourage and discourage conversations and transactions. For instance, we consciously wave at waiters and raise our hands to get a teacher's attention. Much of our opening and closing of channels, however, occurs without our consciously realizing it.

As you observe people conversing, you might notice that they may indicate they are listening by moving their heads. If they agree with what is said, they may nod affirmatively. They may also smile to show pleasure or agreement. If, however, they glance several times at their watch, look away from the speaker, cross and uncross their legs, and stand up, they are probably signaling that they have closed the channel and wish to end the transaction. Be aware that these patterns are not the same in all parts of the world. Head movements, for example, may have varying purposes in different cultures.[8]

There are some cultures in which people move their heads from left to right to signal agreement. Or, in China, the head nod often means, "I'm listening."

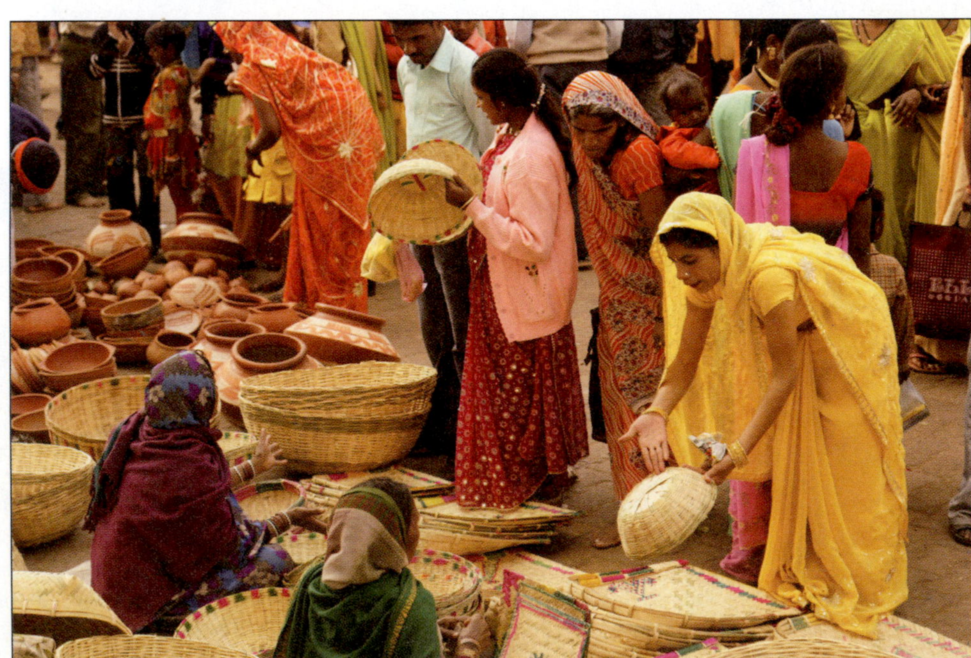

Few of us realize how much we depend on nonverbal communication to encourage and discourage conversations and transactions.

Sources of Nonverbal Signs

We learn to read words through a step-by-step process in which we are taught to use our written, oral, and reading forms of communication. But how do we acquire nonverbal signs? There are two basic sources: innate neurological programs and behaviors common to a culture or a family.

Neurological Programs

Innate neurological programs are those automatic nonverbal reactions to stimuli with which we are born. These nonverbal "automatic reactions" are *reflexive* because of neurological drives. These reflexive drives seem to be tied to our need drives. For example, we blink our eyes automatically when we hear a loud noise (survival need drive) or when a pebble hits the windshield of the car we are driving (survival and territorial need drives). (See pages 119–122.) Our stomach muscles tighten and our hands sweat when we feel insecure (security need drive).

That we are born with some of our nonverbal tendencies is illustrated by the fact that "when the facial expressions of these [blind] children were compared with normal-sighted, normal-hearing children, nearly identical facial expressions were produced for sadness, crying, smiling, laughing, pouting, fear and anger."[9] In addition, "from sneers to full-blown smiles, our facial expressions are hardwired into our genes."[10] "Sighted and blind individuals modified their expressions of emotion in the same way in accordance with the social context."[11] This "seems to confirm that our expressive faces are part of human nature rather than collective learning."[12]

A study of eye-accessing cues indicates "every movement is an important source of body language."[13] Most people, according to neuro-linguistic programming (NLP) research, will look up for visual accessing, down for linguistic accessing, to the left for past experiences, to the right for future perceptions, and straight ahead for present-tense thinking.[14] (See Figure 3.1.) "Some NLP experts consider eye movements to be an aid to accessing inner speech since the eye movements stimulate different parts of the brain."[15] In academia, teachers often make the mistake of misinterpreting students' actions. For example, your professor asks a question, and you struggle to visualize the answer, your eyes moving up or down and to the left or right (depending on whether you are looking for past learned ideas or inventing new material). The professor states, "Well, you won't find the answer on the ceiling." The teacher is potentially wrong. The answer may be found by glancing up and to the left if your normal eye-glance pattern for past tense and picturing concepts is up.[16] A study showed that "children who avert their gaze when considering their response to a question are more likely to come up with the right answer."[17]

A student who knows his or her eye-shift pattern may be able to access past-tense learning by moving his or her eyes in the direction of his or her past-tense triggering and looking up or down, depending on whether he or she is trying to access images or words. So, if you studied for an exam, and while you taking the test you don't immediately recall information that you reviewed, you could shift your eyes in your past tense NLP eye position . . . for most people, to the left . . . and you might be able to access the concept.

Cultural and Intercultural Behavior

Some nonverbal behavior is learned in the same way as spoken language. When we display these culturally taught nonverbal behaviors, they are said to be *reflective*—reflective

The proponents of NLP (Neurolingistic Programming) believe that eye movements are linked to the sensory processing that goes on in a person's mind when he or she is thinking. The eye movement may be a flicker or it may be held for several seconds. This movement happens when a person is organizing incoming sensations, recalling past experiences, or imagining never previously experienced phenomena.

Eyes up and to the left: Recalling something seen before—a visual memory.

Eyes up and to the right: Visualizing something that has not been seen before.

Eyes centered, looking up: present tense visual memory; eyes centered, looking down: present tense verbal memory; eyes centered, staring (no matter whether eyes are up or down): daydreaming or not engaged in decoding any information being sent.

FIGURE 3.1
Eye-Accessing Cues

Source: People who read people. (1979, July). *Psychology Today*. Reprinted with permission from *Psychology Today* magazine, copyright © 2008 Sussex Publishers, LLC. For further information see *The Pegasus NLP* site at http://www.nlp-now.co.uk/tips-n-tech.htm and research on neurolinguistic programming.

of the culture from which they were learned. Culture can affect what is expressed and how it is expressed.[18]

As in reading information about any culture, please be aware that the explanations are based on research generalizations. It must be understood that not every person in the named culture follows the described pattern.

Every culture has its own body language, and the young learn the culture's nonverbal patterns along with those of spoken language. As a research anthropologist indicated, "The important thing to remember is that culture is very persistent. In this country, we've noted the existence of culture patterns that determine physical distance between people in the third and fourth generations of some families, despite their prolonged contact with people of very different cultural heritages."[19]

"Gestures are a powerful language in any culture."[20] A person who speaks more than one verbal language gestures according to the language he or she is speaking. Fiorello La Guardia, New York City's mayor in the 1930s and early 1940s, carried on his political campaigns in English, Italian, and Yiddish—the languages of the major voting blocs in the city. He was observed using one set of gestures for speaking English, another for Italian, and still another for Yiddish. If you fluently speak more than one language, do you notice that your gestures, your facial expressions, and sometimes your volume reflect which language you are using?

Nonverbal gestures and behaviors convey different messages throughout the world. An Arabic male, for example, may stroke his chin to show appreciation for a woman, whereas a Portuguese man does it by pulling his ear. But in Italy a similar kind of ear tugging may be considered a deliberate insult.[21]

Culturally COMMUNICATING

Nonverbal Message Styles

An aboriginal mother wrote to her son's new teachers asking them to examine their own biases and expectations:

> He doesn't speak standard English, but he is in no way *linguistically handicapped*. If you take the time and courtesy to listen and observe carefully, you will see that he and the other Aboriginal children communicate very well, both among themselves and with other Aborigines. They speak *functional English*, very effectively augmented by their fluency in the silent language, the subtle unspoken communication of facial expressions, gestures, body movement, and the use of personal space.
>
> You will be well advised to remember that our children are skillful interpreters of the silent language. They will know your feelings and attitudes with unerring precision no matter how carefully you arrange your smile or modulate your voice. They will learn in your classroom because children learn involuntarily. What they learn will depend on you.

Source: Smith, J. (1997, January 27). Inclusiveness in learning media. Unpublished document. Originally from the *Northian Newsletter*, submitted by Jock Smith, Surrey School trustee and educational counselor for the Department of Indian Affairs to *Focus on Equality,* March 17, 1991.

REFLECT ON THIS:

1. What are the implications for a classroom teacher of knowing this information?
2. What are the implications for you about knowing this information if you become acquainted with an Aborigine?
3. Based on this exposition, what advantages do you think Aborigines have over most Euro Americans when communicating with others?

In communicating nonverbally, people also operate on different action chains. An *action chain* is a behavioral sequence with two or more participating organisms, in which there are standard steps for reaching a goal. If an individual leaves out a step, the chain gets broken, and the person has to start all over again. Different cultures operate under different action chains. For example, to many Euro Americans, being on time normally means making contact within five minutes or so of a designated hour. To a Mexican, however, being on time often means within a reasonable time. A European American businessperson, having been kept waiting for twenty minutes in a Mexico City client's office, may decide to leave the office, feeling that she is being ignored and that the client's lateness is a sign of lack of interest in the business deal. But the Mexican client may not consider himself at all tardy and may be totally confused by the person's quick exit.

European Americans engaged in business dealings with Arabs, for example, should understand and adhere to Arabic customs of hospitality to be successful. The initial meeting with an Arab businessperson is typically devoted to fact finding. No commitments are implied or made, but the initial session is usually lengthy and thorough. Based on their patterns of working quickly so as not to waste time, Euro Americans often feel that the process is tedious. The next meeting is taken up with additional rituals. It is not unusual for a business deal to take as long as thirty days to complete.

Gesture patterns, which have verbal meanings (referred to in nonverbal vocabulary as *illustrators*), also vary. For instance, the thumb-and-forefinger-in-a-circle gesture generally means "okay" in the United States. In France or Belgium, however, it means the recipient is worth zero. The same gesture in Greece and Turkey may be construed as a sexual invitation. And in Brazil, the gesture is obscene. Similarly, an index finger tapping to the temple with the other fingers curled against the palm usually means "you're smart" in the United States, whereas it communicates "you're stupid" in most of Europe. Holding your hand and arm out in front of you, fingers spread means *no* in Lebanon, while in Greece it's a curse called *moutza*. It is an insult in Spain, Nigeria, and Chile.[22]

The use of space also varies widely around the world. Arabs, South Americans, and Eastern Europeans generally favor close conversational encounters, which may make some European Americans feel somewhat uncomfortable and many Germans and Scandinavians totally uncomfortable.

We tend to read nonverbal signs on the basis of our own personal background and experiences, and we assume that others share the same interpretations—an assumption that can be misleading, even dangerous. We must remember that in all forms of communication, an understanding of the receiver is necessary. And, as if matters were not complicated enough, we also must be aware that although cultural patterns are reported to be persistent, not all the people within a given culture share identical patterns.

Emotional Influences on Nonverbal Communication

Emotions have a direct effect on the size of people's personal territory and their resulting nonverbal responses. When people are insecure, they tend to avoid closeness. People who are emotionally upset may even become violent if someone invades their territory. When people are upset, their bodies may become rigid. For example, many people who are nervous about public speaking report that their throats tighten and their stomach muscles contract when they must present a speech. Under great tension, the pitch of the voice also rises because vocal cords tighten.

People under stress sometimes find that others loom larger and closer than they actually are. To a frightened child, an adult can seem like a giant. Because of this, adults who are dealing with upset children should kneel to talk with them. By the same token, police interrogators and trial lawyers know that moving in close to an interviewee may cause him or her to get upset and say something that would be controlled under normal conditions. This invasion of territory may result in the breaking down of defenses.

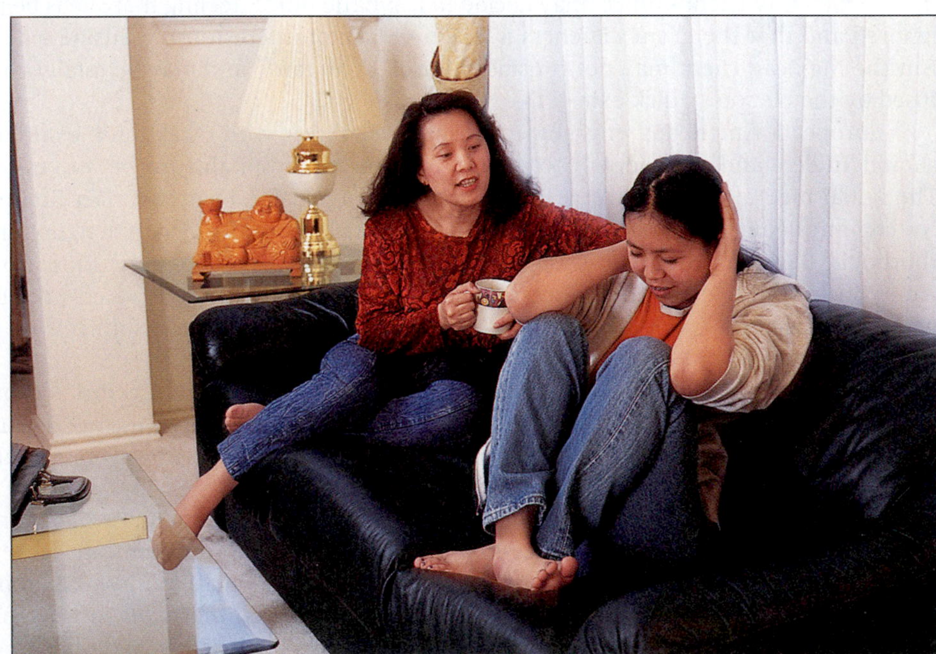

Body shifts can encourage or discourage conversation.

COMMUNICATING in Careers

Nonverbal Communication in Business

Reading and interpreting nonverbal communication in business is a skill worth mastering for more effective communication in the workplace. Just keep in mind that you have to look at nonverbal cues together with other message cues.

A manager that meets with you while sitting behind his desk is either trying to keep the meeting short, or trying to assert his authority over you. Or perhaps he/she doesn't feel like getting up from his chair at that moment.

- Don't give this a whole lot of importance, just observe it.

Looking at a watch, clock, or smart phone. When you are in a meeting with someone who glances at his watch, the clock, or a smart phone very often, it's a sure bet that he needs to cut the meeting short. And perhaps go somewhere, or do something else.

- To avoid jumping to conclusions, just ask if they need to go and continue the meeting at another time, when you have the person's full attention.

Pounding the table or desk. The person is very likely angry. Except in cases when the person is just trying to look stern. It's easy to know if this is the case because the person's face doesn't show anger, it's calm.

- Always look for congruence between the various verbal and nonverbal cues.

Source: Nonverbal Communication in Business by Imelda Bickham, from www.people-communicating.com.

REFLECT ON THIS:

1. What experiences have you had while at a business meeting or in conversing with an administrator or college professor, in which you "read" a nonverbal sign that designated the person was happy, upset, was in a hurry, wanted the session to end?
2. What is the danger of interpreting nonverbal communication rather than just observing it?

Sometimes nonverbal patterns change because of outside influences. For instance, a vast difference exists between normal nonverbal communication and deviant communication, such as that caused by drugs, alcohol, or shock. Patterns change as people lose rational control of their ability to make decisions and value judgments. A person under the influence of alcohol or drugs does not walk, talk, or have the same bodily controls as he or she would when sober. This has resulted in the development of drunk-driver-walking-a-straight-line and touching-the-nose tests, with the assumption being that a sober person can perform these acts but a drunk person can't.

Verbal and Nonverbal Relationships

A link exists between verbal and nonverbal communication. Because they are so tightly interwoven, it is necessary to identify, analyze, and understand their various relationships. The main relationships of nonverbal to verbal communication can be described as substituting, complementing, conflicting, and accenting. (See Figure 3.2.)

Substituting Relationship

Suppose someone asks you a question. Instead of answering verbally, you nod your head up and down. In doing so, you have used the *substituting relationship*. In the Euro American tradition, you have replaced the word meaning "yes" for the action *yes*.

Substituting relationship Nonverbal message replaces the verbal message **Verbal message:** (none) **Nonverbal message:** Nod head vertically to indicate *yes*	**Complementing relationship** Nonverbal message accompanies the verbal message **Verbal message:** "Yes" **Nonverbal message:** Nod head vertically to indicate *yes*
Conflicting relationship Verbal and nonverbal message are in contrast to one another **Verbal message:** "Yes" **Nonverbal message:** Body language indicates *no*	**Accenting relationship** Nonverbal message stresses the verbal message **Verbal message:** "Yes" **Nonverbal message:** Body language indicates *yes*

FIGURE 3.2
Verbal and Nonverbal Relationships

Complementing Relationship

Body language can complement a verbal message. For example, shaking your head horizontally from side to side while saying "no" reinforces the negative verbalization. The simultaneous saying and doing creates a nonverbal *complementing relationship* in which a nonverbal message accompanies a verbal message and adds dimension to communication.

Conflicting Relationship

A person's physical movements sometimes can conflict with his or her verbal message. For example, suppose a professor is confronted by a student after a class session. The student asks, "May I speak with you?" The professor says, "Sure, I have lots of time." While making this reply, however, the professor is packing books, glancing at the clock, and taking several steps away. A conflict exists between the verbal and nonverbal messages.

When actions conflict with verbal messages, forming a *conflicting relationship* between the verbal and nonverbal, the receiver probably should rely more on the nonverbal aspect of communication. Nonverbal clues often are more difficult to fake than verbal ones. When you were young, you might have been surprised to find that your parents knew when you were not telling the truth. There you stood, looking at the floor, twisting your hands, with a flushed face, as you insisted, "I didn't do it." The father of the modern psychology movement is reported to have said, "He that has eyes to see and ears to hear may convince himself that no mortal can keep a secret. If his lips are silent he chatters with his fingertips; betrayal oozes out of him at every pore."[23]

A leading expert in nonverbal communication developed the *Expectancy Violations Theory*,[24] which perceives communication as "the exchange of information that is high in relational content and that can be used to violate the expectations of another, which will be perceived either positively or negatively depending on how much the two people like each other."[25] For example, if you feel comfortable with about three feet between you and the person with whom you are communicating, and the person stays outside of that distance, you are comfortable. But, if the other person gets closer to you than your comfortable distance, you will feel violated and will display that by backing away from the person, breaking eye contact, and/or requesting space.

Most people think they can definitively tell when a person is lying, although research says we cannot.[26] Polygraphs, or lie detectors, read the body's nonverbal reactions by measuring changes in blood pressure, respiration, and skin response—in other words, by attempting to detect a conflicting relationship between the verbal and the nonverbal. "Most psychologists agree that there is little evidence that polygraph tests can accurately detect lies,"[27] though the American Polygraph Association estimates the accuracy is about 80 percent.[28] A report by the National Research Council contends that "almost a century of research in scientific psychology and physiology provides little basis for the expectation that a polygraph test could have extremely high accuracy."[29] Because of this, polygraph findings are generally inadmissible as evidence in courts.

A new technique, functional magnetic resonance imaging (fMRI), "scans the brain and could well morph into a forensic tool far more potent than the flawed polygraph test."[30] While MERMER, a system of brain fingerprinting that records messages emitted by the brain before the body physically reacts, has been developed.[31] An Iowa judge ruled brain fingerprinting admissible in court after it was tested and peer reviewed.[32]

Socially COMMUNICATING

How to Catch a Liar . . . A University Conundrum

At Penn State University, there were four sophomores taking chemistry and all of them had an "A" so far. They were so confident that, the weekend before finals, they decided to visit some friends at the University of Pittsburgh. They had a great time, but after all the partying, slept all day Sunday and didn't make it back to State College until Monday morning.

Rather than taking the final, they decided that after the exam they would explain to their professor that the reason they missed the test was due to a flat tire while returning to campus. The professor agreed they could make up the final the next day.

The next day they were placed in different rooms and each given a test booklet. They each quickly answered the first problem which was worth five points. Then each turned the page. On the second page was written . . . For 95 points, which tire?

Source: A Penn State urban legend.

REFLECT ON THIS: And, the moral is?

Accenting Relationship

Nonverbal behavior may accent parts of a verbal message, much as underlining or *italicizing* emphasizes written language. In the *accenting relationship,* the nonverbal message stresses the verbal one. Jabbing someone's shoulder with a finger as you turn the person to look at you while commanding, "When I speak to you, look at me!" emphatically accents the verbal message with nonverbal signs.

Categories of Nonverbal Communication

Nonverbal channels can be divided into many categories. Our discussion of these categories centers on kinesics, proxemics, paralanguage, chronemics, olfactics, aesthetics, and gustorics.[33] (See Figure 3.3.)

Kinesics: Body Communication

Kinesics is the study of communication through the body and its movements. We communicate through the gestures we use, the way we walk and stand, the expressions on our faces and in our eyes, the manner in which we combine these variables to open or close channels, and what we look like. Specific areas studied in the area of kinesics are facsics; ocalics; gestics; haptics; posture, walk, and stance; artifactics; and physical characteristics.

FIGURE 3.3 **Categories of Nonverbal Communication**

Face The study of how the face communicates is *Facsics*. Even infants can recognize faces and notice changes in the eyes and mouth.[34] Facial expressions range from communicating our internal states such as anger or fear, to carrying messages to others of whether we want to interrupt what they are saying or are interested and want them to continue to speak. The face sends information about our personality, interests, responsiveness, and emotional states. How we perceive another person is often based on that person's facial expressions as we observe or interact with her or him.

Research about the face and its messages has been conducted through the Facial Action Coding System (FACS).[35] Through this process, we have more data about the face than about any other area of nonverbal communication. What has been determined is that facial expressions, movements of brief duration, are so subtle that they can just pass us by as observers. An upturn of the corners of the mouth, flared nostrils, an eyebrow arching, a dropping jaw, or open mouth are often overlooked and the message is not conveyed.[36]

Eyes *Ocalics* is the study of the eyes. Your eyes are the primary way to receive and send body language. The eyes, unlike other organs of the body, are an extension of the brain. Because of this, it may be difficult for an individual to disguise eye meaning from someone who is a member of the same culture. Eye contact, eye avoidance, and eye blinks all carry messages.

A person's eye blinks have an effect on how he or she is perceived by others. For example, the slowness or rapidity of eye blinks can indicate nervousness. The normal blink rate for someone speaking is 31 to 50 blinks per minute. A classic study indicates that during the presidential debate in 1996 between President Bill Clinton and his Republican opponent, Senator Bob Dole, polls indicated that Dole was considered to be very nervous. A review of the videotape of the debate revealed why people had come to that conclusion. Dole averaged 147 eye blinks per minute, almost three times the normal rate.[37]

▪ **Eyes:** Rapid side-to-side eye movement connotes stress. Steady movement suggests command. When comfortable, Bush shares his narrow gaze with individuals all around the room; when less so, he shares it mainly with supporters. To suggest gravity, disdain or the significance of his words, he often narrows his eyes.

▪ **Mouth:** Bush pushes his lip to the side and bites it when frustrated. Experts disagree on the grin. Some say his smiles at inappropriate moments mean "I don't get it." To others, these read, "Why don't you get it?" He bares his teeth, enunciates slowly, to "educate" on a point he considers key.

▪ **Hands:** Uses an abrupt hand chop to frame short, simple points. Too much jerkiness suggests agitation. Aggressive or frequent pointing says "I'm being defensive; back off." Firm handshakes, upper arm clasps and slaps on the back: jocular confidence.

Photo source: Baltimore Sun

FIGURE 3.4
Nonverbal Clues That Help to Interpret a Message
Source: Cleveland Plain Dealer by Staff Writer. Copyright 2006 by Plain Dealer Publishing Company (Cleveland OH). Reproduced with permission of Plain Dealer Publishing Company (Cleveland OH) in the format Textbook via Copyright Clearance Center.

Experts on nonverbal signs created by the eyes, mouth, and hands offered a guide to viewers of how to nonverbally read President George W. Bush's nonverbal public speaking mannerisms.[38] This is illustrated in Figure 3.4.

A theory known as *pupilometrics* indicates that pupils dilate when the eyes are focused on a pleasurable object and contract when focused on an unpleasurable one.[39] Enlarged pupils signify interest, and contracted pupils reflect boredom. Thus, knowledgeable suitors often watch their date's eyes to tell whether there is a positive or negative reaction to their advances.

Members of different social classes, generations, ethnic groups, and cultures use their eyes differently to express messages. European Americans often complain that they feel some foreigners stare at them too intensely or hold a glance too long. This is because a gaze of longer than ten seconds is likely to induce discomfort in a European American. But lengthy eye contact may be comfortable as long as the communicating people have sufficient distance between them.

When individuals in the European American culture are intent on hiding an inner feeling, they may try to avoid eye contact. Thus, the child who has eaten the candy he was told not to consume, will likely not look at a questioning parent during the interrogation. (European American children are often told, "Look me in the eye and say that.")

Movement The study of the movements of the body, such as gestures, which can give clues about a person's status, mood, cultural affiliations, and self-perception is *Gestics*. Why do people gesture when they talk? Linguists have theorized that speech and gesturing function together and may help us think and form words.[40] In addition, gesturing helps people retrieve words from memory. "When asked to keep their hands still by holding onto a bar, people had a more difficult time recalling words than those whose hands were free."[41] Nods of the head and body shifts can encourage or discourage conversation. Other movements may show internal feelings. For example, those who are bored may tap their fingers on a table or bounce a crossed leg.

As people attempt to communicate, they use gestures.[42] These gestures may be classified as speech independent or speech related. *Speech-independent gestures* are not tied to speech and are referred to as emblems. *Speech-related gestures* are directly tied to, or accompany, speech. These gestures are illustrators, affect displays, regulators, and adaptors.

Emblems are nonverbal acts that have a direct verbal translation or dictionary definition consisting of one or two words.[43] The sign language of the deaf and signals between underwater scuba divers are all examples of the use of emblems. It is important to realize that not all emblems are universal. In fact, they tend to be *culture specific;* in other words, an emblem's meaning in one culture may not be the same as that same emblem's meaning in another. For example, the fig—a clenched fist with the thumb coming through between the knuckle of the index and middle fingers means "good luck" in Brazil, but in Greece and Turkey it is considered an insulting gesture, and in Tunisia and Holland it has strong sexual connotations."[44] "In everyday life, Americans regularly use more than 100 emblems."[45]

Illustrators are "kinesic acts accompanying speech that are used to aid in the description of what is being said or trace the direction of speech."[46] They are used to sketch a path, point to an object, or show spatial relationships. Saying, "*Josh, please stand up* (point at Josh and bring your hand upward), *go out the door* (point at the door), *turn to the left* (point to the left), and *walk straight ahead* (point straight ahead)" is an example of a cluster of illustrators.

Affect displays are facial gestures that show emotions and feelings, such as sadness or happiness. Pouting, winking, and raising or lowering the eyelids and eyebrows are examples of affect displays. People tend to use facial expressions in different ways. For example, many European American males mask and internalize their facial expressions because they have been taught that to show emotion is not manly; Italian males, however, tend to express their emotions outwardly.

Regulators are nonverbal acts that maintain and control the back-and-forth nature of speaking and listening between two or more people. Nods of the head, eye movements, and body shifts are all regulators used to encourage or discourage conversation. Imagine, for example, a conversation between a department manager and an employee who has asked for a raise. The manager glances at her watch, her fingers fidget with the telephone, and she glances through some materials on the desk. The manager's regulator signs indicate that she views the transaction as completed.

Adaptors are movements that accompany boredom, show internal feelings, or regulate a situation. People who are waiting for someone who is late, for example, often stand with their arms crossed, fingers tapping on upper arms, foot tapping the pavement, and checking the time every few seconds.

The body, as a whole, gestures by leaning forward and pulling back. The old adage, "jumping into the conversation," does, in fact, describe the body's action while you are involved in conversations. If you are fairly typical, when you get ready to insert a comment into a conversation, you lean forward, and when you withdraw from a conversation you lean back.[47]

Nonverbal communication is composed of all those messages that people exchange beyond the words themselves

Touch The study of the use of touch as communication is *Haptics.* Touch is defined as the physical placing of a part of one person's body on another's body, such as putting your hand on another person's shoulder. This may be done with or without permission. Your skin is a receiver of communication: pats, pinches, strokes, slaps, punches, shakes, and kisses all convey meaning. A doctor touches your body to ascertain sensitivity and possible illness. You shake hands to satisfy social and business welcoming needs. You intimately touch through kisses and use sexually arousing touch in the act of lovemaking. The messages that touch communicates depends on how, where, and by whom you are touched.

The importance of touch is well documented. Many people find that when they are upset, they rub their hands together or stroke a part of their body, such as the arm. "Throughout life, touch is your deepest and most intimate connection to the ones you love."[48] "Researchers have found that tactile deprivation is terrible for a child and can actually be life-threatening."[49] Most people (except those who have been abused, raped, or brought up in a low- or no-touch family or society) associate appropriate touching with positive messages. Those whose bodies have been invaded without permission, however, as in the case of rape or sexual abuse, often pull back or feel uncomfortable when touched. In fact, touch avoidance is one of the signs counselors sometimes use to aid in the identification of clients who have been physically or sexually abused.

If you have ever wondered why you felt comfortable, or uncomfortable, when you were touched, it could well have to do with your upbringing. Different cultures regard touch in different ways. Some avoid touch, but others encourage it. The same is true within families. For example, in the United States, a moderate-touch society, it is not unusual for a person to touch another with either hand, but, "to touch an Arab Muslin with the left hand, which is reserved for toilet use, is considered a

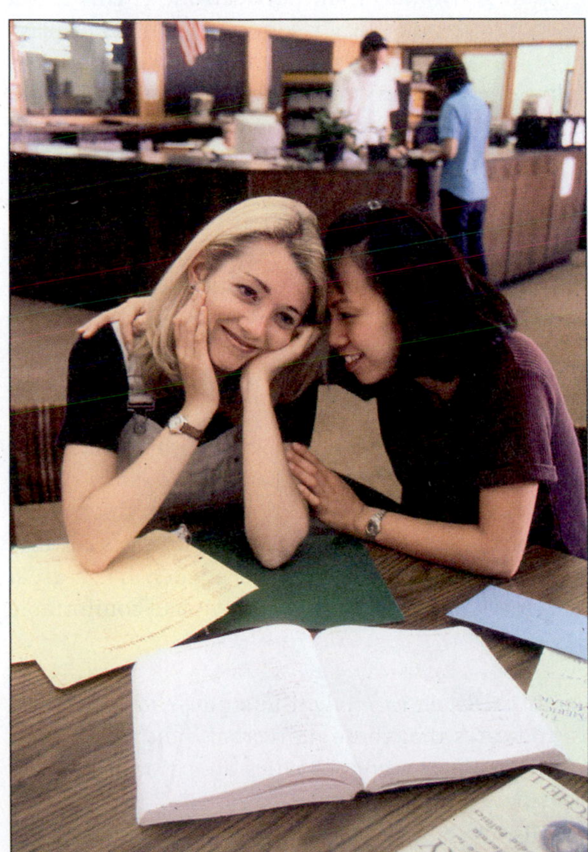

Touch is not only society specific but gender specific.

Culturally COMMUNICATING

A Hands-On Approach

Lingering handshakes, hand-holding, embraces, and sometimes kisses between heterosexual men are the norm in much of the Muslim world. In Senegal, men walk with arms draped around each other's shoulders. In Saudi Arabia, greetings between men are almost always extended with kisses on the cheek. In Afghanistan, men write love poems to friends, and Taliban fighters give one another flowers.

Source: A hands-on approach: Muslim men are affectionate in ways that would make an American male blush. (2007, November/December). *Psychology*, 24.

REFLECT ON THIS:

1. The title of the article from which this activity derived is "A Hands-On Approach: Muslim Men Are Affectionate in Ways That Would Make an American Male Blush." Why would American men blush?
2. Why do you think there is such a difference in views regarding male–male displays of affection in the Arabic world and the United States?

social insult."[50] In the United States, a handshake is appropriate as a business greeting, a bow fulfills the same purpose in Japan, and kissing on both cheeks is an acceptable French custom.

Touching can not only be culture specific but also gender specific. Women in the European American culture tend to engage in more same-sex touch than do men. Female pairs are more likely than male pairs to exchange hugs, kisses, and touches on the arm or back, and to do so for longer duration. Heterosexual men touch one another using only narrowly circumscribed behaviors, such as handshaking or, in instances of extreme emotion (e.g., athletic accomplishments), hugging, butt slapping, or kissing. The acceptability of showing physical affection by women may be one of the reasons lesbians may be less discriminated against than gay men.[51]

European Americans tend to react less to physical displays between women than between men. This is not true in other countries. "Public displays of affection between men have deep historical roots in Muslim culture."[52] In Senegal, men walk with arms draped around each other's shoulders. In Saudi Arabia, greetings between men are almost always extended with kisses on the check. In Egypt and much of the Arab world, it is acceptable for men to hold hands or kiss.[53]

Permission to touch tends to follow an action chain sequence. If you have ever wondered why someone with whom you'd like to be intimate pulls away or gets rigid when one of you is touched, it may well be that you have jumped forward in the sequence too quickly. For a person brought up in a moderate- to low-touch society, there is an appropriate time not to touch, then to touch, then to kiss, and then to fondle. If one person feels he or she is at the no-touch stage, and the partner acts at the fondle stage, strong negative verbal and physical reactions may follow.

Individuals differ dramatically in the degree to which they like or dislike touch. The degree to which an individual dislikes being touched is identified as *touch avoidance*.[54]

If you would like to measure your touch and touch avoidance patterns, fill out the Touch Avoidance Scale.[55] Remember in evaluating your scores that your cultural background, including your nationality, sexual orientation, and gender, has a great deal to do with your score, your desire to touch, and with whom you feel comfortable touching you.

Posture, Walk, and Stance Research in *Body Synchrony*, the study of posture and the way a person walks and stands, indicates that these nonverbal indicators do say something about a person.[56] A person's walk can give us clues about status, mood, ethnic and cultural affiliation, and self-perception.

Even walking follows cultural patterns. Some Europeans coming to the United States often ask why people are in such a hurry, an impression that comes from the quick pace at which European Americans typically walk.

The Touch Avoidance Scale

DIRECTIONS: This instrument is composed of 18 statements concerning feelings about touching other people and being touched. Please indicate the degree to which each statement applies to you by circling whether you (1) Strongly Disagree, (2) Disagree, (3) Are Undecided, (4) Agree, or (5) Strongly Agree with each statement. While some of these statements may seem repetitious, take your time and try to be as honest as possible.

	Statement					
____	1. A hug from a same-sex friend is a true sign of friendship.	1	2	3	4	5
____	2. Opposite-sex friends enjoy it when I touch them.	1	2	3	4	5
____	3. I often put my arm around friends of the same sex.	1	2	3	4	5
____	4. When I see two people of the same sex hugging, it revolts me.	1	2	3	4	5
____	5. I like it when members of the opposite sex touch me.	1	2	3	4	5
____	6. People shouldn't be so uptight about touching persons of the same sex.	1	2	3	4	5
____	7. I think it is vulgar when members of the opposite sex touch me.	1	2	3	4	5
____	8. When a member of the opposite sex touches me, I find it unpleasant.	1	2	3	4	5
____	9. I wish I were free to show emotions by touching members of the same sex.	1	2	3	4	5
____	10. I'd enjoy giving a massage to an opposite-sex friend.	1	2	3	4	5
____	11. I enjoy kissing persons of the same sex.	1	2	3	4	5
____	12. I like to touch friends that are the same sex as I am.	1	2	3	4	5
____	13. Touching a friend of the same sex does not make me uncomfortable.	1	2	3	4	5
____	14. I find it enjoyable when a close opposite-sex friend and I embrace.	1	2	3	4	5
____	15. I enjoy getting a back rub from a member of the opposite sex.	1	2	3	4	5
____	16. I dislike kissing relatives of the same sex.	1	2	3	4	5
____	17. Intimate touching with members of the opposite sex is pleasurable.	1	2	3	4	5
____	18. I find it difficult to be touched by a member of my own sex.	1	2	3	4	5

Directions for scoring:

a. Add up the circled numbers for items 1, 2, 3, 5, 6, 9, 10, 11, 12, 13, 14, 15, and 17: ____________

b. Score items 4, 7, 8, 16, and 18 in reverse so a circled 1 is scored as 5, 2 as 4, 3 as 3, 4 as 2, and 5 as 1, and add them up: ____________

c. Add up items (A) and (B) above to get your score: ____________

A score of 70 or higher indicates a very strong motivation to touch. Less than 14% (about one-seventh) of the population scores this high. If your score is right around 60, your motivation is about average, but still generally positive, since the midpoint between positive and negative on the scale is 54. A score of 50 or lower would place you approximately in the lower 14% in terms of motivation for touch.

Note: Item 14 from the original scale (Andersen & Leibowitz, 1978) has been altered from "when my date and I embrace" to "when a close opposite-sex friend and I embrace." Also, the scoring has been reversed from the original so that a higher score indicates a more positive attitude toward touch.

Source: Anderson, P. (2008). *Nonverbal communication* (2nd ed.). Long Grove IL: Waveland Press, p. 181.

In general, the way you walk and stand tells more about you than you probably realize. When someone enters a room, you may form conclusions about that person. Some people walk with confidence and stand with head high, shoulders back, and jaw set. Others walk slowly with a stance of sloping shoulders, eyes down, withdrawing within their bodies. This posture may indicate a lack of confidence as interpreted in the Euro American culture. Detectives and airline security personnel are trained to pick out suspicious people by the way they walk.

Artifacts The study of those things that adorn the body or environment and send messages to others about us as well as say something about us and our selection of these items is *artifacts*. A person's clothing, makeup, eyeglasses and jewelry carry distinct messages.

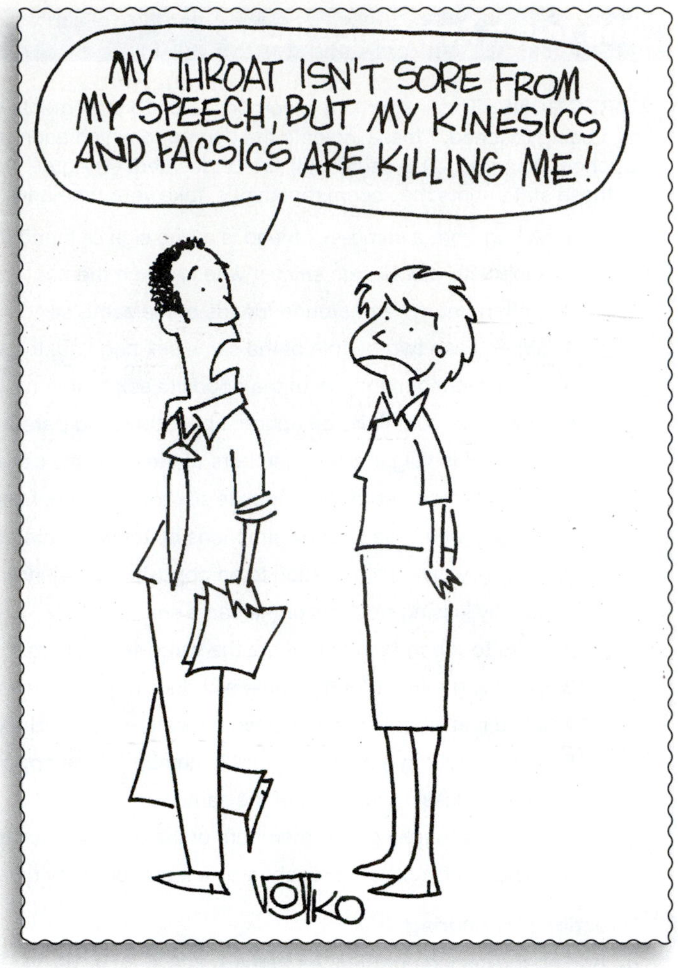

We communicate through the gestures we use, the way we walk and stand, and the expressions on our faces and in our eyes.

Clothing is probably the most obvious of the artifact communicators. It is almost like a substitute body, telling an observer something about who you are. Because you have made a choice about what to wear, it follows that this is the image you want to portray, this is the attitude you want to present about the type of person you are, and this is the way you want others to perceive you. Some pressure has been put on academic administrators to limit clothing choices because wearing certain clothing indicates gang affiliation.[57]

For those interested in climbing the business ladder, the corporate uniform is still the norm for interviews. It is known, for example, that the clothing you wear to a job interview may be a deciding factor on whether you get hired.

In spite of the emphasis on corporate clothing for interviews, casual attire on the job, sometimes referred to as *business casual,* became popular during the last decade of the twentieth century and peaked toward the turn of the century.[58] Business casual attire was meant to create a more relaxed working environment while still appearing professional, but some workers went overboard trading slacks for jeans and shirts for T-shirts.[59] About 70 percent of all U.S companies have adopted some sort of casual dress policy, but there is a trend toward returning to traditional business wear.[60]

Be aware, however, that even though some U.S. companies are allowing casualness, this trend is not universal. Companies dealing in foreign markets know that the business suit, which originally rose in nineteenth-century Europe as a costume to make managerial workers stand out from production workers, is still very much the business garb. In countries such as Japan, England, and Germany, casual is definitely not the "in" style.

Legal professionals also are aware of the effect of clothing worn by themselves and their clients. Lawyers advise clients to dress conservatively and to reinforce their credibility with a professional appearance.

Physical Characteristics A person's *physical characteristics*—for instance, height, weight, and skin color—communicate something about him or her to others. We find some people appealing and others unappealing by how they appear physically.

The prejudice against unattractive people is deeply ingrained in European American society. This attitude may, in part, be the result of the emphasis projected by the advertising industry on attractiveness in their magazine, newspaper, and television ads.

The attitude toward the way people look carries over into the way people are evaluated. Attractive people are often given credit—known as the *halo effect*—for other qualities such as high intelligence and better job performance. Meanwhile, unattractive people may be cast by the *devil effect*—a negative evaluation because of the way they look, regardless of their intelligence or job performance.[61]

Economists recognized the *beauty premium*. "Handsome men earn, on average, 5 percent more than their less-attractive counterparts, good looking women earn 4 percent more. Pretty people get more attention from teachers, bosses, and mentors."[62] "Over his career, a good-looking [professional] man will make some $250,000 more than his least attractive counterpart."[63] "Fifty-seven percent of hiring managers indicate that qualified but unattractive candidates are likely to have a harder time landing a job."[64]

What it means to be attractive differs from culture to culture. For example, judges at international beauty contests have difficulty determining the winner because of the vast physical differences among the contestants and the lack of a universal definition of *beauty*. And, although thinness for women might be an "in" beauty criterion for the white European American culture, that is not necessarily true in African-American culture. In a study of teenage girls, white girls described attractiveness as 5'7", between 100 and 110 pounds, with blue eyes and long flowing hair. However, the black girls in the study named full hips and large thighs as the signs of attractiveness.[65]

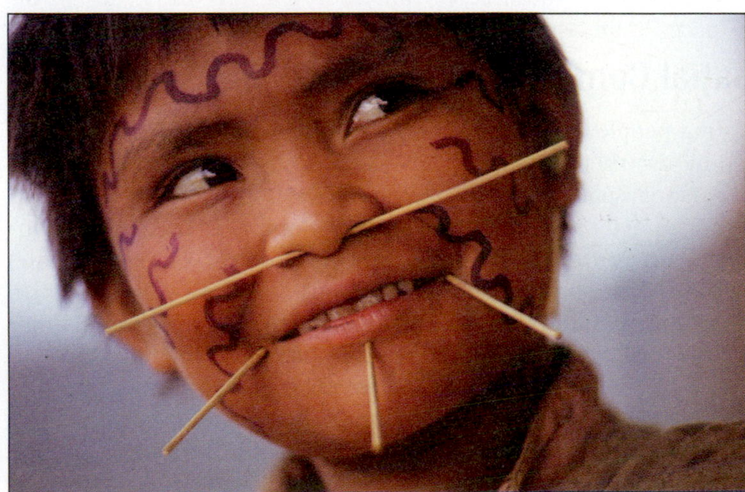

Attractiveness is in the eye of the beholder.

It is generally assumed that females are more vain, more concerned about their physical appearance, and more dissatisfied with their bodies than are males. It is known, for example, that more females than males have eating disorders such as bulimia and anorexia. However, it's not just women who are dissatisfied with their bodies; men seem to be, too. Men's dissatisfaction stems primarily from believing themselves to be less muscular than they really are. Body image is linked to depression, eating pathology, low self-esteem, and using performance-enhancing substances."[66]

A jury's decision can be affected by both the plaintiff's and the defendant's physical appearances. In one study, participants in an automobile-negligence trial heard tape-recorded testimony. The first set of jurors was shown photographs of an attractive male plaintiff and an unattractive male defendant; the second set of jurors saw the reverse. A third panel saw no pictures but heard the testimony. The results: The attractive plaintiff received a 49 percent positive vote from the first jury, the unattractive plaintiff got only a 17 percent positive vote from the second jury, and 41 percent of the third group, which did not see any pictures, ruled for the plaintiff.[67]

It should not be surprising that height can be a communicator. People often are judged purely by their physical presence. Size can affect a man's life. "Short men are discriminated against with respect to job offers and salaries."[68] Men under 5'6" are considered short. People regard them as having less power. Short men may be perceived as *submissive* and *weak;* tall men garner such descriptions as *mature* and *respected.*

A comparison of the starting pay of business-school graduates indicates that tall males received $600 per inch of height more in yearly salary[69] or "1.8 percent increase per additional inch of height."[70] What are the implications? Shorter men may need to be better prepared, be aware that they must exceed in grades and talent, and sell themselves during job interviews. However, success for short men is not impossible. For example, two-term U.S. President James Madison was 5'4"; Attila the Hun, 5'; and, of course, there was Napoleon.

Although European American society seems to show a preference for taller men, tall women often are labeled "ungainly"; short businesswomen, in fact, may have an advantage in not acquiring whatever threatening overtones may attend to increasing height. But very short women may be perceived differently than taller women. A well-qualified 5'1", size 2, master-degreed audiologist reports that her patients often call and ask for "the little girl doctor." Overweight women also find themselves "prejudiced against."[71]

Proxemics: Spatial Communication

A basic difference among people can be seen in how they operate within the space around them—how they use their territory. The study of how people use and perceive their social and personal space is called **proxemics**.

Every person is surrounded by a psychological bubble of space. This bubble contracts and expands depending on the person's cultural background, emotional state, and the activity in which he or she is participating. Northern Europeans—English, Scandinavians, and Germans—tend to have a need for a larger zone of personal space and often avoid touching and close contact. They often structure their lifestyles to meet the need for this space. Thus, the English are stereotyped as being distant and impersonal, not showing great emotion through hugging, kissing, and touching. This stereotype derives from the respect they exhibit for each other's territory. In contrast, many Italians, Russians, Spaniards, Latin Americans, Middle Easterners, and the French prefer close personal contact.

Culture has an effect on how people perceive themselves in space and how they use space.

Culture and Space When people from different cultural backgrounds come into contact, they may assume they have the same concept of space. This, of course, is not true. In fact, "cultures can be distinguished by the distances at which members interact and how frequently members touch."[72] It has been proposed that there are *contact cultures*—those characterized by tactile modes of communication (e.g., Latin Americans, Mediterraneans, French, Arabs)—and *noncontact cultures* (Germans, Japanese, English, North Americans).[73]

Even within our own culture, the space bubble varies according to our emotional states and activity. Although European Americans usually keep well beyond the three-foot personal circle of space, this can change very quickly. If you are on a crowded bus and someone presses against you, you may tolerate it. If, however, you are standing at a bus stop and someone presses against you, you probably will object. This situation brings into play your idea of public distance.

Most European Americans feel most comfortable keeping eighteen inches to four feet space around them. Invasion of this personal territory will cause discomfort.

Your emotional state also can change your idea of space. For instance, when some people are angry, they may grab someone by the front of the shirt, step in close, get "nose to nose," and shout. Others react by running out of the stressing area.

Space Distances An examination of space distances allows for an understanding of space as it relates to culture. Everyone has spatial needs. Studies of space distances as they relate to white middle-class U.S. Americans indicate that there are four classifications that explain their spatial needs: intimate, personal, social, and public. (See Figure 3.5.)[74]

Intimate distance covers a space varying from direct physical contact with another person to a distance of eighteen inches. It is used for our most private activities: caressing, making love, and sharing intimate ideas and emotions. We can often get clues about a relationship by noticing whether the other person allows us to use his or her intimate space. For example, if you have been on a hand-holding/physically touching basis with someone, and suddenly he or she will not let you near or pulls away when you get very close, a change in the relationship may have occurred. If a nontoucher suddenly encourages close body proximity, this also may indicate a change in attitude.

When in other cultures be aware that intimate touch varies. In Arabic cultures, for example, holding hands between an unmarried man and woman is not acceptable in public. An unmarried woman is forbidden to touch a religious Jewish man; not even handshakes are welcome. Note how different these instances are from the intimate distance "rules" of most U.S. Americans.

Personal distance, eighteen inches to four feet, is sometimes called the *comfort bubble.* Generally, European Americans feel most comfortable maintaining this distance when talking with others, and invasion of this personal territory will cause us to back away. If we are backed into a corner, sitting in a chair, or somehow trapped, we will lean away, pull in, and tense up. To avoid invasion of our territory, we might place a leg on the rung of a chair or on a stair. Some of us even arrange furniture so that no one can invade our territory. For example, businesspeople may place their desks so that employees must sit on one side and the boss on the other. In contrast, interviewers have reported a completely different atmosphere when talking to job applicants if the two chairs are placed facing each other about three to four feet apart instead of on opposite sides of the desk.

Social distance covers a four- to twelve-foot zone that is used during business transactions and casual social exchanges. Also part of social distance is the *standing–seated interaction,* in which the person in control stands and the other person sits. Standing–seated positions occur, among others, in teacher–pupil and police officer–arrestee transactions.

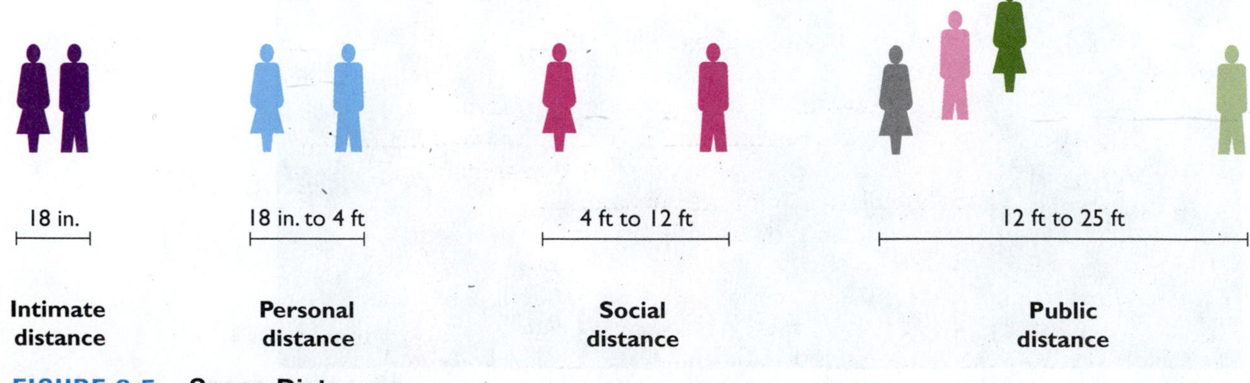

FIGURE 3.5 **Space Distances**

The physical placement of small group members in relation to one another, such as in a tight circle, affects the members' communication and behavior.

Public distance may dictate a separation of as little as twelve feet, but it is usually more than twenty-five feet. Distance is sometimes used by professors in lecture rooms and speakers at public gatherings as well as by public figures who wish to place a barrier between themselves and their audiences.

An important aspect of proxemics is the arrangement of seating and how people are spaced at meetings and in homes.

Small-Group Ecology The physical placement of members of small groups in relation to one another has an effect on their behavior. This *small-group ecology,* which includes the placement of chairs, the placement of the person conducting a meeting, and the setting for a small-group encounter, clearly influences the group's operation. If, for example, people are seated in a tight circle, they will probably feel comfortable and interact more than they would if they were sitting in straight rows. They will be able to see each other's nonverbal reactions, and, because there is no inhibiting physical distance, they will lose their self-consciousness as they become members of the group.

Vocal Cues as Communication

The vocal effects that accompany words, such as tone of voice—but not the words themselves—are *paralanguage* or vocal *cues,*[75] which include the vocal elements that add meaning to your message. A high-pitch and rapid rate when saying "Are you going?" for example, might suggest you're excited and enthusiastic about a trip. In contrast, a low-pitch with a slow, halting rate when saying "Are you going?" might mean that you are sad and disappointed about someone's departure.

Vocal cues communicate nonverbally to the listening ear. The rate (speed), volume (power), pitch (such as soprano or bass), pause (stopping), and stress (intensity) of sounds all contribute meanings. "People spontaneously use a system of communicating when they speak that either reinforces their message or provides additional information not conveyed by the words alone."[76] Sometimes we use our voice in ways that

Socially COMMUNICATING

Voices Weigh In

People can estimate a speaker's weight and age from his voice as accurately as they can after viewing a photo.

Source: "Voice Messages, The Science of Your Sound," (November/December 2006) *Psychology Today*: 15.

REFLECT ON THIS:

1. Did you ever meet someone whom you "knew" only by phone or when listening to him or her on the radio? If so, did the person "look" like what you expected? What clues did you use to come to your first impression?
2. While talking to someone on the phone, does your image of what that person looks like influence how you speak to him or her?

are subtle. Both men and women, for example, tend to use a more pleasant, lower-pitched voice when talking to someone they find attractive in contrast to when they speak to a person they consider unattractive.[77] The vocal changes "happen with little intention on the part of the speaker, although it is possible to use this expression explicitly to dramatize an utterance."[78] For example, "someone will raise his voice slightly at the end of the sentence when saying 'the stock market is going up' or lower it when saying 'the stock market is going down.'"[79]

Vocal cues offer clues to determine the sex, age, and status of a speaker. We also can make some pretty accurate judgments about the emotions and feelings of the people with whom we communicate by their paralinguistic presentation. If you are very angry, the pitch of your voice may go up. And when you are very, very angry, you sometimes say words slowly and distinctly, pausing after each word for special effect.

A study indicates that "sarcasm plays an important part in human interaction."[80] Sarcasm, a bitter, or cutting expression is created not only by the words being used, but by a verbal tone, and sometimes by the body position or facial expression of the speaker.

The voice also may be important in some aspects of persuasion.[81] A faster rate of speech, more intonation, greater volume, and a less halting manner seem to be related to successful attempts at persuasion. If a person sounds assured, the receiver credits him or her with a higher degree of credibility. Television news anchors, for example, work to cultivate an assured broadcast voice.

Vocal cues can provide much information about a speaker, and our overall reaction to another person is colored at least somewhat by our reactions to these cues.

Time as Communication

You communicate to yourself and others by the way you use time. The way people handle and structure their time is known as *chronemics*. Time, as a communication tool, is sometimes greatly misunderstood. Only within certain societies, for example, is precise time of great significance. Some cultures, such as Native Americans and some eastern societies,[82] relate to time as a *circular phenomenon* in which there is no pressure or anxiety about the future. Existence follows the cycle of the seasons of planting and harvesting, the daily rising and setting of the sun, birth and death. In *circular time*, there is no pressing need to achieve or create newness, or to produce more than is needed to survive. Nor is there fear of death. Such societies have successfully integrated the past and future into a peaceful sense of the present.[83] Some societies operate on *linear time*, centered primarily on the future. These societies focus on the factual and technical information needed to fulfill impending demands. In most of Western Europe, North America, and Japan, punctuality is considered good manners.

Time has become a critical factor in the U.S. workplace. Throughout a person's career, punctuality is often used as a measure of effectiveness. A person who arrives late for a job interview probably will have difficulty overcoming such a negative first impression, and employees who arrive late or leave early may be reprimanded and even dismissed.

Time is culture based. European Americans, Euro Canadians, and Western Europeans, in general, are clock bound; African, Latin American, and some Asian Pacific cultures are not clock bound. European Americans traveling abroad often are irritated by the seeming lack of concern for time commitments among residents of some countries.[84] In Mexico and Central America, tours may be late; guides may fail to indicate exact arrival and departure times. Yet in other places, such as Switzerland, travelers can set their watch by the promptness of the trains. Businesspeople may get confused over what "on time" means as they meet those from other cultures. In some Latin America countries, one is expected to arrive late to an appointment. This same tardiness for Germans or European Americans would be perceived as rudeness.[85]

The differences in the use of time have been noted when college students arrive for classes and turn in assignments. For instance, one of your authors found that some of his Arabic and South American students showed few signs of concern for lateness, arriving as much as an hour late for a two-hour class, but also feeling comfortable about asking questions long after the class had officially ended. As one student explained it, "Things just don't start on time, at least U.S. time, where we come from."[86] Some gays and Hispanics have names that refer to their habitual lateness such as *gay-late, mañana time*.[87]

(Note: Remember, as in all generalizations, not everyone in a particular culture follows the same patterns.)

In cultures that value promptness, one of the questions raised about time centers on the person who is constantly late. What does habitual tardiness reveal about the person? Chronic lateness, in a formal-time culture, may be deeply rooted in a person's psyche. Compulsive tardiness is rewarding on some level. A key emotional conflict for the chronically late person involves his or her need to feel special. People must be special in some way, so the person is special by being late. Other reasons include needs for punishment or power or as an expression of hostility.[88]

Procrastination may be about a person's lack of self-confidence concerning completing a task. If a person has aversion to a task, is impulsive, distracted, or lacks motivation, the individual may be a *procrastinator*.[89] Tardiness can also be a sign that a person wants to avoid something or that the activity or person to be met is not important enough to warrant the effort to be on time. Procrastinators are often not valued in a linear time-focused culture.[90]

Smell as Communication

Olfactics is the study of smell. We communicate through our smells. When we put on cologne, we may be intentionally communicating about our personality or emotion.[91] When we use a room deodorizer, we may be trying to send a message to others about our cleanliness.

The sense of smell is extraordinarily precise. "Scents can have positive effects on mood, stress reduction, sleep enhancement, self-confidence, and physical and cognitive performance."[92] "It has been demonstrated that odor remains in our memory much longer than things we see or hear."[93] Our sense of smell is very selective and helps us focus attention[94] and reach conclusions. Some people find certain body odors offensive. This is especially true in a country such as the United States, where we have been taught by advertisers and medical people to wash off natural odors and replace them with neutral, fragrance-free, or substitute smells.[95] Some people make assumptions about a person's social ability and even morality based on the way an individual smells.[96] This is not the case in other cultures such as India and many Arabic countries.[97]

We often make decisions without realizing that these choices are based on odors. There is evidence that people are attracted to mates partly based on smell caused by genetic diversity, for example.[98] Several phenomena provide insight into how smell serves as a nonverbal communication tool: smell blindness, smell adaptation, smell memory, smell overload, and smell discrimination.[99]

Each person has a unique ability to identify and distinguish smells. *Smell blindness* occurs when a person is unable to detect smells. It parallels color blindness or deafness because it is a physiological blockage. It accounts for the fact that some people do not smell differences in the odors of various foods. Because smell and taste are so closely aligned, this can explain why people who are smell-blind may also have taste-identification difficulties.

Smell adaptation occurs when we gradually lose the distinctiveness of a particular smell through repeated contact with it. When you walk into a bakery, you may be aware of the wonderful odors. The clerks who work there, however, may have become so used to the odors that they are not aware of them.

The ability to recall previous situations when encountering a particular smell associated with them is *smell memory.* Smelling a crayon may trigger flashbacks to experiences you had in kindergarten. Smell memory may even have an affect on your academic career, since your sense of smell may be able to "prompt memory when taking a test."[100] Research suggests that "your ability to recall information may be improved by inhaling an odor you breathed while absorbing information."[101] The implications might be to bring a vial of whatever aroma was present when you were studying to your next exam.[102]

Smell overload takes place when an exceptionally large number of odors or one extremely strong odor overpowers you. Walking down a detergent aisle in a store can trigger smell overload for some people; it can also occur when on an elevator with someone who is saturated with perfume.

The ability to identify people, places, and things on the basis of their smells is *smell discrimination.* Smell discrimination allows us to tell the difference between cinnamon and garlic, bananas and oranges, and one person and another.

Effective communicators recognize that smell conveys meaning.[103]

Socially COMMUNICATING

Using Smell to Improve Your Test Taking

An odor has no personal significance until it becomes connected to something that has meaning. On a practical level, that means that you may be able to use your sense of smell to prompt your memory when taking a test. Research suggests that your ability to recall information may be improved by inhaling an odor you breathed while absorbing information—so fire up a stick of incense while studying, then bring a vial of that aroma's essential oil to a big test.

REFLECT ON THIS: Some students have used this technique to improve their grades. See if it works for you. The next time you study for an exam, expose yourself to a particular odor. For example, put your favorite cologne, after-shave, vanilla extract, or some other positive smell on a handkerchief. Smell it occasionally as you study. The day of the test, saturate the handkerchief and bring it to class with you. Smell it during an exam and see if you have any intrapersonal flashback memory that helps you remember answers.

Aesthetics as Communication

The study of communication of a message or mood through color or music is *aesthetics.* When you are driving a car, the type of music on the radio affects your driving, alertness, and concentration. And the music in an elevator is almost never loud and pulsating because such strong sounds would be too emotionally stressful for people in a small, contained area.

As you stroll through the supermarket, you may not even be aware of how music affects you. During a nine-week test, the music in one supermarket was randomly played at a slow 60 beats a minute on some days and at 108 beats a minute on others. On slow-tempo days the store's gross receipts were 38.2 percent higher as people walked at a leisurely pace and purchased more.[104]

Music does many things for the human body, including masking unpleasant sounds and feelings; slowing down and equalizing brain waves; affecting respiration; affecting heartbeat, pulse rate, and blood pressure; reducing muscle tension and improving body movement and coordination; affecting body temperature; regulating stress-related hormones; boosting the immune function; changing our perception of space and time; strengthening our memory and learning; boosting productivity; enhancing romance and sexuality; stimulating digestion; fostering endurance; enhancing unconscious receptivity to symbolism; and generating a sense of safety and well-being.[105]

A study on the impact of rock music tested more than 20,000 records for their effect on muscle strength: "Listening to rock music frequently causes all the muscles in the body to go weak."[106] This relationship may account for the drugged and dreamlike feelings of some people who attend rock concerts. It is theorized that some rock music has a stopped quality that is not present in other types of music—that is, the beat is stopped at the end of each bar or measure. Because the music stops and then must start again, the listener subconsciously comes to a halt at the end of each measure; this may tire the listener.

Music has been credited with easing pain, and a type of music therapy is being used in hospices in working with dying patients. A study found signs that harp music might help regulate a patient's irregular heartbeat.[107] Other researchers believe music can alleviate some of the mental and physical symptoms of disease, including normalizing sick newborns' heart rates and after surgery to reduce patients' anxiety.[108]

Colors also affect people, and many institutions are putting into practice this awareness. For example, hospitals are experimenting with using various colors for their rooms in hopes that the colors may motivate sick people to get well or ease pain. Hospitals also are painting large pieces of equipment, such as x-ray machines, the same color as the background walls so they do not appear as frightening to patients.

Other studies regarding the power of colors to communicate reveal that when otherwise equally matched with their opponent in fitness and skill, male athletes wearing red are more likely to win.[109] The reason, according to scientists, is that red correlates to male dominance and testosterone levels. Anger is associated with reddening of the skin due to increased blood flow.[110] However, the wearing of or sitting next to someone who is wearing red when you take a test could negatively affect your performance.[111] The conclusion reached is, "care must be taken in how red is used in achievement contexts."[112]

Taste as Communication

Every time we place a substance in our mouths, our sense of taste communicates. Sometimes that communication is intentional, such as when you make a friend's favorite food for her birthday celebration. Like our other senses, the sense of taste acts as a medium that carries messages of pleasure, displeasure, and warning to our brains.[113] *Gustorics* is the study of how taste communicates. It encompasses the communication aspects of such factors as the classifications of taste, the role of culture on taste, the role of food deprivation, food preferences, taste expectations, and color and textures as an encourager or discourager of eating and drinking.[114]

Taste qualities have been classified as bitter, salty, sweet, and sour. We receive these signals much the same as we do smells. We come in physical contact with the object that brings about the sense reaction within us. These sense reactions are located not only on our tongue but in various other regions of our mouth and throat. The taste buds of the mouth are the most common tasters.

It is interesting to note that just as some people have smell blindness, and others can't smell all or some odors, some people have *taste blindness*—the inability to taste. This inability to taste can either be a defect in their senses at birth or the destruction of the tasters through an accident or illness. This condition can be long or short term. Another phenomenon associated with gustorics is taste adaptation. *Taste adaptation* takes place when a person becomes used to a taste to the degree that he or she can eat a substance and not taste it. People who eat a lot of very spicy foods may eventually develop an insensitivity to the tang.

Using Nonverbal Communication

Nonverbal communication theories have permeated culture. The field has become an important tool for understanding and evaluating people and places. It has a place in such areas as law enforcement, politics, education, home decorating, and the law profession.

Nonverbal communication has become a weapon in the war on crime. Law-enforcement officers are being exposed to *behavior pattern recognition,* which is training in detecting signs that could indicate a terrorist plot. The officers are taught to look for something outside the normal range of behavior—such as people exhibiting odd or suspicious nonverbal behavior, including wearing heavy or large baggy clothes on a hot day, or going through checkpoints and glancing around excessively or looking nervous—and to listen for verbal stammering when a person is answering questions.[115]

A nonverbal communication consultant who runs *Body Language TV,* a website dedicated to scoring electoral debates, scored hundreds of presentations, taking into consideration gesturing, blinking, smiling and body positions—all nonverbal communication tools states, "We believe that our predictions ring true'[116] "We called California for Brown [Jerry Brown who was elected governor in 2010] over Whitman on the 29th of September after the first televised debate. Oscillating her hands, hand wringing, insincere facial expressions… these were the three big things that did Whitman in. On the other hand, Brown avoided all the negative."[117]

So, should we come to the conclusion that nonverbal communication can be used to predict elections and surveying should be eliminated? "Not necessarily," states the founder of *Nonverbal Solutions,* a consulting group. She explains, "There isn't necessarily a set criteria of positive versus negative body language."[118]

You and Nonverbal Communication

A question arises as to why, if nonverbal communication is such an important aspect of communication, most people aren't aware of it or don't pay much overt attention to its powers. One reason is that most people have not been taught that actions communicate as clearly as words communicate, so they don't look for nonverbal components. Schools don't generally teach courses in the subject, and what we do learn tends to be through subtle cultural communication. You may have been told that if you didn't look someone in the eye as you speak, that person might not believe you, or that you should stand up straight and walk with pride, or that you are judged by what you wear. These messages actually say, "Pay attention to the nonverbals," but most of us don't tie that to the fact that nonverbal communication is carrying messages.

Being aware that nonverbal communication exists, being aware that you need to listen to others with your eyes as well as your ears, and monitoring what you do as a nonverbal communicator will help you to become a more competent communicator.

In Conclusion

IN CONCLUSION

Nonverbal communication is composed of all those messages that people exchange beyond the words themselves. Nonverbal communication is a major force in our lives. There are two basic sources of nonverbals: innate neurological programs and behavior common to a culture. Research shows a relationship between nonverbal and verbal communication. In attempting to read nonverbal communication, we must remember that no one signal carries the whole meaning. Nonverbal communication includes the categories of kinesics, physical characteristics, proxemics, paravocalics, chronemics, olfactics, aesthetics, and gustorics. Through all of these channels, humans are always sending messages, even when no words are used.

LEARN BY DOING

1. Research one of these topics or people and be prepared to give a two-minute speech on what you have learned regarding the topic of nonverbal communication: neuro-linguistic programming, Ray Birdwhistell, Albert Mehrabian, Edward Hall, pupilometrics, biorhythms, Muzak.
2. Give examples of your own recent use of substituting, complementing, conflicting, and accenting.
3. Carefully observe members of your family or think of the nonverbal patterns they display. Can you find any similarities between their patterns and your own?
4. Identify a cultural-specific nonverbal trait and describe it to the class.
5. Make a list of five emblems used by you, by members of your family, or within your culture. Be prepared to demonstrate them. Compare your explanations of what they mean with those of your classmates.
6. Carry on a conversation with a person outside your classroom. As you speak, slowly move closer to him or her. Continue to move in on the person gradually. Observe his or her reaction. Did the person back up? Cross his or her arms? Report to the class on the results of the experiment.

KEY TERMS

nonverbal communication 53
kinesics 61
emblems 64
proxemics 70

CHAPTER 4

Listening

listening process • listening influences • media listening strategies • improving personal listening • listening apprehension

After reading this chapter, you should be able to

- Explain the importance of listening in daily communication
- Contrast hearing and listening
- Define and identify the roles of reception, perception, attention, the assignment of meaning, and response as they relate to the listening process
- List and explain some of the listening influencers
- Describe discriminative, comprehensive, therapeutic, critical, and appreciative listening
- Explain strategies for how to listen to the media
- Identify and explain some of the techniques available for improving personal listening
- Discuss the causes of listening apprehension and approaches to dealing with it

The place: Center Harbor, Maine. The participants? Walter Cronkite [at that time, television's leading news anchorman] and a group of Center Harbor's citizens. What happened? Cronkite piloted his boat toward the dock. Supposedly an excellent sailor, Cronkite noticed a group of people on land, who were waving to him and yelling "Hello Walter, Hello Walter." Cronkite was flattered by the yelling crowd, waved back and took a bow. Suddenly, Cronkite drove his boat aground. He suddenly realized the crowd was actually yelling "Low Water!," not "Hello Walter!"[1]

Like Cronkite, do you hear what you want to hear, or do you hear the words actually spoken? There appears to be enough evidence to indicate that if you are typical, you probably use various strategies that look like listening, but don't quite qualify. Most people will at times feign attention, overreact emotionally, day-dream, use electronic devices, or otherwise zone-out—all when they're supposedly listening.

If you are fairly typical, you have had little, if any, training as a listener. Most elementary schools operate on the assumption that you don't know how to read or write when you come to school, so they teach you how to perform those skills. They also assume that because you can talk and hear, you can communicate and listen. These assumptions are incorrect. Talking and hearing are biological functions. Listening and communicating, like reading and writing, are learned skills. Listening is a complex combination of skills and emotions. As Figure 4.1, the symbol for listening in Chinese, indicates, listening involves a combination of the ears, eyes, undivided attention and the heart.

How effective a listener do you think you are? Are you interested in finding out? If so, try the Janusik/Wolvin Student Listening Survey.

How much of your time do you spend listening? Research shows that the average working person spends 40 percent of his or her time listening. This is in contrast to 9 percent writing, 16 percent reading, and 35 percent talking.[2] "That's right. You listen more than you use any other form of communication. In fact, you spend more time listening than you do reading and writing combined!"[3]

The Importance of Listening

Your academic success, employment achievement, and personal happiness may well depend on your ability to listen effectively.

"Ralph Nichols [considered by many to be the father of listening instruction] believed that effective listening was linked to effective speaking."[4] He went on to say, "It appears

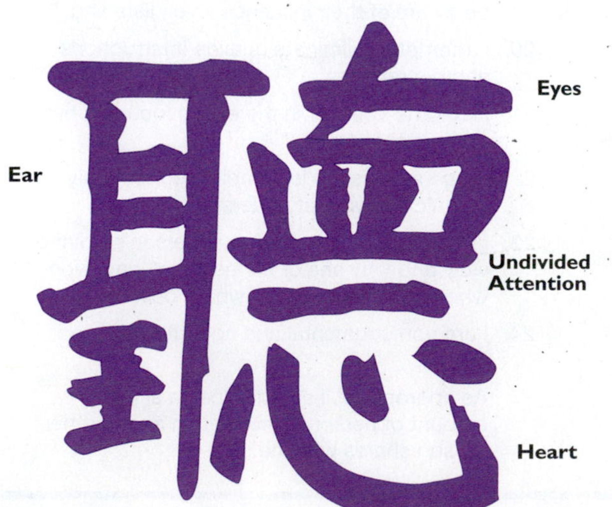

FIGURE 4.1
Chinese Symbol for "Listening"
The Chinese characters that make up the verb *to listen* explain the significance and complexity of the learned skill.

the time is at hand when speech and listening training is to be considered an important area of study throughout the education system."[5]

Listening is an important means for learning at all academic levels. Students listen to the equivalent of a book a day, talk the equivalent of a book a week, read the equivalent of a book a month, and write the equivalent of a book a year.[6] A study showed that students spend 8 percent of their time writing, 6 percent reading, 20 percent speaking, and 50 percent in listening-related activities.[7]

Janusik/Wolvin Student Listening Survey

DIRECTIONS: The process of listening includes the five steps of Reception, Attention, Perception, Assignment of Meaning, and Response. As a process, listening can break down at any of the five steps. This inventory will help you identify your strengths and weaknesses in terms of the steps within the context of the classroom. After reading each of the following statements, code the item with the most appropriate response within the context of the college classroom. Remember, "speaker" can mean the instructor or fellow students, so you may have to average your responses.

(1) almost never, (2) not often, (3) sometimes, (4) more often than not, (5) almost always

____ 1. I block out external and internal distractions, such as other conversations or what happened yesterday, when someone is speaking.

___ 2. I feel comfortable asking questions when I don't understand something the speaker said.

___ 3. When a speaker uses words that I'm not familiar with, I jot them down and look them up later.

____ 4. I identify the speaker's credibility while listening.

____ 5. I paraphrase the speaker's main ideas in my head as he or she speaks.

____ 6. I concentrate on the main ideas instead of the specific details.

____ 7. I am able to understand those who are direct as easily as I can understand those who are indirect.

____ 8. Before making a decision, I confirm my understanding of the other person's message with her or him.

____ 9. I concentrate on the speaker's message even when what she or he is saying is complex.

____ 10. I really want to understand what the other person has to say, so I focus solely on his or her message.

____ 11. When I listen to someone from another culture, I understand that the speaker may use time and space differently, and I factor that into my understanding.

____ 12. I make certain to watch a speaker's facial expressions and body language for further clues to what he or she means.

____ 13. I encourage the speaker through my facial expressions and verbal utterances.

____ 14. When others are speaking to me, I make sure to establish eye contact and quit doing other tasks.

____ 15. When I hear something with which I disagree, I try to get past my disagreement to understand the speaker's point.

____ 16. When an emotional trigger is activated, I recognize it for what it is, set aside my feelings, and continue to concentrate on the speaker's message.

____ 17. I try to be sure that my nonverbal response matches my verbal response.

____ 18. When someone begins speaking, I focus my attention on her or his message.

____ 19. I understand that my past experiences play a role in how I interpret a message, so I try to be aware of their influence when listening.

____ 20. I attempt to eliminate outside interruptions and distractions.

____ 21. I look the speaker in the eye to focus on her or his message.

____ 22. When a message is complicated or highly technical, I work at understanding it.

____ 23. I try to understand the other person's point of view and why she or he feels that way even when it is different from what I believe.

____ 24. I am nonjudgmental and noncritical when I listen.

____ 25. As appropriate, I self-disclose a similar amount of personal information as the other person shares with me.

Janusik/Wolvin Student Listening Survey 

Scoring Directions: Write your responses in the appropriate positions. For example, if you gave yourself a "3" for the first statement, transfer the 3 to the first slot under Reception. When you have transferred all of your scores, add up all five scores for each step. The step with the highest score is your strength. The step with the lowest score is the step that can use the most improvement.

	Reception	Attention	Perception	Assignment of Meaning	Response
	1.____	5.____	3.____	4.____	2.____
	9.____	10.____	6.____	7.____	8.____
	12.____	14.____	15.____	11.____	13.____
	18.____	20.____	16.____	19.____	17.____
	21.____	22.____	23.____	24.____	25.____
Total	____	____	____	____	____

Now add up your scores for all five steps, and use the following as a general guideline:

125–112 You perceive yourself to be an outstanding listener in the classroom.

111–87 You perceive yourself to be a good listener in the classroom, but there are some steps that could use improvement.

86–63 You perceive yourself to be an adequate listener in the classroom, but attention to some steps could really improve your listening effectiveness.

62–0 You perceive yourself to be a poor listener in the classroom, and attention to all of the steps could really improve your listening effectiveness.

Consider:

a. In which step or steps did you excel? What do you consciously do?

b. Which step or steps indicated the most need for improvement? What two specific actions could you take for each step to improve your listening effectiveness?

c. Did you find yourself averaging scores because you were considering both the instructor and peers? What does that say about your perception of both?

COMMUNICATING in Careers

Listening in the Global Marketplace

With continued interaction between companies all over the world, the business world is in a global marketplace. Because of this, there are some listening guidelines that are appropriate for those involved in international sales and service.

1. Listen for your own cultural/individual values.
2. When you are being introduced to someone from another culture, listen for his or her cultural/individual values.
3. Expand your knowledge of the cultural norms of other peoples.
4. Listen with your eyes and mind open.

REFLECT ON THIS:

1. What kind of education do U.S. businesspeople need in order to fulfill the requirements of listening in the global marketplace?
2. Do you think you are prepared to listen in the global marketplace? Why or why not?
3. Shouldn't those from other nations just accept that the cost of doing business with U.S. companies is the requirement to learn Euro American language and nonverbal traditions?

Frequently, listening is considered to be a passive process. But this image is an illusion. A good listener has to be patient, suspend judgment, and analyze what is said. It is an active, rather than a passive, process. Some aspects of poor listening are associated with aggressiveness and a lack of patience, which suggests that a person's perceptions can strongly affect listening skills.[8]

The cost of poor listening can be catastrophic. Federal investigators, for example, observe that poor listening is as much at fault as mechanical problems in airline crashes.[9]

You learn about your culture by listening as your family, clergy, government officials, and the media explain your gender, ethnic, and racial roles. It is also through listening that you gain your language.

As an educated person, you have an obligation to strive to be an effective listener. And to be a responsible listener, you must know what the process is about, what it takes to be an effective listener, how to evaluate your own listening, and how to work toward improving your weaknesses while retaining your strengths.

The Listening Process

Many people wrongly assume that hearing and listening are the same. **Hearing** is a biological activity that involves reception of a message through sensory channels. Hearing is only one part of **listening**, a process that involves reception, attention, perception, the assignment of meaning, and the listener's response to the message presented. (See Figure 4.2.)

Reception

The initial step in the listening process is the *reception* of a stimulus or message—both the auditory message and the visual message. The hearing process is based on a complex set of physical interactions between the ear and the brain. Proper care of the ear is important because auditory acuity enhances the ability to listen efficiently. It is estimated that about 15 percent of U.S. American adults report some level of hearing loss.[10] Also estimated is that 10 percent of U.S. Americans between 20 and 69 years

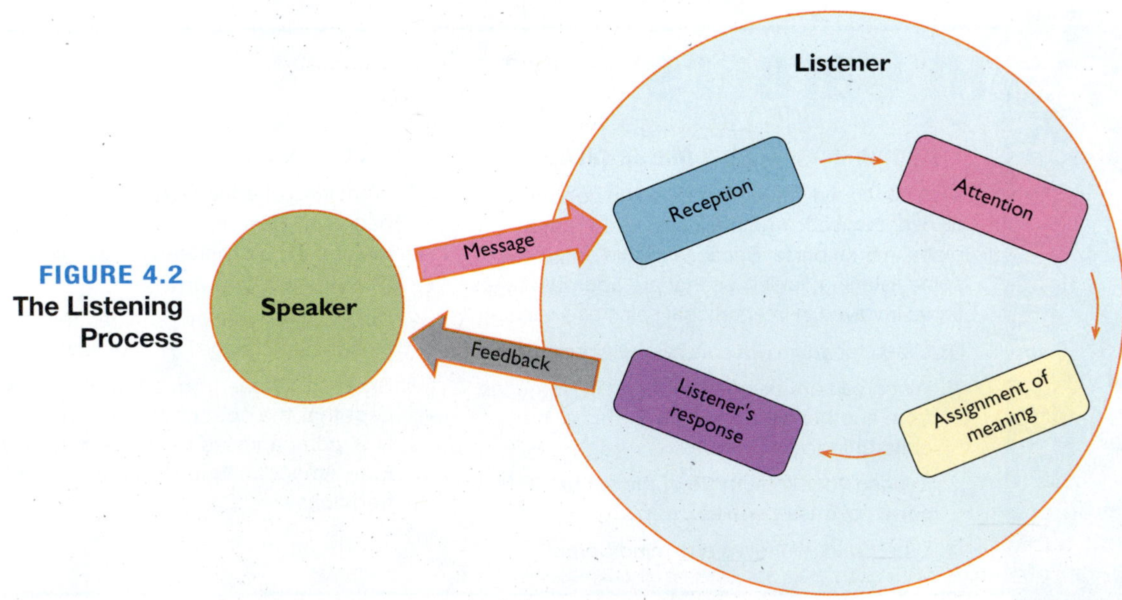

FIGURE 4.2 The Listening Process

have sustained permanent damage to their hearing as a result of exposure to loud sounds and noises on the job or during leisure activities.[11] To keep these statistics from rising, people who work near loud machinery are often required to wear ear protectors. But the workplace is not the only source of potential danger. For example, individuals who expose themselves to excessive amounts of loud music or listen to music through earphones should be aware that they can damage their hearing mechanism.[12] In fact, the use of earphones to listen to music is considered to be a major source of hearing damage.[13] An audiologist warns, "As you enjoy the blaring music in your car, home, or your headsets, or at a concert, be aware that you can be permanently damaging one of your most important biological tools...your hearing mechanism."[14]

In addition to using the hearing mechanism, people listen visually. As you engage in conversations, or as a receiver of public speeches, you should observe facial expression, posture, movement, and appearance, which provide important cues that may not be obvious by listening only to the verbal part of the message. If you fail to look at a person while he or she speaks, you miss much information.

Both speakers and listeners must realize that listeners can recall only about a quarter of what they hear.[15] Thus, speakers must attempt to stimulate listeners by doing "the real thing," simulating a real experience, doing something dramatic, or providing a "hook" that will help the listener's memory. Unfortunately, many speakers don't know this, so you, as a listener, must concentrate when hearing information. Try to get involved in the process and ask questions using the concepts of the interactional model of communication so that you can ensure active listing and comprehending.

Receiving the message through the visual and the auditory channels is but one component of the listening process. The listener also must attend to the message.

Attention

Once the stimulus—the word or visual symbol, or both—is received, it reaches the attention stage of the human processing system.

Role of Attention In listening, *attention* represents the focus on a specific stimulus selected from all the stimuli received at any given moment. In this phase, the other stimuli recede so that we can concentrate on a specific word or visual symbol. Normally your attention is divided between what you are attempting to listen to, what is currently happening in the rest of the environment, and what else is going on in your mind.

The listener's ability to focus attention is limited. Estimates are that the range of attention span of an adult (the amount of time a person can concentrate on a single activity) is from seven[16] to twenty minutes.[17] To informally check this out, during your next classroom lecture, look around after twenty minutes and see how many people are doing other things, such as doodling, looking out the window, daydreaming, playing with their cell phones, or dozing. The implication is that in giving a speech, for example, ensure that, at a maximum, the first twenty minutes include any material that you want your audience to remember.[18] To "prolong attention span, periodically give your audience a rest by telling a story, giving a demo, or doing something else that gives the brain a break."[19]

Cognitive psychologists have come to understand this as a dual-task process of what they call the working memory. A person's *working memory* capacity is made up of both the memory and the attention functions, and listeners shift in and out of the long-term memory to retrieve and to store stimuli while, at the same time, attempting to pay attention to the speaker's message.[20]

The listener's ability to focus attention is limited. After about twenty minutes, people start to doodle, look out the window, daydream, play with their smart phones, or doze.

Role of Motivation/Concentration Undoubtedly one of the most difficult tasks we have to perform as listeners is concentration, put in action by your motivation. For example, if you really want to listen to a speaker, this desire will put you in a more positive frame of mind than will anticipating that the speaker will be boring, thus encouraging concentration on the speaker and subject matter. Realistically, some messages may be boring, but if you need to get the information, careful concentration is imperative. For example, you may not find the chemistry professor's ideas fascinating, but if you do not listen effectively, you probably will fail the next test. You also may find the information so difficult that you tune out. Again, if it is imperative for you to understand the ideas, then you have to force yourself to figure out what you do not understand and find a way of grasping the meaning.

The average U.S. American rate of speech is 130 to 200 words per minute.[21] In conversations, the average rate is 125 words per minute; whereas a speaker before an audience slows down to about 100 words per minute.[22] How fast do listeners listen? Or, to put the question in a better form, how many words a minute can people normally *think* as they listen? Listeners probably average 400 to 500 words per minute as they listen.[23]

Because we can receive messages much more quickly than the other person can talk, we tend to tune in and tune out throughout a message. The mind can absorb only so much material. Indeed, the brain operates much like

Culturally COMMUNICATING

The Haka Race of Taipei, Taiwan's View of Listening

When you listen, you use your ears, eyes, and heart to determine *the* meaning. The eyes are actually more important than the ears. You have to learn to listen to the content, but you have to know what people mean.

Source: "The Haka Race of Taipei, Taiwan's View of Listening" from *Intercultural communication: A text with readings*, 1st Edition by Pamela J. Cooper, Carolyn Calloway-Thomas, Cheri J. Simonds. Copyright © 2007 by Pamela J. Cooper, Carolyn Calloway-Thomas, Cheri J. Simonds. Printed and electronically reproduced by permission of Pearson Education, Inc., Upper Saddle River, New Jersey.

REFLECT ON THIS:

1. What do you think the authors mean by "listen with your heart" as it relates to the meaning of messages you receive?
2. What do you think is meant by "but you have to know what people mean"?

a computer: it turns off, recycles itself, and turns back on to avoid information overload. It is no wonder, then, that our attention fluctuates even when we are actively involved as listeners. Think back to any class you have attended. Do you recall a slight gap in your listening at times? This is a natural part of the listening process. When you tune out, the major danger is that you may daydream rather than quickly turn back to the message. But by taking notes or forcing yourself to paraphrase, you can avoid this difficulty.

Research with compressed speech illustrates the human capacity for efficient listening.[24] In this technique, taped material is speeded up mechanically to more than 300 words per minute. Incredibly, there is no loss of comprehension at this faster rate. Tests even reveal increased comprehension, much as the tests given to people who have been taught to speed-read show an increase in their retention of information. Because of the rapid speeds, the test participants anticipated retention problems and thus forced themselves to listen more attentively and concentrate more fully than they would otherwise have done.[25]

Concentration also requires the listener to control for distractions. As a listener, you probably have a whole list of things that you have to attend to in addition to the speaker's message. Rather than attempting to dismiss them, control your concentration by mentally setting aside these other issues for the moment to give the speaker your full attention. It takes mental and physical energy to do this, but concentration is often the key to successful listening.

Role of Paraphrasing **Paraphrasing**—making a summary of the ideas you have just received—will provide you with a concise restatement of what has been presented. It also will allow you to determine whether you understand the material. If you cannot repeat or write down a summary of what was said, then you probably did not get the whole message or did not understand it. Keep this in mind when you are listening to an instructor and taking notes. Try to paraphrase the material, putting it into your own words, instead of writing down direct quotations. If you cannot summarize in your own words, you should ask for clarification or make a note to look up that particular material later on.

Try verbally paraphrasing the next time you are engaged in a demanding conversation, such as when you are receiving directions. Repeat back to the speaker what you think she or he just said in order to check whether you both received and understood the same things. One of the benefits of paraphrasing is that it eliminates the common complaint that you weren't listening. Giving people back the ideas they have just presented makes it impossible for them to support the claim that you were not paying attention.

Perception

As the message is received and attended to, the listener's perceptions play an important role. Perceiving is an active process. During the act of **perception**, a person takes the material received and attempts to analyze what has been input. Perception is a screening process. The *perceptual filter* strains the stimuli you receive to separate what makes sense from what doesn't so that you can organize and interpret the message.

This filter is your frame of reference through which you screen messages. It is made up of your life experiences, including your background, culture, roles you play (e.g., child, student, parent), mental and physical states, beliefs, attitudes, and values.[26]

As listeners, we use our *selective perception* to narrow our attention to specific bits or pieces of information. The more relevant, or the more novel the stimuli, the more likely it will be perceived by the listener.

The perceptual screen through which you receive and interpret messages is your sensorium [the seat of your senses]. This *sensorium* frames your perceptual filter so that all of your senses are brought to bear as you logically and/or emotionally respond to information. Through this sensorium, listeners perceptually select those messages that will be received, attended to, and interpreted. The perceptual screen is a constant process of tuning in and tuning out stimuli.

Perception plays a major role in how you function as a listener. Essentially, the principle is that "you hear what you want to see and hear." As a result, a patient returning to a physician to get the results of medical tests may have a perceptual mindset that he is very ill. Therefore, he may not hear the physician say, "Your test results are fine," and instead will come out of the doctor's office convinced that he's going to die or that the doctor was not telling him the truth.

Likewise, listeners' perceptual filters frame interpretations so that no two people ever share the exact meaning of a message. Because everyone experiences life differently, every person's perceptual filter is basically different. Thus, we come to understand information in subtly different or even extremely different ways. For example, have you ever attended a class and then, after discussing it with a friend who attended the same class, realized that you each had come to a very different conclusion about what the professor had said?

There is evidence that "women's and men's brains process language differently."[27] A researcher states, "Listening to, understanding and producing speech may be easier for women because [a.] they have more nerve cells in the left half of the brain, which is used to process language, [b.] a greater degree of connectivity between the two parts of the brain, and [c.] more of the neurotransmitter dopamine in the part of the brain that controls language."[28] This may account for the belief that men don't listen well, at least from females who, based on their evolutionary dispositions, operate with the principle of developing relationships and social exchanges.[29]

Socially COMMUNICATING

Linear and Global Listeners in Relationships

Linear listeners prefer what might be termed *deliberate listening*. This is a process of sorting out the acceptable and unacceptable elements of the messages. This doesn't meet the needs of the global listener who needs to be empathized with and contributes to chronic frustration with the linear partner and eventually dissatisfaction with the relationship itself.

Source: Cutter, R. (1994). *When opposites attract: Right brain/left brain relationships and how to make them work*. New York: Dutton Books, p. 65.

REFLECT ON THIS: You are in a relationship with a person whose listening style is not parallel to yours (e.g., he is linear, you are global; she is global, you are linear).

1. What specific things can you do to ensure that you receive the other person's message as effectively as possible?
2. What can you suggest that the other person do to receive your message as effectively as possible?
3. How can you use your relationship partner's message content to adapt to their global/linear listening style?

Assignment of Meaning

Once you have paid attention to the material presented, the next stage in the listening process is to categorize the message so as to assign meanings to its verbal and nonverbal stimuli.

Role of Assigning Meaning The *assignment of meaning*—the process of putting the stimulus into some predetermined category—develops as we acquire our language system. We develop mental categories for interpreting the messages we receive. For instance, our categorizing system for the word *cheese* may include such factors as food, dairy products, taste, and nourishment, all of which help us relate the word *cheese* to the context in which it is used.

The categorical assignment of meaning creates *schema*—scripts for processing information. The mental representations that we carry in our brains—*schemata*—are shaped by the language categories and the way our brains process information. Our individual culture, background, family, education, and experience all serve as the framework for creating the schema that enable us to deal with incoming information. Understanding a discussion of some of the customs and traditions on a college campus, for example, may be difficult for first-year students because they do not have the cognitive schema to relate to the information.

Role of Global/Linear Thinking/Listening Each of us is unique in the way we listen and learn. Some of the differences are based on the way our brains work. A "theory of the structure and functions of the mind suggests that the two different sides of the brain control two different modes of thinking.[30] "Most individuals have a distinct preference for one of these styles of thinking. Some, however, are more

Linear/Global Dominance

Answer all of the questions quickly; do not stop to analyze them. When you have no clear preference, choose the one that most closely represents your normal attitudes or behaviors.

1. When I buy a new product, I
   ____ a. usually read the directions and carefully follow them.
   ____ b. refer to the directions, but really try to figure out how the thing operates or is put together on my own.
2. Which of these words best describes the way I perceive myself in dealing with others?
   ____ a. Structured/rigid
   ____ b. Flexible/open-minded
3. Concerning hunches:
   ____ a. I generally would not rely on hunches to help me make decisions.
   ____ b. I have hunches and follow many of them.
4. I make decisions mainly based on
   ____ a. what experts say will work.
   ____ b. a willingness to try things that I think might work.
5. In traveling or going to a destination, I prefer
   ____ a. to read and follow a map.
   ____ b. get directions and map things out "my" way.
6. In school, I preferred
   ____ a. geometry.
   ____ b. algebra.
7. When I read a play or novel, I
   ____ a. see the play or novel in my head as if it were a movie or TV drama.
   ____ b. read the words to obtain information.
8. When I want to remember directions, a name, or a news item, I
   ____ a. visualize the information or write notes that help me create a picture and maybe even draw the directions.
   ____ b. write structured and detailed notes.
9. I prefer to be in the class of a teacher who
   ____ a. has the class do activities and encourages class participation and discussions.
   ____ b. primarily lectures.
10. In writing, speaking, and problem solving, I am
   ____ a. usually creative, preferring to try new things.
   ___ b. seldom creative, preferring traditional solutions.

Scoring and Interpretation: Give yourself one point for each question you answered *b* on items 1 to 5 and *a* on 6 to 10. This total is your score. To assess your degree of linear or global preference, locate your final score on this continuum:

1 2 3 4 5 6 7 8 9 10

The lower the score, the more linear tendency you have. People with a score of 1 or 2 are considered highly linear. Scores of 3 and possibly 4 show a linear tendency.

The higher the score, the more global tendency you have. People with scores of 9 or 10 are considered highly global. Scores of 7 and possibly 6 indicate a global tendency.

If you scored between 4 and 7, you have indicated you probably do not tend to favor either tendency and are probably flexible in your learning and listening style.

Bear in mind that neither tendency is superior to the other. If you are extremely linear or global, it is possible to develop some of the traits associated with the other hemisphere, or you may already have them.

whole-brained and equally adept at both modes. In general, schools tend to favor left-brain modes of thinking, while downplaying the right-brain ones. Left-brain scholastic subjects focus on logical thinking, analysis, and accuracy. Right-brained subjects, on the other hand, focus on aesthetics, feeling, and creativity."[31]

This *brain dominance* accounts for learning and listening in patterned ways.[32] The Linear Global Dominance questionnaire can help you identify your pattern.

You may be able to improve your communication by adapting to different processing and listening styles. People who are left-hemisphere dominant may listen and learn best when materials are presented in structured ways. They tend to prefer specifics and logic-based arguments. Because they tend to take information at face value, abstractions and generalizations don't add much to their learning. Because they are so straight-line in their learning preferences, they are **linear learners/listeners**.

The right hemisphere of the brain is responsible for intuitive, spatial, visual, and concrete matters.[33] It is from the right hemisphere of the brain that we are able to visualize. People with this listening and learning dominance prefer examples rather than technical explanations. They prefer knowing that the information can be useful and applied. The right-brain–dominant person tends to be creative and rely on intuitive thinking, can follow visual and pictographic rather than written instructions, and enjoys interaction rather than just listening to others talk. Because of their preference for a generalized rather than specific description, right-brain–dominant persons are often labeled as **global listeners/learners**. Global learners may find much of the traditional lecture method of teaching in U.S. schools and universities, a linear methodology, to be dull and frustrating.

Many people are a combination of global and linear learners and listeners. If you fall into this classification, you tend to be more flexible in how you listen and learn than those with extreme style preferences.

It is helpful for you to recognize your listening and learning-processing styles because this understanding can make a difference in the way you approach listening and learning environments. If you know that you need examples and the speaker is not giving them, you should ask for them. If the speaker is not drawing specific conclusions and not speaking in a structured format, and these are necessary for your understanding, then you must probe for information that will allow you to organize the ideas. Don't assume that the speaker knows how you need to receive information; the person probably doesn't. Most classroom instructors teach based on their own listening and learning styles, forgetting that all students don't learn that way. If you are a global listener and learner, this may explain why you had trouble with some math or science classes. On the other hand, if you are a linear listener and learner, literature and poetry classes may have been difficult for you.

For a comparison between linear and global characteristics, see Figure 4.3.

Role of Culture in Assigning Meaning Like brain dominance, a person's culture influences listening and learning abilities. Some cultures, such as many in Asia, stress good listening by being a silent communicator in order to receive messages. People in Japan, for example, are likely to spend less time talking than listening on the job than do European Americans. In addition, some cultures stress concentration, which results in longer attention spans. Buddhism adheres to a principle called "being mindful." This means giving your complete and full attention to whatever you are doing. Training to have long attention spans starts in childhood.[34]

The Theory of High and Low Context Cultures[35] postulates that in *low-context cultures,* such as the United States and Canada, communicators expect to give and receive a great deal of information, since these cultures perceive that most message information is contained in words. In *high-context cultures,* such as Japan and Saudi Arabia, more of the information is situated in the communicators themselves and in the communication

Research shows that the following are the tendencies of people with left-brain or right-brain characteristics. The characteristics listed are for those who have extreme right- or left-brain tendencies. Of course, some people have been taught to adjust to their patterns and may not presently act exactly as described.

Linear-Brain Characteristics

- Prefers maps to oral directions.
- When trying something new, he or she likes to think about it before doing it.
- Likes to do things one at a time.
- Has a serious attitude about things.
- Is time conscious, likes for meetings to start and end on time.
- Likes agendas, program booklets, outlines, lists, written contracts, and agreements.
- Likes neatness in self and others.
- Fairly long attention span, able to concentrate on one subject for a long period of time.
- Is not a risk taker; careful, does not like to make mistakes.
- Likes to follow written directions that are numbered.
- Will ask many questions before making a decision.
- Is sometimes stubborn and very cautious when placed in a problem-solving situation.
- Likes multiple-choice and true-or-false tests rather than essay exams.

Global-Brain Characteristics

- Prefers directions that are explained or demonstrated; doesn't like maps.
- Likes to try things that he or she has not tried before.
- Likes to do several things at once.
- Likes essay tests for which he or she writes out the answer rather than multiple-choice or true-or-false tests.
- Is good at thinking up funny things to say or creative solutions to problems.
- Can tell whether or not someone is happy without the person's telling him or her (good at reading nonverbal signs).
- Often has own concept of time.
- Dislikes structured situations, details, and agendas.
- High tolerance for clutter, disorganization.
- Is a risk taker, does not always fear failure.
- Has a short attention span; daydreamer, mind wanders easily.
- Likes to guess at the answer or use intuition in a problem-solving situation.
- Likes to picture the answers to a problem in his or her head.
- When reading a book, sees the images as if he or she were watching a TV show or movie.

FIGURE 4.3 **A Comparsion of Linear-Mode and Global-Mode Characteristics**

Source: Based on concepts developed by Dr. Paul Torrance and Dr. Bernice McCarthy, Excell, Inc., P. O. Box 6, Fox River Grove, IL.

Some cultures stress being mindful, giving complete and full attention, in order to be a good listener.

setting, so fewer words are necessary. In high-context cultures, it is the responsibility of the listener to understand; in low-context cultures, it is the speaker who is responsible for making sure the listener comprehends all. For example, in some high context cultures, such as the Navajo culture, listening is the most valued communication skill.[36]

Role of Evaluation in Assigning Meaning One of the greatest barriers to effective listening is the tendency to evaluate the stimuli we receive, regardless of whether the stimuli are relevant to the message. In fact, this tendency has long been thought to be the most persistent barrier to communication that we have to overcome.[37] Although assigning meaning to stimuli often requires a quick evaluation, listeners should attempt to avoid instant judgments based primarily on superficial factors. Sometimes if you feel you don't have enough information, or you need to study the information, it may be better for you not to come to a conclusion yet.

A strategy useful to listeners in assigning meaning to messages is to differentiate *factual statements* (those based on observable phenomena or common acceptance) from *opinions* (inferences or judgments made by the speaker).

It also is helpful for the listener to sift through verbal obscurities and work for clarification of meanings. The effective listener asks questions and seeks clarification from speakers.

Listeners also benefit from recognizing what their emotional biases are and how those biases affect interpretations of messages. One way to discover such biases is to draw up a list of terms and phrases that serve as *red flags* (negative reactions) or *green flags* (positive stimulators) that trigger emotional responses. Recognition of such emotional triggers is a good first step toward compensating for the knee-jerk reactions that effectively tune out the speaker or cause you to daydream. Some people have red flag reactions, for example, to such words and concepts as *gay rights, taxes, abortion,* and, yes, *grades*. Some have green flag reactions to such ideas as *vacation, new car,* or *the name of a favorite sports team*.

The assignment of meaning is a complex process involving categorizing, evaluating, filtering through verbal obscurity, and recognizing emotional biases.

Response

Once we have assigned meaning to a message, we continue the information processing with an internal and/or external response—an intellectual or emotional reaction—to the message. It is hypothesized that every stimulus we receive is stored internally somewhere in our brain. In addition, over time the information may be moved from our short-term memory to our long-term memory. Externally, we react to the stimulus by providing feedback to the speaker in order to further the communication.

Role of Memory Techniques Many people find remembering names a problem. In some cases, it may be that you don't remember because you don't listen when the name is spoken, or you don't immediately repeat the name to entrench it in your memory. But there are techniques that you can learn to improve your memory, including name recall. For example, when you are introduced to someone, you must first decide that you want to remember this person's name and then get ready to remember it. If you tend to remember things by pictures, picture the person in a particular setting—perhaps the location where you are meeting him or what she is wearing. You can remember the person either by picturing him with a sign across his chest, emblazoned with his name, or you can tie the person's name to some other mental picture. (This is a good technique for global learners who tend to remember pictures, not words.) If you tend to remember words better than pictures, concentrate

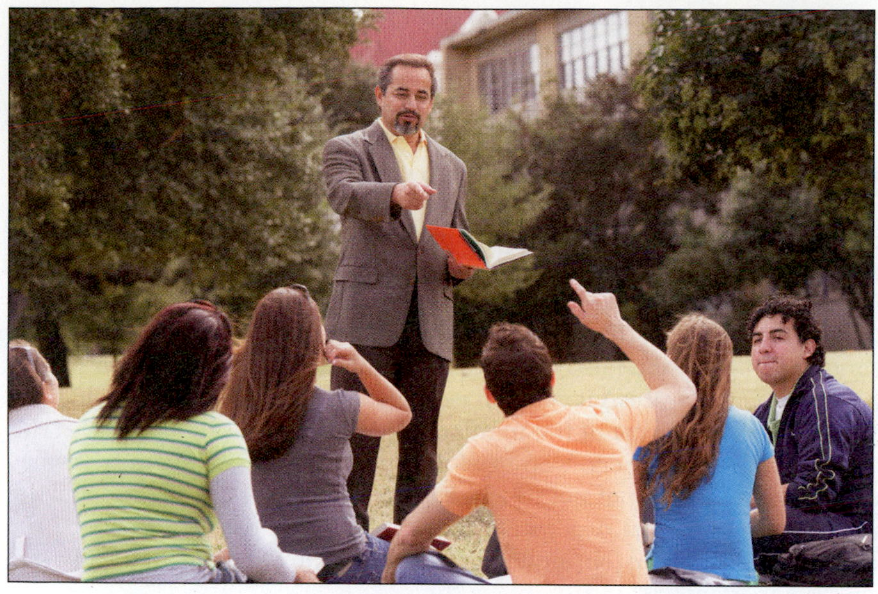

Asking questions enables the listener to ensure that the message he or she has received and interpreted is consistent with the original intent of the speaker.

on the name and repeat it several times to yourself, or select a familiar word with which the name rhymes (a good technique for linear learners since words, rather than pictures, are generally their way of remembering). Finally, repeat the name several times as you speak to the person. If you carry through on this process, the odds of you remembering the name increase greatly.

A memory study found that those "who doodled while listening to a message had a 29 percent better recall of the message's details than those who didn't doodle."[38] "A simple task, like doodling, may be sufficient to stop daydreaming."[39]

Another way of improving listening is to use a 'digital pen. These pens [e.g., Logitech io2 and Livescribe] create files of what you write. It allows you to take written notes as you listen then transfer that information to your computer as a data file. It can force you to actively listen so that you ensure the receipt of correct information. In contrast to digital recording, you are active rather than passive in the listening process.[40]

Role of Questions One area of response that can assist listeners in storing information in long-term memory and, at the same time, provide meaningful feedback to speakers, is asking questions. This enables listeners to ensure that the message they have received and interpreted is consistent with the speaker's original intent.

To be effective, questions must be relevant to the message that the speaker presented. When asking questions, try to figure out what you don't understand. Most commonly, difficulties in perceiving information center on a lack of

Culturally COMMUNICATING

Asian Students and Listening

When some Asian students interact with others, whether it is in a class or in an interpersonal communication event, they expect to understand what is being said, and if they do not, they usually will not express their lack of understanding because in their own cultures, it is their duty to understand without asking questions or making their lack of knowledge or understanding known to others.

Source: "Asian Students and Listening" from *Intercultural communication: A text with readings,* 1st Edition by Pamela J. Cooper, Carolyn Calloway-Thomas, Cheri J. Simonds. Copyright © 2007 by Pamela J. Cooper, Carolyn Calloway-Thomas, Cheri J. Simonds. Printed and Electronically reproduced by permission of Pearson Education, Inc., Upper Saddle River, New Jersey.

REFLECT ON THIS: One of your authors taught at a university in the People's Republic of China. She encouraged class discussion and question–asking during classes. She found that almost none of the students would participate in the discussions or ask questions. What strategies could she have used to get the students to participate?

understanding of vocabulary, a need for clarifying examples, or a need for the material to be presented in a different format or order.

For example, you are taking notes in class and can't paraphrase the instructor's ideas so that you can write them down. One of the mistakes students often make is not to say anything.[41] When asking for information, just don't say, "I don't understand." The instructor won't be able to clarify; you haven't provided the clues needed to be of help. It is common in certain academic subjects for the vocabulary to be new and unusual. If you don't understand the terms being used, ask, "Would you please define [fill in the term]?" Or if you vaguely understand but need something more, you could ask, "Would you please give several examples to illustrate [insert the specific topic]?" (This is often what people who are global learners need to have in order to grasp the idea, because they require examples they can picture rather than memorizing words.) If you don't understand the concept, you could ask, "Could you restate the concept of [fill in the topic] in a step-by-step process?" (This is a technique for linear learners, who need the structure to understand what may be confusing because it was not put in a patterned manner.) In each case, you are specifically centering on what needs to be done to help you gain information. The same techniques work on the job and in other situations in which getting and using information is important.

Role of Feedback Good listeners are conscious of the role of *feedback cues*. Asking questions, nodding or shaking your head, smiling or frowning, and verbalization such as "uh-huh" or "um?" are all forms of listener feedback. Feedback responses can be verbal or nonverbal.

Rather than enter into the listening process passively, assume an active role as a listening communicator, sending feedback such as asking questions, verbally and nonverbally showing agreement, disagreement or acknowledging that you received the message.[42]

Listening Influencers

It should be clear that the process of listening, through which the listener receives, attends to, perceives, assigns meaning to, and responds to messages, is complex. To be effective, the listener must be actively involved throughout this process and work to overcome barriers that may arise. Certain key influencers can facilitate or hinder the process.

Role of the Speaker The speaker's credibility—that is, the listener's perception of the speaker's trustworthiness, competence, and dynamism—can lead the listener to accept or reject a message. Unfortunately, some listeners are so in awe of a particular speaker that they may lose all objectivity in analyzing the person's message. For example, if the speaker is an athletic superstar, the listener may overlook that he is not an expert in the specific subject in question. If the listener accepts the speaker's message simply because he is a celebrity, the receiver may be overlooking the logical weaknesses of the presentation. Listen to the message, not just to the status of the speaker.

The speaker's physical presentation—animation, appearance, clothing—can have an instantaneous effect on listener attention. A speaker who is dynamic and humorous may be able to get past the critical listening abilities of certain listeners. Compare the presentational style of several of your professors who use the lecture method to conduct class. To whom do you pay the most attention? Whom do you consider the better teacher? If you are fairly typical, the answer is the one who is not only knowledgeable, but the most animated, humorous and/or dramatic.

Noise (interference in the communication process) can diminish the effectiveness of the speaker–listener interaction.

Role of the Message Another major influencer is the message itself. If the presentation is not clearly organized—if the arguments are not well ordered—the listener may have difficulty concentrating on and staying tuned in to the message.

The tone and the treatment of the message can also affect a person's listening abilities. Some religious speakers, for example, are known for their ability to put fear into the minds of their listeners when they prophesy eternal damnation. Listeners must ascertain whether the message is appropriate for them and whether they believe in the prophecies presented.

Role of the Channel The communication channel can influence listening ability. Some people are more auditory, while some are more visual in orientation. The public speaker, for example, who couples the message with clear visual aids may assist listeners in comprehending the material. Electronic channels versus face-to-face presence also can have an effect. For instance, television and the Internet have changed the nature of political campaigning. Historically, candidates had to appear in person before an audience, where listeners could have some physical contact with them. Now, sound bites, thirty-second spots, YouTube videos, and debates in which listeners can actively participate in the experience have made for drastic differences. Likewise, candidates are making increased use of voice mail and the Internet, including blogs and social networks, to reach potential voters.

Students have reacted both positively and negatively to varying channels of communication. For example, the concept of distance learning, in which television sets and/or computer screens replace a live instructor, has met with mixed reactions. Some like that the instructor cannot call on the listener, that the message can be viewed whenever the receiver wants to listen or watch, and that they can replay the material for reinforcement. On the other hand, some students think that using the linear model of communication in which there is a separation between the listener and speaker causes a sterile environment and eliminates the possibility for feedback and adaptation.[43]

Socially COMMUNICATING

Listening by Quieting Your Inner and Outer Voice

The first thing to notice about our intrapersonal communication is how it can interfere with the process of listening effectively to others. We need to quiet our inner voice, as well as our outer voice, if we are to fully comprehend what others have to tell us. We cannot fill a full cup. If we are to truly listen to friends and colleagues we must first empty our own cup (our mind) of thoughts so we have room for the ideas of the speaker. The process of quieting the mind takes personal effort and discipline.

Source: Borisoff, D. & Purdy, M. (1991). *Listening in everyday life: A personal and professional approach*. Lanham, MD: University Press of America, p. 25.

REFLECT ON THIS: The authors encourage you to "quiet [your] inner voice." That is easy to say, but hard to do. What specifically can you, as a listener, do to quiet your inner voice so that it doesn't interfere with receipt of the message?

Role of External and Internal Variables Noise (any sort of interference) in the communication channel can diminish the effectiveness of the listener. Static on your smart phone or distortions on the television screen can interrupt good listening. Noise from the environment also affects listeners. If the lighting is poor or the room temperature is too cold or too hot, the listener may have greater difficulty concentrating on the speaker's message. Control of or adjustment for the distraction may be necessary—for example, moving to a different place in the room so that you can see or hear the speaker more readily, adjusting the auditory or visual channel, or negotiating with the speaker to move to a better environment.

Listeners are influenced not only by a vast array of external factors but also by internal ones. Receivers are affected by their physical state (general or psychological health), experiences (background, life history, training), attitudes (predispositions), memory, and expectations. The listener's culture also can be influential. People from different cultures have different ways of attending to each other, as indicated by the amount of eye contact, distance between each other, and the degree of patience. For example, in some South American cultures, it is perceived as bad manners to look directly into the eyes of a speaker, especially if the presenter is an authority figure. Some Arabic and Asian cultures stress standing very close to people while conversing, often touching or holding hands, which causes many European Americans to be uncomfortable, thus making concentration difficult.

The positive or negative attitude the listener carries into a listening situation (in conjunction with expectations for the experience) is important. For example, a listener who goes to a training session convinced beforehand that it will be a waste of time will probably refuse to suspend judgment and listen comprehensively.

The listener's positive or negative attitude extends to himself or herself as a listener. Just as speakers have self-concepts, so too do listeners. Most people have had very little praise for good listening but have probably heard negative messages such as, "Keep quiet and listen" and "Why don't you ever listen to me?" These negative messages can create a negative attitude in people about their listening abilities.

Role of Time The listener has to have the time, and be willing to take the time, to listen with discrimination and comprehension. Well-intentioned listeners find it useful to recognize that they are busy and distracted. You must be willing, however, to mentally set aside or *bracket* the other internal factors competing for your attention ("Yes, I do have to finish that memo") and focus on the speaker and his or her message at the moment ("...but first I need to listen to...").

Purposes of Listening

We listen on a number of levels, for a variety of purposes: to distinguish among sounds, gain ideas, discriminate among ideas, aid others, and appreciate sounds or symbols. Awareness of the purposes of listening sometimes helps a listener select the listening techniques that best fit the desired outcome.[44]

> **COMMUNICATING in Careers**
>
> **Business Listening: Don't Multitask**
>
> Don't multitask if you are supposed to be listening. For example, if you are on a conference call, don't try to read your e-mails at the same time. You wind up listening to only part of what someone says, or pretending to listen while you think about or do something else. You also sacrifice important nonverbal cues and information about their intent, their confidence level, and their commitment level. Even if you think that you can get enough of what people say while multitasking to serve your immediate purpose, you should assume as a general rule that people notice when you don't listen to them attentively.
>
> *Source: How to listen (attentive listening skills).* Retrieved from businesslistening.com
>
> **REFLECT ON THIS:** Have you ever tried to multitask while listening? For example, have you ever driven your car and listened to a friend, or conducted business on a cell? Do you know of any instances of anyone being in an auto accident because of texting and driving simultaneously?

Discriminative Listening

In **discriminative listening**, we attempt to distinguish auditory and visual stimuli. Through discrimination, we can come to understand differences in verbal sounds (dialects, pronunciation) and nonverbal behavior (gestures, facial reactions). By understanding such differences, we gain sensitivity to the sights and sounds of our world. We can then determine, for example, whether a person is being sarcastic, cautious, negative, or uncooperative because we realize that the same set of words can be taken in a variety of ways.

Discriminative listening also is important when we come in contact with some of the nonhuman features of our everyday lives. We may listen, for instance, to household appliances to determine whether they are functioning properly. People in professions such as music, medicine, and technology often find listening discrimination to be their most important listening skill. Examples of professional discriminative listening are: "Is the piano in tune?" and "I think I hear an irregular heartbeat."

It is interesting to check your own level of listening discrimination. Read the directions for the rest of this paragraph. *Directions:* Close your eyes for about one minute. Listen to the sounds around you, then open your eyes and answer these questions: What sounds did you recognize? What sounds were unfamiliar to you? What effect did these sounds have on you as you processed them? Now, carry out the directions.

Is it important for you to be a discriminative listener? Daily you encounter sounds to the point that you just screen out most of them. However, if your vehicle's engine is making an unusual whining noise, you should know that you need to get it to a service technician right away. Or listen to your own voice as you are involved in a conflict. When the pitch and volume increase, these changes may indicate that you are getting stressed and could become verbally or physically abusive.

Comprehension Listening

In **comprehension listening**, the objective is to recognize and retain the information. Some techniques have been found to enhance listening comprehension. In the academic setting, knowing how to take notes effectively is a vital skill. "Students spend roughly 80 percent of their weekly in-class activity listening to lectures."[45]

"Notes provide students with an external storage mechanism."[46] They allow students to encode information into memory because in order to take notes, they must pay attention to, organize, and interpret lecture information. The problem with most students' note taking is that "in lecture situations, some students seem to want to record everything said by the lecturer."[47] What students need to know is how to select, organize, and interpret lecture information.[48]

There are various strategies to aid in the selection and organization of material and to concentrate on getting the main points of a message rather than all of the supporting details. That is, listen to an instructor by focusing on the main points rather than on the elaboration and details, sorting the main points and the supporting details. This can be done, for example, by drawing a vertical line down the middle of the paper, putting the main points in the left-hand column, and noting the supporting ideas in the right-hand column. Using abbreviations of commonly used words saves time in writing, which allows for more listening time. For instance, if the early part of this chapter ("The Listening Process") was given as a lecture, effectively taken notes might look like those in Figure 4.4.

The student whose notes are shown obviously thought there were sufficient cues for understanding the material so that examples were not essential. Nevertheless, many note takers like to provide examples to help clarify material. Each note taker has to determine how much detail and how much reinforcement are necessary for comprehension of the material.

Some communication experts[49] recommend a technique called *clarifying and confirming* to improve concentration. This strategy calls for the listener to ask for

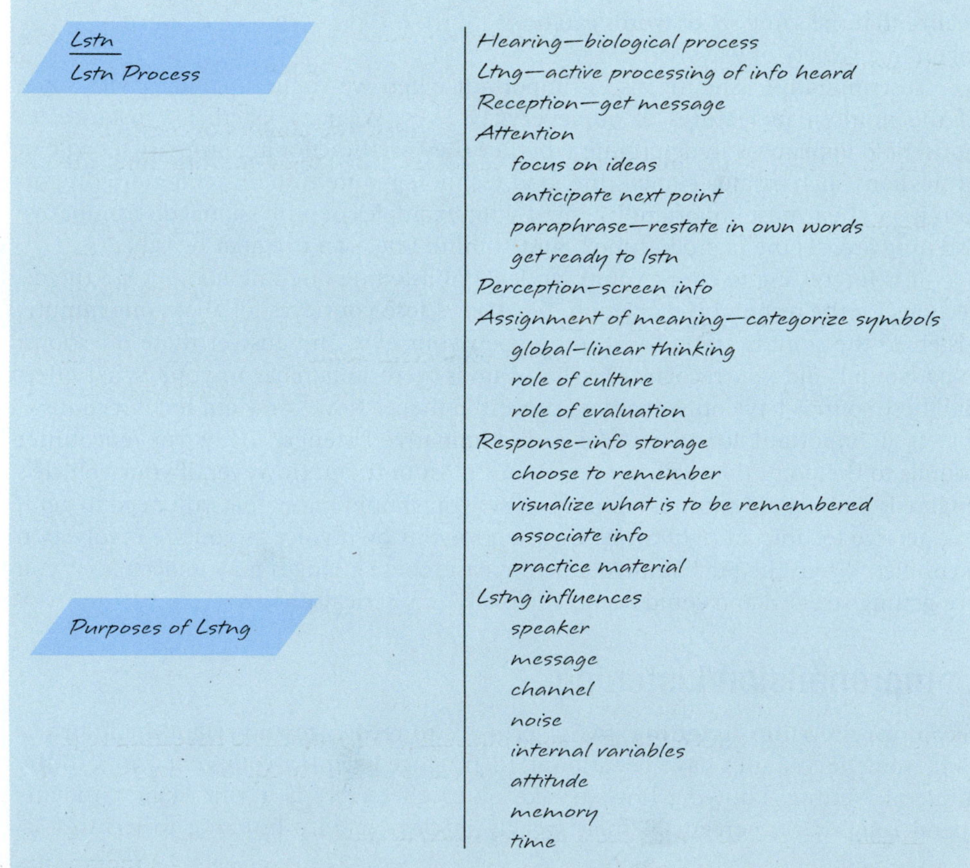

Lstn
Lstn Process
Hearing—biological process
Ltng—active processing of info heard
Reception—get message
Attention
focus on ideas
anticipate next point
paraphrase—restate in own words
get ready to lstn
Perception—screen info
Assignment of meaning—categorize symbols
global—linear thinking
role of culture
role of evaluation
Response—info storage
choose to remember
visualize what is to be remembered
associate info
practice material
Lstng influences
speaker
message
channel
noise
internal variables
attitude
memory
time
Purposes of Lstng

FIGURE 4.4
Note-Taking Format

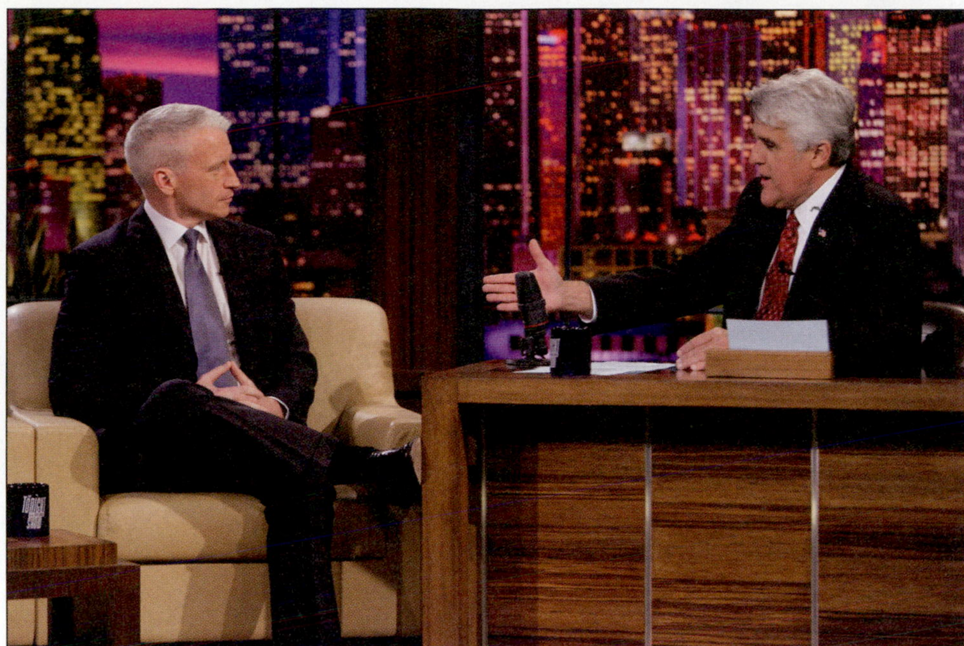

An effective media interviewer uses paraphrasing, verbal feedback, internal summaries, and bridging.

additional information or explanation. This system works well when added to a technique known as *bridging:* relating one part of the message to another. Good radio and television talk-show hosts use this system when interviewing guests. They use paraphrasing (repeating ideas), verbal feedback ("uh-huh" and "that's an interesting idea"), internal summaries (summarizing one topic before going on to the next), and bridging (indicating what topic or idea she'd like to talk about next by referring to a quotation in a book or one just made by the speaker). The abilities of clarifying, confirming, and bridging are important tools for individuals going into listening professions such as counseling, social work, police interrogation, newscasting, and reporting.

Remembering the main points at a later time also may require the development of a number of memory techniques. Some research indicates that a person can lose as much as half of any given information after the first day without taking notes and reviewing them.[50] Because it is so easy to lose information in memory storage, good listeners work to preserve the information presented. Some students have found, for example, that they retain ideas best if they review the information immediately after it is presented and then go over it daily rather than waiting until the night before an examination to cram.

Using comprehension and discriminative listening as the foundation, people listen for special purposes: to provide a therapeutic setting for a person to talk through a problem, critically evaluating a persuasive message, or appreciating aspects of a particular message.

Therapeutic Listening

Listening at the therapeutic level is important for those in such fields as mental health, social work, speech therapy, and counseling. **Therapeutic listening** requires a listener to learn when to ask questions, when to stimulate further discussion, and when, if ever, to give advice.

In daily life, people often need a listener when dealing with a problem. The listener can help the speaker talk through the situation. To be effective in this role, therapeutic listeners must have *empathy* for the other person—the ability to understand that person's problem from her own perspective by momentarily putting themselves into her shoes and attempting to see the world as she sees it. This is difficult for many people to do, as there is a tendency to want to solve the other person's problem and help rid her of the pain.

How can you learn to be an effective therapeutic listener? Resist the temptation to jump in with statements such as "The same thing happened to me" or "If I were you, I would..." Don't diminish the person. Saying, "That's no big problem" doesn't help lessen the hurt. In addition, remember that there is nothing wrong with silence. Listen patiently. The person in pain may need time to feel the ache and get in touch with her thoughts and feelings.

A direct device that can be helpful is for the listener to help the speaker generate a list of possible alternatives from which that person may choose. Allowing the person to choose, rather than you giving him your solution, will allow the person to develop a commitment to carrying out the action.

Critical Listening

Critical listening centers on the listener evaluating the message that has been received. A critical listener assesses the arguments and appeals in a message and then decides whether to accept or reject them. Judgments should take into account such factors as:

- *The personal appeal of the speaker.* The speaker's credibility stems from the position held (e.g., sports celebrity), expertise (e.g., professor), trustworthiness (e.g. judge), and dynamism (inspirational speaker). The critical listener needs to recognize how much this credibility is influencing how the message is being understood and analyzed.
- *The speaker's arguments and evidence.* Does the speaker present a logical argument supported by substantive and relevant data?
- *The speaker's motivational appeals.* How is the speaker attempting to get the listener involved in the message? What appeals to the listener's needs are used to get the listener to respond to a persuasive message?
- *Assumptions on the part of the speaker.* Does the speaker assume that something is a fact before it has been established as such? Just because someone says, "It is readily apparent that..." doesn't make it so.
- *What is not said.* In some cases, the speaker implies rather than states ideas, so the listener is forced to read between the lines to supply the message. "You know what I mean" is a remark to which the listener should be alert. What do you really know from what was said?

Sales pitches, advertising messages, campaign speeches, and persuasive briefings all require critical analysis.

As a communication student, you probably will be called on to critique the speeches of fellow students. In this mode of critical listening, your role is to provide information to help speakers improve their work. Offer comments on what the speaker does effectively as well as what the speaker needs to improve. Deal with content (topic choice, structure, supporting materials, clarity, and interest) and delivery (animation, vocal dynamics, and eye contact).

Appreciative Listening

Appreciative listening takes place when a person engages in enjoyment of or sensory stimulation to a message, such as listening to humorous speakers, comedians, or music videos.

Listening Apprehension

Not only are some people apprehensive when they speak, but they may also be apprehensive when they must or are given the opportunity to listen. **Listener apprehension**, "the fear of misinterpreting, inadequately processing, and/or not being able to adjust psychologically to messages sent by others,"[51] is a concern for many people. It may be a short-term fear, such as the anxiety associated with knowing you are going to receive a negative evaluation, or the fear of the person who is going to talk to you or what he might say. For example, in the context of physician–patient interaction, the difference in power roles between you as a patient and the doctor as the expert may interfere with your ability to listen to your physician calmly and accurately. You also might be afraid of what the doctor might say, so you dread listening.

Listener apprehension also may be a long-term disability. There are individuals who have lived their entire lives being told they are poor listeners and have come to believe it. There are others who have a hearing or vision disability and fear that they will miss the core of the message in listening situations.

Listening anxiety may make it difficult to understand, process, and remember a message. It may make a person less able to interact effectively, less willing to communicate, and less confident about communication abilities. Further, if a listener is emotional about the content of the message, that emotional response may take so much attention energy that it can increase apprehension.

If you experience listening apprehension, here are some suggestions that might help:

- Realize that worrying isn't going to make you a better listener, so if you can't avoid the situation, then you must force yourself to participate and accept that you will do the best job you can.
- Repeat back the speaker's ideas so that you can assure yourself that you are receiving the message and that you are letting the other person know that you are listening and understanding.
- Prepare questions and formulate ideas in advance if you know you are going to be evaluated or will need to defend yourself or your ideas.
- If there has been an agenda, memo, or outline of what will be discussed, such as for a meeting or a class, go over the material ahead of time and get ready to listen.
- Get ready for the session. If you are at work, have the ideas researched. For the classroom situation, read and prepare the assignment.
- Prepare notes to use during the discussion. That way you won't have to worry about not having anything of value to say.

Improving Your Listening

Effective listening is a complex process. Despite its complexities, you can improve your skill as a listener.[52]

Here are some suggestions to help listeners develop greater skills:

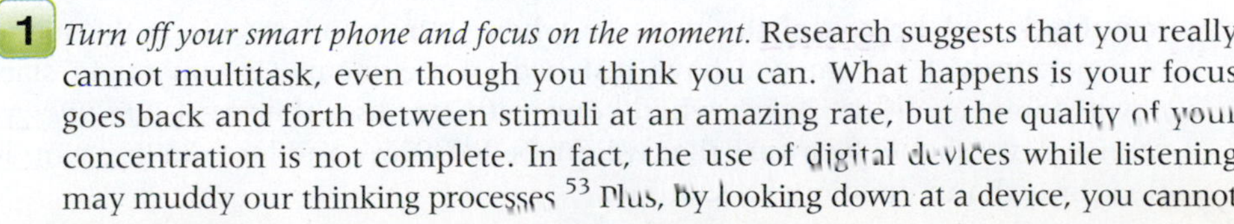

1 *Turn off your smart phone and focus on the moment.* Research suggests that you really cannot multitask, even though you think you can. What happens is your focus goes back and forth between stimuli at an amazing rate, but the quality of your concentration is not complete. In fact, the use of digital devices while listening may muddy our thinking processes.[53] Plus, by looking down at a device, you cannot

gather all the nonverbal visual cues the other person is sending you. You may think you are fully listening to your friend talk while you text another friend, but that's just not the case.

2 *Recognize that both the sender and receiver share responsibility for effective communication.* If you are sending a message, you should define terms, structure your message clearly, and give your receiver the necessary background to respond effectively. As a receiver, you should ask questions and provide feedback if you cannot understand the speaker's point. If possible, repeat the major ideas so that the speaker can check to be sure you have grasped the meaning.

3 *Suspend judgment.* One of the greatest barriers to human communication is the tendency to form instant judgments about information we encounter. As listeners, we are prone to assess speakers prematurely, before we have even comprehended the entire message. Thoughts such as "I don't like his voice" and "This is a boring lecture" set up barriers to effective listening. Good listening requires setting aside these judgments and listening for the message.

4 *Be a patient listener.* Avoid interrupting or tuning out until the entire message has been communicated. We often find ourselves beginning to act before we have totally understood what is being said. This is especially true of global listeners, who often act intuitively on perceived information.

Think about how difficult it is to assemble a new product until you thoroughly comprehend the instructions. Or remember the times you filled out a form, only to realize later that you put down your first name when the directions said your last name should come first. Patience in listening will help you avoid having to go back over messages you missed the first time or did not understand because you did not let the whole message come through.

5 *Avoid egospeak.* **Egospeak** is the "art of boosting our own ego by speaking only about what we want to talk about, and not giving a hoot in hell about what the [other] person is speaking about."[54] When you jump into a conversation and speak your piece without noticing what the other person is trying to communicate or listen only to the beginning of another's sentence before saying, "Yes, but...," you are engaging in egospeak. As a result, you do not receive the whole message because you are so busy thinking of what you want to say or are saying it.

Several techniques can be used to control egospeaking. First, monitor your body. Individuals who are about to interrupt have a tendency to lean forward as if to jump into the conversation and poise an arm and hand so that they can thrust them forward to cut in. If you feel your body taking these actions, be aware that you are about to egospeak—and don't.

Another way to deter yourself from egospeaking is to repeat the speaker's ideas before you give your point of view. Be aware that if you can't summarize, you may not have listened long enough to gain the message. In future conversations, see if you can repeat the message of the speaker to yourself before you jump in.

6 *Be careful with emotional responses to words.* Inciting words, red and green flags, are those words or phrases that trigger strong feelings, either positive or negative, within us. How do you react to the words *recession, rapist,* and *spring vacation?* Words like these often send us off on tangents. In an everyday situation, you may block out the rest of the message when your friend mentions the name of a person with whom you have just had an argument. Or you might start daydreaming about the beach when your instructor uses the word *sunshine.* As receivers, we should be aware that we can be led astray and lose our concentration through our emotional responses.

7 *Be aware that your posture affects your listening.* When you listen to an exciting lecture, how do you sit? Usually you lean slightly forward, with your feet on the floor, and look directly at the presenter. If you slump down and stare out the window, it's unlikely that you're actively participating in the communication act taking place.

Have you ever left a classroom and felt totally exhausted? You may have been concentrating so hard that you became physically tired. After all, good listening is hard work. An effective listener learns when it is necessary to listen in a totally active way and when it is possible to relax. An analogy can explain the concept. When you're driving a car with an automatic transmission, the car shifts gears when it needs more or less power. Unfortunately, people don't come equipped with automatic transmissions; we have to shift gears for ourselves. When you need to concentrate, shift into your active listening position: feet on the floor, posture erect, and looking directly at the speaker to pick up any necessary nonverbal clues. Once you feel that you understand the point being made (a test is the ability to paraphrase what has been said), you may want to shift your posture to a more comfortable position. When a new subject arises or when you hear transitional words or phrases such as *therefore* or *in summary,* then you shift back into your active listening position.

8 *Control distractions.* All of us are surrounded by environmental noise—the sound of machinery, people talking, music playing—that can interfere with efficient listening. If the message is important to you, try to adjust the interference or control it. If possible, turn off the machinery, or move away from it. Tell someone who is speaking to you while you are talking on the telephone that you cannot listen to both people at the same time. Remember that there is little point in continuing the attempted communication if you cannot hear the other person or that person cannot hear you.

9 *Tune in to the speaker's cues.* An effective speaker provides the listener with verbal and nonverbal cues. You should recognize *transitions* (words indicating a change of idea or topic: "therefore" or "finally"), *forecasts of ideas* (statements that show a series of ideas: "There are three ideas that…," or "The next point is…"), and *internal summaries* (restatements of ideas that have just been explained: "and so I've illustrated that…"). These are all vehicles for furthering your grasp of the major points the speaker is presenting.

The rate, volume, pitch, and pauses that the speaker uses also can help you understand the points being developed. By stressing words, pausing before an idea, or increasing the volume of a phrase, the speaker is telling you that something is important or significant.

The speaker's physical movements can carry a meaning that may reinforce or contradict a verbal message. For example, a speaker who uses a forceful gesture or enumerates points with the fingers can assist listeners in following the main points. You often have to listen with your eyes as well as your ears to pick up all the cues to help you understand the real message.

10 *Paraphrase.* Paraphrasing can be one of the most effective ways to sharpen concentration, because it requires careful focus and storage in short-term memory. By repeating the ideas in your answer, you let the speaker know what you have received. If your paraphrase is not correct, the speaker can clarify to help you understand what was really intended.

11 *Visualize.* To engage in successful communication, a good technique, especially for the global learner and listener, is to visualize the speaker's points or what he is doing when certain concepts are presented. Visual associations are a useful way to improve storage and retrieval in long-term memory. For example, a student relayed to a former instructor that even today when she hears certain topics discussed, she visualizes where the instructor stood in class and can remember what he said.

Not all the listening you do is one-on-one. People spend a great deal of time receiving media messages, including listening to iPods, cell phones, televisions, and radios. You need to understand how these messages influence the way meaning is framed and shared by society. One media specialist recommends these strategies for listeners to increase their media literacy:[55]

- Think about how realistic or how fantasized the images are.
- Think about what is communicated in the presentation. Is it reasonable? Is it biased? Is it trying to manipulate you by appealing to your weaknesses?
- If you tend to believe the appeal, ask yourself why you are opening yourself to that belief.
- Be aware of when someone is trying to change your point of view. Apply this awareness by challenging the contentions before you go along with the idea.
- Recognize that much of what is on the media seeks to manipulate you to buy products or services.
- Recognize that commercials and factual news are not the same.
- Recognize that situation comedies, dramas, and other fictionalized stories are not reality. Real life doesn't always have happy endings, cures are not always found for diseases, and life doesn't go from beginning to end in thirty or sixty minutes.

In Conclusion

IN CONCLUSION

Listening is a central part of the communication process. It is a process of receiving, attending to, perceiving, assigning meaning to, and responding to messages. We listen to discriminate among auditory and visual stimuli, comprehend information, provide therapeutic support to other communicators, critically evaluate messages, and appreciate messages.

Various strategies can be undertaken to improve a person's listening skills, including shared responsibility for effective communication with the speaker, suspending judgment and being a patient listener, avoiding egospeaking, being careful with emotional responses to words, being aware that your posture affects your listening, making a conscious effort to listen, controlling distractions, tuning in to the speaker's cues, learning how to use paraphrasing, and using visualization.

People spend a great deal of time processing television, radio, smart phone, and voice messages; therefore, they need to understand how words, images, and sounds influence the way meanings are created and shared.

LEARN BY DOING

1. Analyze your own listening. Name one listening behavior you have that does not match the characteristics of a good listener as described in this chapter. Devise a plan for how you will change this listening behavior.
2. Now that you are aware of some of the principles of effective listening, put them into practice. At the next speech or lecture you attend, sit up, concentrate on what the speaker is saying, and focus all your attention and energy on comprehending the material. Make internal summaries and paraphrase to assist yourself. After the session is over, analyze your listening behavior and determine what you can still do to improve your comprehension.
3. Make a list of your "red flags" and "green flags." Go back and review these terms. Why do you think they incite you? If class time is available, your instructor will divide the class into groups of four to six students. Discuss your "red flags" and what implications they have for your communication.
4. To learn how to paraphrase, do this three-step activity:
   a. Indicate whether you thoroughly agree (TA), agree (A), disagree (D), or thoroughly disagree (TD) with each of these statements:
      (1) Prayer should be allowed in the public schools.
      (2) Stem cell research should be sanctioned and financially supported by the federal government.
      (3) Homosexual marriages should be legally sanctioned.
      (4) College students should not have required courses outside of their major area of concentration.
      (5) Gun ownership and possession should be outlawed in the United States for everyone except those entrusted with the defense of citizens (e.g., police, armed forces personnel, security guards).
   b. Your class is divided into groups of four to six students. Your task is to get everyone in the group to accept one of the attitudes (TA, A, D, or TD) for each of the preceding statements. You must paraphrase during the entire discussion. You may not give your opinion until you have summarized the statement of the person who preceded you. One member of the group acts as referee and says, "Foul" if anyone speaks without summarizing. (If time does not allow for a discussion of all five questions, your instructor will select one for discussion.)
   c. Now make a list of the positive aspects of paraphrasing as a listening technique; then list the frustrations it causes.
5. Your instructor will play a short video of a political candidate or office holder. Each class member is to critically listen to the speech. You may, as the speech proceeds, take notes. At the end of the speech, list the major points the speaker made and his or her "back-up statement" for each of those points. There will be a class discussion that will first list the major points and their back-ups (comprehensive listening), followed by a critical listening evaluation of the back-ups.

KEY TERMS

hearing 84
listening 84
paraphrasing 87
perception 87
linear learners/listeners 90
global listeners/learners 90
discriminative listening 97
comprehension listening 97
therapeutic listening 99
critical listening 100
appreciative listening 100
listener apprehension 101
egospeak 102

CHAPTER 5

The Self and Perception

intrapersonal communication • self-perception • basic needs theory • communication apprehension

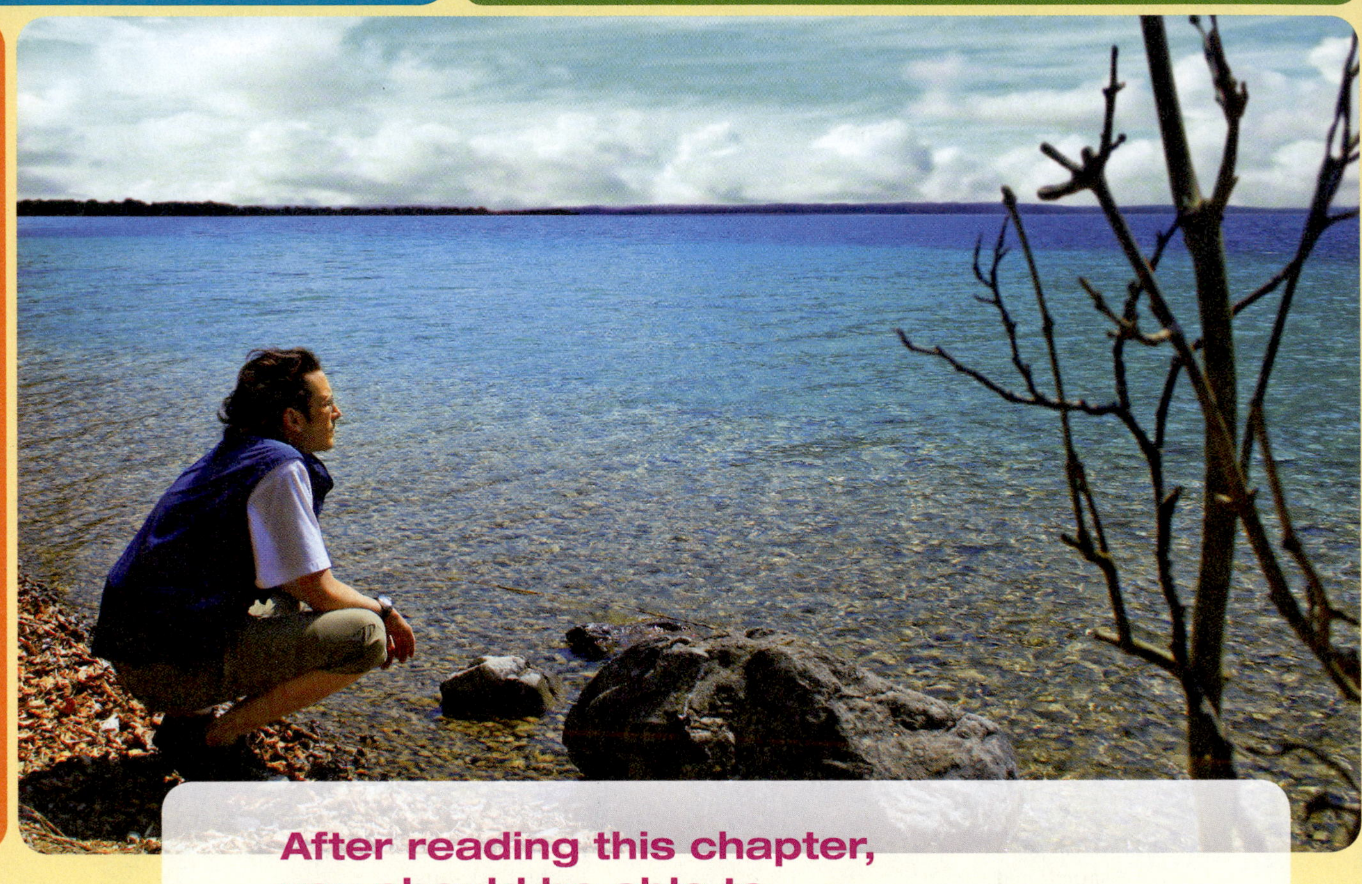

After reading this chapter, you should be able to

- Define and explain the concept of intrapersonal communication
- State and discuss the theory of basic drive forces as they affect inner communication
- Explain self-concept and its role as a guiding factor in a person's actions
- Define self-talk and explain its relation to our communication accomplishments
- List some options and sources for improving self-perception, self-confidence, and self-esteem (or all of them)
- Define and explain the causes, results, effects, and aids for communication apprehension
- Evaluate how culture has an effect on self-communication and the development of self-perception
- Explain the role of perception on communication

In the late 1960s, a professor of speech and a group of his graduate students started to use the research and theories of the social sciences (psychology, sociology, and anthropology) to examine what people did as communicators. Their work is credited as laying the foundation for the development of speech communication as a social science.[1]

The professor believed that people displayed their psychological underpinnings in the way they internally processed thoughts and ideas. It was his contention that by studying people's inner communication researchers and educators could improve what he called an individual's intrapersonal communication.[2]

Intrapersonal communication is inner speech, "communication [that] takes place within a single person, often for the purpose of clarifying ideas or analyzing a situation. Other times, intrapersonal communication is undertaken in order to reflect upon or appreciate something."[3]

To put this on a personal level: You talk to yourself when you debate during a test which of the multiple-choice answers is correct. Your body can "speak" to you nonverbally when muscles in the back of the neck tighten when you get emotionally upset or when your stomach churns just before giving a speech. Intrapersonal communication may occur below your level of awareness, such as when you dream or daydream.

One way of understanding your self-communication and, if necessary, improving your communication skills, is by understanding your self-talk.

Self-Talk

The starting point of any communication is **self-talk**—communicating within yourself. "You communicate with yourself when you think, when you make decisions, when you engage in any type of communication activity."[4]

We all engage in this inner dialogue. Sometimes you are conscious of your vocalizing aloud within your head, but self-talk is often silent thinking, an internal whisper of which you are scarcely aware, or your automatic nonverbal reactions. Even though it may be quiet, its impact can be enormous. "Your behavior, your feelings, your self-esteem, and even your level of stress are influenced by your inner speech."[5] Everything that you do begins as self-talk. Self-talk shapes our inner attitudes, our attitudes shape our behavior, and of course our behavior—what we do—shapes the results we get.[6] The self-talk often triggers confidences and inquiries you have about yourself, which then affect your interpersonal communication decisions.

You may be wondering if you really do talk to yourself. If you blog,[7] keep a journal,[8] daydream,[9] tell yourself positive affirmations,[10] imagine conversations you want to have,[11] then you talk to yourself.

Communicating Culturally

Do I Have a Place in This Society?

What does it mean to be Black? ... My mom worked long hours and she worked so very hard all her life so that she could send me to a private school. I did in fact have some Black friends but not as many as I would have liked. Does this mean I don't consider myself Black? NO! Not at all. I see myself as Black and I love being Black. But I don't know much of Black history. What I know is just the surface, and what I NEED to know is the core. What makes me sad is, I am considered to be the White girl in my family. It saddens me because they don't know my struggle deep inside. Yes, I wish I were strong in being more "ethnic," but I'm not and that scares me. Am I blind? Do I not have a place in this society?

—Lanitra, *College Student*

Source: Ting-Toomey, S., & Chung, L. C. (2005). *Understanding intercultural communication*. Los Angeles, CA: Roxbury Publishing Company, p. 84.

REFLECT ON THIS:

1. Do you perceive President Barack Obama, the child of a mixed (white and African) marriage, to be black, African American, white, or some other designation?
2. Golfer Tiger Woods considers himself "Cablinasian"—Caucasian, black, Indian, and Asian—because of his racially diverse background. Do you agree with his "title" for himself?

Think of the inner struggles you have concerning whether you will believe something, will take a particular action, or will make a certain decision. Awake or asleep, you are constantly in touch with yourself. You think, daydream, dream, fantasize, and feel tension. These are all forms of inner speech.

There is controversy over whether inner speech and symbolic thought are the same thing. A major theorist in thinking and speaking postulated that "inner speech was solely thinking silently to oneself, while symbolic thought is used to make associations between or among words or concepts, thus creating word meanings."[12] For our purposes, "the term *inner speech* refers to silent intrapersonal spoken language used to generate symbolic and conceptual thought while in the process of creating word meanings."[13] This inner speech allows us to silently produce words that remind us of things we need to do, things that have happened, or things we want to do. We tend to think, self-talk, continually. The inner voice rarely stops.[14]

Imagined Interactions

A type of self-talk is *imagined interactions*, when you mentally picture or hear people communicating. Perhaps you rehash a conversation you already had and how you wish it had played out. You may think about what you will say in an upcoming interaction with your professor or best friend. Imagined interactions are a type of mental practice for communication and probably reduce fears and contribute to effective communication.[15]

Do you perceive your digital world as imagined or real interactions?[16] Are your virtual conversations as real as your face-to-face conversations? Are your Facebook friends real friends? When you tell a story to an online group, are you speaking to real people?[17] Your view of real versus imagined says a great deal about you as a person and a communicator. Do you confront reality or attempt to escape into a fantasy world?

Digital Communication

In **digital communication**, electronic transmission is made of information that has been encoded by digitally processing. When personal computers became available in the 1980s, scholars began to analyze the perception about those computers as a "second self."[18] You may perceive what is stored on your electronic device (e.g., notebook, Droid, iPad) to be an extension of yourself, your brain, even your personality. The applications, saved files, and stored photos may be ways you extend yourself through an electronic device. If this is your perception, then your digital storage is intrapersonal communication. It is communication within the self. It's a way to communicate with yourself.[19] This means that before the invention of the digital devices this type of intrapersonal communication was not possible.

Self-Concept

Self-concept, your idea or picture of yourself, "is the accumulation of knowledge about the self, such as beliefs regarding personality traits, physical characteristics, abilities, values, goals and roles."[20] Your concept of your self-esteem begins in infancy and is acquired as you interact with cultural forces such as your family, media, friends, teachers, and the others with whom you come in contact. Although you may think of your self-esteem as being a single unit, those who study self-esteem have been able to identify four areas of esteem: physical, moral-ethical, family, and social. The *physical* refers to how you perceive your body. Do you evaluate highly such aspects as your height, weight, or attractiveness? *Moral-ethical* relates to your evaluation of your belief system, your moral behavior. The *family* aspects of your self-esteem relate to your views of your family relationships, the functional system of your family, how you were treated by your parents or whoever was responsible for your upbringing. And the *social* aspects of your self-esteem are your evaluations of yourself as you regard yourself in social situations—your pleasing others and your treatment of others. The sum total of these add up to your total concept of your self-esteem.

Are you interested in probing into your self-esteem? If so, try the Analyzing My Specific Self-Esteem activity.

Your concept of self is important because how you act and communicate with others is connected closely with your self-perception.[21] Your self-esteem rises and falls, acting as an internal barometer of how well you perceive you are doing in your personal, social, and career environments. The degree to which you are comfortable with yourself has been found to affect many areas of your psychological functioning.[22] Those with high levels of self-esteem, for example, tend to be less anxious in social situations than those with lower self-perceived esteem. They also tend to be less likely to be depressed, irritable, or aggressive.[23]

From the communication perspective, your self-concept often determines what you will say and to whom you will say it. For example, if you perceive yourself to be a good communicator, then you are likely to feel confident in your communication. But if you label yourself as shy or apprehensive, then you may find it difficult to express yourself. At the heart of this dynamic process is the premise that if you do

Analyzing My Specific Self-Esteem

DIRECTIONS: Indicate the degree to which each item is true or false for you.

If it is completely false, mark the item 1.

If it is mostly false, mark the item 2.

If it is partly false and partly true, 3.

If it is mostly true, 4.

If it is completely true, 5.

____ 1. I am satisfied with my weight.

____ 2. I am satisfied with my looks.

____ 3. I am satisfied with my height.

____ 4. I am satisfied with my moral behavior.

____ 5. I am satisfied with the extent to which I am religious.

____ 6. I am satisfied with my relationship with a Supreme Being.

____ 7. I am satisfied with my family relationships.

____ 8. I am satisfied with how well I understand my family.

____ 9. I am satisfied with how I treat (treated) my parents.

____ 10. I am satisfied with how sociable I am.

____ 11. I am satisfied with the extent to which I try to please others.

____ 12. I am satisfied with the way I treat other people.

Scoring:

Add items 1, 2, and 3:__________ . This is your *physical self-esteem score.*

Add items 4, 5, and 6:__________ . This is your *moral-ethical self-esteem score.*

Add items 7, 8, and 9:__________ . This is your *family self-esteem score.*

Add items 10, 11 and 12:__________ . This is your *social self-esteem score.*

Scores in any category between 12 and 15 indicate high self-esteem; scores between 3 and 6 indicate low self-esteem; and scores from 7 through 11 indicate moderate self-esteem.

COMMUNICATING in Careers

A Business Professional Shares Her Views on Self-Concept

Profile: Linda Eaton, senior consultant, Franklin Quest Company, Salt Lake City, consultant to many of the Fortune 1000 companies.

How does a person develop a strong self-concept?

A great self-concept is acquirable. Martin Seligman's *Learned Optimism* is a great guide for businesspersons to use to assist them in the development. It basically stresses that positive people (a) take credit for their actions, (b) take responsibility, and (c) identify negative experiences as learning opportunities, not things that happen to them (a "victim") but rather things they had a hand in shaping.

Is there a correlation between positive self-confidence and leadership?

Leaders have positive self-concepts, a vision, and the confidence to develop and share that vision. Leadership builds on the belief in the self and a positive self-concept.

How does a person's self-concept affect businesspeople in the changing work environment, especially as it relates to downsizing and mergers?

As George Bernard Shaw once said, "Luck is the marriage of opportunity and preparation." A downsizing, a merger, or an acquisition is not necessarily a good or a bad thing. Those with strong self-concepts view their jobs as a vehicle for self-development, and therefore are less negatively emotionally impacted by change.

Source: "A Business Professional Shares Her Views on Self-Concept" from *Business communication in a changing world* by Roy Berko, Andrew Wolvin, and Rebecca Ray.

REFLECT ON THIS:

1. In this era of corporate downsizing, mergers, and layoffs, how do you think a person who has a positive self-concept will react versus a person with a negative self-concept?
2. Think of a person you know who has a positive self-concept. How do you think he or she developed that attitude?

not accept yourself, probably no one else will, either. A lack of confidence is easily detected by those with whom you interact.

Research shows that there are seven signs that are common among those with a weak sense of self. Most people have some of these, but the person with a negative self-belief system displays many of these signs.[24]

- *Sensitivity to criticism.* This is displayed by a person not liking it when people point out any shortcomings.
- *Inappropriate response to flattery.* Most people accept flattery—in fact, they are honored by it. Those with negative self-esteem, however, tend to refuse to believe anything positive about themselves because it is inconsistent with their own perceptions. Do not, however, mix up modesty with negative reactions.
- *Hypercritical attitude.* People who do not feel good about themselves often have trouble feeling good about anyone else.
- *Tendency toward blaming.* Some people project their perceived weaknesses onto others in order to lessen the pain of thinking of themselves as inferior.
- *Feelings of persecution.* People with low self-esteem tend to believe the world is against them and constantly picking on them.
- *Negative feelings about competition.* Many of us like to win, but in order to avoid the feeling of loss, those with weak self-perceptions avoid competition because they believe they cannot win, and not winning will reinforce their negative self-views.

- *Tendency toward seclusion and timidity.* People who think they are inferior believe that they may not be as intelligent or talented or attractive or sociable as others, so they tend to avoid social situations. Or, if they do participate, they avoid speaking up so as not to embarrass themselves or reinforce their negative self- perceptions.

Some people worry about appearing too self-confident and being considered a braggart. Accepting yourself as a worthy person does not necessarily mean that you are boasting. Sometimes you have to "blow your own horn" because no one else knows how to play the tune. You know yourself better than others and know more about yourself and your skills and talents than others do. There is a difference, however, between tooting your own horn and playing a symphony (e.g., the distinction between sharing your accomplishments with others and going on and on about them or exaggerating). In this vein, consider this advice:

Your self-concept can work for or against you. "We have a choice each time we think, to think positively or negatively. Many of us don't believe it, but that absolutely is our choice. Once we understand that our private thoughts are ours alone to determine, we can select to program ourselves with empowering, confidence-building thoughts."[25]

Confronting Negative Self-Thoughts and Beliefs

Consider the vulture, an unattractive bird with sharp claws and a pointy beak whose favorite activity is picking on the weak, the helpless, and, preferably, the dead. It dives into the flesh and picks away at it. The *psychological vulture* does much the same thing. It attacks a person's perceived weaknesses and eats at the person's self-worth.

Are you interested in finding out about your vultures? If so, try the Identifying Your Vultures activity.

Psychological vultures tend to nest in six areas: *intelligence* vultures ("I'm dumb," "I'm no good in math"); *creativity* vultures ("I can't draw as well as Zander," "I can't sing like Eric"); *family* vultures ("I'm the odd-ball in the family," "My brother is the favorite child"); *relationship* vultures ("I'm no good at meeting people," "I'm shy"); *physical* vultures ("I'm too short/tall/fat/thin"); and *sexual* vultures ("I'm not sexy," "Only a person who was desperate would want to have a relationship with me").

Identifying Your Vultures

DIRECTIONS: List as many negative statements about yourself as you can for each statement. (Don't be concerned if you can't fill in all the blanks, but try to be honest!)

My *intelligence* (e.g., "I'm dumb," "I'm no good in math.")

____

My *creativity* (e.g., "I'm not imaginative," "I can't sing.")

____

My *family* (e.g., "I'm the odd-ball in the family," "My brother is the favorite.")

____

My *physicality* ("I'm too fat.")

____

My *sexuality* ("I'm not sexy.")

____

Me and my *relationships* ("I can't make friends," "Nobody likes me.")

____

The more positively you perceive yourself, the more likely it is that you will have self-confidence—that is, a sense of competence and effectiveness.

COMMUNICATING in Careers

How to Keep Your Composure

Your boss or coworker says something that irritates you—and you want to lash back. But you don't want to lose your cool at work. How can you keep your composure without experiencing a lot of stress?

Some suggestions:

- Step away and do what's called "a perception check." Ask yourself what you're really upset about. Does the situation revive something that happened to you as a child?
- Try to understand why the person behaved that way. You might realize that the intent was not vindictive.
- Let your feelings out on paper. Don't edit or censor a thing. Then look over what you've written and destroy the piece of paper. You'll feel better.
- Talk with coworkers you can trust. You'll release some emotions—and you might also get an objective assessment in the situation.
- Try to determine if you're overreacting. Ask yourself: "If this happened to my best friend, would I think that she or he was no good?" Your answer should help keep things in perspective.
- Before you decide to confront the offender, ask yourself these questions:

  "What will I gain by taking this action?"

  "Will I achieve my goals with this particular person?"

Source: "How to Keep Your Composure" by Nancy Monson, from *New Woman*. Copyright © by Nancy Monson. Reprinted with permission of the author. www.nancymonson.com

REFLECT ON THIS: Have you ever been in a work or school situation where knowing these principles would have been of value? If so, describe the situation. Which of these principles would have been of value? Why?

The results of self–put-downs are obvious: A person avoids the areas where the vultures lurk. Depending on the perceived vultures, he or she avoids such things as math classes, drawing, dates, singing, and going to social events. He or she wears large clothing to cover up their body or makes excuses for not participating in parties.

Your self-talk can work for or against you. How do you use self-talk to kill off your vultures? A theory regarding changing your self-defeating self-talk encourages:[26]

- Pat yourself on the back by saying something good and true about yourself. You can surely think of something for which to compliment yourself.
- Pat someone else on the back by saying something good and true about her or him. Not only will you feel good about yourself for complimenting another person, but you'll also find that compliments beget compliments.
- Recognize your self–put-downs. To make sure you catch them, you may want to ask a friend for help. Be sure to identify both the obvious and the subtle ones (and don't argue when your friend points them out). This step is crucial: You can't cure what you don't recognize! Once you start focusing on the positives, the negatives tend to go away. Negative self-talk can't survive if you don't feed it.[27]

The *replacement method* has been used with athletes to overcome negatives. In one study, basketball players were divided into three groups for foul-shot practice. The first group used imagery (internally picturing that they were shooting and making their shots) and negative-message elimination but did not practice shooting. The second group practiced shooting, and the third group did both corrective imaging and practiced shooting baskets. Although all three groups improved, the first and third groups improved by the same amount, and the second group improved less. "Positive self-talk really can turn your life around and make any life more successful."[28]

In addition to self-talk and self-concept, another important aspect of self-communication is how we process the information we receive.

Cognitive Processing

Your culture, background, family, education, and experiences all serve as the framework for shaping how you deal with incoming information and affect the way you decide on what actions to take or avoid. While what goes on inside our heads is a complicated and elusive aspect of communication, you cannot analyze or improve your own communication without considering the perceptions you hold, which influence your interaction in social contexts. We tend to cluster around people who have similar views and make us think or feel good about ourselves and our ideas. For example, are you part of a Facebook group where most members look at the world in pretty much the same way? Probably yes. Do you listen to talk radio and news shows that parallel your views? These actions may be cutting you off from hearing other viewpoints, which may enhance your depth of understanding.

The act of *cognitive processing* is how we deal with information in relationship to our values, attitudes, and beliefs. Each of us carries with us *values* (what we perceive to be of positive or negative worth), *attitudes* (our predispositions), and *beliefs* (our convictions). Most people try to keep their actions parallel to their values, beliefs, and attitudes. If things are in balance, we feel fairly good about ourselves and the world around us. If they are not, we may intrapersonally become confused and frustrated, which may cause us to act negatively toward ourselves or others. This imbalance happens, for example, when you know that a certain action you are about to take is wrong based on your value system. Your "internal voice" cries out, "Be careful! Don't do that!" Before the event, you may have a sleepless night as you toss and turn with the internal voice speaking messages, or you may dream about the negative things that are going to happen as a result of your taking the action.

The *imbalance* between your values, attitudes, and beliefs is called *cognitive dissonance*.[29] Cognitive dissonance often leads to a *guilty conscience:* The real or perceived fear that we are going to get caught, get punished, or otherwise be "found out." For example, an individual who believes cheating is wrong yet cheats on a test may feel cognitive dissonance following the act, no matter what grade she receives.

If you become aware of cognitive dissonance before you act and decide not to do the deed, you could chalk it up to your conscience warning you and saving you from a perceived disaster. If you take the negative action and then brood about the action afterward, then you may need to accept that you took the action, there is nothing you can do about it now, and go on from there, with the internal pledge to not do it again. Your internal voice, through its self-talk technique, often continues to shout at you until you put the imbalance to rest. For example, apologizing to a person you've insulted may make you feel better.

Perceptions

Based on your perceptions you came to a conclusion of whether something is right, wrong or you can't assign a value to it because of lack of strong feelings or evidence.

The perceptual process follows a step-by-step order. First, your senses collect the evidence, then you organize the cues, then you interpret those cues. Remember, the senses often work below your level of awareness, so you may not even know you are collecting and processing. For example, you may look at someone, collect visual and auditory information, and come to a conclusion of whether you like or dislike the person. This activity may take only an instant, but the evaluation is done. Looking at unfamiliar food, smelling a scent in the environment, or feeling a texture, all lead us to make identification or value judgments. How do you decide what to buy in a store? Sometimes it is a logical decision. Sometimes it is an instant emotional reaction to what you perceive.

A common occurrence in communication is jumping to conclusions, which is assuming we understand what another person thinks, feels, or perceives.[30] We may assume, for example, that a homeless person is uneducated and dangerous, someone only interested in taking money from public funds and not working. None of this may be true, but your past experiences or teaching allows you to reach those conclusions. A few sensory inputs and off you go to conclusion-land. Before jumping to conclusions, before believing biased individuals, find out the facts. A classical example of jumping to conclusion without the facts, or ignoring the facts, is exhibited by *birthers*, people who, seemingly based on nothing but the statements of right wing talk show hosts, came to the conclusion that Barak Obama was not eligible to be President because he was not born in this country. Though there is an official Hawaiian document showing Obama's birth date, city, name, and the names of his parents and their races, the birthers refuse to allow facts to override their preset ideas.[31]

Understanding how our perceptions work, realizing that our conclusions, based on those perceptions, may be right or wrong, allows us to open ourselves to examine our self and our conclusions in constructive ways.

The Self

How a human being views himself or herself will determine most of that individual's actions and choices in life.[32] Thus, the more positively you perceive yourself, the more likely it is that you will have *self-confidence*—that is, a sense of competence and effectiveness.

Each of us possesses a real self, an ideal self, and a public self. (See Figure 5.1.) The *real self* is what you think of yourself when you are being most honest about your interests, thoughts, emotions, and needs. For many people, the real self is dynamic and changing. This accounts for why you may feel as if you are in constant turmoil, searching for who you are, questioning your motives for doing and not doing certain things.

The *ideal self* is who you would like to be or think you should be. This is the "perfect you," perceived as being "perfect" by yourself or others (or both). It's often the you the significant others in your life (relatives, employers, the media, advertising) have told you that you should be, or who they want you to be.

The *public self* is the one you let others know. It is the person that you have decided to let others see. It is based on the concept that "if others believe the right things about me, I can get them to like me; I can persuade them and generally get my way." It acknowledges that "if others believe the wrong things about me, I can be rejected and blocked from my goals. Not only actors and politicians shape their public selves, we all do."[33]

Recognition of the importance of self-esteem and self-concept has a long tradition in the Euro American culture. Psychologists, educators, and communication theorists have examined the self and self-esteem based on observing and studying what we intrapersonally communicate about ourselves and what we interpersonally communicate to others.

The classic theory about the self is that it is composed of four aspects: the *spiritual,* what we are thinking and feeling; the *material,* represented by our possessions and physical surroundings; the *social,* represented by our interactions with others; and the *physical,* our physical being.[34] Much of our self-talk centers on how we perceive the four aspects.

Another theory stresses that the self evolves from the interactions we have with other people and how we intrapersonally integrate these interactions into our self-thought. This evolution takes place in stages. For example, a child aims for a sense of self as a separate person while developing gender identity; the adolescent tries to establish a stable sense of identity; the middle-aged person emphasizes independence while adjusting to changes in body competence; and the elderly person seeks to come to terms with aging.[35] As we go through these changes, our self-communication reflects the alterations that are

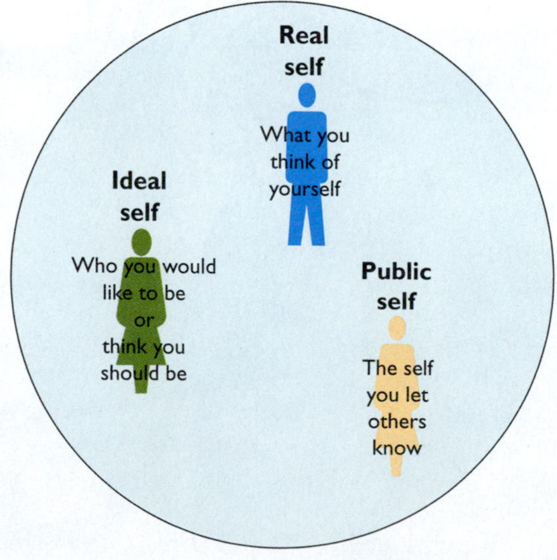

FIGURE 5.1 **Your Many Selves**

taking place, and for this reason we experience over our lifetime multiple concepts, rather than a single one, of who we are. Thus, at any one time in our lives, we may perceive ourselves to be a different person than we were at another time. You are probably not the same person today that you were five years ago, and you are not the same person today that you will perceive yourself to be five years from now.

Self-concept also seems to be situational. Who you are with one person or in one place may not be the same as who you are with someone else or in a different place. In one relationship, you may take on the role of student, and in another the role of friend. At work you may be the leader, and at home the follower. Many of these role-plays are based on our intrapersonal perception of who we should be or who we need to be with these people in this environment.

It is important that you understand yourself and your perceptions of yourself. This is the basis of self-awareness, which is the basis for much of your self-talk.

Understanding Yourself

Most people have only a general idea of who they are and what they really believe in. This explains why many of us don't understand why we think the thoughts we do and are intrapersonally motivated to act in particular ways.

It is often of great personal value to attempt to discover the you who is within you—the you who carries on your self-talk, cognitively processes, and acts on your self-concept.

It has been said that you are what you are based on your verb *to be*.[36] Are you interested in finding out your verb "to be?" If so, try the Perceiving My Verb "To Be" activity.

A good part of our lives is devoted to communicating our pleasure or lack of pleasure as we exploit our conquests, stress our influences, and reinforce our accomplishments.

Perceiving My Verb "To Be"

DIRECTIONS: Complete these statements:

I am ______________________________.

I would like to be ______________________________.

I like to ______________________________.

I believe that ______________________________.

I have been ______________________________.

I wouldn't want to ______________________________.

The quality I possess that I am most proud of is ______________________________.

My biggest flaw is ______________________________.

Something that I would prefer others not know about me is ______________________________.

When you are finished responding to these items, write a two-sentence description of yourself based on the answers to the statements you completed.

____

____

____

If you completed this activity, your two-sentence summary is your view of your perceived "to be." You have used your intrapersonally stored data to examine your past experiences *(I have been/done),* current attitudes and actions *(I am),* and future expectations or hopes *(I would like to be/do).* If you were honest and revealed what you really think and feel, you have just gained a glimpse of your perceived self.

Another way of looking at yourself is through the model known as the **Johari Window,**[37] which allows you to ascertain your willingness to disclose who you are and allows others to disclose to you. From an intrapersonal perspective, the Johari window helps you understand a great deal about yourself.

If you are interested in finding out your willingness to disclose, try the "Johari Window" Questionnaire.[38]

Based on your answers to the questionnaire, use Figure 5.2 to plot your scores. Compare your pattern with those in Figure 5.3 to ascertain your self-disclosure/receive-feedback style. What is revealed are the four common styles people use in receiving and giving personal information and feedback.

Johari Window Questionnaire

DIRECTIONS: Before each item in Part I, place a number from 1 to 6 to indicate how much you are *willing to reveal.* A 1 indicates that you are willing to self-disclose nothing or almost nothing, and a 6 indicates that you are willing to reveal everything or almost everything. Use the values 2, 3, 4, and 5 to represent the points between these extremes.

Before each item in Part II, place a number from 1 to 6 to indicate how *willing you are to receive feedback* about what you self-disclose. A 1 indicates that you refuse or resist feedback, and a 6 indicates that you consistently encourage feedback. Use the values 2, 3, 4, and 5 to represent the points between these extremes.

PART I: Extent to which I am willing to self-disclose my

____ 1. goals
____ 2. strengths
____ 3. weaknesses
____ 4. positive feelings
____ 5. negative feelings
____ 6. values
____ 7. ideas
____ 8. beliefs
____ 9. fears and insecurities
____ 10. mistakes
____ Total

PART II: Extent to which I am willing to receive feedback about my

____ 1. goals
____ 2. strengths
____ 3. weaknesses
____ 4. positive feelings
____ 5. negative feelings
____ 6. values
____ 7. ideas
____ 8. beliefs
____ 9. fears and insecurities
____ 10. mistakes
____ Total

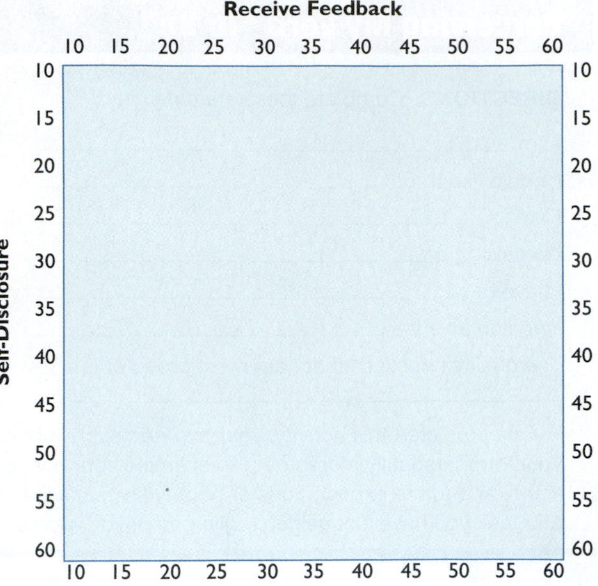

FIGURE 5.2
Plotting Your Johari Window
Circle the number on the top line of the square, designated "Receive Feedback," that corresponds to your score on Part II of the Johari Window Questionnaire. Circle the same number on the bottom line of the square. Connect the two circles with a straight line. Then circle the number on the left side line of the square, designated "Self-Disclosure," that corresponds to your score on Part I of the Johari Window Questionnaire. Circle the same number on the right side line of the square. Connect the two circles with a straight line.

- *Style I* people spend little time disclosing or giving feedback. They tend to be perceived as good listeners and fairly shy or quiet; sometimes they are labeled as introverts.

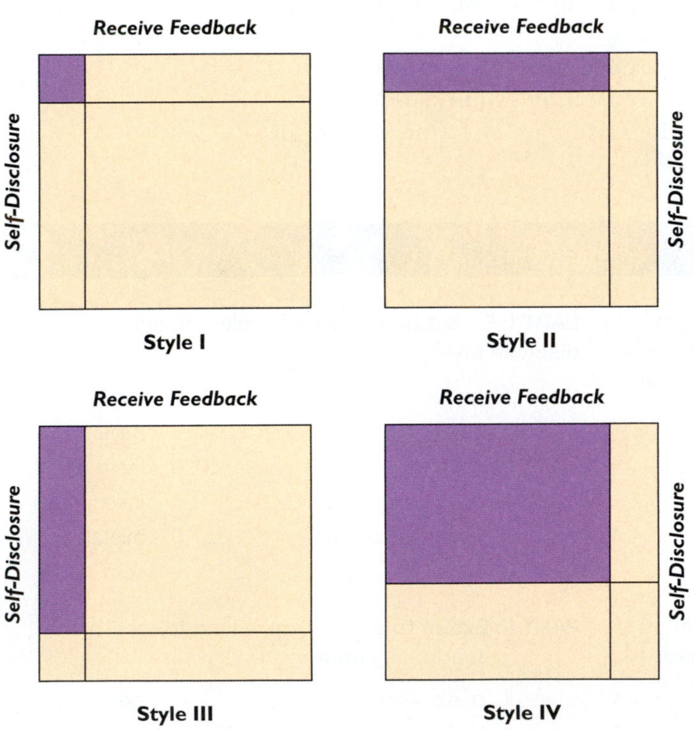

FIGURE 5.3 Johari Style Indicator

Source: "Johari Style Indicator" from *Group Processes: An Introduction to Group Dynamics*, 3rd Edition, by Joseph Luft. Copyright © 1984 by Joseph Luft. Reprinted with permission of The McGraw-Hill Companies, Inc.

- *Style II* people spend a great deal of time listening and not much time sending out personal information. After you have been with a Style II type of person for a while, he or she tends to know a great deal about you, but you don't know much about him or her. This is the style that generally describes introverts.
- *Style III* people give a great deal of personal information but don't like to receive very much. They tell you about themselves and are often perceived as great talkers but not very good listeners. You tend to know a great deal about them, but they don't know much about you.
- *Style IV* people like to give and get information. People who are very open and easily share themselves with. Because these people share, they are known to themselves and to others. They are often referred to as extroverts; they are outgoing and interactive.

If your four-sided figures are approximately the same size, you do not have a predominant self-disclosure/receive-feedback style.

What you should gain from the Johari window exercise is an understanding of not only your perception of yourself and how it affects your intrapersonal communication but also how others may perceive you based on your willingness or unwillingness to disclose and receive information.

In application terms, Style II people and Style III people would appear to make excellent partners in relationships as one likes to disclose and the other to receive but not disclose. The problem with this combination may be that after a while the Style III person realizes that he does not know much about the Style II person, and the Style II person realizes that while she knows a lot about her partner, the partner knows practically nothing about her. The relationship is sometimes perceived as not being balanced.

Style IV people often scare those who are Style I individuals. A Style IV person dominates the conversation by telling about himself and probing to find out about the other person, who really doesn't necessarily want to learn about the other person nor reveal anything about herself. This can be unnerving to Style I individuals.

Need Drives Affecting Communication

We are each born with certain biological tools that allow us to communicate: a brain, sound-producing organs (mouth, tongue, larynx), and a receiving apparatus (ears, eyes). According to *ethnographers*—researchers who study cultures—we are born with need drives that must be satisfied. Some communication theorists think that these intrapersonal drives are the basis for our communication: what we think, what we express, what inspires us to act the way we do, and how we react to the way others express and use their drives. This concept explains why we communicate in ways that go beyond our usual understanding of communication.[39]

The basic forces that determine human behavior are survival of the species, pleasure seeking, security, and territoriality.[40] These drives are not manifested equally in every person. One person may have a pleasure need that is stronger than any of the other forces, whereas another may have strong needs for security and territoriality.

Survival

A person who is threatened screams out for help; when a pebble flies against the windshield of your moving car, you duck. These are examples of attempts to ensure *survival*. These actions are *reflexive*—inborn reactions that we instinctively use to communicate our fear of a possible ending of our existence.

Our ability to communicate selectively gives us a distinct survival advantage. For example, we can call for help, plead, explain our needs, or try to convince attackers that their action is unwise. In addition, we are aware of our own evolution. Because of this, we can communicate about how we reproduce, what causes us to die, and how we can attempt to alter conditions to prolong our lives and those of our descendants. We have been able to communicate these ideas from person to person and thus build on the experience of the past in developing intrapersonal understanding.

Pleasure Seeking

We are basically *pleasure-seeking* beings. A good part of our lives is devoted to communicating our pleasure or lack of pleasure. We talk about our awards, citations, and good grades to communicate to others that we have succeeded, thus satisfying our pleasure need.

People find different events pleasurable, and each of us may find both pleasure and pain in a single event. Moreover, we may find pleasure in satisfying not only our own needs but also the needs of others or in fulfilling our long-term goals as well as our immediate desires. What pleases one person may well torture another. One person happily gives a speech before a large audience; another is petrified by any speaking situation.

If given the opportunity, we choose to communicate in those situations in which we perceive we will get pleasure. You raise your hand to answer a question in class if you think you know the right answer. We are constantly sending ourselves intrapersonal messages relating to whether some experience was or was not pleasurable, or whether a perceived activity will render pleasure.

Security

You enter a classroom for the first meeting of a class. You see a place that is unfamiliar, people you do not know, a professor who is an unknown entity. You feel insecure. Your desire to participate and your comfort in this situation can be affected directly by the messages you send yourself.

The need for *security* causes us to seek equilibrium, a balance. When security is absent, when we feel a lack of control, most of us are uneasy and cautious.

We choose to communicate in those situations in which we perceive we will get pleasure.

Our concept of ourselves in situations of security or insecurity motivates our verbal and nonverbal communication. Fear causes the vocal pitch to rise, the body to shake, and the stomach to churn. We find ourselves afraid to speak, or speaking incessantly, or stammering. But as we become more comfortable in a situation and learn the rules of the game, we find ourselves acting quite differently because we send ourselves positive messages. The first day of class, for instance, you may not say a word. But as you acclimate yourself to the situation, you may feel secure enough to participate.

Hearing intrapersonal messages of fear of the unknown explains why some people will not wander down the unmapped paths of life. The messages they send themselves center on the warning "Beware of the unknown, the uncomfortable."

Territoriality

We intrapersonally define a particular *territory,* whether physical or perceptual. We defend it from invasion and use it for protection. We mark off land by defining it precisely with a deed indicating length, width, and location. We mark our territory with fences, signs, and numbers that specifically say "This belongs to me." We tend to feel most secure when we are in our own territory, and we often identify ourselves by our hometown, our school, and our social groups, all of which are territorial markers.

Communicating Socially

Chicagoans Protect Their Territory

In an urban version of wild animals marking their territory, Chicago residents use chairs and other objects to tell anyone who passes that someone has taken the trouble to dig out enough snow to park a car—and that person expects the spot to remain available when the vehicle returns. "It's an unwritten rule of etiquette," said an attorney about to place a bright blue folding chair on a spot he'd dug in front of his home. "And you bear the consequences if you break it." One woman found this out when, not wanting to walk a long way by herself in the dead of night, she moved the chairs, and parked and went to bed. When she came back, her tires had been slashed. She later said, "I don't move people's chairs anymore."

Source: Babwin, D. & Johnson, C. (2011, February 6). Chicago revives post-storm etiquette: Making parking spots. *[Cleveland] Plain Dealer*, p. A6.

REFLECT ON THIS:

1. Explain the actions discussed as they relate to the Ethnographic Theory of Needs.
2. Some Chicagoans refer to the actions as "following the law of the street." Do you agree with this nonordinance passed law?

We mark off territory by marking it with objects, fences, signs, and numbers.

We act differently in different territories. When friends come to visit you, conditions are not the same as when you go to visit them. The friend you invite over for dinner does not act the same at your house as when you go to his house for dinner. In the same way, there is a definite difference between playing an athletic game at home and playing it on the road. The home team is estimated to have an advantage of 2.33 points in the National Basketball Association, 2.58 point in the National Football League, 3.85 in college football, and 3.70 in college basketball.[41]

In addition to physical territory, we have ideas and areas of expertise that we identify as ours. Inventors obtain patents to protect their inventions; writers copyright their books. Both are attempts to establish a territory and to communicate the boundaries to others.

The more insecure a person is within a territory, the greater is that person's intrapersonal fear of losing the territory. Once people have defined something as theirs, they will tend to defend it. Thus, an invasion of someone else's territory is likely to invite a counterattack.

Clearly, one's basic drives have a significant influence on intrapersonal communication.

Communication Apprehension

Many people call it *shyness*, but in the field of communication, the anxiety is identified as **communication apprehension**.[42] The communicatively anxious person is aware of the anxiety because intrapersonal messages clearly warn of the fear. The messages warn of unfavorable outcomes, and the person experiences a sense of impending doom.

Although many think of communication apprehension only in regard to public speaking, it is actually much broader.[43] Worries, concerns, and fears interfere with efficient listening, communicating in groups, talking in class and on the telephone, and verbalizing during interviews.

Individuals who are considered to have high communication apprehension often think and feel that one or more of their basic needs is being attacked. They may feel so endangered that they perceive their very existence is endangered (survival need). Because they do not think that the experience of communicating is or will be positive, they do not perceive it as positive (pleasure need). They often are so uncomfortable thinking about communicating in conversations, or giving speeches, that they are off-balance and up-tight (security need). Going into a setting (territorial need) where communication will take place (e.g., a classroom where a speech must be given or a job site where a report must be presented) may be unnerving.

"Shy people have inaccurate self-concepts."[44] They often believe that they are inadequate when they are not. "They tend to blame themselves for failure and credit others for success. They tend to erase themselves: they avoid eye contact, speak softly or less than others, and rarely take a strong position on a topic."[45] People who are shy seem inclined to use mediated communication over face-to-face and are more likely to develop online relationships than less apprehensive people do.[46]

Almost 95 percent of the population reports having apprehension about communicating with some person or group in their lives.[47] Of those, 30 percent classify themselves as extremely shy, so introverted that they choose careers or go into jobs and lifestyles that center on avoiding one-on-one or group communication situations.[48]

Shy people avoid interacting directly with others because of the availability of non-face-to-face tools such as e-mail, Facebook, and Twitter. Thus, they avoid practicing the very skills that they need to hone.

Communication apprehension may be situation specific or general. For example, some people only feel fear when confronted with giving a speech. A survey indicates that 40.6 percent of respondents identified their major fear to be speaking before groups, exceeding fear of heights, death, and loneliness.[49] On the other hand, some people report perceived discomfort only in one-on-one conversations or in groups. Others indicate experiencing apprehension in any speaking situation.

Are you interested in finding out whether you considered yourself communicative apprehensive and, if so, in what situations? If so, take the Personal Report of Communication Apprehension (PRCA-24).

Personal Report of Communication Apprehension (PRCA-24)

Directions: This instrument is composed of twenty-four statements concerning feelings about communicating with other people. Indicate the degree to which each statement applies to you by marking whether you (1) strongly agree, (2) agree, (3) are undecided, (4) disagree, or (5) strongly disagree. Record your first impression.

____ 1. I dislike participating in group discussions.

____ 2. Generally, I am comfortable while participating in a group discussion.

____ 3. I am tense and nervous while participating in group discussions.

____ 4. I like to get involved in group discussions.

____ 5. Engaging in a group discussion with new people makes me tense and nervous.

____ 6. I am calm and relaxed while participating in group discussions.

____ 7. Generally, I am nervous when I have to participate in a meeting.

____ 8. Usually I am calm and relaxed while participating in meetings.

___ 9. I am very calm and relaxed when I am called upon to express an opinion at a meeting.

____ 10. I am afraid to express myself at meetings.

____ 11. Communicating at meetings usually makes me uncomfortable.

____ 12. I am very relaxed when answering questions at a meeting.

____ 13. While participating in a conversation with a new acquaintance, I feel very nervous.

____ 14. I have no fear of speaking up in conversations.

____ 15. Ordinarily I am very tense and nervous in conversations.

____ 16. Ordinarily I am very calm and relaxed in conversations.

____ 17. While conversing with a new acquaintance, I feel very relaxed.

____ 18. I'm afraid to speak up in conversations.

____ 19. I have no fear of giving a speech.

____ 20. Certain parts of my body feel very tense and rigid while I am giving a speech.

____ 21. I feel relaxed while giving a speech.

____ 22. My thoughts become confused and jumbled when I am giving a speech.

____ 23. I face the prospect of giving a speech with confidence.

____ 24. While giving a speech, I get so nervous I forget facts I really know.

Scoring:

18+ scores for items 2, 4, 6; minus the scores for items 1, 3, 5 = Group discussion score

18+ scores for 8, 9, 12; minus the scores for 7, 10, 11 = Meetings score

18+ scores for 14, 16, 17; minus the scores for 13, 15,

18 = Interpersonal conversations score

18+ scores for 19, 21, 23; minus the scores for 20, 22,

24 = Public speaking score

Add your group, meetings, interpersonal, and public speaking scores = Total score

The interpretation of your scores can be found on page 464.

The Effects of Communication Apprehension

There are some demonstrated effects of communication apprehension.[50] In classroom situations, communicatively anxious students rarely volunteer, if at all.[51] They often drop classes that require oral communication or miss class when oral participation is necessary. These behavior patterns can affect both learning and grades.[52] Some anxious college students even fail to graduate when they have only one course to complete—a required course in speech communication.[53]

People with communication apprehension often choose college majors that require few, if any, oral presentations, such as research or technical fields. In the workplace, if they must participate orally—whether one-on-one, in a group, or in a public setting—they fail to do so, thus missing out on promotions and pay increases because they are handicapped by their fear.[54]

In interpersonal situations, people with communication apprehension talk very little about themselves and seem overly concerned that the other person understand and agree with them.[55] They are also nonassertive, tending to yield to the other person and submitting themselves to others' directions. Insofar as perceptions of communicatively anxious people are concerned, after interacting for only a short period of time with strangers, communicatively anxious people are perceived as less socially attractive, trustworthy, and satisfied than people who are not communicatively anxious.[56]

Although they may have as much desire for social relationships as those who are not communicatively anxious, people who are afraid to communicate have fewer steady dates than those who are less anxious.[57]

Help for Communication Apprehension

Approximately 10 to 15 percent of babies are born with inhibited temperament. Biologically these children, referred to as being shy, react more intensely to the stimuli around them than other children do.[58]

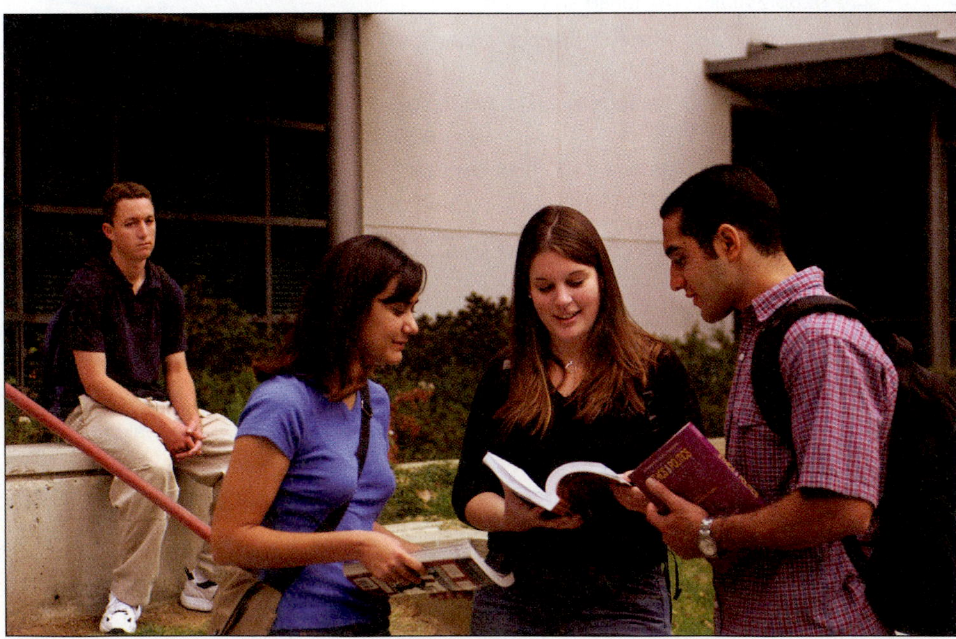

The communicatively anxious person is aware of the anxiety because intrapersonal messages clearly warn of the fear.

Communication apprehension is not a mental disorder.[59] Except for those children born with high anxiety, communication apprehension is an attribute a person applies to himself or herself, and it can be removed. The easiest way to do this, of course, is for the person to declare that he or she doesn't want or need the title. Sound silly and oversimplistic that you can declare yourself no longer a communication apprehensive? It's not. A change of self-perception can result in a change of action. Just as some people declare, "I will no longer smoke" and they never light up again, people have successfully overcome shyness by declaring that their self-perceived social phobia is over.[60] Doing this is very difficult for many to do, however, so be reassured that aid is available to those who want to rid themselves of the title. Such actions as skill training, systematic desensitization, cognitive modification, a willingness to communicate, and drug therapy are forms of help.

Skill Training One of the factors that is perceived to be a problem among communicatively anxious people is their lack of oral communication skills. Not knowing how to structure or organize a speech, how to start and continue a conversation, or how to participate in a group can manifest itself by triggering the negative aspect of two basic human needs—security and pleasure.

"Socially confident people deliberately learn specific skills, like displaying friendly body language, understanding the predictable format for conversation with new people, and focusing on the topic rather than on how they are perceived."[61]

Systematic Desensitization People's fear of humiliation and embarrassment when they are around unfamiliar people or of being evaluated negatively by others are

Socially COMMUNICATING

What Is Your Life Script?

How fixed beliefs define our roles:
Our fixed beliefs define the roles we play in life. The scripts that are running follow a play's script of lines, actions, and attitude. We follow life scripts according to what our fixed beliefs tell us. Are you telling yourself that you are a tragic character or heroic character? Are you playing the loving mother, abusive husband, frustrated artist, business leader, student leader, or college athletic all star?

Why scripts are dangerous:
Whatever your fixed beliefs are, you have practiced your script for so long that you believe what it says about your potential. This is why life scripts are dangerous. We begin to perceive them as being set in stone. We even allow them to shape the way we expect things to turn out. Fixed beliefs also influence the casting, location, and wardrobe of our script. Who is "right" for the part in our script and who isn't? What type of living arrangement and attire are the character we are playing, etc.?

When life scripts become limiting:
Because our scripts are based on fixed beliefs, we tend to resist any challenges or changes to them. If we are happy and fulfilled, but our script says that we should feel sad and hopeless, we tend to panic because we script. It just doesn't feel right and besides, the happy role belongs to someone else, doesn't it? This is an example of why most fixed beliefs are also limiting beliefs. They limit our scripts by dictating what we can't do, don't deserve, and aren't qualified for.

Source: McGraw, P. (n.d.). Retrieved from www.dr.phil.com

REFLECT ON THIS:

1. Name two entries in your life script.
2. What are two of your fixed beliefs?
3. At this point in your life, how set is your life script?
4. Are you willing to change any or all of your life script?
5. What would get you to change any or all of your life script?

major apprehension inducers.[62] Through systematic desensitization, people are taught first to recognize tension in their bodies and then how to relax.[63] As many as 80 or 90 percent of the people treated professionally by this system report the complete elimination of their apprehension.[64]

Cognitive Modification The basic concept behind cognitive modification is that people have learned to think negatively and must be taught to think positively. The first step in this process is for people to learn how to recognize when they are thinking negatively and to identify their own negative statements about their communication. Then they learn to replace negative statements with positive ones. Rather than saying, for example, "I really say stupid things," they may change their response to "I can present clear ideas; it isn't that hard." The last stage of the training is to practice substituting positive statements for negative ones. This may sound very theoretical, but in reality, it works. The success achieved by using this technique is quite high.[65]

Drug Therapy "Pasted on bus shelters nationwide, a poster asks passersby to imagine being allergic to people."[66] The purpose of the billboards is to alert individuals with social anxiety disorder that, in extreme cases, there may be some help for dealing with the problem by using drug therapy as a support for psychological and speech communication assistance. These are available only through medical professionals and should be prescribed only after carefully medical and psychological evaluation.[67]

The Role of Culture on Self-Communication

The basis for your identity is anchored in your *social orientation,* which includes all aspects of your culture: your nationality, race, gender, sexual orientation, and religion.[68] How your culture deals with and teaches about boastfulness, orientations toward life, spirituality, relationship to nature, attitudes toward others, and what it means to be a successful communicator affects your development of self-concept.

In this discussion of cultural tendencies, please be aware that the statements are assertions based on research findings. This means that any individual member of a culture may not follow the patterns described. Testing looks for norm patterns—patterns of the general members of the group. If you are a member of the culture being discussed, for example, you may fall outside of the described statistical sample.

Aspects of Culture That Affect the Self

Varying cultural concepts affect a person's concept of self. These include self-credentialing and self-humbling; relationship to the spirit world, nature, and other living things; doing or being orientation to life; attitudes toward others; and, high and low context communication.

Self-Credentialing/Self-Humbling Societies In cultures that stress a *self-credentialing verbal mode,* emphasis is placed on drawing attention to or boasting about one's accomplishments. For example, "In the Swiss and U.S. cultures, individuals are encouraged to sell themselves and boast about their achievements."[69] The same pattern is found in Arab and African cultures.[70]

In *self-humbling verbal mode societies,* people see the importance of lowering oneself via modest talk, verbal restraints, and the use of self-deprecation. Native Americans and those from some areas of West Africa, may have difficulty understanding and applying the concept of self-credentialing because of their linguistic patterns of underplaying, rather than overplaying, their sense of self.[71]

Your self-concept is obviously based on different criteria, depending on if you are from a self-credentialing or a self-humbling verbal society.

Doing or Being Orientation to Life Middle- and upper-middle-class African Americans, Asian Americans, Latino Americans, Jewish Americans, and European Americans focus on a *doing oriented approach to life.*[72] They tend to be achievement oriented. Much of the self-image of a people who believe in the doing orientation is based on their financial gains and/or obtaining the respect of others through accomplishments. Their concept of self is often based on what others think or say about their deeds.

On the other hand, Africans, Native Americans, Hindus, and Buddhists are more in tune with the *being oriented approach to life.*[73] In this orientation, a person may strive for life goals, but this is not something to use as an evaluation of a person's self-worth or self-value. They often do not talk about their accomplishments, and therefore the idea of self-worth is a nonissue.

Attitudes toward Others Some societies have respect for all. Societies, for example, where Buddhism is practiced are likely to avoid evaluating the lifestyle and beliefs of others. This is in opposition to those societies where there are strong religious traditions such as by Muslims, Orthodox Jews, fundamentalist Christians, and traditional Catholics. These religions teach that there are good versus bad behaviors, desirable and undesirable practices. This creates an atmosphere where those who are pointed out as being deviant or different have challenges in developing positive self-images.

Gay men and lesbians, for example, in the United States, because of years of exclusion by the general society and its laws, and some religious teaching, have found it necessary to hide who they are. Thus, a gay person's self-concept may have been negatively influenced.[74]

High-Context/Low-Context Communication In *low-context communication societies,* the emphasis is on the expression of ideas through explicit verbal messages.[75] In *high-context communication societies,* the emphasis is on how the verbal message can best be conveyed through indirect language and the nonverbal channels of silence and subtle tone of voice.

The British, Germans, Danes, Swedes, Euro Americans, Canadians, and Australians tend to be low-context communicators, using the low-context mode.[76] The speaker is expected to construct a persuasive message that the listener can easily decode.

The Arabic and Spanish language systems tend toward a more status-based, high context verbal model. Other high context nationalities are Japan, China, South Korea, Vietnam, Nigeria, Mexico, Kuwait, and Saudi Arabia.[77]

In comparing the two contexts, "The Japanese disclose less because they highly value harmony, group interest, formal relationships,

COMMUNICATING

The Stolen Generation: Positive Self-Concept Denied

"For the indignity and degradation thus inflicted on a proud people and a proud culture, we say sorry."

Australian Prime Minister Kevin Rudd, apologizing to members of the "Stolen Generation" of Aborigines, an estimated 100,000 children who until the 1970s were forcibly taken from indigenous parents under now discredited assimilation policies.

Source: Perspective. (2008, February 25). *Newsweek, 25.*

REFLECT ON THIS:

Do you think the President of the United States should make an apology to:

1. Japanese Americans who were imprisoned by the U.S. government during World War II?
2. African Americans for being enslaved?
3. Gays and lesbians for the discrimination against them caused by laws restricting their rights and the lack of protection for their rights?

private selves and nonverbal forms of disclosure, while U.S. Americans emphasize informal relationships, personal interests, greater social spontaneity, public selves and direct expressions."[78]

These communication styles influence the formation of self-concepts. For example, praise or criticism are given for acting the way in which a culture dictates, as well as setting up how one should perceive himself or herself as a social being. In the United States, respect is given for extroversion.

Most people in the United States believe extroverted people are better communicators because U. S. Americans value assertiveness and expressive communicators.[79] In the United States, introversion is considered a disadvantage. On the other hand, in Japan, where being thoughtful and a good listener is revered, communication apprehension, as defined by Euro American standards, is a positive way of acting.

In Conclusion

IN CONCLUSION

The basis for communication with others is the ability to communicate with oneself. The internal messages that we send to ourselves are called intrapersonal communication. Each person's culture, background, family, education, and experiences serve as the framework for his or her perceptions which shapes how the person deals with incoming information and affects the way he or she decides on what actions to take or avoid. How a human being views himself or herself will determine most of his or her actions and choices in life; however, most people have only a general idea of who they are and what they really believe in. Some communication theorists believe that the intrapersonal drives we are born with are the bases for our communication: what we think, what we express, what inspires us to act the way we do, and how we react to the way others express and use their drives. Most people experience and subsequently deal with some form of communication apprehension. Culture has a strong affect on self-concept and self-perception.

LEARN BY DOING

1. Prepare a list of ten questions an interviewer should ask to get an accurate picture of who you really are. These questions should allow the interviewer to understand your personal history, beliefs, and future plans. Phrase the questions so that they require more than a one- or two-word reply. Your instructor will then match you with another member of the class. You will interview each other using the questions that each of you has prepared. Then introduce each other in a two- to three-minute presentation to the class. After the class presentation, answer the following questions:
   a. What did it feel like to reveal myself to a stranger?
   b. Did I conceal things about myself during the interview? If so, why?
   c. How did I feel and what did I do while my partner was introducing me to the class?

2. Bring to class a painting, poem, or piece of music you like. Share it with the class or a small group, and indicate why you have positive feelings about it. What does your choice indicate about you? Did you find it difficult to share something so personal with strangers?
3. State whether you agree or disagree with these statements: "A person is changeable and can alter behavior patterns if she or he really wants to do so." "No one can change anyone else; only the individual can change himself or herself." Explain the reasons for your answers.
4. Get one of your friends to fill out the Johari Window form (see p. 117) as if she or he were you. Compare that person's answers with yours. What did you learn about yourself from this activity?
5. Make a shield like coat of arms out of a piece of cardboard large enough for the class to see. Draw or cut out and paste at least four pictures, symbols, or words on the coat of arms that represent you: your beliefs, attitudes, bodily image, hobbies, future plans, past successes or failures. The class will be divided into groups. Each person is to explain his or her coat of arms and why he or she selected these things as self-representations.
6. Think of two people you know well. List both your and their beliefs regarding gun ownership, abortion, and the Tea Party. What about your or their backgrounds has lead each to those perceptions? Do you think media has affected these views? Are there any cultural connections that set the perceptions?

KEY TERMS

intrapersonal communication 107
self-talk 107
digital communication 108
self-concept 108
Johari window 117
communication apprehension 122

CHAPTER 6

Interpersonal and Electronically Mediated Communication

the self • compliance • power • relationships • masculine-feminine communication • harassment • bullying • mediated communication

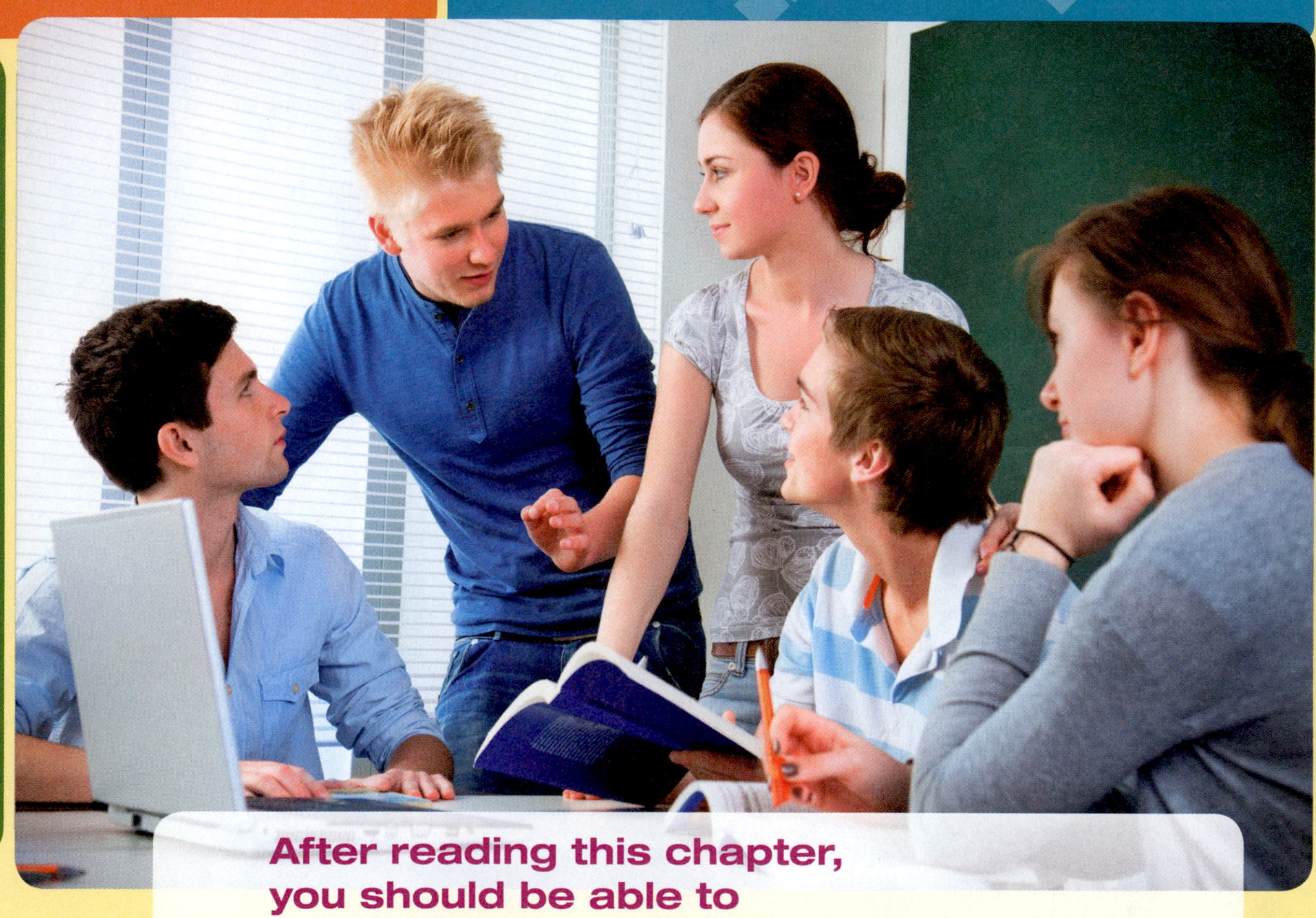

After reading this chapter, you should be able to

- Illustrate how self-disclosure plays a role in both self-understanding and understanding of another person
- Explain the roles of trust, approval seeking, emotions, and power as they relate to interpersonal communication
- Compare and contrast the similarities and differences in the communication of males and females and their potential effects on interpersonal communication
- Analyze the role of sexual harassment in the workplace
- Describe the role of bullying as a verbal and nonverbal communication weapon
- Define what relationships are and demonstrate how they develop, continue, and end
- Evaluate the causes of relational conflict
- Explain the role of, positive and negative aspects of, and how to be a better online electronically mediated communicator

The concept of interpersonal communication developed in the early 1950s.[1] As a result of research on the subject, the field of speech expanded from study focused on public speaking into the broader field of communication, encompassing such areas as self-disclosure, approval seeking, relational communication, family communication, small-group communication, nonverbal communication, conversational communication, intercultural communication, organizational communication, and conflict resolution.[2]

The term *interpersonal communication* can be defined as "communication that is based on communicators' recognition of each other's uniqueness and the development of messages that reflect that recognition."[3] It also can be described as an interactional process in which two people send and receive messages. Two primary themes underlie this process: communication necessitates give and take, and communication involves relationships and information.

Because there can be no interpersonal communication unless the communicators give and take information, the basis for interpersonal transactions is the sending and receiving of messages in such a way that they are successfully encoded and decoded. The more experiences the communicators have in common and the more openness they have between them, the more likely it is that their communication will be successful.

Our interpersonal relationships bring together the most important people, roles, contexts, and energies we experience. Interpersonal communication functions to combat loneliness, shape self-concepts, confirm experiences, renew personal and intrapersonal growth, and aid us in understanding who we are and how we relate to others.

Having good interpersonal relationships at work increases a person's commitment to the job.[4] On the personal level, family and relational communication is dependent on your being a competent interpersonal communicator. Interpersonal communication is at the core of collegiate success. Your interpersonal abilities can affect your academic success, relational rapport, and social connectedness.

Basic Concepts of Interpersonal Communication

As you read about interpersonal communication, keep these basic concepts in mind:

- *Communication takes place within a system.* As we enter into communicative relationships with others, we set a pattern by which we will interact. For example, in a family, there are flow patterns of message sending and receiving: who speaks to whom, who controls the interactions, who has the power to praise and punish. If you examine any relationship you are in, you will recognize communication.

  A change in the system results in a change of the communication. If someone in the system changes roles (e.g., a teenager leaves for college) or outside factors change the communication patterns (e.g., a grandparent moves in), that changes the system.

  There may be resistance to changing the system because this may also shift the power structure. If your supervisor, spouse, lover, or friend likes being in control, and you are proposing a change, problems may arise. At the other extreme, there also may be situations in which the system requires adjustment so that a person is forced to assume responsibility after having been dependent on someone else. The communication system remains unchanged as long as the status quo is maintained.

- *We teach others how to treat us.* Each person plays a role when a system is developing. If both people accept their roles, then those roles become part of the system. If a role is rejected, then it does not become a rule. Often we wonder why people treat us as they do. In many instances it is because when they treat us in a particular way, we didn't object; therefore, it becomes the pattern. For example, a habitual physical abuser at one point hit someone who didn't object. Consequently, the next time the abuser found a need to aggress, he or she repeated the action. The cycle is set unless the abused takes action to teach the aggressor a new way to act or leaves the relationship.
- *We communicate what and who we are.* Every time we communicate, we tell a great deal about ourselves. Our selection of words, the tone of our voice, and the gestures we use combine to give a picture of our values, likes and dislikes, and self-perceptions. We give clues to our background by our pronunciation patterns and the attitudes we express. As receivers, we form conclusions about senders and react to these conclusions based on our own culture—our background, experiences, and beliefs.
- *Much of our interpersonal communication centers on our wanting others to act or think or feel as we do; in other words, much of it is an attempt at persuasion.* In our interpersonal relations with parents, children, and friends, we often attempt to alter or reinforce behavior, gain compliance, give advice, or elicit some type of action. We use phrases like, "What I think you should do" and "That's wrong, the right answer is."
- *Meaning is in people, not in words.* In communicating with others, we must be aware that what a particular symbol means to us is not necessarily what it means to the other person. A homeowner hearing the word *grass* may think of the *lawn.* A drug counselor probably thinks of *marijuana.* Unless some basis for understanding exists, ineffective communication may be the result. Thus, we must define terms and give examples, keeping our audience in mind and adjusting our messages accordingly.
- *We cannot not communicate.* Communication does not necessarily stop simply because people stop talking or listening. Suppose you do not answer a question your instructor has asked. Or you sit quietly at the dinner table instead of joining in the conversation. In these cases, you are still sending messages, although your lips are silent. Remember that much communicating is done below the verbal level. You may think that if you do not actively participate, you are not sending messages—but you are! In many instances, your body is communicating nonverbally, and the very fact that you are not saying something may be interpreted as if you were telling the other person that you are not interested, don't care, or disagree.
- *People react to our actions.* We constantly are demonstrating the *action–reaction principle.* When we smile, others are likely to smile back; when we display anger, others tend to do the same. Try an experiment. The next time you walk down a hallway or a sidewalk, smile as others come toward you. You probably will find that the people you pass smile back, often saying *hello*—action–reaction.
- *We do what we do because in the end we expect to achieve happiness.* When we choose to enter into communication, we do so hoping to gain from the experience, but certainly to be in no worse psychological shape than when we entered. Consequently, many people try to avoid any situation in which they feel they may get negative feedback or be unsuccessful in communicating their ideas.

- *We cannot always have the same understandings and feelings as others.* As we communicate, we must recognize that because of differences in cultures, the only areas we share are those in which we have a common experiential background. To illustrate this, let us assume that all our knowledge and experience is contained within one circle and that all the knowledge and experience of the person with whom we are communicating is contained within another circle. The only commonality—the only place where our ideas, concepts, beliefs, and vocabulary will overlap—is where we have had similar exposure. Figure 6.1 illustrates this idea. Only in the area where the circles overlap are there any common unities.

    If we add a third person to the conversation, the problem becomes even greater, as Figure 6.2 illustrates. Here, there are areas of overlap that exist between persons A and B, between persons A and C, and between persons B and C. But notice the small area of overlap among all three. The difficulty of communicating with large groups of people can easily be demonstrated when this process of drawing representative circles is continued.

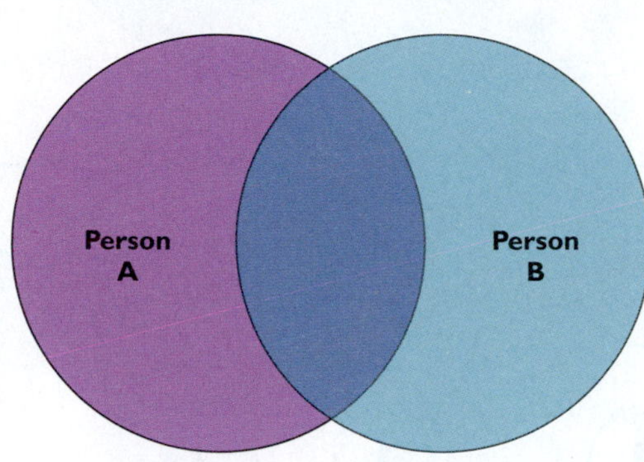

FIGURE 6.1 **Commonality of Experiences between Two Persons**

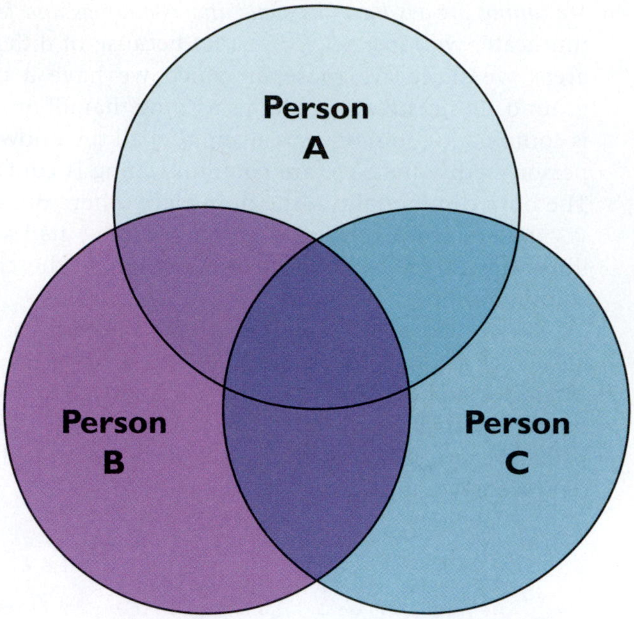

Person A
Person B
Person C

FIGURE 6.2
Commonality of Experiences among Three Persons

SO WE ALL AGREE
YES!
DEFINITELY!
VOTKO

Self-Disclosure

Self-disclosure is "intentionally letting the other person know who you are by communicating self-revealing information."[5] This revealing can be accomplished through verbal or nonverbal messages.

Whether the atmosphere is supportive or defensive is a large factor in determining how much will be revealed and how vulnerable you will allow yourself to become. The amount and type of disclosure will also be based on the relationship between the people involved. The deepest level of self-disclosure occurs when two people open themselves in such a way that each can be hurt by the other's actions. In addition, your attitude toward disclosing is an important factor. Think back to the Johari Window activity that you did in Chapter 5 (see pages 117–118). Are you a discloser or a concealer?

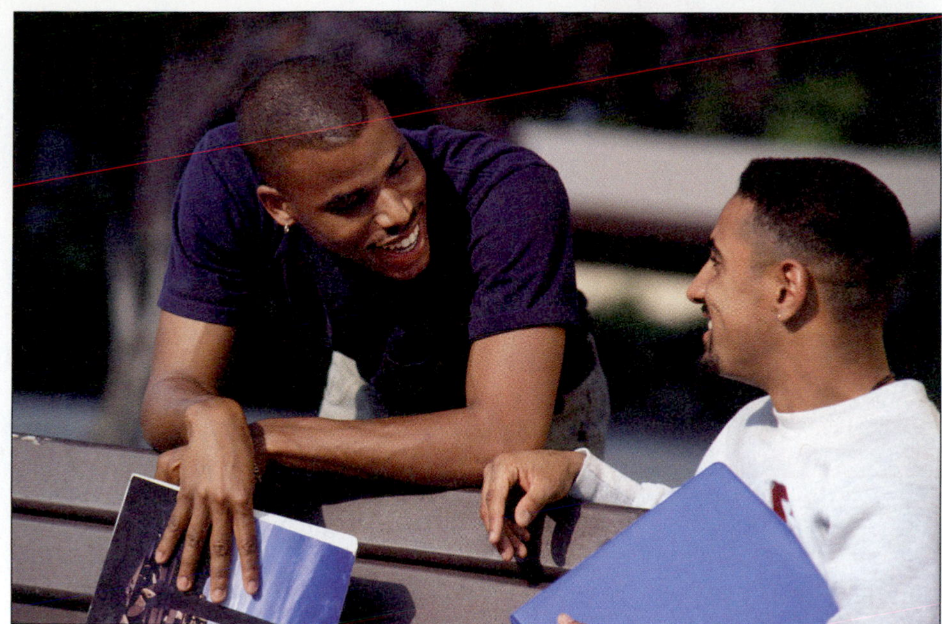

Self-disclosure is "intentionally letting the other person know who you are by communicating self-revealing information."

Self-disclosure allows others to understand you, and it allows you to understand yourself. As you talk about yourself, the other person is not the only one exposed to you; you may also learn something about yourself.

Storytelling can be a type of self-disclosure as you tell about your experiences, values, or dreams. Research has suggested that storytelling helps a person make sense of a situation, such as during a counseling session, but it can also reduce stress, and it is an excellent tool to use during conversations to share information about yourself.[6]

Culturally COMMUNICATING

Ethnic Self-Disclosure: Euro Americans and Afro-Americans

In the area of ethnic self-disclosure, European Americans tend to self-disclose more with people they do not know than do African Americans. However, in close friendship situations, African Americans tend to self-disclose more and at a deeper level than do European Americans.

In addition, African Americans repeatedly emphasize the importance of *acceptance, problem-solving,* and *lifetime support* in close friendships; in comparison, European Americans emphasize *confiding in each other* and being *free to be myself;* Mexican American interviewees emphasize terms such as *mutual sharing* and *mutual understanding* in explaining close friendships.

Source: Ting-Toomey, S., & Chung, L. C. (2005). *Understanding intercultural communication*. Los Angeles, CA: Roxbury Publishing Company, p. 299, referencing Hecht, M., & Ribeau, S. (1984). Sociocultural roots of ethnic identity. *Journal of Black Studies, 21*, pp. 501–513; Collier, M. J. (1991). Conflict competence within African, Mexican and Anglo American friendships. In S. Ting-Toomey & F. Korzenny (Eds.). *Cross-cultural interpersonal communication*. Newbury Park, CA: Sage.

REFLECT ON THIS:

1. What do these descriptions tell you about each of the three cultural groups described?
2. Describe why individuals from different cultures may not understand each other.

Socially COMMUNICATING

First Impression

Try this simple tip to help you project a good first impression: Notice the color of a person's eyes as you shake hands. *Why it works:* You'll gain strong eye contact in a way that shows you care.

Source: Dawson, R. (n.d.). *Secrets of power persuasion*. Englewood Cliffs, NJ: Prentice-Hall. Communication Briefings. Retrieved from www.briefings.com

The Self and Others

Your image of yourself makes up your "I."[7] The *self-perceived I* is the image you project, the way you perceive yourself. It is revealed through the words, ideas, actions, clothing, and lifestyle you choose. All of these communicate your "I" to others.

Those with whom you come into contact also build their own images of you for themselves, and they sometimes communicate this image to you. For example, friends comment about what they like and dislike about you; teachers and parents praise and criticize. These collective judgments by significant others develop into a "Me." The *other-perceived Me* is the person that others perceive you to be. It may be the same as or different from your self-perceived I.

One of the best ways to understand how the I–Me dichotomy affects your communication is to examine the entire process as a mathematical formula. Under ideal conditions, we come as close to I = Me (I equals Me) as we can. Just as in algebra, when the equation balances, there is no basic error. If your perception of self (I) and the perception of you that significant others hold (Me) are basically the same—if these perceptions balance—then you maintain your equilibrium and continue to function as before. As a result, you continue to communicate in the same manner as previously. (See Figure 6.3.)

When the I and the Me are not in balance (I ≠ Me), you have four options for how to communicatively react:

1. *You can accept the perception and alter your communication actions.* You attempt to make the specific changes the significant other has indicated. In the play *Our Town,* George, one of the play's young lovers, must decide whether to alter his behavior as a result of a conversation with his girlfriend, Emily. She tells George that he is spending all his time playing baseball and that he has become stuck-up and conceited. As the conversation continues, George offers to buy Emily an ice cream soda to celebrate not only their recent election as class officers but also his good fortune in having a friend who tells him what he should be told. The scene ends with George's promise to take Emily's advice and change his ways.

   You can change on your own, or you can get help from mental health professionals, friends, or relatives. You have probably known someone whose personality changed, because of an alteration of attitudes and ideas as expressed through verbal and nonverbal communication.

2. *You can accept an evaluation by acknowledging that it exists, but you feel the recommended change is not desirable.* Consequently, you accept the evaluation but do not change. For example, a member may take the leadership role after a group makes no progress toward accomplishing its goal. Another member may accuse the newly emerged leader of exerting too much power. Because the group made no previous progress and is now well on its way to fulfilling its goal, the newly emerged leader may decide to accept the evaluation but not make any changes in her behavior pattern.

3 *You can reject the input.* You consider the information, decide it is not true, and do nothing about making changes. This happens, for example, when a student in a communication class, rather than accepting comments about his speech presentation, refuses to consider any suggestions. It can take place in a work environment when an employee fails to make the adjustments presented by a manager. Be aware that the rejection can have consequences, such as failing a class or being fired.

4 *You can ignore any evaluation.* You don't seek out criticism, and if someone attempts to give it, you can refuse even to listen to what is said. Ignorers use statements such as "Don't even bother to tell me what you think—I'm not interested" or "Let me be me." Sometimes you block out all criticism because you find it potentially depresses you or forces you to think about who you really are. Think, for example, of people who adopt the attitude "I am what I am, and I'll be that way no matter what you say!"

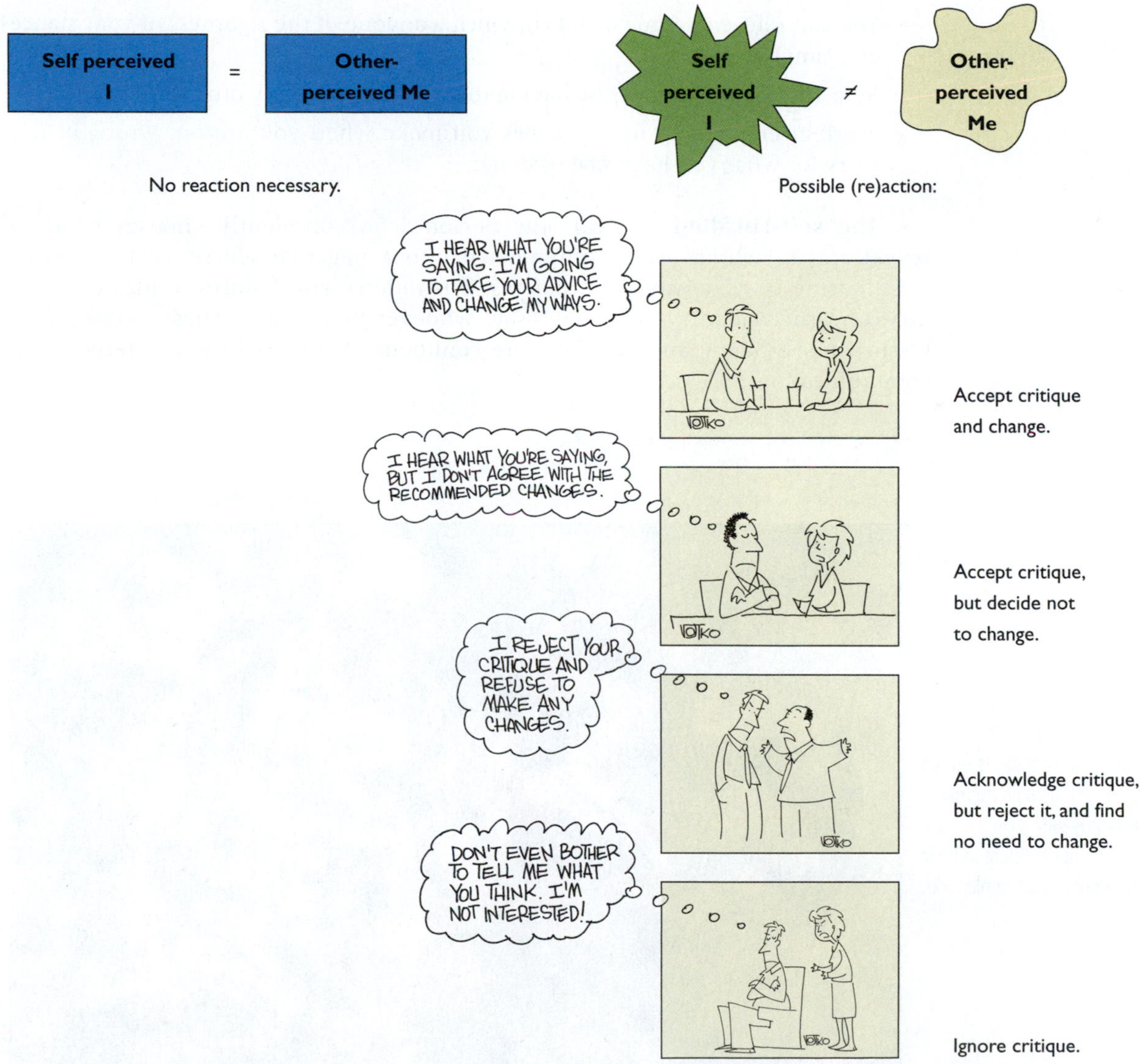

FIGURE 6.3 I = Me or I ≠ Me

Seeking Approval

A great deal of interpersonal communication is spent trying to get the approval of others. Some people are so controlled by others and the fear that others (friends, relatives, employers) won't like them that they almost become immobile. Thus, not being able to make decisions for themselves, they turn over their destiny to others.

If you want to eliminate approval-seeking behavior as a major need in your life, keep these guidelines in mind:

- If you think someone else is trying to control you by withholding approval, say so.
- When you are faced with disapproval, ask yourself, "If they agreed with me, would I be better off?"
- Accept that some people will never understand you and that this is acceptable.
- You can refuse to argue or try convincing anyone of the rightness of your stance and simply believe it.
- Stop verifying your ideas by having them substantiated by others.
- Work at eliminating the apologies you make when you are not wrong or not sorry for what you have said or done.

The **self-fulfilled person**—the person who confidently chooses what to reveal and to whom—is not intimidated into a negative self-concept and realizes that there will always be problems, frustrations, and failures in life. They are not concerned about what "they" say, whoever "they" are. These people have learned to be happy and are therefore confident of their ability in interpersonal communication.

The self-fulfilled person is not as concerned with gaining approval, but is happy with who they are and therefore confident in their interpersonal communication.

Gaining Compliance

In our relationships with other people, we often need to get others to do something for us, agree with us, or otherwise engage with us. As a result, it is sometimes necessary to apply the skills of persuasion to our interpersonal communication to *gain compliance*. Physicians, for instance, must work to get patients to comply with their recommended treatment plan. Teachers must persuade students to do the work required in a course. Parents rely on persuasive strategies to gain their children's compliance with their wishes.

Research on compliance-gaining strategies reinforces how much securing compliance is a transactional, give-and-take process. Some of the strategies that have been found to work effectively include:[8]

- *Pregiving.* In pregiving, you give the person something he or she may want in order to help convince the person to act as you might want him or her to act. For example, you could give your significant other a gift and then request agreement with your plan to vacation in the mountains.
- *Liking.* In order to assist in the persuasive interpersonal act, you may try to put the other person in a receptive mood by being friendly to him or her. For example, you could offer to help a coworker with a project she is doing so that she has positive feelings toward you and might, therefore, be open to a suggestion that she assist you on your next project.
- *Promise.* In proposing assistance or conformity with your view, you might make a promise. For example, a candidate running for public office might promise that in exchange for your vote he will attempt to get funding for the local YMCA, which is one of your favorite projects.
- *Threat.* You could include in your proposal the intention to use influence or control over the other person if he or she doesn't conform to your request. A teacher does this, for example, when she discusses academic work with a student and warns that the student will fail if he doesn't pass the next test.
- *Self-feelings.* You might include a statement of guilt in your proposal. A parent does this when, for instance, he tells his son that he will feel bad, and so should the child, if the child doesn't stop being a bully on the playground.
- *Esteem.* One of our basic needs is pleasure, and people often strive to achieve personal recognition as part of that need. Indicating that there is a reward, recognition, or praise that could result from conforming with your request may sway the person to your side. For example, as a manager at a business, you might indicate to a worker that she could be a candidate for the Employee of the Month Award, which carries a $500 stipend. This incentive might inspire her to work harder.
- *Debt.* You may decide to indicate to a person who is indebted to you for a past favor that he "owes you one" in order to get him to comply with your request. For example, you could ask a friend to drive you to the airport and include the comment that he owes you a return favor since you gave him your sociology class notes when he had missed class.

Of course, these strategies can backfire if you aren't careful about when and how you use them. As always, you must consider the ever-present factors of communication, the participants, the setting, and your purpose in evaluating which, if any, of these strategies you will use. It's necessary to assess how the other person will respond to your appeals. Realistically, people might consider your using any of these tactics as being manipulative, so be ready for a potential rejection. The bottom line is that you should determine what is the best strategy, make sure that you plan your proposal and compliance-gaining strategy carefully, approach the persuasion ethically, and consider what the ramifications of your actions may be before you proceed.

Emotions as a Factor in Interpersonal Communication

A theory that relates to how the brain works suggests that our brain contains both logical and emotional segments.[9] The logical part of the brain contains the information we are taught: reasoning patterns, the rules of civilized behavior, and cultural rules. The emotional part of the brain regulates our feelings, creativity and intuition. It tends to trigger first. This explains the concept that we instinctively act; then we logically reason to conclusions.

It has been estimated that most of our actions are emotional, leaving only a small percent intellectual.[10] If you say, "I feel" you indicate that you are acting or reacting emotionally. "I think" says you have thought it over, considered the consequences and come to a logical conclusion.

Any message we communicate is made up of both logic and emotion. You probably have grown up believing that you can control your emotions—that anger, fear, and hate, as well as love, ecstasy, and joy, are things that happen to you but can be stuffed (held inside). This pattern of conduct is especially true if you are a typical European American male. If you were brought up to believe that it is good to control your emotions, whether love or hate, that nice people do not display their emotions, or that men do not cry, then this statement may startle you: *There is nothing wrong with expressing your feelings; it is normal and natural!*

One of the most feared interpersonal displays of emotion is anger, yet anger is a natural, normal emotion. To react with anger to a situation or set of events is not bad. Anger serves as an emotional defense mechanism to relieve the stress of an overly stressful situation. Suppressed anger leads to ill health, emotional disturbance, and a general feeling of unhappiness.[11]

Expressions of anger, however, can be constructive or destructive. Letting out your anger by saying how you feel while not verbally or physically attacking another person can be a positive outlet. But physically or verbally abusing a person is not a positive way of showing emotions. If we use someone as a scapegoat, blaming him or her for our own shortcomings, we are not being fair to ourselves or the other person. Each of us must assume responsibility for our feelings and for our reactions to them.

Power as a Factor in Interpersonal Communication

"**Power** is the ability to control what happens—to create things you want to happen and to block things you don't want to happen."[12] Power is the ability to choose for yourself or to control the choice of others.

Defining *power* as the ability to control what happens and to make choices clarifies several preconceptions. First, the power to choose is not bad. The view of power as bad may stem from its abuse (often in the form of winning at someone else's expense), from the perception that it contradicts the belief that all humans should be equal, or from its waste (as when there's really no opportunity to gain anything and large amounts of resources are being thrown away in the process, such as when a person spends time and money on a former romantic partner who does not intend to begin a new relationship with him). In fact, power—the ability to make choices—is desirable, not bad.

Every person may be more or less powerful or powerless, depending on the situation and its participants. Thus, you have power, and you are powerful—maybe not with everyone, at all times, and in every circumstance, but certainly with some people, at some times, and in particular settings. For example, a father may be powerful at home when dealing with his four-year-old son but powerless in a work situation in which his boss has made it clear that all decisions must be approved by her.

Interested in finding out how powerful you think you are, how powerful you feel? If so, do the How Powerful Do You Feel? questionnaire.

People who feel powerless often lack the ability to make choices about their relationships, such as deciding which to maintain and which to terminate. They may feel that they don't have the ability to make choices, and therefore they settle for unsatisfying relationships. Also, people who feel powerless in one situation may take out their hostilities and frustrations in other situations. For example, a parent having problems with her boss at work—and who feels powerless to do anything about it—may be unusually harsh with her children.[13]

How Powerful Do You Feel? Questionnaire

Think of one of your important relationships and keep it in mind as you respond to the following questionnaire. Each item has two alternatives. Your task is to divide 10 points between the two alternatives according to how well each describes you. You may give all 10 points to one alternative and none to the other; split the points evenly, 5 and 5; or assign any other combination of 10 points that seems appropriate.

1. When the other person says something with which I disagree, I

____ a. assume my position is correct.

____ b. assume what the other person says is correct.

2. When I get angry at the other person, I

____ a. ask the other person to stop the behavior that offends me.

____ b. say little, not knowing quite what to do.

3. When something goes wrong in the relationship, I

____ a. try to solve the problem.

____ b. try to find out who's at fault.

4. When I participate in the relationship, it is important that I

____ a. live up to my own expectations.

____ b. live up to the expectations of the other person.

5. In general, I try to surround myself with people

____ a. whom I respect.

____ b. who respect me.

Scoring:

Add all of your *a* responses. *a* = ____________

Add all of your *b* responses. *b* = ____________

Each of the two totals, *a* and *b*, indicate how powerful you feel in the relationship you chose. The total number of points is 50, so one score could be 50 and the other zero, although that is unlikely.

If your *b* score is greater than your *a* score by 10 or more points, you probably feel somewhat powerless in your relationship because you see the other person's choices as more important than your own.

If your two scores are within 10 points of each other, you are probably unsure of your own power and your potential to influence others.

If your *a* score is greater than your *b* score by 10 or more points, you most likely feel quite powerful and in control of the choices you make in a relationship.

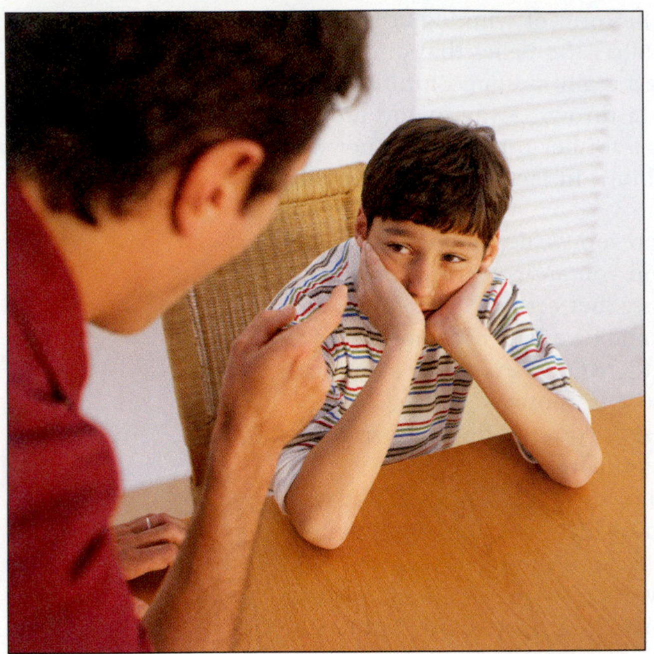

Every person may be more or less powerful or powerless, depending on the situation and its participants, such as the power a parent has with a child.

Many European Americans are raised to believe that they have great power over their own lives and even over the lives of others. Not only do they want power and think that they deserve it; they also do not want other people to have power over them. They may leave home so that their parents will not have power over them. Women, homosexuals, and minority groups ask for power so that they can have freedom from internal and external restraints. In short, some Euro Americans are generally taught not to be powerless. This, of course, is not the case with all cultures or even all Euro Americans. Most of the world's people, in fact, believe that an outside source or fate—be it "God," "the gods," or "nature"—controls their lives. Muslims use the expression "It is Allah's will," and Hindus believe that their karma is being acted out. In such instances, these people do not feel powerless per se, but instead they believe in a philosophy of "what will be, will be." It is not their mission to seek power, nor in most instances do they rebel against the fact that they do not have power. In most situations, they hold the view that the legitimacy of power is irrelevant.[14]

People telling others about their power is not a universal trait. There are cultures, such as those in parts of Asia, in which people do not talk about themselves. First, too much self-focus is considered a form of bragging or boasting. Individuality is "systematically repressed."[15] Second, cultures that have a nonverbal rather than a verbal tradition believe that people possess intuitive *feelings* about each other and therefore do not have to state what is "known" by both parties. If an individual has power, others will just know it. In these cultures there is a belief that "it is the heart always that sees, before the head can see."[16]

Have you ever considered that there are different types of power and that you may possess all or none of these? The types include expert power, referent power, reward power, coercive power, and legitimate power.

Expert power is your capacity to influence another person because of the knowledge and skills you are presumed to have. Are you knowledgeable about how to throw a curve in baseball or bake the world's best chocolate-chip cookies? To build expert power, you need to communicate or demonstrate your expertise to others. You can do this by mentioning your background and training, demonstrating that you are well informed on various topics, and accomplishing tasks competently.

Referent power is probably the most important source of power because it's based on personal loyalty, friendship, affection, and admiration. The key to securing this power base is to demonstrate your friendliness and trustworthiness. For example, emphasize the similarities between yourself and the other person, such as your background, goals, attitudes, and values. It also helps to communicate your support for the other person, give her or him the benefit of the doubt, and create symbols that bind you together, such as inside jokes and a special language.

Reward power requires that you be perceived as the best or only source of desired rewards. To a child, for example, parents may be the ultimate possessors of reward power. Instructors and bosses also have reward power in the form of grades and pay increases.

Coercive power is based on possible negative outcomes that are used as weapons. To exercise coercive power, you need to (1) know what consequences the other person fears most, (2) acquire the weapons, (3) communicate that you have them, and (4) persuade the other person that you're willing to use them. A boss who threatens to fire an employee unless she works overtime without pay is exercising coercive power—power that forces the person to decide between two options, neither of which is desirable. In this case, the employee can either work for free or get fired.

Legitimate power stems from one person's perception that another person has the right to make requests of him or her because of the position that the other person occupies or because of the nature of the relationship. For example, in an academic relationship, students perceive that the professor has the right to make requests of them such as asking them to do homework and take tests. In a committed relationship, companions often feel that their partners have the right to ask favors of them. To increase your legitimate power, you must either move into a new position or role that has more authority (e.g., become the boss), change the nature of the relationship (from acquaintance to friend), or persuade another person that you have more authority by changing the expectations associated with your position.

When you are involved in interpersonal communication, you must recognize that you can lose a great deal by failing to realize the consequences of what you say and to whom. If a person has the power to control you, you must be willing to pay the price for any show of strength you may make. The price of challenging the power can include losing a job, failing a class, or getting a traffic ticket. If, however, you are in a position of power, you can, if you so desire, demand obedience based purely on your ability to manipulate, reward, and control.

Ideally, the use of power is controlled to the extent that it becomes a tool of cooperation rather than a weapon of punishment. In fact, a way of showing exemplary leadership is by giving away power.[17] A Hindu proverb says, "There is nothing noble in being superior to another man; true nobility is in being superior to your former self." Realistically, however, you must recognize that many people do not hold this attitude, and you should take this into consideration in your dealings with others.

Besides power as a communication factor, gender considerations affect much of your interpersonal communication.

Male/Masculine–Female/ Feminine Communication

Is there a difference between males and females as it relates to communication? While scholars accept that there are many similarities, there also appears to be enough evidence that indicates that differences between male and female communication do exist—enough so that the different tendencies deserve to be discussed.[18] As a female researcher states, "I know it's not politically correct to say this and I've been torn for years between my politics and what science is telling us. But I believe that women actually perceive the world differently than men."[19]

From the sexual perspective, biological research has "produced a body of findings which paints a remarkably consistent picture of sexual asymmetry. The sexes are different because the brain, the chief administrative and emotional organ of life, is differently constructed in men and in women. It processes information in a different way, which results in different perceptions, priorities and behavior."[20]

These biological underpinnings can have a profound effect on communicating. For example, scientists suggest that the differences in emotional response between men and women may be partially explained by the differences in the structure and organization of the brain. Because the two halves of a man's brain are connected by a smaller number of fibers than a woman's, the flow of information between one side of the brain and the other is more restricted. It is proposed, therefore, that a woman can express her emotions better in words because what she feels has been transmitted more effectively to the verbal side of her brain.[21]

Parallel to this view are findings about gender. "Sex refers to one's biological or physical self [male/female] while gender refers to one's psychological, social, and interactive characteristics [man/woman]."[22]

This research shows that much of gender "is socially constructed." Because of the lessons we learn about ourselves and our world, people may develop differently. As children, and later as adults, females and males often are treated differently, so it hardly is surprising that our ways of knowing and ways of being are distinct.[23] "From infancy on [in the Euro American culure], males generally learn masculine traits—independence, self-absorption, competition, aggression."[24] "Females learn feminine traits—dependence, other-absorption, nurturance, sensitivity."[25] However, recognize that there are some children who are born with, learn, and use reverse gender roles.

Another factor to keep in mind is that the terms *men's traits* and *women's traits* really refer to "masculine traits" and "feminine traits." In fact, it has been suggested that discussion of male and female communication should refer to "mannish tendencies" and "womanish tendencies."[26]

Keep in mind that any generalization runs the risk of stereotyping and that gender tendencies are not sexual descriptors. Someone whose gestures, walk, voice pitch, and language better fit the stereotype of what a member of the opposite sex uses does not make the user sexually that gender. Research shows that how a person is raised as a female or male may affect the way the individual communicates with others. It has also been ascertained that how a person expresses his or her gender may be displayed in both face-to-face and online communication.[27]

Are you interested in finding out how you perceive yourself on a masculine/feminine scale? If so, try the BEM Sex-Role Inventory questionnaire.

How Men and Women Communicate Differently

In this discussion of male and female tendencies, please be aware that the statements are assertions based on research findings. This means that any individual male or female may not follow the patterns described. Testing looks for norms or patterns of the general members of the group. You or someone you know, for example, may fall outside of the statistical sample description for the particular gender or sex being described.

Accepting that males and females generally communicate in somewhat the same patterns, it can also be reasoned that communication between men and women can be cross-cultural communication. It appears sometimes that the dual communication patterns can be as confusion ridden as talk between people from two different countries. Because men and women often approach one another from distinct worlds, the simplest phrase can carry separate, and sometimes conflicting, meanings to members of the opposite sex. Men and women sometimes use language to contrary purposes and effect. Women tend to use language to create intimacy and connection, whereas men tend to use language to preserve their independence and negotiate their status.[28]

BEM Sex-Role Inventory Questionnaire

Indicate the degree to which each statement is true of you.

Write 1 if the statement is never or almost never true of you.

Write 2 if it is usually not true of you.

Write 3 if it is sometimes but infrequently true of you.

Write 4 if it is occasionally true of you.

Write 5 if it is usually true of you.

Write 6 if it is always or almost always true of you.

____ 1. I am self-reliant.
____ 2. I am cheerful.
____ 3. I am independent.
____ 4. I am affectionate.
____ 5. I have a strong personality.
____ 6. I am sympathetic.
____ 7. I act as a leader.
____ 8. I am eager to soothe hurt feelings.
____ 9. I am analytical.
____ 10. I am warm.

The odd-numbered items represent a stereotypical "masculine" personality and the even-numbered items represent a stereotypical "feminine" personality. Add your responses to the odd items to obtain your "masculine" score. Then add your responses to the even items to obtain your "feminine" score. Total scores above 22 in either category are considered high and scores below 22 are considered low.

If you scored high on masculine and low on feminine, you would be classified by this instrument as having those personality characteristics that research shows are indicative of a person called "masculine." If you scored low on masculine and high on feminine, you would be classified by this instrument as "feminine." High scores on both lead to classification as "androgynous," a balance of both masculine and feminine personality characteristics, and low scores on both lead to classification as "undifferentiated." These classifications exist apart from your biological-sex categorization. Both males and females fall into all four personality categories.

Source: Adapted from Bem, S. L. (1974). The measurement of psychological androgyny. *Journal of Counseling & Clinical Psychology,* 42, 155–162.

How do these differences develop? Research shows that girls and boys grow up in different worlds of words. Though there have been some alterations in the patterns in recent years, boys and girls tend to have different ways of talking to their friends. Boys tend to play in large groups that are hierarchically structured; there is a leader and/or a competition for leadership; there are winners and losers in the games they play, as well as complex rules. The emphasis is on skill and who is best. Girls tend to play in small groups or pairs and usually have a best friend; intimacy is the key. Everyone gets a turn, there are usually no winners and losers, and girls are not expected to boast about their successes. Girls generally express their preferences as suggestions. Boys might say, "Gimme that!" and "Get out of here!" Girls might say, "Can we do this?" and "How about doing that?" Gender differences in language can be observed in children as young as age three.[29]

Both male and female styles are valid in their own ways. Misunderstandings arise because the styles are different.

There are patterns of communication that can generally be identifiably male and female. For example, which of these do you think tend to be true, false, or questionable? As stated earlier, *please be aware that the "answers" that follow these assertions are based on generalized research findings. This means that any individual male or female may not follow the patterns described.*

- Women use more words to make their point.
- Men are more competitive in their speaking.
- Men tend to be more task-oriented.
- Women are more supportive conversationalists.

- Men are more direct in their communication.
- Women disclose more personal information to others than men do.
- Women have larger vocabularies than men for describing emotions and aesthetics.

The myth that *women use many more words per day than men* is questionable. The numbers usually quoted vary from 7,000 a day for women to 2,000 for men; other counts are as high as 24,000 for women and 10,000 for men. Recent research, using an electronically activated recorder, however, says the "data fails to reveal a reliable sex difference in daily word use. Women and men both use on the average about 16,000 words per day, with very large individual differences around this mean [average]."[30]

Yes, *men are more competitive in their speaking.* They have generally been socialized to "take charge" and get things done. Typically men engage in *competitive turn taking,* grabbing the floor by interrupting another speaker. Women often have been conditioned from childhood to believe that to interrupt is impolite. Indeed, research on male–female communication patterns found that 96 percent of the interruptions and 100 percent of the overlaps in mixed pairs in daily conversations were performed by men.[31]

Yes, *men do tend to be more task-oriented; women tend to be more maintenance-oriented.* Men tend to want results at any cost. Women typically are more concerned about the process used, about keeping things going smoothly, and about doing business in the least disruptive manner. Women characteristically use tentative phrases such as "I guess" and turn direct statements into indirect ones. For example, a woman may say, "Don't you think it would be better to send that report first?" A man will typically say, "Send the report."[32] Men will say, "What's next on the agenda?" and "What's

What we say and what we'd like to say are not necessarily the same.

the bottom line?" Women tend to ask, "You haven't spoken; what do you think?" or "How does everyone feel about this?"

Yes, *women are more supportive conversationalists.* They are much more likely to check the connection of conversations. Women tend to ask more questions and work harder than men do to keep the conversational ball rolling. In fact, women ask questions three times as often as men do. Women often feel that it is their role to make sure that the conversation goes well, and they assume that if it is not proceeding well, they have to remedy the situation.

Yes, *men tend to be more direct.* When men want something, they ask for it directly; women tend to be more indirect.[33] A man may ask a woman, "Will you please go to the store?" He wants something; he feels that he has the status to ask for it and get it. But a woman asking a man may say, "Gee, I really need a few things from the store, but I'm so tired." A man may well describe the manner in which a woman makes a request as "beating around the bush," and he may ask, "Why, if you want something, don't you just ask for it?" Women also tend to use more **tag questions**—questions added onto the end of statements, such as "That movie was terrific, don't you think?" The intent is to get the partner to enter the conversation. Men sometimes construe the tag question as continuing what has already been discussed.[34]

Yes, findings suggest that *women disclose more personal information than men do.* In their vocabulary selections, females tend to be people-oriented and concerned with internal psychological and emotional states, whereas men are self-oriented and concerned with action.

Yes, *women have larger vocabularies for describing emotions and aesthetics.* In the United States, women are typically taught to express their feelings; many men have been taught to hide or disregard their feelings. Therefore, women tend to have a larger repertoire of words to describe what they are feeling. Women also have broader vocabularies that can finitely separate aesthetics such as colors. Men, for example, will describe the color as red; women might describe specific shadings such as ruby, magenta, or rose. Other factors also seem to be present in male–female patterns:

- Women and men communicate emotions differently through touch.[35] Anger, sympathy, and happiness, for example, appear to be communicated nonverbally based on gender differences.
- Men and women use digital media differently. For teen girls, that translates to 80 texts a day and for boys, 30 texts a day.[36] Females are more likely to send cell phone pictures than males are.[37] Women use social networking sites more than men do.
- Although a woman may complain that a man doesn't listen, research suggests that men and women listen equally well. Often men are less expressive listeners—less head nodding, less "uh-huh"—so they only seem to be listening less well.[38]
- "Men are more interested in visual stimulation, or physical details. Women are more interested in tactile sensations, emotional overtones, and intimacy."[39]
- Men prefer to talk about actions rather than emotions.[40]
- Men tend to pull away and silently think about what's bothering them; women tend to feel an instinctive need to talk about what's bothering them.[41]
- Men are motivated when they feel needed; women are motivated when they feel cherished.
- Men primarily need a kind of love that is trusting, accepting, and appreciative; women primarily need a kind of love that is caring, understanding, and respectful.[42]

A Sexual Harassment Quiz

How much do you know about sexual harassment? Here are some questions based on court rulings in sexual harassment cases. Answer "true" or "false."

1. A single incident or statement does not normally constitute sexual harassment.
2. If a person participates voluntarily in an unwelcome sexual relationship, sexual harassment is not an issue.
3. The courts recognize that fear of retaliation can prevent a victim from communicating that a harasser's conduct is unwelcome—even though the victim is expected to communicate this fact.
4. For vulgar language or sexual flirtation to be considered as creating a hostile environment, behavior has to adversely affect the working environment—in the judgment of a reasonable person.
5. If a sexual harassment problem is common knowledge at work, the employer is presumed to know about it.
6. Displaying "girlie" pictures can constitute a hostile work environment—even though some workers think they are harmless.

Answers:

1. True. Usually a sustained pattern is necessary—unless the incident was severe or physical. 2. False. The Supreme Court has ruled that volunteering is not a defense. 3. True. 4. True. 5. True. 6. True.

Whose communication patterns are right? Neither gender holds the key to being a competent communicator. For the past decade, some people have believed that men need to change since it is perceived that women are more effective communicators and more sensitive to human needs. In fact, a review of communication books leads to the conclusion that feminine patterns of being supportive, talking through issues, and not interrupting are positive; however, the task orientation, the directness, and the lack of tentativeness of males also gain points. Some communication theorists feel that one approach to a "best" communication pattern centers on a person who acts with *androgyny*—a person who communicates with both masculine and feminine patterns. That individual has the largest repertoire of communication behaviors to call on. For example, this person may behave both emphatically and objectively, and both assertively and cooperatively, which increases the person's adaptability—one of the qualities of the competent communicator.

Sexual Harassment and Bullying

Issues that can affect both males and females are sexual harassment and bullying.

Sexual Harassment

Sexual harassment may be described as "unwanted and unwelcome behavior, or attention, of a sexual nature that interferes with your life and your ability to function at work, home or school"[43] It includes sexual advances, forced sexual activity, statements about sexual orientation or sexuality, requests for sexual favors, and other verbal or physical conduct of a sexual nature. The behavior may be direct or implied."[44]

How much do you know about sexual harassment? Do you want to find out? If so, try the Sexual Harassment Quiz.

"Approximately 15,000 sexual harassment cases are brought to the EEOC (Equal Employment Opportunity Commission) each year."[45] As might be expected, the majority of complaints come from women; however, the number of complaints filed by men is rapidly increasing.[46]

Communication is the primary medium through which sexual harassment is expressed. It is the means by which those who are harassed respond to harassment.

The causes of sexual harassment at work can be complex, and steeped in socialization, politics, and psychology. Work relationships can be quite intimate and intense. Supervisors and employers can grow accustomed to the power they have over their employees. Such closeness and intensity can blur professional boundaries. "No occupation is immune from sexual harassment; however, reports of harassment of women is higher in fields that have traditionally excluded them, including the blue collar environment such as mining, firefighting [and law enforcement], and white collar environments such as surgery and technology."[47]

Men's perceptions of what their behavior communicates are vastly different from women's. The harasser may see himself as intending to exercise his power, protect his professional turf, boost his self-image, and demonstrate his friendliness and helpfulness. The person who is harassed may want to stop the harassment; deter future incidents; preserve her reputation; avoid retaliation; maintain rapport; and preserve self-respect, physical safety, and psychological well-being.[48]

Sexual harassment takes place not only in the workplace but also on college campuses. Students at one university reported that as many as 89 percent of women experienced sexual harassment at least once and that many experienced it more than once.[49]

Some colleges, whether due to legal pressure or acknowledging a need to protect students, have undertaken action programs. For example, "Five years after Notre Dame College [Ohio] came under fire because a dean waited weeks before reporting two allegations of sexual assault, the college now says it's taking a leading role in developing policies regarding sexual misconduct on campus. Notre Dame now trains students, faculty and staff to deal with all forms of harassment, has revamped its campus security department and has a website dedicated to information on sexual misconduct and a detailed student code of conduct."[50]

Although "sexual harassment is experienced primarily by women,"[51] this does not mean that men are not also victims. "While some people may think sexual harassment of male employees is a joke, the issue is real,"[52] states an Equal Employment Opportunity spokesperson. The EEO reports that 16 percent of the reported cases are women on men or men on men harassment. A landmark case took place in 2008 when six male Cheesecake Factory restaurant staffers claimed they were subjected to repeated sexual harassment, including allegations of sexual fondling, simulated rape, and even being physically dragged into the restaurant's refrigerator. The company settled the dispute by paying $340,000 to the victims.[53]

Sexual harassment has not changed over the years. "What has changed is that people now are more willing to label these behaviors as being sexual harassment, people are more willing to talk about it, and people are more angry about it."[54]

Responding to Sexual Harassment[55]

One of the questions often asked regarding sexual harassment is "What should I do if I am a recipient of unwelcome behavior?" In general, if you question a person's actions as being inappropriate,[56] you should:

- *Trust your instincts.* If you think it is harassment, it may well be harassment.
- *Don't blame yourself.* You are the victim, not the perpetrator. A common ploy by harassers is to intimate that the victim brought the harassment on or encouraged

the actions or advances by the type of clothing she or he wore, the way the person looked at the harasser, or the type of language she or he used. In almost all instances, this is a ploy to turn the innocent person into the guilty party.

- *Get emotional support.* Turn to a mental health professional, an expert in harassment, or a support telephone service or hotline that deals with harassment.
- *Say "no" clearly and early to the person whose behavior and/or comments make you uncomfortable.* Don't allow him or her to continue with the actions or verbalizations. Call a halt to it immediately by saying emphatically, "I will not allow you to … (speak to me like that, *or* put up with that type of talk, *or* allow you to touch me)."
- *Document every incident in detail.* Write down everything that happened, including exactly what was said and done, with dates and times and any other supporting evidence. Share the information with another person to verify that the acts have taken place. If possible, get a witness to attest to the action(s).
- *Find a way to speak out.* Make a statement to someone in the personnel or human resources department of your organization or university. Also alert your supervisor or campus counselor.
- *Seek out supportive individuals.* More and more businesses and institutions are designating safe zones: a person or department responsible for providing resources for persons who perceive that they have been harassed.
- *Seek out institutional and company channels and use them.*
- *File a charge with a local, state, or federal antidiscrimination agency if necessary.* As with any other legal action, it will be your responsibility to prove the harassing actions or verbalizations. Be sure you can document the accusations.

If someone tells you that he or she has been or is being harassed, you should:

- *Listen without judging.*
- *Validate that sexual harassment is wrong.*
- *Offer to help explore resources and support the recipient's efforts to seek help.*
- *Be prepared for displaced anger because the recipient may not be able to channel it appropriately.* In some instances, a person who is feeling stressed attacks the nearest source, so don't be surprised if the victim turns her or his wrath on you, even if you are trying to be helpful. The person is not really attacking you but is just acting out of frustration.
- *Offer affirmation to the recipient that whatever feelings are being expressed are his or her right to have.* Victims sometimes are confused and don't trust their own judgment. They need affirmation as to their rights and responsibilities.
- *Reassure the recipient that you care and are there to be supportive.* Offer to be of assistance in whatever way you can, but be aware that you are not the person who was harassed.
- *Do not take matters into your own hands; rather, help the individual find the appropriate channels either inside or outside the company or other institution.* Unless you are a lawyer or a mental health professional, be aware of your limitations.

Bullying

It is often perceived that **bullying**, verbally or physically attacking someone, takes place in junior and senior high school. However, research shows that employees are bullied and belittled in many U.S. workplaces.[57] "Managers at about one out of four workplaces reported bullying. And three out of five said uncivil behavior, such as berating employees and 'the silent treatment,' had happened."[58]

"About three out of four workers report these experiences, but most don't complain to higher-ups, so a lot of bosses wouldn't necessarily know what's going on."[59] "In larger corporations the abuse can be buried in corporate layers, and if bosses don't dig deep, they won't find it."[60]

The consequences of the bullying are multileveled, whether at work, school, or online. "Verbal abuse at work fosters depression, insomnia, and alcohol and drug abuse. It also lowers productivity, motivation, and job satisfaction."[61] It can have the additional effect of causing conflicts in home environments as employees carry home their frustration and anger.

The actions that someone who is being bullied should take are the same as those one should take to remedy sexual harassment—the person should indicate to the bully that she or he will not accept that type of action, document the incidents in detail, find a way to speak out to those who are responsible for protecting an employee in the workplace (a union, governmental agencies, the organization's human resources office), and file charges.

Relationships

Throughout our lives, we find ourselves in relationships with other people: parents, siblings, friends, and coworkers. This reality makes it extremely important that we understand how relationships develop, how they continue, what constitutes a positive relationship, how to communicate effectively within the structure of a relationship, and how to deal with relational endings.

Interpersonal relationships are social associations, connections, or affiliations between two or more people. They can vary from intimacy and sharing to establishing a common ground, and are usually centered on something shared in common. Relationships may be described with such terms as *romantic, friendship, business partners,* or *family.*

Mediated communication has prompted new thinking about relationships. On Facebook, for example, people often acquire many "friend" relationships. People may have many, many friends online. The question is, what is the quality of these "friendships"? Is it possible for a person to nurture hundreds of relationships simultaneously? Or is the acquiring of lots of people who are called friends, nothing more than a way of thinking that someone is popular and well liked because they have many people who are listed on their Facebook account? A study indicates that a very small or an overly large number of Facebook friends raises doubts about the Facebook user's attractiveness.[62]

Even the beginning aspect of relationships, the meeting of another person, has been changed by Facebook and other social networking sites. Besides the traditional Match.com and eHarmony.com sites on the Internet, AreYouInterested.com, a dating application can be found on Facebook and the Apple iPhone.[63]

Development of Relationships

Relationships vary so greatly that it is almost impossible to formulate any rules about them. Nevertheless, some general principles explain how they develop.[64] Within the first moments of a relationship, decisions are being made that can determine the functions and goals of the association. Whether the relationship will be primarily

Intimacy depends on clear communication, maintaining a balance of independence and interdependence, and knowledge of the sequential patterns of relational development and maintenance.

task-oriented, friendship-oriented, or intimate-oriented more often than not is established with the initial interaction.[65]

When two persons meet for the first time, their levels of uncertainty about each other and themselves are fairly high. Initial encounters can cause uncertainty in the future as well because predicting behavior is always difficult, and little or no information has been exchanged between the two.[66]

COMMUNICATING in Careers

Mutuality In Business Relationships

You can't forge any kind of sincere, lasting relationship on an expectation of *quid pro quo* (I give to you if—and only to the same degree that—you give to me). We have to be willing to freely give to the other person without expectation of return.

But, there is a limit to the give. There needs to be at least some take. If a relationship is devoid of reciprocity—or *mutuality*—it's going to quickly deplete us. We'll inevitably want to shout, "Hey, enough about you, what about me!"

Source: Herz, A. (2007, January 25). A mutuality in business relationships. *Legal Sanity.* Retrieved from www.legalsanity.com/2007/01/articles/key-lawyering-skills/mutuality-in-business-relationships/

REFLECT ON THIS: Think of a relationship in which you have been involved.

1. Apply the principle in paragraph 1 to that relationship.
2. Apply the principle in paragraph 2 to that relationship.
3. Based on your experiences and applications, do you think this theory is true?

Powerful barriers to establishing intimate connections exist: *fear of exposure* (the decision not to tell certain things because they may be perceived as weaknesses or make you an undesirable partner); *fear of abandonment* (if the relationship begins, what happens if the other person decides to leave?); *fear of reprisal or attack* (what if something goes wrong, and the other person physically or verbally assaults me?); *fear of loss of control* (based on not being able to make decisions for and about oneself); *fear of loss of individuality* (the potential loss of *me* as *I* and *you* become a *we*); and *fear of creating a power imbalance* (the potential for relinquishing power to the partner, thus losing your own power).

Think back to your first meeting with a good friend, your spouse or lover, or a coworker. What happened during that first encounter? Why did you decide to pursue the relationship? Did your attitudes change as you got to know the person better? How long did it take you to decide to pursue the relationship? We ask questions each time we encounter others and decide how far to allow the interaction to go.

It also is recognized that developing intimacy is difficult. Intimacy depends on accepting one's self as well as others, communicating clearly, maintaining a balance of power, maintaining a balance of independence and interdependence, and knowing the sequential patterns of relational development and maintenance.

Role of Culture in Relationships

In any relationship, culture has an effect. Differences between the participants' religions, nationalities, and race can be a factor in forming and retaining relationships. As each person enters into a relationship, whether it is friendship or a bonded coupling, they bring with them their backgrounds concerning such factors as language, food preferences, modes of religious beliefs, methods of conflict resolution, sexual patterns, and much more.

Whenever there is a clash between individuals' cultural patterns, there is likely to be conflict. The potential for *intercultural-intimate conflict* centers on "any antagonistic friction or disagreement between two partners due, in part, to cultural or ethnic group membership differences."[67] In Figure 6.4, Alan (who has a strong African American identity) and Sara (with a strong sense of Jewish identity) illustrate the point.

Some of the conflict sources include attitudes toward *individualism/collectivism* (Is each member of the relationship important, or is the relationship the most important?); *value orientations* (What is important and what is unimportant concerning relationships with other family members, religious affiliations, and the rules of having or not having a religious system of ethics?); *power* (Who is responsible for making decisions? Is the system matriarchal or patriarchal?); and *certainty/uncertainty* (To what degree can each participant stand uncertainty in his or her life regarding rules of relational operation and how decisions are to be made?).

Stages of Relationships

Relationships have a sequential pattern. The **Knapp's Relationship Escalation Model**[68] is a communication-based explanation of how relationships develop and continue. Knapp describes the escalation stages as initiation, experimenting, intensifying, integrating, and bonding.

ALAN: How can you know what it means to be discriminated against? You grew up in a comfortable, safe neighborhood. You got to choose whether or not you revealed to others that you were Jewish. My ancestors were brought here as slaves.

SARA: I can't believe you're saying this stuff. You know that I lost great-aunts and great-uncles in the Holocaust. You don't have any monopoly on suffering. What right does the past give you to say how we lead our lives?

Alan and Sara's identity conflict issues—cultural, racial, and religious identities—obviously tapped into very intense, core emotions in their own identity construction. They will need time to really get to know the identity of each other and to find meaningful ways to connect to each other's cultures as well as their own.

Source: Reprinted by permission from Ting-Toomey, S., & Chung, L. C. (2005). *Understanding Intercultural Communication.* Copyright © 2005 by Oxford University Press Inc.

FIGURE 6.4 Different Identities Can Affect Relationships

The *initiation stage* tends to be short, sometimes only 15 seconds. Think of the first time you met someone who later became your friend. You exchanged basic information such as each other's names. You may have observed each other's appearance or mannerisms. This stage is critical in determining whether there is interest on the part of either person to progress to the next relational level—the relational escalation level. Evaluations are made as to physical appearance, clothing, strength of the handshake, or sincerity of the smile. Whether the person gets good or bad "vibes" (feelings about the person) may be the determinant of interest.

The *experimenting stage* centers on asking questions of each other in order to gain more information, which will allow for determining whether there is interest in furthering the relationship. More demographic information may be investigated (e.g., Where do you go to school? Where are you from?). Light probing about belief systems and attitudes may be included. Relationship development online may go faster than in face-to-face situations, and for people who are shy, they may actually find online relationships to be more comfortable than ones that are face-to-face.[69]

In the *intensifying stage,* self-disclosure becomes more common. The relationship often becomes less formal, the interactants start regarding each other as individuals, personal nicknames and knowledge below the surface level are known. There is growing awareness about attitudes, beliefs, family, and other friendships. There is often common "language" about activities that have been co-experienced.

The *integrating stage* normally includes such terms as *best friends, couple, boyfriend–girlfriend/boyfriend–boyfriend/girlfriend–girlfriend,* or *engaged* associated with the duo. Others perceive the dyad as a pair, as they have developed a shared relational identity.

During the *bonding stage,* a formal, sometimes legal, announcement of the relationship takes place. Terms that describe this phase include getting engaged, going through a marriage or civil union, or forming a business partnership. Other actions that may indicate that the couple is bonded may include living together, or having or adopting a child. Very few relationships in one's life reach this level.

Much of our interpersonal communication centers on our wanting others to act or think or feel as we do, in other words, much of interpersonal communication is an attempt at persuasion.

Continuing a Relationship

People make judgments about interpersonal contacts by comparing relational rewards and costs—**Social Exchange Theory**.[70] As long as rewards are equal to or exceed costs, the relationship will usually become more intimate; however, once costs exceed rewards, the relationship may begin to stagnate and eventually dissolve.

If one person believes that the investment *(relational costs)* of such factors as money, time, and emotion is met with such factors as security and affection *(relational rewards)*, then that person will want to continue the relationship. If one person is doing all the giving and the partner is only taking, then the relationship will probably end.

With this in mind, examine a relationship that you have. You have continued to associate with this person because you receive at least as much as you are giving from knowing and being with the person. In contrast, if you have taken the initiative to end an association with someone, you probably believed that you were giving too much and not receiving enough; the relationship was tilted against you, or it was one-sided.

Positive Relationships A good relationship allows freedom of expression and reflects acceptance of the idea that the feelings of both people are important. We should remember, however, that any alliance experiences times of uncertainty and anxiety. The persons may change as individuals, what appeared to be fulfilling the economic model may no longer do so, and the reason for the relationship may cease to be.

We also must recognize that we cannot achieve happiness through someone else. If it is to be found, it must be found within ourselves. Unfortunately, this desire to find happiness in someone else causes us to try changing people we supposedly love when in fact we should allow them to be themselves and do what they feel is best for themselves. Love is the ability and willingness to allow those for whom you care to be what they choose for themselves without any insistence that they satisfy you. Unfortunately, this idea is easier to present as a concept than to live as a reality.

Communication is the key to creating and maintaining relationships.

Most of us spend a great deal of our time trying to alter and change the people we supposedly love.

Research shows that couples who are happily married argue no less vigorously for their own positions than do those who are not happily married. But happily married couples come to agreement fairly readily through one partner conceding to the other without resentment or compromise. Unhappily married people tend to get caught in a situation that seems like cross-complaining. Neither partner is willing to come halfway to resolve a dispute; each must continue to have his or her own way.[71] Interestingly, one approach that may help in difficult interpersonal communication situations is texting, which one person can use to get the conversation started because the mode makes him or her feel less anxious or less inhibited and more in control.[72]

One approach to successful relational communication centers on five guidelines for making a relationship flourish:

1. *When you are speaking, get into the habit of using "I" messages instead of "you" messages.* Indicate what you are feeling or how you are reacting to the situation rather than accusing the other person. Say "I feel ... " or "I think ... " rather than "You did ... " or "You make me ... . " Report facts to back up your contentions. Rather than saying, "You are always late," try "I get angry when you tell me you will be here at 2:00 and you arrive at 2:45."
2. *Respond to what the other person has said.* When you go off on a tangent without first having replied to the original statement, you are catching the other person unaware.
3. *Give the other person freedom of speech.* If you want to have the opportunity to state your view, you must also be willing to hear out the other person.
4. *Set aside frequent talking time for just the two of you.* We often get so busy that we forget to talk to each other. Don't assume the other person knows what you are thinking.
5. *Do not put labels on either yourself or the other person.* Name calling doesn't solve issues; stating the issue and discussing it can possibly solve it or at least get it out into the open. Moreover, when people get angry, labeling can become the source of attack and conflict. Saying, "You're stupid," is an invitation to a battle.

Also, watch out for some specific communication patterns that cause conflict in intimate relationships. Included among these are blaming, putting someone down, and teasing. In the case of teasing, what can start out as fun usually has an underlying message behind it that is not humor.

Game playing can result in relational trouble. Such activities as trying to make a person measure up to preset expectations, making an individual prove how much he or she loves you, and forcing someone with whom you have a relationship to follow your wishes can result in conflicts that are irreconcilable.

Another problem is *relational fusion,* which takes place when one partner defines, or attempts to define, reality for the other. In other words, the controller dictates what is good, right, and acceptable for the partner. If the partner allows that to happen, the pattern for the future can be set. Then, when the defined partner wants to break the pattern, abuse may result.

People who are unhappy in their relationships tend to talk at each other, past each other, or through each other, but rarely with or to each other. Just because you're talking doesn't mean you are communicating. Although couples may spend time talking to each other, many lack the skills to get their messages across effectively, express their feelings, or resolve conflicts without hurting each other or provoking anger.

Communication in Relationships All relationships have a structure, and each person has a role. As long as no one changes the system, and each member of the relationship maintains the assigned role, the structure is working. But if someone wants alterations, wants to do things that are not normally done, then the system can become a *dysfunctional system*. A system that is operating to the general satisfaction of the participants is a *functional system*. Assume, for example, that you are dating someone. You and that person look forward to your times together. When conflicts do arise, you are capable of working out the problems without destroying the relationship or building up bad feelings. In contrast, a dysfunctional system is one in which its members are confused about the roles they are to play. For example, if a woman who has been a stay-at-home mother decides to go to college, there will have to be a redistribution of her former chores in the family, and the family's old system of operation will be thrown out of kilter. Some members in the system may not want to change roles. The husband may not want to do the cooking or child care, or the children may resent not having their mother around. Before the system can become normal again, a new balance has to be established. This does not mean that the system has to return to the past mode of operation, but a mode of operation in which a pattern of cooperation exists must be instituted.

This does not mean to suggest that dysfunctional systems are not operational. The individuals in the relationship may continue to function quite effectively as they make changes. The usual result of the dysfunction, however, is confusion because each person lacks clarity about what role to play and what rules to follow. For example, questions and protests may arise as to who is responsible for the tasks formerly done by the mother and wife who is now going to college. Common complaints may include "Why should I have to make the meals now?" or "I've never cooked before, and it's not fair for that job to be shoved on me."

The need to reestablish a system is not necessarily disastrous. In fact, most relationships go through adjustments on a regular basis. As a system is being *recalibrated*—restructured—growth can take place. People learn to assume new roles, develop new respect for each other, or make a new team effort. On the other hand, chaos may result as people fight for new role identities, defend their emotional territories, or feel compelled to make changes not to their liking.

In a positive relationship, the participants attempt to adjust to alterations in the normal patterns so that the dysfunctional period is kept to a minimum. This adjustment usually takes place because the partners have developed effective communication skills and a positive method for solving problems.

Relational Conflict[73] One of the concerns of individuals who are in any type of relationship—be it friendship, family, bonded, or work—is whether there will be *relational conflict.* Conflict in any relationship is normal. However, when conflict is unresolved, it can be difficult for people to continue their relationship.

Typically, relational conflict has four recognizable stages: tension development, false ignoring, resentment, and unforgiveness. Recognizing these stages can assist individuals in attempting to save the relationship.

During the first stage, *tension develops.* Causes might include disagreements regarding finances, division of labor, intimacy, respect, or behavioral quirks. For instance, one partner may be irritated because he or she cleans up after the other person. These disagreements are normal, but are not always discussed, so one partner holds the conflict in his or her thoughts while the other is clueless about the issues until there is an explosion.

In the resentment stage of conflict, the person who is offended distances himself or herself emotionally and shares little information.

The second stage of conflict is *false ignoring,* the decision to stop talking about the topic of disagreement or to pretend nothing is wrong. This occurs when attempts to discuss the topic have proven to be fruitless. That is, either no behavioral change has been forthcoming, or any discussion of the issue has quickly ended in anger and/or hurt feelings.

Resentment, the third stage, is the end result of repeated disappointment. The person who is resentful distances himself or herself emotionally and shares little information regarding his or her thinking. Sometimes both partners feel resentful at the same time, which only intensifies the strain. If this situation continues long enough, often one partner will without warning demand to terminate the relationship (e.g., divorce, firing of an employee, moving out on a roommate, or violence in the form of battering or murder).

As the relational conflict develops, some couples maintain an uneasy truce with each other, telling themselves, "If we are not raising our voices at each other, things are going relatively well." Ordinarily, most people cannot maintain an uneasy truce indefinitely.

The fourth stage, is *unforgivenes*. In this stage, one partner has crossed over (in the other partner's mind) from being a misguided person to being "bad." If one or both partners do something that the other considers unforgivable (e.g., committing infidelity or physical abuse), trust and respect are not possible. Forgiveness, although possible at this stage, is often not considered an option.

Heading into the downward spiral of relational conflict can be avoided through honest and open communication. Some people can recognize the decline, resolve to talk about the relationship problem, and work it out on their own. Others have difficulty helping themselves due to a lack of conflict-resolution skills because they have not had good parental modeling or have not taken a communication course such as the one you are taking, which teaches the necessary skills. In some cases, professional assistance by a relational therapist may be required.

Stages of Terminating Relationships[74] Relationship endings go through varying stages. **Knapp's Relationship Termination Model** describes how, at any stage of the model, participants may work toward ending the relationship. The ending stages are differentiating, circumscribing, stagnating, avoiding, and terminating.

The *differentiating stage* is highlighted by one or both of the partners being aware that he or she needs to assert independence. This may result in one or both persons realizing that "we" is no longer as important as "me." In terms of Social Exchange Theory,[75] the negatives of being in the relationship are exceeding the rewards being received. This imbalance could be a warning sign that the relationship needs to be recalibrated or that it is beyond help.

Circumscribing stage is illustrated by the diminishment of volume and quality of the intercouple communication. Again, this awareness can be used as a sign that the relationship needs to be discussed and maybe recalibrated.

During the *stagnating stage,* the individuals may start to avoid discussing the relationship because one or both think they know what the other will say and are afraid of the consequences. The relationship may take on the air of suspended animation, with little or no mutual feelings or actions taking place. If there has been a sexual component to the relationship, those actions may cease or become automatic rather than meaningful. Often, words of endearment start to disappear during this stage.

The *avoiding stage* is noted by the partners physically separating. Little or no discussion takes place, as it is often thought that the relationship is on a strong downhill slope and is basically over.

The *terminating stage,* the final stage, may come naturally, such as at the end of the semester when roommates move out, or arbitrarily, through divorce or legal separation.

A breakup of a relationship can be hurtful. And this hurt usually comes with the realization that there has been heavy emotional and sometimes physical investment. At such times, we feel loss, question who we are, feel alone, search for the reason for the break, and sometimes experience guilt. These emotional difficulties are compounded when one party wants to terminate the relationship and the other does not.

Relationship endings can take many forms. In some cases, the people decide on a mutual split, go their separate ways, and feel little regret. In other cases, as, for instance, when your best friend moved, you tried to keep in touch for a while, and then your interests and need for each other faltered, and eventually memories faded away.

Sometimes, it is possible to leave a relationship, if not on a positive note, at least with a feeling of not being rejected or with some positive gain from the experience. This sort of ending is most likely to occur in a face-to-face meeting in which the participants take time to discuss their own observations and inferences about the relationship and each other without attacking the other person. Although this is seldom done, it can be an insightful experience.

Some intimate relationships end with the individuals agreeing to "still be friends." This is very difficult. Being friends is not the same as being in an intimate relationship. Much time and effort often have gone into the relationship, and reverting to a shallow version of the former relationship is almost impossible. Unfortunately, the endings of many relationships tend to be charged with tension and hostility and feelings of loss, failure, or rejection.

The role of electronically-mediated communication as a means of interacting with others, including the development of relationships, is an important interpersonal communication issue.[76]

Electronically Mediated Communication

Online dating sites have grown in popularity over the years so that today eHarmony claims responsibility for more than 5 percent of the weddings in the U.S. each year.[77] A typical U.S. American teenager sends more than 1500 text messages a month.[78] Facebook has more than 500 million regular users.[79]

Through social networking sites, we can reconnect with old friends, make business contacts, keep up with loved ones at a distance, say "hi" to others, and even build our social status.[80] Active users log on to Facebook four times a day to check in with their families and friends[81] and give status updates about life's ups, downs, and tedium. How savvy we are with social networking, our number of friends, group membership, whether we have virtual relationships, and how we network affect how we perceive ourselves and how others perceive us as social beings.[82]

Electronically mediated communication (EMC)—also referred to as digital communication or mediated interpersonal communication[83]—is a pervasive force in our lives. EMC includes all forms of communication using digital devices such as cell phones, e-mail, instant messages, YouTube, blogs, and social networks (e.g., Facebook, MySpace, Twitter). These tools have become substitutes, in many instances, for faxes, voicemail, letters, and even face-to-face interactions. Electronically mediated communication includes group communication, such as teleconferencing, online meetings, Webinars, and public archives of e-group discussions. In contrast, private and conversational communication that is mediated includes person-to-person e-mail, texting, Skype, and instant messaging between two people.[84]

Although EMC is made possible through an electronic vehicle, in reality it is about intrapersonal and interpersonal communication,[85] not just about computers and smartphones. The technology doesn't communicate. You communicate as you use the technology.

Smartphones and Personal Digital Assistants

Smartphones are an important part of interpersonal communication in modern life. In addition to serving as telephones, personal digital assistants may be cameras, video recorders, wireless e-mail devices, address and calendar books, Internet servers, and audio systems.[86] Your electronic communication device serves you as interpersonal communication[87] because the device facilitates your social communication network (e.g., school, work, family, friends, external world of the Internet). [88]

As a result of the popularity of smartphones, interpersonal communication has changed dramatically. Rather than connect in face-to-face conversation, many people rely on cell phones, e-mail, and text messaging to replace or facilitate face-to-face interaction. Digital devices offer the advantages of a quick, easy, and instant means of communicating, so you truly can stay connected.

A trend in cellular connection centers on fewer homes having landline telephones, especially in Americans aged 25 to 29.[89] "Wireless is the new norm."[90]

In spite of the positives, smartphones can be distracting. A cell phone can interrupt face-to-face conversations and meetings. Driving and using a cell simultaneously can be dangerous. It has been discovered that even though conversing involves different parts of the brain than those used for driving, the ability to drive is impaired by cell phone conversation.[91] In addition, it is believed by some communication theorists that digital devices are diminishing "our ability to communicate face-to-face."[92] "Many people are more comfortable texting than calling and 'friending' on a social network rather than greeting someone in person."[93]

The smartphone requires a unique style of communication. Some useful advice for communicating via cell phone includes:[94]

- Don't interrupt a face-to-face conversation to answer your cell phone or respond to a text message.
- Go to a private area to engage in a cell phone conversation so people around you won't have to be engaged in the conversation too.
- Put the volume level of your cell phone on low and speak softly when talking into the instrument; don't engage in "cell yell!"
- If you are expecting an important call or text, let those in your conversation know that you may have to excuse yourself.
- Avoid discussing personal matters if you are in a public space (i.e., retail store, sidewalk) where others might overhear you.

The Internet

The use of the computer as an interpersonal communication tool has grown at an astronomical rate. It is estimated that 77.4 percent of U.S. Americans use the Internet.[95] It is estimated that internationally, almost two billion people (28.7%) use the Internet.[96] It is fast becoming the basic feature for communication in the personal and organizational global civilization.[97]

Positive Aspects of Internet Use Some people use the Internet to improve themselves by taking courses. Others use the Internet to look for employment and to conduct business *(e-commerce)*. Some have turned to chat rooms to supplement their psychological needs. People in remote areas can find others who can be of assistance. For example, an isolated gay youth or a woman with breast cancer can find interactive voices on the net.

Through the Internet, people who would never come together under traditional face-to-face circumstances have the opportunity to connect online. This interaction with strangers can offer unique opportunities for growth and confrontation of prejudices.

The Internet offers enormous flexibility. The noninvasive nature of e-mail allows each individual to handle communication in her or his own time and own way. A person can take a break from working at his or her desk, and still communicate with someone via e-mail. They can go online with their cell, iPhone, or Blackberry when desired.

E-mail and texting are fast. Most people can text a message faster than they can make a phone call. It also can be time saving because text messages tend to be brief and to the point with little or no side conversations, such as happens during phone calls.

In most business situations, work is being conducted through computers. Even what was once a tradition of face-to-face decision making has become a subject for collaborating by electronic mail through such programs as *GoToMeeting*, a web conferencing tool that enables coworkers, customers, and prospects to view any application running on your PC in real time.[98]

Socially COMMUNICATING

"A Little Mouse Killed Me"

I committed suicide a year ago. Well, Internet suicide. As suicides go, it was very quick. I told no one. I left no signs. Chat buddies only found out via instant messages in chat rooms I used to visit. Their condolences were the type of dialogue you commonly find in chat rooms. For example, "He was a good man" was never used to pay homage. Instead, offerings were more along the lines of "Man, he was so hot" or "He will be missed, I heard he was a top."

I remember holding the weapon in my hand, thinking, do I really want to terminate this alter ego that has been a self-indulgent validation tool for so many years? I struggle with the thought. I even recall the last words that go through my head: "Are you sure you want to delete this screen name?" Then, with one simple tap of my finger, I'm dead. A little mouse killed me.

Source: Thom. (2002, September 13). A little mouse killed me. *Sex and the Internet*. Retrieved from online partner.com

REFLECT ON THIS:

1. This entry appeared on a gay online source. Besides the source note, what wording was your clue to this being a gay-oriented commentary?
2. Have you ever thought you wanted to delete any of your personal internet accounts? If so, why didn't you?
3. What would you lose by eliminating your personal MySpace or Facebook account?
4. What would be the gain in eliminating a personal Internet or MySpace or Facebook account?

It is interesting that the use of e-mail outside of the business world has become a generational divide. As many older people are using e-mail to keep in contact, the younger generation has turned to texting and social networking sites for their personal contact.

In the collegiate environment, not only can the Net be used for research and making contacts with other students to find assignments and share class notes, but students can also contact instructors who otherwise might not be available face-to-face, and faculty members can send individual or group mailings to students.

The Internet can open avenues of academic communication. Sometimes out of fear of negative face-to-face reactions, or cultural patterns that restrict a student from speaking directly to an authority figure, or out of shyness, students may not approach professors. For example, some Asian students have been brought up not to lose face by admitting they don't know information, or cause others to lose face, such as asking questions of authority figures who may not know the answers. These students feel more comfortable asking for information online.

Colleges have created virtual classrooms that bring together distance education students, allowing them to work online without ever stepping onto a conventional campus

Negative Aspects of Internet Use In spite of all the positive features of the Internet, it still has its negative aspects. Most people will use the Internet with discretion and will experience few, if any, problems. However, there are some individuals who become so involved in Internet usage that they use it to the point of neglecting personal and work responsibilities, and become socially isolated. For example, a survey indicated that 13 percent of college students thought that their computer use interfered with personal functioning.[99] Internet interference can include use of e-mail, Facebook, chat rooms, instant messaging, Internet pornography, fantasy sports, MySpace, gambling sites, eBay and computer games.[100]

Negative aspects of Internet use include cyber addiction, negative social impact, cyber bullying, cyber stalking, inappropriate use, and diminishment of writing skills.

Cyber Addiction **Cyber addiction** is considered the major negative aspect of Net usage.[101] It is classified as an addiction because it fits into the addiction cycle,[102] which is *need* that leads to *use* that leads to *trouble* that leads to *repeating the action* to satisfy the *need*. The problem has caught the attention of the American Psychological Association, which is considering whether to include it in its newest official manual of psychological disorders.[103] It is estimated that about 10 percent of college students have some form of cyber addiction.[104] Men are more likely to become addicted to online games, cyber porn, and online gambling, while women are more likely to become addicted to chatting, Instant Messaging, eBay, and online shopping.[105]

Symptoms of cyber addiction include lying about or hiding your level of Internet usage, being preoccupied with using the Internet, and neglecting almost everything else in your life.[106] The person's "drive to compulsively use the Internet [including all cyber tools] is similar to that of other impulse-control disorders, characterized by the repetitive and irresistible urge to perform a pleasurable act that will lead to personal and professional problems and become otherwise intrusive in one's life."[107]

Are you interested in finding out if you are a cyber addict? If so, do the Are You a Possible Cyber Addict? questionnaire.

Even if you are not cyber addicted, ask yourself, "Is my online time disrupting my face-to-face relationships? Are digital devices allowing me to hide from

A person who spends a great deal of time with social networking sites needs to ask if the online time is disrupting face-to-face relationships.

appropriate face-to-face interaction? Are other aspects of my life suffering because of my use of the Internet?"

Those who are obsessive in their use of electronic media may experience such consequences as lost jobs, academic problems, marital strife, mounting debts, broken trust, and being caught in lies and cover-ups.[108]

Are You a Possible Cyber Addict? Questionnaire

Directions: How many of the following statements describe your tendencies regarding the use of the Internet or your smartphone?

1. Given a choice, I would generally choose to go on the Internet than go to a social event.
2. I often stay on the Internet for longer periods of time than I originally intended.
3. I have made repeated, unsuccessful efforts to control, cut back on, or stop engaging in my use of the Internet.
4. I am restless or irritable when attempting to limit or stop engaging in my use of the Internet.
5. Using the Internet is a way for me to escape from problems or relieve feelings of helplessness, guilt, anxiety, or depression.
6. I return to the Internet day after day in search of a more intense or higher-risk experience.
7. I lie to friends, family members, therapists, or others to conceal my involvement on the Internet.
8. I commit illegal or unethical acts online (e.g., downloading pornography, gambling, creating a computer virus, or exchanging test or homework answers).
9. I have jeopardized or lost a significant relationship, a job, or an educational or career opportunity because of online behavior.
10. I have incurred significant financial consequences as a result of engaging in online behavior.

Scoring Guide: Answering *yes* to three or more of these indicates problematic online addictive behavior.

The psychological "causes" of excessive usage may be long or short term. For example, in the short term, a college freshman who feels isolated after leaving the security of home may turn to electronic media to counteract her social isolation until she gains school friends and feels secure in her new environment. Long-term causes center on a person having an addictive personality, being compulsively shy, or being obsessive-compulsive. In these cases, the users find the computer or cell phone a safe haven for satisfying their needs and hiding from direct eye-to-eye contact.

If you think that you are overdoing the computer connectedness, ask yourself, "What could I do instead of spending all my time online?" If your answers indicate that your time would be better spent in other pursuits, but you simply can't motivate yourself to cease your overuse, realize that you can choose to act differently and that there are ways to make changes. You might want to consider learning how to control the computer so that it doesn't control you. Set specific start and stop times when you can use the computer. If you can't control the time on your own, you may ask a family member or friend to help. Or have a friend enter a new password and turn on the device for you. You may also connect your computer to a timer that reminds you to stop. If you can't do this on your own, you may want to get involved in some face-to-face therapy or search out a support group for cyber addicts.[109]

Cyber Bullying **Cyber bullying** is harassment that takes place using an electronic medium."[110] In some cases, cyber bullying is even more cruel than the in-person kind "because the cyber bullies can often hide their true identities."[111] If the bullying leads to a person committing suicide, it is referred to as *bullicide*.[112]

Although commonly thought to be a tool of teens and preteens, the cyber bullying has been found on college campuses as well as in the rest of the adult world. The death of a Rutgers University freshman, who had been cyber bullied, stirred outrage and remorse on campus from classmates who wished they could have stopped the teen jumping off a bridge. A video of the boy having sex with another male was broadcast live on the Internet. Not only did it aid in destroying one person's life, it will have an influence on the lives of the two people who committed the act. "Collecting or viewing sexual images without consent is a fourth-degree crime. Transmitting them is a third-degree crime with a maximum prison term of five years."[113] The act, at the time, may have been "fun" for those who took the pictures, but they are still responsible for their actions.

Cyber bullying has become so pervasive that municipalities have passed measures to make online harassment a crime.[114]

Cyber Stalking **Cyber stalking** is "sending multiple e-mails or texts, on a systematic basis, to annoy, embarrass, intimidate, or threaten a person or to make the person fearful that she or a member of her family or household will be harmed."[115]

Given the enormous amount of personal information available through the Internet, a cyber stalker can easily locate private information about a potential victim with a few mouse clicks or key strokes.[116]

In order to protect yourself from cyber stalking, you might want to follow these suggestions:

1. Create a gender-neutral name, not one that reveals your interests or your gender.
2. Remove gender and personal information from your user profiles.

3. Make your e-mail signature dull, businesslike, and gender neutral.
4. Check your e-mail headers, which may be sending information without your knowledge.
5. If you find yourself being victimized online, ignore the stalker. Erase the message and block the person's identification. Even responding to say "Leave me alone" just encourages him or her. "Your best bet is to hope that your cyber stalker will get bored by your lack of response."[117]

Inappropriate Use of EMC When a person feels threatened, he or she prefers mediated (e-mail or instant messaging) over face-to-face communication, perhaps because he or she can send messages under hidden or assumed identities. Research finds that individuals who believe they are more competent using online communication over face-to-face communication have a higher fear of negative evaluation by others.[118]

Some people persist in using mediated communication in spite of how inappropriate the form may be for certain types of communication. For example, there have been cases of those who break up a relationship by text message, or fire someone via e-mail.

Diminishment of Writing Skills A person's writing skills may deteriorate if she or he uses texting to correspond. Devotees may exhibit bad writing habits that include:

- Dashing off notes without stopping to think about what they're writing or to whom they're writing, resulting in misspellings, little audience analysis, and poor grammatical constructions
- Using *e-lingo* and *e-bbreviations*—computer shorthand and Internet nonverbal indicators—such as LOL, BRB, JK, :(, and :)—without concern for whether or not the receiver understands them. For example, using LOL (laughing out loud), BRB (be right back), JK (just kidding), :((sadness) and :) (happiness).

Ways to Be a Better Interpersonal Online Communicator

How can you be a competent interpersonal cyber communicator?

- Know that you may not always get a response to your e-mail messages. Many people receive a large volume of e-mail, may delete days' worth of mail, may select the "No Mail" option, or may be selective about responding when busy. You might have to repeat your message or alter your channel of communication—using a telephone or fax—to make sure that the message has arrived.
- Some e-mail users become irritated with comments that continue back and forth needlessly. Watch for cues that indicate that a correspondence has reached its climax. Such statements as "That about does it for this topic," "We seem to have concluded this," or "I'll get back to you when I have something more to say," are forecasters of conversational closings.
- Be aware that there is no such thing as a private e-mail conversation. In many businesses, a device that allows managers to monitor e-mail has been integrated into the organization's computer system. If you don't want others to know the sites you are visiting or the content of your personal messages, don't use your business computer or a home computer to which others have access.

- Your computer provides "cookies" to most Internet sites so that companies, law enforcement, and those being stalked can track back to you and/or your computer. The illusions of Internet safety and anonymity are just that—illusions.
- Be aware that if you are using a university or company computer, the organization owns your e-mails, and your e-mail messages are encoded by their computers and are kept on the organization's Internet provider. A rule of good sense is "Don't say anything on the Internet that you would be ashamed to have your family, boss, or best friend read."
- Harassment charges can be lodged regarding e-mail. For example, if you send a private e-mail to a friend that contains gender-centered jokes, or if you send racist humor to another person, you can be charged with harassment.
- Remember that you can't recall e-mail. Once it is sent, it is sent. If you are angry or upset, don't pound your feelings out on the keyboard, or if you do, consider whether you want to wait awhile and then delete the message once you have vented your frustrations. Is today's message really what you will want to say tomorrow?
- Before you cyberbully, extinguish the message. You are libel for any abusive, aggressive, or deliberately antisocial e-mail you send.
- Remember that "there is no intonation, affect, facial expression, as e-mail offers only bare words."[119] To make your e-mail more expressive, pretend you are writing a novel. Include in your message any necessary descriptive information so your receiver can picture what you are talking about and know the feelings you are expressing.
- If you use e-bbreviations, make sure the person receiving the message will understand their meaning. If not, don't use them.

Socially COMMUNICATING

Flash Mobsters Use Social Networking to Coordinate

The July 4 [2011] fireworks display in the Cleveland suburb of Shaker Heights [Ohio] was anything but a family affair.

As many as 1,000 teenagers, mobilized through social networking sites, turned out and soon started fighting and disrupting the event.

Thanks to websites like Twitter and Facebook, more and more so-called flash mobs are materializing across the globe, leaving police scrambling to keep tabs on the spontaneous assemblies.

Flash mobs started off in 2003 as peaceful and often humorous acts of public performance, such as mass dance routines or street pillow fights. But in recent years, the term has taken a darker twist as criminals exploit the anonymity of crowds, using social networking to coordinate everything from robberies to fights to general chaos.

In London, rioting and looting over the weekend [August 6-7, 2011] was blamed in part on groups of youths using Twitter, mobile phone text messages and instant messaging on BlackBerries to organize and keep a step ahead of police.

On June 23 [2011], a couple dozen youths arrived via subway in Upper Darby, outside Philadelphia, and looted several hundred dollars of sneakers, socks and wrist watches.

Dubbed "flash mob robberies," the thefts are bedeviling both police and retailers, who say some of the heists were orchestrated or at least boasted about afterward on social networking sites.

In recognition of the problem [group robberies of stores], the National Retail Federation issued a report last week recommending steps stores can take to ward off the robberies. There have even been legislative efforts to criminalize flash mobs.

The National Retail Federation said 10 percent of 106 companies it surveyed reported being targeted in the last year by groups of thieves using flash mob tactics.

Source: "Flash Mobsters Use Social Networking to Coordinate" by Eric Tucker and Thomas Watkins, from *The Associated Press*, August 9, 2011.

Social Networking

In 2010, *Time* magazine named Mark Zuckerberg, the founder of Facebook, its Man of the Year. Why? "Zuckerberg has undoubtedly altered the way more than half a billion people connect."[120] "Zuckerberg has changed communication forever."[121] He has forced us to decide whether we meet face-to-face or use electronic media and find a balance between direct interacting and using media. He's added a new dimension to the act of entering and exiting relationships, including "making breaking up too easy to do online."[122] As a cyberdating expert states, "There's nothing worse than finding out on your Facebook wall that you're no longer in a relationship."[123]

If you are a typical college student, you spend much time **social networking**, talking online in such communities as Facebook.com, MySpace.com, and Twitter.com. These sites allow you to interact with other students from down the hall, across the campus, or around the world.

Who uses Facebook? "Women spend more time on social networking sites than men—averaging 5.5 hours per month, compared with 3.9 hours for men."[124] This statistic went up to more than 7 hours a month in 2010,[125] and is much higher for avid users.

Facebook Facebook has become so well known among students that a common comment on some college campuses is "Facebook me," much like previous generations said, "Give me a buzz [phone me]" or even "e-mail me." In fact, the verb, *facebooking*, has reached the status of being entered into standard dictionaries.[126]

Facebook is a hot-button issue. It has been praised and damned. Specifically, positive aspects of Facebook include:

- Provides more detailed information about acquaintances so you can talk about pertinent topics when you are face-to-face.
- Offers people who aren't socially outgoing the opportunity to meet others and for everyone to potentially create a positive self-image.
- Allows people to create social networks and stay connected with past and present friends or to reconnect with past friends.

Socially COMMUNICATING

Gay Users Applaud Facebook Options

Jay Lassiter is no longer "in a relationship." Lassiter is still with his partner of nearly eight years, but since Facebook expanded its romantic-status option, Lassiter's profile there echoes his relationships' legal status: "Domestic partnership."

It may not be a life altering change. But, Lassiter notes: "It's high time. It's an affirming gesture. It's sort of one tiny step for gays, but a giant leap for gay rights."

Facebook's addition of civil unions and domestic partnerships to the list of relationships of its users "acknowledges the relationships of countless loving and committed same-sex couples in the U.S. and abroad, Facebook has set a new standard of inclusion for social media."

"As Facebook goes, so goes the world."

Source: From Jocelyn Noveck, New Facebook status options applauded by gay users, *Associated Press*, February 18, 2011.

REFLECT ON THIS:

1. Do you think Facebook should have added an option that is not legal in many U.S. states?
2. Discuss how the Facebook decision may be a life altering change for some people.

- Removes the requirement of being able to meet someone only face-to-face. Instead of a handshake, people can check status updates.
- Gives a sense of connecting with a person's day-to-day activities.
- Allows surveys and event listings to be accomplished easily.

In contrast, negative aspects of Facebook include:

- Because personal information is available to anyone, stalking or harassing someone can be done with little effort. For example, in an attempt to rattle him, the week before an Ohio state high school football championship game, fans of one of the schools began a poke campaign against the opposing team's quarterback, which resulted in hundreds of entries on his Facebook site.[127]
- *Facebook addiction,* chronic obsession with using the site, can take place. Some people's lives literally revolve around Facebook.[128]
- Identification with certain interest groups may lead to negative evaluations by prospective employers or campus authorities.
- Potential future employers can find out information about an interviewee that may exclude the person from employment or force the person to explain his or her actions.
- Students can get in trouble with university administrators for incriminating and inappropriate information or pictures that are violations of school policy or the code of conduct. For example, students may get into trouble over photos of drinking or other behaviors against university policy.[129] A professor created furor by posting hate speech against homosexuals on his blog,[130] and students got in trouble because of racist comments posted on Facebook accounts.[131]
- Though you enter Facebook with the promise of fun and free service, you may not realize that you are paying "for it by giving up loads of personal information" which is sold to advertisers that want to send you targeted messages.[132]
- Be aware that your privacy is not private on Facebook. Though the organization states that is wants to give "a simple control to determine whether their information was visible to only friends,"[133] there have been many breaches to that pledge. "The company keeps changing the rules."[134]

Protecting Yourself on Facebook Because there can be negative results from being a Facebook participant, you can avoid some of the problems by protecting yourself by realizing that the Web is not secure. Do not put anything on your page that you would not want everyone to know.

Do not post private information such as your land or cell phone number, address, class schedule, date of birth, social security number, or social plans. In spite of warnings not to list sensitive information, a recent investigation of Facebook accounts found that "41% of users divulge personal information."[135]

Be careful about even listing yourself on Facebook if you do not want to be contacted or traced by others. Anyone who searches the Internet can gain access to members' names and photos.[136]

Recognize that employers use sites like Facebook, MySpace, LiveJournal, and Friendster to check on potential hires. How would you feel about your potential employer seeing what you have posted? Before going to a job interview, check over your Facebook account. Be prepared to answer questions about your listing.

Google yourself to see how your name or identity is used. Subscribe to www. pubsub.com to keep track of your name and identity on the Web.[137]

Don't assume that if you remove a blog or site, it is gone. For example, one of your authors went to www.alexa.com and entered the name of his website that had been "erased" several years ago. The materials were still "active."

Overwhelmed by the number of Facebook friends you have? Nervous about how your Facebook entries will affect your future? You can close your Facebook account, defriend specific cyber relationships, or go to www.seppukoo.com, "a site that aims to subvert Facebook by offering its users a glorious end and a memorial page to match."[138] In five easy steps on seppukoo.com, you can deactivate and commit ritual suicide. (If you change your mind later, you can always log back on again and be instantly restored.)

Text Messaging

It should come as no surprise to college students that "American cell phone users are sending more text messages than they are making phone calls."[139] For the second quarter of 2008, U.S. mobile subscribers sent and received on average 357 text messages per month, compared with making and receiving 204 phone calls a month. The new statistic is a clear indication that U.S. Americans have jumped onto the texting bandwagon as evidenced by the fact they send and receive 110 billion text messages per day.[140]

Texting, a short message that takes place between two or more mobile devices, is a quick and easy way to keep in touch. Because it can be used anywhere, and it is silent and discreet, you can text without anyone knowing it and not disturb anyone.

Besides personal use, this technology has all the makings of something that could become a highly effective means of communication between various segments of society. Organizations are starting to understand the value of texting. An analysis of the poor communication at Virginia Tech during the 2007 massacre, in which 32 students were killed on the VT campus, has brought about communication patterns on many college campuses that alert students via texting of potential or real dangers on campus.

Texting Issues In spite of its positive effects, texting can cause difficulties that include poor academic achievement, physical danger, physical impairment, academic cheating, texting addiction, and diminishment of writing skills.

Academically, students may lose their ability to correctly spell words, use appropriate grammar, and develop complete thoughts with a back-up of ideas. Teachers have found that some students have actually started to turn in assignments in texting format and language.[141] A professor at Syracuse University cites an example of a student who left him this note: "hi prof how are u culd u tell me my sm grade—tim[.]"[142]

Physical danger can result from texting. For example, a study indicates that "the collision risk of driving while texting was 23 times greater than when not texting."[143] An 18-year-old who was text messaging while driving was killed and killed the driver of another car when her auto drifted into oncoming traffic.[144] But, even though 95 percent of drivers said that texting was unacceptable behavior, 21 percent said they had recently texted or e-mailed while driving.[145] The reason given for putting their lives in danger, "It's convenient."[146] This attitude, and the rising number of accidents, have resulted in states and municipalities banning texting while driving. In another instance, a teen fell down an open manhole while texting, walking down the street and not paying attention to where she was going.[147]

Socially COMMUNICATING

It

"It takes your eyes off the road an average of five seconds at a time. At 55mph, that's like driving the length of a football field—completely blind. It's like driving after having 4 beers. It makes us 23 times more likely to crash. It results in car crashes that kill an average of 11 teens each day. It results in 330,000 distracted driving injuries a year."

What is "it?" TEXTING!

Source: Wellington: Students pledge to "X the Text." (2011, February 8). Based on material from Allstate Insurance and Channel One Pledge. Retrieved from http://www.allstate.com/auto-insurance/teen-text-pledge

REFLECT ON THIS:

1. Are you surprised by these statistics?
2. Will knowing these facts affect whether you will text and drive?
3. Would you be willing to sign a pledge that you will not text and drive?

There may be a temptation to use texting for cheating in academic settings. Since students can text an outside-of-class accomplice to look up materials while taking exams, many academic institutions forbid students from bringing or activating phones during classes.

Texting has, in some cases, become an inappropriate substitute for communicating face-to-face with others. The use of electronics can be for convenience, to avoid looking at the person as bad news is delivered, or to avoid any chance of a direct response. It can become a device to vent feelings and take actions that would normally be done in person. Sometimes the person receiving a venting, argumentative, or insulting text does not accept the action as being appropriate. For example, after a heated exchange in the locker room following a Tennessee Titan's 2010 loss, quarterback Vince Young, texted an apology to his coach. This resulted in coach Jeff Fisher stating, that it was "probably not the best move since talking face-to-face is a 'man thing.'"[148]

Texting can be addictive.[149] As a clinical psychologist states, "Anything that you can become obsessed with, and you do so much that you don't do the things you need to do with family, friends, school, job—that can be an addiction. And texting absolutely can qualify,"[150] There are people who are so obsessed with their text messages that they must check their phones constantly, thus not listening attentively in class, not eating properly because of the need to be available for quickly answering messages, and losing sleep because of the need to be present so that they don't miss a message.[151] There can be physical damage from too much texting. The tendons connecting the thumb to the palm can became so inflamed that surgery is needed to correct the problem.[152]

Be careful what you tweet, text, or post. A famous rocker found out the hard way that you are responsible for what your fingers punch out. Courtney Love hurled a stream of insults at the designer known as "Boudoir Queen." "That tirade, along with others the Hole front woman unleashed on social media platforms including MySpace and Etsy.com during the next four days, form the basis of a groundbreaking lawsuit; the first high-profile defamation trial over a celebrity's comments on Twitter." [153] You may not be a rock star, but you are responsible for what you tweet and text.

In Conclusion

IN CONCLUSION

This chapter dealt with interpersonal communication, especially self-disclosure and relationships. Interpersonal communication is an interactional process in which meaning is stimulated through the sending and receiving of messages between two people. Our interpersonal communication is made up of both logic and emotion. The role of power is important in any relationship. There is a sequential pattern for developing and exiting a relationship. People make judgments about interpersonal relationships based on comparisons of rewards and costs. In a functional system, members are clear about the roles they are to play. Males and females may not communicate in the same way. Electronic mediated communication (EMC) is an integral part of our daily communication on campus, at home, and in the workplace. Senders and receivers of EMC should be responsible communicators, and be aware of the potential pitfalls of relying on electronic communication, including its effect on interpersonal communication.

LEARN BY DOING

1. Think of an interpersonal problem you have had. On a 3″ × 5″ card, describe your role and the role taken by the other person. The class will be divided into groups of three. Read your card to the other two people in your group, and find out how each of them would have handled the situation. After the discussion, tell them what you did and what the outcome was.
2. Relate to the class a recent personal experience that illustrates the action–reaction principle.
3. Think back to a relationship you had that has ended. Examine it from the standpoint of the costs and rewards theory (Social Exchange Theory) discussed in the chapter.
4. What do you consider the most difficult part of developing a relationship? Give examples to back up your contention.
5. Relate an experience you had in which power was an important element in a relationship. Was the power used to aid or destroy the relationship? If the power structure had been eliminated, would the relationship have been the same? Why or why not?
6. Relate a personal experience in which your emotions totally dominated your logic, and you said or did something for which you were sorry later.
7. Discuss this statement: "Sometimes you have to blow your own horn because no one else knows how to play the tune."
8. Be prepared to take a stand on these topics:
   a. Men are being verbally bashed by women as women attempt to get what they call *equal rights*.
   b. Stereotyping males and females by their communication patterns is a disservice because it teaches people how others act and sets those patterns for others to follow.
   c. The pop-psychology treatment of male and female communication has trivialized the valid research on the subject.
9. Select one of the following topics, and relate a personal experience or an incident a friend or relative has had: developing personal relationships online, cyber addiction, people changing demographics online, e-lingo, e-bbreviations, and Facebook problems.

KEY TERMS

self-disclosure 134
self-fulfilled person 138
power 140
tag questions 147
sexual harassment 148
bullying 150
interpersonal relationships 151
Knapp's Relationship Escalation Model 153
Social Exchange Theory 155
Knapp's Relationship Termination Model 158
electronically mediated communication (EMC) 160
cyber addiction 162
cyber bullying 164
cyber stalking 164
social networking 167
texting 169

Interpersonal Skills and Conflict Management

conversations • direction giving • empathy • information seeking • conflict resolution • criticism

CHAPTER 7

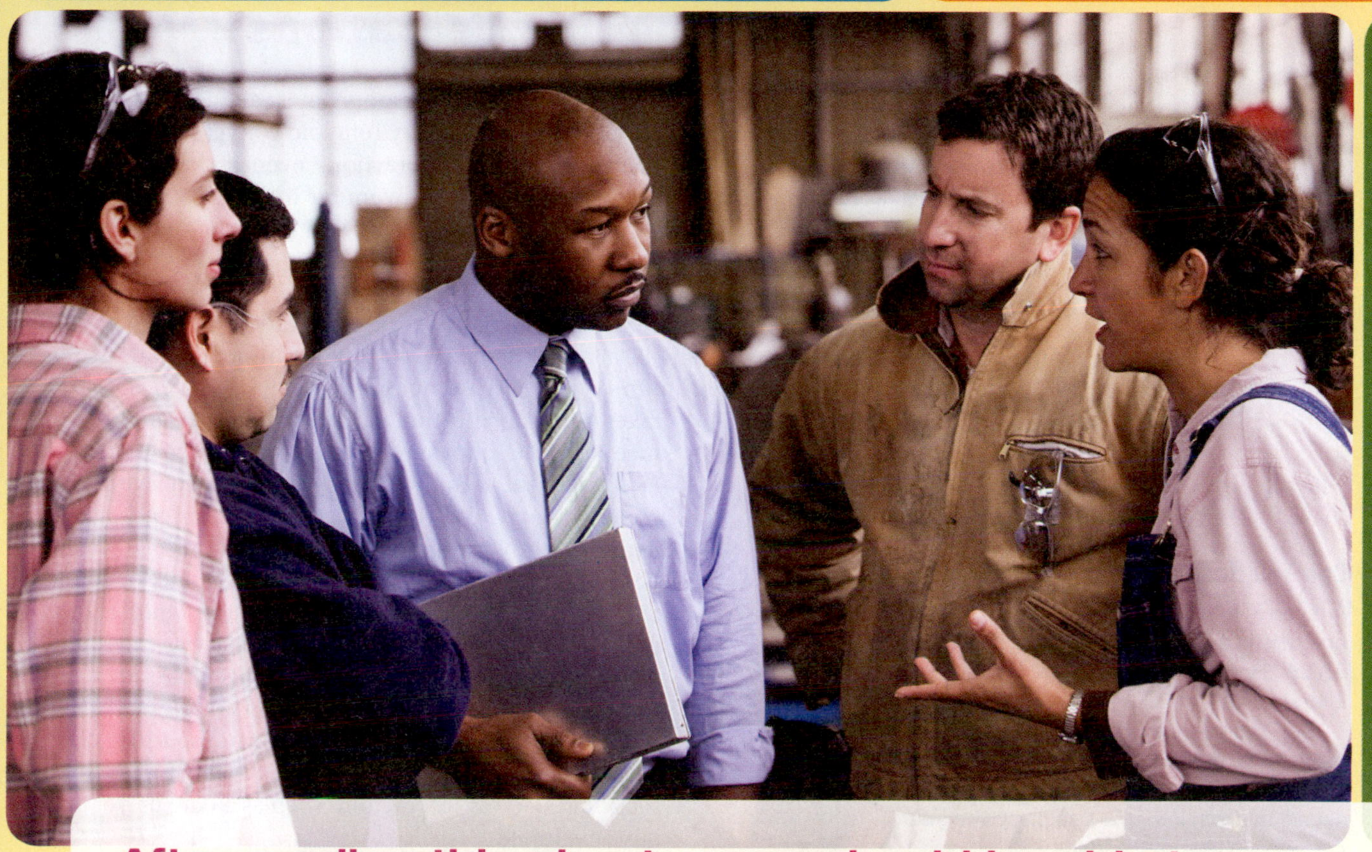

After reading this chapter, you should be able to

- Explain the presentational, listening, and nonverbal concepts of conversation
- State the rules for giving details, organizing ideas, and using appropriate terms in giving directions
- Define empathy and explain how to communicate empathically
- Discuss the process of ascertaining information, asking for change, and questioning
- Apply the process of apologizing
- Define interpersonal conflict
- Evaluate anger and explain it as a negative and positive emotion
- Explain negotiation, avoidance, accommodation/smoothing over, compromise, competition, integration, and fighting fair as they related to conflict
- Differentiate the win-lose, lose-lose, and win-win styles of negotiation
- Demonstrate the simple, empathic, and follow-up assertions, and DESC scripting
- Explain techniques for handling rejection and criticism
- Analyze the role of culture as it relates to conflict resolution, apologizing, and criticism

Every day you participate in the act of interpersonal communication. You converse with friends, negotiate with members of your family, become involved in conflicts, and send messages to and receive messages from your instructors. To participate successfully in all of these interactions, you need to master certain interpersonal skills, including how to participate in conversations, give directions, make requests, ask and answer questions, resolve conflicts, accomplish goals, and handle rejection and criticism. You should also be aware of the cultural influences that affect these concepts.

Participating in Conversations

A **conversation** is an interaction with at least one other person. Almost all of us possess basic conversational skills. Nevertheless, some people try to avoid conversations. Others have difficulty starting and maintaining social interactions even if they are not communicatively apprehensive. Still others need improvement in their conversational skills.

Conversational Presentation Skills

Conversations usually start with small talk and then move to more in-depth sharing. **Small talk** is an exchange of information with someone on a surface level. It takes place at informal gatherings, parties, and meetings. The information exchange centers on *biographics* (e.g., name, occupation or college major, hometown, college attended or attending) or slightly more personal information (e.g., hobbies, interests, future plans, acquaintances). Small talk usually lasts for about fifteen minutes, and then in-depth conversation starts. The ground level of communication has been passed when people start talking about personal matters, such as attitudes, beliefs, goals, and specific ways of behaving, or express the desire for a social or business interaction, such as a date or a business lunch.

You will find that people usually like to talk about themselves and their experiences. For example, you can ask about where a person lives, what it is like to live there, and what his or her job is. You can ask whether a person likes her or his college and how she or he chose it. The key to good conversation is to hit on a common interest between you and the other person.

Other approaches can help you become a good conversationalist. Keep track of current events, watch nonverbal clues, show interest. If you disagree and want to state your opinion but do not want to offend, try to be tactful. You can say, for instance, "I see your point. Have you considered ...?" Another approach is to make a comment about an aspect of the situation you

Socially COMMUNICATING

Can You Hear Me Now?

Are you in a friendship or relationship with someone who is a gabber, and you are not (or visa versa)? Here are some tips that will help your interactions:

Set aside a time to talk each day. No phone calls, texts, media interruptions.

If you are a talker, slow down. Break your speaking down into bite-size pieces so your partner can absorb the ideas.

Ask questions. Conversation is not a monologue. Remember you are talking *with* a person, not *at* them.

Ask for a break. The nontalker should feel free to say, "Let me have a quick breather. I'm running out of listening gas. Let's come back to this in a few minutes."

Use technology as a supplement, not a substitute. Sending quick tweets, does not substitute for face-to-face conversations.

Source: From E. Bernstein, She talks a lot, he listens a little, *The Wall Street Journal*, November 16, 2010.

REFLECT ON THIS:

1. Of what value is knowing this information?
2. Do you think these recommendations are too theoretical or can you put them into practice?

are both in or an observation about the person you are talking with. Say something positive about the person's appearance, request advice, or ask a question.

A vital part of being a good conversationalist is to understand that a person's name is usually important to him or her. As you are introduced or the person reveals his name, repeat it immediately. Then, as the conversation proceeds, use the person's name several times. For example, "That's really interesting, Ian." Several interchanges later, add, "I never thought of it from that perspective, Ian." This reinforces the person's name in your memory and also lets the person know that you are interested in him.

Questions are powerful devices for building conversations. In using questions, remember:

- *Questions encourage people to open up by drawing them out* (e.g., What university do you go to? What's your major? I've been considering switching my major to communication; do you think that's a good idea?).
- *Questions aid you in discovering the other's attitudes* (e.g., Why did you decide to be a communication major?).
- *Questions keep the conversation to the topic at hand.* Ask a follow-up question that probes for more information about the topic (e.g., What do you feel the future job market is for communication majors?).
- *Questions can be used to direct the conversation.* A question can change the topic, probe for more information, and keep the conversation going.
- *Questions help you gain information and clarify meanings.* If what the person says is not clear, ask for definitions or examples or for the basis of information.
- *Ask questions that require the person to give more than a yes or no response*. For example, ask "What's your favorite movie?" rather than "Do you like movies?" This gets the person to talk and opens up the possibility of *follow-up questions,* where you probe for additional information. For example, you might respond, "Wow, Ian, that's my favorite movie as well," and then elaborate on why and probe why it is his favorite movie.

One of the biggest problems for people who are nervous about conversations is staying calm and not giving themselves negative intrapersonal messages like "I'm really messing this up." Periods of silence are all right. If the other person does not want to talk to you, that is his or her issue, not yours. If you convince yourself that you cannot carry on a conversation and that the other person is superior to you, then you become your own worst enemy.

Specific suggestions for conversational improvement include:

- Turn the spotlight on the other person. Discover the person's interests. People are usually flattered by your interest in them.
- Listen closely for a nugget to explore that will interest you both. Follow these up with such comments as "What did you mean by that?," "Oh, that must have been exciting," or "It sounds as if that was tough on you."
- Keep it light. Stay away from controversial subjects on your first meeting.[1]

Remember that some people are difficult to get to know and that there are some people you may not want to get to know any better. The small talk at the start of a conversation often gives you and a new acquaintance an opportunity to determine whether a closer relationship merits exploring.

The Effect of Culture on Conversations

Be aware that not all people converse in the same way. In the United States, people are constantly coming into contact with individuals from other cultures. European Americans often speak in thought patterns emphasizing *analytical thinking,* which dissects events and concepts into pieces that can be linked into chains of statements backed up by facts and/or examples. Analytical thinking is not typical for all cultures, however. *Holistic thinking,* which doesn't dissect events or concepts, is more typical in some South American and Asian cultures and for people descended from those cultures.[2] Storytelling and the use of parables are common. Although the stories may be interesting, they sometimes confuse European Americans, because stories don't prove the original contention or answer posed questions, and often don't come to conclusions, but leave it up to the listener to ascertain the point(s) being made.

In addition, European Americans generally are open to approaching others, often start conversations with strangers, and are responsive to people who approach them. Those from other cultures may not be as open to invasion of their ideas and personal space. Asians and Native Americans are generally more "standoffish" toward strangers, more reluctant to approach them, and respond less favorably to conversations initiated by people they do not know.[3]

Conversational Listening Skills

Listening is a very important part of conversations. People who can converse well with strangers are invariably good listeners. To be a good conversationalist, maintain eye contact. You might want to force yourself to discover the color of your conversational partner's eyes. This ensures that you are making eye contact. Learn how to paraphrase the speaker's ideas, but be sure to allow the speaker to finish a point before you repeat your understanding of what was just said or respond to it. Interruptions can be very annoying, especially to those from mannerly cultures such as Japan.

Listening in conversations requires some strategies:

- *Conversations should be two-sided, with both people having the opportunity to participate.* Sometimes, people ask questions only so that they can give their own answers. If you are interested in a conversation, not in giving a personal speech, find out what others think and address their ideas. An "I-I" conversation can be very unsatisfying.
- *Don't assume.* Too often we assume one thing and later find we were mistaken. Because physical and oral first impressions are not always accurate, give the other person a chance to prove he or she is worthy of your conversation or repugnant enough to cast aside.
- *Before speaking, ask yourself what message is needed.* Some people do not like to participate in small talk because it appears to offer no opportunity for in-depth discussion or because finding out little tidbits about people in whom they are not interested seems a waste of time. These contentions may be true, but you cannot get to know a person to the degree necessary to have an in-depth conversation until you get to know him or her on a basic level and build rapport. People who start right off by stating strong viewpoints and getting too personal often are rebuffed.

Conversational Nonverbal Skills

Nonverbal communication plays an important role in conversation. For example, quick glances away may indicate that the person is anxious to leave, and the same may be implied when that person glances repeatedly at a smart phone, looks around the room, or shifts from one foot to the other. If, however, the person leans forward, is intently looking at you, or is directly facing you, then the interaction is probably positive. Consider whether to continue or end the interaction based on the other person's comments as well as both of your nonverbal cues.

Giving Directions

We often find ourselves giving other people *directions*—for example, instructions for accomplishing a task, achieving an effect, or getting somewhere. In giving directions, include all the necessary details, organize the ideas in a specific order, and use clearly understood terms.

How many times have you asked someone for directions and been given only a very general description? Others assume that because they know what they are talking about, you do also. "Go down the street to the corner and make a right" may be very clear if you know what street and which corner the person means. Unfortunately,

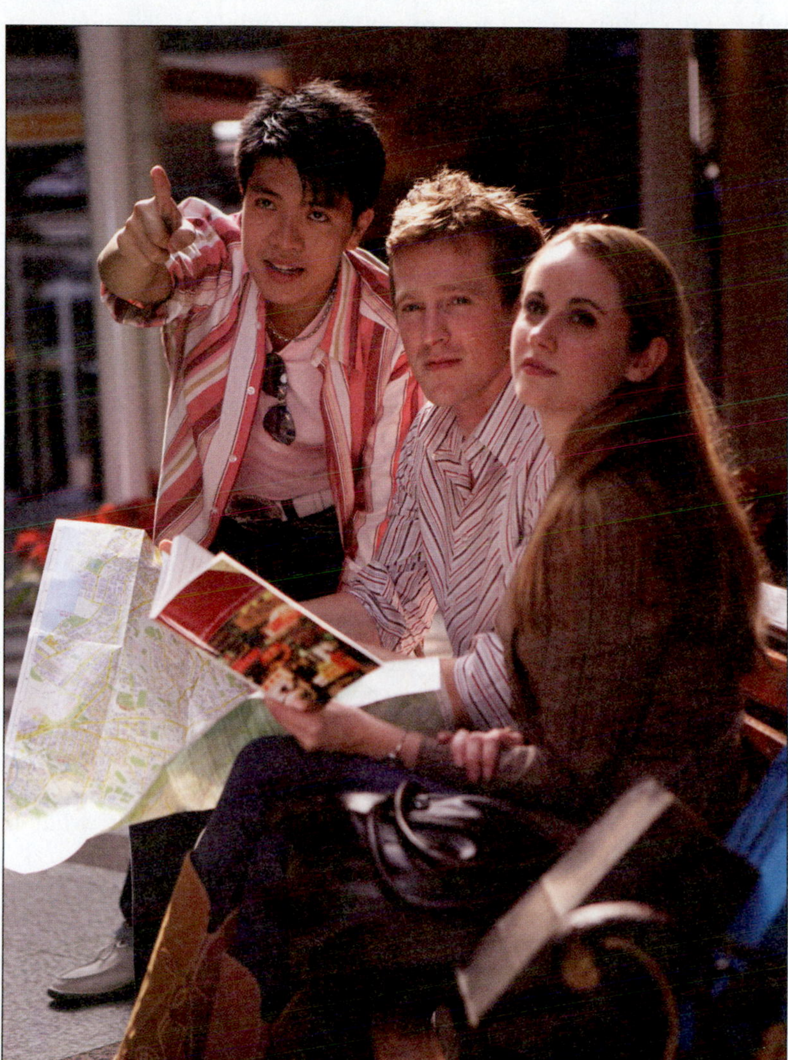

We often find ourselves giving other people directions.

such is not always the case. When directing a person, use specific language that indicates spatial relationships ("Place the block two inches to the right of ... ").[4] Start with a point of reference and follow a specific order (e.g., north to south or from top to bottom). Be careful not to give too many details as overloading can be confusing.

When providing directions, try to be as specific and clear as possible. Include such information as names, references (north, south; left, right), descriptions (the size of the item, a map, a sketch of what it looks like), and warnings about where confusion may set in. The procedure should be the same whether you are giving travel directions, assembly information, or a recipe.

Organizing Ideas

Directions are easiest to follow when they are given in a chronological or a spatial order. In a chronological order, you indicate the step-by-step procedure by telling what is to be done first, second, third, and so on. This is a good method to use when explaining how something should be assembled.

Spatial orders involve providing descriptions according to geographic directions. A travel plan from the auto club indicating the exact place where you start and the place-by-place order of the cities you will go through is an example of directions that are in spatial order. Automobile navigation devices follow this procedure.

Knowing if someone is a linear or global thinker (see Chapter 4, pp. 89–90, for details and a test to determine your style) can aid you in deciding how to package the directions. Linear thinkers prefer maps and written-out directions. Global thinkers prefer pictures and oral directions with specific landmarks (e.g., the identification of indicators such as restaurants and gas stations by description or name).

Requesting

Requesting is the process of expressing a desire for something. It centers on asking, expressing a desire, or soliciting for something wanted.[5] Requests usually fall into one of two categories: requesting information or asking questions.

Requesting Information

When you request information, specify the exact nature of the information you want. If you ask the research librarian, for example, to tell you about Lucerne, Switzerland, she or he can give you volumes of information. But what specifically do you want to know? Maybe you are interested in finding out the local sites to visit or the most recent population statistics. Try to be as specific as possible.

If you are not presenting the request in person, indicate how you wish to receive the reply: by telephone, e-mail, fax, letter, text messaging, or in person. If the information must be received by a deadline, be sure to specify this as well.

Make sure that both you and the other person understand exactly what is wanted and how the request is to be processed.

Asking Questions

People often do not ask questions because they are afraid to do so, do not know how to ask them, or do not know what to ask. The reluctance to ask questions is a major communication problem in academic, personal, and professional environments.[6] Students may sit in class not understanding the concepts being presented. However, when the instructor asks if there are any questions, they fail to take advantage of the opportunity for clarity. Employees, when given instructions for accomplishing a task, may not ask for clarification, even though they don't understand the directions. Personal relationships may be endangered because participants don't understand what another person is saying but won't state their lack of knowledge. Gaining the skills involved in *asking*—seeking out information by inquiring—will help you to eliminate misunderstandings, aid you in ensuring receipt of your intended message, reassure you that you gained the proper information, and convince the sender that you really do understand. Remember that if something is important to understand, it is important enough to ask questions.

When you ask questions that probe for information, word the queries in a way so that the listener will know exactly what you need. To do this, determine what it is that you do not understand. Ask a specific question that will clarify your dilemma. If you cannot identify what you do not understand, recognize that confusion usually centers on the need for restatement, definition, or clarification.

Socially

COMMUNICATING

The Interpersonal Edge: Be Influential

Next time you're in a frustrating conversation, stop talking and start listening to what the other person wants and feels. Next, stop presenting your point of view and repeat back in your own words the other person's point of view.

Will Rogers [the philosopher and comedian who was one of the nation's best-known celebrities in the 1920s and 1930s] observed, "In order to be qualified to change my opinion, you must first demonstrate you understand it."

Source: Skube, D. (2011, January). The interpersonal edge. *The Costco Connection*, p. 67.

REFLECT ON THIS:

1. Do you think the author's suggestions will/will not work? Why or why not?
2. Why is Will Rogers' quote so relevant today?

Asking for Restatement Sometimes in explaining, people state their ideas in such a way that the concepts are unclear. This confusion may be caused by the order in which the ideas were presented. For example, an explanation of an accounting procedure that does not tell the first step, the second step, and so on, will probably lead to confusion. In this case, ask for the ideas to be presented in a step-by-step sequence. This is especially true if you are a linear listener and learner. Linear listeners generally need a clear step-by-step structure to organize the ideas, thus leading to clarity.

Asking for Definitions Unclear vocabulary is a major problem in understanding information. Asking someone to define terms often clears up the misunderstanding. Many professionals forget that the average person does not have much expertise in the subject and therefore does not have access to technical terminology. This is usually the problem, for example, with physicians who use medical terms to explain a patient's illness. An explanation appropriate to the layperson's vocabulary is necessary.

Each time you are introduced to a new subject area, you must learn its vocabulary. Chemistry, psychology, and communication, for example, all have specialized vocabularies. Students who do poorly in these subjects often do so because they are weak in the subject's vocabulary. In asking for a definition, be specific. Ask, "What does [fill in the word] mean?"

Asking for Clarification Sometimes the basic information in a message is simply not enough. In this case, clarification can be achieved through the use of examples, illustrations, and analogies. For example, while listening to a lecture, you will find that the first few sentences dealing with each new concept tell the idea, and the rest of the statements enlarge the idea. Sometimes, however, senders forget to give examples, illustrations, or analogies. If the illustrations used are not clear, ask for new or additional ones. This is especially true if you are a global listener and learner. Global listeners generally need examples to clarify and make abstract ideas concrete.

As you sit in class, participate in a medical examination, or are being trained to operate a piece of equipment, try to paraphrase what the speaker is saying. If you cannot do so, you probably do not understand the message. In that case, ask questions—specific questions!

Expressing Empathy

When a friend shares a feeling of being sad or troubled, do you (a) start giving advice of what you would do, or (b) tell the person you've gone through the same thing and to ignore it, or (c) listen from the other person's perspective. If you answered a or b, you are indicating a lack of empathy.

Empathy is "the ability to put oneself into the mental shoes of another person, to understand her [or his] emotions and feelings."[7]

It is theorized that by the age of two, U.S. American children tend to display basic empathic responses through touching, crying or verbalization.[8] Individuals who have difficulty expressing empathy, whether verbally or nonverbally, "may be so busy worrying about themselves and their own issues that they don't have time to spend empathizing with others."[9]

Empathy is the ability to put oneself in the mental shoes of another person, to understand her/his emotions and feelings.

A study comparing college students of varying eras indicates that "the current group of college students, 'Generation Me,' are the most self-centered, narcissistic, competitive, confident and individualistic in recent history."[10] Many of these qualities create effective interpersonal communicators, but the lack of empathy may create problems for Generation-meers, when it comes to lasting friendships, relationships, and building trust.

As the lead researcher explains, "It's not surprising that this growing emphasis on the self is accompanied by a corresponding devaluation of others."[11] "If you have never felt a certain feeling, it will be hard for you to understand how another person is feeling. This holds equally true for pleasure and pain. If, for example, you have never put your hand in a flame, you will not know the pain of fire."[12] "Reading about a feeling and intellectually knowing about it are very different than actually experiencing it for yourself."[13]

"The person who has actually experienced the widest range and variety of feelings—the great depths of depression and the heights of fulfilment, for example, is the one who is most able to empathize with the greatest number of people from all walks of life. On the other hand, when we say that someone 'can't relate' to other people, it is likely because they haven't experienced, acknowledged or accepted many feelings of their own."[14]

What has caused this lack of feeling for or making an effort to understand others? Some might blame the addiction to social media, where sending off quick texts, often without even really understanding or taking into consideration what the other person is saying, causes a lack of connectedness. Have you ever quickly read an e-mail or text, sent off an answer and not thought about what the other person was really saying or asking for? Have you posted something on a friend's Facebook wall, and then realized you haven't taken his or her feelings into consideration?

Using electronic media often eliminates the verbal clarifications, the nonverbal aspects of one-on-one conversations, such as facial expression and body movements and positions. These often give us clues as to what the other person really is saying. The use of symbols to try and clarify what we feel often doesn't work.[15]

In addition, the lack of empathy may be affected by "this generation of college students who grew up with video games, and a growing body of research is establishing that exposure to violent media numbs people to the pain of others."[16] Those who are not in touch with their own feelings are not likely to have a sense of conscience. They may feel no remorse, no guilt for causing harm to others. They may not be able to even be aware that they are causing pain in others.

How do you communicate empathy? The first step is to acknowledge that the other person needs your support, in the form of listening, taking his or her feelings into consideration, not giving advice from your perspective, asking what you can do, not diminishing their loss or hurt. Phrases like, "That happened to me" or "Don't worry about it, the pain will go away in time" or "What you should do is ..." are not displaying empathy. You might say, for example, "I can see that this is bothering you" or "I can understand why you would be upset" or "Is there anything you'd like me to do?" (Only state the latter if you are willing to fulfill a request.)

You "can also show empathy through a simple sign of affection such as hug or a touch. Though empathy is usually used in reference to sensing someone else's painful feelings, it can also apply to someone's positive feelings of success, accomplishment, pride, achievement etc. In this case a high five would also be a sign of empathy."[17]

Dealing with Interpersonal Conflict

When you hear the word *conflict,* what do you think? If you are fairly typical, your list includes such terms as a *fight, dissension, friction, strife, and confrontation.* These terms tend to be negative, and many of us have been taught to think of conflict as a totally negative experience—something to be avoided. In truth, conflict in and of itself is a natural process that can be negative or positive, depending on how it is used. The Chinese word for *conflict* or *crisis* is made up of two components. (See Figure 7.1.) The top figure stands for "danger" and the bottom section stands for "opportunity." Most people recognize the danger part in a crisis or conflict, but few recognize the opportunity. Conflict can promote relational changes, bring people together, precipitate personal growth, or aid in gaining personal and relational insights.

Conflict Defined

"A **conflict** is any situation in which you perceive that another person, with whom you're interdependent, is frustrating or might frustrate the satisfaction of some concern, need, want, or desire of yours."[18] "The source of conflict or crisis could be your

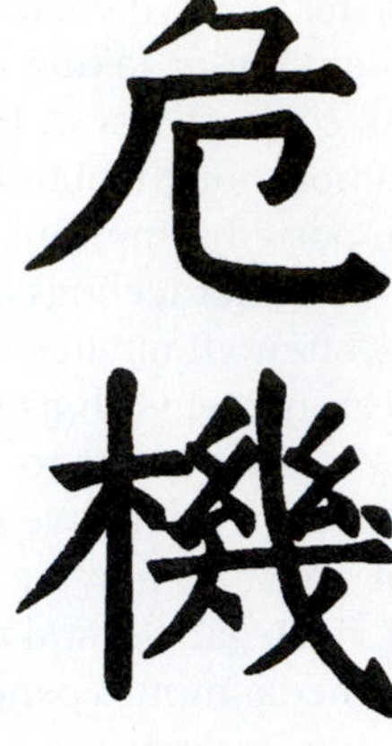

FIGURE 7.1

In Chinese, the words *danger* (top) and *opportunity* (bottom) are components of the word *crisis*.

perception of a limited resource (such as money) or an individual difference between you and the other person (such as differences in how you and the other person define your relationship)."[19] Conflict is part of everyone's life.

When you experience conflict, you probably feel angry and frustrated, in emotional turmoil. "But, it's not just emotional turmoil. Physiological changes are happening inside your body. To ramp up for battle, your body goes into fight-or-flight mode, a primitive, automatic survival response."[20] So, the answer is to avoid conflict, right? Wrong. "Conflict is inevitable. It is normal and natural. Conflict is not only inevitable, it's good. It means that two people have different perspectives. When you learn the verbal skills for fair fight, the relationship grows."[21]

The process of conflict begins when one person perceives that another person has caused him or her to experience some type of frustration, thus they experience interference from each other in accomplishing their goals.[22] This frustration, if put into words, would sound like: "I *want* [your personal concern, need, want], *but* [the person perceived as frustrating you] *wants* [his or her concern, need, want]." From these statements comes a conflict or crisis situation in which incompatible thoughts are present. These thoughts prevent, block, or interfere with each other or in some way irritate the participants.

Some people try to avoid conflict at any cost. Indeed, one study indicated that "students try to avoid about 56 percent of their conflicts. They become skilled at turning away from conflict."[23] This sort of behavior may not be desirable. If handled constructively, conflict can be healthy because it allows for the communication of differing points of view, which can lead to important awareness and changes.[24]

Just as conflict can serve a useful function, so too can it be detrimental. Conflict is detrimental when it stops you from doing your work; threatens the integrity of a relationship; endangers the continuation of a relationship or your ability to function within it; causes physical, mental, or sexual abuse; or leads a person to give up and become inactive in a relationship or life in general.

Since most of the readers of this book will be dealing with conflict in the predominantly Euro American society, an investigation of that society's conflict patterns will be undertaken. However, even if you are European American, remember that because the United States and Canada are nations of immigrants, a great number of the people with whom you come in contact have strong other-cultural ties and may follow the patterns of their native cultures. In addition, not all people within a culture act exactly the same. The patterns described are based on research but probably don't describe the actions of everyone in a specific culture.

Causes of Conflict

Think back to instances when you were involved in a conflict. What preceded the conflict? What were the causes of the conflict that ensued? Four major issues have been identified as the root causes of conflicts.[25] These issues center on goals, allocation of resources, decision making, and behaviors.

- *Goals to be pursued.* Communication often centers on someone's desire that you do what he or she wants you to do while you are interested in doing what you want to do. A friend asks you to do her a favor that you don't want to do. A boss insists that the only right way to perform the employee's job is the boss's way. These are examples of goals one person is trying to set for someone else.
- *Allocation of resources.* You only have so much time. You only have so much money. When someone asks you to expend your resources, you may get stressed. This stress can lead to conflict. For example, you have a term paper due in two days. A friend asks you to go to a party with her. You indicate that you are on a short calendar. She insists that you have lots of time and that the party will be fun. Or remember the time when you asked your parents for a new laptop? They refused and explained that money was short, but that meant little, as your needs were the most important issue. A battle followed. Often the acting out of these conflicts escalated with your saying something like, "You're cheap" or "Everyone else's parents get them what they need."
- *Decisions to be made.* Decisions that are appropriate for one person may not be appropriate for another. This situation becomes a source of conflict when Mia attempts to force Sheiva to go along with Mia's decision. Another source of conflict centers on how decisions are made. People generally don't want to go along with decisions that concern them but that don't include their input. Employers who impose working hours on employees without obtaining the employees' input

Sometimes in conversation, a person gets caught between two opposing points of view.

may find themselves at the center of a storm. Teenagers may rebel over what they consider to be imposed solutions to their problems. Conflicts may erupt concerning what person she can date, and even what she can wear out of the house.

- *Behaviors that are considered inappropriate.* Each of us has certain parameters by which we live our lives, and we often expect others to follow our lead. If a person deviates from that course, we may consider the person's behavior inappropriate. A person displaying a lack of manners in a restaurant, wearing inappropriate clothing, or drawing unnecessary attention to himself or herself may be the cause of conflict. "You embarrass me when you act like that" may be the statement that stimulates conflict.

Levels of Conflict

As with all other ascending levels of emotions, conflict develops sequentially and can be understood by examining the levels it travels through. These steps seem present in every type of conflict, ranging from neighborly spats to family disagreements, marital problems, labor negotiations, and international incidents. (See Figure 7.2.)[26]

Level 1: No conflict. The individuals face no key differences in goals.

Level 2: Latent conflict. One person senses a problem and believes that goal differences exist. Yet the other gives no sign of noticing such differences or tries to deny that differences exist.

Level 3: Problems to solve. The people express concerns that focus on interests. They choose to confront the problem and have the courage to face the risks associated with that confrontation. The goals do not include personal attacks that move the conflict toward a destructive orientation.

Level 4: Dispute. There is a problem to solve that carries with it a needs-centered conflict. The individuals fight about an issue but insert frequent personal attacks that move the conflict toward a destructive orientation.

Level 5: Help. When people can no longer manage their dispute because it has gotten out of control, they often seek help. The help can be from friends, relatives, or a professional such as a mental health worker, conciliator, mediator, arbitrator, or adjudicator. It is best if the third party is neutral and invited to participate rather than one who intrudes. The assistance can be directive or nondirective, but unless required to do so by law, the third party should manage the procedure, not solve the conflict. Individuals forced into a solution, such as in court-decreed divorces and child custody cases and arbitrated labor–management conflicts, almost always hold resentments.

Level 6: Fight or flight. If the help fails or the parties become so angry that they don't think of asking for help, they either move against and try to defeat or destroy one another (such as in declaring war) or they try to escape from the situation, such as when a teenager runs away from home. It is at the fight stage that physical and verbal aggression, battering, or even murder may take place. At the flight level, getting divorced or quitting a job may be the chosen action.

Level 7: Intractability. When people remain at the fight-or-flight level for a long period of time, sustaining the conflict becomes more important than resolving it. That is, the conflict gains a life of its own. People abandon hope for a constructive solution. The conflict may continue until the parties destroy one another or lose the will to continue to fight.

Level 1
No conflict

Level 2
Latent conflict
- One person senses conflict
- Other person does not agree

Level 3
Problems to solve
- People express concerns
- People confront problems
- Avoid personal attacks

Level 4
Dispute
- Problem to solve carries needs-centered conflict
- Individuals fight about issue, but personal attacks move conflict toward destructive orientation

Level 5
Help
- People may get help when dispute becomes unmanageable
- Help can come from friends, mental health professionals, conciliators, mediators, arbitrators, or adjudicators
- Third party should be neutral and invited
- Help can be directive or nondirective
- Third party should manage procedure, not solve dispute (unless required to do so by law)
- Persons forced into solutions almost always resent them

Level 6
Fight or flight
- If help fails or help is not sought:
  - people move against one another
  - people try to defeat one another
  - people try to destroy one another
  - people try to escape the situation
- Fight: physical or verbal aggression, battering, or even murder take place
- Flight: Getting divorced or quitting job may be action chosen

Level 7
Intractability
- When people remain at Level 6 for a long time, sustaining conflict becomes more important than resolving it
- Conflict may continue until people destroy one another or give up

FIGURE 7.2
Levels of Conflict

Role of Personal Anger in Conflict

Explaining reactions to conflict, a person may say, "He made me mad" or "I was so angry I couldn't control myself." These are statements expressing the emotion of anger.

Anger is the feeling of being upset with yourself or others (or both). "Anger is a signal, and one worth listening to. Our anger may be a message that we are being hurt, that our rights are being violated, that our needs or wants are not being adequately met, or simply that something is not right."[27] With the possible exception of anger caused by illness, angry episodes tend to be action events. You can be angry at yourself because you allowed yourself to be taken advantage of, for not standing up for your rights, or for doing something that you now know was not the right way to act. Or your anger may be aimed at another or others for what you perceive he, she, or they did to you, or said to you or about you, or didn't say or do.

Anger is not a condition with a single cause; it is a process, a transaction, a way of communicating. You communicate to yourself first that something is wrong, and then, in some cases, you communicate that knowledge to others. Sometimes your anger is below your level of awareness; you know something is wrong, but you don't know what it is. Anger assumes meaning only when you are aware of it or express it to yourself or others. Anger is emotional, not logical. You get angry emotionally, and you often express that emotion by attacking yourself or someone else. Anger isn't a problem, but the way you express that anger can make it into a problem.

When you get angry, there are various forms that the expression may take (see Figure 7.3). Your actions may follow an internal or outward form that has negative implications, or you could take a positive action by asserting yourself in a clear, direct, and expressive way. The negative implications tend to follow a pattern—first, internal and/or external actions, then passive resistance, acting out, and, finally, violence. The expression of anger may stop at any step of the process.

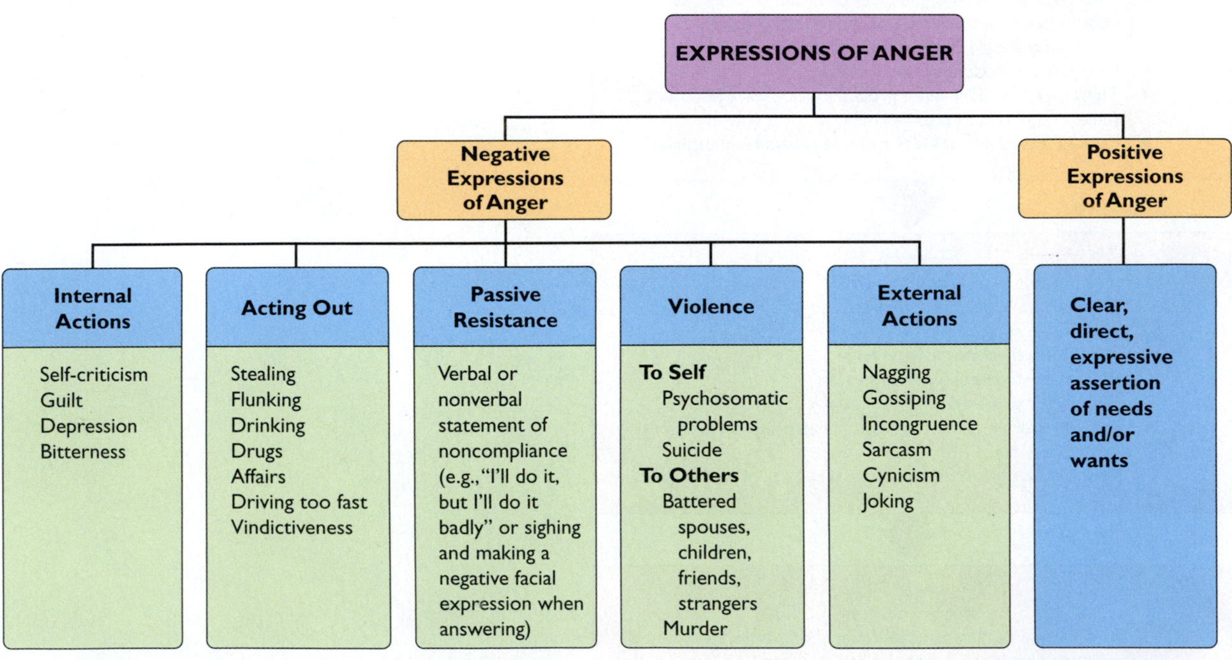

FIGURE 7.3 Forms of Expression for Anger

Source: "Forms of Expression for Anger" by Judith K. Beede and Sandra J. Nowakowski. Reprinted with permission of the authors.

Anger can be *implosive.* You can beat yourself up in various ways: negative self-talk; overuse of drugs, alcohol, or food; self-mutilation; or suicide. Or anger can be *explosive:* You attack others through physical or verbal abuse, cut off verbal or social contact, remove love, restrict financial support, or disown them.

Once you are aware of the feeling of anger, you can identify what it is and its cause by putting your thoughts into words. Think back to the last time you were feeling angry. Using that information, fill in the blanks in this statement: *I want/wanted* ___________ ___________ , *but* [name the person(s)] ___________ ___________ ___________ *wants/wanted* or *didn't want/doesn't want to* ___________ ___________ ___________ . For example, "I wanted to leave to go to dinner, but Michael kept wasting time." Being able to verbalize what is bothering you often makes it possible for you to understand what is happening and decide what to do about it.

Normally we perceive anger to be a negative feeling. On the other hand, it can be positive if you use the anger to alert yourself to what's wrong, figure out how to deal with it constructively, and act in a responsible way.

There are some techniques that can affect your interpersonal expression of anger so that it can be a constructive rather than a destructive action. Consider, for example:[28]

- *Do not react immediately when you are angered.* The count-to-ten technique is often effective. It stops you from acting on only your emotions and allows you to think through the ramifications of your actions.
- *If possible, don't make important decisions in the heat of an angry moment.* A moment of emotional stress is not the time to fire anybody or tell your spouse or lover that your relationship is over.
- *Use the extra energy generated by anger to act constructively.* When you experience anger (or its first cousin, fear), your body activates its *fight-or-flight mechanism*

Anger assumes meaning when you express it to yourself or others.

(stay and battle it out or run away). This results in an increased flow of adrenaline that makes you temporarily stronger than usual. But instead of beating up someone, go for a fast-paced walk.

- *Apologize if necessary.* If you really behave badly during a fit of anger, an apology to those who have been affected is in order. A simple "I'm sorry; I was angry" will probably do. Sometimes you need to go further and make an "I" statement of what motivated your outburst (e.g., "I really get upset when I feel my ideas are being totally ignored. I'm sorry I left the meeting. I'd appreciate it if next time you'd let me finish my entire presentation before telling me that it is not a good idea").

Dealing with Another Person's Anger in Conflict

To deal with someone else's anger, one expert advises, "Don't let them dump on you; it only encourages their craziness."[29] Instead, you must determine what is the best behavior for you and then carry it out. *We teach people how to treat us.* If you give in to another's emotional blackmail (e.g., threats that he will leave you or stop being your friend), you have set a pattern by which that person can control you in the future. And the more you give in, the more the person will use the same ploy again.[30]

Remember that in a conflict situation, the other person often is attacking you when you may not be the cause of the problem or cannot solve the problem. It may be simply that you are the first person who wandered on the scene after an incident happened. The best approach is to allow the person to vent her frustrations while you remember that the attack is not really against you and try not to react personally. If the person continually uses you as her scapegoat, recount factually what the pattern has been and that you will not allow yourself to be a scapegoat. State the facts and how you want to be treated. It's hard to argue with facts! You could say, "Yesterday you yelled at me when Maria didn't get her report in on time and when Derek didn't reach his sales quota. I wasn't responsible for either of those things. I know you were angry, but I'd appreciate it in the future if you discussed other people's problems with them, not take your anger out on me."

Disagreements actually can end up being constructive if you follow the basic principles of fighting fair.[31]

Fair Fighting

In **fair fighting**, participants work toward an amicable solution to the problem and keep in mind that although the issue is important, the relationship is also important, such as with marital or other relational partners, children and parents, and friends. Some fair-fighting strategies include:

- *Get as much information as you can, and attempt to adjust to the problem based on this information.* Fact, rather than hearsay, may show that the supposed cause of the conflict is not the actual cause.
- *Keep arguments in the present tense.* Do not argue about what happened in the past; that can't be changed.
- *Do not try to make the other person change things that cannot be altered.* We cannot trade in our relatives, extensively alter our physical appearance, or become a totally different person.

- *Do not start a fight when it cannot be finished.* It is not appropriate to start a stressful discussion when a person is walking out the door on the way to work, or on a tight schedule, or when one or both parties are extremely tired.
- *The setting can affect a conflict.* Disagreeing in public or in front of individuals who are not part of the conflict is not a good strategy. It can bring about embarrassment not only to the participants but also to the observers.
- *A fight can take place only if both parties participate.* If the conflict is getting out of hand or has gone on too long, then one party should stop participating. The length of a constructive argument is normally about twenty minutes; people get tired, and their reasonable intentions break down after that. When the participants start repeating the same arguments, they have run out of concepts regarding the issue, and it is not uncommon, at that point, for one of the participants to start attacking the other person rather than dealing with the issue.[32]
- *Listen to your body.* If you are aware of your voice getting louder or your body tightening up, or you are making fighting fists, you should either physically leave or limit your role to that of a passive listener for a while.
- *Identify realistically what you need to get out of the transaction.* Often we enter into a conflict situation without having identified our goals, which means we have no clarity of purpose and don't even know if the conflict is over.[33]

Mastering these strategies for fair fighting can help resolve potential conflicts.[34]

- *Sit down.* Sitting down puts your logical mind back in control and avoids the possibility of physically attacking the other person. It also gives a quick break to the tension. Ask whoever you are in the conflict with to also sit down.
- *Show you are listening.* After collecting the information, summarize what you heard, for example, "You're saying it happened because of X, Y or Z." If you've listened effectively both of you are now understanding what the other person's perspective is. If you haven't paraphrased effectively, the other person can correct you and there is understanding of the cause of the situation which lead to the conflict. If you perceive the situation differently, now that you understand the other person's perspective, you can present your view.
- *Make an agreement.* The goal of a conflict is not to win but to agree on a future plan of action so that the error, mistake, or problem doesn't erupt again. "Research shows that if you participate in coming up with a solution [or at least an understanding that you have to agree to disagree] you are much more likely to comply with it."[35]

Individual Approaches to Dealing with Conflict

People react differently in dealing with conflict. Some people pull back, some attack, and others take responsibility for themselves and their needs. Most of us use a primary style for confronting conflict. Are you interested in determining your usual conflict management style? If so, do the Conflict Questionnaire.

Knowing your style and its ramifications can be helpful in determining whether you are pleased with your interpersonal communication conflict management style. If you are not, you may need to acquire the skills to make a change in your habitual pattern. The styles of conflict management are avoidance, accommodation/smoothing over, compromise, competition/aggression, and integration. (See Figure 7.4.)

Conflict Questionnaire

We each have a general pattern by which we deal with conflict. To learn your approach to dealing with conflict, circle T (true) or F (false) to indicate how you would respond in each of the situations. Although you may not agree with either choice, you must select either T or F. Read quickly, and react quickly.

Directions: Circle T (true) or F (false) to indicate which of the following statements best describes how you would respond in each of these situations. Although you may not agree with either choice, you must select either true (T) or false (F). Your first instinct will be your best response.

		1	2	3	4	5
1. When there is a difference of opinion, wants, or needs, I would rather explore our differences than try to convince the other person that I am right and he or she is wrong.		F				T
2. When there is a difference of opinion, wants, or needs, I would rather disagree openly and explore our differences than agree with the other point of view simply to have someone agree with my point of view.					F	T
3. When asked to perform an unpleasant task, I would rather postpone the task indefinitely than follow orders without discussion.			F	T		
4. When there is a difference of opinion, wants, or needs, I would rather try to win the other person over than withdraw from the conversation.		T		F		
5. Sometimes it's easier to agree and appear to go along with something without discussion than to avoid making any comment on a controversial subject.			T	F		
6. During a disagreement, I would rather admit that I may be half wrong than try to convince the other person that I am 100 percent right.		F		T		
7. When there is a difference of opinion, wants, or needs, I would rather give in totally than try to change the other person's mind or opinion.		F		T		
8. I would rather postpone a potential disagreement than explore our different points of view.				T		F
9. During a disagreement, I would rather meet the person halfway than give in totally.			F		T	
10. Sometimes it's easier to agree without discussion than to try to convince the other person I'm right.		F	T			
11. During a disagreement, I would rather admit that I am half wrong than not say anything and withdraw from the conversation.				F	T	
12. When asked to perform a task I don't want to do, I would rather postpone it indefinitely than make someone else do the task.		F		T		
13. During a disagreement, I would rather try to win the other person over than to split our differences.		T			F	
14. When there is a difference of opinion, wants, or needs, I would rather explore our differences and reach a mutually satisfactory solution than withdraw from the conversation or conflict.		F		T		
15. When asked to perform a task I don't want to do, I would rather postpone the task indefinitely than discuss my feelings and attempt to find a solution we can both agree on.				T		F
16. During a difference of opinion, wants, or needs, I would rather try to convince the other person that I am right than explore our differences.		T				F
17. During a disagreement, I would rather admit that I am half wrong than explore our differences.					T	F

(continued)

Conflict Questionnaire (continued)

18. Sometimes it is easier just to agree without discussion than to give up half of what I believe to reach an agreement.			T		F	
19. When there is a difference of opinion, wants, or needs, I would rather explore our differences than give in without a discussion.			F			T
20. During a difference of opinion, wants, or needs, I would rather try to win the discussion than sacrifice my point of view by not discussing it.		T	F			
21. During a disagreement, I would rather try to find a solution that satisfies both of us than to let the other person find a solution without my input.			F			T
22. During a disagreement, I would rather try to win the other person over than give in totally.		T	F			
23. When asked to perform a task I don't want to do, I would rather agree to perform just half the task than to find a solution that is mutually satisfactory.					T	F

Scoring Instructions:

1. Count the number of items circled in each of the five columns. Record your totals in the boxes below. Multiply each score by 10.

	1	2	3	4	5
× 10 =					

2. Chart your score on the graph below. Place an X next to your score for each of the five strategies. Draw a straight line connecting the Xs from one column to the next. This will give you your conflict management strategy pattern.

	1	2	3	4	5
	Competition/ Aggression	Accommodation/ Smoothing Over	Avoidance	Compromise	Integration
120					
110					
100					
90					
80					
70					
60					
50					
40					
30					
20					
10					
0					

Avoidance Some people choose to engage in **conflict avoidance**—not confronting the conflict. They sidestep, postpone, or ignore the issue, no matter how unpleasant.[36] Although seemingly unproductive, avoidance may actually be a good style if the situation is a short-term one or of minor importance. If, however, the problem is really bothering you or is persistent, then it should be dealt with. Avoiding the issue often uses up a great deal of energy without resolving the aggravating situation. Avoiders usually lose a chunk of their self-respect since they so clearly downplay their own concerns in favor of the other person's. Avoiders frequently were brought up in environments in which they were told to be nice and not to argue, and eventually bad things would go away. Or they were brought up in homes where verbal or physical abuse were present, and to avoid these types of reactions, they hide from conflict.

Accommodation/Smoothing Over People who attempt to manage conflict through **conflict accommodation** put the needs of others ahead of their own, thereby giving in. Accommodators meet the needs of others and don't assert their own.[37] The accommodator often feels like the "good person" for having given the other person his or her own way. This is perfectly acceptable if the other person's needs really are

Let's assume that I want to go to the movies and you want to go to a rock concert. This is a chart about the choices I make when you and I want different things.
COMPETITION/ AGGRESSION
I go to the movie. (I want to go to the movie so I do what I want, when I want to do it. Your wants are not important to me.)
INTEGRATION
I go to the movie, you go to the concert and we meet afterwards at our favorite restaurant for a midnight snack. (We are both happy with this plan.)
I want to go to the movie. I like the freedom to see what I want, when I want.
COMPROMISE
We agree to go to the movies tonight and a rock concert next week. (We are both happy with this plan.)
AVOIDANCE
I don't say anything and go to the concert with you. (I don't want to make problems.)
ACCOMMODATION/ SMOOTHING OVER
I tell you that our friendship is more important than the movie so I'll go to the concert with you. (I may not go where I want; but, I'm "kind of" okay with that.)

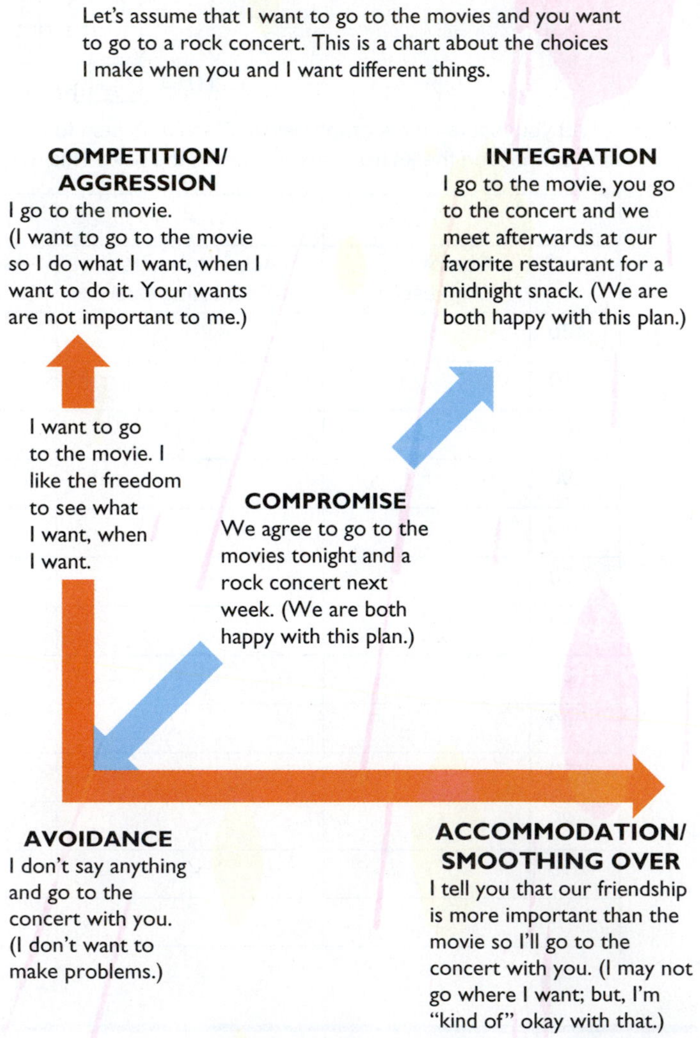

FIGURE 7.4
Personal Styles of Conflict Management

Source: From National Conference for Community and Justice, Northern Ohio Region, adaptation of "Activity 1," handout developed by Mary Adams Trujillo and Laurie Miller and distributed at the workshop "Responding to Conflict Around Issues of Difference," February 19, 1999, Cleveland, Ohio.

more important. But unfortunately, accommodators tend to follow the pattern no matter what the situation. Thus, they often are taken advantage of, and they seldom get their needs met. Accommodators commonly come from backgrounds where they were exposed to a martyr who gave and gave and got little, but put on a happy face. They also tend to be people who have little self-respect and try to earn praise by being nice to everyone.

A form of accommodation known as **conflict smoothing over** seeks above all else to preserve the image that everything is okay. Through smoothing over, people sometimes get what they want, but just as often they do not. Usually they feel they have more to say and have not totally satisfied themselves.

As with avoidance and accommodation, smoothing over occasionally can be useful. If, for example, the relationship between two people is more important than the subject they happen to be disagreeing about, then smoothing over may be the best approach. Keep in mind, however, that smoothing over does not solve the conflict; it just pushes it aside. It may very well recur in the future.

Those who use this technique as their normal means of confronting conflict often come from backgrounds in which being nice was considered the best way to be liked and popular. And being liked and popular was more important than satisfying their needs.

Compromise **Conflict compromise** brings concerns out into the open in an attempt to satisfy the needs of both parties. It usually means "trading some of what you want for some of what I want."[38] The definition of the word *compromise,* however, indicates the potential weakness of this approach, for it means that both individuals give in some degree, give something up to reach a solution. As a result, neither usually completely achieves what she or he wants. This is not to say that compromise is an inherently poor method of conflict management, but it can lead to frustration unless both participants are willing to continue to work until both of their needs are being met. Those who are effective compromisers normally have had experience with negotiations and know that they have to give to get, but they don't have to give until it hurts. Those who tend to be weak in working toward a fair and equitable compromise believe that getting something is better than getting nothing at all. Therefore, they are willing to settle for anything, no matter how little.

Competition/Aggression The main element in **conflict competition** is power. Its purpose is to "get another person to comply with or accept your point of view, or to do something that person may not want to do."[39] Someone has to win, and someone has to lose. This forcing mode, unfortunately, has been the European American way of operation in many situations—in athletic events, business deals, and interpersonal relations. Indeed, many people do not seem to be happy unless they are clear winners. Realize that if someone wins, someone else must lose.

The value of winning at all costs is debatable. Sometimes, even though we win, we lose in the long run. The hatred of a child for a parent caused by continuous losing, or the negative work environment resulting from a supervisor who must always be on top, may be much worse than the occasional loss of a battle. In dealing with persons from other cultures, European Americans sometimes are perceived as being pushy and aggressive because of the win at all costs attitude. Many sales, friendships, and relationships have been lost based on the win-at-all-costs philosophy. Many of the aggressive behaviors in the personal lives of professional athletes are directly credited to their not being able to leave their win-at-all-costs attitude on the athletic field.

Integration Communicators who handle their conflicts through **conflict integration** are concerned about their own needs as well as those of the other person. But unlike compromisers, they will not settle for only a partially satisfying solution. Integrators keep in mind that both parties can participate in a win-win resolution and are willing to collaborate. Thus, the most important aspect of integration is the realization that the relationship, the value of self-worth, and the issue are equally important. For this reason, integrative solutions often take a good deal of time and energy.

People who are competitive, who are communication apprehensive, or who are nonassertive find it nearly impossible to use an integrative style of negotiation. They think that they must win, or that they cannot stand up for their rights, or that they have no right to negotiate. In contrast, people who tend to have assertiveness skills and value the nature of relationships usually attempt to work toward integration.

Avoidance, accommodation, and smoothing over are all nonassertive acts; the person's needs are not met. *Competition is an aggressive act* in that the person gets his or her needs met at the expense of others. *Integration is assertive*, since the objective is to get one's needs met without taking away the rights of someone else. *Compromise*, depending on how it is acted out, *can be either nonassertive or assertive*.

Communication Approaches to Managing Conflict

The communicative approaches to managing conflict are assertive communication, negotiation, arbitration, litigation, and mediation.

Assertive Communication

Have you ever found yourself saying, "I didn't want to come here, but she made me," or "I ordered this steak well done, and it's rare. Oh well, I guess I'll eat it anyway"? If so, the communication skill you probably were missing was the ability to be assertive.

Assertive Behavior Defined **Assertive communication** takes place when a person stands up for and tries to achieve personal rights without damaging others. It begins by acknowledging that you have a right to choose and control your life. A person who is assertive takes action instead of just thinking about it. Rather than saying, "Why didn't I tell her?" or "If the waiter was here now, I'd say ... ," the assertive person takes action at the appropriate time. "Assertive people say 'no' when they don't want to do something, express their feelings without hurting others and initiate and terminate conversations."[40]

The root of many communication problems is the lack of assertion. You know you are being taken advantage of and are upset because others are getting their needs met and you aren't. You may know how you feel but are afraid to state your needs because you're afraid somebody won't like you, you'll get in trouble, or you don't know exactly how to go about making your needs clear.

Assertion, Nonassertion, and Aggression As illustrated in Figure 7.5, the goal of assertive behavior is to communicate your needs through honest and direct communication.[41] **Assertiveness** does not mean taking advantage of others; it means taking charge of yourself and your world.

In contrast, the goal of **nonassertive behavior** is to avoid conflict. Nonassertive statements include "Think of others first," "Be modest," and "Let's keep the peace."

	Nonassertive	Assertive	Aggressive
Characteristics of the behavior	Does not express wants, ideas, and feelings, or expresses them in self-deprecating way Intent: to please	Expresses wants, ideas, and feelings in direct and appropriate ways Intent: to communicate	Expresses wants, ideas, and feelings at the expense of others Intent: to dominate or humiliate
Your feelings when you act this way	Anxious: Disappointed with yourself. Often angry and resentful later	Confident: You feel good about yourself at the time and later.	Self-righteous: Superior, sometimes embarrassed later
Other people's feelings about themselves when you act this way	Guilty or superior	Respected, valued	Humiliated, hurt
Other people's feelings about you when you act this way	Irritation, pity, disgust	Usually respect	Anger, vengefulness
Outcome	Don't get what you want; anger builds up.	Often get what you want	Often get what you want at the expense of others. Others feel justified in "getting even."
Payoff	Avoids unpleasant situation, conflict, tension, and confrontation	Feels good; respected by others. Improved self-confidence. Relationships are improved.	Vents anger; feels superior.

FIGURE 7.5 A Comparison of Nonassertive, Assertive, and Aggressive Behavior

Source: "A Comparison of Nonassertive, Assertive, and Aggressive Behavior" by Phyllis DeMark. Copyright © by Phyllis DeMark. Reprinted with permission of the author.

The consequence of nonassertive behavior is that you do not get what you want. Because of this, anger may build, and you may be alienated from yourself and others.

The goal of **aggressive behavior** is to dominate, to get your own way. If you are aggressive, you are likely to make such statements as "Win at all costs," "Give them what they gave you," and "They only understand if they're yelled at." Aggressive behavior may well get you what you want, but it can also lead to alienation, thereby putting emotional distance between you and others that can lead to loneliness and frustration. *Direct aggression* is the outward expression of dominating or humiliating communication—for example: "That's the way it's going to be, and if you don't like it, that's tough. I'm bigger, and I'm stronger. You lose!" *Passive aggression* attacks or embarrasses in a manipulative way. This can be done by pretending that there is nothing wrong but, at the same time, derailing any attempt to solve a problem that isn't to your liking in a way that doesn't appear to be aggressive. Devices for passive aggression include using sarcasm that sounds like teasing, withholding something from the other person (some service, compliance with a request), or being sweet and polite but in fact controlling what is being done. Passive aggression is a common cultural pattern in places where direct aggression is considered bad manners, such as England, China, and Japan. In the United States, the direct aggressive sign would read, "No Dogs Allowed. This Means You and Your Mutt!" In Britain, where direct aggression is generally frowned upon, the sign would say, "We Regret That in the Interest of Hygiene, Dogs Are Not Allowed on These Premises."

Principles of Assertiveness To learn to use assertive communication, you might keep these basic principles in mind:

- *People are not mind readers.* You must ask for what you want. You must share your feelings if you are hurt, have been taken advantage of, or need assistance.
- *Habit is no reason for doing anything.* "That's the way it always has been," and "Our family tradition is ..." are patterned statements. But the presence of a past pattern does not mean that change cannot occur.
- *You cannot make others happy.* Others make themselves happy, just as you make yourself happy. Much of our guilt has come from parents and friends who make us believe that if we do not act as they want us to, then we are causing them unhappiness.
- *Remind yourself that parents, spouses, friends, bosses, children, and others will often disapprove of your behavior and that their disapproval has nothing to do with who or what you are.* In almost any relationship, you will incur some disapproval.
- *Whenever you find yourself avoiding taking some action, ask yourself, "What's the worst thing that could happen to me?"* Before you let fear act on you, determine what the consequences of the action, the communication, may be. If you would prefer to avoid these consequences, then by all means avoid the situation. But in most instances you will probably realize that the potential consequences aren't that bad.
- *Do not be victimized.* A *victimizer* is a person or establishment that interferes with another person's right to decide how to live his or her own life, and a *victim* is a person who is denied that right. Recent cases of sexual harassment illustrate that women and men have been made victims because they would not stand up to a victimizer. Victimization may be enacted by others, but it also can take the form of *self-victimization,* in which a person prevents himself or herself from deciding how to live. Self-victimizers often go through life thinking of themselves as failures or losers with no capability to achieve anything worthy.

When people are functioning as assertive human beings, they use available resources to get out of victimizing situations and victimizing relationships. They report a sexual abuser or leave situations in which they are being victimized. These are communicative actions that say, "I am too valuable a person to be taken advantage of."

- *Worrying about something will not change it; only action will.* Worrying will not alter the past, the present, or the future. Instead, you must take some action to relieve yourself of anxiety.
- *Adopt the attitude that you will do the best you can, and if someone else does not like it, that is her or his problem, not yours.* You are responsible to only one person: you. If others cannot and will not accept that idea, that is their problem, not yours. This does not mean that you should not seek out information and advice from those whose opinions you respect; instead, it means that you do not need to seek reassurance for everything you do, think, and feel.
- *When you decide to be assertive, be aware of the consequences.* Actions have consequences. If you threaten to quit your job if you do not get a raise, you should be ready to start looking for another employer. Don't make a threat unless you are willing to accept the responsibility for the results of the action.

Assertiveness Skills If you are not already assertive, you may have decided that you would like to be. Or if you are basically assertive but have not been extremely

1. *Simple assertion:* State the facts. If someone shoves ahead of you in the supermarket, you say, "I was here first."*
2. *Empathic assertion:* You recognize the other's position but state your own needs. "I know you're probably in a hurry, but I was here first."*
3. *Follow-up assertion:* Repeat a description of the person's behavior, then state your own position. "I was here first. I'd like you to go to the end of the line."*

* Remember that assertions should be made in a nonaccusatory oral manner.

FIGURE 7.6 Three Types of Assertive Responses

Source: "Three Types of Assertive Responses" based on a concept by Judith Spencer. Reprinted with permission.

successful at it, it may be that you lack sufficient techniques to handle a variety of situations. In either case, some strategies can be of assistance to you.

One assertiveness strategy is composed of simple, empathic, and follow-up assertions. The use of this technique follows several stages. (See Figure 7.6.) When you feel the need to be assertive, start with a **simple assertion** in which you state the facts relating to the existence of a problem. This may be enough to solve the problem because people are often unaware that something is bothering you or that they have done something you consider wrong. A simple assertion alerts them to the problem. If they act to eliminate the problem, the solution is at hand.

Sometimes, however, you need to recognize the other person's position but state your own needs. This is an **empathic assertion**. It may follow a simple assertion or be the first step in the assertive process. By recognizing the other person's problems or rights, you may find that she or he understands that you are not on the attack and may then become quite cooperative.

A **follow-up assertion** is used when the simple or empathic assertion is not successful in getting the desired action. It takes the form of a restatement of the simple or empathic assertion and then a statement of your own position, which may include a direct statement of the action you need or want.

Do not assume that by being assertive, you will always get your way. You may not, but you definitely have a better chance than if you are nonassertive. And you probably won't get the negative reactions that you might receive if you were aggressive.

DESC Scripting **DESC scripting** is a way of dealing with interpersonal conflicts that centers on the process of **D**escribing, **E**xpressing, **S**pecifying, and stating **C**onsequences. This system allows you to "analyze conflicts, determine your needs and rights, propose a resolution to the conflict, and, if necessary, negotiate a contract for change."[42]

The process of DESC scripting also allows you to plan ahead, if desirable, to avoid being unable to think of what to say. Most people, especially those who are communicatively anxious, tend to feel more secure if they know exactly what they are going to say. This system enables them to rehearse and eliminate bad scripts or self-defeating statements. There are four steps of DESC scripting:

1 *Describe.* Describe as specifically and objectively as possible the behavior that is bothersome to you—for example, "I was told these repairs would cost $35, and I've been given a bill for $100."

2 *Express.* Say what you think and feel about this behavior—for example, "This makes me frustrated because I feel I was not told the truth."

3. *Specify.* Ask for a different, specific behavior—for example, "I would like my bill adjusted to the original estimate."
4. *Consequences.* Spell out concretely and simply what the punishment will be for not changing the behavior. The consequence should be something that you are willing to do and are capable of doing. Threats that go beyond reasonableness will be ignored. For example, a positive consequence statement would be, "In the state of Ohio, I know you legally can charge me only $50 over the amount of the estimate. If the change isn't made, I'll contact the state's Consumer Protection Office and lodge an official complaint." (Since this is the law, you can carry through.)

DESC scripting can be used for requesting an adjustment, asking for information or help, clarifying instructions, reconciling with someone, saying *no* to unreasonable demands, protesting annoying habits, and dealing with unjust criticism.

Negotiation

Whether it's with an employer, family member, friend, or salesperson, we all negotiate for things each day. We negotiate for a higher salary; better service; solving a dispute with a coworker, roommate, or spouse; extending a homework assignment due date; or deciding where to go on a date.

Negotiation is the act of bargaining to reach an agreement with at least two people or groups working on a mutual problem.[43] It is a process in which the participants search for an agreement that satisfies all the parties. When negotiating, both parties must be explicit about what they want and why. In order to negotiate, it is important to understand the principles and styles of negotiation.

Negotiation is the act of bargaining to reach an agreement with at least two people working on a mutual problem.

The Principles of Negotiation[44] Every time you deal with someone you have to decide what you owe that person (if anything) in terms of fairness, candor, and the use of pressure tactics.

You should keep in mind four principles of negotiation during the process:[45]

- If possible, prepare in advance.
- Reframe the questions and the arguments.
- Respond; don't react.
- Identify and alter tactics.

Whenever possible, *prepare in advance*. Consider what your needs are and what the other person's needs are. Consider outcomes that would address what you both need and want.

If you are interested in getting the best for both sides, *commit yourself to a win-win approach,* even if the tactics used by the other person seem unfair. Be clear that your task will be to steer the negotiation in a positive direction. Realistically, some people go into the negotiation prepared to battle to the end and will do anything to get their way or their idea accepted. Entering with this attitude almost always ensures that the negotiation will not go smoothly and that the odds of getting to an amicable agreement will be slim.

During the proceedings, if you need clarification or want to ensure that the other person understands what you or he or she has proposed, *restate what you heard in your own words or ask a question to reframe,* such as, "I just want to make sure I understand your proposal. Do you believe that if the fraternity eliminates its pledging procedures, it will increase membership?" Or "What I heard you suggest was a 5 percent salary increase." Or "You want me to loan you my car for two weeks in exchange for your paying the rent this month?"

Try to manage your emotions. Remember that you want to reach an agreement that is acceptable to both parties. Win-win negotiation is not an "I win; you lose" situation. Attack the problem or the issue, not the other person.

It is often difficult for people to admit that they are wrong or that their ideas have not been accepted. So, if it is appropriate, *make it possible for the other party to back down without feeling humiliated by identifying changed circumstances that could justify a changed position on the issue*—for example: "Since we've been negotiating, we seem to have made some adjustments in our requests. As I understand it, the proposal now is that you are willing to take less in alimony if I am willing to grant partial custody of Mark." This is better than saying, "I told you that you wouldn't get full custody and all the money!"

Maintain the relationship while trying to resolve the issue. A statement such as "Our friendship is more important than solving this issue" may, in fact, help solve the issue as well. Focus on being partners solving the problem rather than opponents by using statements such as "If we really work at this together, I'm sure we can come up with a solution that satisfies both of us."

Invite trading (e.g., "If you will do … , then I will do … ."). Trading allows both sides to feel that they have participated in the final outcome.

Once a person has proposed a solution, he or she may push for that solution simply because it is "my" idea. To eliminate this possibility, explore best and worst alternatives to negotiating an acceptable agreement by making a list of the alternatives without discussing their positive or negative implications. Often, just making the list opens up new possibilities and clarifies the ideas for all parties.

If attacks or aggressive methods are present, name the behavior as a tactic. For example, if someone starts making personal attacks, you can say, "I realize this is stressful, but name calling isn't going to get us to an agreeable solution."

Take a break. If things are getting heated, it might be wise to cool things off by saying, "I think it's getting a little intense. I think it's time for us to take a break."

Change locations or seating arrangements. Meeting in a person's home or office makes that person feel that he or she is in charge. Perhaps adjourning to another setting may change the dynamics of the discussion. If you think this might be true, suggest the change. Or change your seat so that you are sitting across from someone whom you want to address directly.

Go into smaller groups. Often, meeting in large groups can lead to chaos. Meeting in smaller groups tends to work better. For example, one of your authors was chairperson of a salary and fringe benefits committee for many years. The two sides each consisted of six people. Whenever no progress was being made, your author suggested that the chairpersons meet privately. In a short time, a negotiated settlement was reached.

Sometimes it is wise to *call for the meeting to end now and resume later,* perhaps "to give an opportunity for reflection."

Select the appropriate negotiation technique. The following are the most common approaches:

- *Spiraling agreements.* Begin by reaching a minimum agreement, even though it is not related to the objectives, and build, bit by bit, on this first agreement.
- *Changing of position.* Formulate the proposals in a different way, without changing the final result.
- *Gathering information.* Ask for information from the other party to clarify its position.
- *Making the cake bigger.* Offer alternatives that may be more agreeable to the other party, without changing the terms.
- *Commitments.* Formalize agreements orally and in writing before ending the negotiation.

Culturally COMMUNICATING

U.S. and Japanese Negotiation Styles

Brett and Okumura studied the negotiation styles of U.S. and Japanese managers. They reasoned that because U.S. culture is individualistic and egalitarian and Japanese culture is collectivistic and hierarchical, managers from the two cultures would exercise different styles of negotiation. Their results showed that Japanese negotiators paid significantly more attention to power during negotiations than did U.S. negotiators. Brett and Okumura also found a difference in the two cultures' focus on self-interest during negotiations. The U.S. American negotiators were much more focused on self-interest than were the Japanese. The two researchers also found that joint gains in negotiations were significantly higher in intracultural negotiations than in intercultural ones. In other words, when U.S. managers negotiated with other U.S. managers, there were higher gains than when U.S. managers negotiated with Japanese managers. The same result was found among Japanese managers.

Source: Brett, J. M., & Okumura, T. G. (1998). Inter- and intracultural negotiation: U.S. and Japanese negotiators. *Academy of Management Journal, 41*, pp. 495–510; Neuliep, J. W. (2003). *Intercultural communication: A contextual approach*. Boston: Houghton Mifflin, p. 320.

Negotiating Styles Each of us has developed a negotiating style. Children may lie on the floor and kick their feet or cry, or they may ask nicely. Teens may pout or plead, or they may do whatever is asked, knowing that this is the only way to get something they want. As an adult, you might scream or threaten, thinking this tactic will get you your way, or you may offer to do someone a favor in return for getting what you want.

We learn our style by trying out various approaches and figuring out which one works best with which individual in what setting. Since one pattern does not work in all situations, if you are a good negotiator, you recognize that you must fit the approach to the individual. This method goes back to the concept that in any communicative situation, there are always participants, a setting, and a purpose that set the parameters for the communication.

Much of your strategy settles on whether you are interested in a win-lose, lose-lose, or win-win resolution. (See Figure 7.7.)

Win-lose negotiations center on one person's getting what he or she wants while the other comes up short. In **lose-lose negotiations**, neither person is satisfied with the outcome because neither gets what he or she wants. In a **win-win negotiation**, the goal is to find a solution that is satisfying to everyone. Although the latter seems to be the ideal for which most people strive, some may aim for a different option. There are times when people feel they must win at all costs, and if they cannot win, then the other person is not going to win, either.

If you are interested in a win-win resolution, take these concepts into consideration:

- *Set up a conducive climate for negotiating.* If the atmosphere is positive, the negotiation will probably go forward. If the atmosphere is negative, however, there may be no way of avoiding a win-lose or lose-lose situation, both of which are fostered by competition. Are you really interested in amicably settling the issue? If so, make an effort to be cooperative. Try to set up a "we" rather than a "you versus me" atmosphere.
- *Consider the impact of the setting.* Trying to negotiate in front of others often places a strain on the participants that can result in a less than desirable solution. If the participants feel rushed, tired, or under pressure to meet a deadline, this feeling can influence both their thinking and their emotional attitude.
- *Keep the discussion focused.* Avoid attacking the other person; rather, stick to the topic.

Arbitration

Arbitration is an alternative process for deciding disputes.[46] Instead of being decided by a judge or jury, cases are decided by a third party who is an expert in a particular field. The third party hears evidence and then makes a decision on how the conflict will be resolved. In arbitration, both sides have previously agreed that they will abide by the decision. Instead of being decided in a courtroom, as in litigation, cases are dealt with in an office and decisions are final, with no right to appeal.[47] Arbitration advocates think this system is better than litigation due to its speed (litigation can take years), costs (a lawsuit may run into tens of thousands of dollars), and informality (no presence of a judge, jury, or observers).

Win-lose negotiation	Lose-lose negotiation	Win-win negotiation
• One person gets what s/he wants • Other comes up short	• Neither person is satisfied with the outcome	• All parties try to find a solution that is satisfying to everyone

FIGURE 7.7 Options for Negotiation Resolution

Arbitration is an accepted pattern in such circumstances as disputes in professional baseball, in which a player who does not agree with the salary and/or contract offered by the team that holds the rights to his playing can apply for arbitration. Some workers and corporations and professors and their institutions will agree to binding arbitration as a means of avoiding a work stoppage or settling a strike.

Litigation

Litigation is adversarial communication in which a dispute is settled by presenting evidence to a judge or a jury, who decides who is right. Litigation is usually conducted by lawyers who call witnesses and question them to reveal information while following a prescribed set of rules that have been established by law and interpreted by the person in charge, usually a judge.

Mediation

Mediation is a process in which a neutral person who has no vested interest in the outcome facilitates communication between parties and, without imposing a solution on the parties, enables them to understand and resolve their dispute.[48] Mediation is becoming a communication technique that many courts are mandating instead of litigation in such matters as custody, divorce, and neighbor disputes. It tends to work well in situations in which the parties want to have a win-win outcome and are not interested in litigation.

The basic principle in mediation is to get those in conflict to communicate with each other so that they can reach a win-win decision, thus ensuring that the dispute will remain settled.[49] It is imperative in mediation that the participants keep the discussion in the present tense and discuss how to solve the issue. Therefore, mediation rules usually indicate that the first session may be used by disputants to blame each other, but then they are not to revert to blaming each other again for the rest of the time but instead should work toward agreement.

Since most people are not trained to deal with each other in a nonconfrontational manner when they are involved in a conflict, a mediator acts as both guide and teacher in getting the disputants through the process. Mediators are specially trained in specific communication techniques and are often licensed to perform the act of mediation.

The Role of Culture in Conflict

A person's attitudes, dispositions, and beliefs, which are developed by his or her various cultural influences, lay the foundation for how that individual approaches conflicts. *Remember, as in any discussion of culture, variations exist within specific cultures so that not everyone in a cultural group reacts in exactly the same way, but there are patterns based on how research illustrates generalized patterns.*

The conflict styles discussed so far in this chapter basically reflect the research on Euro Americans and nations such as Australia, Great Britain, and Canada. This research reflects that the rights of individuals are strongly stressed. In most Middle Eastern and Mediterranean cultures, which are considered *conflict-active societies,* conflict is accepted as an important part of life, and men generally take great delight and pleasure in haggling and arguing. Besides in personal matters, haggling is expected when purchasing goods in many Central and South American and Arabic countries.[50]

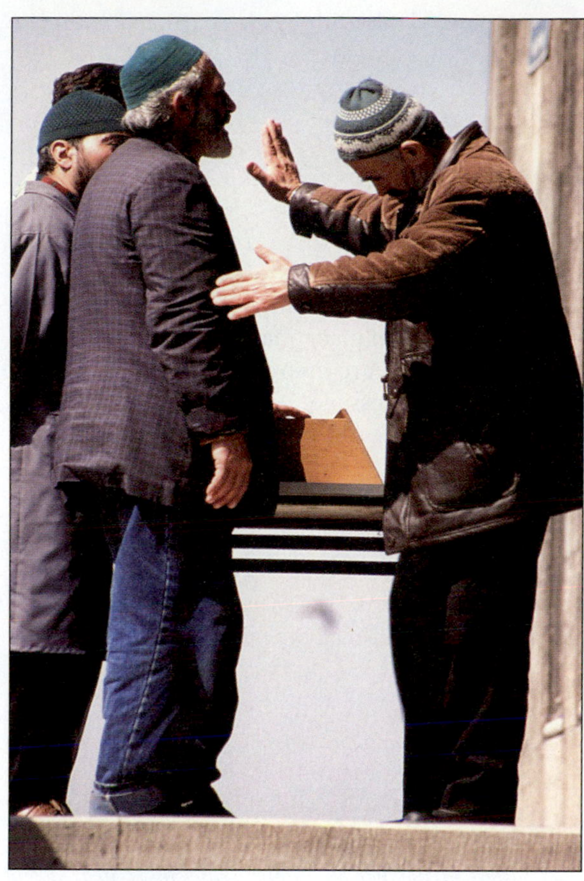

In most of the Middle Eastern and Mediterranean cultures, conflict is accepted as an important part of life, and men especially take great delight in haggling and arguing.

In nations where the group is stressed over the individual, such as Guatemala, Ecuador, Panama, and Venezuela, care is taken not to directly confront individuals. People from *conflict-avoidance societies* believe that face-to-face confrontations are to be avoided.[51] Many Asians find haggling and confrontation distasteful.[52] For example, a Chinese proverb states, "The first person to raise his voice loses the argument." Asian culture doesn't encourage people to tell you what you're doing wrong. Many Asians avoid conflict at all cost and will not risk loss of face through telling you directly what is on their minds.[53]

The conflict-avoidance aversion in Japan includes not resolving disputes with lawyers. It is estimated that the Japanese have only one lawyer for every ten thousand people; in the United States, a conflict-active society, there is one lawyer for every fifty people.[54]

Another factor that affects the conflict style is face. *Face* concerns "socially approved self-image and other-image."[55] It is expressed as *facework,* "the verbal and nonverbal strategies that we use to maintain, defend or upgrade our own social self-image and attack or defend the social images of others."[56] In countries where face is stressed, such as in China, Japan, Korea, Taiwan, and Mexico, direct confrontations are generally avoided. The use of self-defensive, controlling, dominating, and competitive styles in managing conflict is discouraged.[57] Avoidance, accommodating, and compromise styles are more appropriate. Using a competition/aggression style will probably cause embarrassment. Recently, one of your authors was in a Vietnamese restaurant. A patron at another table yelled to the young waiter, "I've been waiting for my check. Get it now!" The young man bowed his head, shuffled away and didn't come back into the dining room. Another server brought the bill.

In some cultures, conflicts are not directly dealt with by the participants in the disagreement. The decision is turned over to others, such as the elders, village leaders, or the tribal chief.

Criticism

Criticism—the act of judging—is typically considered to be a negative act by the receiver. Few of us handle criticism well. In many instances we attempt to deny or dismiss it. Criticism often triggers within us memories of being corrected by our parents, teachers, coaches, or clergy. It may make us feel inadequate and unacceptable.[58]

But like it or not, sometime in your life, you are going to be the recipient of criticism. To handle criticism as constructively as possible, without feeling the need to justify yourself, get angry, withdraw, or counterattack, you can try these strategies:

- *When criticized, seek more information.* If someone accuses you of having done something, ask for specifics. For example, if a friend says that you are selfish and do not respect anyone's feelings, ask for specific examples that led to the comment.
- *Paraphrase the ideas of the person making the criticism to clarify them for both of you.* Repeat the accusation, and ask if that is what the accuser really meant. That way, you will be dealing with exactly what has been said.
- *Ask yourself what consequences will result from your not altering the behavior being criticized.* Will you personally gain from making the changes, or is the criticism based solely on satisfying the needs of the criticizer?
- *Listen to the person; if the criticism is just, accept the opinion.* Use such techniques as agreeing with the truth, agreeing with the odds (if it is a projection into the future, agree with the odds for its occurrence), agreeing in principle (if the criticism comes in the form of an abstract ideal against which you are being unfavorably compared, you can agree with it in principle without agreeing with the comparison), or agreeing with the critic's perception (agreeing with the right of the critic to perceive things the way he or she does). For example, if you are accused of spending too much time studying and not enough socializing, and you feel this is true, why not simply agree rather than arguing that you have a right to spend your time as you wish?[59]

In dealing with criticism, recognize that much of it is well intentioned. Often, family members, friends, and your supervisor are telling you how to change for (what they perceive is) "your own good." This does not mean that they are right or wrong or that you have to take their suggestions. Remember that none of us has

COMMUNICATING

in Careers

Feedback: Try This Response to Criticism

Benefit from both positive and negative feedback with STAFF:

- ***S****ay thanks.* Even if the feedback is negative, avoid the urge to defend yourself. If you agree, say so and thank the person. If you don't agree, say nothing except "Thank you."
- ***T****hink about what the person said.* Walk away and take time to honestly answer this question: "Was the feedback accurate?" Don't waste time trying to think of ways to defend yourself or to criticize your criticizer.
- ***A****sk for more information, if you feel you need it*. Even if you disagree with the feedback, it can help to know the reasons for it. Also, you both need to agree on the problem and how serious it is before moving to the next step.
- ***F****ind out what you need to change*. Ask for specifics. If the other person has none, and if you feel you deserved the criticism, try to think of how you might do better. But also consider this: The lack of specifics could also mean the criticism was unfounded.
- ***F****ollow through on any changes you've agreed to try on your own.*

Source: "Feedback: Try This Response to Criticism" by D. Hudson, *Office hours*. Reprinted with permission of Briefings Media Group.

There are times when people feel they must win at all costs and if they cannot win, the other person is not going to win either.

a crystal ball allowing us to see into the future. Your desires, needs, and goals are ultimately your responsibility, and you can do as you wish as long as you are also willing to accept the consequences.

The Role of Culture in Criticism

The discussion, so far, regarding criticism, centers on Euro American attitudes and techniques regarding commenting on the actions of others as well as attempting to guide the other person toward correcting or improving his or her actions or deeds. These concepts are not universal.

The Asian concept of face enters into the act of criticism. "Direct criticism of individuals in the Chinese culture, particularly in front of others needs to be handled delicately."[60] What is considered constructive criticism in many Western societies can cause deep embarrassment with many Asians. For example, a communication professor teaching Chinese students in Hong Kong found that whenever anyone did offer some form of criticism it was striking that everyone's head in the class went down. Even if the criticism was couched with praise, the reaction was the same. Both criticism and praise, the teacher found, brought attention to the individual, and that individual attention was not part of the collective concept of being part of a group. Interestingly, the instructor found that by allowing the students to prepare the speech as a group, and having one person selected by and representing the group, allowed for constructive criticism, since the group, not the individual, was being evaluated.[61]

Apologizing

Have you ever angrily said something to another person? Have you ever offended someone by being sarcastic or joking around when your remark was perceived to be serious and not funny? Have you ever acted inappropriately toward someone whom you really like? If the answer to any of these is *yes,* what did you do about it?

We all have said or done something we know has hurt or offended a personal friend, a significant other, or even a stranger. For many people brought up in the European American culture, **apologizing**, saying you are sorry, although it is a key to getting along with others, is a difficult task. How you react to having offended someone has a great deal to do with your background. If you've been brought up to fight for being right, not to give in, or to hold a grudge, you are not likely to consider apologizing. If you've been brought up to believe that the feelings of others supersede your own feelings, then making an apology is probably an automatic reaction.

Questions arise as to when it is appropriate to apologize and how to do it. For many people, it is both hard to know when to apologize and difficult to apologize. You may be ashamed of your negative actions or have too much pride to admit to another that you did something wrong. Sometimes, even though you may want to apologize, you just may not know how. But remember that apologizing often solves the small problems and keeps them from getting bigger.

Traditionally, an apology has three parts. First, the person who has done the wrong states what he or she did. For example, the person could say, "I yelled at you after you told me that the idea I had presented at the meeting was wrong." Second, the perpetrator explains why he or she took the action. For example, the person could say, "I spent a lot of time on that solution, and I felt I had to defend myself." Third, a statement of remorse is made. For instance, the person could say, "I was upset, but I shouldn't have yelled at you. It didn't do anything to help deal with the task on which we were working." The reason the second step is optional is that you may not know why you took the action, or an explanation may incite further anxiety. If either of these situations is the case, it may be wise to skip that part of the process.

Does the process sound too formulaic or unnatural? It may well be, especially if you aren't in the habit of apologizing, but it lays out a pattern for verbalization that can and does work. Once you adopt the style, you may make adjustments to fit your own personality and situations, but at least you now have a format for the apology process.

The person who has been wronged may reject your apology. That is not your problem. If you offer an apology, and the apology is sincerely worded and felt, then whether the other person accepts or rejects the action is not the issue. You have fulfilled your obligation. You have recognized that what you did or said was wrong and have taken an action to let the other person know that you are remorseful. You can only be responsible for one person's actions—your own. You cannot make the other person act as you would like him or her to act. Therefore, acceptance of the apology is out of your hands. Don't go into the process of apologizing to receive forgiveness. Go in accepting that you are doing the right thing.

Here are some additional tips that may make it easier to say you're sorry:[62]

- *Repair the damage.* To be complete, an apology should attempt to correct the injury. If you damaged someone's property, offer to fix it. If the damage is emotional, you might ask, "I'm really sorry. What can I do to make it up to you?" There may be nothing concrete you can do, but the offer is usually enough and shows your sincerity. You might follow up by saying something appropriate, such as "I'll try to be more considerate in the future. In the meantime, how about if I buy you a cup of coffee."
- *Take responsibility.* The starting point of any change of behavior is self-admission. Admit to yourself that you have offended someone.
- *Use good timing.* If possible, apologize right away for little things. For example, if you bump into someone, say you're sorry right away. However, if you have done something more serious, like insult a friend out of anger, you may need some time to figure out exactly what to say. A quick apology might not give you time to realize what you've done, why you did it, and what the ramifications might be.
- *Show your regret.* The other person needs to be aware that you recognize that what you did was wrong. Be specific in your regret. For example, "I feel bad that

I told your secret. You trusted me, and I betrayed your trust. I shouldn't have done that."

- *Choose an appropriate conduit.* What's the best conduit for an apology? Letters, e-mail, text messaging, voicemail, the phone, and speaking face-to-face are all message channels that are available. The first four are definitely impersonal. Using them may be easier and might save you from facing the person directly, but they are usually not as effective as other channels. Resort to using them only if there is no way to meet face-to-face. If a person lives far away, then there may be no choice. If that's the case, using the phone is probably a better alternative than a written presentation. At least hearing the tone of your voice can be a clue to the honesty of your message. If you do apologize by voicemail, "it is best to plan exactly what you want to say, and keep it to 30 seconds, never more than a minute."[63]

  A face-to-face apology is often best because you can display your honesty. It can be a humbling experience, as you must see the other person's expressions, show yours, and probably hear a verbal reply. As one expert states, it is worth the anxiety because "you will be respected by the person you are addressing as well as by yourself more if you are able and willing to make your apology in this manner [face to face]. Smiles, laughter, hugs, handshakes, and other displays of appreciation and affection are added benefits for both parties that are all possible when apologizing this way!"[64]

- *It's not about who "won" or who "lost."* Remember, life is not a war unless you or the other person makes it a war. Stubborn pride often leads to a loss of friends and can result in physical confrontations. "An apology is a tool to affirm the primacy of our connection with others."[65]

The Role of Culture in Apologizing

There is no universal "truth" regarding apology. The concepts just discussed so far are those typical in the Euro American culture.

Research shows that "the Japanese typically apologize far more frequently than Westerners."[66] Although, in many instances, those from Western countries seem reluctant to admit their own failure, this is not the case in Asian countries, where the concept of "apologizing is considered a virtue."[67] This may come from the individualistic concept in Western cultures where the person is solely responsible for his actions and is often reluctant to acknowledge that responsibility, thus appearing to have done something wrong. In many Asian/Eastern countries, the collective concept of a person as part of a group, and not wanting to insult any member of that group, comes into play. When one apologizes and shows one's remorse, he or she is not blaming others, not embarrassing them so that they lose face. The attitude is expressed in the proverb "The more you feel sorry, the more deeply you bow,"[68] meaning that you are showing respect for the other person. It is also interesting that in English, we have basically one word for apology, whereas the Japanese have at least seven, each indicating a deeper degree of remorse.[69] Not only are there nationality differences but there are also gender differences. For example, in the Euro American culture, females both offer and receive more apologies then men.[70] Also, males and females often perceive apologies differently. "Men may regard apologies as signals of social distance or as devices to be used only in cases of relatively serious offenses ... women's motivation for apologies may be related to their perception of what is necessary to maintain the relationship with the person offended."[71] In addition, "males were more likely to apologize to strangers than to friends, but females were likely to apologize to friends and to strangers."[72]

In Conclusion

IN CONCLUSION

Every day we participate in interpersonal communication. The basic principle of good conversation is to find a common interest between yourself and the other person. Directions include instructions for how to accomplish a task, achieve an effect, or get somewhere. Requesting is the process of seeking out information or change. Conflict is natural, the inevitable result of individual differences, limited resources, and differences in role definitions. Apologizing is saying you are sorry. The communicative approaches to resolve conflict include assertive communication, negotiation, arbitration, litigation, and mediation. Knowing how to handle criticism is an important communication skill. Culture impacts all aspects of interpersonal communication.

LEARN BY DOING

1. Select a place on your campus, and write directions from your classroom to that place. Your instructor will divide the class into pairs. One partner gives the directions orally to the other partner without revealing the chosen destination. See if by following your directions, your partner can figure out the place you selected. Then reverse roles.
2. Select an object and write a description of it without revealing its identity. Then read your description to your classmates. At the end of the entire description, they will attempt to name the object. When everyone has read his or her description, discuss why the class members could or could not identify certain objects.
3. Do this activity over a period of several days, completing the tasks in the order given. When you are finished, share your experiences with the class, and discuss what you learned about the process of assertiveness. In the discussion, figure out why activities a and b were assertive acts.
   - **a.** Do something you have wanted to do for yourself but for some reason have not (e.g., call a friend you have wanted to talk to for a while). This is an assertive act. Record what you did and how you felt.
   - **b.** Do something you have wanted to do for someone else but for some reason have not (e.g., visit an ill relative). This is an assertive, selfless act. Record what you did and how you felt.
   - **c.** Think of something that someone is doing that bothers you. Using the DESC or the simple/empathic/follow-up assertion format, tell that person how you feel, remembering to be assertive, not aggressive (e.g., tell your roommate you would appreciate her not borrowing your clothes without asking). This is an assertive act. Record what you did and how you felt.
4. Think of a specific situation in which you should have been assertive but were not. Why did you not assert yourself? How could you have asserted yourself? What do you think might have happened if you had asserted yourself? Use your answers as the basis for a discussion on assertiveness.

KEY TERMS

conversation 174
small talk 174
empathy 180
conflict 181
anger 186
fair fighting 188
conflict avoidance 192
conflict accommodation 192
conflict smoothing over 193
conflict compromise 193
conflict competition 193
conflict integration 194
assertive communication 194
assertiveness 194
nonassertive behavior 194
aggressive behavior 195
simple assertion 197
empathic assertion 197
follow-up assertion 197
DESC scripting 197
negotiation 198
win-lose negotiation 201
lose-lose negotiation 201
win-win negotiation 201
arbitration 201
litigation 202
mediation 202
criticism 204
apologizing 205

CHAPTER 8

The Interview

types of interviews • organization of interviews • participating in interviews

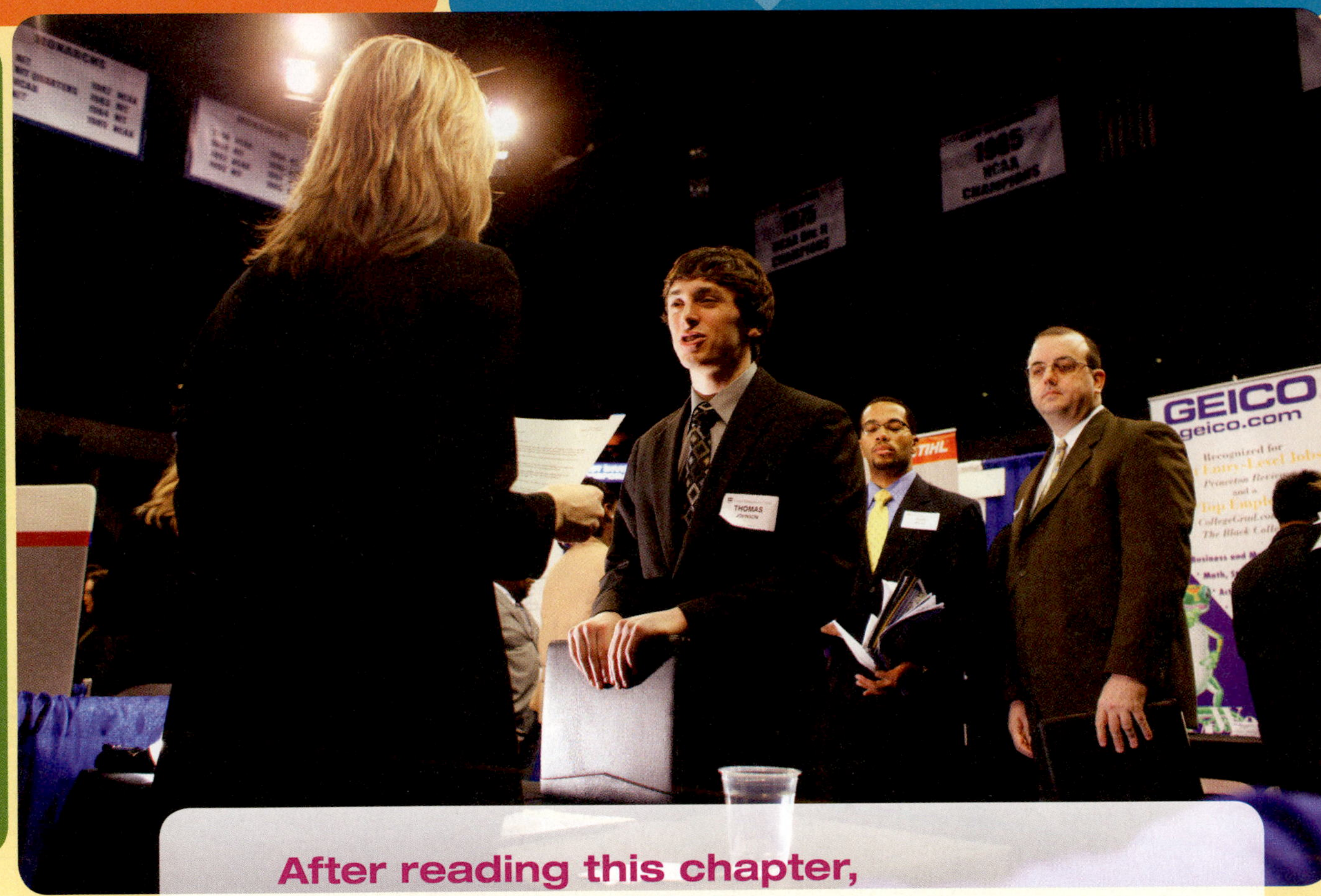

After reading this chapter, you should be able to

- Define what an interview is and identify the types of interviews
- List and explain the different purposes for interviews and how those purposes affect what happens in the interview
- Demonstrate the organizational structure of an interview
- State the principles of preparing for and functioning as an interviewee and an interviewer
- Identify and illustrate the types of questions used in an interview

Some people believe that interviewing is a skill they need only for a job search. Not so. As a college student you may need to interview an expert for information for a term paper. You may be interviewed for your scholarship application or an internship. If you decide to go to graduate or law school, there are usually entrance interviews. If you are a human resources, media, or health careers major, a great part of your professional life will involve your being responsible for planning and conducting interviews. If you want to be an effective communicator, part of your package will include good interviewing skills as both an interviewer and interviewee.[1]

The Interview and the Role of the Participants

An **interview** is a purposeful conversation between two or more persons that follows a basic question-and-answer format. The participants in an interview are the **interviewer**, the person responsible for arranging for and conducting the interview, and the **interviewee**, the person who is the subject of the interview. In some instances, there may be a team of interviewers or a number of interviewees.

Role of the Interviewer

The interviewer is responsible for the interview's arrangements and takes the lead in conducting the process. This person usually establishes the time, location, and purpose of the meeting. The interviewer usually prepares an **interview agenda**, which outlines the procedures that will be followed to achieve the interaction's purpose.

A good interviewer tries to build a climate of trust and support and is aware of and adapts to the verbal and nonverbal cues of the interviewee. The interviewer also should be a good listener so that she or he can adapt to the needs and concerns expressed by the interviewee.

Interviewers should be aware that it is the purpose of the interview to find out about the interviewee, and therefore the interviewer should not talk too much. It is wise to remember, as an interviewer, that your role is not to dominate by telling your beliefs, unless you are involved in a reprimanding, persuasive, or appraisal interview. If, as the interviewer, you say such things as, "You agree with me, don't you?" or "What I believe is ..." you may well be leading the interviewee, which is not your role.

Developing an Interview Agenda To accomplish the purpose of an interview, the interviewer usually develops an agenda. It includes the format for the interview. The traditional format, regardless of the interview's purpose, is divided into the opening, the body, and the closing.

A checklist of questions he or she wants to cover is developed. To do this, the interviewer must determine the type of information that is desired from and about the interviewee. For example, in the following job interview outline, the interviewer has decided there are four categories of information needed: educational background, experience, job-related outside activities, and communication skills. These categories and the questions within them are set up in a format consistent with the communication goal.

The order of questions often takes the form of a *funnel schedule* in which the questions are sequenced to take the interview from more general to more specific information. An interviewer can arrange the questions in each category with a range from those that are easiest to answer to those that are more difficult. He or she might decide to ask those that require factual information first, followed by those that probe attitudes. The interviewer should provide transitions at the end of each category of

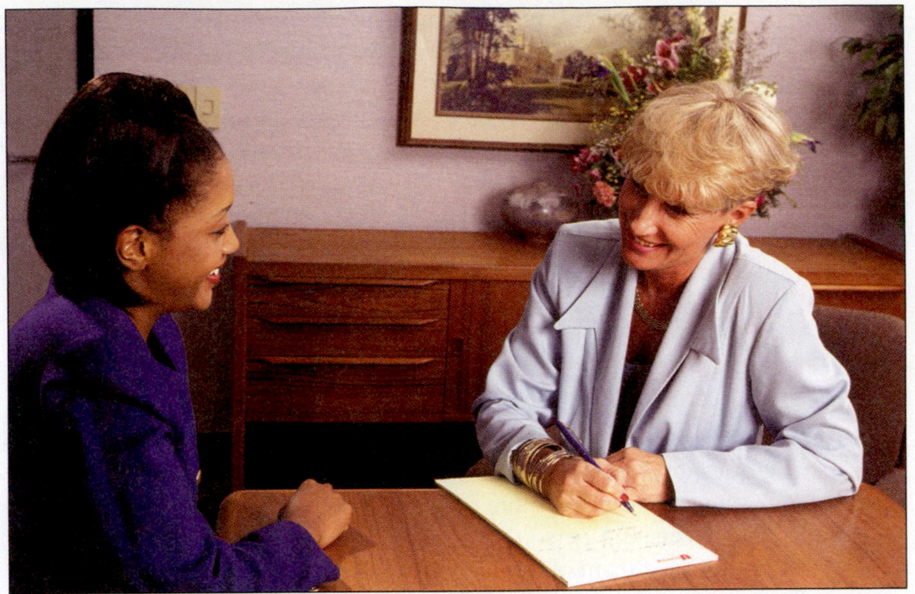

A good interviewer works at establishing a rapport with the interviewee by providing a climate of trust and support.

questions so that the interviewee knows when the questions are changing directions. Specifically, the interviewer could say, "Now that we've covered your educational background, let's turn to your past on-the-job experience."

In this agenda, the interviewer is a corporate personnel director seeking to hire a civilian computer programmer to work on a military base. The interviewee is a computer programmer.

I. Open Interview
   A. Specify details of position
      1. Duties
      2. Workdays, hours, benefits, and pay
   (Transition to next topic) "I'd now like to examine your educational background."

II. Education
   A. Why did you choose computer science as your educational major?
   B. Which courses do you feel best prepared you for this position?
   C. Why?
   (Transition to next topic) "Let's now examine how your experiences relate to this position."

III. Experience
   A. Describe one problem for which you devised a solution on your last job.
   B. If you were rushing to meet a deadline, how would you complete the assignment while keeping quality high? Give an example from your last job.
   (Transition to next topic) "Let's move on to discussing your skills as they relate to this position."

IV. Job-Related Activities
   A. In which computer language or languages are you fluent?
   B. Which language do you like the most? Why?
   C. What specific computer-security measures do you feel should be carried out to protect military information?
   (Transition to next topic) "You appear to have good communication skills. Let's now find out how you apply them to a specific task."

V. Test of the Ability to Display Clear Communication Skills
   A. We cannot read the VTOC on any of a string of disk drives. The CE is stumped and strongly suggests that it is a software problem. You are 100 percent sure that it is a hardware problem, not a software issue. If I am the CE, convince me that I am wrong and you are right.
   B. If I were to offer you the following two jobs, which would you choose and why?
      1. One with a $65,000 salary and a job description and responsibility level with which you are not very happy.
      2. One with a $50,000 salary and a job description that fits the type of position you really want.

   (Transition to next topic) "I'd like to wrap up the interview by restating some of the major ideas we've discussed, find out if you have any questions, and tell you about what our procedure is for informing potential employees of their status."

VI. Conclude Interview
   A. Summarize briefly.
   B. Ask for any questions.
   C. Tell interviewee when to expect to hear from you regarding the final hiring decision.

Opening the Interview Interviewees generally are nervous at the start of an interview. They are in an unfamiliar environment, are stressed, have little control over the process, and have a strong desire to impress. This places the responsibility on the interviewer to make the interviewee comfortable. The interviewer can ease some of the stress by providing a welcome which, in Western culture, includes a smile, a handshake, and establishing clear goals and a procedure for the process.

In interviewing, the participants usually have a preset purpose.

Body of the Interview In the body of the interview, the interviewer asks a variety of questions in an attempt to accomplish the purpose of the session. Types of interview questions include:

- *Direct questions* are explicit and require specific replies—for example, "Where did you last work?"
- *Open questions* are less direct and specify only the topic—for example, "What is your educational background?"
- *Closed questions* provide alternatives, narrowing the possibilities for response, and probing for opinions on opposite ends of a continuum—for example, "Do you think knowledge of a product or possessing communication skills is the most important asset of a salesperson?"
- *Bipolar questions,* a form of closed question, require a yes or no response—for example, "Would you like to work for this company?"
- *Leading questions* encourage a specific answer—for example, "You wouldn't say you favor gun control legislation, would you?" This is a leading question because it implies how the interviewee should answer the question.
- *Loaded questions,* a type of leading question, are designed to elicit an emotional response. Asking a job applicant who was an officer of the union at a previous job to defend this company's policy of nonunion affiliation would, for example, be a loaded question.
- *Yes-response questions,* another form of leading question, are stated in such a way that the respondent is encouraged to agree with the interviewer—for example, "You would agree with me, wouldn't you, that this company's policies are fair?"
- *Mirror questions* are intended to follow up on the initial questions and get a person to reflect on what he or she has said and expand on it. For example, the interviewer may say, "I've worked for this corporation for years, and I'm getting nowhere." A mirror question might be, "So you think you're not moving ahead in the corporation as rapidly as you would like?" Such a probe may encourage the interviewee to disclose more about her or his feelings.
- *Probes* are used to elicit a more detailed response—for example, "Why do you feel that way?" "Tell me more." The probe encourages the interviewee to discuss his or her point with more direction and depth.

Concluding the Interview When the interview is nearing its end, the interviewer should give the interviewee an opportunity to make statements or ask questions. The employment interviewer might say, "You are one of three candidates for the position. Before we conclude, do you have any questions?"

An interview's conclusion should summarize what has been accomplished. If appropriate, a discussion of the next step to be taken after the interview has ended.

Role of the Interviewee

The interviewee, the person who is being interviewed, should prepare for the session by knowing the purpose of the meeting, role and responsibilities, expectations, and the information needed. As an interviewee, anticipate what you will be asked and think about how you can best respond. But don't assume that your only role is to answer questions. It is fairly common during interviews for the interviewee to be given the opportunity to probe for information.

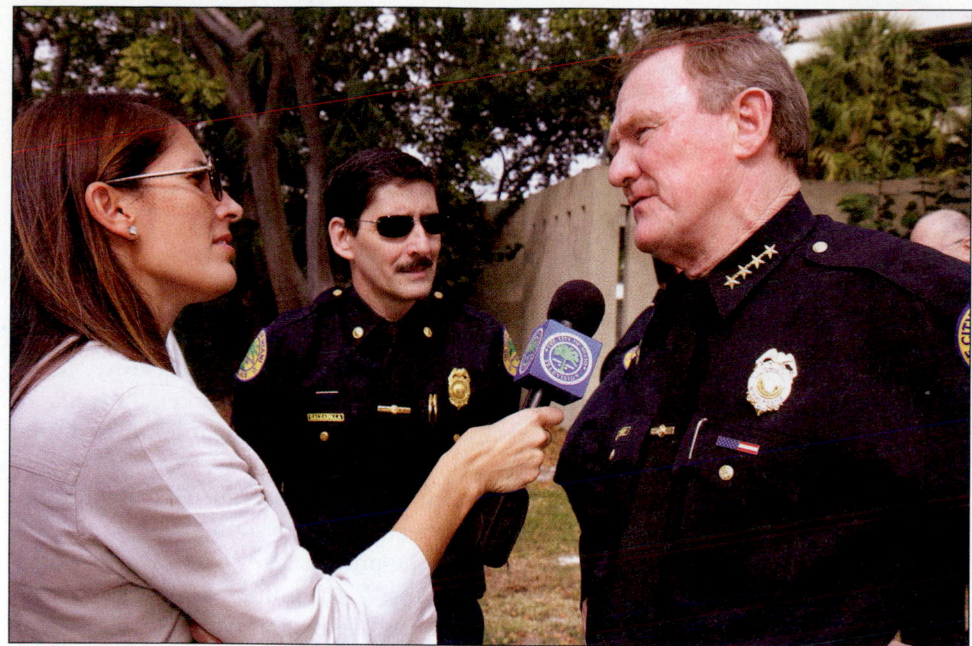

The interviewee should prepare for the interview by knowing the purpose of the session, role and responsibilities, expectations, and the information needed.

Answering Interview Questions The interviewer carries the burden of determining the sequence of questions. The interviewee's responsibility is to answer with accuracy, clarity, and specificity. Not all interviewers are trained in interviewing techniques, so if that seems to be the case, as the interviewee, you may need to show some leadership to make sure the interview goes well. Be aware, however, that interviewer-interviewee roles carry specific behavioral expectations.[2]

Your answers should be backed up with supporting material for clarification and evidence. Here are some suggestions for answering interview questions.

- *If you don't understand the question, ask for clarification.* For example, you might ask, "Would you please restate the question?"
- *Restate the question in the answer.* If asked, "What are your responsibilities in your present job?" the interviewee might begin with, "In my current job, I … ." In this way, the questioner knows you are listening, and you are responding specifically to the question.
- *Answer one question at a time.* Too often interviewers group questions together. In general, it is best to answer one question at a time to make sure that the questioner knows specifically which piece of information you are giving. For example, should the interviewer ask, "Would you describe the working conditions and what you like best about your job?" You could divide your answer into two parts, such as "My working conditions are …" and "I like the fact that at my job I can … ."
- *Try to turn negative questions into positive answers.* A commonly asked job interview question is "What do you think your greatest weakness is?" This negative can be turned into a positive by stating, for example, "I am aware that I am rather compulsive about my work, so I spend a great deal of time making sure that what I do is done correctly."

Types of Interviews

There are numerous types of interviews. The commonly used formats are employment, information gathering, oral history, problem solving, counseling, persuasive, appraisal, reprimanding, interrogatory, and media. Although not all the varieties may be relevant to you at this point in your academic or employment career, you may well be called on to participate in them in the future. Therefore, it is useful to investigate some considerations of each type.

Employment Interview

The most crucial interview for many people is the **employment interview**. It is a way of finding out about a specific job field and entering the job market, a means for changing positions, getting promotions, achieving salary increases, and a way of find a new occupation when you leave a job.

How long does the interviewing for the process to be concluded? The length of time it takes to find a career job varies widely according to your major, your geographic location, and the economic times. Often the process takes 6 months or more.[3]

"Technology is streamlining the hiring process."[4] According to a career services professional, "One of the most common requests we're getting these days from employers is for students to have their resumes and portfolios available online."[5] Rather than read hard copy cover letters and resumes, and do face-to-face interviews, resumes are scanned to ascertain if the candidate has the basic requirements, then telephone and video interviews are used to cut down the costs and time needed for the interviewing process.

The first step in obtaining the right job is totally completing your application well in advance of your desired employment date, then checking back regularly. As one potential employer says, "When I talk to a potential employee, I often say I'm not sure we have a relevant opening, but to check back Monday. That's my first screening—to see if the person contacts me Monday morning."[6]

Your ability to communicate effectively is often important in getting hired. Stress these skills in your cover letter and interview:

- *Listening* (the ability to listen, to paraphrase, to give appropriate feedback)
- *Leadership* (the ability to set clear goals and lead others in a constructive manner)
- *Language abilities* (the use of acceptable standard language grammar and vocabulary)
- *Ability to develop a logical argument* (provide support for arguments and display a clear pattern of organization to the thoughts presented)
- *Social skills* (exhibit a positive attitude, being strongly motivated to succeed, and appearing to have a personality that fits into the specific organization's culture)

Culturally COMMUNICATING

Interviewing Non-native Speakers of English

Long pauses and disjointed sentences are generally perceived as indications of a lack of knowledge. However, during an interview, non-Native English speakers may be struggling to understand questions or find the right words for the answer.

Telephone interviews are particularly challenging because immigrants cannot use nonverbal cues to enhance their understanding.

To alleviate this problem, interviewers should consider providing non-native English speakers the questions in advance. This may limit the interviewer's ability to evaluate the person's ability to answer questions quickly, but if this is not a requirement of the job, then this is no problem.

The interviewee may want to explain their limited English language knowledge and request questions in advance.

Source: "Interviewing Non-native Speakers of English" from www.upwardlyglobal.org. Reprinted with permission of Upwardly Global.

- *Communication style* (the use of appropriate verbal and nonverbal communication skills that fit the position and the organization's culture)
- *No personal woes* (no matter how desperate you are for the job, keep your problems out of the interview process. "You want to demonstrate resilience in the face of unpredictable obstacles"[7])
- *Show you've done your homework about your potential employer by explaining how your background relates to the specific organization and its needs*[8] (Make sure you have a good answer for the question: "What do you know about our company?")

Interviewers often ask questions that develop more than a superficial level of information, thus revealing an in-depth view of the potential employee. For example, besides asking about educational background and experiences, questions might include:

- Tell us about a time when you had a conflict with your supervisor or professor and how you handled it.
- What are your specific life goals?
- What are the most important rewards you expect in your career?
- Do you prefer working alone or in teams? Give an example from school or a job that illustrates your answer.
- How would a good friend describe you?

Interviewer Role in Employment Interviews In an employment interview, the interviewer's purpose is to find out about the job applicant as well as selling the organization or the position.

Legal ramifications may result from the failure to have clear criteria and procedures because of federal, state, and municipal employment laws. Since interviewers vary widely in their selection decisions, and are highly idiosyncratic in their approach to employment interviews, selection interviewers are advised to develop selection criteria, determine how the criteria will be assessed, and establish a criteria-based interview guide.[9]

It is important, as an interviewer, to recognize and adapt to cultural differences as they relate to an interview. Those whose first language is not English, who are not familiar with Euro American nonverbal customs such as greeting procedures, or whose life experiences do not include the spotlight being shone on them may be uncomfortable in the interview process.[10]

Sarcasm, slang, abstract terms may make interviewees unable to respond and react in the expected manner. If the job does not include the need to speak English, such as the person is being interviewed for a customer service position to specifically handle Spanish speakers, then it may be wise to have a translator present to help in the interview process. Some useful guidelines for managing cultural variations in interviews include:

- Be aware that slight changes in words can alter meanings, that languages have different grammatical patterns, and that words may take on different meanings when processed through the perceptual filter of a non-native English speaker.
- Define technical terms and abbreviations. Being part of a profession gives a person the privilege of knowing the terminology of that vocation. Those outside that profession cannot be expected to know or understand that specific jargon.
- Gain as much knowledge as you can concerning the cultural background of the person you are interviewing.

Culturally COMMUNICATING

Job Interviewing in the United Kingdom

- The job *interview* is a time of mutual assessment. You may be confronted by a panel of three or more selectors for the purpose of assessing your technical competencies.
- *Punctuality is expected*, so arrive at least 10 minutes before the job interview.
- *Prepare yourself*—find out information about the company you want to work for.
- Remember to bring with you copies of professional and academic qualifications. An extra CV can be handy too. You will never get a second chance to make a first impression!
- The meeting begins with introductions and hand shakes. Shake hands with everyone present when arriving and leaving. Titles are important—particularly Dr., Professor and even those such as Mr., Mrs. and Ms. Normally those present do not exchange business cards at the job interview.
- Remember that it is best to avoid body contact and to keep a wide distance when conversing. One should also avoid emotional responses, loudness, overuse of hand gestures and patting on the back!
- Do not sit until invited. Talk effectively demonstrating your knowledge of the industry and/or the company, do not interrupt the interviewer and criticize former employers. Answer questions respectfully and directly, and avoid arrogance or boasting.
- Prepare for all kinds of *questions* about yourself, your skills, qualifications, experience and hobbies, and answer them as fully as you can, avoiding yes and no answers. Also ask interviewers questions about the internal operations, responsibilities, and even benefits.
- UK companies make extensive use of Assessment Centres. The tendency among some companies is to use them even at the beginning of the selection process, before the interviews. During such tests, which can last up to three days, intelligence, social and communication skills, and management qualities are tested.
- United Kingdom Job Interview Dress Code: It is important to demonstrate at the job interview good appearance as well as good manners. Dress neatly and conservatively. Men usually wear black, blue, or gray suits and ties. Women wear dresses or conservative skirt suits, with simple accessories.

Source: "Job Interviewing in the United Kingdom" from JobEra.com. Reprinted with permission. http://www.jobera.com

REFLECT ON THIS: What about these suggestions do you perceive to be different from being interviewed for a job in a U.S. company?

Interviewee Role in Employment Interviews The interviewee has the responsibility to provide information about his or her background and experiences and, at the same time, convince the recruiter that he or she is the best applicant for the position. As the job seeker, don't overlook the importance of preparing for an employment interview.

Preparing for the Employment Interview One of the first steps in preparation is to research and understand the position for which you are interviewing and the nature of the organization.

An excellent source for finding information about most positions is the *Occupational Outlook Handbook*. Another source is *Choices Planner*. They provide up-to-date information regarding job responsibilities, employment outlook, educational requirements, and starting salaries.

In examining organizations, learn about their function, mission and goal, products and services, size, and local and international locations. For many organizations, a Google search will suffice. In addition, ask the interview contact source to send you information about the organization.

Normally, if you are applying for a job at a new place of employment, you will be asked to provide a résumé and a letter of interest so that the recruiter has background information. A résumé and cover letter ought to be tailored to the specific company and position for which you are applying. There are many excellent sources for finding information on techniques for preparing effective résumés and cover letters including:

- The book *What Color Is Your Parachute?*[11] is available in many libraries and collegiate career counseling centers.
- *Congo Resume* is an online source for cover letters and résumés which charges for its services.
- A free source is About.com which has a section entitled, "How to write a cover letter."

When using online help, however, remember that you don't want your application materials to look exactly like everyone else's. As one public relations professional said: "The first thing I do is reject everyone who has obviously used the Microsoft resume template. I expect PR professionals to be able to think for themselves."[12]

Because of the increasing use of the electronic screening of applications, make sure to include the exact key words used in the position announcement or job description. For example, if the announcement says, "Operational knowledge of Word and Excel required," state in your cover letter and in the résumé: "I have operational knowledge of Word and Excel," not, "I am computer literate." Electronic scanners will pick up the designated words and ignore the other terms, no matter how close the meanings.

In many ways, the online application creates a barrier for potential employees because they may be screened out by a computer or other automatic process without being able to really sell themselves. It can be frustrating because you cannot talk to a person to clarify who you really are and why you are qualified for the job. You may not be permitted to attach materials such as a cover letter, resume, or a portfolio. You have to comply with the procedures of the organization who is listing the job, so make sure that you include what you can, within the guidelines.

Another important aspect of preparation is to be ready to answer the questions posed. Here is a list of

COMMUNICATING in Careers

3 Job Interview Myths

According to career coach David Couper, there are many surprising myths surrounding job interviews. Three of these are:

Myth 1: The interviewer is prepared. He may have barely glanced at your resume and given no thought to your qualifications.

What you can do: Identify a problem that is stated or hinted at in the job ad. In the interview, if he doesn't bring up the subject, you do and show how you can solve that problem

Myth 2: The interviewer will ask the right questions. Many interviewers prepare no questions beyond "Tell me about yourself."

What you can do: Prepare several effective sound bites (succinct examples) that highlight your past successes and skills. Sneak those in when a question remotely refers to that success or skill.

Myth 3: The most qualified person gets the job. "Less-qualified but more outgoing candidates may win over an interviewer's heart."

What you can do: Don't give one word answers. Prepare explanations and examples to discuss. Find out about the interviewer, for example, check her LinkedIn profile, and find a reason to compliment her for a professional accomplishment or her company's success. Smile and make eye contact.

Source: "3 Job Interview Myths" by Charles Purdy. Copyright © 2011 by Charles Purdy. Reprinted with permission of the author. Charles Purdy is the Senior Editor for Monster Worldwide.

the most-asked interview questions for entry-level positions and some ideas about how you might answer them:[13]

1. *"What are your future plans?"* Connect your response to the goals of the organization with which you're interviewing. For example, since your pre-interview investigation revealed that the company is growth oriented, you might state, "Since I have strong training and experience in computer graphics, I really want to be part of an organization that is exploring new and creative ways of entering into the graphics field."

2. *"In what school activities have you participated?"* Highlight any activities that demonstrate your leadership abilities and how you are good at time management, assuming responsibility, and multitasking. An appropriate answer would be "I served on the Student Government Council for two years. This activity allowed me to assume leadership, balance school work with other responsibilities, and develop skills in working well with others."

3. *"How do you spend your spare time?"* Be selective in what you disclose. Focus on those activities that reflect your physical, intellectual, and community service activities that are applicable to the position. Consider including your religious or ethical activities only if you perceive that the organization and interviewer are aligned with your views. Usually, it is wise to avoid making political comments or talking about social activities, especially those that would put you in a bad light. A solid answer might be "I enjoy working out at the gym, going to professional sports games, working with Habitat for Humanity, and volunteering as a Big Brother." If your list is not strong, you might add wishes for the future by stating, "I have been busy getting my degree, but as soon as I have a job, I'm planning on becoming involved in Habitat for Humanity and volunteering as a Big Brother."

4. *"In what type of position are you most interested?"* Try to tailor your response to this company and this position. If you are interviewing for an entry-level position, it would be appropriate to state, "As a recent college graduate, I am interested in your opening because it will give me the necessary basis for understanding the field of accounting." If the interviewer asks, "Is that your career goal?" you could respond by saying, "Realistically, I need to know more information about the field, which I can acquire in this position, before I can make decisions about the future." This response doesn't close doors on your ambition and indicates that the job is at your appropriate level. Avoid saying, "I'm willing to do anything." It makes you sound desperate and unfocused.

5. *"Why do you think you may like to work for our company?"* In answering this question, refer to your pre-interview research about the company and reflect on those features of the firm that are attractive to you and that the organization also stresses. For example, you could say, "I'm very excited that your company is so innovative in product development. I also like your connection to our community and the way the company encourages employees to participate in community service projects."

6. *"What jobs have you held?"* Include those positions that are relevant to the job for which you are interviewing. Even if you have only had part-time jobs, you can successfully weave those into your answer. If you are interviewing for a customer-service position at a bank, try stating something like "While working my way through school I was employed in Home Depot's customer-service department, I learned about organizations and their rules. I think this background will be helpful in this job."

7 *"What courses did you like best? What courses did you like least?"* Be sure in answering these questions that your response doesn't contradict what your transcript reveals. If you got a D in Introduction to Physics, you might have to substantiate why you received that grade. If you are interviewing for your first teaching position, you could say, "I've always wanted to be a history teacher, so I was really pleased with the fact that my university had a top-notch history department and a strong education program. As for what courses I liked the least, science isn't my favorite subject. Given a choice, I would always take a history class over a science course."

8 *"Why did you choose your particular field of work?"* Demonstrate that you have passion for the field, not that you just fell into it for lack of anything else to study or do. An acceptable answer might be "When I was in junior high, I came home and asked my father what career someone goes into if everyone is always asking for advice and when he gives it, they take it. My dad said, 'Sounds like a psychologist to me.' So I set my goals right then to become a psychologist, and here I am today interviewing for a position on your mental health staff."

9 *"What are your strengths? Your weaknesses?"* Interviewers know that in communication and job preparation courses, students are prepped to answer interview questions. The general rule is that when answering these questions, try not to sound conceited but let the interviewer know of your strengths as they relate to the potential job. And try to turn your weaknesses into strengths. Consider saying something like "I've been told over and over that my strength as a person is my ability to analyze what's going on around me. I work creatively and efficiently. My creativity sometimes gets me into trouble because I think of solutions that others haven't considered. If they are fairly traditional, they might think my ideas are off the wall. In the long run, however, my ideas do give people some options to think about."

10 *"What is your ideal work environment?"* Ideally, you should reflect about your ideas for what comprises a good work routine, your preferred supervisory style, and the role you like to play in creating a good working setting. You might say, "I tend to work best when I'm given clear directions and then am trusted to carry out the tasks" or "As a former athlete, I've learned to be a team player. I work well with others and feel comfortable to play the role of either the follower or the leader."

Sometimes interviewers ask off the wall, yes, even weird questions. For example, these are real inquiries posed during interviews:[14]

- If you were shrunk to the size of a pencil and trapped in a blender, how would you get out? (Reportedly asked at a Goldman Sachs interview.)
- Rate yourself on a scale of 1 to 10 how weird you are. (Reportedly asked at a Capital One interview.)
- If you could be any superhero, who would it be? (Reportedly from AT&T interview)
- An apple costs 20 cents, an orange costs 40 cents, and a grapefruit costs 60 cents. How much is a pear? (Reportedly from Epic Systems interview)

How do you answer these types of questions? Try to be creative. The interviewer may be trying to find out if you panic under stress or how resourceful you can be. In the case of the pencil in the blender, an answer such as, "I'd write 'Help, I'm trapped in here, get me out' on the side of the blender" would show purposeful thinking.

For the superhero question, choose a superhero who does good for the community would illustrate your desire to help others. If the job is one that requires creativity, such an advertising agency, an uncanny response will probably receive a positive reaction, but if you are interviewing at a law firm, bizarre is probably not a quality for which they are looking.

If you are interested in an in-depth examination of employment interviewing and practicing for an interview, you might go to JobBankUSA.com. In addition, an interviewing coach suggests that you "list all the questions you think the interviewer might ask, particularly the questions you are most afraid you will get, and prepare a short answer to each."[15] Buy a deck of three-by-five cards, put each question on a card and have a friend drill you as if you're learning the multiplication tables with flash cards.[16]

Dressing for the Employment Interview Your clothing communicates a great deal about you. Therefore, a consultant who advises businesspersons on what to wear states, "Walk through a door into an office, and instantly people draw a dozen conclusions about you, from how much money you make (or should make) to how trustworthy you are."[17] "An initial salary of 8 to 20 percent higher is a result of upgrading a mediocre business appearance to one that is crisp and effective."[18] Make sure you have prepared a professional look from your haircut to your polished shoes.

Although some organizations have turned to a more relaxed look, this doesn't normally apply to clothing choices for employment interviews. If you want to succeed, you must package yourself to turn off the least number of people and turn on the greatest number of opportunities. This generally translates into the clean, pressed, conservative, trustworthy look for traditional organizations. Anything goes when

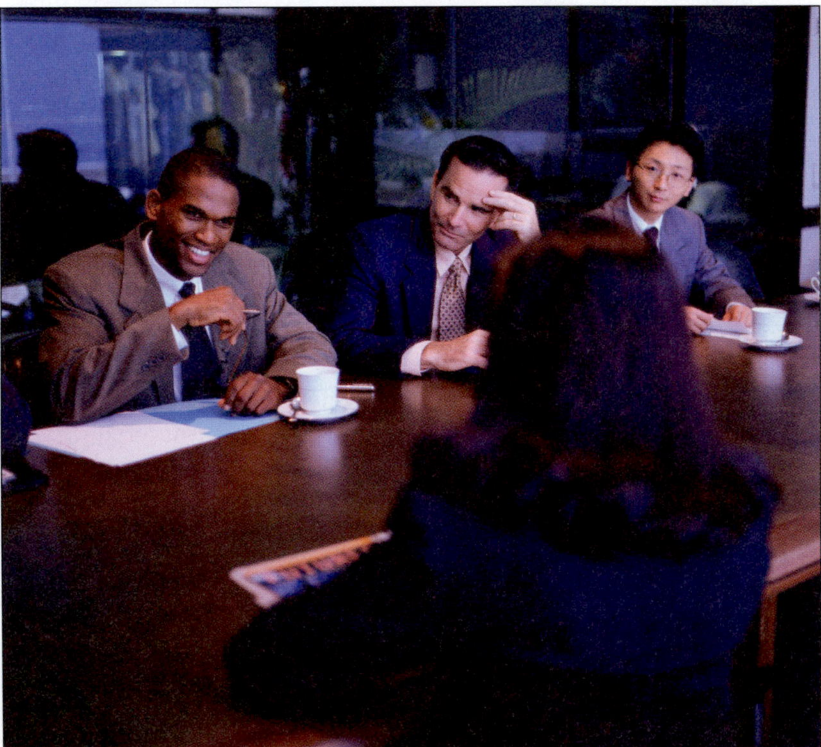

Although some organizations have turned to a more relaxed look, this normally doesn't apply to clothing choices for employment interviews.

you are interviewing for a job at places like Facebook or Apple, but they are the exceptions.

For men, that means solid color suits (navy or dark grey), color-coordinated long-sleeved shirts, tie, dark socks, and conservative leather shoes.[19] In other words, leave the Nike running shoes and wrinkled shirt at home.

For women, navy, black, or dark grey suits are recommended with a color-coordinated blouse and a skirt long enough to allow for comfortable sitting.[20] Shoes should be conservative.[21] Women should go for a professional look and avoid too much cleavage, a skirt that is too short, see-through clothes, over-accessorizing, and casual wear (e.g., lip-flops, spaghetti straps, sundresses, sunglasses).[22]

Because fashion changes so quickly you probably should ask for advice from a member of your college's Career Planning and Placement office. For both men and women, a portfolio or briefcase is recommended, a neat and professional hairstyle, manicured nails, and limited jewelry (no earrings for men).[23] Items that should be left at home include body-piercing jewelry and iPods. Don't forget to turn off your cell phone (if you use "vibrate," it may distract you and interrupt your flow of thought).[24] A list of top twenty interview fashion faux pas includes unnatural hair colors, sunglasses on top of your head, ear buds, and backpacks. The fashion faux pas list also suggests that women avoid more than one set of earrings, long fingernails with bright polish, heavy makeup, and patterned hosiery. Men should avoid short-sleeved shirts.[25]

Context is important, so adjust your clothing and accessory choices to match the culture of the organization for which you are interviewing. Hallmark Cards, for example, is known as a company with an interesting mix of conservative suits (the business employees of the corporation) and more "artsy" dressers (those who work in the creative side of Hallmark).

Remember that your appearance is just one aspect of how you communicate nonverbally during an interview. If you have an interview over lunch, for example, your food and drink choices and your manners communicate. Selecting extremely expensive entrees, drinking alcoholic beverages, even if the interviewer does, and showing poor manners, will probably negatively affect your employment chances.

One business executive takes prospective employees for a walk during interviews and says, "If they don't walk as fast as I do, I wonder how hardworking and motivated they will be."[26]

Actions During the Employment Interview What should you do during the interview? In general, it is wise to keep in mind the following advice:[27]

- *Be prepared to tell the employer your specific job preferences.* This gives you a chance to explain your training and strengths, and it displays knowledge about the organization and what positions are available.
- *Stress your qualifications without exaggeration.* Be specific as to what you actually did. Rather than saying, "I did office work," say, "I entered data using both Word and Excel, did Internet searches to be used in product development, and edited letters and advertising copy before they were sent."
- *Avoid criticizing former employers and fellow workers,* when you discuss your previous jobs. If you complain, you may well be perceived as a malcontent.
- *Be honest.* Few people lie well. Even if you can, employers will hire you for what they see and hear, and if you are not the person you have pretended to be or cannot perform at that level, you'll be terminated.

- *Ask appropriate questions*—for example, ask about what your initial duties will be and what kind of training you will receive.
- *Take notes* with a professional looking pen and notepad or an electronic device during the interview, which you can use to remind yourself of questions you want to ask or refer to later.
- *Be careful of interrupting as ideas pop into your mind.* Be patient, jot down questions you want to ask and wait for an appropriate time to probe.
- *Avoid negative mannerisms.* Use good eye contact. Avoid chewing gum, playing with your pen, checking your cell phone, texting, constant throat clearing, slouching, finger drumming, nail biting, or resting your chin in your hand.
- *Ask about the next step.* If the employer does not definitely offer you the job or indicate when you will hear about it, ask when you may call to learn of the decision.[28]

Dealing with Legal Restrictions During the Employment Interview An important consideration for both the interviewer and the interviewee are the legal issues that relate to the selection process.[29] Both the interviewer and the interviewee should know the federal guidelines as to what questions can and cannot be asked in employment interviews. Unfortunately, the laws are constantly being changed, so a review of the current standards must be made. At the time this book was published, these were some of the regulations:[30]

An interviewer *may* ask:

Are you a veteran? How did your military service provide you with skills you will need on this job?

How many years' experience do you have?

What are your career goals?

Who were your prior employers?

Why did you leave your previous job?

What languages do you speak?

Do you have any objection if we check with your former employer for a reference?

An interviewer may *not* ask:

How old are you?

Are you married?

Are you a U.S. citizen?

Do you take drugs, smoke, or drink?

What religion do you practice?

What is your race?

Are you pregnant?

Unfortunately, in spite of these guidelines, job applicants are subjected to inappropriate questions. Some interviewers haven't been trained in interviewing and simply don't know what is appropriate, while others don't care.

What should you do if an illegal question is asked? You might be direct about your concern, "I'm not trying to be difficult, but I was told in my Business Communication class that asking that question is illegal. I'm afraid if I answer it we could both get into trouble. So, if it's all right with you, I'll not respond." Another approach is to compliment the questioner but refuse to answer the question—for example, "That's an interesting question. Normally I'd love to answer it, but in my communication class, the professor told us that we aren't legally allowed to answer that question." On the other hand, if you think your answer will be positively perceived, you may want to go ahead and answer.

If you believe that you have been discriminated against in the interviewing process because of gender, age, sexual orientation, or any of the other classifications approved by your state or legislative district, you have the right to take action. If you plan to make a complaint to a governmental agency or lodge a law suit, be certain that you can document the questions that were asked and/or the procedure that was followed.

Types of Employment Interviews

Employment interviews may be classified according to their purpose and format: second interview, behavioral interview, employment stress interview, off-site interviews, telephone job interviews, online interviews, video interviews.

Second Employment Interview Many organizations use the initial employment interview as a recruitment tool to gain a pool of applicants for a particular position. The candidates whom the company wishes to consider seriously may be invited to a second interview.

Second employment interviews provide more detailed information about the position and, at the same time, further determine the candidate's fit to the organizational climate and the job. This stage may also test the potential employee through a job task or a test of an ethical dilemma.

This is the appropriate stage of the interview process to ask questions about salary, benefits, retirement plans, and projected plans of the company.

Behavioral Interview As part of the initial or second employment interview, a prospective employee may be asked to participate in a **behavioral interview**, which is designed to allow employers to know what skills you, the applicant, may have and how these skills would translate into performance on the job. In applying for a teaching position, an applicant should be prepared to teach a class. In business organizations, the interviewer may ask you to talk in detail about your abilities or demonstrate job-related skills. For instance, you might be asked about a time that you assumed leadership, such as, "How did you do this?" or "How did you perform?" You also might be asked to perform a specific function, perhaps to edit a document if you are applying for an executive assistant position.

If you know you are going to participate in a behavioral interview, you might want to review the types of skills needed for the position and what skills might be tested, and then prepare for the test by rehearsing your abilities.

Employment Stress Interview The **employment stress interview** is designed to determine how you might function under pressure. Because many employment positions operate in a crisis management mode, an employee's ability to handle stress can be a necessary criterion for employment. You may face two or more interviewers who are firing questions at you, or the interviewers may act in ways that induce stress, such as standing very close to you while interviewing or asking you personal questions that are intended to embarrass you. They may ask rapid-fire questions, interrupt before you are finished with an idea, or belittle your answers. These are all meant to see how you react.

The key to handling this type of interview is to stay as calm as you can, realizing that this is a type of game intended to rattle you. Assume the attitude that

Walk though the door into an office for a job interview, and instantly people draw a dozen conclusions about you, from how much money you should make to how trustworthy you are.

you personally are not under attack. You win the game when you don't allow the harassment to bother you.

The stress interview may be of value to you as a potential employee. It may be an indication that this is not the right job for you. If you can't handle the stress, you may not be happy with this position.

Telephone Job Interview At many organizations the *telephone job interview* has replaced the first personal interview that an applicant used to have with a company.[31] This is done in an attempt to save time and money. Weeding out undesirable candidates; cutting down on airplane, hotel, and meal costs; and eliminating the interruption of the normal organizational routine are regarded as offsetting the lack of face-to-face interaction. Some think that this is a positive step because it eliminates the interviewer's possible prejudice toward certain people regarding their race, physical appearance, or disabilities.

As a result of this trend, the principles of employment interviewing must be adapted to how best to use the telephone. Here are some suggestions for being a participant in a telephone interview:

- *Confirm the time of the interview* and be sure your telephone is going to be available.
- *Select a quiet setting,* one in which you will not be interrupted. If other people use the phone, tell them not to place a call between *x* time and *y* time. Make your

setting secure by informing others not to enter your space and, if possible, put up a sign asking for privacy and quiet.

- *Prepare your desk* or working space with items you may need. These might include a pencil, a pad for taking notes, your résumé, and any materials to which you might want to refer, such as the organization's financial report or research notes you've made about the company.
- *Use a land line,* if possible, so that you don't run the risk that your cell phone signal will fade or a battery will expire during the interview.
- *Try to maintain a positive attitude and high energy* throughout the interview. Smile as you answer the phone. Sit erect in the chair, feet on the floor, to ensure an active listening posture. Or you may want to stand, which can help you project your voice.[32] Don't play with anything on the desk. Concentrate on the phone and the caller. Don't get distracted by objects in the room.
- *Hold the phone in one hand*—instead of with your shoulder—and use your free hand to gesture or take notes. Animated speakers are vocally more expressive.
- *Listen carefully*. Write down the name(s) of the interviewer(s) during the introductions. Refer to the interviewer(s) by name when addressing them. Directing questions and answers to specific people is imperative if there is a team of interviewers.
- *Ask questions.* You may prepare these questions in advance, or you can generate them during the interview. Because the interviewer can't see you, you can write down the questions as they occur to you so that you don't have to interrupt the interviewer's flow of questions. If the interviewer clarifies something you have been curious about, remove that question from your list.

Online Interview Another cost-saving technique is to conduct *online interviews,* using cyberspace for recruiters to meet with candidates. The interview may take place through meeting software, with or without the use of web cameras.

From the standpoint of the interviewee, unless you lack technical skills (e.g., poor computer abilities), the online interview should be no greater challenge than the face-to-face interview. The same type of questions will normally be asked and your strategies to sell yourself as effectively as possible will be essential.

Video Interviews The use of *video interviewing* is growing. It started with high tech companies, but diverse employers are increasingly aware of the benefits of web based video interviewing. There is consistency—all candidates are asked the same set of questions. Following the interview, hiring managers have the opportunity to replay, review, and rate the interviews online, so they can compare candidates without having to remember who said what or review their notes.[33]

InterviewStream (www.interviewstream.com), is one of the sites used for screening of candidates.

In order to make your video interview most effective, keep these factors in mind:[34]

- *Dress* the same as you would for an in-person interview.
- *Look straight at the camera* when speaking.
- *Use web-based social networking sites* such as MySpace, Facebook, or LinkedIn to promote yourself. Link your interview video to the networking site.

- *Link* your electronic resume to your video so that it can be accessed by a prospective employer.[35]
- *Be professional* and make sure that any photos or video clips used are not outrageous or unprofessional.
- *Search for yourself on Google and Facebook* and eliminate any negative materials.
- *Tailor* your electronic resume and social networking materials to fit that of the organization to which you are applying (e.g., creative to an advertising agency, conservative to legal firms).
- *Use spell check and a grammar program carefully* in preparing your cover letter and resume. Before sending your materials read them aloud. You often catch mistakes when you read aloud. Also, have someone else read the material for spelling and grammar errors.

Virtual Interviews *Virtual interviewing* is another approach to screening job candidates.[36] Some companies have established websites where recruiters and job seekers can create computer-generated images of themselves *(avatars)* and use their computer to navigate through the interview site. When it is the interviewee's turn, he or she enters the "virtual world called Second Life, and meets the interviewees by either typing questions and answers or talking."[37] Much like an online video game, virtual

In virtual conferencing, each participant interacts with others through the use of an avatar, which is a computer user's three-dimensional model or picture which represents himself/herself.

interviewing requires the technical expertise to create your avatar and to be comfortable moving and conversing in this futuristic format. According to a human resource person who has used the process, the advantage over online interviewing is, "You get to know a candidate better. You see what they chose to wear, you see what they laugh at or what they interact with."[38]

Managing a virtual interview takes practice with the browser and software. Despite glitches that you would expect in any computerized format, some technology employers like it because it offers a measure of one's computer expertise and adaptive style.[39]

After the Interview Be sure to respond within 48 hours to the interviewer, with a thank-you e-mail or handwritten note. Include a comment about something you learned from the interview as a way to make your note memorable.[40] As one executive explained, "Whether or not a person follows up an interview promptly is our first screening device."[41] In addition to your note, you can forward or deliver hardcopies of any additional materials, such as examples of your work, a list of references, or other items you discussed during the interview.

Information-Gathering Interview

In an **information-gathering interview**, the interviewer sets out to obtain information from a respondent. This type of interview is important to journalists, law-enforcement authorities, health-care workers, students, businesspeople, and mental health professionals. As a student, for example, you may want to conduct an information-gathering interview to collect data to use in a speech or a term paper. Reporters and news people depend on information-gathering interviews to obtain information.

Conducting an Information-Gathering Interview Information-gathering interviews may be transacted in person, by telephone, or through e-mail. Some guidelines for conducting information-gathering interviews include:

1. *Make an appointment.*
2. *Preplan the questions* you want to ask.
3. *Send your list of queries to the interviewee in advance of the session,* if possible. However, avoid sending the questions if you wish to catch the interviewee off guard and get a spontaneous response.
4. *Use the five-Ws-and-an-H approach* developed by journalists for getting facts: who, what, when, where, why, and how? *Who* has to do with the person or persons involved in an event. *What* asks for a description or explanation of the event. *Where* indicates the place the incident happened. *When* provides such information as the date and time of the occurrence. *Why* is an explanation of the reason the event took place. And *how* centers on the exact details of what occurred.
5. *Actively listen* during the interview. Ask follow-up questions. Make sure that you understand and get all the information you need; you may not be able to do a follow-up session.
6. *Take careful notes.* If you are going to use quoted material, repeat back what the person has said to be certain you have the information correctly recorded. Or

to ensure that you have the exact information, use a digital audio recorder. Be sure to ask permission when you make your original appointment as to whether recording equipment can be used.

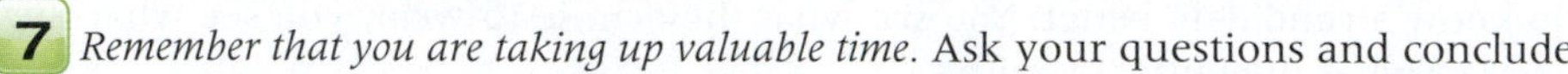

7 *Remember that you are taking up valuable time.* Ask your questions and conclude.

8 *Stay focused.* Be aware that certain people can be highly evasive, hard to pin down. You just have to persevere and keep after them: "I understand what you're saying, but you haven't answered my question." If this person has something to hide or if the information could be used in a legal action, then it well may be impossible to find out exactly what you want.

Being the Subject of an Information-Gathering Interview You may find yourself being asked to give information. If so, be sure that you understand the questions being asked and that you don't feel pressured into answering against your will.

If your employer requires an exit interview when you leave your job, for example, you will be asked to discuss why you are leaving and what problems you see in the organization. You will want to be candid yet tactful in your exit interview. Don't say anything that can be used against you if you plan to list the company on a resume as a source for an evaluation. Be aware that though you may get satisfaction from venting your negative feelings and thoughts, since you won't be at the organization to benefit from the changes that might result from your comments, you gain little except emotional release and the fall out could be great.[42]

If you are a witness, say, to a traffic accident, you may be asked to provide information as to what happened. If you are unable to give facts, make sure the interviewer is aware that you are communicating your opinion. There is a vast difference between saying, "The driver turned left on the red light" and "I couldn't see the light clearly, but I think it was red when the driver turned left." It is advisable, if you know you could possibly be called as a witness, to write down or voice-record everything you can remember as soon as you can, immediately following the incident. Time often alters memory.

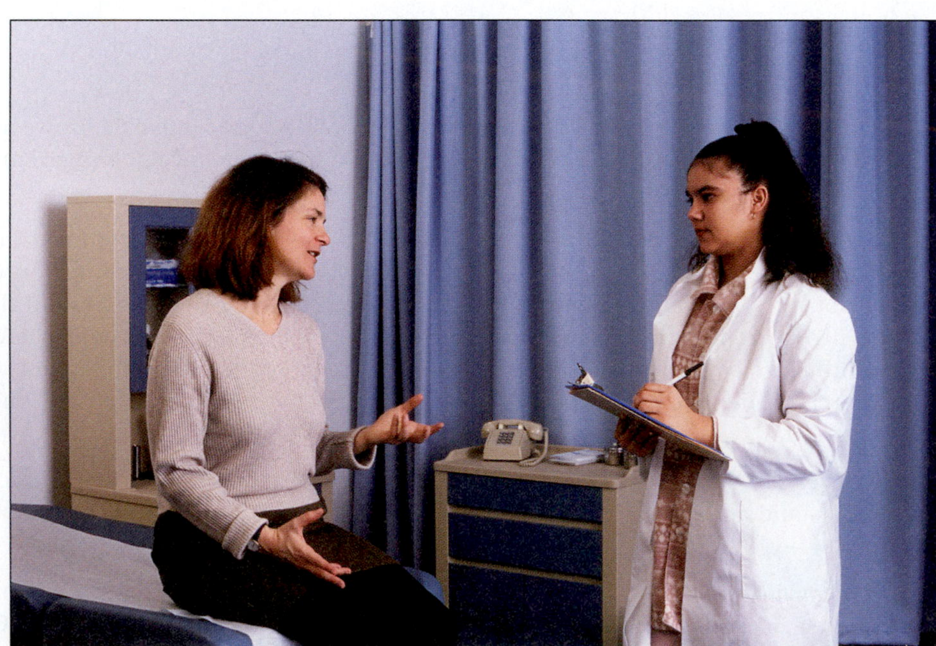

In an information-gathering interview, the interviewer sets out to obtain information from a respondent.

You need to make a decision about what and how much you are willing to share when being interviewed. Do not allow yourself to be pressured into an answer you may regret later. Remember that even in a court of law, you always have the Fifth Amendment right not to reveal information that may be used against you.

As the interviewee, you legitimately may be concerned about how your responses will be used. You may want to stipulate that the information may not be used until you are given a copy of the article or speech in which the ideas are to be used.

Oral History Interview

A valuable application of informative interviewing is the **oral history interview**. It is a way for families to preserve their history by interviewing members of the family who have stories and customs they can share on audio files or DVD. Organizations are using the oral history interview to establish and maintain an archive of people and their stories. Knowledge of historical events is also stored this way, as in the Shoah Project, a series of interviews done with Jewish survivors of the Holocaust.

An oral history is best conducted in an informal atmosphere so that the interviewee feels free to tell his or her story. It's usually important to make a recording of the session in order to preserve the authenticity of the events in the words of the participant. People may experience a sense of discomfort when they know they are being video- or audio-recorded, but most people forget about the mechanical devices once the interview is underway. If, in spite of assurances, the interviewee is still stressed by the presence of the recorder, turn it off, take notes, and try for a recorded session at another time.

Socially COMMUNICATING

Capturing Oral Histories

If you've decided to capture some oral histories, it's good to start with your oldest relatives first. Because most of them won't write down their life stories, they'll need your help. They often lack the writing skills or health, or perhaps even the energy to spend weeks putting their lives on paper or computer. What a blessing it is, then, both for them and for you, to be able to audio- or video-record their life histories.

In speaking to family members:

- Start with a question you know they'll like to answer—you want to relax them quickly.
- Stifle the impulse to interrupt—let the narrator tell his or her story and do your best to simply listen.
- Let there be pauses—you'll often find that the interviewee has something more to say just when you were about to move on to another topic.
- Save questions about details for later—let them answer your broad questions completely before following up with questions about details, clarifications, or possible contradictions.
- Do more than just listen—listen for clues to whole new topics that hadn't occurred to you before; if you don't want to interrupt the flow, jot notes to remind you to get back to these new topics later.
- Pursue truth and accurate information—you might occasionally need to ask a question several different ways or clarify how the interviewer knows something.
- Allow tangents—let them ramble; there can be goldmines in their ramblings and they'll be more natural than if you cut them off.
- Keep your opinions to yourself—this is their interview, not yours.
- Save sensitive matters until late in the interview—if you broach them too early, your interviewee may close up or even end the session.
- Watch for signs that it's time to take a break—look for signs of fatigue and be sensitive to the needs of the interviewee; plan on no more than 2 hours for a session.
- Ask for other family records or a show-and-tell of materials near the end.

Source: "Capturing Oral Histories" from Ancestors: Writing History from www.byub.org. Provided courtesy of BYU Broadcasting, Brigham Young University.

The interviewer should normally start by asking for the person's name, age, and any other relevant background information such as place of birth. Establishing a chronological order, starting as far back as the person can remember, often helps the speaker organize his or her thoughts. This is usually wise when interviewing the elderly, as their long term memory is usually better than their short term memory.

If a pattern is not followed, there is a danger that random ideas may be presented, much history left out, and details omitted. Use prompts such as "What happened next?" is a good device for keeping on a chronological path. If the person objects to this method or can't remember things chronologically, you might try a topical arrangement, such as discussing individuals in the person's life or referring to specific stories you've been told and asking for clarification or amplification.

As the interviewer, you must learn to be comfortable with silence, repetition and confusion. Sometimes people need time to think or to make a decision as to whether they want to share certain information. They also may not remember instantly, or need to say something several times to clarify their ideas.

You should also be prepared to participate in the interview. You might want to model an answer by stating, "I remember a story about how you and your sisters finally got Grandma's Russian tea biscuit recipe written down. I'd love to hear that story again. What happened?" You might be able to fill in any gaps of information by asking questions about things that you've discovered in family documents and genealogy records.

As you proceed with the interview, be aware that an older person might tire easily. If that's the case, divide the session into segments with breaks. Each time you reenter the interview, remind the person what was discussed at the last session. In order to stimulate memory, you might say, "You were saying something about your grandfather Kwan. I'm curious about when he was born and where he grew up."

The conclusion of the oral history interview should include an expression of appreciation and a discussion of what will be done with the information. If it is appropriate, present the interviewee with a final copy of the report or video.

Problem-Solving Interview

In a **problem-solving interview,** the interviewer and interviewee meet to solve a personal or work related dilemma. The end goal is to develop a solution that can solve the problem, won't cause bigger problems, and can be put into effect.

In working toward the solution, the interviewer usually proposes a series of steps to assist in addressing and solving a problem. There are many formats for this to take place. For example, as illustrated in Figure 8.1, "a problem-solving cycle" could be the format employed.

An effective problem-solving format commonly relies on a give-and-take in which the interviewer and interviewee shift roles, following the transactional model of communication. Questions are used to seek information, probe thoughts, and discover points of view.

Socially COMMUNICATING

Helping Others Solve Problems

Would you like to encourage others to work on problems that are bothering them? The key is to get them to open up and express themselves. Here are two approaches:

- Ask open-ended questions—such as those that begin with "what," "which," "why," "how," etc. Also use open-ended comments—such as "Tell me more." Examples:
  —"How do you feel about ...?"
  —"What do you think of ...?"
  —"Give me a complete picture of how you see things."
- Mirror others' feelings by reflecting what they say or imply. Examples:
  —"I sense that you're ..."
  —"When you talk that way, it seems to me ..."

Source: Adapted from Weiss, D. H. (n.d.). *Why didn't I say that?! What to say and how to say it in tough situations on the job*, by AMACOM. American Management Association, 135 W. 50th St., New York, NY 10020.

REFLECT ON THIS: Which of these approaches do you think is best? Why?

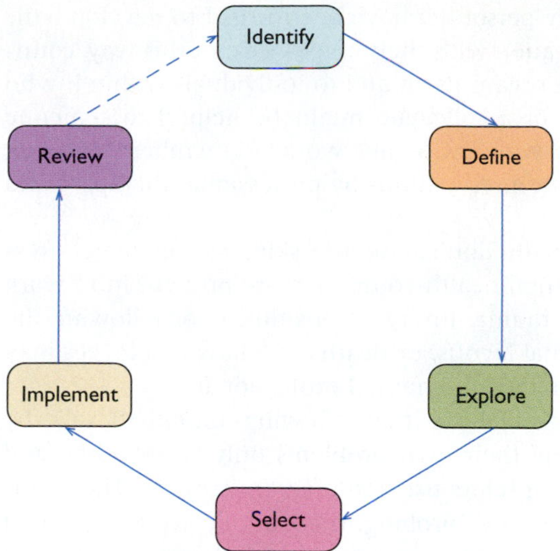

In the first stage — **identify** — recognizes that there is a problem to solve. This may be an emergency or it may be a minor difficulty which has been nagging away for some time; it may not even be a 'problem' but an experiment, an attempt to find out a new way of doing something.

Whatever the initial stimulus, finding a problem then triggers the next stage which is to **define** it more clearly. Here the issue is often to separate out the apparent problem (which may only be a symptom) from the underlying problem to be solved. Defining it also puts some boundaries around the problem; it may be necessary to break a big problem down into smaller sub-problems which can be tackled — 'eating the elephant a spoonful at a time'. It can also clarify who 'owns' the problem — and thus who ought to be involved in its solution, if the solution is to stick for the longer-term.

Having analyzed the nature of the problem, the next stage is to **explore** ways of solving it. There may be a single correct answer, as in crossword puzzles or simple arithmetic — but it is much more likely to be an open-ended problem for which there may be a number of possible solutions. The challenge at this stage is to explore as widely as possible — perhaps through the use of brainstorming or other group tools — to generate as many potential solutions as possible.

Next comes the selection [**select**] of the most promising solutions to try out — essentially the reverse of the previous stage since this involves trying to close down and focus from a wide range of options. The selected option is then put into practice [**implement**]— and the results, successful or otherwise, reviewed [**review**].

On the basis of this evaluation, the problem may be solved, or it may need another trip around the loop. It may even be the case that solving one problem brings another problem to light.

FIGURE 8.1 A Problem-Solving Cycle

Source: Tidd, J., Bessant, J., & Pavitt, K. (2005). *Managing innovation*. Managing-innovation.com. Retrieved from http://www.managing-innovation.com/tools/Problem%20Solving%20Cycle.pdf

Counseling Interview

The **counseling interview** is designed to provide guidance and support to the interviewee. It is used by mental health professionals, friends, managers within organizations, and family members, among others.

One approach to the counseling interview centers on the concept that it should not include any evaluation by the interviewer. Using this approach, in talking to a friend who is doing poorly in school, instead of saying, "You're failing all your classes and the problem is, you are not studying enough," you might say,. "You have been saying that you are failing most of your classes. I've also heard you say that you don't spend much time studying." Such *nondirective techniques*—not taking an active role in a solution or accusing someone of something—can work only if the troubled person accepts that a problem exists, has the skills to identify what is wrong, and wants to deal with it. Realize that no matter how good your intentions are, a person will not do what they don't want to do unless they buy into the process.

In some organizations, supervisory personnel have been urged to develop basic counseling skills to improve communication with their employees. In this way, counseling can provide a service to both the organization and to individuals within it who have particular problems. A manager or a colleague might be helpful to someone who has a problem that is interfering with his or her work. Remember, however, that serious psychological issues warrant interventions by professional therapists and counselors.

Because nontrained persons normally don't have the skills to conduct a stress reducing intervention, professional mental health counselors are brought in to work with personnel who have undergone trauma. Interventions during or following the downsizing of an organization, individual layoffs, or deaths of fellow employees may be required. These types of interventions require mental professionals.

Some mental health professionals believe that allowing unlimited talk by patients who are not capable of solving their own problems only wastes time and leads to even more problems. These counselors use a *directive intervention*: The counselor takes a stand that there should be active probing, that specific activities should be carried on outside the counseling session (e.g., writing a letter to or directly confronting a person who has abused the client), that there should be role playing and activities during counseling (e.g., releasing emotions by envisioning that the victimizer is sitting in a chair nearby so the client can tell the imagined person exactly how he or she feels), and that specific counseling techniques such as therapeutic hypnosis could be used.[43]

Professional therapeutic interviews go through a series of stages: The objectives of the counseling are spelled out; the interviewee elaborates on his or her emotional and logical perceptions of the problem; the problem is explored and the interviewee's perceptions are examined to establish their validity; further probing is done to continue to clarify the problem and the interviewee's perceptions concerning the problem; the interviewee's options are discussed; the options are examined; and a plan of action is put into effect as to what the interviewee will do if necessary. If all the steps have not been accomplished in a single session, further sessions are planned.

Persuasive Interview

The purpose of a **persuasive interview** is to change or reinforce a person's beliefs or behavior. The selection and organization of persuasive points depends on the initial position of the interviewer. If she or he agrees with the interviewee's beliefs or purpose, then the task is to reinforce the agreement. For instance, if a person comes to a volunteer agency already convinced that she wants to volunteer, then the volunteer coordinator does not have to persuade her to give her time to the cause, but may need to persuade her to be dependable in volunteering.

If the interviewee disagrees with the interviewer's beliefs or purpose, then the interviewer should find some points of agreement and try to build on these before leading the interviewee into areas of controversy. For example, a management consultant may have to begin with praise and recognition for some aspect of a company's management program before attempting to persuade its executives that their organization needs to develop better internal communication.

The uncertain or neutral interviewee may require more background information before persuasive appeals can be introduced. If, for example, a voter does not know anything about your preferred candidate for mayor, you will have to provide that person with some background information on the candidate before giving any reasons to vote for her or him.

Compliance-gaining strategies can be used in an attempt to influence people to do what you would like them to do. Among the more familiar techniques are asking for a favor, calling in a debt, and triggering guilt. Health professionals recognize the value of some of these strategies to assure that patients will take the full course of a medication, for instance, by reinforcing how much the patients have at stake in the outcome of the treatment. On the other hand, as many psychologists, teachers, and parents have found out, a student, child, or patient will only willingly do something that they want to do. If forced to take an action against their will, they may rebel in antisocial ways.

Sales Interview The sales process is a persuasive interview. The sales interview process is generally culture specific. The techniques are different according to the cultural group (e.g., nationality, gender, and race). In many Middle Eastern cultures, for example, an exchange of personal information and the establishment of a friendship are imperative for a successful sale. In Turkey, where one of your authors purchased several carpets, the sales process included having tea, talking about families, and then being shown the products. Haggling or negotiation is part of the customs of some cultures, such as those in many parts of Mexico, Arabic countries, and South America, where the buyer and seller are expected to negotiate the final price.

On the other hand, in the United States, Canada, Japan, and most European countries, the procedure is quite different. The **sales interview** usually begins with the salesperson establishing rapport, arousing interest, and getting the customer involved. The salesperson then explores the customer's needs through probing, careful listening, and observing. The next step is to present the product or service and illustrate how it will meet the customer's needs. This is followed by an acknowledgment and responding to of the potential buyer's objections. Finally, on closing the sale, the salesperson reiterates the reasons to decide favorably, asks for a commitment, and paves the way for future business.

If a sales pitch is legitimate, and the product or proposal is going to meet your needs, then your acceptance may be in order. But remember that many salespersons

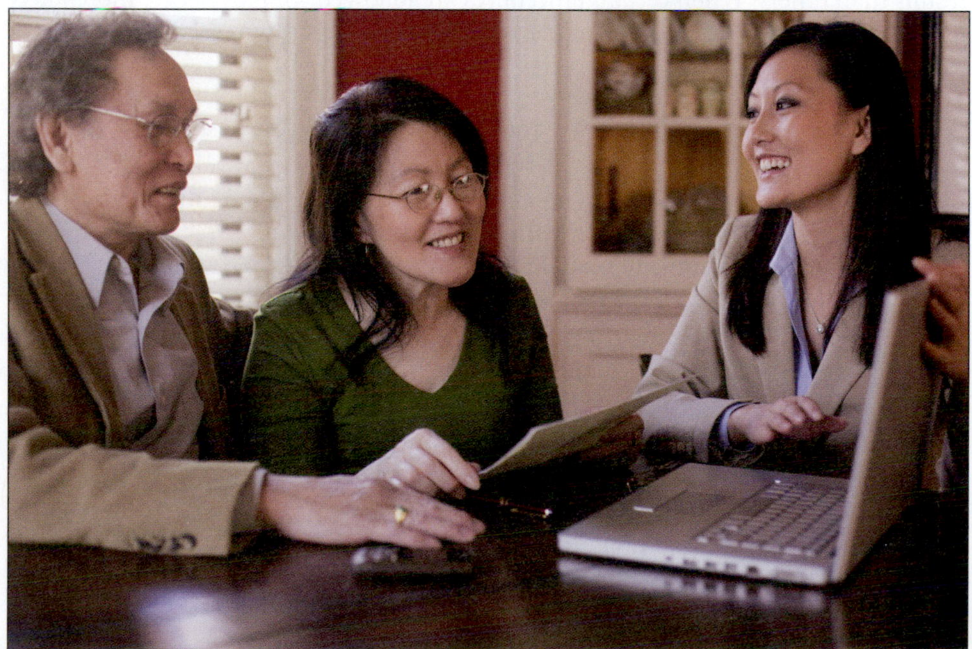

The sales interview usually begins with the salesperson establishing a rapport, arousing interest and getting the customer involved.

are trained to close a sale in order to make a commission or reach a quota; thus, they have strong motivations to do whatever they can to disarm and manipulate you. Don't be intimidated by appeals to guilt (e.g., "I've spent a lot of time with you when I could have been helping other customers, so ...") or pressure (e.g., "This deal is only good for today"). Be especially careful signing contracts, such as a health club membership. Read the contract carefully before you sign it for hidden costs and add-ons. If you don't understand the terms, take the document to a lawyer for clarification.

If you are or become a salesperson, and you want to counter the often negative perception of sales personnel, keep in mind that trust can be built by showing knowledge of the product, concern using sales techniques that are not manipulative, being sincere without being condescending, and showing concern for the costumer's finances and welfare.

Appraisal Interview

In an **appraisal interview**, sometimes referred to as a *performance review,* the interviewer helps the interviewee realize the strengths and weaknesses of his or her performance. In the academic arena, an appraisal interview, for example, takes place when you meet with an instructor to review your English theme, science project, or in-class speech.

In the workplace, employees are often rated on their performance. Many governmental units, business organizations, nonprofit agencies, and educational institutions have formal systems of personnel assessment. Performance appraisal interviews are useful in improving individual performance by (1) clarifying job requirements and standards, (2) providing feedback on an employee's progress in meeting the requirements, and (3) guiding future performance on the job.[44]

Unfortunately, appraisal interviews may be misunderstood, abused, and too frequently used only for negative criticism instead of positive reinforcement. But when handled well, an appraisal interview can present methods for change while reinforcing the positive aspects of a person's performance.

Certain techniques in performance appraisal have been found to yield better results than others. When certain procedures are followed, employees are more likely to view the appraisal process as accurate and fair. These procedures include:[45]

- *Discussion encouragement.* Employees are likely to feel more satisfied with their appraisal results if they have the chance to talk freely and discuss their performances.
- *Constructive intention.* It is very important that employees recognize that negative appraisal feedback is provided with a constructive intention (i.e., to help them overcome present difficulties and to improve their future performance).
- *Performance goals.* Goal setting is an important element in employee motivation. Goals can stimulate employee effort, focus attention, increase persistence, and encourage employees to find new and better ways to work.
- *Appraiser credibility.* It is important that the appraiser (usually the employee's supervisor) be well informed and credible. Appraisers should feel comfortable with the techniques of appraisal, and should be knowledgeable about the employee's job and performance.

As in many phases of organizations, electronic methods have been incorporated into appraisals. One such device, *Halogen eAppraisal,* is intended to enhance the appraisal process and save time and money, while aligning employee goals and developing a high-performing workforce.[46]

Just as it requires skill to present constructive criticism in a performance appraisal, so too does it take ability to receive criticism. Unfortunately, criticism can engender a great deal of defensiveness. People are ego centered; most people have a need to be right. Even when we recognize we are wrong, we may want to defend our actions. Think of some of the tryouts for *American Idol* when the contestants' interviews include not only questioning, but also a display of their singing abilities. Often, when someone receives a negative evaluation they show extreme negative reaction, even when the interviewer, the judges in this case, are clear on why they are giving a negative evaluation.

Performance appraisals, from the viewpoint of the receiver, may be most productive when the interviewee

- *Listens carefully to the criticism.*
- *Paraphrases the criticism.*
- *Asks for specifics.*
- *Monitors nonverbal behavior* and is aware of the physical signs that indicate possible upset: hand twisting, teeth grinding, face flushing, wiggling in the chair or shifting from foot to foot if standing, or feeling sudden tightness in the back of the neck or the temples.
- *Responds by agreeing to take the steps necessary to change the situation*, or, if he or she feels the criticism is not legitimate or beneficial, seeking a different solution or refusing to take the recommended actions and indicating why in a reasonable manner.

Remember that if you refuse to accept the recommendations or input, you may be punished for that action: fired, denied a promotion, put on warning for insubordi-

COMMUNICATING in Careers

If You Must Criticize Someone

Here are some suggestions for giving criticism in a way that motivates others to do a better job:

- See yourself as a teacher or coach—as being helpful. Keep in mind that you're trying to help someone improve.
- Show you care. Express your sincere concern about sharing ways the other person can boost his or her success.
- Pick the right moment to offer criticism. Make sure the person hasn't just been shaken by some incident.
- Avoid telling people they "*should* do such and such" or "*should* have done such and such." "Shoulds" make you appear rigid and pedantic.
- Avoid giving the impression that you're more concerned with seeing your recommendations put into practice than in helping the other person improve.
- Show how the person will benefit from taking the actions you suggest.
- Give specific suggestions. Being vague might only make the situation worse by creating anxiety and doubt.

Tip: Be sure you can take criticism yourself. If not, you may not be perceived as a credible source.

Source: "If You Must Criticize Someone" from *How to love the job you hate* by Jane Boucher. Reprinted with permission of the author. Jane Boucher is an Executive Coach, Professional Speaker, and Author. Contact: Jane@janeboucher.com or 937.416.9881 for more information.

REFLECT ON THIS:

1. What is the hardest part of giving criticism? Why?
2. What is the hardest part of receiving criticism? Why?

nation, or fail a course. Therefore, if you choose to take such an action, be sure you are willing to accept the consequences.

The goal of performance appraisal in any field is to improve performance, but improvement can result only if a specific plan is established during the interview. For this reason, the performance appraisal interview should conclude with a concrete plan in which both parties jointly explore several possible actions; concentrate on one or two specific actions; specify to whom those actions will happen and what will happen; provide for follow-up on the work; and set out in writing the plan to be followed.

Reprimanding Interview

In a **reprimanding interview**, the interviewer helps the interviewee analyze problems caused by the latter so that corrections can be made. A reprimand is usually scheduled after a serious negative incident or after an appraisal interview where the person failed to change the problematic behavior.

The *inverted funnel schedule* is usually most appropriate for a reprimand. In this format, the interview starts with a specific statement of the problematic performance so that there is no question as to what the difficulty is. After revealing the problem(s), the discussion should move to what barriers are interfering with an acceptable level of functioning.

In reprimanding interviews, communicators will want to attempt to avoid accusatory statements and stick to factual statements. They should ask questions that permit each person to express feelings or thoughts, and explain behaviors, stay away from verbalizing conclusions during the body of the interview, and try to conclude the interview on a neutral note.

Because the interviewer can be held legally liable for any type of punishment that is given, she or he must use factual evidence as a basis for any final decision. Common causes of legal actions include statements which indicate sexual bias, age discrimination, and verbal harassment. Asking a neutral party to attend—such as a person from the human resources department—can be a good idea. Evidence should be documented and available for any legal action that may follow.

Interrogation Interview

An **interrogation interview** is designed to secure information from an interviewee through extensive use of probing techniques. Lawyers, credit personnel, tax specialists, and law-enforcement officers use such interviews. Because of the circumstances, the interviewer is sometimes dealing with an interviewee who is reluctant to respond to questions. Consequently, through the phrasing of questions and the manner in which they are verbally and nonverbally presented, the interviewer often uses psychological pressure to elicit responses. Specific types of interrogations include the law-enforcement, security, legal, and media interrogations. Others include the medical and psychological intake interrogations.

Law-Enforcement Interrogation Patrol officers and police investigators are commonly involved with *law-enforcement interrogation*, a format designed to scrutinize an interviewee and, in the case of an arrest, to secure a confession to a crime. As a result, the interviewer may work to create a climate of stress during the interview to pressure the interviewee into admitting wrongdoing.

Investigators who use this interview format must keep their emotions under control throughout the interrogation. Whatever your personal feelings toward the person being questioned, or the conclusion that you have reached, keep those

The courtroom interviewee must be on guard to answer only the questions for which he has factual information.

feelings and thoughts to yourself. In spite of this recommendation, realistically, there are situations in which strong emotions may be required to extract the necessary information.

Because the interviewee in a police investigation is likely to be quite hostile, the questioning strategy is very important. A good interrogator works to break through the hostility and get the information needed to complete the case. The interrogator should begin this process by informing the suspect of his or her rights. The U.S. Supreme Court's far-reaching *Miranda* decision requires that police officers inform suspects that they have the right to remain silent, that anything they say may be used as evidence against them, and that they have a right to have an attorney present at the interrogation.

An interrogator should establish credibility and take control of the situation. By using different types of questions, the officer constructs a picture of the incident depicted by the suspect. Lies are difficult to maintain. By noticing contradictions or improbable statements, an interrogator may be able to undermine the suspect's story, which weakens resistance and self-confidence and makes compliance with the investigator's demands easier.

Interrogation became an issue during the presidency of George W. Bush due to the controversial treatment of prisoners at Guantanamo Detention Center. It was alleged that the tactics being used were illegal and against international law.[47] Forms of interrogation intended to get prisoners to speak and reveal information included water boarding, a controversial interrogation technique that simulates drowning.[48]

It should be noted that interrogation techniques displayed by television and movie detectives and police officers can be misleading. License is often taken with legalities which would not be allowed in real-life situations.

Security Interrogation Interrogation interviews extend to a variety of security interviews. Post-9/11 security needs in the United States increasingly demand that officials put in place security screenings and barriers to ensure the safety of citizens. As a result, you may find yourself to be an "instant interviewee" if stopped by a Transportation Security Association (TSA) employee at an airport screening station. Respond honestly to the questions and try not to "over talk," which is a common pattern of people under stress.

If you are applying for a sensitive position, you might be asked to take a polygraph test. Contrary to what you may be told, it is your option as to whether you desire to subject yourself to the test. In most states, polygraph results are not admissible in court. In addition they have questionable accuracy, but if you refuse to submit yourself to the interrogation you may be thought guilty because of your refusal.

Legal Interrogation Interrogation in court is a firmly established practice. Some trial lawyers attempt to trap a witness by asking questions that elicit information outside his or her factual knowledge. For this reason, witnesses should be on guard so they do not place themselves in the position of answering questions on the basis of opinion rather than proof.

For example, one of your authors appeared as a character witness for a former student who was on trial for possession of illegal drugs. The prosecutor asked, "Do you think that the defendant has ever used drugs?" and "Would you say that there is a drug problem at the school the defendant attended?" In both questions the prosecutor was asking for information beyond the factual knowledge of the witness. The answers given were, respectively, "I have no way of knowing whether the defendant has used illegal drugs," and "I don't know what you mean by 'drug problem,' and if I did, I would have no way of knowing whether the school has such a problem." The witness was not trying to be evasive or hostile, but the questions were posed for the purpose of leading the witness to conclusions that the prosecutor could then use to influence the jury.

The courtroom interviewee always must be on guard to answer only those questions for which he or she has accurate, factual information. Saying, "I think ..." or "I believe ..." or "It could be that ..." may get you in trouble.

Media Interviews

The **media interviews** take place when an interviewer asks questions of a guest. The most popular examples are talk and news show. Formats vary greatly: one guest and one host, one host and open lines for listeners to phone in, or multiple guests with a single or several hosts. Such shows may cover a wide range of topics.

The host's responsibility is to set the format and tone for the program. Some choose the attack-dog approach, others the nice-person role; some are looking for facts, others to incite reaction; some hold strong biases, while others try to be more centrist. There is no one way to format such shows; therefore, the techniques vary greatly. Some hosts ask questions and politely wait for the guest to answer. Others interrupt, badger, and incite. Some hosts insist that all calls be screened; others let any call come through.

If you appear on such a show as a guest, be sure you know and approve of the format. Know if you will be asked to submit questions in advance and whether the host or the listening audience will do the asking. Agree in advance on the topic, and set any guidelines of what subjects you are and are not willing to discuss. Some guests have been amazed by both the type of the questions asked and the manners of those who ask them.

The type of media interview in which most ordinary citizens will participate is the by-stander interview. An incident such as an auto accident or flash mob takes place and you, as a person who happens to be present, is interviewed by a member of the news media. First, determine if you want to be interviewed; realize that you and your answers may appear on television or the radio. If you agree, give factual answers. If asked your opinion, be aware that you could be libel for slander if you defame someone. This is not to say you should not participate, but be aware that your minute of fame may have consequences.

In Conclusion

IN CONCLUSION

The interview is a communication form used extensively to accomplish many goals. Effective participation requires that interviewers and interviewees recognize that an effective interview involves an opening that enables both parties to establish rapport and clarify their objectives, a body of questions and responses that accomplishes the communication objectives, and a closing that concludes the conversation and identifies any further steps to be taken.

Interview communicators participate in many different types of interviews, including the employment, the information-gathering, the oral history, the problem-solving, the counseling, the persuasive, the appraisal, the reprimanding, the interrogation, and the media interview.

LEARN BY DOING

1. Make an appointment with a person who is or was employed in your current career field or desired career. Interview the person to determine what academic courses she or he took to qualify for the job, what specific skills are required for success in the career, what the specific job responsibilities are, and what helpful hints he or she can give you about being successful in the field. Report to the class on both the results of the interview and what you learned about the interviewing process.

2. You are paired with another student according to your academic major. Each student independently researches job descriptions within the field of employment opportunities: communication skills, special talents, and abilities that are needed; types of organizations employing people trained in the field; working conditions; and salary. You are given time to complete your research. You and your partner then conduct a five- to seven-minute information-gathering interview concerning the selected career during one of your class periods. One of you acts as the interviewee and the other as the interviewer. Before the interview, develop an interview agenda and questions. If your professor prefers, the interviews can be audio- or video-recorded and submitted for evaluation.

3. Write down five items you want an interviewer to know about you; then write a sentence about how you plan to convey each of these items. The class is then divided into groups of three, each group having an interviewee, an interviewer, and an observer. After a five-minute interview, the observer states what he or she believes the applicant has communicated. The interviewee shares the list of five items, and then the entire group discusses how the interviewee might have communicated any items he or she failed to get across. Then change roles and repeat the process until all three members of the group have had a chance to be interviewed.

4. You are paired with another student. You are to select a subject of mutual interest and ask each other a series of questions about the topic. You should first ask each other a direct question, then an open question, then a closed question. Repeat the procedure three times to practice the types of questions. Continue the interview by asking a leading question, a loaded question, and a yes-response question. Follow up with a mirror question and a probe.

5. Select an ad from a newspaper or online for a job you would be interested in applying for. It should be one for which you are qualified now. Use the advice given in this chapter on how to prepare to be interviewed, and write a paper with specific examples describing what you would do to get ready for the interview.

6. Your instructor will assign groups of two people in your class various segments of Richard Bolles's *What Color Is Your Parachute?*[49] to read. Each pair conducts an information-gathering interview about the segment read. These interviews may be done in front of the entire class, outside the classroom, or in dyads while the class is in session. If either of the latter is done, each team is asked to share observations in a class discussion after the interviews have been completed.

7. There are numerous family history software programs such as *Reunion, The Family Tree Software* by Leister Productions. Online sites are also of value. For example, search "Oral History Internet Resources" in Yahoo! or Google. The Indiana University Oral History Research Center offers a pamphlet on how to organize and conduct oral history interviews. Using these sources, prepare a list of statements that expand beyond the text's discussion on how to conduct a family history interview. Be prepared to share your list with your classmates.

8. Go to www.western.edu/career/Interview_virtual/Virtual_interview.html, the website of Virtual Job Interviews, and practice your job interviewing skills. Be prepared to participate in a group discussion or to give a short speech about your experience.

KEY TERMS

interview 211
interviewer 211
interviewee 211
interview agenda 211
employment interview 216
behavioral interview 225
employment stress interview 225
information-gathering interview 229
oral history interview 231
problem-solving interview 232
counseling interview 233
persuasive interview 234
sales interview 235
appraisal interview 236
reprimanding interview 238
interrogation interview 238
media interview 240

The Concepts of Groups

group defined • stages of the group process • group decision-making techniques • voting • the role of setting in groups • mediated meetings

CHAPTER 9

After reading this chapter, you should be able to

- Define what a group is and compare and contrast large and small groups
- Explain the advantages and disadvantages of group decision making
- List and define the kinds of groups
- Explain and illustrate the norming, storming, conforming, performing, and adjourning group phases
- Apply the Six-Step Standard for Decision Making and the Berko 1-3-6 Decision-Making Technique
- Define voting and explain the four common voting methods: consensus, majority, plurality, and part of the whole
- Analyze the role of the setting in group actions
- Explain the various types of mediated meetings

Think back over the last several weeks. How often have you been involved in group activities or heard others speaking about attending a meeting of some type? If you are typical, you probably came up with a considerable list. Businesspeople hold conferences, scientists work in teams, educators serve on committees, families meet and discuss mutual joys and problems, students attend classes, and form study groups, citizens serve on juries, and athletes play on teams. All of these are examples of groups in action.

In the United States, people join groups for various reasons. You may join because you are required to do so, such as in a work environment or classroom when there is a group project. You may affiliate because you like the members of the group. This is a common reason that individuals join fraternities or sororities. You may join because you believe in the causes that the assemblage espouses, such as Save the Whales or the Human Rights Campaign. These groups gain membership because of their stances. Some people join because of the meaning or identity a group gives their lives. For example, you might join a particular group because of your philosophical or religious leanings. Some people affiliate because they think they can gain contacts or socialization from the other members. Joining the American Society for Training and Development, for instance, is a way of making business contacts. Facebook can help you connect to others.

Groups Defined

A **group** traditionally has been defined as "a system which is characterized by interconnectedness of its constituent parts [the individuals who make up the group]."[1] A group is more than a collection of individuals. A group has a goal and a purpose, and the members interact with each other.[2] An aggregate of people standing in line at the bus stop is not a group. They do not have a collective goal. On the other hand, the Egyptians who, in 2011, collectively marched against what they thought was the government's oppression, was a group, since the assemblages had a purpose and the participants influenced each other.

Groups often are classified by their size. **Small groups** usually consist of three to twelve persons; **large groups** normally have more than a dozen. Research shows that participation rates are affected significantly by differences in group size. For example, six-person juries offer greater vocal participation than do twelve-person juries.[3]

Group Versus Individual Actions

Groups, by the very nature of their collective identity, offer participants both advantages and disadvantages over working alone.

Advantages of Groups

The group process provides an opportunity for input from many people with different points of view. Groups also offer the advantage of challenging ideas before they are put into action. Since a group may be composed of people with varying backgrounds and interests, an idea probably will receive the scrutiny of many evaluators before it receives group acceptance. Because any one person's experiences are limited, the aggregate viewpoints should result in a better thought-out decision. Groups can help individuals resolve conflict and feel a part of an organization.[4] Social networking groups such as those formed on Facebook, can help individuals create social capital through their connections. Individuals may develop better social relationships (bonding) or a broader network of resources through people (bridging relationships).[5]

In addition, taking part in group action can lead to greater commitment among participants to the decisions reached. Workers who discuss new procedures, for instance, may approach their tasks of producing or selling products or services with more enthusiasm because they helped to develop the procedures.

The *risky shift phenomenon* maintains that decisions reached after discussion by a group display more experimentation, are less conservative, and contain more risk than decisions reached by people working alone before any discussion is held. A group of managers who come together to solve a problem of worker morale, for instance, is more likely to adopt a more creative strategy than any manager acting alone.[6]

Disadvantages of Groups

Although the group process offers important advantages, it also has some disadvantages. For example, group decision making takes much longer than individual decision making because there are discussions among many people with diverse points of view. The group process also requires participants to give up some individuality for the purpose of compromising with other group members.

Yet another disadvantage of the group process may surface when people blindly commit themselves to group cohesion at the expense of careful analysis. This phenomenon, **groupthink** is "the mode of thinking that persons engage in when concurrence-seeking becomes so dominant in a cohesive in-group that it tends to override realistic appraisal of alternative courses of action."[7]

Although it happened over half a century ago, the disastrous Bay of Pigs invasion in Cuba in 1961 is still considered a classic example of groupthink. President Kennedy's group of advisers blended so well as a group that they felt that any negative comments about the proposed action would be perceived as being so disloyal to the group that even those who disagreed didn't speak up.

The decision of the George W. Bush administration in 2003 to attack Iraq was another example of groupthink.[8] The president had surrounded himself with a vice president and cabinet members who were hawkish and pro-war. Condoleezza Rice, who was appointed as Secretary of State during George W. Bush's second term as president, in testimony before the 9/11 commission in 2004, stated, "What emerged [at that time] was a picture of an organization with great discipline and a strong belief in orderly structures and clearly articulated concepts and policies. But it is also a top-down bureaucracy, with little capacity for hearing variant viewpoints or testing its theories against the practical wisdom of front-line operatives."[9]

To prevent groupthink:[10]

- Recognize the problem of groupthink and that it stems from pressure to conform to group norms.
- Seek information that challenges an emerging concurrence.
- Develop a norm in the group that legitimizes disagreement.
- Be aware that although cohesion is normally a positive aspect of group maintenance, the more cohesive a group is, the greater is the danger of groupthink.

Members of any group must be aware that although participation in the decision-making process can lead a person to greater commitment to his or her work or to the decision made, in some cases social loafing may take place. *Social loafing* occurs when group membership leads people to work less than they would individually. An individual who thinks that his or her own contribution to the group cannot be measured may tend to slack off.[11] A problem sometimes confronted by students is their participation in a group project in which one or more members do all the work, with social loafing being practiced by the rest. The question arises about who should and should not get credit for the final outcome of the project when social loafing takes place.

Types of Groups

We communicate in various types of groups, including work teams, study groups, support groups, committees, focus groups, families, public meetings, and town meetings. As you consider these types of groups, realize that each type may exist partially or totally in a virtual environment.

Work Teams

In the professional setting, people may be involved in a number of groups. One of the most prevalent groups in U.S. industry is the **work team**: small groups of workers who function as teams to make and implement decisions about their own work.[12]

As organizations work to accomplish their goals, they have found, based on the success of the Japanese and the Swedes, that it is important to set up work teams. For a work team to achieve its goals, management must commit to empowering the

COMMUNICATING in Careers

Work Groups: How to Get Hot

Unlike most work teams, *hot groups* become so emotionally involved with their task that they actually behave like people in love. The excitement of the task and the interaction that comes with it can be an enormous turn-on. As a result, hot groups often set performance records and even volunteer for extra work.

Sounds like every manager's dream—but there's a catch. Such groups are hard to create, and when they do arise they are often short-lived. Their unorthodox work habits and tendency to isolate themselves from the parent organization can incense management, hastening their demise.

But other times they hit the jackpot. Consider Apple Computers, started by a hot group of free-spirited twenty-somethings striving to build a computer for the masses rather than large businesses. Taking on corporate goliath IBM spurred them to create the revolutionary Macintosh.

Alas, there's no simple formula for spawning hot groups. Like hothouse flowers, they're exquisitely sensitive to their environment and wilt for no apparent reason. But you can optimize conditions for their growth:

- *Offer workers a thrill.* Crises and intense competition are the most powerful external motivators of hot groups. Any provocative project, however, can excite passion and intensity.
- *Feed the soul.* Hot groups are inspired by the search for truth and the feeling that they're making a difference. "Their task has to have meaning to people, society, and the organization. That's why hot groups are particularly common in research institutions.
- *Provide a connective leader.*—Such leaders are willing to share both the work and the glory.
- *Banish bureaucracy.* Freedom is essential for hot groups. Workers quickly lose enthusiasm when entangled in red tape.

Source: "Work Groups: How to Get Hot" from *Business communication in a changing world* by Roy Berko, Andrew Wolvin, and Rebecca Ray.

team: training the members to work in a group and allowing the group the time to carry out its functions and the decisions it makes.[13] Organizations have found that the use of work teams leads to improved employee morale, greater responsiveness to and flexibility in meeting customer needs, and better quality of services and production of goods.

Study Groups

Study groups are established to enable individuals to work together to study and learn with the assistance of others. Students planning to take the Graduate Record Examination or LSAT (Legal SAT) for example, often join together to work toward learning the materials on the test.

To be productive, a study group should follow some basic principles. These include:

- Limit the participants.
- Meet on a regular basis in a location that lends itself to studying, not to socializing or interruptions, and insist that smartphones be turned off.
- Insist that all members of the group attend all meetings and participate.
- Require that each member be prepared for sessions.
- Allow each member to take a turn in leading and providing explanations.

Support Groups

A **support group** is a system that allows people to interact with others who share similar goals or problems. The purpose of a support group is to increase people's knowledge of themselves and others, assist people in clarifying the changes they most want to make in their lives, and give people some of the tools necessary to make these changes.[14] Support groups may be face-to-face or online.[15]

Study groups enable individuals to work together and to learn with the assistance of others.

People come together in groups to cope with a wide variety of issues, including dealing with preventive and remedial aims (e.g., Alcoholics Anonymous), learning coping skills (Adult Children of Alcoholics), offering support for grieving (Mended Hearts), and being the parent or friend of a gay man, lesbian, or transgendered person (P-Flag). Support groups can be particularly effective online because participants are not bound by geographical location, and the online discussion offers a sense of anonymity.[16]

In the counseling setting, support groups may be more effective than individual counseling because groups can provide the empathy and knowledge of other people who have had similar experiences and can share their thoughts and feelings.[17] Support groups are considered an effective means for working through trauma caused by rape, incest, physical abuse, battering, physical illness, and phobias. In a landmark study, a Stanford University doctor found that "women with advanced breast cancer who attended weekly support group meetings lived twice as long as women with the same diagnosis who did not participate in support groups."[18]

Committees

Most organizations rely heavily on committees. Because it is often difficult for a large group of people to accomplish much more than voting on policy matters, it may become necessary to send certain tasks to a **committee**: a small group responsible for study, research, and recommendations about an issue. The committee's actions usually are brought back to a larger group for action. Unfortunately, some individuals use the "refer to committee" technique as a ploy to make sure the issue is never discussed again. They know that referring a subject to committee often means no one will actually deal with it or that it will be forgotten.

To ensure that committees work effectively, these guidelines may help:

- Have clear objectives.
- Include diverse members.

One of the most prevalent groups in industry is the work team.

- Be sure that everyone is allowed a voice in the deliberations.
- Balance the needs of the committee with the needs of the rest of the organization.
- Cooperate and work as a team.
- Assume the responsibility for study, review, guidance, direction, and evaluation, but allow the implementation to be handled by management.

Focus Groups

Organizations often have to discover information to help lead them to make decisions. One of the ways, for example, that advertising agencies discern market trends, logo favorites, or attitudes of particular potential groups of consumers is to use **focus groups**,[19] which are designed to test reactions to a particular product, process, or service offered by an organization. A randomly selected group of participants who are representative of the user or consumer group are brought together with a professional facilitator to discuss, for example, a new product. The reactions are carefully recorded and quantified in a report to the organization as input for decision making. Before advertisements are released for viewing they are often evaluated by a focus group, composed of individuals who represent the demographic description of the desired audience.

The Family as a Group

Although you may not have ever thought of it as such, the family is a group.[20] Families are groups operating as a system by the very nature of their purposes and functions: decision making, interpersonal relationships, and mutual dependency.

A *family* is an assemblage of people who have legally been declared a group or who have defined themselves as such. Typical kinds of families are natural families (a married couple with or without children), blended families (families created by divorce and remarriage or death and remarriage), single-parent families (one parent with a child or children), extended families (a cluster of relatives who may also

Families are groups operating as a system.

COMMUNICATING in Careers

A Business Professional Shares Her View on Work and Groups

As a qualitative research consultant, I work for companies all over the country in their development of product lines and/or their advertising campaigns. In addition to in-depth interviewing, I make extensive use of focus groups to get reactions of typical consumers to proposed products or ads. The focus groups are an important part of my work, because the dynamics of the group enables me to get to a deeper level of response from the representative participants. I find that the synergy of the group helps the individual participants respond to products or ads both in the thinking and the feeling levels.

Source: "A Business Professional Shares Her View on Work and Groups" from *Business communication in a changing world* by Roy Berko, Andrew Wolvin, and Rebecca Ray. Copyright © 1997 by Bedford/St. Martin's. Reprinted with permission of the publisher. All rights reserved.

REFLECT ON THIS:

1. How do you think synergy helps in generating feedback?
2. Do you think that focus groups are of any real help to advertising and product development companies?

include friends), and self-declared families (e.g., heterosexuals living together, homosexuals living together, communal groups, religious cults).

There is no one best way for a family to operate. Some families learn to operate under stress and chaos. Some have open channels of communication and operate in cooperative harmony. Most family communication follows a structure that resembles a sculptural mobile. The parts (family members) are segments of the same unit, and any reverberation of a problem goes through the system and throws off the mobile's balance. How well the family functions depends on the members' abilities to communicate with one another and balance the various parts of the system. (See Figure 9.1.)

Family discussions center on answers to basic communication questions. What are members allowed to talk about (e.g., death, alcohol use, sex, money)? What words can be used to talk about certain subjects (e.g., death is "passed on"; alcoholism is "Daddy is sick")? Where can members talk (e.g., in the kitchen, in the bedroom, "only in our own house—this is nobody else's business")? Who can talk about it (e.g., mother and father only; father talks, others listen)?

Most families typically enforce rules randomly and lack consistency in their methods of operation. In some families, however, rules of communication are established and upheld at all costs, resulting in praise, cooperation, abuse, punishment, and/or banning.

Public Meetings

In addition to the use of internal group interactions, some organizations find it necessary to conduct **public meetings**, in which members or interested individuals may attend the sessions. Corporations must hold stockholders' meetings. Government organizations, such as school boards and city councils, may need to conduct their meetings in public to ensure that the decisions they reach are in the best interests of the public they serve and to fulfill the legal requirements of many states to hold open meetings.

Public meetings can follow a number of formats. The members may discuss the issue among themselves and then let the audience ask questions. Or there may be a series of experts or witnesses in a **symposium** format, in which participants give prepared speeches with no interaction among themselves or with the audience. These presentations are often followed by a **forum**, a question-and-answer session during which the participants field questions from each other as well as from any audience that is present.

Public meetings require skillful moderating. It is important not to let just the most outspoken people dominate a discussion so that only one point of view is expressed. "It is imperative that a diversity of participation take place in order to lend credibility to the final decisions or actions."[21] This interaction can be done by having clear rules that indicate who can speak, how long he or she can speak, and how the process of keeping the meeting in order will be implemented. Most public meetings operate under *parliamentary procedure*, most commonly those practices set forth in *Robert's Rules of Order*. It is wise to have a parliamentarian present, a person well versed in the rules of order and meeting management, to assist the group in following the rules.

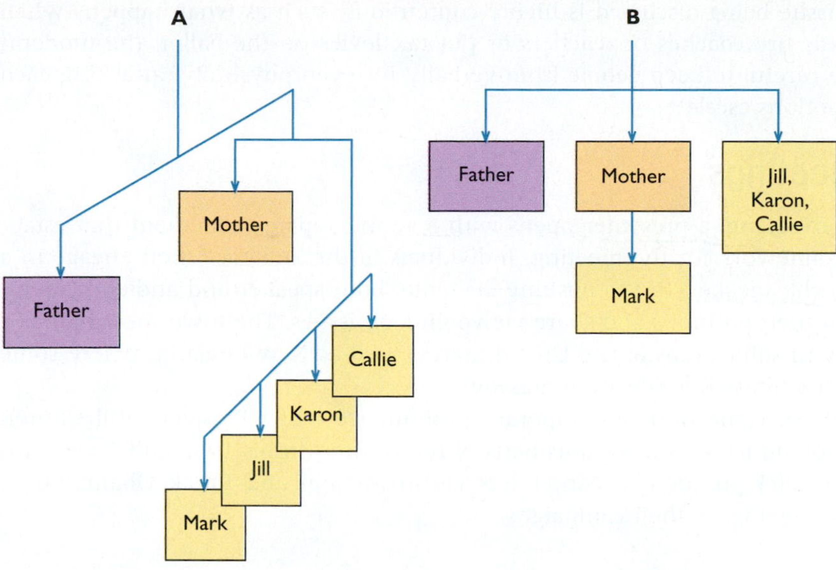

FIGURE 9.1 A Sculptural Drawing of a Family System
Each member of a family is important in developing the group's system. In an unbalanced system (A), for instance, as illustrated in this mobile, John (the father) has a total power. He controls the finances and is an alcoholic whose actions dominate the group's actions. Members of the family are in constant turmoil trying to live in a system where chaos reigns due to John's erratic behaior.

In example (B), Maria, John's wife, and Mark, his son, have formed an alliance to keep peace and harmony in the family, making sure that John's actions have less influence. They have worked with a counselor to get John to join Alcoholics Anonymous. Jill, Karon, and Callie, the three youngest daughters, have little real power, but their presence is important, for John has been made to feel guilty concerning his former physical abuse of the young girls. This system functions because the family members have worked out a pattern for how the rules, customs, and traditions of the group will work, thus the mobile is in balance.

Some families learn to operate under stress and chaos.

If the issue being discussed is highly contentious, such as what happens when school boards fire coaches or teachers or put tax levies on the ballot, the moderator must be careful to keep people from verbally (or even physically) attacking each other as emotions escalate.

Town Meetings

In a **town meeting**, a presenter opens with a short prepared statement that establishes the framework for the meeting. Individuals in the audience then engage in a forum with the speaker. In the ensuing dialogue, both speaker and audience members explain their positions and share viewpoints on issues. The town meeting has a long history in some areas of the United States, such as New England, where some communities still use it for decision making.

The format came into contemporary prominence when President Bill Clinton conducted town meetings in various parts of the country in his 1992 and 1996 campaigns. The 2008 presidential contenders (John McCain and Barak Obama) used many town meetings in their campaigns.

Group Operations

As groups operate, they are continually evolving. Normally they go through six phases: forming, norming, storming, conforming, performing, and adjourning.[22]

Group Forming

Groups start by going through a process known as *group forming.* The membership can come together because they are appointed to accomplish a task. A supervisor, for instance, may want a selected number of her employees to develop a set of guidelines for conducting a survey. Groups can assemble because some individuals have a common mission they wish to accomplish and bring together a number of people to carry out the task. For example, the groups formed spontaneously through the messages sent via Facebook and on Twitter in Egypt and Libya during the 2011 uprisings, were flash mobs formed for a purpose.

Group Norming

Group norming occurs when people in a group establish rules and procedures, as well as get to know the other members.

During this stage, *group norms*—the rules by which the group will operate—are developed. The obligations of the members, what they can and can't do, and the mode of operation are decided. These norms can be explicit (written and agreed on, as in a constitution) or implicit (understood but not formalized).[23]

The source of the group's norms may be influenced from outside the group. They may be rules preset by others, such as when a local chapter of a sorority is given rules by the national organization; developed by group members based on their past experiences or through trial and error; or influenced by a member or leader who has either experience in the group process or strong enough persuasive skills to influence others. Whatever the means, setting boundaries is a critical group function.

Group procedures that should be determined include:[24]

- *Plan an agenda.* Group meetings normally follow an *agenda:* a list of the topics to be discussed or the problems that must be dealt with in the order in which they will be acted on.

Normally groups go through six phases: forming, norming, storming, conforming, performing, and adjourning.

- *Handle routine housekeeping details.* Such details include taking attendance and agreeing on the rules for decision making.
- *Prepare for the next meeting.* An ongoing group must decide when it will reconvene. It is sometimes necessary to designate who will be responsible for certain details for the next session.

Group Storming

Although it might be ideal, and make group decision making much easier, groups seldom work toward their goal without some disagreements. Most groups, during either the process of setting rules or working toward their goal, enter into a period called **group storming**, when conflicts erupt. The disagreements may be caused by a power struggle among those interested in being the leader, conflict over the rules of operation, or personality conflicts among group members. Conflict can develop in support groups too, over issues about criticism and the value of allowing disagreement in face-to-face or online discussions.[25]

Storming can be a positive aspect of group operation since it often alerts the group to underlying problems. It brings the conflicts into the open, allows the members to possibly deal with them, and can permit the establishment of an open communication environment. Although storming is common, don't assume that something is wrong if a group you are in doesn't go through storming. Just be sure that the lack of storming is not caused by groupthink (see pages 245–246).

Types of Group Tension Two types of social tensions are at the base of storming. *Primary group tension* refers to the normal jitters and feelings of uneasiness that group members experience when they first congregate. Think of an experience you've had when entering a group for the first time—for example, entering a class on the first day or going to work on a new job. Group interaction at this point is usually of low intensity. Often there are periods of silence, discussion of frivolous topics, tentative statements, and members being overly polite. Interruptions tend to evoke apologies. There is a tendency, especially among European Americans, to want to get through this "meaningless stuff" quickly and get down to business. However, people in other cultures are interested in this relationship stage and are willing to put time into it. It is fairly common in Japan and in Arabic countries, for example, for social interactions to take initial precedence over getting down to work.

Your strategy as a competent communicator is not to avoid primary tension but to let it take its natural course. Primary tension tends to be short-lived and cause for little concern unless it escalates to an unmanageable level. With time, it normally disappears.

The other type of social tension is referred to as *secondary group tension;* it is the stress that occurs within a group later in its development. Frequent causes of this problem are having to make a decision, shortage of time to accomplish the task, differences of opinion, and difficult members.

Signs of secondary tension include abrupt departure from the group's routine, a sharp outburst by a member, a sarcastic comment, or hostile exchanges between members. Extreme secondary tension can be unpleasant. If it is left uncontrolled, the group's existence may be threatened. By seeing other group members as your peers, you may be able to effectively resolve tension.[26] The goal is not to eliminate the tension, but to use it in a positive way. Tension can be energizing—a source of creative thinking—and, if effectively dealt with, can bring a group together.

Role of Power One of the major triggers of storming is the role of power. *Power* is the ability to influence another's attainment of goals. Power can center on controlling another person or persons, influencing the efforts of others, and/or accomplishing a goal.

All groups have a power structure. It is usually held by one person, but it may be shared, such as the co-captains of a football team. The person may exert power because he or she has information or expertise that will allow the group to reach its goal. For example, a group dealing with a financial crisis may turn for advice to the person most knowledgeable about economics. In some cases, power centers on legitimate authority. The person who is appointed chairperson of the committee by the company president holds the position legitimately and therefore can act as the leader no matter what the feelings of the group. Sometimes the power figure has the ability to give rewards or punishments. A parent, for instance, often has the ability to decide on allowances and curfew times, thus putting her or him in a control position over children.

Another type of power centers on personal qualities. Some people have the likeability to become a power source. It is believed that our most effective leaders, whether presidents or athletic coaches, are those who get others to follow them because of their charisma.[27]

The person(s) who holds power may exert it in a positive way by helping the group come to good decisions. On the other hand, some leaders are tyrants (e.g., World War II German dictator Adolf Hitler), whose main interest is in controlling others. Or they may be incompetent or have psychological problems that interfere with their exerting positive leadership.

Unresolved Storming Do not assume that all groups make it through the storming stage. Some find that because of poor leadership, the personalities of the members, the inability to decide on norms, or the lack of clarity of purpose, they simply cannot work their way through storming. In this case, the group may disband, continue to operate in a storming fashion, or members gradually fade away and the group folds when members stop coming to meetings because nothing is being accomplished.

Storming Strategies In order to deal with storming so that it does not remain an unresolved issue, consider following these guidelines:

- *Provide a get-acquainted period* before the first meeting so that group members meet each other informally.
- *Schedule an informal chat period* before each meeting so that there is no pressured interaction among participants.
- *Remind the group that disagreement can help* to achieve a superior outcome and that the purpose of the assemblage is to achieve the group goal, not individual goals.
- *Tolerate, even encourage, disagreement and deviance.* The trick is to keep disagreement within tolerable limits. Be aware, however, that some people can't tolerate any disagreement. They may have a history of physical or verbal abuse and panic when bickering starts, fearing it will escalate into a full-fledged war. Others have been brought up to avoid fighting at all costs.
- *Use humor*, joking, and shared laughter to lighten the mood, if appropriate.
- *Stick to attacking the issues*, not the person who disagrees with your stand. Don't keep repeating the same argument over and over.
- *Be an active listener.* Even though you have a clearly defined viewpoint, be aware that the other person believes his or her viewpoint is as valid as yours. If you really listen, you might find that the other's view has some validity.
- *Look for possible places to compromise.* Be careful, however, that in reaching a compromise, you don't water down the solution so much that it will not achieve its goal of relieving the problem.
- *Monitor the leadership.* If it is efficient, good. If not, work for change by replacing the leader, develop new rules of operation, or trying to negotiate for a change in the way the leader operates.

Group Conforming

Groups that work their way through the storming stage are those that can go on to work together. This coming together is called *group conforming*. The group will know that it is in the conforming stage when such issues as norms, the group's purpose, and how to handle the role of power have been settled. The group is now ready to work toward the agreed-on mission, recognizing that it may revert back to storming and will then have to work again toward conforming.

Group Performing

Group performing is the action stage of group process. During this phase, the members clearly start to work toward goals. They have developed a history and know each other, have worked out their mode of operation, and have agreed to move forward to accomplish their task and maintenance roles.

All decision making in a group is influenced by both task and maintenance dimensions. These are not independent entities that stand in opposition to each other; they are interrelated.

The *task dimension of groups* includes decision making, informing, appraising and examining, problem solving, and creating interest in staying on track. Some consider accomplishing the goal the entire purpose of the group and concentrate solely on making sure that the group stays "on task." However, most groups also need to attend to the *maintenance dimension of groups:* meeting the interpersonal needs of the members. The main purpose of maintenance is developing *group cohesion:* the interconnectedness of the members.

As social beings, most people like to be with others, interact with them, and express opinions and feelings. Ignoring these aspects of group process by concentrating only on task functions can lead to an empty experience for some of the participants.

Group Adjourning

Groups may also find it necessary to go through *adjourning:* going out of existence. In business settings, certain groups are constituted to accomplish a particular task. At the completion of the task, the group disperses. Study groups are formed to prepare the participants for a test or complete a project. Once the task is completed, the group's purpose is completed. Such adjourning requires no specific action other than awareness that the task is done.

On the other hand, some groups have no specific end goal but are ongoing as they keep in existence by continuing to perform their duties (e.g., groups such as fraternities, sororities, and service clubs have the objective of continuing to work forever). But even these groups may come to an end. Members may lose interest; people may leave the organization, therefore depleting the membership; or group members determine that the group no longer has a purpose. In these cases, the members vote the group out of existence or simply stop holding meetings. It is advisable that group members take formal action to bring the group to an end. Otherwise, they may think that they have not reached a true ending and feel incomplete, similar to not completing the process of saying good-bye to someone who dies suddenly.

Making Group Decisions

One of the most prominent functions of the group communication process is decision making. Traditionally in the European American culture, effective decision making tends to follow a step-by-step procedure that allows group members to explore the dimensions of a problem, seek out solutions, and select a solution the members think is most appropriate.

Developing a process leads a group to consider the rules of operation to be followed to reach decisions. Formal organizations, such as city councils and sororities and fraternities, develop a constitution and bylaws clearly spelling out procedures. A set of parliamentary guidelines, such as *Robert's Rules of Order,* usually is adopted as a framework for handling procedural agreements and disagreements.[28] Individuals who chair formal meetings should learn these rules of order. Less formal organizations may allow the leader of a group to determine the operational procedures. Whatever method is used, however, it should be agreed on before any formal work is undertaken how action will occur.

Formulating an Agenda

For the members of a group to be aware of the order in which items will be handled, an **agenda**—the order of business for a meeting or discussion—is prepared. It allows the group to cover topics systematically and accomplish the task in the most efficient way possible. An agenda should be used like a road map. It should contain just enough detail to allow the group to travel the path to the task but should not be so rigid that it does not allow for any detours.

Most meetings follow an agenda to complete the group's business. A common format is:

I. Calling the meeting to order
II. Reading the minutes of the previous meeting
III. Presenting committee reports
IV. Discussing unfinished business
V. Proposing new business
VI. Adjourning the meeting

Sometimes the agenda specifies not how the meeting should be run but rather how to go about solving a specific problem. The participants start their work by wording a *discussion question*—the issue or problem that will be dealt with. For example, if the group's purpose is to decide what type of grading system should be used on campus, the question could be "What should be done to solve the problem of inconsistent grading policies on campus?"

Some guidelines are useful for wording a discussion question:

- *Propose the issue in a question form.* Since the major issue of a problem-solving discussion is a question of what the group should do to solve a problem, the discussion should center on answering the question.
- *Keep the question clear and short.*
- *Word the question so that it does not show bias.* You cannot honestly discuss a question that states the expected conclusion.
- *Word the question as an open-ended question so that it cannot be answered with a yes or no.* Allow for other alternatives.

In some instances, the group is formed because the dilemma is clear and the group's task is to solve the wording of the problem. On the other hand, some groups may be given a general idea of what is wrong and need to begin by formulating a specific discussion question. One way to plan a discussion question is for each member to prepare one in advance. Then the group can meet to share individual questions and blend them into a question on which the group can agree. No discussion of the issues should take place while the question is being determined.

When the question is agreed on, a format for a discussion is in order. This step in the process involves developing a discussion agenda. Assume that you are in a group that is going to discuss the question "What can be done at XYZ Corporation to solve the problem of computer hardware and software incompatibility?" Your problem-solving agenda could look like this:

I. What is the problem?
    A. What terms do we need to know to deal with the problem?
        1. What is computer hardware and software?
        2. What is meant by computer hardware and software incompatibility?

B. How does this problem concern us?
   1. As professionals?
   2. As consumers?

II. What are the causes of the problem?
   A. Is the desire for profits the cause of computer hardware and software incompatibility?
      1. Is competition among leading companies a cause of incompatibility?
      2. Is the purposeful creation of more profitable products a cause of incompatibility?
   B. Does the swiftly growing and changing nature of computer design cause incompatibility?
   C. Does a lack of standards contribute to incompatibility?

III. What are possible solutions?
   A. Would government guidelines bring about greater compatibility?
   B. Would public encouragement of hardware and software compatibility solve the problem?
   C. Would forming a group of manufacturers bring about greater compatibility?
   D. Could groups dedicated to enforcing standards solve the problem?

IV. What is (are) the best solution(s)?
   A. Which of the solutions proposed is workable?
   B. Which of the solutions proposed is desirable?
   C. Which of the solutions proposed is practical?

V. How can the best solution(s) be put into effect?

Following such an agenda allows for complete discussion and contributes to a well-thought-out solution.

Voting

In addition to developing a system for conducting business and arriving at results, a group has responsibilities for determining how decisions will be made by members. **Voting** takes place when members are given an opportunity to indicate agreement, disagreement, or no opinion on an idea or candidate. The purpose of voting is to ensure that members know the outcome of the discussion and the decision made. It is imperative that the method of voting be agreed on before the group starts working toward the solution to avoid conflict when it comes time to vote.

There are four common voting methods:

1. *Consensus.* The word *consensus* means "all."[29] Thus, in a consensus decision, every member of the group must agree on a proposal before it can be put into action. This is often the method used for decisions in which dire consequences can result from the outcome of the action. For example, most juries operate by consensus. In consensus, a member not voting is considered the same as a negative vote, as it stops an "all in favor" outcome. The terms is often misused to indicate general agreement.

2. *Majority vote.* Majority vote is often misunderstood. It does not solely mean more than half. In *majority voting,* the winner must receive more than half of the votes, excluding those who do not vote or who abstain (i.e., do not want to vote).[30] For example, if there are ten people in a group and all vote, it will take six votes for a majority to rule. If, however, one of the people abstains, then it will take five votes for passage according to the majority method.

Voting takes place when members are given an opportunity to indicate agreement, disagreement, or no opinion on an idea or candidate.

3 *Plurality.* The word *plurality* means "most."[31] Often when more than two options are available, a group may turn to plurality voting. If, for example, three candidates are running for an office, in plurality voting the one getting the most votes is declared the winner. In the same way, if five ideas have been proposed as solutions to a problem, the solution selected will be the one receiving the greatest number of votes.

4 *Part-of-the-whole voting.* This method occurs when a specific number or percentage of those who are eligible to vote is required to bring about some action. For example, some of the rules of operation of an organization can be changed only if 75 percent of those eligible to vote agree to the change. A group has the right to set any number or percentage it wishes to allow action to take place. These numbers need to be set before starting the decision-making process.

The method selected for voting can have a profound effect on the outcome of a proposed action. In a historic case, the proposed federal Equal Rights Amendment was not enacted as a U.S. constitutional change, even though more than a majority of the states approved its inclusion. This happened because the part-of-the-whole method was used, and a two-thirds vote by the states' legislatures was needed but was not obtained. Thirty-five states ratified, three short of the required number. If a majority voting system had been used, the amendment would have passed. Juries, which use consensus, require all twelve jurors to agree on the vote. If the vote is eleven to one, which is clearly a majority, there is no decision. This lack of ability to reach a consensus results in a "hung" jury, one unable to reach a decision.[32]

Decision-Making Techniques

In European American culture, there are a number of approaches to structuring a decision-making discussion. All of these center on two concepts. First, "effective group decision-making requires an analysis and understanding of a problem before members search for solutions,"[33] and, second, "effective decision-making groups normally engage in creative exploration of unusual, even deviant, ideas during initial discussions."[34] These two steps ensure that the group works toward solving an agreed-on problem and that all the resources and creativity of the members are used. Two methods of decision making are the Six-Step Standard Agenda and 1-3-6.

Six-Step Standard Agenda for Decision Making

The *Six-Step Standard Agenda for Decision Making*[35] is a direct outgrowth of the traditional reflective-thinking process, which stresses that a problem be identified and analyzed, solutions sought, and a solution selected and implemented.[36] The procedure for this method is comprised of six steps:

Step 1: Problem identification. A question is worded that states the problem. The query may be a *question of fact* (whether something is true, and to what extent); a *question of value* (whether something is good or bad, right or wrong, and to what extent); or a *question of policy* (whether a specific course of action should be undertaken in order to solve a problem).

Step 2: Problem analysis. Collect the information needed to identify the problem. Gather the facts, determine how serious the problem is, determine what harm is associated with the problem, decide whether the harm is serious and widespread, and identify what causes the problem.

Step 3: Solution criteria. Before the solutions are addressed, determine what criteria will be used to evaluate possible solutions. One of the most common sets of criteria centers on workability, practicality, and desirability. *Workability* is whether the solution will solve the problem. *Practicality* is whether the solution can be put into effect. *Desirability* is whether harm will be caused by implementing the solution.

Step 4: Solution suggestions. Brainstorm for possible solutions to the problem.

Brainstorming consists of generating possible solutions without evaluation of them at the time of their proposal. Guidelines for brainstorming include:[37]

- Don't evaluate ideas while brainstorming.
- Don't clarify or seek clarification of an idea during the collection.
- Encourage zany ideas. Some of the best solutions are those that haven't been tried before or are out of the mainstream.
- Record all ideas without reference to who contributed the idea.
- Encourage participation by all group members.

Step 5: Select a solution. Explore the positives and negatives of all the ideas collected during brainstorming, and apply the agreed-on criteria. Another method of selecting the solution is to apply an evaluation technique known as *RISK,* which has these basic steps:[38]

- Think of any risks, fears, or problems associated with the solution.
- Brainstorm potential negative consequences either individually or as a group.
- Post all potential consequences on a chart or whiteboard for all members to see.

- Give time for additions to the list.
- Discuss each negative point again.
- Weigh the risks and consequences against the perceived benefits.
- Make a decision to implement, delay for further study, modify, or kill the proposal and search for better alternative(s).

Step 6: Solution implementation. Put the solution into effect and monitor it by follow-up testing and observation to make sure it is working. If it is not working, repeat steps 4 through 6.

Nominal Group Technique for Decision Making

The *Nominal Group Technique for Decision Making* centers on brainstorming without direct group interaction in the initial stage. This technique encourages idea generation from all individuals but avoids criticism, destructive conflict, and long-winded speeches.[39]

The *Berko 1-3-6 Decision Making Technique* is a format for using the nominal group technique.[40] It takes place after the specific decision to be made or problem to be solved is agreed on by the group, and members are ready to work toward solution. The technique gets its name from how the participants work: alone (1 person), then in a group of (3), and then in a group of (6). The steps, illustrated in Figure 9.2, are:

Step A: Each individual in the group lists what he or she thinks should be done to solve the problem or the best possible decisions regarding the issue. This process is a brainstorming session.

Step B: Participants are divided into groups of three. Each group combines its members' lists. No items are deleted, but possibilities are combined and solutions or decisions reworded. There should be no discussion of the value of the ideas during this step.

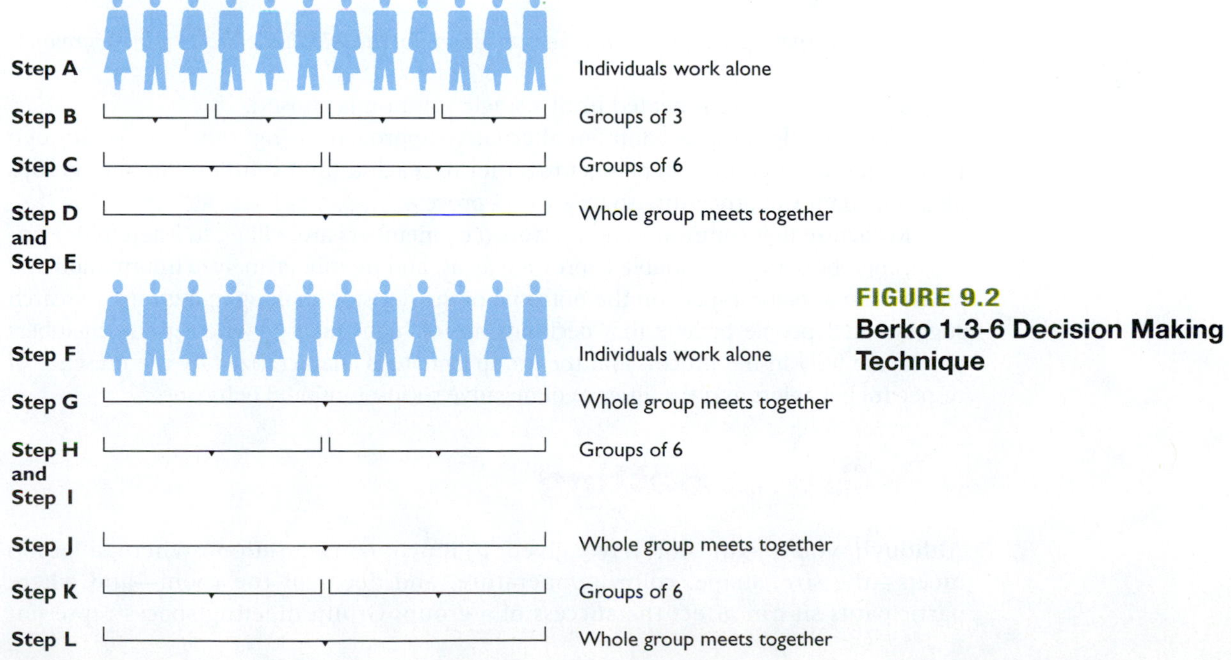

FIGURE 9.2
Berko 1-3-6 Decision Making Technique

Step C: Each subgroup meets with another one, and they combine their lists. Again, duplicate ideas are eliminated and solutions or decisions reworded. No evaluations are made.

Step D: The whole group reassembles. A spokesperson for each subgroup reads its list aloud. All items are written on a long sheet of paper or on a whiteboard. (It is important that everyone in the room be able to read the lists.)

Step E: The items are numbered.

Step F: Each person prioritizes the entire list, ranking in order all items with no ties. The most important or best solution or decision should be numbered 1, the next 2, and so forth. Each person's rankings are recorded on a sheet of paper.

Step G: The rankings are collected and tallied. The top items are identified, the final number of which should be a proportion of the number of items generated in step D. If thirty or more items were generated, the top ten would be a reasonable final list. For fewer items, about one-half to one-third of the total is appropriate. (Determine this in advance to avoid conflict over how many should be included in the final list.)

Step H: Individuals select their top choice and then are randomly divided into subgroups of no more than six persons. If possible, a representative of each of the subgroups in step C should be in each of the newly formed units. (This is not imperative, but in cases where there is lack of clarity in a statement, the individual from the subgroup that generated the idea may be able to clarify its meaning.)

Step I: Each subgroup selects what it considers the best solution using the individual selections from step H. At this step, evaluations are made. Statements may be reworded, but no new solutions may be introduced.

Step J: Spokespersons for each subgroup report on the decision of the subgroup. If all subgroups have selected the same solution, the process is completed. If not, solutions that received the support of at least one subgroup are retained and the others eliminated.

Step K: Subgroups reassemble and select what they consider the best solution from those remaining on the list.

Step L: A spokesperson for each subgroup reports on the selection of his or her subgroup.

Steps K and L are repeated until a single solution is chosen.

Some smaller groups adopt an alternative approach, using only steps A through F, and then have all members meet together to reach a final solution. Smaller groups also can adapt the procedure to be a 1-2-4 process.

Recognize that communication factors (i.e., members are willing to listen to one another, members are comfortable expressing ideas, and members analyze information and ideas) have a major impact on the outcome of the decision making in a group. Research suggests that people believe that decisions are of high quality "when group members participate fully in the process and the group climate is characterized by the presence of respectful behaviors and the absence of negative socio-emotional behaviors."[41]

Group Setting

Although you might not have given it much consideration, where a group meets—the size, shape, color, temperature, and decor of the room—and where participants sit can affect the success of a group. Group meeting spaces represent a particularly important type of microenvironment that can influence the quality and quantity of communicative interaction, the participants' perceptions of each other, and the task performance of a given group.[42] Two specific variables in group settings that can affect group action are seating choices and the configuration of the tables.

Seating Choice

Where you sit at a meeting may determine whether you are selected or perceived as the leader, how much you will participate, and how others perceive you. This is an important concept for you to consider if you aspire to be the group's leader. For example, the person who sits at the head of a rectangular table significantly increases his or her chances of being perceived as the leader.[43]

Studies about seating have arrived at these findings:

- The person who is seated in the dominant position at a table, such as at the center of the table, is in the power position. For example, if you saw the television show *The Apprentice,* you probably noticed that Donald Trump, who had the power to hire or fire, was seated in the boss position illustrated in Figure 9.3. He placed the apprentices opposite him so that he could test their ability to communicate their expertise, defend their decisions, and counter arguments presented by others.

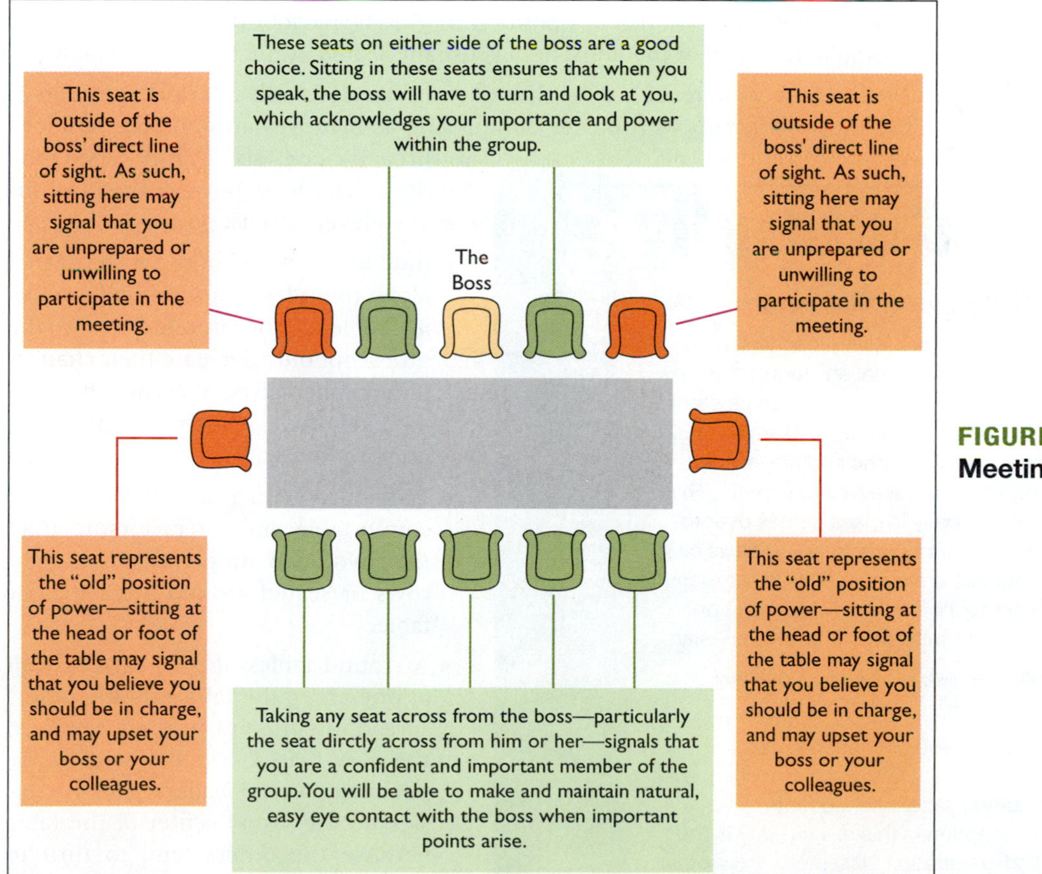

These seats on either side of the boss are a good choice. Sitting in these seats ensures that when you speak, the boss will have to turn and look at you, which acknowledges your importance and power within the group.
This seat is outside of the boss' direct line of sight. As such, sitting here may signal that you are unprepared or unwilling to participate in the meeting.
This seat is outside of the boss' direct line of sight. As such, sitting here may signal that you are unprepared or unwilling to participate in the meeting.
The Boss
This seat represents the "old" position of power—sitting at the head or foot of the table may signal that you believe you should be in charge, and may upset your boss or your colleagues.
This seat represents the "old" position of power—sitting at the head or foot of the table may signal that you believe you should be in charge, and may upset your boss or your colleagues.
Taking any seat across from the boss—particularly the seat dirctly across from him or her—signals that you are a confident and important member of the group. You will be able to make and maintain natural, easy eye contact with the boss when important points arise.

FIGURE 9.3
Meeting Seating

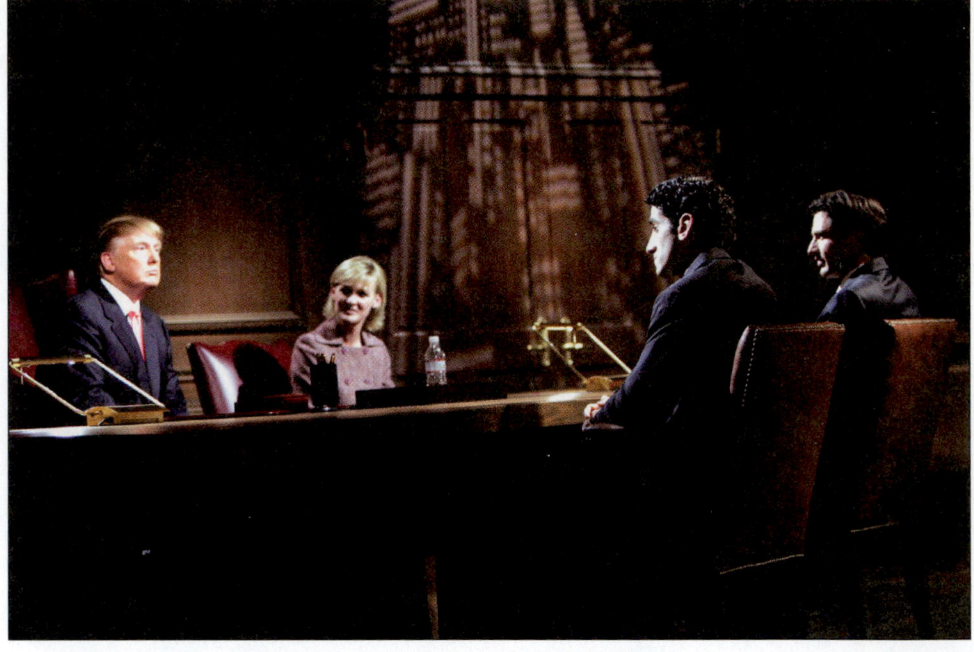

On the TV show *The Apprentice,* Donald Trump was usually seated in a power position, with the apprentices opposite him and forced to look at him.

- Traditionally leaders are expected to be found in a power position, "usually at the head or end of the table,"[44] or where the participants are forced to look at the leader, such as Trump's position in *The Apprentice*. At family dinners, for example, the head of the household is usually seated at the head of the table.
- At a round conference table, whoever sits at the twelve o'clock position is the most powerful, with power diminishing as it moves around past positions at three o'clock, six o'clock, and nine o'clock. The least powerful person sits at the eleven o'clock position.[45]
- Individuals who choose to be seated along the sides of a rectangular table, if the leader is at one end or the other, not only decrease their chances of being perceived as leaders but also are likely to be perceived as individuals with low status.[46]
- People seated in a circle will feel more comfortable and interact more than they would if they were in straight rows or seated around a rectangular table.
- At round tables, if several people sit at one arc of the table and the others spread themselves around the rest, the two seated together tend to be perceived as the leaders. This is considered the visual center of the table because the others tend to turn to face the two seated together.[47]

Culturally COMMUNICATING

Culture's Effect on Classroom Discussions

One of the significant challenges facing teachers in an increasingly multicultural educational environment is how to increase the participation level in class of some ethnic minority students. Japanese students, for example, initiate and maintain fewer conversations and are less apt to talk in class discussions than are other students. This reticence to participate verbally in class carries over to small group situations. Contributions to group decision making by ethnic minorities are consistently lower than nonminorities. In 76 percent of the small groups in one study, the member who contributed the least was Asian.

Source: Rothwell, J. D. (2004). *In mixed company* (5th ed.). Belmont, CA: Wadsworth/Thomson Learning, p. 225.

REFLECT ON THIS: Have you ever been in class with first-generation (i.e., recent immigrants, exchange students, visiting scholars) Japanese students? If so, did they follow the description in this discussion? Is the same true of other first-generation classmates from other cultures?

In classrooms arranged in rows, students who participate the most tend to form a triangle from the center of the room. For example, in a room with six rows of chairs, most class participation tends to come from those seated in the first four seats of the row closest to the front, the three seats behind them, the two seats behind them, and the one seat behind them. The least participation comes from the very back corners and those seated in the end rows.[48]

Table Configuration

Table configuration or shape is an important variable in group interaction. Rectangular arrangements foster more and better communicative interaction than do T-shaped or L-shaped seating arrangements, and a round configuration is better in this regard than a rectangular table. The round configuration is the most neutral.[49] At rectangular tables, communication usually flows across the table rather than around it.[50]

People seem to be aware of the different perceptions related to different seating positions. Interestingly, when asked in one study to select seats to convey different impressions, respondents chose end positions to convey leadership and dominance, the closest seats to convey interpersonal attraction, and seats that afforded the greatest interpersonal distance to indicate they did not wish to participate.[51]

Effect of the Physical Environment

The physical environment should fit the purpose of the meeting. An informal meeting may take place around the water cooler or copy machine. For more formal meetings it should be remembered that a meeting can unravel if the room is too large or small, if it is too warm or cold, and if the lighting or the acoustics are not conducive to seeing and hearing one another. Groups often function more effectively if snacks are provided. Attention to these kinds of details will pay off in member satisfaction with the group and contribute better to the group process and product.

On the other hand, the *meet-while-standing theory*[52] requires a meeting place without any furniture. The concept is that people forced to stand will make decisions more rapidly because the participants get tired and want to finish their business and find someplace to sit.

Mediated Meetings

Mediated meetings, are electronically held teleconferences, video conferences, web conferences that allow for meetings to be held anyplace where someone who needs to participate in a meeting is located. Groups no longer have to meet in a conference room; they can meet in cyberspace.[53]

Types of Mediated Meetings

There are four basic types of mediated meetings:

1. *Teleconferencing* consists of telephone conference calls and speakerphone meetings.
2. *Video conferencing* are meetings conducted with one-way video and two-way audio as well as interactive two-way video and two-way audio.

3 *Web conferencing* consists of meetings in which participants log on to a central conference database through their personal computers. It is similar to their sending or receiving e-mail. Computer meetings can take place as a *real-time conference,* in which all participants are at their computers at the same time, or as an *asynchronous conference,* in which participants contribute to an online conference database at different times. These meetings may go on for weeks, depending on their purpose.[54]

4 *Virtual conferencing* takes place when participants are connected to a platform such as *Second Life,* an Internet-based virtual world that enables its users, called "Residents," to interact with each other through avatars, which are a computer user's representation of himself or herself, which takes the form of a three-dimensional model or a two-dimensional icon or picture. Residents can explore, meet other "residents," socialize, and participate in individual and group activities. Avatars and objects can chat, send and receive e-mails as well as instant messages. This modality is popular for meetings among younger organizational members, as they perceive it to be much like playing computer games.[55]

Positive and Negative Aspects of Mediated Meetings

As with any other method of operation, there are advantages and disadvantages with each type of mediated meeting. Understanding these differences can help potential users or participants.

Teleconferencing Most organizations have the equipment and procedures in place for multiway calls. Speakers can be on land lines at their job site, but could also be at home, in an auto, or on their smartphones. Therefore, one of the major advantages of **teleconferencing** is the ease of use. On the other hand, participants typically are sitting, and they may feel isolated. If there are several people in a single room with a speakerphone, regulating who will speak can be difficult. Participants cannot observe their co-participants' nonverbal feedback, so it is hard to read feedback cues. Other drawbacks are that member participation may be inconsistent, members can do other things while participating, such as work at their desks or on computers, and not pay strict attention. It is also difficult to share visual elements such as charts or diagrams unless they have been distributed in advance or can be faxed or emailed to others while the discussion is ongoing.

Video Conferencing Voice-sensitive cameras and audio systems, flat-screen monitors, and a set of speakers, the equipment for **video conferencing** is often readily available in organizational headquarters or hotels and conferencing centers.[56] Systems such as *Halo* and *Telepresence Solutions* have made conducting sensitive contract talks and other high-level meetings possible.[57]

Video conferencing is effective for introducing new products to a team of salespeople or potential users, having collaborative meetings among project members in distant places, holding corporate town meetings when employees are at various worldwide sites, conducting training sessions, and participating in trade shows without leaving the office.[58]

Some suggestions for effective video conferencing are:[59]

- Speakers should be close enough to the microphones so they can be easily heard.
- Participants should control the noise of papers, tapping on the table, and other distracting habits that microphones will pick up.

Group videoconferencing is distinguished by its interactive capabilities, the ability to originate from any number of locations, and the ability to reach multiple worldwide locations simultaneously.

- High-quality graphics must be prepared to fit the television format.
- Audio or materials that are too complex to be seen on video should be mailed or faxed to participants in time to be used for reference during the session.
- Participants should identify themselves continuously during the process.
- Participants should announce when they leave or enter the discussion.
- Wait until the camera is on you before speaking.
- Limit the agenda to no more than one hour. If it is longer, a break should be scheduled.
- Select the appropriate participants: people who are willing to work with media and are not being forced to do so.
- Make sure the technology is operating properly and the participants know how to work the equipment.
- Have an orientation with the participants before the actual presentation in order to answer questions about the procedure and the media.
- Prepare and distribute a written agenda in advance of the session.
- Since there may be a voice delay in videoconferences, be careful to wait and not talk over someone.[60]
- Be aware that presentations "should be shorter [than in face-to-face meetings] because it's easier to lose people's attention."[61]

Web Conferencing **Web conferencing** is fairly inexpensive. Most employees have computer workstations, and the only other costs are special computer programs, if they are desired. The conferences can take place wherever a computer can be activated. General training is minimal because most people are computer literate. Participants report that dynamic interactions often take place as people get involved in each other's messages.[62]

The fact that the conference can take place over an extended period of time can be an advantage. "Members of asynchronous conferences often report being able to mull over their comments before entering them, resulting in deeper and more thoughtful discussions."[63]

Web conferencing has weaknesses as well as strengths. Some view computer meetings as impersonal, more time consuming because it takes longer to type a thought than to speak it, and unsatisfactory for those who are uncomfortable with computer technology.[64]

An additional weakness is that there is a delay in message sending and retrieval and a tendency to use short and incomplete messages. Moreover, there is no nonverbal presence; the interactions are dependent on the keyboarding speed of the participants; overlapping messages can cause confusion; and with numerous participants, direct interactions become very difficult.[65]

Attempts to overcome the negative aspects of Web conferencing have led to the development of *groupware:* specially designed software that meeting participants use to perform tasks such as brainstorming and decision making.[66] In a typical meeting in which groupware is used, each participant sits at a computer terminal. The participants may be at a single site or spread around the world. The leader begins the meeting by inputting to participants what problem must be solved or what decision must be made. Participants input ideas and cast votes on their individual screens, which are integrated by the groupware.[67]

"Most research suggests that groupware does improve the quality of meetings." It is reported to save time, help build consensus, and guide the uninitiated through meeting procedures.[68] On the other hand, it doesn't automatically make meetings more productive. Slow typists complain that they can't participate or that decisions are made before they can respond. It limits the amount of discussion that can take place. Extroverts complain that they can't participate enough. And because of the ease of operation, so many ideas may be presented that the volume becomes unmanageable.

GoToMeeting is one of the most commonly used groupware. It is a Web conferencing tool that allows you to meet online. It is easy to use and cost effective. Patented technology enables co-workers, customers, and prospects to view any application running in real time. With the flexibility to meet in person or online, the program's distributors contend, "you'll be able to do more and travel less."[69]

Virtual Conferencing **Virtual conferencing**, use of virtual worlds to conduct group interactions through virtual sessions, have positive aspects, there are negatives as well. Individuals not familiar or comfortable with computer gamesmanship or computer manipulations often are not comfortable being cast into a virtual world. In addition, there are numerous laws which must be followed in order to bring the activity into international compliance. There also are technical issues in using virtual meetings, such as system instability and incompatibility. Electronic crashes, communication problems between the main program servers and individual computers, may cause bottlenecks in which the server goes down, and leaves the user with an unworkable program. There has also been a loss of data due to program glitches. Equipment requirements may also a problem. In 2011, *Second Life,* the most commonly used program for virtual conferences, required 300kbps of Internet bandwidth for basic functionality, with 1mbps providing better performance. In addition, there have also been cases of data theft.

Before using any of the mediated meetings formats, be sure you understand both the advantages and disadvantages of the system.

In Conclusion

IN CONCLUSION

A meeting should be a purposeful interaction; therefore, no matter the setting or the technique, the basic questions always to be asked are (1) why the meeting is being held? (2) who should attend? (3) when the meeting should take place? and (4) what materials need to be prepared and present for accomplishing the purpose?

Groups are an assemblage of persons who communicate in order to fulfill a common purpose and achieve a goal. Group members influence one another, derive some satisfaction from maintaining membership in the group, interact for some purpose, assume specialized roles, and depend on one another. Groups often are classified by size, with small groups containing three to twelve persons and large groups more than a dozen. One of the most prominent functions of the group communication process is that of decision making. There are advantages and disadvantages to both participating in a group and having groups make decisions, versus working alone. Groups normally go through six phases: forming, norming, storming, conforming, performing, and adjourning. Where a group meets and where participants sit can affect the success of a group. Besides face-to-face meetings, organizations are using mediated meetings, which include teleconferencing, virtual conferencing, Web conferencing, and video conferencing.

LEARN BY DOING

1. Be prepared to defend or counter this statement: "The advantages of working in a group outweigh the disadvantages." Go beyond the arguments given in the chapter and use personal examples to develop your answer.
2. Consider a group in which you have worked that was *not* successful in reaching its goal or that had difficulty in reaching its goal. What specifically was the problem? How could the problem have been solved?
3. For your next examination in this class, students will be divided into study groups to prepare for the test. After the exam, a class discussion will be held on the value or lack of value of study groups.
4. Mentally revisit a group in which you have participated. Write a short paper (which may be given as an oral presentation) analyzing its norming, storming, conforming, performing and adjourning stages.
5. Your class will be divided into groups. Each group is to contact at least two representatives of an organization that is conducting mediated meetings. Interview them in person, by telephone, or online about the pros and cons of conducting mediated meetings. Write a short report on your findings. You will present a group report to your classmates on your findings.
6. Be prepared to discuss this situation: You are a member of a classroom group that is to investigate the concept of groupthink, write a collective paper, and give an oral group report. The class has been told that everyone in the group will get the same grade for the project. There are six people in the group. One person fails to show up for any group meetings, nor does he research his segment of the paper, so others do that research. When it comes time to hand in the paper and give the oral report, what should the group do regarding the errant member?

KEY TERMS

group 244
small groups 244
large groups 244
groupthink 245
work team 246
study group 247
support group 247
committee 248
focus groups 249
public meetings 250
symposium 250
forum 250
town meeting 252
group storming 253
agenda 257
voting 258
brainstorming 260
mediated meetings 265
teleconferencing 266
video conferencing 266
web conferencing 267
virtual conferencing 268

Participating in Groups

culture and groups • role of participants • leaders and leadership in groups • resolving disagreements in groups

CHAPTER 10

After reading this chapter, you should be able to

- Explain how people from different cultures possess varying attitudes about being group participants, applying procedures for working in groups, making decisions, following procedural structure, and using information
- Discuss the role of gender as a factor in group activities
- Define and explain the role of the participants, the leaders, and the leadership in groups
- Compare and contrast the role of disagreement in the group process
- Evaluate the role of the hidden agenda in the group process
- Define the autocratic, participatory and free rein leader types
- Analyze why a person would want to be a group leader and demonstrate how he or she would proceed to acquire the leader or leadership role

Groups are made up of people. Those who comprise a group play the roles of leaders, leadership, and participants. **Participants** are those members of a group who interact to bring about the actions of the group. **Leaders** are those who guide the group. **Leadership** refers to those who influence the group to accomplish its goal.

Members of groups, whether they are assuming a participant or leader role, come to the group with cultural influences. These influences affect the way in which group members function.[1]

Cultural Differences in Groups

Each of us is a product of the culture in which we were brought up. We learn the customs and patterns of our culture, and these carry over into all phases of our lives. Research shows that people from different cultures possess varying attitudes about making independent decisions and being group participants, applying procedures for working in groups, making decisions, following procedural structure, and using information.

Be aware that any discussion of culture includes generalizations. These are based, whenever possible, on research findings and expert observations. They are in no way intended to lead to the conclusion that all members of that culture conform to the generalized patterns.

Cultures and Groups[2]

"A dominant perception in American culture assumes that the world is material [something to be used] rather than spiritual [an idea or essence to be appreciated and saved], and should be exploited for the material benefit of humanity."[3] The Euro American point of view strongly affects how people from that culture work in groups and the purposes for which groups are formed. Euro Americans tend to use groups to

Culturally COMMUNICATING

Cross-Cultural Considerations

These guidelines can help you speak the right business language when you deal with those from other cultures:

- **Find out** if the culture you'll do business in is *high contact*—expects lots of details—or *low contact*—prefers a broad overview.
- **Realize that** you may have to ask permission to take meeting notes. *Reason:* Some in other cultures object because they feel it may "pin them down."
- **Assume that** in most cultures it's safer to let your counterparts bring up business issues first. That allows them to set the pace and provides signals you can use to adjust your behavior.
- **Be more** formal. Use titles and last names—and be sure to pronounce them correctly.
- **Talk clearly,** avoid slang and sports terms, and learn and use a few key phrases in the others' language. *Examples:* "Good morning," "Yes," "No," "Please," and "Thank you."
- **Adjust your** tempo to your counterparts' concept of time. Some cultures have little concern for punctuality.
- **Learn to** read cultural differences in nonverbal signals. *Example:* A smile can signal embarrassment in some cultures.

Source: "Cross-Cultural Considerations" from *Speaking the language of business overseas,* Prudential Relocation Global Services. Reprinted with permission of Briefings Media Group.

get things done (e.g., commerce, getting products produced) rather than for strengthening the bonds of the members of the group (e.g., creating good will, supporting the emotional needs of the members).

People in the United States are highly individualistic.[4] This *individualism*, which stresses personal loyalty before group loyalty, has a strong historical base. The United States was founded by adventurers and dissidents. In this culture, membership in groups (except those that are mandatory because of a person's work or academic environment) tends to be voluntary. While recognizing that there may be traditions, such as membership in a particular religion, European Americans tend to decide for themselves whether they want to belong to a group. You, for example, choose whether to participate in a social group or a fraternal organization. After you become part of the group, if you don't like being a member, you can resign. Because of this ability to join and leave a group, allegiance may not be a lifelong commitment. This, however, is not the case in other parts of the world. For example, in many East Asian countries, Confucianism is the basic philosophy of much of the population. The *Confucian principle of i* requires that a person be affiliated and identify with a small and tightly knit group of people over long periods of time. These long-term relationships work because group members aid and assist each other when there is a need; sooner or later those who assisted others will have to depend on those they aided. This mutually implied assistance pact makes for group interdependence.[5]

Not only does the attitude toward being in groups vary by culture but there also is a difference in the training required in certain cultures for group participation. Because they participate in groups to a limited degree, many European Americans need to learn about group operational methods when they enter into organizations. The same is true of people from other countries having a high degree of individualism, such as Australia, Great Britain, Canada, New Zealand, and Denmark. In contrast, people from *collective societies*, in which group adherence is stressed, have a clearer sensitivity about how groups operate, since they are encased in groups all their lives. Many of the areas and countries that are collective are found in Asia (Japan, China, Vietnam) and South America.

The Confucian principle of i requires that a person be affiliated and identify with a small and tightly knit group of people over long periods of time.

Cultural differences also are reflected in the way a person works in a group. In many East Asian countries, there is a strong distaste for purely business transactions. This is carried over into meetings, where the tendency is to mix personal with public relationships. Business meetings, for example, may take place over a long period of time in order for people to establish personal relationships, engage in activities like sports and drinking, foster an understanding of the personalities of the participants, and develop a certain level of trust and a favorable attitude.

A good example of a nation that stresses group culture is Japan, where individualism is submerged and expression occurs in hidden ways.[6] This, of course, is almost the opposite of how European Americans operate. In the United States, individuals work in groups to get *tasks* accomplished. In Japan, the individual's sense of identity *is* the group. This is based on a long history of ruling families who created a social structure that bound families, villagers, and strong leaders together. In the United States, the stress has been on rugged individualism, with the group coming second to the individual. In Japan, the word for describing a group is *we*. In the United States, groups often are divided between "us" and "them." For instance, administrators and faculty members are part of the same group—the university—but often find themselves on opposite sides when making institutional decisions.

Contrasts in Cultural Group Decision Making

If the assumption is made that one of the important tasks of a group is decision making, another cultural variation comes into play. It is important to realize, when working in decision-making groups, that there are vast cultural differences in how people think, apply forms of reasoning, and make decisions.

In the Western view, it is generally believed that people can discover "truth" if they apply the scientific method to the decision-making process. The traditional Western problem-solving sequence has four segments: identify the problem, search for solutions, test those solutions, and put a solution into practice. The final decision is often based on a majority vote of the membership, with those who will have to implement or live with the decision often not part of the decision-making team. For example, few students are included in university discussions on curriculum requirements. In Japan, on the other hand, those affected by the decision are often included in the process.

Other societies use different decision-making approaches.[7] For example, for the Chinese, though this has relaxed some during the present opening of the country to the free enterprise system, decision making is more authoritative than consensual; decisions are made by higher authorities without the inclusion of subordinates. Although subordinates are consulted informally, the leader makes the final decision.

Work groups in Mexico tend to use a *centralized decision-making process*. Mexicans often view authority as being inherent within the individual, not his or her position. Making trade-offs is common for Mexican negotiators, including adding issues that are not part of the original business at hand.[8]

Cultural Contrasts in the Role of Information for Groups

Even information or ideas that are used for making decisions may differ among cultures. European American negotiators tend to compartmentalize issues, focusing on one issue at a time instead of negotiating many issues together. In the United States, negotiating toward the final decision usually takes on a form of *proposal– counterproposal negotiating,*[9] in which a plan or solution is presented and then a counteroffer is made. For example, in a group meeting concerning salary negotiations, the employees propose a particular salary and explain why they think this is the appropriate amount. Management then typically makes an offer of a lesser amount and offers counterarguments. This process continues until an amount is agreed on. The negotiations may be accompanied by a threat of the workers going out on strike, an action unheard of in some other cultures.

The French, on the other hand, seem to have no problem with open disagreement. They debate more than they bargain and are less apt than Euro Americans to be flexible for the sake of agreement. They start with a long-range view of their purpose, as opposed to Euro Americans, who work with more short-range objectives. This format was evident in the French stand against the war in Iraq, where the question of the long-range purpose of the war was a point of contention between the countries.

"Japanese negotiators tend to make decisions on the basis of detailed information rather than persuasive arguments."[10] "The Japanese and most Asian cultures view [the] Euro American version of powerful speech as immature because it indicates insensitivity to others and is likely to make agreement more difficult."[11]

Because this book is directed primarily at individuals who will find themselves most often participating in groups in the U.S. culture, the material in this chapter deals mainly with participant and leader conventions and patterns typical in the United States. However, because of the multiculturalism of this country, you likely will be working with people and in social situations with individuals from a variety of cultural backgrounds. Also, with the internationalization of business, it is becoming more and more common for businesspeople from the United States to be working in international settings, so knowledge of other cultures' group procedures can be helpful.

Male and Female Roles in Groups

Besides cultural differences based on nationality, the roles of males and females in European American culture can play an important role in leader and participant operational modes.[12]

Is gender a factor in group tasks or maintenance?[13] Generally, though the concept insights reactions from some individuals, studies on leader, leadership, and the group process indicate that differences do occur in the way men and women operate in a group.[14] For example, "women are more likely than men to engage in caring, personal communication."[15] In addition, "women tend to exceed men in collaborative, participative communication that enables others."[16] *As in any instance when using research about any group, keep in mind that the results represent a norm and there are exceptions to the rule. You, for instance, may not follow the patterns, or perhaps you know people who don't.*

Other studies about males and females in groups indicate that "subordinates judge male and female leaders to be equally effective, and judge both masculine and feminine styles of communication to be important in leaders."[17] In fact, one study concludes that "men and women are 99% similar and only 1% different in their communication."[18] However, "when judging a group member's expertise, men and woman are not viewed through the same lens. Men more than women are encouraged by groups to contribute their expertise, partly because group members, both males and females, don't initially think of women as experts."[19] Although men are considered to be more competitive than women,[20] "women are becoming more competitive as they enter the workforce in larger numbers."[21] As for presenting and defending ideas, "men are more argumentative than women, meaning men are more likely to advocate controversial positions during group discussion or to challenge the positions on issues taken by other group members. Women are inclined to view verbal aggressiveness and argumentativeness as strategies of dominance and control."[22]

There apparently has been a shattering of the glass ceiling (an invisible barrier of discrimination that has traditionally excluded women from top jobs in corporate and professional America), as there has been a significant change in the leader role of women in the United States. Almost half (49 percent) of all managerial and professional positions in the United States are now held by women.[23]

Research in educational groups[24] indicates that students believe classes led by women are more discussion oriented, and classes taught by men are more structured and emphasize content mastery. In addition, male college professors are perceived to be less supportive and less innovative than female instructors. It also has been shown that "male students initiate more interactions with teachers than female students initiate, and that males tend to dominate classroom talk."[25]

The Group Participant

Participants in groups have various responsibilities to themselves and to the group. They normally perform communicative maintenance and task roles, form networks by which they relay messages, and must deal with other members. Researchers who study the role of the follower in a group remind us that, although there is considerable focus on understanding the dynamics of good leadership in a group, we need to remember that effective group dynamics has to start with good followership. For example, what distinguishes an effective follower from an ineffective follower is enthusiastic, intelligent, and self-reliant participation without star billing in the pursuit of an organizational goal. Further, exemplary followers are those who communicate as team members, actively engaging in the work of the group, critically assessing group decisions, and contributing creative ideas that enhance the group's goals.

Group actions are based on proposing actions, putting forth ideas, and proposing solutions to problems.

Responsibilities of Group Members

Participants should remember that an entire group is responsible and accountable for final decisions. Thus, being a member of the **silent majority** (those who say nothing during the decision-making process) does not release you from accountability for that decision. For example, if the group decides that each member should pay fifteen dollars more in dues, you must pay the extra fee, even though you may not have said anything during the discussion and may not have even voted on the issue. Despite your lack of participation, if you expect to remain a member of the group, you cannot announce after the decision is made, "I didn't say anything and I didn't vote, so I don't have to pay!"

All group members should be knowledgeable. In the Western logic system, although personal beliefs are important, expert opinions and facts reveal what authorities believe and what testing has proved, and this is the basis for sound decision making. In other words, the use of supporting evidence can help ensure that your conclusions have substance and will probably be perceived as having credibility. Consider how you can apply evidence such as statistics, testimony, and illustrations to your discussions. Your participation is enhanced if you use this research to support your comments clearly and concisely.

Some groups are plagued by people who insist on dominating the discussion and the decision-making process. These people may, at worst, destroy the group and, at best, irritate members and make decision making difficult. Although it is sometimes very difficult when you have strong opinions and believe you are right and others wrong, each participant should try to respect as much as possible the rights of the others. This does not mean you should not participate if your views differ from those of others. It does mean, however, that a point can be reached where continued bickering can be destructive to the group's mission. Suppose that after presenting your point of view, it appears that your ideas are not going to be accepted. Your task, then, is either to try to work toward reaching a compromise into which you can enfold your ideas or to accept the fact that you have done everything you could to get your viewpoint presented and accepted but have failed to achieve your goal.

Being a member of the silent majority does not release you from accountability for a decision.

It is important not to assume that rejection of your idea is a rejection of you personally. Unfortunately, many people have difficulty making this distinction. Not understanding this concept causes people to "fight to the death" for acceptance of their beliefs. This may lead the rejected person to start attacking others rather than sticking to the issues. Personal attacks often do little to get your stand accepted; rather, they cause alienation within the group. Personal issues lead other people to take stands not on what solution is right or wrong but on who is right or wrong. This choosing up of sides often divides the group, causing internal rifts and destroying the chances for group cohesion and goal accomplishment.

Normally, group members should take an active role in communicating with each other so that the entire group can benefit. Of course, there are times when, for whatever reason, you may feel that you do not want to participate. You may think that you do not have the necessary information, or that you might not have strong enough feelings to interject, or that your beliefs have already been presented by someone else. Whatever the reason, if you knowingly and willingly don't participate, this is your privilege. However, choosing not to participate is an act of abdicating responsibility as a group member.

Participants in a group discussion, much like therapeutic listeners, also must try to set aside their own prejudices and beliefs so as to listen and respond to what others have to say. This ability to suspend judgment is difficult. Deal with conflicts by adopting an openness to compromise and conciliation—that is, if you think this is in the best interests of the group process and you can live with the compromise. Remember that compromises can result in giving up beliefs and moving to watered-down solutions, unsatisfying to all concerned. Do not allow a verbal bully to force you into a compromise or to adopt a solution you feel is not in the best interest of the group. Note that the focus is on the best interest of the *group*, which may not necessarily be in *your* best interest!

Communicating as a Group Member

As a group member, you perform varied communication activities. Foremost are speaking and listening. In the process of participation, you probably evaluate information, propose concepts, and agree and disagree with the ideas of others. Group interactions seem most effective when participants are aware of their maintenance and task roles.

Performing Group Maintenance Tasks Group participants have a responsibility to attend to the maintenance functions of the group, because a productive group is one in which members feel positive about participating. "*Group maintenance* focuses on the social dimension of the group. The central communicative function of maintenance roles is to gain and maintain the cohesiveness of the group."[26]

In order to effectively perform your group maintenance, you would be wise to:

- *Treat others with respect.* No doubt you realize that you will not always agree with everyone. There should be an understanding that disagreement can be helpful because it opens the decision-making process to a variety of viewpoints and allows differences of opinion to be aired, but that disagreement is not an invitation to discourtesy.
- *Maintain a positive attitude.* Having positive attitudes about what you are doing makes for a more committed group member.

  If group members have pride in their group and show commitment to it, the odds go up for group success. If this is not the case, maybe one of the tasks of the group should be to investigate why there are negative attitudes. Dealing with this issue may make working in the group more pleasant and increase the productivity of the membership.

- *Encourage others.* Being encouraging rather than discouraging can keep communication channels open. Communication stoppers such as "That won't work," or "That's ridiculous" will have the effect of shutting down communication.
- *Pay attention to nonverbal messages.* The effective group communicator attends to group members' nonverbal messages. Be aware of when your body is relaxed and when it tenses due to your discomfort because of the length of the discussion or your own reactions to what's transpiring in the group. Is it time to speak up? Is it time for you to stop talking? Be aware that your gestures, pace, and fluency can affect others. Be aware that people who are connecting with each other tend to face one another, looking directly in each other's eyes. When someone is turning away from an idea or a person who is presenting the idea, he or she will often literally turn away. Also, be aware that not all cultures use the same nonverbal signs. Just because someone is nodding his head and smiling does not mean the person is agreeing with you. It is common in some Asian cultures, due to the politeness factor, to show agreeable signs, even when disagreeing. Also because someone is slouched in a chair does not mean that person is not paying attention. It may be his normal seating position or a cultural pattern, not discourtesy.
- *Assume an active role.* Taking an active role in a group through volunteering ideas, showing willingness to work on subgroups and committees, and making supportive comments is important for helping a group to work cohesively.

Performing Task Roles Besides maintenance roles, participants need to perform *group task roles,* making sure the group accomplishes its goal.

In order to effectively perform your group task role, you would be wise to:

- *Initiate ideas.* Group actions are based on someone proposing actions, putting forth ideas, and proposing solutions to problems. Initially, people in most groups tend to be a little shy about presenting ideas. But as the group moves from norming to participating, this reluctance to put forth ideas is overcome. If others in your group aren't proposing ideas, make a suggestion. This may encourage them to participate. If you know that suggestions will be sought, and you know the topic of the discussion or the nature of the problem, come to the meeting prepared to propose ideas.
- *Encourage diverse ideas.* Another important aspect of task roles is to encourage diverse ideas. Conservative thinkers hold to the tried and true. They tend to recreate past solutions to problems. Creative idea generators go beyond the norm and search for different solutions. Their ideas may seem crazy at first, but many seemingly outrageous ideas have satisfied major needs. Historically, space travel, the invention of the computer, and even the light bulb were all "far-out" ideas. Don't be stifled by the tried and true; think creatively, even if you risk being called a dreamer or an idealist. Join Alexander Graham Bell, Mark Zuckerberg, George Washington Carver, Madame Marie Curie, and other inventors, scientists, and explorers who have made a difference.
- *Use reasoned thought.* One of the important roles of task communication is to operate on the basis of reasoned thought. Being able to support sound ideas, develop well-thought-out concepts, separate fact from opinion, criticize weak or unsubstantiated ideas, use critical thinking, offer evidence, and integrating ideas are important obligations of a constructive task communicator.
- *Stay open-minded.* In general, most of us come to a conclusion, believe it is correct, and defend it no matter what. But ideally we should be open to the possibility that someone else's ideas may be as valid as, if not more valid than, ours. There

are often ideas we haven't thought of, approaches we haven't been exposed to, ideas that challenge our beliefs.

- *Be aware of hidden agendas.* Be aware that not all members of a group will be as open, caring, and responsible. Some members of a group enter the task process with a **hidden agenda**: an objective or purpose that goes beyond the constructive interests of the group as a whole. When individuals work for their own unstated ends rather than for the group's objectives, the result is usually counterproductive. A hidden agenda is apparent, for example, when a department manager, discussing budget allocations, promises to support any plan that divides the resources equitably among departments but then opposes every plan presented. In this case, the manager has a hidden agenda: perhaps the manager wants most of the funds for his department and thinks a delay will tire the participants and lead to a decision that favors that department. The manager is trying to manipulate the group.

  Listen carefully to the proposals and arguments of other members and be alert to the possibility of hidden agendas.

- *Be cognizant of time constraints.* A group participant should be sensitive to time factors, both to ensure that time is used wisely and that the group is not manipulated by a clever user of time. If you use a great deal of time and dominate a discussion with too many statements or lengthy comments, you run the risk that you will be tuned out or that your contributions will be so overpowering that the group process will be lost in your dominance. Use time effectively, and make sure that you allow others the time they need.

  Be wary of the participant who knows the meeting is coming to a close and that time is short, yet suggests a new, untested solution that has not been discussed. This is a device commonly used by individuals who know that when time pressures become a dominant factor, group members may act impulsively. If someone suggests a solution late in the discussion, make sure it is not acted on immediately, before the group has time to think about the advisability of taking the proposed action.

Dealing with Manipulative Group Members

Most people in groups are cooperative, participate, assume leader and leadership roles in noncontrolling ways, and are willing to be open-minded. Unfortunately, there are some people who create dissent, are self-centered, attack others rather than deal with the issues, and won't stick to the agenda. They "will do whatever it takes to get what they want, including manipulation."[27]

It is theorized that 90 percent of the people who are members of groups are reasonable most of the time. There are conflicts and differences of opinion, but people contribute to the good of the group and work things out. About 9 percent of the members are somewhat difficult to work with. These people have hidden agendas and disagreeable personalities. Then there is the remaining 1 percent. Their consistent obstructive nature gets in the way of any attempt to deal cooperatively with them.[28]

To deal with the 90 percent, applying the concepts presented in this chapter on effective group communication should be sufficient to work toward task and maintenance accomplishment.

As for the 1 percent—the impossible people—there is very little you can do to work constructively with them. Reasoning with them or giving in to their demands accomplishes little. These individuals are out to make life miserable for themselves and everyone around them. They tend to be so self-absorbed that there is no way to work things out, short of giving in. But giving in only encourages their behavior, which escalates their negative actions because they know that eventually the group will give in to their tantrums and negativism again. They may have psychological problems, such as being paranoid, which causes them to believe everyone is against them. Or, they may be desperate for attention. The psychological principle here is, "people want attention, and if they can't get it positively, they will get it negatively."[29]

One coping method is, if it is possible, to expel the impossible ones from the group such as removing a disruptive student from class, or having an athlete who breaks the rules "thrown out of the game." Another is to ignore them. A third is to recognize that they must have their say, but it is no one's obligation to listen. Unfortunately, if one of these is the group leader—the supervisor, the professor, the parent—the problem is compounded. Even group experts and psychologists have no recommendations for what participants should do if this is the case. Quitting a job, withdrawing from the class, or leaving a group may be your only salvation if things get too bad.

That leaves the 9 percent who are considered difficult group members. Difficult people are those who cause problems regarding the task or maintenance functions of a group—actions such as frequent disruptions, long speeches, irrational requests, insulting behavior toward others, and interruption of participants.

Before taking any action, be sure that the scenario is actually taking place and that the person is in fact difficult. Sometimes we perceive a person to be difficult because his or her ideas are different from ours. Is the person really difficult, or is the problem yours?

Here are some ways to know if someone is trying to manipulate the group:[30]

- *Buttering up.* Manipulators will often make members of a group feel good so they can then ask for something they want. What you can do: return the compliments before saying, "No."
- *Guilt.* Guilt trips work because victims succumb to the demands because they feel that have to, not because they want to. What you can do: ask if they want you to do something. If they say yes, indicate that you are not comfortable taking that action. Don't be pushed around out of false fears of not being liked or whatever else the guilt tactic was.
- *Repetition.* If a person asks you over and over to do what they want you to do they think that they will eventually wear down your resistance. What you can do: continue to repeat over and over that you will not change your mind.
- *Selective memory.* You agree on a plan, everyone is in agreement, and the manipulator pretends to remember the agreement from another perspective. What you can do about it: Call them out on the fact that they conveniently changed the game plan to fit their needs.
- *Bullying.* When these people don't get their way, they make you out to look and feel like the bad person. They accuse you of being wrong and threaten to tell something about you to others, physically threaten you, or psychologically unnerve you. What you can do: Be firm, tell them that their bullying tactics are inappropriate and unacceptable.

The bottom line is the need for you to be consistent and not be manipulated.

Experts seem to agree that to deal with difficult people, five general axioms should be followed:[31]

1. *Don't placate the troublemaker.* Allowing the disrupter to manipulate the group in order to keep the peace rewards the troublemaker for objectionable behavior and only encourages similar future actions. For example, the person might interrupt a vote by saying, "I don't want us to vote at this point. It's not fair to cut off discussion until we have all had our say." You could respond by saying, "The

motion to call for the vote was made and seconded. The result was unanimous—except for your vote. Therefore, we have followed parliamentary procedure, and we will go ahead with the vote." To give in to the person would encourage him or her to continue to be an obstructionist in the future.

2. *Refuse to be goaded into a reciprocal pattern.* Resist the temptation to fight fire with fire. Someone might say to the chairperson, "You and your people are always making decisions that cause problems for this group. You need to be more honest in dealing with the rest of us." The person's intent is to get the chairperson upset and have her or him apologize or back down. The chair should not be pulled into such goading. The chair might state, "Although I disagree with your comment, I intend to be respectful toward the committee as a whole. Let's proceed with the vote."

3. *Try to convert disruption into a constructive contribution.* There is a difference between being disruptive and being constructive. Use the person's idea to ask for other ideas. Doing this takes the discussion away from the person and allows others to speak. If, for example, a member of a committee indicates that the decision-making process of the group was tainted by a lack of input, the chair might state, "That's an interesting point of view. Let's review the minutes of the meeting and reexamine the arguments for and against the selected decision." Doing this not only stops the disagreement but it may also alert the group to whether or not groupthink has occurred.

4. *Confront the difficult person directly.* If her or his tirades or other actions are disruptive, tell the person so. Continual disruptions and other negative actions that stop task and maintenance progress are not in the best interest of the group and need to be dealt with. Ideally, the confrontation should be assertive, factual, and focused on the issue—in other words, state exactly what the person has done. For example, instead of saying, "You are always making stupid and irrelevant remarks," state, "The last two times we have discussed the issue of selecting a new membership campaign, you changed the subject to why you believe the club should have more social events and why you believe you should be serving on the finance committee. Neither of these statements had anything to do with the topic being discussed, and they didn't help us solve the issue at hand."

5. *Separate yourself from the difficult person if all else fails.* Some individuals leave no other option but ostracism by the group. Quitting the job or leaving the group may be your only recourse. Before quitting, make an assertive statement that clearly indicates why you find the person's actions disruptive to the group and why you find yourself unable to continue working with the person. Make sure that your statements contain only facts that led you to your conclusion.

You can control only your own communication behaviors and your own responses to others' communication. Unless you are in a total power control position, you cannot change or control the actions of another person, so concentrate on dealing with yourself, and avoid getting frustrated.

The Group Leader and Group Leadership

The strength of a group is found not only in effective participation but also in meaningful guidance and decision making. The leader of a group is the person who is recognized as being responsible for guiding it through its tasks. (See Figure 10.1.) The leader may be *elected* (e.g., president of the speech honor society), may be *appointed*

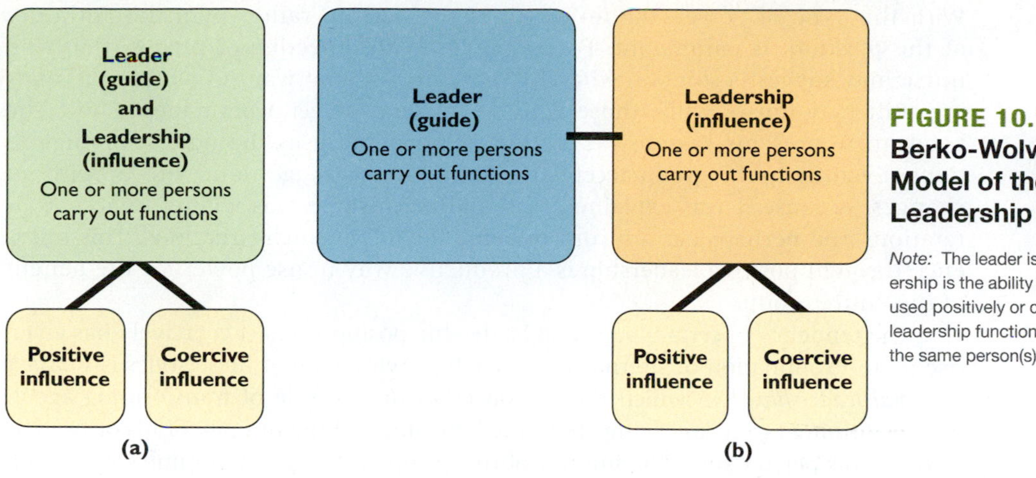

FIGURE 10.1
Berko-Wolvin-Wolvin Model of the Leader/ Leadership Relationship

Note: The leader is the group's guide. Leadership is the ability to influence, which can be used positively or coercively. Both leader and leadership functions can be carried out by (a) the same person(s) or (b) separate persons.

by an outside source (e.g., the board of trustees appoints the university president), may *volunteer* (e.g., a person volunteers to chair the social committee), or may *emerge* by taking control (e.g., a parent in a family). A group also may have more than one leader; for instance, a group may have several chairpersons. Furthermore, in some groups, the recognized leader may not be the only one guiding the group; other members may share this function by being appointed or assuming such responsibility. "Leadership is everyone's business."[32]

The ability to influence others' opinions and actions is known as *leadership*. (See Figure 10.1.) It can be demonstrated by one or more people in a group, and the use of the power that derives from leadership can be viewed as enforcing obedience and/or the ability to influence others to perform.

Leadership power stems from various sources in the dynamics of a group. A classic study on leadership power[33] identified five sources by which leaders gain power: (1) *legitimate power*, inspiring a sense of responsibility in followers; (2) *reward power*, providing followers with things they desire; (3) *coercive power*, taking away rewards or administering sanctions and punishments; (4) *expert power*, providing others with information and advice; and (5) *referent power*, providing others with self efficacy, worth, or approval. In one sense, then, leadership power can be described as enforcing obedience through the ability to withhold benefits or inflict punishment. In this sense, power is coercive.

Coercion, the act of forcing another person to take an action he or she does not want to do, centers on offering a selection of choices, all of them undesirable. For example, in a meeting of nurses to discuss whether shifts should be rotated, many of the participants may not want to do this. But if the head nurse is in favor of rotating shifts, then the power of the position may come into play. He may say that it's his responsibility to determine staff assignments and that anyone who cannot accept his proposal can request a transfer to another department or quit. Thus, the decision has been made through coercive power because neither of the options offered may be desirable to the nursing staff. Similarly, in a family, a mother can control the members by stating, "As long as you are living in my house, you will do as you are told or get out." This form of "arm-twisting" leadership often causes resentment, leading to attitudes such as "I'll get back at her for forcing me to do something I don't want to do" or "I'll do it, but I'll do it poorly."

But leadership power can also be identified as the ability to influence others to perform or produce results. This kind of power does not use force or coercion.

With this type of power, the influence of the person, rather than the authority of the position, is paramount. For example, in the meeting of nurses, the head nurse may suggest a solution whereby those nurses who want to work on a rotating shift may do so, while those who do not may select a permanent shift. The head nurse presents reasons for his two options and asks the others for suggestions. Eventually the group accepts the head nurse's suggestion, with or without changes, because it was explained well and because he was willing to accept alterations and perhaps has a record of being flexible in such situations. This influence through positive leadership is a productive way to use power for the benefit of the entire group.

The tendency of certain people in leadership positions to act coercively has given rise to an examination of alternative leadership styles. One of these styles is *transformational leadership,*[34] in which the person takes on the role of transforming agent. A transforming agent can change both the behavior and the outlook of his or her followers. This person keeps the interest of the group and its goals in mind rather than forcing her or his will on the group. Therefore, she or he gives up the command-and-control model of leadership.[35] This approach closely resembles the way most managers operate, getting others to perform or produce by offering rewards or punishments

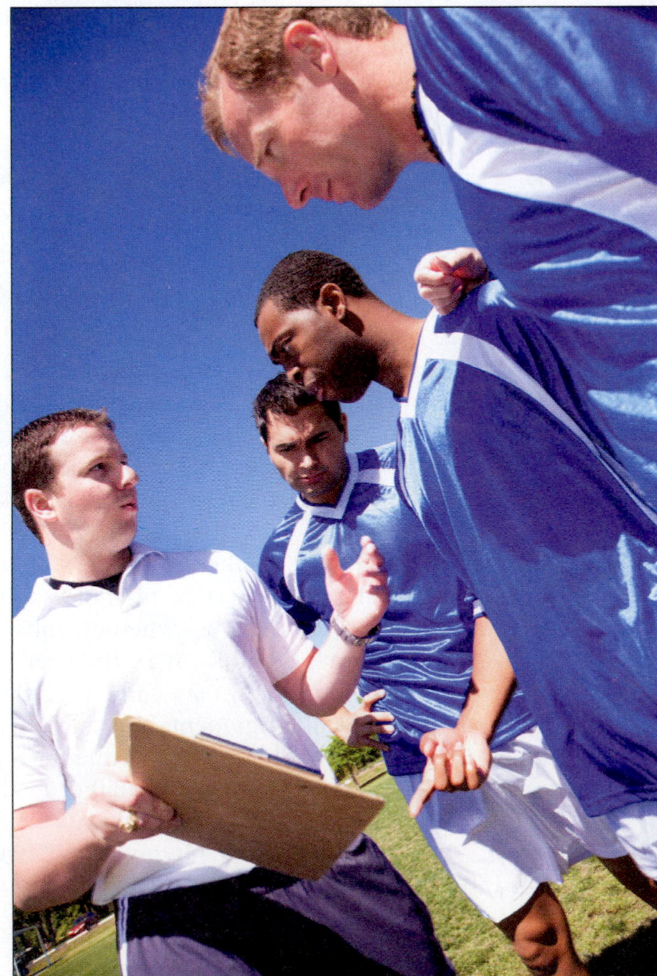

The leader of a group is the person who is recognized as being responsible for guiding the group through its tasks.

in the process. Transactional leadership may be well suited to short-term goals of a group, but the group, to be successful, may require a more visionary approach in the long run.

Another style is *super leadership*, in which people lead themselves and thereby release the self-leadership energy within each person.[36] Such an approach is especially appropriate in today's scaled-down organizations, in which not all qualified employees have the opportunity to move up the corporate ladder into management or executive positions. This leadership format allows everyone to develop his or her leadership skills and to stay productive in changing an organization.

Types of Leaders

Do you know what type of leader you are? Interested in finding out? If so, do the Leadership Style Quiz.

Leadership Style Quiz

Circle the response that reflects your first reaction. There is no right or wrong answer.
As a leader, I tend to....

	Always	Often	Sometimes	Never
1. Make my own decisions	4	3	2	1
2. Tell others what to do	4	3	2	1
3. Suggest a decision to others	4	3	2	1
4. Persuade others to do things my way	4	3	2	1
5. Participate just like any other person	4	3	2	1
6. Provide resources to others	4	3	2	1
7. Gather other's feedback before deciding	4	3	2	1
8. Rely on my own judgement	4	3	2	1
9. Make sure the majority rules	4	3	2	1
10. Turn decision over to others	4	3	2	1
11. Ask others to brainwash choices	4	3	2	1
12. Share my own ideas	4	3	2	1

Add the numbers together from the following set of questions. The highest number will show what leadership style that seems natural for you. *You should strive to understand different leadership styles of ways you might use them for different situations.*

Add the numbers you circled for the following questions	Total	Leadership Style
Question 1,2,4,8	________	Autocratic
Question 3,7,9,11	________	Participatory
Question 5,6,10,12	________	Free Rein (laissez-faire)

Leaders use their power to influence the process of group effort in various ways. These characteristics can be categorized. Three basic types of leaders have been identified as:[37]

1. An **autocratic leader** dominates and directs a group according to personal goals and objectives, regardless of how consistent or inconsistent these goals are with group members' goals. This leadership style is direct and controlling. When in a group led by an autocratic leader, participants tend to be more oriented toward productivity and goals. The strength of an autocratic leader is that things get done and decisions are made quickly. They are task oriented. Members of the group may feel manipulated by this type of leader since their input is not sought out nor welcomed.

2. A **participatory leader** facilitates a group according to the goals of its members and allows them to form their own conclusions. This leadership style encourages input from others. Emphasis is on how the decision is reached and that everyone has a voice. Participatory leaders tend to make decisions in a slow, thoughtful process. This type of leadership requires that the participants be good listeners and cooperative. The advantage to this type of leadership is that everyone feels included. The disadvantage is that it requires time and patience, which are sometimes in short supply when there is pressure to get a job done and a solution in place.

3. A **free rein leader** (often called *laissez-faire leader*) is nondirective and empowers group members to do their own thing. This style centers on the leader being relaxed and supportive. The participants are free to take the actions they wish to take. Details tend not to be a major concern, and there are few rules. This leadership style is dependent upon the good will and motivation of the participants to assert themselves, be responsible and take action on their own. This style works well for some groups, but others find it frustrating because of the lack of structure and dependence on everyone doing their part without being told or held accountable.

Evidence suggests that no one style is consistently more effective than another. Each approach works under certain conditions. The key to leader effectiveness is matching the appropriate style to the group environment. Thus, if group members are very task oriented and are empowered to make decisions, they may be productive working with a free reign leader. This style may be disastrous, however, if group members are unable to function productively on their own. A participatory leader works well with a group that requires minimal supervision. If group members cannot accomplish their tasks because they lack self-discipline, an autocratic leader may be needed to direct activities and assign specific responsibilities.

Socially COMMUNICATING

What's a Leader?

If your actions inspire others to dream more, learn more, do more and become more, you are a leader.

John Quincy Adams

REFLECT ON THIS:

1. Do you know of a leader who fulfills this quotation?
2. What qualities of leadership did the person you identified in question one possess?

Patterns of Leader/Leadership Emergence

If a leader is not appointed for a group, one of the questions that arises is—how should a person interested in becoming a leader proceed?

Research shows that when an official leader is not assigned within a group, the individual members accept the responsibility of carrying out the roles of the leader, and perhaps even assume the unofficial title of leader.[38]

"The general tendency is for groups to accept as a leader the person who provides the optimum blend of task efficiency and sensitivity to social considerations"[39]—in other words, someone who has talent and popularity. Proving your leadership ability centers on demonstrating your competence, being accountable for your actions, and satisfying the group members' expectations.[40]

Leaders tend to conform to the group's norms, values, and goals while displaying the motivation to lead. They know the rules of order, have charisma, are positive about themselves, encourage others to communicate, and are supportive listeners.

Why People Desire to Be Leaders

Recognizing that a great deal of responsibility is laid at the feet of leaders, that leaders often find themselves the target of attacks, and that they are blamed if things don't go right, why would anyone want to be a leader? Why would people who already have wealth and power want to, for example, take on the job of President of the United States, in which they open themselves to ridicule and stress? Why would someone want to become the president of your college's student government? People seem to want to be leaders for various reasons:

- *Information.* The leader is privy to special information. Many leaders like to be "in the know."
- *Rewards.* Leaders receive praise, attention, payment, power, and special privileges for being in their positions. Being a corporate executive who makes several million dollars a year can be highly satisfying in spite of the responsibilities and time constraints. Some people also like to be in the public eye. For example, a number of corporate and business leaders do advertisements for their companies in order to gain ego attention.
- *Expectations.* Certain people have enough faith in themselves to believe that they can accomplish a task or that they have better solutions than someone else. Listen to politicians campaigning for office. They have platforms that attempt to explain why they are more capable of making things better than are their opponents.
- *Acceptance.* Some people equate the title of president, chairperson, or boss with being accepted, liked, and admired.
- *Status.* Acquiring status in one group can bring status in other groups. That is, a record of having been a leader often is the basis for selecting someone for another leader position. Other students may consider you a person of high status because of your campus leadership. A potential employer may see on your resume that you held a leadership position in a student group and offer you a job because you will be able to use the same skills as an employee.

Leader/Leadership: Communicative Perspective

There is a fundamental link between human communication and leadership. Influential leaders such as Winston Churchill, Golda Meir, Martin Luther King Jr., Sitting Bull, Gandhi, Mao Tse Tung, John F. Kennedy, Ronald Reagan, and César

Chavez were all compelling communicators. "Historically speaking, there seems to be a correlation between those presidents we think of as great communicators and those who are considered successful presidents."[41]

A communicative perspective emphasizes the leader as a catalyst for communication.[42] Leaders not only must use words well but also must be aware of their own nonverbal communication as well as the verbal and nonverbal communication of the group members. In addition, the leader has to listen and explain clearly while moving the group toward their task. A leader's goal is not to win a popularity contest but rather to get the task of the group completed.

Effective Leader Questioning

One of the most important responsibilities of a leader is to monitor the proceedings and interject appropriate questions to stimulate discussion, clarify ideas, and resolve conflict. Here are some ways to deal with common problems.[43]

- *Issue: Drawing out a silent member*
  Question to ask: "Does anyone who hasn't spoken care to comment?" Or "Amad, what is your opinion of ...?"
- *Issue: Calling attention to points that have not been considered*
  Question to ask: "Does anyone have any information about this matter?" Or "Lamont, would you care to explore this angle of the topic in more detail?"
- *Issue: Keeping the discussion focused on the subject*
  Question to ask: "That's interesting, but just how does this point fit in with the issue being considered?"
- *Issue: Using conflict constructively*
  Question to ask: "Since we do not seem to be able to resolve this difference now, could we move on to the next point?"

Emergent leaders exhibit a significantly higher rate of participation than do nonleaders.

- *Issue: Suggesting the need for more information*
  Question to ask: "Is it agreeable to the group if we ask a subcommittee to investigate and bring back the needed information to our next session?"
- *Issue: Calling attention to the source of information*
  Question to ask: "Where did this information come from?"
- *Issue: Preventing a few from monopolizing the discussion*
  Question to ask: "May we hear from someone who hasn't expressed an opinion?"
- *Issue: Suggesting the need for closing the discussion*
  Question to ask: "We're scheduled to finish discussion in about five minutes. Is there a final comment?"

Responsibilities of Leaders

Regardless of style, a leader has the responsibility for guiding the group toward accomplishing its task and maintaining the group as a functioning unit. An effective leader needs to know when to sit back and let the group work on its own, when to step in and make suggestions, when to warn about such potential problems as groupthink, how to motivate the building of cohesion, and how to instruct on the need to evaluate ideas critically and express doubts. In other words, an effective group leader needs to know her or his responsibilities and how to carry them out.

A leader has responsibilities before, during, and following a meeting:[44]

In Preparation for a Meeting

- Define the purpose of the meeting.
- List specific outcomes that should or must be produced from this meeting.
- Establish the starting and ending times of the meeting.

The effective group communicator should attend to nonverbal messages.

COMMUNICATING in Careers

A Business Professional Shares Her Views

What does it take to be a good group facilitator?

Most of my work as a group moderator is to be a good listener so that I can be sure that all of the group members do participate actively and so that I can provide a thorough report of the group's responses to the client. Since a focus group meets for a rather short, prescribed time frame, I have to establish trust with the members, build rapport, and develop cohesion within the first three minutes. It is important to communicate an unconditional positive regard for each member in the group. I have to "work" the group in order to engage all of the members early on in the process so that they will feel committed to the group and its goal. A focus group can't just be a serial interview of each participant; I have to understand how groups function and work to accomplish my group objectives.

Source: "A Business Professional Shares Her Views" by B.G. Rosenthal, Qualitative Research Consultant, from *Business communication in a changing world* by Roy Berko, Andrew Wolvin, and Rebecca Ray.

REFLECT ON THIS: How does a leader "establish trust," "build rapport," and "develop cohesion"?

- Notify members of the purpose and the agenda, their necessary preparations, and the time and place of the meeting.
- Seek member input in planning the agenda.
- If specific resource persons are needed, advise them and prepare them for the meeting.
- Make necessary physical arrangements.
- Get necessary work items (e.g., pencils, paper, charts, data sheets, reports).

During the Meeting

- Describe the importance and purpose of the meeting.
- Make an effort to establish a climate of trust and informality (if appropriate).
- Stimulate creative thinking (if appropriate).
- Stimulate critical thinking.
- Provide summaries and transitions, and watch time limits.
- Promote teamwork and cooperation.
- Equalize opportunities to participate and influence.

Follow-Up to the Meeting

- Remind members who agreed to do after-meeting work.
- If minutes are kept, see that they are written and distributed.
- If the group decision should be forwarded to another person, see that this is done immediately.
- If work is necessary before a future meeting, be sure it is done.

IN CONCLUSION

Groups are made up of people. People from different cultures possess varying attitudes about making decisions or being group participants. Participants are those members of a group who interact to bring about the actions of the group. Leaders are those who guide the group. Leadership refers to those who influence the group to accomplish its goal. Group members, their leaders, and their leadership perform task and maintenance roles.

LEARN BY DOING

1. Your class will be divided into groups. Each group is to take twenty minutes in which to agree on what a time traveler should take into the future, using this information for the decision:[45]

   A time machine travels to the year 5847. By then, the world has been destroyed in a nuclear holocaust, and all that remains are a few men and women living a primitive existence and having no record or memory of the past. The traveler in the time machine decides to rebuild the world but can make only one trip back and forth in time. On the trip, which can encompass any years between the dawn of humanity and this year, the traveler may collect such useful items as living things, printed materials, food, toilet paper, and so forth. The only limitation is one of weight: excluding the weight of the time traveler, no more than 200 pounds of material may be carried through time. What should the time traveler take into the future?

   After the small-group discussion, the class meets to discuss these questions:

   a. What effect did differences in members' backgrounds have on the group's decision?

   b. What was the role of the leader in the group?

   c. What was the greatest problem the group encountered in reaching its decision? Could this have been resolved? How?

   d. What inferences about how groups operate can be drawn from this experience?

2. The purpose of this exercise is to illustrate how groups operate and the roles of members of a group.

   a. Before coming to class, indicate whether you thoroughly agree (TA), agree (A), disagree (D), or thoroughly disagree (TD) with each of the following statements. You must select one of the four options for each of the statements.

      (1) Prayer should be allowed in public schools.

      (2) Corporations have an obligation to their stockholders to make profits; this obligation supersedes all other obligations.

      (3) The positive value of Facebook outstrips its negative aspects of the social network site.

      (4) Every member of an organization should be permitted to present views at a meeting, regardless of how long this process may take.

(5) The changing ethical structure of current society has led to confusion and a breakdown of traditional morality.

(6) Television is a major factor in desensitization of people to violence.

(7) Texting while driving should be legally forbidden.

(8) War is an inevitable result of international conflict.

(9) Same-sex persons should be allowed to legally adopt children.

b. Your instructor will assign each member of the class to a group. Each group is to elect a leader who will be responsible for leading the discussion. Each group will be assigned one of the topics to discuss. If you finish your discussion of your topic, proceed to the next numeric topic (e.g., if you are assigned 5, and complete your discussion, discuss 6, etc.). The group must reach consensus—total agreement—on one of the four responses (thoroughly agree through thoroughly disagree). Group members may rewrite a statement if it will help them come to consensus.

c. At the end of the discussion, each person will write answers to these questions:

(1) What one thing did the leader do that helped the group in reaching its goals?

(2) What one thing could the leader have done that would have helped the group in reaching its goals?

(3) One thing I did as a participant that pleased me was ...

(4) One thing I did as a participant that I should not have done was ...

(5) This group did/did not work well because ...

d. After each student has completed step c, each group will meet and discuss each member's answers. Be prepared to report back to the class of your group's overall strengths and weaknesses and the process of group decision making.

3. Using the discussions that were held for either activity 1 or activity 2, each person in your group is to write an analysis of each of the group members, including himself or herself, by identifying the specific roles each played as leader, leadership, or participant. Share your lists with the members of the group, and discuss the observations.

KEY TERMS

participants 272
leaders 272
leadership 272
silent majority 277
hidden agenda 280
leadership power 283
coercion 283
autocratic leader 286
participatory leader 286
free rein leader 286

Public Speaking: Planning the Message

CHAPTER 11

definition of public speaking • a listenable speech • ethics of public speaking • planning difference types and modes of public speeches

After reading this chapter, you should be able to

- Define public communication/public speaking
- Formulate a listenable speech
- Explain the ethical responsibility of a public speaker, including the implications of plagiarism and fabrication
- Explain the role of the participants, setting, and purpose/topic in public communication
- Define and explain the roles of prior, process, and post speech analyses
- Clarify the role of the statement of the central idea of a public speech
- Discuss how to develop impromptu (or ad lib), extemporaneous, manuscript, and memorized presentations
- Compare and contrast the advantages and disadvantages of the impromptu, extemporaneous, manuscript, and memorized modes of presentation

For many, the thought of giving a speech is exciting. For others, standing before an audience conjures up feelings of terror. No matter what your attitude is, you can learn to be a competent public speaker. Really!

The act of **public communication** involves a transaction between a speaker and an audience. You may think that public speaking is something you do not need to be concerned about, but this is not the case. In fact, "a surprising number of persons ... do speak to audiences of ten or more people fairly frequently."[1] No matter what your college major or current position, odds are that you will be doing some type of public speaking.[2]

The Listenable Speech

The *listenable speech*[3] is one that is formatted to be easily understood by listeners. Just as writers should be concerned about the readability of their text, speakers should strive to prepare and present speeches that are listenable.

A study of what makes a speech listenable determined that an effective presentation requires language that fits the intellectual level of the listeners; follows a clear pattern such as chronological, problem solving, or cause to effect; includes phrases that tell a listener what is coming; and the statements made are backed up with facts or examples in such a way that the audience can understand and basically accept what is being presented.[4] Listeners seem to prefer a conversational style public speaker.[5]

Key elements of a listenable presentation are a logical structure that includes an introduction, a statement of a central idea, a body that consistently follows a pattern

Listening to a speech can be an exciting, interesting, or uplifting experience.

Communicating Culturally

Kenyan Public Speaking Patterns

While public speaking classes are placing increasing emphasis on diversity, this emphasis frequently stops at advising students to find culturally relevant examples for their speeches and to be sensitive to potentially offensive phrases or visuals. Cultural influence on rhetorical practices of societies goes much deeper. A recent study examines the public speaking patterns of Kenya, and compares those findings to the content of American speeches.

"Most frequently mentioned areas of difference between American and Kenyan public speaking were establishment of speaker credibility, structure of the speech, selection of supporting materials, audience demographic factors, and the purpose or occasion of the speech."

Major speech patterns of Kenyans include: The personal pronoun "I" is used very rarely as there is a strong spirit of collectivism. The country's poloychronic time usage (lack of adherence to strict time limits) means that speeches often go beyond the allotted time. Being a high context culture, Kenyans center on indirectly conveying messages through the use of proverbs and analogies, without clear consequences or conclusions reached.

As a result of these patterns, speeches by Kenyans often do not normally include extensive research, offering, instead, a personal anecdote to illustrate ideas. The stories used will not necessarily be connected to the main point, leaving the audience to infer the meaning. Proverbs are used in subtle ways, with the speaker being credited as being wise or experienced for knowing the proverb. Song may be used in the middle of a speech. African speeches are filled with audience responses, with the speaker letting a sentence hang and waiting for the audience to fill in the blank or lead the audience in chanting specific phrases. Speeches may not follow any particular structural pattern. African speeches are often circular, wandering and then returning to the subject.

Source: "An Exploration of Kenyan Public Speaking Patterns with Implications for the American Introductory Public Speaking Course" by Ann Neville Miller, from *Communication Education 51*(2) 2002.

REFLECT ON THIS: Of what importance is this material to professors and students in U.S. college public speaking classes in which Kenyans are enrolled?

of development, and a conclusion that summarizes the presentation; is a suitable length; and uses examples that are appropriate for that particular audience.[6]

To prepare a listenable speech, you need to know yourself as a communicator. What is your style? What is your comfort level? What format will you be using (i.e., stand-up speech, table-top briefing, video cast)? Who are the listeners? What do they know about you and your topic? Why should they care about you and your topic?[7]

Let's now investigate the specific details of how to prepare a speech so that you will be able to make a listenable presentation.

Preparing a Speech: An Overview

The quality of a speech performance normally correlates positively with the total preparation time, the amount of research done, the time and effort spent in developing speaking notes, the effort put into preparing visual aids, and the time spent rehearsing out loud.[8]

Although there is no universally agreed-on best way to prepare a speech, here is a process that works well for many people:

Step 1: Decide on a topic or accept the topic assigned to you.

Step 2: Formulate a statement of the central idea.

Step 3: Collect research that develops the statement of the central idea.

Step 4: Finalize the statement of the central idea, the specific purpose, and the goal that adapts to the listeners and setting of the presentation.

Step 5: Formulate and organize the body of the presentation so that the goal can be achieved.

Step 6: Prepare the necessary aids, such as audio, visuals, and computer-generated graphics.

Step 7: Develop an introduction that previews and a conclusion that summarizes the main points of the presentation.

Step 8: Polish the introduction and conclusion. The introduction should grab the attention of listeners and orient them with any necessary background. The conclusion should wrap up the presentation and clinch the purpose expressed in the central idea.

Parameters of Public Speaking

Any act of communication is based on three parameters: the participants, the setting, and the purpose of the communication. In a speech, these three parameters affect the topic selected, the language used, the types of examples and illustrations chosen, and the aids needed to support and/or clarify ideas.

The *speech participants* are the speaker and the members of the audience. The *speaking setting* encompasses where the speech is given, what the time limit is, when the presentation is made, and the attitude of the audience. The **purpose of the speech** centers on the speaker's expected outcomes for the presentation.

Ethics of Public Speaking

A major concern of any communicator should be the matter of ethics. An ethical public speaker:

- Does not knowingly expose an audience to falsehoods or half-truths that may cause significant harm.
- Does not premeditatedly alter the truth.
- Presents the truth as he or she understands it.
- Raises the listeners' level of expertise by supplying necessary facts, definitions, descriptions, and substantiating information.
- Employs a message that is free from mental as well as physical coercion by not compelling someone to take an action against his or her will.
- Does not invent or fabricate statistics or other information intended to serve as a basis for proof of a contention or belief.
- Gives credit to the source of information and does not pretend that the information is original when it is not.
- Shows respect for human dignity.

An ethical speaker takes his or her audience into consideration. If the speaker does not do so, the results could be very embarrassing. For example, on January 18, 2011 "Alabama Governor Robert Bentley told a church crowd just moments into his new administration that those who have not accepted Jesus as their savior are not his brothers and sisters."[9] Complaints by the Anti-Defamation League ("the nation's premier civil rights/human relations agency"), stated, "His comments are not only offensive, but also raise serious questions as to whether non-Christians can expect to receive equal treatment during his tenure as governor."[10] In addition, "he is dancing dangerously close to a violation of First Amendment of the U.S. Constitution, which forbids government from promoting the establishment of any religion."[11] After much other negative national attention, Bentley apologized with the statement, "If anyone from other religions felt disenfranchised by the language, I want to say I'm sorry."[12]

Clint McCance, vice president of the Midland School District in Pleasant Plains, Arkansas, resigned his seat after he "fumed over a gay rights group's Spirit Day ... when the group urged supporters to wear purple to raise awareness about harassment and bullying against gay youth."[13] McCance stated, "The only way I'm wearing it [purple] for them is if they all commit suicide."[14] He also stated, "I also enjoy the fact that they [homosexuals] often give each other AIDS and die." Education officials in Arkansas and nationally condemned McCance's statements. Clearly, Bentley and McCance showed ethical failure.

Two specific areas of ethical concern in public speaking are plagiarism and fabrication.

Plagiarism

Plagiarism occurs when a speaker uses the ideas and words of others as his or her own without giving credit to the originator of the material. It can be as seemingly innocent as overhearing someone's idea of a solution to a problem, presenting that idea in your speech, and not giving credit to the originator of the idea. Or the speaker can copy an entire essay someone else prepared and present it as a speech with no reference to the source.

There are unscrupulous people who encourage plagiarism by supplying opportunities to participate in the act. For example, online theme and speech sales organizations sell prepackaged presentations. Be aware that using one of these in a classroom can result in your failing a course or even being expelled from school, plus the personal embarrassment of being identified as a cheat.

Also be aware that there are federal laws regarding the illegal use of someone else's materials, especially if the ideas are copyrighted. Materials published in a book or magazine are almost always copyrighted, as are many entries online.

One of your authors was at a national convention and attended a session at which a graduate student presented a teaching activity that she credited as being her own. She supplemented her speech with a drawing. During the question-and-answer session, the author asked if this was the speaker's own material. She assured him that it was original and developed specifically for this presentation. He knew better. Following this session, the author was to present a workshop on creative teaching and had a copy of an instructor's manual, published several years previously, which he had written and that contained the *exact* exercise, complete with the *exact* drawing, which he pointed out to the presenter. You can imagine how difficult and embarrassing it was when the plagiarist was forced to make a public apology.

Every idea you present in a speech does not have to be original; however, if the concept comes from another source, you are obligated as an ethical speaker to give credit. ESPN anchor Will Selva was forced to apologize for taking copy from a newspaper column and passing it off as his own. Selva stated, "I made a horrible mistake"[15]

Digital technology makes cutting and pasting easy. Thus, many students who have grown up with easy access to information which is hanging out in cyberspace, don't understand that they are responsible for quoting the material and searching out the sources. In fact, about 40 percent of one college's undergraduates admitted to copying a few sentences in assignments.[16]

"At Rhode Island College, a freshman copied and pasted from a website's frequently asked questions page about homelessness—and did not think he needed to credit a source in his assignment because the page did not include author information. And at the University of Maryland, a student who was reprimanded for copying from *Wikipedia* in a paper on the Great Depression said he thought its entries—unsigned and collectively written—did not need to be credited since they counted, essentially, as common knowledge."[17] Both students were wrong and academically punished.

The consequences for plagiarism can be severe. "At some colleges, students who plagiarize are expelled."[18] At one prestigious southern university, thirty-three students were expelled after a professor employed software that he had designed to detect plagiarism.[19]

Communication instructors at many institutions are scanning manuscripts and speaker outlines through turnitin.com, an online "proprietary system that instantly identifies papers containing unoriginal material and acts as a powerful deterrent to stop student plagiarism before it starts."[20] Besides stopping the total copying of someone else's materials, such a search also discourages students from just stringing one online cutting of materials to another without interjecting any of their own ideas.

All plagiarism, intentional or unintentional, is stealing! Someone else has done the work; you are taking credit for it. That is not ethical.

Fabrication

Fabrication is making up information or guessing at information and making it appear true. If research doesn't reveal the desired statistics you need for proving a point of a speech, you shouldn't just make them up. Don't assume that listeners are stupid. They read, and they watch television; they can be experts on the particular topic about which you are speaking. How would you feel if you had fabricated statistics and, during the question-and-answer session following your presentation, an audience member indicated that the information was not accurate and had proof to back up the inaccuracy? How would you feel if during a business briefing your employer was made aware by an audience member that the material you were using was made up, not accurate, and had no substantiation?

"From George Washington's 'I cannot tell a lie' to Richard Nixon's 'I am not a crook' to Bill Clinton's 'I did not have sexual relations with that woman,' our nation boasts a notable speaker history of dishonesty and indiscretion. Over the past several years, sports fans have been treated to a barrage of lies, fibs, mistruths and fabrications about who did what, when, where and how."[21] Major league baseball received negative publicity when "Barry Bonds, baseball's all-time leading home run hitter was indicted by a federal grand jury on charges of perjury and obstructing justice for allegedly lying about using steroids."[22] This was followed by information that "Alex Rodriquez lied about his steroid use."[23] Baseball wasn't the only sport in which participants made public statements about their issues that turned out to be fabrications including "Michael Vick lied to the National Football League Commission about his dog-fighting ring,"[24] "Olympic gold medallist Marion Jones lied about drug use,"[25] and "Rosie Ruiz, won the Boston Marathon at a record pace, but was found to have gotten on a subway to complete the race."[26]

Things have gotten so bad in political races that the [Cleveland] *Plain Dealer* started a column entitled *PolitiFact Ohio,* which each day examines the statements of local and national politicians. In an article entitled, "Flawed data persist on cap and trade," the columnist quoted politician after politician who used facts which had proven to be wrong, and had been publicly reputed. The writer concluded that these people's rhetoric should be labeled, "pants on fire," the most heinous of ratings given.[27]

Telling half-truths because you haven't completed your work or you didn't have enough time for proper research is no excuse for making up information. Fabrication is lying, and lying is unethical.

As an ethical public speaker, you must understand that you are a moral agent. When you communicate with others and make decisions that affect yourself and others, you have a moral responsibility.

Analyzing the Parameters of Speeches

To give effective speeches, analyze the parameters in three stages: prior analysis, process analysis, and postspeech analysis. The majority of the work takes place in the *prior to the speech analysis,* before the speech is given. But observing the audience for feedback (the *process of the speech analysis*) and paying attention to reactions following a speech (the *postspeech analysis*) are also very important.

Prior to the Speech Analysis

In determining what you are going to say, you need to consider several factors. This information will aid in selecting or refining a topic, developing the speech, selecting appropriate language, and deciding what information to include in the presentation.

Audience analysis, consists of assessing the demographic, psychographic, and rhetorographic characteristics of your prospective listeners.

This **audience analysis** consists of assessing the demographic, psychographic, and rhetorographic characteristics of your prospective listeners.

Demographics *Demographics*—your listeners' characteristics based on their descriptions and backgrounds—include such factors as age, gender, religion, ethnicity, education, occupation, and race.[28]

- *Age.* Make sure that the examples and language you use are appropriate for the age level of the group you are addressing.
- *Gender.* Knowing whether the audience will be made up primarily of males or of females may help you in deciding how to approach the topic or what types of examples to use. It is important not to stereotype all men or women as being universally the same; however, using examples that are appropriate to the gender makeup of the group can draw in the listeners. Further, be aware that sexist statements can turn listeners against the speaker.
- *Religion.* A speaker can establish or destroy a common bond with specific religious groups through language and examples. If the group is all of the same religious belief, using examples of people or principles of that group could lead to the acceptance of your views, just as an inappropriate reference might turn listeners against you.
- *Ethnic background.* Appropriate ethnic references, if they fit the topic, can enhance a speaker's credibility. For positive reactions, to all but bigoted groups, select references that put the ethnic group in a positive light.
- *Educational background.* Understanding the educational background and training of your listeners is important so you can choose material appropriate to their level.
- *Occupation.* Occupational interests and experiences often serve as the communication bond for speakers and listeners.
- *Racial background.* Like ethnic background, the racial composition of your audience may be a critical consideration. Just as it is important not to make stereotyped statements when addressing all men or all women, so too is it important not to make assumptions about any particular racial group, especially if you, the speaker, are not of the same race as your listeners.

Psychographics *Psychographics*—the audience's attitudes and beliefs—are an important consideration. This profile can be determined by analyzing the listeners.

- *Attitudes. Attitudes* are the predispositions that your listeners bring to the communication event. They will have attitudes toward you as the speaker based on their perceptions of your trustworthiness, competence, and presentational style.

Culturally COMMUNICATING

Student Listening Preferences: Audience Analysis

- *U.S. student preferences*: In a recent cross-cultural study of student listening preferences, American students reported liking messages that are short and to the point. They tend to prefer speakers with whom they can identify (women more so than men).
- *German student preferences*: German students prefer precise, error-free messages; disorganized presentations frustrate and annoy them. They are much less concerned about identifying personally with the speaker.
- *Israeli student preferences*: Israeli students prefer complex and challenging information that they can think over and evaluate before they form judgments and opinions. The length of the message is relatively unimportant.

Source: "Cultural Listening Styles" from *Public speaking: Concepts and skills for a diverse society,* 3rd Edition by C. Jaffe.

The setting for public communication may be affected by its emotional climate—the overriding psychological state of the participants.

Your listeners may have attitudes toward the occasion. Usually they are part of a voluntary audience, participating in the speech event because they want to be there; but if they are a captive audience (e.g., students enrolled in a required class outside of their major, a required training seminar), it is important for you to take that into consideration. Audiences that are required to listen to a speech are less receptive, and you may need to add humor or drama to get and hold their attention. You may want to recognize that you realize that they are not there voluntarily and empathize with them.

Additionally, your listeners will have attitudes toward your subject. If they agree with you—for example, they are pro-choice when you are speaking on that subject—then they will probably need less persuading. On the other hand, if the majority of the audience is pro-life, you are going to have to use devices to change their attitudes. In this case, you may want to anticipate that the pro-life audience may verbally attack you in the question-and-answer session, so you might prepare for that eventuality by anticipating the questions that may be asked and preparing counterarguments.

- *Conservative/Liberal.* In dealing with issues such as abortion, the death penalty, genetic engineering, homosexuality, and school prayer, you are taking on topics about which the listeners may well have an emotional investment that comes out of their conservative or liberal disposition. It is helpful to know the predispositions of your listeners as you select arguments and appeals to get them to believe as you do, or to stay open to ideas counter to their belief system.
- *Political affiliation.* The listeners' political affiliations usually correspond to their conservative/liberal dispositions. You may want to know if your listeners were primarily independent voters or registered members of a particular political party before putting together your message in order to trigger the responses you desire by appealing to their loyalties.

Rhetorographics Just as you analyze your audience, so must you analyze the *rhetorographics*—the place, time limit, time of day, and emotional climate—for the speech.

- *Place.* The place can affect the tone and topic of a speech. Such factors as the size of the room, temperature, lighting, furniture arrangement, and physical comfort or discomfort of the audience all affect your communication. Do the acoustics of the room enable the listeners to hear you clearly? Is there a microphone? When using presentation software, can you dim the lights or do you have to turn them off completely? How is the seating arranged?
- *Time.* Both the time limit and the time of day affect a speaker's performance. Whatever the reason for the time limit, a speaker has an obligation to stay within the prescribed boundaries, so it is important to prepare so that you don't ramble.

  The time of day can affect an audience. Early morning and late night hours, for instance, often are difficult times to hold the attention of an audience. You might want to plan a shorter speech if you know you are speaking near the end of the day or at the finish of a conference.
- *Emotional climate.* The setting for public communication may be affected by its *emotional climate*—the overriding psychological state of the participants. A community recently devastated by a tornado, for example, would have a high level emotional climate. Thus, a speaker called on to present a speech in such a setting would have to adapt his or her message to the tragedy and deal with the fears, bitterness, and trauma that the audience has been experiencing.

From the information obtained in the prior analysis, you should be able to reach a reasonable conclusion about a topic that will fit you and the audience as well as the language and the supporting materials needed to develop such a speech.

Applying the Prior Analysis Assuming you have completed your prior analysis, how do you use the information?

Topic Selection Typically, speakers are asked to make presentations because of their knowledge, experiences, or expertise. For example, a businessperson is told to present a new plan for reorganizing her department. Or a speaker decides that he has something to say and finds an audience who should and will listen to the message.

On the other hand, sometimes a speaker is given limited leeway in selecting a topic. In the academic setting, for example, to help students learn how to plan and prepare speeches, instructors may restrict students on what topic to use for a class assignment.

If you are given latitude in selecting your topic, know that you are your best resource. An examination of your life experiences and interests can be useful for selecting topics. For example, consider your hobbies and special interests, places you have lived or traveled, or the skills you have. Some people like to develop a speaking inventory to help them in the topic identification process. To develop such a list, fill out the Your Speaker Inventory.

Socially COMMUNICATING

Focus on Why

When preparing a presentation, conduct a "so why?" test. Pretend you're a member of the audience and ask, "So why do I need to know this?" If you don't have a clear answer, your audience won't either.

Source: Communication briefings. Simple steps to a powerful presentation. *Quill*, 100 Schelter Road, Lincolnshire, IL 60069.

Your Speaker Inventory

One of the keys to giving an effective oral presentation is to choose a subject you are interested in and about which you have some knowledge. To learn your interest and knowledge base, fill out this speaker inventory:

1. Hobbies and special interests ____________
2. Places I have traveled ____________
3. Things I know how to do (sports I can play, skills I have) ____________
4. Jobs I have had ____________
5. Experiences (accidents, special events) ____________
6. Funny things that have happened to me ____________
7. Books I have read and liked ____________
8. Movies and plays I have seen and liked ____________
9. Interesting people I have known ____________
10. People I admire ____________
11. Religious and nationality customs of my family ____________
12. Talents I have (musical instruments played, athletic abilities) ____________

In order to assist you in preparing classroom speeches, a list of topic ideas is presented in the Appendix. After selecting a general topic, many speakers new to public communication have difficulty narrowing the topic to fit the audience and the time limit. One of the best ways to do this is to probe into the various aspects of the subject you have selected by asking yourself questions about the selected theme:

- What is your topic?
- Where does the topic come from?
- How have attitudes and knowledge about the topic changed in recent years?
- What are some subtopics of the subject?
- Why is it significant?
- What are major events related to the topic?
- What can you say about your topic that will be useful to your audience?
- What makes you to want to talk about this topic?
- What/how does your topic/solution cause or eliminate problems?
- What/how does it cause or eliminate problems?

Obviously, not all of these questions can be applied to every topic, but by asking these questions you should be able to narrow the general topic to subtopics so you can have a specific focus for your presentation. (See Figure 11.1.)

Another way to narrow a topic is to Google the subject. For example, in one  Google attempt of the term *baseball,* a single page listed, "Negro baseball leagues," "Little League baseball," "heroes of baseball," "the science of baseball," "minor league baseball," and "baseball cards." A search on "baseball cards," further narrowed the topic to "vintage baseball cards," "the best in baseball cards," "trading baseball cards online," and "Topps baseball cards."

A student athlete and sports management major used questions to select the general topic of *baseball* for a five-minute informative speech for his class. He knew he needed to narrow the topic and take into consideration the demographic, psychographic, and rhetorographic information about his audience. He began with these questions:

What is it?	Baseball is a sport that is played on the professional and amateur levels.
Where does it come from?	Baseball was invented in the United States and has a long history.
How has it changed?	Rule changes of baseball include adding of the designated hitter; differences in types of balls, glove and bats used; the banning of performance-enhancing drugs.
What are some subtopics of the subject?	Strategies including giving of signals to the batter and the pitcher; the differences between major and minor leagues; how a player gets to be a major league player.
What are major events of its past?	Black Sox scandal; excessive payment to players; major stars being suspended for use of strength-enhancing drugs

Based on the questions, his audience analysis, and his own knowledge and interests, he narrowed his specific topic choices to:

1. The controversy regarding the use of performance-enhancing drugs.
2. How signals are given to the batter and the pitcher.

Since the topic of performance-enhancing drugs was currently an issue in the press, that many student athletes were in the class, that several parents in the class had teenagers who were playing sports, and he had heard briefings on the performance-enhancing drugs, he selected the topic, performance-enhancing drugs. He will discuss what the drugs are, why athletes take the drugs, and the two major reasons why student athletes should not use these drugs.

FIGURE 11.1 Narrowing the Topic of a Speech

Source: Concept conceived by Tony Zupancic. Notre Dame College, South Euclid, OH.

Using the information presented so far, let's examine the process leading up to the presentation of the speech:

- Picking a General Topic: An Example

  Chan is a twenty-year-old college sophomore. In filling out his speaker inventory, he discovered that many of his interests and knowledge center on his having worked at McDonald's restaurants for the past four years. He is now in the management training program and is in college to fulfill requirements for becoming a district manager. He would like to talk about McDonald's! He now has a general topic. The next question is, What specifically will he speak about? The answer takes further analysis.

- Using Demographic Information: An Example

  Chan remembers that during the first day of his communication course, everyone was introduced. Almost all of the students are health care, pre-medicine, social work, preschool, education, and psychology majors. He is one of two business majors. A number of the older students have young children. The topics he considers include how a McDonald's restaurant is managed, what his job consists of, his possible future employment with the restaurant chain, and the Ronald McDonald House program. He would feel comfortable talking about all of these, but which would be best for this audience? Based on the major academic fields of the audience, he eliminates managing the restaurant and possible employment; these would be more appropriate for business majors. He eliminates speaking about what his job consists of because it is of interest to him but probably not to anyone else. Chan realizes that everyone in his class—no matter what their majors—probably cares about kids. He selects the Ronald McDonald House program because it deals with health care and social service issues and is aimed at working with children and parents, which fits the audience demographics.

- Using Psychographic Information: An Example

  Chan reconsiders his choice based on psychographics. It doesn't appear, from what he can tell of the class, that any political or conservative/liberal disposition would be negatively stirred by his topic selection, so he decides to stick with his Ronald McDonald House choice.

- Using Rhetorographic Information: An Example

  Chan now needs to test his topic regarding place, time limit, time of day, and emotional climate. The classroom doesn't seem to have any negative effect on the topic selection, although he is aware that his idea of showing snapshots isn't going to work in the large room, with a class of thirty students, so he decides to use PowerPoint graphics instead. There doesn't seem to be any existing emotional climate he has to deal with. The time limit of the speech, however, is going to be a factor. He has a maximum of five minutes to speak. There is no way he can inform the class about all the activities of Ronald McDonald House in that time, so he is going to have to limit the breadth of the topic. He decides to tell the purpose of Ronald McDonald House and give two personal examples of children he has assisted as an active volunteer with the local project.

Language Selection Like the topic, the language selected for use during a speech must be adapted to the audience. The average thirteen-year-old's vocabulary is not the same as a college graduate's, for example. By the same token, certain terms that are common to a specific occupational or cultural group may be baffling to individuals who are not members of that group. And a person who is well versed on a specific subject can easily forget that the audience may not have the same knowledge.

It is important to adapt your vocabulary to the level of the audience. Be careful not to talk down to your listeners and not to use language that is so technical or abstract that they do not understand.

- Selecting Appropriate Language: An Example

  Chan, in thinking about the subject, the audience, and language, realizes that he has to make sure not to use terms that are unfamiliar to those not working at McDonald's or unfamiliar with the facility. For example, he must avoid calling the site "Willie's Place," the volunteers' nickname for it. (The first person to portray Ronald McDonald was the now TV personality Willard Scott, who has been strongly identified with the agency.)

Statement of Central Idea In developing a message, a speaker should know specifically what she or he wants to communicate. Thus, before even starting to put together the actual presentation, public speakers find it useful to compose a **statement**

of central idea, which defines the subject and develops the criteria by which to evaluate the material to be included in the speech. A statement of central idea centers on what you want the audience to know, to be able to do, to believe. The statement of central idea typically consists of three parts: the goal of the speech, the statement of the topic, and the method or process used to develop the speech.

The *goal of the speech* is expressed in terms of its expected outcome. To *inform* (impart new information and secure understanding or reinforce information and understandings acquired in the past) or to *persuade* (to get the listener to take some action, to accept a belief, or to change a point of view) are the speech goals.

The *topic of the speech*—the subject—should be stated as specifically as possible.

The *method of speech development* encompasses how you plan to approach the presentation. A topic that requires an in-depth study of one fact—for example, how cast members are chosen for a theatrical production—presents a detailed development of a single issue. If the topic requires a complete survey of ideas, a number of topics may need to be covered—for example, how a play is cast, rehearsed, and performed. Just as in language selection, the method of development depends a great deal on your determination of how much your listeners know about or, need to know about the topic you have selected.

Key words can assist in developing a statement of central idea for an informative speech—for example, *by explaining, by summarizing, by contrasting, by describing, by demonstrating,* and *by analyzing.*

In a persuasive speech, key phrases in developing the statement of central idea can include *to accept that, to support, to agree with, to contribute to, to serve, to share,* and *to vote for.*

Here are two examples of the statement of central idea prepared by an informative speaker:

- To inform the audience why competency testing is being used as a determination for high school graduation by discussing the three major reasons for use of testing.
- I want the audience to know of the important effect that Latino music has had on changing the self-image of Hispanic Americans. To do this, I will list and explain the effects on Hispanic Americans brought about through the cross-cultural popularity of Ricky Martin, Jennifer Lopez, and Selena.

Here are two examples of persuasive statements of central idea:

- I want the audience to fill out and sign living wills. To do this, I will list three reasons for them to take the action.
- To persuade the audience to accept the concept that getting help from a mental health professional can be a positive act by examining the five most common reasons people seek mental health help and the statistics showing the success rate of treatment for those problems.

By keeping these factors in mind, you can avoid some of the major pitfalls of neophyte speakers: not finishing the speech in the time limit, not accomplishing the speech's purpose, and not allowing the audience to gain the information.

- Writing the Statement of Central Idea: An Example

Chan is now ready to prepare his statement of central idea: "To inform the audience about the Ronald McDonald House project, by explaining the purpose of the project and presenting two examples of children who have been aided by Ronald McDonald House." He checks to make sure his statement contains a goal (to inform), a topic (the Ronald McDonald House project), and a method of development (explaining and presenting). Chan is now ready to develop his speech.

The speaker's preparation also extends to doing a careful prior analysis of the audience and the setting, and drawing up a statement of central idea that will be appropriate to his or her level of expertise and knowledge and to the intended listeners.

Process of Speech Analysis

As the speech is being presented, actively analyze the feedback you are receiving. This process of speech analysis is important to the accomplishment of your speaking goal. Speakers frequently need to adjust the materials as they present. For example, A gay rights activist heckled President Obama at a California fundraiser during the lead-up to the 2010 election, urging the President to "move faster on a proposed repeal of the military's don't ask-don't tell policy."[29] The crowd then began chanting Obama's signature campaign chant: "Yes we can! Yes we can! Yes we can!" Obama said to the audience, "When you've got an ally like Barbara Boxer [California Senator who had voted against don't ask don't tell when it was passed during the Clinton administration] and you've got an ally like me who are standing for the same thing, then I don't know exactly why you've got to holler, because we already hear you." Obama remarked to applause, 'I mean, it would have made more sense to holler at the people who oppose it [the repeal of don't ask, don't tell].'"[30]

Verbal interruptions are not typical. More typical are nonverbal cues of attentiveness and agreement, or of boredom or hostility, conveyed through posture and facial expression. Some speakers are sensitive to the *cough meter.* If you have lost your audience's attention, you may hear an increasing number of people clear their throats, cough, and become physically restless.

Effective process analysis requires that you interpret cues accurately and then adapt to them. Be careful not to assume, for instance, that one person nodding off represents boredom on the part of all of your listeners. However, if most of the audience looks bored, you should be concerned.

You can adapt to the feedback in various ways. For example, if you think the audience does not understand a point, add an illustration, clarify your terms, or restate the idea. If you sense that the audience is not attentive, change the volume of your voice, use a pause, move forward, or insert an interesting or humorous story. Another technique used in the classroom or training session is to ask questions of audience members to involve them in the presentation.

Most people don't feel totally comfortable in departing from their preplanned notes during a speech. The more confidence you have in your speaking abilities and the more comfortable you are with the topic, the more willing you will be to adjust to the feedback. Some people make mental notes about what is happening and then try to figure out afterward what went wrong so they can adjust their material or presentational style for their next speech. Besides noting what is going on during the speech, post-speech analysis can be of help in perfecting your speaking skills.

Post-Speech Analysis

Post-speech analysis enables you to determine how your speech affected the audience, which offers you useful information for preparing and presenting future speeches. A direct way to conduct a post-speech analysis is to have a question-and-answer session. The questions your audience asks may reveal how clear your presentation was. The verbal and language tone of the questions may reflect the general mood of the listeners, telling you how positively or negatively they received you and your message. Informal conversations with members of the audience after the speech also can reveal a great deal.

Other post-speech techniques include opinion polls, tests, questionnaires, and follow-up interviews. These techniques are often used by professional speakers, such as politicians, to evaluate their presentations.

Part of your preparation for a speech is to decide on the mode of presentation you will use when presenting the speech.

Modes of Presentation

Four basic *modes of speech presentation*—the preparation method and reference aids to be used during the speech—are impromptu, extemporaneous, manuscript, and memorized. Within those modes, presentations are typically face-to-face. Today the presentation may also included online or mediated formats.[31]

Impromptu or Ad Lib Mode

Sometimes a speaker uses information acquired from experience, speaks with little or no preparation, and organizes ideas while he or she is communicating. This approach is referred to as **impromptu speaking.** Some speech theorists distinguish this from **ad lib speaking**, in which a speaker has no time to organize ideas and responds immediately when answering a question, volunteering an opinion, or interacting during a question-and-answer session. The impromptu mode gives a speaker a short period of time to decide what to say; therefore, the speaker does not communicate quite as spontaneously as when ad libbing. For example, when a teacher asks a question in class and gives students a minute or so to think of the answer, students use the impromptu mode when responding. Getting called on and being required to give an immediate answer is an ad lib.

These forms of speaking offer the advantage of being natural and spontaneous and tend to represent a speaker's true feelings and thoughts because so little time is available to develop defenses and strategies.

Sometimes a speaker uses information acquired from past experiences, speaks with little or no preparation, and organizes ideas while he or she is communicating.

Both of these modes are weakened, however, by the lack of time a speaker has to develop organized and well-analyzed statements. Another drawback, which derives from the impossibility of doing research, is the speaker's lack of opportunity to use statistics, examples, or illustrations to explain ideas clearly unless he or she is an expert on the topic. Still another liability is the speaker's tendency to be short or ramble, and or use phrases such as "you know" and "stuff like that" to gain thinking time or gloss over nonspecific information. Finally, lack of preparation also can result in oral uncertainty—a speaker's inability to present a coherent speech.

Putting together an impromptu speech requires quick work and immediate decisions. The process is the same as preparing for any other type of speech, except that there is less time to get ready. As you try to organize your thoughts, keep these ideas in mind:

Step 1: Determine what topic you wish to present.

Step 2: Word a statement of central idea that represents the topic.

Step 3: List the major headings that develop the statement of central idea. If paper is available, jot down the ideas. Write these in the vertical middle of the sheet of paper so you have time to add the introduction about them later, if time is available. Leave space between the major headings so that if you have time for developing subpoints, you will be able to write them in.

Step 4: Arrange the major headings according to one of the methods of organization—time or space order, problem solution, or a topical approach (see Chapter 13 for a discussion of organizational methods). Use the list you developed in step 3 and number the order of each heading.

Step 5: Decide on an introduction. Most ad lib/impromptu speakers tend to use a question or a reference to the topic, but often you can think of a story that relates to the topic. Because you probably will not have time to write out the whole introduction, jot down several key words so you will remember what you want to say.

in Careers

Facing a Last-Minute Speech

If you have to present with little notice, follow these tips:

- Write down a single phrase describing what you need to communicate to your audience. Then, write three actions, reasons, or qualities supporting that phrase. *Example*: If you want to communicate how to increase sales, three actions to do so could be: make more cold calls, ask for referrals, and survey customers. Mention the points during your speech. *Tip*: Write them on the back of a business card for easy reference.
- Answer the questions who, what, when, where, why, and how. *Example*: If you're talking about change that will occur in your organization, tell the audience who will be in charge of the change effort, what the change is, why it's necessary, when it will occur, where it will take place, and how it will be achieved.
- Refer to a current event or personal story and link either to your main point. Audiences will remember these more easily than facts or figures.
- Use an analogy to help get your message across. *Example*: If speaking about a new product, say, "Our new widget is like a stealth fighter because it gets the job done, and you don't even know it's there."
- Memorize four or five quotations about motivation, communication, or teamwork and include them in your talk.

Source: "Facing a Last-Minute Speech," by S. Deep and L. Sussman, adapted from "Smart Moves for People in Charge," *Communication Briefings*. Reprinted with permission of Briefings Media Group.

Step 6: Restate the major points you made as the conclusion.

Step 7: If you have time, go back to see if you can think of any illustrations, examples, or statistics that develop the major ideas you want to present. Write them in at the appropriate place in the outline. If there is no time, try to think of some as you speak. Make sure that you clarify or define any words that may be unfamiliar to your listeners.

Extemporaneous Mode

People who have more time to prepare for their presentations often use the mode of **extemporaneous speaking**, developing a set of *talking points*, in notes or an outline, to assist them in presenting their ideas.

The extemporaneous mode offers significant advantages: time to find the information needed to help accomplish the statement of central idea; the security of having notes or an outline to refer to throughout the speech; the use of quotations, illustrations, and statistics in written form for backing up ideas; and a more spontaneous and natural oral presentation and physical presentation than are likely in the manuscript or memorized mode.

As with any other presentational format, the extemporaneous mode of delivery has some disadvantages as well. For example, a speaker who does not allow sufficient time for preparation and rehearsal may get mentally lost during the presentation. Furthermore, if a speaker refers to the notes or outline too frequently during the speech or has too many notes, she or he may fail to interact with the audience. And because extemporaneous material is not written out word for word, there will be no permanent written record of the speech.

Preparing the Extemporaneous Speech Most speakers use either notes or an outline when they present an extemporaneous speech. Notes can consist of a list of words that guide the speaker through the presentation or a series of phrases or sentences to act as clues.

Many speakers start out with a **speech planning outline**, a brief framework used to think through the process of the speech. This outline contains the major ideas of the speech, without elaboration. It is a means of thinking through the things you wish to say and putting them in a structured order. Some speakers use this for practice and while speaking. Others prepare a **speech presentation outline** in which they flesh out the outline with examples and illustrations and write in internal summaries and forecasts. (An outlining tool for formatting a speech can be found on this textbook's website.)

Outlining The basic concept in *outlining* is that the speaker has a clear step-by- step structure of what will be said and in what order. Some speakers simply list the headings and subordinate points in a sequential order. Others use a formal outlining method.

Numerous rules have been developed for how to structure an outline.[32] Some speech instructors are very specific as to what the outline is to look like, indicating that the discipline of developing the outline aids the speaker in making sure that all parts of the speech are well developed and ordered. Others are more flexible and believe that the outline helps the speaker become comfortable with the material and remember what he/she need to say so strict outlining rules do not have to be followed.

An outline generally has a balanced structure based on four major principles: parallelism, coordination, subordination, and division:[33]

- *Parallelism.* Whenever possible, when preparing an outline, you should express coordinate heads in parallel form. That is, nouns should be made parallel with nouns, verb forms with verb forms, adjectives with adjectives, and so on (*Example:* Nouns: *computers, programs, users;* Verbs: *to compute, to program, to use;* Adjectives: *home* computers, *new* programs, *experienced* users). Although parallel structure is desired, logical and clear language should not be sacrificed simply to maintain parallelism. (For example, there are times when nouns and gerunds at the same level of an outline are acceptable.) Reasonableness and flexibility of form are preferred to rigidity.

- *Coordination.* In outlining, those items that are of equal significance should have comparable numeral or letter designations: An *A* is equal to a *B,* a *1* to a *2,* an *a* to a *b,* and so on. Coordinates should have the same value. Coordination is a principle that enables a writer to maintain a coherent and consistent outline. Here is a sample of good coordination:

A. Types of alternative electric energy sources
   1. Nuclear power plants
   2. Wind turbines
   3. Solar energy

B. Evaluation of programs
   1. Safety
      a. Nuclear power plants
      b. Wind turbines
      c. Solar energy
   2. Cost of building and maintenance
      a. Nuclear power plants
      b. Wind turbines
      c. Solar energy
   3. Effect on the community
      a. Nuclear power plants
      b. Wind turbines
      c. Solar energy

- *Subordination.* To indicate levels of significance, an outline uses major and minor headings. Thus, in ordering ideas, you should organize the outline from general to specific or from abstract to concrete—the more general or abstract the term, the higher its level or rank in the outline. This principle allows your material to be ordered in terms of logic and requires a clear articulation of the relationships among the component parts used in the outline. Subdivisions of each higher division should always have the same relationship to the whole. Here is a sample of a good subordination form of major headings:

A. Nuclear power plants
   1. Positive features
   2. Negative features

B. Wind turbines
   1. Positive features
   2. Negative features

C. Solar energy
   1. Positive features
   2. Negative features

- *Division.* The purpose of the divisions is to detail the major ideas by adding clarifiers, examples, and illustrations. Some outlining purists contend that "for every *A* there should be a *B* and for every *1* there must be a *2*."[34] In general, this makes sense. If you are subdividing an idea—that is, breaking it into parts—then by definition, you must have at least two sub-ideas. This does not mean, however, that if you are supporting an idea with an example, you must have two examples. Here is a sample of good division form:

  A. Computer storage
    1. Mainframe
    2. Micro
      a. Zip drive
      b. External hard drive
      c. Flash drive
      d. Portable hard drive

  B. Computer uses
    1. Institutional
      a. Individual
      b. Shared
    2. Personal

- *Form.* The most important rule for outlining form is to be consistent! Most speech outlines use either a topic structure or a sentence structure.

  A **topic outline** has words or phrases for all entries and usually has little or no punctuation after entries. One advantage of this format is that it presents a brief overview of the ideas. In addition, speakers often find that they will speak more and read less with the abbreviated material on the page.

  A **sentence outline** has complete sentences for all entries and usually has correct punctuation. One advantage of this format is that there is a more detailed overview of the ideas to be presented. Therefore, it may give the speaker more security since whole ideas rather than word clues are presented.

  An outline can use a combination of Roman numerals and letters or a decimal form. An outline composed of Roman numerals and letters follows this format:

  I.
    A.
    B.
      1.
      2.
        a.
        b.
  II.

  An outline composed of decimals would follow this format:

  1.0
    1.1
    1.2
      1.2.1
      1.2.2
        1.2.2.1
        1.2.2.2

Here are some additional guidelines specific to speech outline format:

- *Include internal summaries and forecasts.* Internal summaries restate each major point before proceeding to the next major point. Forecasts tell the listener what is coming next. To ensure that they remember to include these in the oral presentation, many speakers write the statements into the outline.
- *Write notes in the margins to remind yourself of necessary information.* If you need a reminder to slow down in certain sections or to use a visual aid to emphasize a point, write yourself a note in the margin of the outline. Use a color of ink that stands out. Although the marginal notes are not an official part of the outline, they are yet another device to help make the speech effective and to help you feel comfortable and gain confidence.
- *Avoid over outlining.* To avoid having an excessive number of notes, limit the quantity to those you absolutely need to trigger your thoughts. In determining what is essential, you are wise to consider this analogy. The first time you drive to a particular site, you may need a detailed set of directions complete with route numbers, road markers, and indications of exact mileage. On your second trip, you need less information, and by the third trip, you need almost none. So it is with your use of notes and outlines. You should have enough information to feel comfortable and free to navigate through the presentation with no fear of getting lost. The only way to discover the extent of your readiness is to take several test drives through your speech to ascertain how much prepared information you really need to have with you in the form of written prompts.

Mind Mapping An alternative to using an outline for the extemporaneous mode of presentation is mind mapping. **Mind mapping** is a method of arranging materials visually rather than in list form. This is a mode often favored by global thinkers/listeners who are stimulated by pictures rather than words (see pages 89–90 for a discussion of global thinkers/listeners).

To mind-map, the potential speaker makes a list of all the ideas to be included in the speech. Then major headings are selected, each major idea is placed in a circle,

Mind mapping is a method of arranging materials in a speech visually rather than in list form.

and the subpoints are grouped around the major heading circles and connected to the circles with spokes. The speaker indicates the major heading, then orally flows from one spoke to another. When one circle and its spokes are finished, the speaker proceeds to the next circle and discusses its topical spokes. Let's say you are planning on speaking about a visit to Washington, DC, the nation's capital. You make a list of the things you did and the sights you saw (Figure 11.2). You then set the major theme ideas in circles and group the subhead ideas around those major themes (Figure 11.3). This drawing forms the basis for the speech.

Subject: Visiting Washington, DC

- Smithsonian Museums
- Georgetown
- Kennedy Center for Performing Arts
- Tyson's Corner Center
- Korean Memorial
- Metro
- *Outdoor things to do
- Vietnam Memorial
- Ford's Theater
- Jefferson Memorial
- Beltway
- Bureau of Engraving and Printing
- The White House
- Capitol Building
- Mazza Gallery
- *Indoor things to do
- Holocaust Museum
- Washington Monument
- Arlington Cemetery
- National Zoo
- FBI Building
- Parking lots
- *Transportation
- Roosevelt Memorial
- Corcoran Art Gallery
- Lincoln Monument
- The Mall
- *Shopping
- Tidal Basin
- Pentagon
- Old Town Alexandria
- Smithsonian Gift Shops
- Fashion Mall at Pentagon City

Outdoor Things to Do

- Arlington Cemetery
- National Zoo
- Korean Memorial
- Vietnam Memorial
- Lincoln Monument
- Jefferson Memorial
- Roosevelt Memorial
- Washington Monument
- Tidal Basin
- The Mall

Shopping

- Old Town Alexandria
- Mazza Gallery
- Smithsonian Gift Shops
- Fashion Mall
- Georgetown
- Tyson's Corner Center

Indoor Things to Do

- Smithsonian Museums
- Kennedy Center for Performing Arts
- Bureau of Engraving and Printing
- The White House
- FBI Building
- Corcoran Art Gallery
- Pentagon
- Capitol Building
- Holocaust Museum
- Ford's Theatre

Transportation

- Beltway
- Parking Lots
- Metro

*Main topics

FIGURE 11.2 Mind-Mapping Procedure

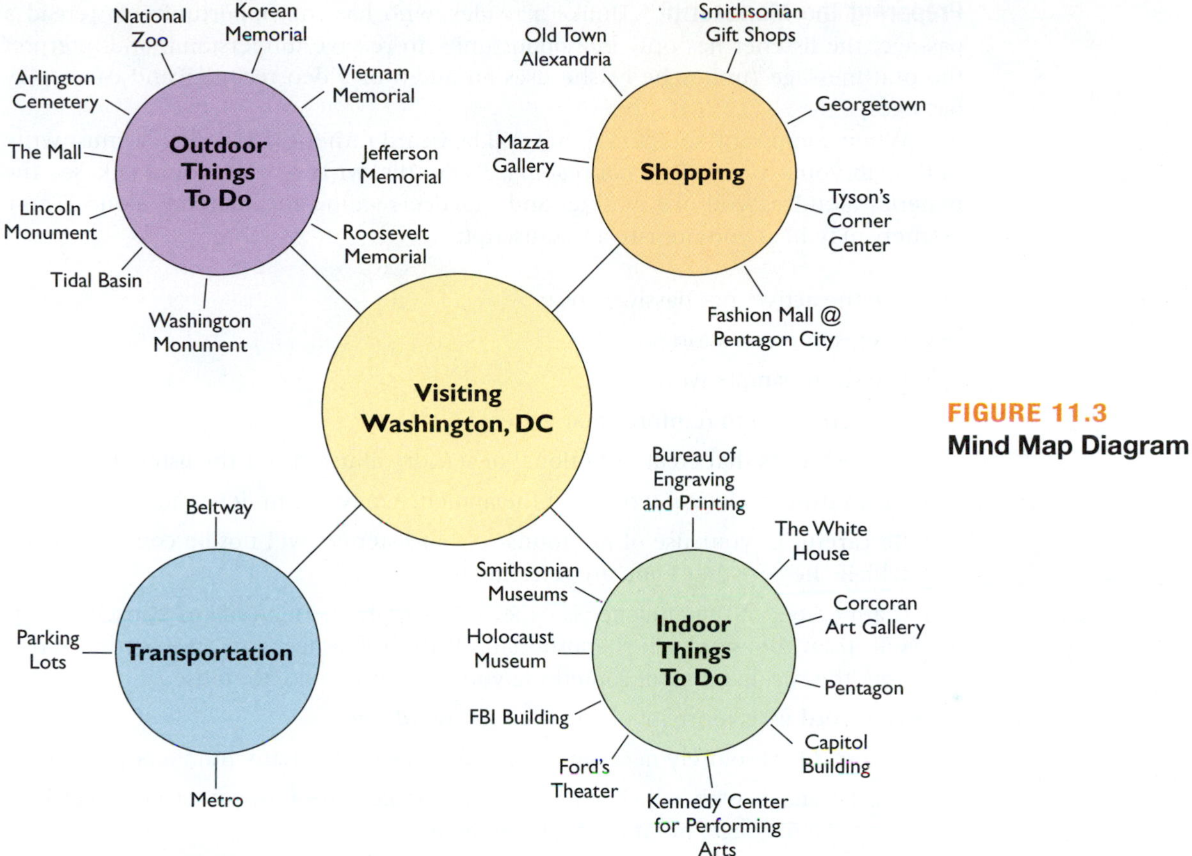

FIGURE 11.3
Mind Map Diagram

Manuscript Mode

In the **manuscript speech mode**, the material is written out and delivered word for word. This method offers the advantages of providing accurate language and solid organization. In addition, it gives the speaker a permanent written record of the speech.

But the manuscript mode also has some disadvantages. Because the manuscript provides a word-for-word record of the speech, the speaker cannot easily adapt it to suit the audience during the presentation. The speaker is stuck with the message as written. As a result, the speaker must depend entirely on prior audience analysis to ensure that the message is tailored to the listeners.

The manuscript mode of delivery also requires the ability to read effectively from the written page. An effective speaker should use extensive eye contact, vocal inflections, and physical actions to maintain rapport with the listeners. Unfortunately, many people are not very good oral readers. They read monotonously, make reading errors, get lost in the script, and fail to establish good eye contact. Many novice speakers turn to the manuscript mode because they feel more secure with it. However, manuscript speeches, are often dull and boring.

Accomplished speakers generally use the extemporaneous mode rather than the manuscript mode because it allows them to interact more freely with their audience and to adapt to feedback. At times, however, preparing an exact word-for-word presentation is necessary. For example, the manuscript mode must be used when speakers are going to be quoted, when they must meet specific time requirements, when they need precise word selection, or when it is important to have a written record of the presentation for future reference.

Preparing the Manuscript Unlike a reader, who has the opportunity to reread a passage, the listener has only one opportunity to receive, understand, and interpret the oral message (unless he or she uses an audio or video recorder and can replay passages).

When composing something that will be heard rather than read, you must write as though you are speaking, not reading. To do this, write as you would talk, say the material aloud as you are writing, and practice reading the material aloud. These pointers may help you prepare a manuscript:

- Use the active, not passive, voice.
- Keep sentences short.
- Use short, simple words.
- Use repetition to reinforce major ideas.
- Express ideas that create emotional or sensory allusions for the listener.
- Avoid using technical terms that the audience may not understand.
- Be careful in your use of pronouns so that listeners will not be confused about which "he" or "they" you are referring to.
- If a member of the audience is expected to apply the material to himself or herself, then the word *you* is appropriate. If the reference is to an experience that you, the speaker, had or something you are going to do, then use *I*.
- The word *we* is more involving than the word *you*.
- Unless it is absolutely necessary not to do so, round off any numbers you use.
- Use language with which you are comfortable. The purpose of language is to convey a message, not impress the audience.
- Remember the rule for wording a bumper sticker: Express specific ideas by employing a few well-chosen words.

Memorized Mode

In the **memorized speech mode**, a speech is written out word for word and then committed to memory. Public speakers seldom use this mode of communication because it is potentially disastrous. Whereas speakers who use the extemporaneous or manuscript mode can refer to written information, those who use the memorized mode have nothing available for reference as they speak. Forgetting one idea can lead to forgetting everything. Also, the memorizer may be so concerned about getting the exact word in exactly the right place that the meaning of the words becomes secondary. The few advantages of the memorized mode include the ability to select exact wording and examples, the opportunity to look at the audience extensively during the entire speaking process, and the ability to time the presentation precisely. The disadvantages of memorized speaking usually so overshadow its advantages that few people choose to use this mode.

In Conclusion

IN CONCLUSION

The act of public communication involves a transaction between a speaker and an audience. As in any other act of communication, the participants, the setting, and the purpose of the communication affect a public speech. These three parameters may affect the topic selected, the language used, the types of examples and illustrations chosen, and the aids needed to support and clarify ideas. To investigate the parameters, an audience analysis is done through prior speech analysis, process of speech analysis, and postspeech analysis. The public speaker can use one of four basic modes of presentation: impromptu or ad lib, extemporaneous, manuscript, and memorized.

LEARN BY DOING

1. You have two minutes to introduce yourself to your classmates. Make two outlines for the presentation. The first should follow the traditional format, the second the mind-mapping format. Practice the presentation using the footnotes. Which one appears to be a format you would be comfortable using?
2. What questions would you ask a person who has invited you to give a speech on the topic of your choice to a club or organization? Why did you pick these questions?
3. Use a topic related to your academic major to develop a statement of central idea for an informative speech to be presented to a group of classmates. Then prepare another informative statement of central idea for the same topic but for a nonclassroom audience. Based on the different statements of central idea, how will the speeches vary?
4. Prepare a statement of central idea informing a group of high school students about your college for a speech of fifteen minutes. Now write a statement of central idea for the same speech in which you will have only five minutes to speak. Why did your statement of central idea change according to the time frame?
5. On a 3″ × 5″ card, list three topics you think you could speak about for a minimum of two minutes. Your instructor selects one of these for you to give an impromptu speech about. You have two minutes to get ready. You may use any notes you can prepare within that time.

KEY TERMS

public communication 294
purpose of the speech 296
plagiarism 297
fabrication 298
audience analysis 300
statement of central idea 305
impromptu speaking 308
ad lib speaking 308
extemporaneous speaking 310
speech planning outline 310
speech presentation outline 310
topic outline 312
sentence outline 312
mind mapping 313
manuscript speech mode 315
memorized speech mode 316

Public Speaking: Developing the Message

reference sources for developing public speeches • identifying and analyzing support material

CHAPTER 12

After reading this chapter, you should be able to

- Identify the sources used to develop public speaking messages
- List basic reference sources used for the development of public speeches
- Illustrate the value of using and the method for finding books, magazines, newspapers, journals, indexes, government publications, special-interest group publications, and nonprint media
- Record research information
- Evaluate the validity of research material used to develop a speech
- Analyze the role of support material in the development of a speech
- Identify and evaluate means of presenting and focusing supporting material

Listening to a speech can be an exciting, interesting, or uplifting experience. It also can be frustrating, boring, or confusing. The differences between positive and negative experiences often are based on whether the speaker has defined terms, organized the speech clearly, offered clarifying examples, explained abstract concepts, presented proving statistics, drew in the audience emotionally, restated ideas, and illustrated thoughts with supplementary aids.

Sources of Information

Most of the information we use to develop messages is based on personal experiences, personal observations, or learning acquired through school, the media, and reading. As we are exposed to information, we retain a certain amount of it, and this knowledge forms the core of our communication. We select words and examples from this storehouse that we use to organize messages. Sometimes, however, we need information that is not in this core to develop a message. In such cases, you need outside sources to aid you.

Since the advent of the World Wide Web, some speech researchers have relied on doing a Web search for materials and using only what is revealed in a quick search. Be aware that search engines (e.g., Google, Yahoo, Bing, Opera) find only so much and some of that is of doubtful value.

As you search for sources of information to support your points, you should make every effort to locate **primary sources of information**: sources that represent the original reports of the observations or research. A peer-reviewed journal article is an example of a primary source. In other words, the scholar who conducted the research is the one writing the article. A presentation about a speaker's personal experience and a book written about an author's experiences are also examples of primary sources. The information is direct or "first hand." When the original work is not available, you may find it necessary to go to **secondary sources of information**; sources that report, but did not originally generate, the observations or research. The text of a new governor's State of the State speech is of more value for quoting than the summary written by a political reporter for the local paper. But, if the governor's speech is not published or available, the summary might have to do.

The expansion in digital networks in the United States' research and educational communities has opened up tools for millions of researchers.[1] It's not like the experience of past years when a student had to trudge off to the library to find information. Computers and smart phones have made web data available, not only in the library, but also at coffee shops, dorm rooms, or while sitting in the park.

Sources of information that speakers seek include books, magazines, newspapers, special journals, indexes, government publications, and the publications of special-interest groups. Many of these sources are available electronically. Additional sources include nonprint materials such as digital recordings, records, films, CDs, DVDs, videotapes, charts, models, and YouTube videos, as well as interviews with knowledgeable people in a particular field.

Books

Personal, academic, and public libraries can be the sources of much information; nevertheless, you must know how to find the materials you need. In libraries, books are shelved according to a numerical system and can be located by looking in the electronic catalog under the title, the author's name, or the general subject to find the index number. You can go to your library's online catalog, select the books you want, and have them delivered to the library location near you.

Some of the books can be downloaded as audio sources to an MP3 device. Many print books can be transferred to a Kindle, IPad, and other devices.

Books are of great value in supplying information, but they can become out of date. It generally takes at least a year for an average book to move from the author's draft through the printing process and onto the shelves of a library. Some subjects change little, and in these areas books are a good research source. But for quickly changing subjects, more up-to-date sources are needed for a thorough investigation.

Magazines

Most news magazines are designed to provide recent information quickly. Some of the news magazines are published weekly, so their information is as current as is the publication date. For example, a story in *Time* about Hosni Mubarak as Egypt's leader was viable on January 11, 2011, but past tense on February 11 of that year.

The growth of the Internet has decreased the number of magazines available as the advertising dollars once invested in magazines are now being funneled to online sources. At one time the only way to access a magazine was to locate a copy of the publication. Now, many magazines can be electronically accessed or they have online versions available to the public.

Be aware that there are magazines whose purpose is to spread sensational scandal and gossip. These tabloids are seldom sources for factual information.

Researchers must be aware that because the writers for magazines often gather their data quickly because of publication date pressure, some inaccuracies may occur. In addition, the editorial staffs of magazines sometimes have political and ideological biases

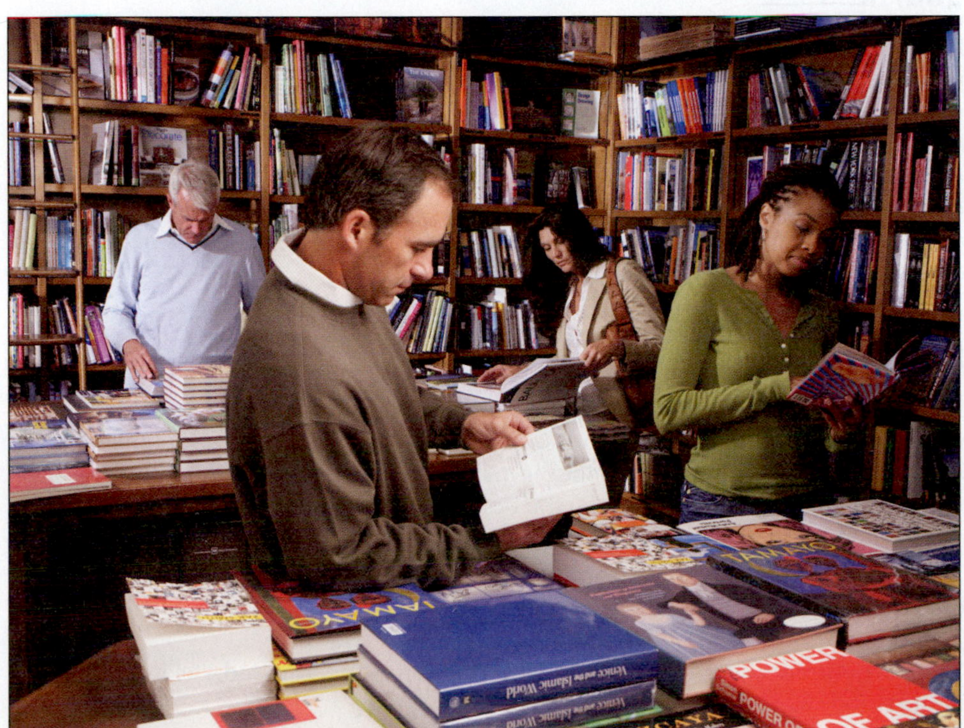

Besides using computer searches, sources of information that speakers seek out include books, magazines, and newspapers.

that may temper what they write or influence what subjects they include. Knowing, for example, that the *New Republic* supports liberal social causes and social democratic policies, while *The National Review* has a conservative editorial stance, allows the researcher to be aware of the biases of the information available.

To find information in magazines, one electronic index is the *Readers' Guide to Periodical Literature*,[2] a publication that indexes magazine articles by subject, title, and author. The *International Index* and other databases provide popular and trade magazine articles.

Newspapers

Newspapers, like magazines, are becoming rarer and rarer in paper form. Most libraries do not keep past issues of newspapers, except for those that have been recently published, but some store past publications on both microfilm and microfiche, or make them available through electronic databases.

More and more newspapers are publishing a digital version of their daily news. For example, the *New York Times* publishes a daily paper, but also publishes nytimes.com. Some of the digital versions often contain more material than the print version as it is cheaper to put information online than invest in newsprint.

Be aware that sometimes newspapers are the only source for finding certain materials. If, for example, you are looking for the specific past history of an event that happened at your college, checking the institution's collection of past newspapers may be the only source, since historically, collegiate publications and newspapers were not transferred to online archives nor were the events publicized in any other source. The same may be true for locating information about a small town's past. The area's newspaper may be your sole source. Unfortunately, many small town newspapers have no digital record.

Journals

Professional organizations often publish journals reporting research and theories in their specific fields. The National Communication Association, for example, publishes *Communication Education, Quarterly Journal of Speech, Communication Monographs, Journal of Applied Communication Research, The Communication Teacher,* and *Critical Studies in Mass Communication.* Thus, students who are interested in finding out about some area of communication can refer to these journals that are published in hard copy as well as available through Communication and Mass Media Complete. This is an Ebscohost database, the world's most-used reference resource.

Indexes

Encyclopedias, atlases, and bibliographical guides are indexes that provide descriptive information in certain categories. An index usually contains a minimal amount of information on many topics. Indexes may be a good starting point, but if you want in-depth material, they may not be the best sources. Often, electronic indexes link to additional information about the particular topic.

Wikis

Wikis are Internet sites that offer free information. Users can add, delete, or edit the information.

The best known Wiki is the online encyclopedia *Wikipedia*,[3] which is used by "36% of online American adults."[4] Be aware that it allows "anyone with an internet connection to create or alter any entry."[5] Because of the lack of an editorial board or screening panel, some wikis publish material that is factually questionable and cannot be corrected. A scientist, for example, found a number of factual inaccuracies in her subject of expertise, but when she submitted information to *Wikipedia*, they did not accept her input.[6] One of your authors, who was in on the founding of a new theatre some years ago, heard a speech by the newly appointed manager of the theatre. The information the manager presented was incorrect. When, following the speech, he asked the speaker about the source of her information she responded, "*Wikipedia*." Rather than search through the theatre records, she took the "easy way" and found wrong information.

Based on potential inaccuracy, most communication professors do not allow students to use *Wikipedia* as a source for speech and term paper research. A student, when asked if he would recommend the use of *Wikipeida* as a source for research, said, "Are you going to put the fate of your grades in the hands of total strangers who are able to make up things about a topic they might know nothing of? I think not!"[7]

Government Publications

The U.S. government publishes materials, available at minimal cost, on a variety of subjects. These can be found at bookstores in federal buildings in many major cities of the country and also can be accessed through the U.S. Government Printing Office's homepage. In addition, many major universities are designated as government depositories; all government documents are housed in those campus library systems.

Special-Interest Group Publications

Special-interest groups such as the American Cancer Society and the American Society for Training and Development publish information regarding their research and programs. A telephone call, email, or letter to such an organization often brings a response. Many of these materials can also be accessed through an organization's homepage on the Web. To find the name of an organization, its e-mail address, and/or its website, look in *Gale's Encyclopedia of Associations*.

Nonprint Media

Much information is available from nonprint media. Libraries and audiovisual departments of colleges and universities have collections of recordings, records, films, filmstrips, videotapes, DVDs, and CDs from commercially and locally prepared sources covering a variety of topics. These sources usually are cataloged in a manner similar to that used for books and periodicals. Some nonprint materials are available for general circulation, but others must be used on the premises.

Local and national radio and television stations and networks often sell audio or visual copies of their programs or provide streaming programs on the Internet. For example, ABC News and National Public Radio have catalogs of program recordings and videos available for sale.[8]

Interviews

Interviews can be used to find information that is not available from written or electronic sources. After all, what better way is there to find out, for example, how the budget of your college is developed than by talking to the institution's budget director? Such interviews can be conducted in a variety of ways. If someone is not available for a face-to-face meeting, try an email, instant messaging, or telephone session. You can submit a series of questions to be answered in-person, via the telephone, fax, or through e-mail.

Computer Searches

Almost every source suggested so far can be searched via computer. In fact, the Internet is the most popular source for the researching of information.[9]

Although most students enter the name of the topic they are searching for in Google or Yahoo!, this doesn't always give access to the best source. Just because something pops up first does not mean it is the best or even valid. It may simply mean that that item has been accessed the most or has paid for a top position. Note that in most research you do, one of the first sources that pops up is *Wikipedia*, because it is so often used. As just discussed, it is a source which has potential accuracy problems.

Don't just grab the initial offering. You often need to search further. You need to evaluate the source to determine whether or not the information is valid. Online research also requires knowledge of what computer-based retrieval system to use, as well as how to access information.

Computer-Based Retrieval Systems A *computer-based retrieval system* is an electronic database, which allows the researcher to retrieve content from subscription periodicals and other types of reference works and publications. LexisNexis, ProQuest, Ebsco Host, and Wilson Indexes are just a few of the databases available.

Searches may be used for a variety of purposes, including gathering research or references, compiling a reading list, acquiring statistical information, or simply keeping abreast of developments in a field. A major advantage to this method is the time saved, as a computer retrieves information in minutes that would otherwise take longer to compile. The search can locate references that many conventional searches may not. Another feature is the timeliness of the material since these databases are updated frequently.[10]

These databases give citation information, abstracts, and often full-text articles, so you can find the articles you need. Because these databases contain generic and academically based sources, you are likely to get much higher quality information than you would from a general search of the Internet.

Conducting a Database Search Once you have the database you plan to search, you need a method to find what you need. There are several steps in conducting an effective computer search. The principles apply no matter what database or index you use.[11]

1. *Select a database* that is relevant to the kind of information you seek (e.g., education sources: Education Full Text [www.hwwilson.com]; general information: Academic Search Premier [EBSCOhost]).
2. *Try key terms.* Realize that you may need to narrow or broaden the use of subject terms. Search by author, title, publication name, key words, or subject.
3. *Examine the hits* you have for clues to what is working and what isn't working. If you have trouble finding the necessary sources, check to be sure you're using the right words by consulting the database's thesaurus.

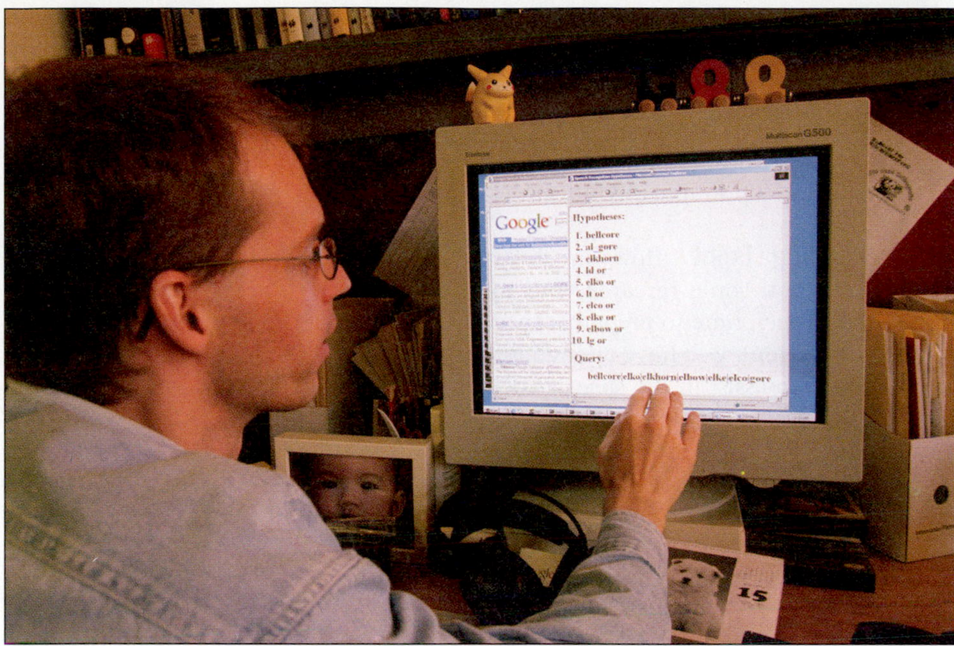

Online research requires knowledge of what search engine to use as well as how to access information.

4 *What do you do if your search gives too many hits?*

(a) Select only English-language articles (or articles written in whatever languages you read).

(b) Narrow to recent dates.

(c) Notice the key terms of articles that are what you need, and narrow to using only those terms.

(d) Select full-text articles so you can read the whole article without further searching.

(e) Conduct a *Boolean search,* a search that combines multiple words connected by *and* or *or.*

5 *What do you do if your search gives too few hits?*

(a) Look at the key words for any article that is on the right track.

(b) Link to the references inside any article you like.

(c) Look up in the database other key terms that might be appropriate.

What if you're not satisfied with your search?

Remember, you just need one good article to help you find more. See what key words were used to index the article, which will help lead you to similar sources. Look at the article's reference list, and you may find other articles of interest directly linked inside that database. Many databases will link you directly to other sources written by the author you found. Most major databases also offer tutorials that will give you suggestions about increasing the effectiveness of your research. Don't forget that a college reference librarian can provide assistance in your search.

6 *Mark the sources.* When you find sources you like, check the boxes or mark them.

7 *Save your sources* by printing, emailing them to yourself, or saving. You can set the database to give you American Psychological Association (APA) or other frequently used formatting so that your reference list is facilitated for you. If you found abstracts, then the database may have a "find it at ..." your library link to assist you in finding the full articles. If you found full text sources, you can link to the information you need.

8 *Cite your sources.* Make sure you collect the source of the material so you can specifically cite the source in your speech and can include it in your reference list.

Set a Stopping Point How much time will you spend on your research? Theoretically, you could research your topic for minutes or years. Realistically, you have only so much time to prepare a speech. Set a logical stopping point. This is usually when you think you have enough information to create the speech and have the aids you need to assist in the speech's development. If necessary, as you prepare the speech itself, you can go back and find any additional support to plug any holes in your message. Of course, this theory is based on the supposition that you have left yourself enough time to research, prepare, practice, and adjust the speech. If you are a procrastinator, you may be rushed to find material and not find appropriate or accurate sources.

Recording Your Research When you do research, keep a record of where your information came from so you can refer to the source to find additional information, answer questions about a source, or give oral footnotes during a speech. When you write a term paper, you must footnote *quotations*—material written or spoken by a person in the exact words in which it was originally presented—and *paraphrases*—someone else's ideas put into your own words. You do the same in public speaking, except orally. As you read through the following materials be aware of the amount of information that you will need to collect and record in order to develop an appropriate oral footnote.

In a speech concerning male–female communication, this **oral footnote** would be appropriate:

> Dr. Julia Wood, in discussing nonverbal behaviors of women and men in her book, *Communication, Gender, and Culture,* states, "Nonverbal behaviors expected of women emphasize communality—building and sustaining relationships and community. Nonverbal behaviors considered appropriate for men emphasize agency—displaying power and initiative, achieving."[12]

In some instances, it might be necessary to establish a quoted author as an authority. You do this because you think the audience doesn't know the author's credentials or the person, or because you want to reinforce the author's credibility. In this case, for an oral footnote, you could say:

> Julia T. Wood is one of our nation's eminent communication scholars and professors. The Council for Advancement and Support of Education (CASE) in Washington, DC, and the Carnegie Foundation for the Advancement of Teaching in Princeton, New Jersey, named Julia Wood Professor of the Year for North Carolina. Her interest in gender led her to teach graduate-level courses in Feminist Research in Communication and a seminar in Communication in Personal Relationships. In her book, *Gendered Lives, Communication, Gender, and Culture,* Dr. Wood states, "Nonverbal behaviors expected of women emphasize communality—building and sustaining relationships and community. Nonverbal behaviors considered appropriate for men emphasize agency—displaying power and initiative, achieving."

In recording your research, you may select from a variety of formats. The most commonly used patterns are those of the Modern Language Association (MLA) and the American Psychological Association (APA).[13] There is an APA style guide on the inside back cover of this text.

When actually inscribing your bibliographical information and notes from your research, you need to be careful to keep track of where you got the material. Notes can be taken on cards, sheets of paper, or as part of the computer files of your database research. Whichever method you use, be sure to transcribe the source of the material, including the author, title, publication, where the material was obtained (newspaper, book, the Internet), the date of the publication, the publisher and city, and the page number.

COMMUNICATING in Careers

Endnoting

Having trouble assembling and formatting your footnotes and endnotes?

Endnote X4 is a computer program that guides a researcher in how to compile and manage source citations by creating bibliographic databases. As the conceivers indicate, "The Internet is a vast resource—and it is growing at an ever increasing rate. As a researcher, sifting through the overwhelming number of websites in the search of scholarly information can be a challenging experience. This guide focuses on how to locate information efficiently and evaluate that information for quality of content."

Source: From http://endnote.com

One method of recording the research is to use a running bibliography. The list is numbered so that it can be used while you are taking notes. For those who are unfamiliar with formats for coding bibliographical entries, patterns for (1) a book, (2) a newspaper story, (3) a magazine or journal article, and (4) an online article are presented.

References

1. Wood, J. T. (2011). *Gendered lives: Communication, gender, and culture* (8th ed.). Belmont, CA: Thomson Higher Education, p. 152.
2. Knowlton, S. R. (1997, November 2). How students get lost in cyberspace. *Washington Post,* 18.
3. Tyre, P., & Scelfo, J. (2006, July 31). Why girls will be girls. *Newsweek,* 46–47.
4. Bryner, J. (2008, March 20). *Clueless guys can't read women.* Retrieved from www.msnbc.msn.com/id/23726891/

The American Psychological Association (APA) style is most frequently used in the field of communication. Because APA cites are by author, you can simply keep track of the source of information using the author, year, and page like this (Woods, 2011, p. 152). If you obtain your references from a database like EBSCOhost, you select this procedure to create your reference list: (1) select the APA option, (2) use the print function without actually printing, (3) copy and paste the references into a Word file, (4) then select the "Sort Text" function to alphabetize your list.

As you do your research and record information, you can refer to the source by the author's last name, thus eliminating the necessity for continually writing out the same bibliographical material. You can refer to Wood's male–female quotation, for example, as Woods-152 (Woods in the bibliography, page 152). If the material is directly quoted, put quotation marks around it. If it is paraphrased, the use of quotation marks is not used, but make sure you remember that the material is not your original idea but from another source.

Keyboard a *running bibliography* and enter the reference material by keyboarding or scanning it. Double-space between entries. After assembling all of your research, you can print out the material. Then cut the reference material into strips, separate them by topic, write or outline directly from these slips of paper or arrange the slips on sheets of blank paper and attach the slips to the pages with transparent tape, and use these as an outline for the speech. An alternative is to connect the strips and then duplicate them on a copy machine, thus creating a working outline. The advantages of using or copying the actual slips of paper center not only on saving time but also having all your footnote sources available if you are asked about them during the question-and-answer session.

If you used note cards or another system, keep track and arrange references in alphabetical order. In a reference list, everything used and cited in your speeches needs to be in the reference list.

Supporting Material

Supporting speech material should clarify a point you are making in the speech or offer evidence of the validity of the argument presented. The challenge for the speaker is to find material that supports the main point being discussed so that the listener pays attention because she or he is interested. Characteristics that constitute the most memorable material are (1) simple, (2) unexpected, (3) concrete, (4) credible, (5) emotional, and (6) story based so that the listener will be engaged as the point is developed.[14]

The forms of support you select depend on your purposes, but the most common are stories, specific instances, exposition, statistics, analogies, and testimony.

Stories

Stories are the most interesting form of supporting material. "The delivery of the message is enhanced with stories because stories help us reach our deepest level of understanding."[15]

Humans connect with each other through the stories they tell. Speakers who use stories tend to be perceived as being more engaging. For this reason, many politicians

President Barack Obama used a story to add "humanness" and to engage his listeners in his speech following the shooting of Congresswoman Gabrielle Giffords.

attempt to enhance their credibility and listenability by telling stories to illustrate that the plan they are presenting has worked in specific cases or that the "pain" they are feeling comes from their examining the plight of a particular person or family. For example, President Barack Obama, in his speech following the attempted assassination of Congresswoman Gabrielle Giffords in Tucson on January 8, 2011, added a touch of humanness with a story about two of the victims of the shooting: "George and Dorothy Morris—Dot to her friends—were high school sweethearts who got married and had two daughters. They did everything together—traveling the open road in their RV, enjoyed what their friends called a 50-year honeymoon. Saturday morning, they went by the Safeway to hear what their congresswoman had to say. When gunfire rung out, George, a former Marine, instinctively tried to shield his wife. Both were shot. Dot passed away."[16]

Stories may be hypothetical or factual. If the illustrations are hypothetical, the speaker should make this clear by saying something like "Suppose you were ..." or "Let us all imagine that ... ." A medical technician can use a hypothetical illustration, for instance, by taking a listener on an imaginary trip through the circulatory system. In contrast, a factual illustration is a real or actual story. A speaker developed a speech on safety codes with this illustration:

> Where Memorial School stands today, Jefferson School once stood. One day a devastating fire struck Jefferson School. Eighty students and four teachers lost their lives in that tragic fire, and hundreds of others were seriously injured. The reason so many were trapped was a building design flaw. The doors of the school opened in, not outward. When the students tried to get out the door, several tripped in front of the door, blocking the movement of the door inward. The new Memorial School can never eradicate the memories of those who died during the tragic fire, but it is built with doors that swing out, now a building design requirement in the State of Ohio.

Stories can be powerful tools of persuasion. "Narratives—from novels to sitcoms—pervade our lives and can affect what we believe about topics as sweeping as historical events or as personal as safe sex."[17] A speaker, for example, who is giving a speech about why the classroom audience should sponsor her in an upcoming Multiple Sclerosis Walk told the story of her daughter's brave ongoing battle with the crippling disease.

Be careful when using stories. Don't assume that your telling of a story is factual proof of your contention. Stories are *illustrations*, devices for explanation, clarification, and attracting attention. They are not generally intended to offer proof.

Stories can be powerful tools of persuasion, but should not be used as factual proof of your contention.

Specific Instances

Condensed examples that are used to clarify or prove a point are *specific instances*. If you want to develop the idea that speech communication is an interesting major for college students, for example, you can support your point with specific instances of careers that employ communication majors: speech writing, teaching, research and training in business and industrial communication, political campaigning, health communication, and public relations.

Socially COMMUNICATING

Putting Humor in Its Place

Humor has a place in your presentations and your work with others. Even if you feel you can't tell a joke, you can still make humor work for you.

Humor should be relevant to the message you are giving. Link it to a point you are making, and make it the type of humor that is in good taste.

- Analogies are one way to use humor. Linking your present situation or problem to something else often provides an opportunity for humor. The link can be either logical or illogical and could even be a personal anecdote.
- Another way to use humor—and an easy one for the person who falls into the "cannot-tell-jokes" category—is to use funny quotes. Get a book of humorous quotes.

Also: Have you seen an amusing cartoon in the paper or in a magazine? Describe it. Show it on a screen.

Some specifics on using humor:

- When you are telling jokes or quips, don't pre-announce them. Just insert them here and there.
- Avoid anything offensive or sarcastic. If in doubt, leave it out.
- Remember that sometimes things occur—such as power failures, dead mikes, etc.—during presentations. Have a joke or comment ready for emergencies.

Source: "Putting Humor in Its Place" by Stephenie Slahor, Ph.D. Reprinted with permission of the author.

Exposition

An *exposition* gives listeners the necessary background information so that they can understand the material being presented. Sometimes, for example, a speaker needs to define specific terms, give historical information, explain the relationship between herself or himself and the topic, or explain the process that will be used during the presentation. In using exposition, the speaker must also anticipate or alter a message, if necessary, to aid listeners' understanding.

The speaker, realizing an obligation to aid the audience in understanding the message, may feel a need to define terms and ideas that will be used in the presentation. For instance, a speaker who wants to explain the advertising campaign to be used in marketing a product may find it necessary to clarify such terms and phrases as *bandwagoning* and *plus-and-minus factor in surveying*.

An audience may need historical information as well. For example, in order for listeners to understand the rationale for the United States agreement to back the United Nations intervention in the Libyan civil war in 2011, they would need to have quotations from President Obama himself or from members of his administration.

Listeners may need a bridge between the speaker and the topic to understand why the speaker is discussing the subject or to establish the speaker's expertise. For example, a student nurse who is explaining the nursing program he recently completed should share his educational background with the audience.

In addition, indicating the process to be followed during a presentation or the results the speaker wants to achieve may be helpful to listeners. An outline of the major points to be made can be distributed or displayed, or the speaker can explain what she or he will do and will want the audience to do as the speech proceeds.

Statistics

Any collection of numerical information arranged as representations, trends, or theories makes up *statistics*. For example, in discussing the changing U.S. workplace, a speaker might state statistics found from a U.S. government site.

"By 2050, the U.S. population is expected to increase by 50 percent and minority groups will make up nearly half of the population. Immigration will account for almost two-thirds of the nation's population growth."[18]

Before accepting statistics as proof, the wise speaker asks:

- Who says so?
- How does he or she know?
- What is missing?
- Did somebody change the subject?
- Does it make sense?[19]

When statistics have been accurately collected, are properly interpreted, and are not out of date, their use is a valid aid in reaching conclusions.

Statistical Surveying Statisticians have developed methods for collecting data—*statistical surveying*—that can be used with some degree of assurance that the resulting information will be correct.[20] Ideally, to discover everyone's opinion on a particular issue, everyone should be asked, but of course this is usually impossible for large groups of people. Thus, to make educated guesses, statisticians have devised methods of random sampling that allow less than the entire population to be surveyed. These methods recognize the probability of error, and a speaker should indicate this fact when giving the statistical results of a survey.

Proper Interpretation of Data If a particular group or person is trying to get a specific result, that tester may keep testing until she or he gets the desired conclusion or ignore results that do not agree with the goal. For this reason, be wary of statistics

In using statistics in a speech, remember that a person can only retain a limited amount of information.

that are taken out of context, are incomplete, or do not specify the method used to collect the data. Ideally, statistics should be reliable and valid. *Reliability* means that each time the test is run, it shows the same results. *Validity* means that the process followed is correct. Sometimes people accept information that has not been shown to be both reliable and valid because they are desperate for a source to back up claims. For example, a student speaker's statement of central purpose was, "To persuade the audience by relating the research that proves that gender identity can be changed by sociological interventions." She based her entire speech on the work of Dr. John Money, a gender identity specialist. Unfortunately, after finding Money's original research she stopped her search. She missed that fact that numerous follow-up studies could not duplicate his supposed success and that he, in fact, had manipulated evidence so that his findings were neither valid nor reliable.[21]

Currency of Data Studies and surveys conducted in the past may have been perfectly accurate at the time they were done. This does not mean that they are accurate now. It is important that you use or receive the latest data and not allow yourself to be influenced by information that is out of date.

Reporting the Data Remember that a person can retain only a limited amount of information. Thus, extensive lists, complicated numerical combinations, and long numbers may well be lost if you do not help listeners by simplification or visualization. For example, a long list—such as the figures representing the cost of each material used to produce a piece of machinery—can be written on a chalkboard or poster or projected on a screen. In this way, listeners view as well as hear, and they can refer to the numbers as needed.

Simplify numbers. A statistic such as $1,243,724,863 is difficult to comprehend, but the phrase "approximately $1.25 billion" is within the grasp of an audience. If a statistic is important enough to include in a speech, you must be sure that the listener can understand the information.

Analogies

A speaker may use an *analogy* to clarify a concept for listeners; that is, the speaker compares an unfamiliar concept to a familiar one. For example, in the section of this text dealing with the processing capacity of the human cortex, an analogy was drawn between a cybernetic process and a computer process. This comparison was not intended to indicate that the cortex and the computer are one and the same, but to demonstrate that if a reader understands the functioning of a computer, he or she may also understand the basic operation of the cortex.

Remember that an analogy is effective only if listeners are familiar with the object, idea, or theory being used as its basis. Contrasting a patient on an operating table to stars in the sky may confuse listeners who are unfamiliar with either astronomy or surgical techniques.

A speaker also should be careful not to overextend the comparison or contrast. A college president once developed an inaugural speech by comparing the school to a football team. The analogy compared faculty members to team players, students to spectators, the president to the coach, and on and on and on! After a while, the listeners became confused and stopped paying attention; the intended effect was lost.

Testimony

Testimony may be a *direct quotation* (actual statement) or a *paraphrase* (reworded idea) from an authority. Speakers provide testimony to clarify ideas, back up contentions, and reinforce concepts. Thus, a speaker may turn to this type of supporting material when it is believed that an authority is more knowledgeable than the speaker about the topic being discussed or that the opinion of an authority will make listeners more receptive to a particular idea.

An *expert* is a person who, through knowledge or skill in a specific field, gains respect for his or her opinions or expertise. We trust experts' opinions because their knowledge has been acquired through personal experience, education, training, research, and/or observation. We also respect people who have academic degrees, who are licensed or accredited, or who are recognized by peers as leaders in their fields. Many useful quotations are available to speakers on www.quotationspage.com.

Selected quotations should be true to the intention of the source. Before you accept testimony as support, assess its validity by asking some basic questions:

- Is the material quoted accurately?
- Is the source biased because of position, employment, or affiliation? A quotation by the chairperson of the board of directors of a major tobacco company that cigarette smoking may not lead to cancer should be suspect because of the speaker's biased position.
- Is the information relevant to the issue being discussed?
- Is the source competent in the field being discussed? For example, what qualifies an actor to recommend changes in U.S. foreign policy?
- Is the information current, if currency is important?

In addition to locating information, a speaker must assess its validity. Sources of information often reflect biases.[22] Thus, when doing research for a presentation, it is a good idea to pay attention to these factors: Who was the author of the material? What are his or her affiliations? Is there anything in the person's background which would make you believe that the person's political, employment, organizational affiliations would lead to untruthful, manipulated or misleading views?

A classic example of how testimony and statistics can lead to misguidance is the now debunked autism study which linked the measles, mumps, and rubella vaccination to autism. As it turned out, "the study to link a childhood vaccine to autism was based on doctored information about the children involved."[23] The original study was done on only 12 children (not a large enough sample to reach such a conclusion) and could not be duplicated (lack of reliability).[24] Why did people believe this shoddy research? They wanted to do so. Parents, desperate for some explanation of why their children were sick, were willing to latch on to any news. In this case, the original story was picked up by the media and spread quickly. It was only when an investigative reporter, "was able to go behind the face of the 1998 paper [the original date of the now denounced Dr. Andrew Wakefield's journal article], identify the subjects, and access original patient data"[25] that the research was debunked.

Use of the World Wide Web

Researchers should realize that the World Wide Web (WWW) is not always a perfect search source. As one Internet expert states, "The Internet makes readily available so much information that students think research is far easier than it really is. Students are producing superficial research papers [and speeches], full of data—some of it suspect—and with little thought."[26]

Since some Internet sources are inaccurate, you'll want to check for validity. Look for sources noted for generally doing accurate investigation, such as universities, scholarly organizations, and the government. If you are looking for statistics for a speech about rape, for example, find recent information from your local police department, the FBI, or a local rape crisis center. In addition, associations such as the American Psychological Association and the American Counseling Association have homepages that can lead to information that has been published after being reviewed by experts in the field. Other sites that report reviewed documents are Library Spot (www.libraryspot.com), Bigchalk (www.bigchalk.com), and the Library of Congress (www.loc.gov).[27]

Here are some additional tips for finding credible information.

- Check the Uniform Resource Identifier (URL) extension. Typically, a government site's information is reliable (.gov, .MO, .UK). Higher education sites tend to be valid (.edu), although be careful of student conceived sites. Nonprofit sites are often reliable, and are often indicated with a .org extension. Commercial or individual sites are the most suspect (.net, .com). Be careful about a tilde (~) in the url because the page may belong to an individual with no direct responsibility to the main website.
- Look for the author's credentials.
- Look for credentials about the organization that published the information and its potential biases.
- Look for a date. Information about some topics gets out-of-date quickly. What was true last year, may be irrelevant today. For example, in speaking about political trends, a speaker using information from October, 2010 would have stated that the Democrats controlled the White House and both the House and Senate. By January of 2011 (three months later) that information was wrong.
- In general, information from government agencies and educational institutions is perceived to be credible because they tend to have less of a vested interest in persuading people to a particular point of view. For instance, the Central Intelligence Agency's *World Factbook* offers an exhaustive collection on the population, geography, government, and economy of other countries (www.cia.gov/publications/the-world-factbook).
- Subscription-based sites that provide reliable, advertising-free information also can be dependable sources. Publications with long-standing reputations such as the *New York Times* and the *Economist* are generally considered credible sources.
- Avoid Urban Legends. Online sources such as www.snopes.com, www.UrbanLegends.about.com, BreakTheChain.org, Scambusters.org, and TruthOrFiction.com are valuable in checking out truth versus *urban legends* (hoaxes, and stories that have been repeated over and over without any factual base). For example, students in a public speaking class were assigned to give a speech on a topic that may or may not have involved urban legends. Some of the topics included the fashion of males wearing sagging pants and the religious book that Barack Obama used when he was sworn into office as a senator from Illinois.

Following each speech, the students voted to tell whether they believed that the material was true, false, or undetermined. How many of the statements did you think were true?[28]

Claim: The fashion of wearing sagging pants was originally a prison mode for signaling sexual availability.

Status: False. Although sagging pants were first worn in the U.S. prison system, this was not a style originating with imprisoned homosexuals intent on advertising their interest in casual flings. Sagging pants became the behind-the-bars fashion thanks to ill-fitting prison-issue garb: Some of those incarcerated were provided with clothing a few sizes too large. That oversizing, coupled with the lack of belts available in prisons, led to a great number of prisoners whose pants were falling off their waists. Belts are not permitted in most correctional facilities because all too often the lifeless bodies of inmates have been found hanging from them.

Claim: When Barack Obama was sworn into office as a senator from Illinois he did not use *The Bible,* but used *The Koran.*

Status: False. During his run for the Democratic presidential nomination, lots of rumors circulated about Obama. *The Koran* rumor was one of them. In fact, as a Christian, Obama did use *The Bible.* The circulators mixed up Obama with Keith Ellison, a Muslim congressman from Minnesota, who did use *The Koran* at his swearing-in ceremony.

- Be leery of Blogs. Blogs (short for WebLogs) are a type of journal where a person can post whatever he or she wants. Be especially careful when using blogs as a research source. "In size and scope, blogs are low-budget, one-person operations that could not be more different from the country's newsrooms. There is no editorial layer—no reporters, editors, copy editors, or producers constantly verifying and tweaking what is reported before it is seen by the public. There is no call to be objective and strike a balance in the stories."[29] In other words, you have no way of knowing whether the information on a blog is truthful, has been well researched, or is total fantasy.

For a recap of how to evaluate Internet sources, see Figure 12.1.

The 9 Cs provide criteria in evaluating Internet resources.

1. **Content.** What is the intent of the content? Are the titles and author identified? What is the date of the document or article? Do you have the latest version?
2. **Credibility.** Is the author identifiable and reliable? Is the content credible?
3. **Critical thinking.** Can you identify the author, publisher, edition, as you would with "traditionally" published resources?
4. **Copyright.** If the material falls under the copyright laws, is the credit given?
5. **Citation**. Is credit given to the author? Does the format of the citation follow a standard style?
6. **Continuity.** Will the Internet site be maintained and update? Can you rely on this source over time to provide up-to-date information?
7. **Censorship.** Does your search engine or index look for all words, or are some words excluded?
8. **Connectivity.** Does access to the resource require a graphical user interface? Are you familiar with the tool and the applications required to access the material?
9. **Context.** How does the Internet Information fit in the overall information context of your subject?

FIGURE 12.1 The Nine Cs for Evaluating Internet Sources

Source: Adapted from "The Ten C's for Evaluating Internet Sources," McIntyre Library, University of Wisconsin-Eau Claire, and "Evaluating Internet Research Sources" at http://www.virtualsalt.com/evalu8it.htm.

Be careful to search for quality information as it will be central to the quality of your communication. "Use credible information providers. Identify sources. Authenticate what they say. Then ask yourself: Is this gold or garbage?"[30]

Techniques for Presenting Supporting Material

Four means of presenting and focusing supporting material are internal summaries, forecasting, signposting, and use of supplementary aids.

Internal Summaries

As a listener, have you ever been on the receiving end of a message and found yourself totally confused because of the amount of material involved? To avoid listener confusion, summarize each segment of a presentation by providing an **internal summary**, a short restatement of what has just been said in the section that you are about to leave, before proceeding to the next segment. For example, after spending several minutes proposing that the United States should adopt a more aggressive foreign policy, the speaker could bridge out of that unit with the internal summary, "Our nation, then, needs to pursue a more vigorous, definitive approach to its international relations."

Forecasting

A **forecast** is a statement that alerts the audience to ideas that are coming. An example of a forecast is, "Let's now examine the three examples of how to create a secure computer password." This forecast alerts the audience to get ready to listen for the three points.

Signposting

An additional vehicle for presenting supporting material is signposting. In **signposting**, a speaker reviews where the listeners have been, states where they are presently, and forecasts where they are going. This aids the listener by recapping what has been presented and telling where the speech is going. An example of a signpost is, "We've seen how the effects of cholesterol could result in clogged arteries. I've just reinforced this idea by presenting information from the American Medical Association proving the theory to be correct. Now, let's examine what you can do to lower your cholesterol and, therefore, lessen your chances of having a stroke or heart attack."

Supplementary Aids

Many speakers find **supplementary speech aids**—visual, audio, audiovisual, and computerized—valuable in augmenting the oral segments of their presentations. Aids are intended to facilitate listener understanding, not to function as decorative touches; therefore, a speaker should ask two questions before using aids: Is the aid relevant to the presentation? And will listeners better understand the material through the use of an aid?

In a speech, statistical differences can be greatly enhanced by the use of charts. In a classroom, supplementary aids can be used to teach particular techniques. For example, student nurses sometimes inject needles into grapefruits so they can learn how to give shots, and a videotape of an interrogation can supplement a discussion on how to question suspects for law enforcement students. These aids are intended to supplement the speaker's voice and nonverbal communication and reinforce the credibility of the speaker and the material.

Visual Aids Today's public speaker needs to understand the principles of effective public presentations and the appropriate use of technology. Sometimes speeches are given face-to-face with an audience. Sometimes speeches are given totally via electronic media. And sometimes today's speeches incorporate both face-to-face and mediated communication. Although speakers tend to use technology as visual aids, there are many options available to the public speaker.

Visual aids appeal to our sense of sight. And since so many listeners are visual in orientation, visual support of a speaker's message can be a key to enhancing comprehension. As in using any supplementary aid, speakers must be sure that the visual aid truly *aids* the presentation; that is, be sure that it doesn't just replace you and your message. Some speakers use the basic rule that if something can be said orally, without any assistance, then an aid should not be used. Others contend that right-brained listeners (see pages 89–91) often depend on visual stimulation both in order to comprehend and to pay attention. Too many speakers bring in a huge number of pictures or PowerPoint slides and proceed to overwhelm listeners with no real purpose. Be aware that PowerPoint can be effective, but there are other types of visual aids that will help develop your speech.

A speaker can choose from a variety of visual aids:

1. *Real objects*. To demonstrate the process of swinging a hammer, why not use a real hammer? Or use an actual form to show how a traffic ticket is filled out. These are examples of using real objects as visual aids.
2. *Models*. At times, it is impossible to use real objects. In such cases, a scale model (in exact proportion to the dimensions of the real object) or a synthetic model

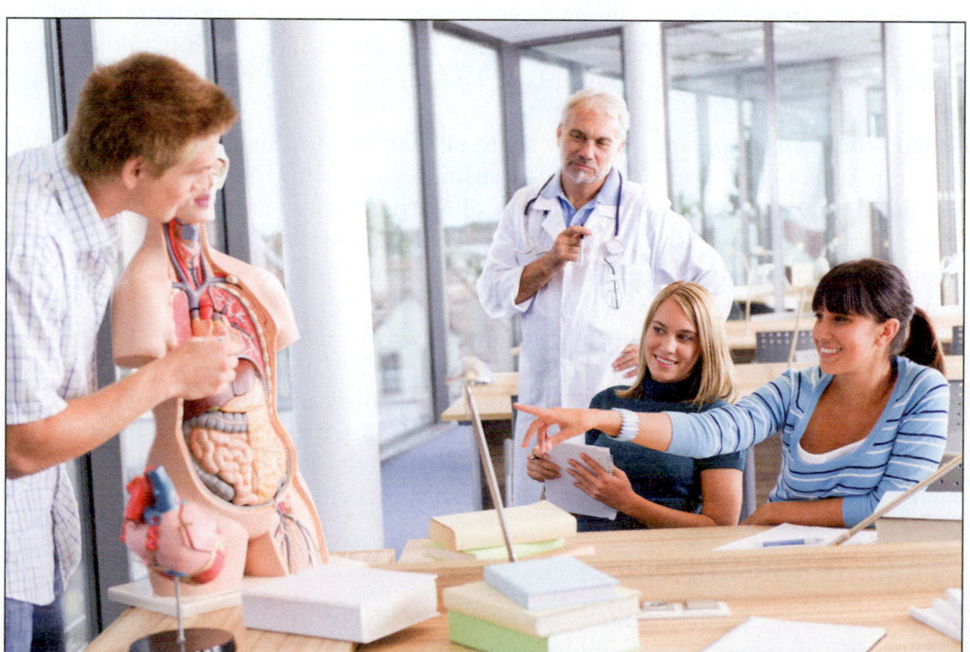

Visual aids appeal to our sense of sight. As in using any other supplementary aid, speakers must be careful that visual aids truly enhance and support the presentation.

(not in proportion but nevertheless representative) may be used. For example, although a Boeing 757 jet cannot be brought into an aviation classroom, a scale model certainly can be.

3 *Photographs, pictures, and diagrams.* A photograph of a death scene and the victim can be shown to a jury in a murder trial in order to reconstruct the scene or the violence.

4 *Charts.* A chart is a visual representation of statistical data that gives information in tabular or diagrammatic form. For example, a series of columns representing the number of doctors available to a hospital compared with the number needed presents a striking visual image of the problem.

5 *Cutaways.* It is often difficult to look inside certain objects. A cutaway allows us to see what we normally would have to imagine, thus enabling us to visualize and understand better. To show the layers of materials used to construct a house, a wall is cut in half so that we see the siding, the insulation, the studding, the wallboard, and the wallpaper.

6 *Mockups.* A mockup shows the building up or tearing down of an article. For example, a biology textbook may include an outline drawing of the human body on a page with a series of clear plastic sheets attached. Each of these plastic overlays shows a specific drawing that, as it is flipped onto the original sketch, adds an aspect of the human anatomy.

7 *Flip charts, whiteboards, and smartboards.* You may be presenting in a classroom or training room with little or no technological support. In such a setting, make use of the board or bring a flip chart with blank pages so that you can list your major points or illustrate numbers as you speak.

8 *Presentation graphics.* Presentation graphics are visuals that are projected using a projector while the speaker is discussing each point. The slides enable the speaker to illustrate visually with statistics, cartoons, short quotations, maps, and other materials.

In order to supplement computer-generated materials in lengthy presentations, it often is helpful to provide listeners with a copy of the slides with blank space for taking notes.

Audio Aids *Audio aids* appeal to our sense of hearing. Such devices as CDs and tape recordings may be the only way to demonstrate particular sensations accurately for listeners. For example, playing a segment of Martin Luther King's "I Have a Dream" speech is an excellent way to demonstrate his dynamic oral style, as is playing a Beattle's song to illustrate the distinctive sound of that group.

Audiovisual Aids *Audiovisual aids* such as films, videotapes, and tape–slide presentations combine the dimensions of sight and sound. A video clip of a seeing eye dog assisting her person can illustrate the support that such animals can provide. In the same way, a videotape of an executive's speech is an excellent way to illustrate his vocal and physical mannerisms. Inserting a YouTube clip that illustrates a point being made, can add both credibility and interest to a speech.

Presentation Software

A speaker who uses presentation software effectively can provide listeners with multimedia messages, stimulating their visual and auditory senses since it provides speakers with the opportunity to outline a speech, create slides with or without animation, import visual graphics, photos, video or audio clips, and Internet connections.

Most people are used to stimulating visual media. A computerized presentation allows for varying the visuals through a variety of media and media techniques. The inclusion of visuals will tend to hold an audience member's attention better than just words. It will also give a visual impression that the listener can retain.

Besides the advantages, recognize that there are also drawbacks to using presentation applications:

- If the projection equipment is substandard, it may be necessary to turn out the lights so the audience can see visuals, a move that creates a sleep-inducing environment and makes it difficult for people to take notes.
- There is a risk of putting so much on the screen that the material becomes overwhelming.
- A speaker can get so carried away with the program's technological abilities that the medium becomes more important than the message.

In planning the use of presentation software, remember that it is designed to assist your oral presentation, by clarifying, reinforcing, illustrating, not to replace the speech. As a result, you will want to plan carefully how best to incorporate the visuals so that they reinforce or clarify your oral points. Recognize that some speakers rely far too extensively on visuals, putting their entire presentation on the screen. Remember that audiences are expected to comprehend the software presentation while still focusing on what the speaker is saying. Some presentations may bombard the audience with an over-stimulating media presentation, while others lull the audience to sleep with dark, wordy slides. Keep in mind the purpose of supplementary aids and expectations of your audience. People are used to simultaneously texting, searching the Internet, watching a video, and more. How will you use presentation software so it effectively accomplishes your communication purpose?

Using Presentation Software Effectively There are numerous presentation graphics programs, including PowerPoint (the most commonly used product), Prezi, Visual Understanding Environment (VUE), and Apple's Keynote, which can enhance your speech by helping clarify ideas and get and hold the listener's attention.

No matter which software you use, you'll want to give careful consideration to the design elements of your presentation.[31] For clarity, keep these suggestions in mind:

- Use simplicity in design.
- Your presentation visuals are an extension of your ideas. After carefully constructing your speech outline and planning documents, make sure the visuals follow the same organizational format.
- Keep in mind the rule of 5 × 5, which suggests using five words per line and no more than five lines

Communicating Socially

The Controversy over PowerPoint

In 2007, one of the most elegant, most influential, and most groaned about pieces of software in the history of computers was 20 years old.

While PowerPoint has served as the metronome for countless crisp presentations, it has also allowed an endless expanse of dimwit ideas to be dressed up with graphical respectability.

Graphics guru Edward Tufte says the software "elevates format over content, betraying an attitude of commercialism that turns everything into a sales pitch."

Robert Gaskins, one of the inventors, states that "a PowerPoint presentation was never supposed to be the entire proposal, just a quick summary of something longer and better thought out." He cites as an example his original business plan for the program: 53 densely argued pages long. The dozen or so slides that accompanied it were but the highlights.

Source: Gomes, L. (2007, June 20). PowerPoint turns 20, as its creators ponder a dark side to success. *The Wall Street Journal*, B1.

per slide. The idea is to make sure you use content that enhances your presentation, without being too wordy.

- Avoid writing out your speech and putting that on the slides.
- Make sure the font is large enough to read easily.
- Select fonts and colors for readability. A clean-looking font that people are used to reading on a screen is a good idea, such as Arial or Verdana. Limit the number of different fonts and use a consistent format between slides.
- Phrases are easier to grasp than full sentences, but full sentences may be useful to express complete thoughts or to remind yourself of a complicated point.
- Bulleted and numbered lists and topic outlines are useful to remind you (the speaker) of your ideas and to help focus the audience on those ideas. If you've ever experienced a "death-by-PowerPoint" speech, however, you know that too many words and not enough visual interest on slide after slide can be dull and distracting.
- Avoid distracting or overwhelming animation schemes. They may be entertaining at the start, but quickly become distracting.
- Carefully select colors, backgrounds, and designs. Backgrounds that are both light and dark on the same slide, for example, create readability problems. Use high-contrast print and colors that can be easily seen (avoid putting black print on a dark background or light print on a light background).
- Add interest devices, such as appropriate and relevant visuals, cartoons, video, maps, graphs, sound, Internet links, and charts.
- Consider preparing a single slide or visual that lists the main points of the speech to use as an overview of the body of the speech or to show at the end as you present a summary.
- A final slide of visual and content sources used in the speech (reference list) can be helpful.

In Conclusion

IN CONCLUSION

The sources of information available to a speaker include personal experiences, personal observations, and accumulated learning, plus information derived from research and interviews. Research information may be found in library databases, books, magazines, newspapers, journals, indexes, government publications, publications from special-interest groups, and the Internet. Additional information can be found in nonprint media and interviews. When doing research, keep a record of where the information came from. Supporting material is used in a speech to clarify the speaker's point or to demonstrate that the point has some probability of being true. Supporting material can include illustrations, specific instances, expositions, statistics, analogies, and testimony. Four means for presenting and focusing supporting material are internal summaries, forecasting, signposting, and the use of supplementary aids. Presentation software, such as PowerPoint, can provide support to a speech.

LEARN BY DOING

1. Select a controversial subject area (e.g., abortion, euthanasia, legalization of drugs, confiscation of handguns), and identify an authority on the subject. Interview that person (in person or via the phone or email), and give an oral presentation to the class about your interview. You should clearly state the interviewee's stand concerning the issue and the reasons for the stand. After all of the presentations have been made, participate in a class discussion on the value of the interview as a means for collecting data for a speech.
2. Use the information collected from the interview in activity 1 to research the same topic. Look for the views of other authorities on the subject. Prepare a presentation in which you compare and/or contrast the results of your interview with the results of your research.
3. Make a presentation to the class in which a supplementary aid is absolutely necessary for the listeners' comprehension of the message (e.g., a description of Van Gogh's style of brush stroke, the music of Michael Buble in comparison with that of Josh Groban, the architectural styles of the Maya of the Yucatan).
4. Research each of these items and compile a set of notecards or notes and a running bibliography as explained in the chapter:
   - **a.** The name of one book about the teachings of Aristotle
   - **b.** A magazine article about nuclear-waste disposal
   - **c.** The longitude and latitude of Omaha, Nebraska
   - **d.** Three encyclopedia entries about the building of the White House
   - **e.** The name of a journal exclusively about nonverbal communication
   - **f.** The definition of the word *cacophony*
   - **g.** The 1950 population of the United States
5. Use the format explained in the chapter to make three bibliographic notes for a speech with the purpose statement "to inform the class of the effects of the Salk polio vaccine." Two are to be quotations and one should be a paraphrase. Use a different source for each entry. Use APA style.
6. Find a factual or hypothetical illustration that could be used for the speech described in activity 5.

7. What background information do you think would be needed by members of your class if you were to present the speech in activity 5?

8. Locate and footnote three sources of testimony concerning the effects of secondary smoke on nonsmokers.

9. Find a humorous story that you could use as an introduction for a speech about the U.S. educational system, gender similarities or differences, or sports.

10. Prepare a three- to five-minute speech that depends on the listeners' viewing visuals through presentation software (e.g., Apple Keynote, PowerPoint, Prezi).[32]

KEY TERMS

primary sources of information 320
secondary sources of information 320
oral footnote 326
supporting speech material 328
internal summary 336
forecast 336
signposting 336
supplementary speech aids 336
visual aids 337

Public Speaking: Structuring the Message

structure of a speech • types of introductions and conclusions • statement of central idea • the overall structure of a speech • question-and-answer session • culture and speech structure

CHAPTER 13

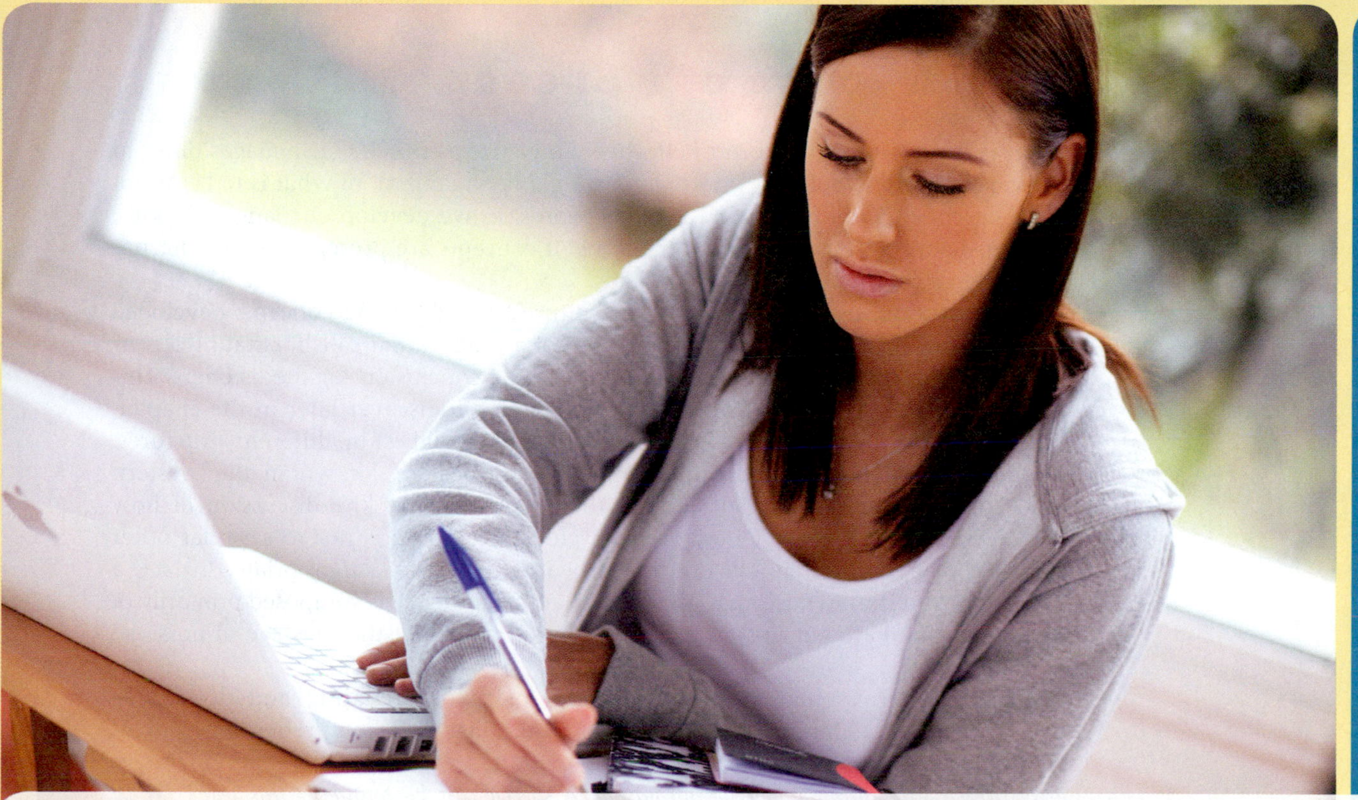

After reading this chapter, you should be able to

- Explain why it is important to structure speeches carefully
- Structure a speech to meet the needs of the listeners
- Analyze and apply what makes an effective introduction, central idea, body, and conclusion for a speech
- List and give examples of introduction attention getters for a speech
- Identify the purpose and types of orienting materials
- Explain the purpose of and develop a central idea for a speech
- List and give examples of the methods of issue arrangement for the body of a speech
- List and give examples of the methods for concluding a speech
- Identify and illustrate the methods for the overall organization of a speech
- Make transitions into a question-and-answer session
- Explain how culture has a role in speech organization

Have you sat through a class lecture and found yourself thoroughly confused because the instructor kept jumping from idea to idea and then back to a previous one while discussing still another thought? If so, you were experiencing organizational confusion.

Listeners have limited and fluctuating attention spans, constantly tuning in to and out of a speaker's message. Consequently, it is important for a speaker to present a carefully structured message that enables listeners to get back on track when they tune back in to the speech. If the major points in the speech are well supported with statistics and examples, listener understanding will be enhanced.

Structure of a Speech

What is the basis for the need to effectively organize a speech? "Languages differ in the very assumption of how information should be organized, of what is to be or not to be described and expressed."[1] In other words, as we develop our language skills, we hear ideas presented in certain patterns. If concepts are presented in an alternative pattern, it can cause listener problems.

Historically, speakers from Western cultures, based on the concepts developed by the Greek rhetorician Aristotle, make use of a process that calls for stating a contention, supporting that contention, and drawing a conclusion for the listeners. This is accomplished in a step-by-step manner. As you will discover later in the chapter, other cultures are exposed to, and therefore tend to listen best in, different structures. Because this book is written primarily for public speakers for whom the Western mode of reasoning and organization is the general format, the discussion of how to structure a speech will follow Western guidelines.[2] This is not to say that other formats or approaches should not be learned or used when appropriate. In fact, a European American whose analysis shows that the audience is composed primarily of individuals who are not European Americans should adapt the message, if possible, to that audience.

The Western system requires a careful plan for preparing and developing effective presentations.[3] The plan should foster listening comprehension, aid in eliminating confusion, produce a well-supported presentation, and maintain attention. (*An outlining tool for formatting a speech can be found in this text's http://mycommunicationlab.com/*).

To make the most effective use of this plan, it is helpful to look first at the basic elements (introduction, central idea, body, and conclusion) of a speech and how each of these four elements are put together.[4]

1. *Introduction*—attention-gaining and orienting material.
2. *Central idea*—the purpose of the presentation and a specific statement of its main idea.
3. Body—the major points to be expressed in the presentation. The body of the speech may be organized into as many divisions as necessary to develop the intent of the message.
4. *Conclusion*—a summarizing and possibly a motivating statement.

The Introduction

The purposes of the **introduction to a speech** are to gain the listeners' attention and orient them to the material that will be presented.

Attention Material

It is imperative to gain your listeners' attention at the start of the speech. If a speaker fails to convince the audience to listen immediately, getting them to tune in later is almost impossible. Attention-getting techniques include personal references, humorous stories, illustrations, rhetorical questions, action questions, unusual or dramatic devices, quotations related to the theme, and a statement of the theme.

Personal References Introductions containing personal references give a speaker's reasons for undertaking a presentation on a specific topic. For example, to introduce a presentation that appeals for funds, a speaker may relate the personal experience of receiving aid from the Muscular Dystrophy Association or a member of the college's football team could tell the importance to him of fan support when he is playing.

Communicating Culturally

A Navajo (Diné) Speech Introduction

Not all cultural groups begin their speeches by first gaining attention, next relating to audience interests, then establishing their credibility. Speakers at Diné Community College (formerly Navajo Community College) first answer the listeners' question, "Who are you and what's your clan affiliation?" Students thus begin their classroom speeches by telling their names (who they are) and identifying their clan affiliation (knowing this helps listeners understand the roots of their life). Until this personal, identifying information is shared, neither the speakers nor their listeners can feel at home.

Source: "A Navajo (Diné) Speech Introduction" from *Public speaking: Concepts and skills for a diverse society,* 3rd Edition by C. Jaffe.

Humorous Stories People like to laugh and enjoy themselves; therefore, humorous stories can be an effective way to start a presentation. The humor should fit the audience and the occasion, be relevant to the material being presented, and set the desired tone.[5]

The humor should parallel the intent of the speech. A speaker, for example, could begin a presentation with a humorous anecdote: "A railroad agent in Africa had been bawled out for doing things without orders from headquarters. One day headquarters received a telegram from the agent which read, 'Tiger on platform eating conductor. Wire instructions.'"[6] From this story, listeners would expect a speech about worker empowerment or creative decision making.

It is important to consider, too, whether humor is appropriate to your own communication style. Some people are not very comfortable telling funny stories or jokes, and that discomfort will be revealed to the audience. Other speakers have a good ear (and memory) for relaying humorous anecdotes and find the form successful.

Likewise, a humorous introduction may not always be appropriate for the audience or the topic at hand. A briefing on the state of affairs in war-torn Afghanistan, for instance, certainly does not call for a light, humorous opener.

Humorous stories often are an effective way to start a presentation.

Illustrations Illustrations such as stories, pictures, and slides help make ideas more vivid for listeners because they create a visualization or image of the topic to be discussed. For example, showing pictures of the results of a new skin-grafting process for burn victims clearly illustrates the topic to be discussed. Similarly, a speaker who is going to talk about the need for well-equipped police cars can begin a speech by saying, "Picture yourself on a dark road some night with car trouble or maybe even an injury that prevents you from driving.

COMMUNICATING in Careers

Try These Speech Starters

Successful presenters use these techniques to quickly establish a connection with their audiences:

- Quiet a talkable group with the silent treatment. Just stand there and look at them until all the eyes—and the ears—in the room focus on you. At the precise moment that occurs, hit them with a statement that gives them a good reason to keep listening.
- Imply that you need their help. *Example:* "I have something on my mind, and I'd like to share it with you to see what you think."
- Dramatize what you're planning to tell them. *Example:* "I'm deeply troubled by something, and I'm wondering if the same thing is also troubling you."
- Ask them how they feel about the topic of your presentation. *Example:* "I'm fed up with the tax system. Are you?"
- Say something that will involve them. *Examples:* "I'm going to ask you to think about an important topic." "I'd like you to do something for me."

Source: Steve Adubato, PhD, Emmy Award-winning author and communication trainer, Bloomfield, NJ. Adubato, S. (n.d.). *Business News New Jersey,* Snowden Publications, Inc., 104 Church St., New Brunswick, NJ 08901. © Communication Briefings, www.briefings.com, 1101 King Street, Alexandria, VA 22314. Used with permission.

Speakers like multi-Emmy award winner Jon Stewart know that humor is an excellent device to get and hold an audience's attention.

Suddenly you see the headlights of a car. It could belong to almost anyone. But wouldn't you feel relieved if it turned out to be a police officer with all the equipment you needed?"

One form of illustration is a historical reference in which the speaker tells a story or uses instances of historical happenings that draw the listeners' interest into the topic of the speech. For example, a speaker at the dedication of the newly renovated Stamp Student Union on the University of Maryland campus began with a series of historical events that had occurred in the old student center during the past fifty years, including that in 1963, Bill Cosby met the woman who was to be his wife; in 1979, Kermit the Frog delivered a homecoming speech; in 1992, author Alex Haley presented his last lecture, and in 2008, a presidential nomination debate took place in the venue.

Rhetorical Questions Questions for which no outward response is expected are *rhetorical questions.* For example, a speaker may say to an audience, "Have you ever asked yourself what you would do if someone tried to rob you?" In this case, the speaker does not intend to count how many people in the audience have or have not asked themselves the question. Instead, the purpose is to have audience members ask themselves the question so as to build their curiosity or interest.

Although they are sometimes overused, rhetorical questions can be an effective method of getting the audience to ponder a topic and to engage them right from the start.

Action Questions *Action questions* are a means of getting the audience involved in a speech and making listeners think and respond. For example, a speaker started a presentation by asking, "How many of you have been involved in an auto accident?" After the hands went up, the speaker said, "For those of you with your hands up, do you remember that instant when you knew the accident was going to happen and you couldn't do anything about it? What flashed through your mind?" After getting some answers from the audience, the speaker said, "Yes, a common response is helplessness and fear." Thus, the speaker involved the audience and was able to move their attention to the next segment of the speech, which centered on how to overcome the feelings of helplessness caused by fear and despair.

Unusual or Dramatic Devices Unusual or dramatic devices get the audience's attention because of their curiosity or shock value. In one dramatic opening, a medical lab technician set up equipment and drew blood from a student volunteer to show how blood is analyzed.

Quotations Related to the Theme Speakers sometimes begin by quoting a famous person or expert, reading an account of a specific event, reciting a section of a poem or play, or reading a newspaper editorial. The quotations should be relevant to the topic and be read meaningfully.

A speaker started her speech by stating, "Robert Frost in his poem *A Road Not Taken wrote,* 'Two roads diverged in a wood, and I, I took the one less traveled by, And that has made all the difference.'"[7] She went on to say, "That's the story of my life...when confronted with decisions, I have continually taken the road less travelled."

A mistake many speakers make in presenting a quotation is to select an appropriate piece and then speed through the reading or fail to stress the meaning.

Stating the Theme Theme statements indicate to the audience exactly what the speaker is going to talk about. Unfortunately, many untrained speakers start out their presentations by saying, "Today I am going to tell you about..." This is not a creative or attention-getting opener.

Unusual or dramatic devices get attention because of their curiosity or shock value.

A more creative theme statement is likely to get the audience's attention. For example, a police officer started her presentation by saying, "There is a right way and a wrong way to respond to a police officer who has stopped you for speeding. Even though this is a stressful situation, you need to make the right choices when communicating with the officer. Let's look at those choices."

Orienting Material

Orienting material gives an audience the background necessary to understand the basic material of the speech. It is designed to tie the material to the central idea, provide necessary information, establish personal credibility for the speaker, and make the subject important to the listener. Orienting material can include such clarifiers as providing a historical background, defining terms that will be used in the presentation, tying the speaker's personal history to the subject, using statistics to identify how many people are affected, and illuminating the importance of the ideas to the listener.

Historical Background Often a speaker has to explain what led up to the present time so an audience can gain the necessary historical background. For example, a speech intended to persuade the audience to vote for a renewal of a school levy ought to include the facts that illustrate the history of the levy.

Defining Terms Although terms usually are defined at the place they are used in a speech, sometimes the very nature of a speech depends on the audience's having an understanding near the start of the presentation. For example, in a speech about agoraphobia, its definition as an emotional illness that manifests itself in a person's not wanting to appear in public should appear near the beginning of the presentation. Only terms that are universal to the speech should be included in the orientation.

Personal History and/or Tie to the Topic A speaker can gain credibility if she or he has some personal tie or experience related to the topic. A speaker intending to demonstrate the steps in mouth-to-mouth resuscitation could refer to his Red Cross training and his background as a lifeguard. This documentation establishes the speaker's authority to speak about the subject.

Importance to the Listeners One of the most critical parts of the orienting material is relating the subject to the listeners in some way. Listeners pay attention to ideas and issues that are relevant to them, so it is helpful if the speaker makes that link at the outset. One good strategy is to show the importance of the topic based on the interests of the audience. For example, "'Last year, 34.8 million self-prepared tax returns were received electronically by the IRS.'[8] Many of these forms were completed incorrectly, meaning lost refund dollars. Hopefully, your tax form was not one of these."

The Central Idea

The **statement of the speech's central idea** is intended to keep the speaker on course for developing a purposeful and well-organized speech. It also indicates the response the speaker wants from listeners. If, for example, the central idea of a speech

Speakers who don't have a clear purpose risk not getting their point across to the audience.

is stated as "There are two reasons why we should all vote for the school bond issue on November 4," both the speaker and the audience are clear about the topic (school bond issue), the method of developing that topic (two reasons), and what is desired from the audience (vote for the levy).

The importance of stating the central idea in a speech cannot be overemphasized. Speakers who skip this important part of the speech deprive the listeners of the clue they may need to determine the exact point of the speech. The central idea should be presented as a statement so the audience knows exactly what to expect. A speaker who uses a question (e.g., "Should the federal government provide financial aid to private educational institutions?") is not indicating to listeners what the main point really is. But a speaker who presents the point as a statement ("There are three reasons that I believe the federal government should not provide financial aid to private educational institutions") is clarifying the stand that will be advocated and how the body of the speech will be organized.

In some persuasive speeches, when listeners initially may disagree with some aspect of the speaker's purpose, a speaker might choose to start with common ground and unfold ideas that move listeners from initial disagreement to some acceptance of the speaker's proposal, thus moving the presentation of the central idea to a later place in the speech.

The Body

The **body of a speech** develops through major points as well as any subpoints needed to develop the speaker's central idea. The major points are placed in a structured format. In this way, the listeners should have little trouble understanding the message.

One of the questions often asked by those learning the techniques of structuring and organizing a speech centers on how many points to use in the body of the speech. "Cognitive psychologists tell us we learn better when we portion blocks of information into 3 to 7 major units."[9] Most communication instructors "recommend 3 to 5 major points."[10]

Traditional Methods of Arrangement for the Body of a Speech

The **method of issue arrangement for the body of a speech** in the Euro American culture traditionally takes one of six forms: spatial arrangement, time arrangement, topical arrangement, causal arrangement, comparison–contrast arrangement, or problem–solution arrangement. The method selected acts as a guide for sequencing information for listener clarity.

Spatial Arrangement Many people organize information automatically even though they are not aware of it. Suppose some friends are visiting you at your college. They have never been on your campus before, so they ask you to tell them about the institution. You start by describing the buildings located on the south end of the campus and then proceed to talk about all the other buildings, noting their

The body of a speech develops through major points as well as any subpoints needed to develop the speaker's central idea.

locations from south to north. You have organized your presentation according to the **spatial method of issue arrangement**. You have set a *point of reference* at a specific location and followed a *geographic pattern*. The pattern can be left to right, north to south, or from the center to the outside. This is a common method for giving directions or describing something by its location.

We can see how spatial arrangement can be used for the body of a speech.

Note: In all of the outlines presented only the body of the speech is shown. In a regular speech outline, I—Introduction and II—Statement of Central Idea would precede the body, with IV—Conclusion following the body.

The central idea for this speech is "to inform the audience of the financial tax base of Maryland by examining the state's patterns from west to east." Here is a possible outline of the body of the speech with major headings spatially arranged according to geographical location:

III. Financial Tax Base of the State of Maryland
   A. Western Maryland
      1. Cumberland
      2. Hagerstown
   B. Central Maryland
      1. Baltimore
      2. Rockville
      3. Potomac
   C. Eastern Maryland
      1. Annapolis
      2. Ocean City

Time Arrangement The **time method of issue arrangement** orders information from a beginning point to an ending one, with all the steps developed in numerical or time sequence. Research shows that using a time method of issue arrangement increases a listener's retention of a speaker's information.[11]

Time arrangement can be used to develop the body of the speech whose central idea is "to inform the audience of the accomplishments of the last four Chinese dynasties." The outline of the body for the speech would read:

III. Four dynasties mark the end of China's experience with monarchy and foreshadowed modern times.
   A. AD 960–1280: Song (Sung)
      1. Paper money invented
      2. Primitive printing press developed
      3. Scholars active
         a. Books printed
         b. Painting reached zenith
   B. AD 1280–1368: Yuan
      1. Became part of an empire that stretched to Europe
      2. Silk Road reopened
      3. New religions introduced
   C. AD 1368–1644: Ming
      1. Agricultural methods of production developed
      2. Great sea expeditions undertaken
   D. AD 1644–1911: Qing (Ching)
      1. Tobacco and corn industries developed
      2. Lost Korea, Taiwan, and the Pescadores Islands

Topical Arrangement Ideas can be organized on the basis of their similarities or other relationships. Thus, in using a **topical method of issue arrangement**, a speaker explains an idea in terms of its component parts. For example, in speaking about dogs, a speaker may discuss cocker spaniels, poodles, and then collies, developing ideas about each breed (the component part) completely before going on to the next one. The speaker also can organize the presentation of ideas by talking about the temperament of each breed, and then about the sizes of each breed, and finally about the coloring of each breed. In this way, the speaker is organizing ideas by classifying the animals according to specific identifiable characteristics (the component parts) and then developing each subsection into identifiable patterns of information.

Although there is no set sequence in which topics must be presented in the topical arrangement, main points might be made in their order of relevance, importance, priority, or even given alphabetical order. The key to an effective topic arrangement is for the speaker to create and communicate a rationale for the main points.

As illustrated in the following example, with a plan of exposing the audience to the topics and the order in which they will be discussed, you might say in the (II) Statement of Central Idea segment of the speech, "There is a misconception among Americans that since there has been a decrease in AIDS, the epidemic is over. Some of this reasoning is based on a lack of knowledge about the disease. I think a refresher course in AIDS is necessary, so today I'm going to define AIDS/HIV, reveal the origin of HIV, and give a brief history of HIV in the United States."

III. HIV/AIDS
   A. What is HIV/AIDS?
      1. Viral infection
         a. Gradually destroys the immune system
         b. Results in infections that are hard for the body to fight
      2. Occurs by the transfer of fluids
         a. Blood
         b. Semen
         c. Vaginal fluid
         d. Pre-ejaculate
         e. Breast milk
      3. Routes of transmission
         a. Unprotected sex
         b. Contaminated needles
         c. Breast milk
         d. Transmission from an infected mother to her baby at birth
   B. Origin of HIV
      1. Scientists identified a type of chimpanzee in West Africa as the source of HIV infection in humans
      2. Virus most likely jumped to humans when chimpanzee meat was eaten
      3. Virus spread across Africa to other parts of the world
   C. History of HIV in the United States
      1. First identified in 1981
      2. During early 1980s, 150,000 people a year were infected with HIV
      3. AIDS cases began to fall dramatically in 1996
         a. New drugs
         b. Awareness of how disease is spread

4. About one-quarter of people with HIV or AIDS do not know they are infected
    a. Put themselves at risk
    b. Put others at risk
5. Living with HIV today

Causal Arrangement The **causal method of issue arrangement** shows how two or more events are connected in such a way that if one occurs, the other will necessarily follow. In other words, if one incident happened, it caused the second incident to happen. This is a good method to use when a specific observable result can be understood by determining what happened.

This outline was developed for the body of a speech whose central idea was "To list and discuss the theory that a series of identifiable events can result in the development of agoraphobia": (The definition of agoraphobia was presented in Ib of the introduction.)

III. Series of Events Resulting in the Development of Agoraphobia
- A. Sequence of events
    1. First event
        a. Physical symptoms such as heart palpitations, trembling, sweating, breathlessness, dizziness
        b. No apparent cause for the physical symptoms
    2. Second event
        a. Duplication of physical symptoms in a place similar to the site of the first event
        b. Increasing awareness of fear of going to certain places
    3. Third event
        a. Symptoms occurring when there is a thought of going to a place similar to the site of the first event's occurrence
        b. Feeling of being out of control when thinking of leaving the safety site (usually the home)
- B. Result: agoraphobia
    1. Personality changes
        a. Frequent anxiety
        b. Depression
        c. Loss of individual character
    2. Emotional changes
        a. Impassiveness
        b. High degree of dependence on others
        c. Constant alertness

Note that the events leading up to the final result are listed, with the final result discussed last. An alternative form would have been to give the final result first and then list the events leading up to it. The former method is called *cause(s) to effect;* the latter is *effect from cause(s).*

Comparison–Contrast Arrangement Suppose you are asked to explain the similarities between a community college and a four-year institution. Your explanation could follow the **comparison method of issue organization,** in which you would tell how the two types of institutions are alike. In the case of the colleges, you could talk about the similarities in curriculum, staff, facilities, activity programs, and costs. If, however, you are asked to tell the differences between the two, you would use the **contrast method of issue arrangement,** developing the ideas by giving specific examples of differences between the two types of institutions. A speech based on the **comparison–contrast method of issue arrangement** shows both similarities and differences.

Here is the body of a speech with a central idea of "Informing the audience of some similarities and differences between high-context and low-context society's communication patterns":

III. Similarities and differences regarding high- and low-context society's communication patterns
   A. Similarities
      1. Both high- and low-context communication societies express ideas in verbal messages
      2. Both high- and low-context communication societies express ideas in languages
      3. General consistency within each society as to the context of the system used
   B. Differences
      1. Expression of intentions
         a. High-context emphasis is on how intention or meaning can be conveyed through the social roles or positions of the participants by both verbal and nonverbal means
         b. Low-context emphasis is on how meaning is best expressed through explicit verbal messages
      2. Value base of expression
         a. High-context emphasis is on collectivistic values
         b. Low-context emphasis is on individualistic values
      3. Verbal style
         a. High context—indirect verbal style
         b. Low context—direct verbal style

An alternative way of presenting the material would be to explain by examining how the communication of high- and low-context societies are different. The outline for that speech would be:

III. There are differences between the way high- and low-context communication takes place
   A. High-context societies
      1. Collectivistic values
      2. Spiral logic
      3. Indirect verbal style
      4. Verbal reticence or silence
   B. Low-context societies
      1. Individualistic values
      2. Linear logic
      3. Direct verbal style
      4. Verbal assertiveness or talkativeness

Problem-Solution Arrangement The **problem–solution method of issue arrangement** is used when a speaker attempts to identify what is wrong and to determine how to cure it or make a recommendation for its cure. This method can be used to think through a problem and then structure a speech. A person dealing with the problem of child abuse, for instance, may wish to begin by analyzing the problem: the influence of family history, the lack of parental control or knowledge, and the different types of child abuse. Such an analysis could then lead to a consideration of various solutions, such as stricter legislation mandating penalties for child abuse, stronger enforcement of child abuse laws, improved reporting procedures, and greater availability of social services to parents and children alike.

When you develop a problem–solution message, your sequence should state the problem, its cause, its possible solutions, and the selected solution. This organization allows your listeners to share a complete picture of your reasoning process.

Here is an example of a speech outline using problem–solution for the body of a speech with the central idea "to inform the audience what anger is and some methods of coping with anger":

III. What is anger and how can it be dealt with?
  A. Anger defined
    1. Anger is an emotional state that may range in intensity from mild irritation to intense fury and rage
    2. Anger can have such physical effects as an increase in heart rate and blood pressure
    3. Biological influences
      a. Temporal lobe epilepsy
      b. Temperament
      c. Substance abuse
      d. Chemical imbalance
    4. Psychological influence
      a. Cognitive style
      b. Interactional style
      c. Coping style
  B. Treatment for anger
    1. Venting
      a. Free expression to the anger
      b. Volcanic reactions
    2. Ventilation
      a. Talking out of feelings rather than acting them out
      b. Talking feelings out in a positive way
    3. The lifesaver technique
      a. Suck on a lifesaver until it's all gone before your respond to your anger
      b. Delays action and gives the mind a chance to change from the emotional to the logical state
    4. The Keep My Cool Technique
      a. Label the anger
      b. Respond, don't react; emotions come and go
      c. Reconnoiter—identify the who, where, why, and what
      d. Review your options
      e. Respond by ventilating
      f. Reward yourself

A more detailed presentation of the speech can include discussions of testing each of the solutions. This can be accomplished by including subdivisions under each of the statements of the solution to explore whether it is *workable* (developing why the suggestion will solve or help solve the problem), *desirable* (explaining why the suggestion will not cause greater problems), and *practical* (indicating if and how the suggestion can be put into practice).

An alternative form of the problem-solution method is the *see-blame-cure-cost method*. In this approach, the evil or problem that exists is examined (*see*); what has caused the problem is determined (*blame*); solutions are investigated, and the most practical solution

Socially Communicating

Openers and Closers: Using Stories and Jokes

The Roman gladiator, Androcles, developed quite a reputation for staying alive. He was frequently thrown to the lions, and, just as frequently, he returned alive. He always used the same approach. Just as the lion was about to eat him, Androcles would whisper in his ear, and the animal would appear to lose his appetite and slink away with a defeated look.

Finally, the Roman emperor called him to his court. "Androcles," he said, "I can take it no longer. I need to know your secret." "It's this way, your highness," Androcles said. "I merely remind the lion that when he has finished dinner, he'll be asked to say a few words. I'm living proof that lions don't like to give after-dinner talks!"

The key is to make sure the story fits your topic and can lead right into it. After this story, I say, "I know a lot of people, too, who don't like to make after-dinner talks, or after-lunch talks, or before-lunch talks,..."

Source: Bjorseth, L. D. (2007). Improving your public speaking: Openers and closers. *The Sideroad.* Retrieved from www.sideroad.com/Public_Speaking/improve-public-speaking.html

is selected (*cure*); and what finances, time, or emotions will have to be expended (*cost*) are examined.

Major and Internal Methods of Arrangement

For each speech, the speaker usually selects one major method of development, always keeping in mind that other methods may be used as necessary to present subdivisions of the complete idea. For instance, in developing a presentation on the causes of World War II, a speaker may decide to use a chronological arrangement as the major method of development and a spatial method for some of the subtopics of the presentation. Thus, the speaker may talk about the political and social changes in the 1920s in England, France, Germany, Russia, and Japan; then proceed to tell about events in the early 1930s in these countries; and then discuss happenings in these countries in the mid-1930s. In this way, the audience can develop a listening pattern that allows for clarity of comprehension through the decade span and then the location.

No matter which pattern you use to develop a message, maintain that pattern consistently throughout your presentation. Otherwise, your audience will be confused by sudden shifts or failure to follow a sequence to its logical conclusion.

The Conclusion

Depending on the purpose of a speech, the **conclusion of a speech** can be used to summarize and/or motivate listeners to take a prescribed action.

Summary

Whatever the purpose, a presentation should end with a *summary* that restates the major points to recap what has been covered. The guide for developing the summary is to refer to the major headings in the body of the speech and indicate how they develop the statement of central idea.

Clincher

Many speakers, speechwriters, and speech coaches agree that all speeches should end with a summary of the major points, followed by a *clincher to the speech,* which gives the speaker one more chance to reinforce the major ideas presented and then wraps up the presentation with a final message to clinch the selling of the central idea. The outline of the conclusion section of a speech that includes a clincher would be:

IV. Conclusion
 A. Summary
 B. Clincher

Clincher techniques are similar to attention-getting introduction methods—for example:

- *Personal reference.* A speaker who established expertise at the start of a speech can reestablish his or her authority in the conclusion.
- *Humorous story.* A humorous story can summarize the speaker's ideas. For example, a presentation about public speaking anxiety could end with "The mind is an amazing thing; it starts working the moment you are born and never stops until you get up to give a speech."
- *Illustration.* A drug counselor can end a speech on substance abuse with a story about a client's success in turning away from the drug scene.
- *Rhetorical question.* A speaker who posed a rhetorical question at the beginning of a presentation can conclude by answering it.
- *Unusual or dramatic devices.* A speaker concluded a speech about the necessity of proper dental hygiene by passing out a small cup of disclosing solution and small mirror to each member of the audience. She then asked each of them to rinse out their mouths with the solution, which turned plaque and other substances on or between the teeth bright red. This activity effectively illustrated the importance of proper brushing—and the value of unusual or dramatic devices.
- *Quotations.* A quotation that restates the major theme of a presentation can be used in ending it. A speaker could summarize a speech against the death penalty, for example, by reading the vivid description of an execution presented in Truman Capote's classic book *In Cold Blood.*
- *Repetition.* Closing a speech with repetition ties it back to the introduction. It makes for a circular presentation, which many speakers find to be the most effective concluding device because it clearly wraps up the speech by coming back to the statement of central idea which laid out the topic and format for the speech.

Alternative Methods for Organizing the Speech

"In addition to the traditional patterns usually taught in U.S. public speaking classes, communication theorists are constantly looking at other organizational patterns."[12] These methods include those used by women, ethnic, religious, and racial speakers, as well as some concepts developed by those who perceive that there may be some alternative ways to structure the bodies of speeches to allow for ease in both preparation and receipt of the message. The search for alternatives centers on the idea "that many speakers are uncomfortable with the standard organizational patterns due to cultural backgrounds or personal inclinations."[13] As a speaker, you should choose that organizational pattern that will best meet your communication goals and your listeners' needs.

In organizing a speech, you, the speaker, must make careful decisions about the type of introduction, statement of central idea, methods of arranging the material in the body of your speech, and various techniques you can use to conclude.

Alternative methods for organizing include the partitioning, unfolding, and case methods.[14]

Partitioning Method

The **partitioning organizational speech structure** is a deductive format in which, as the speech proceeds, the speech is partitioned into a number of points. In developing the speech, you state your point and then develop each point with supporting details. This format lends itself to informative speaking (see Chapter 15).

When using this type of organization, you start with the introduction (I), state the central idea (IIA), then preview the points you will be making in the speech (IIB), and then specifically tell the audience the main issues you will be covering in the body of the speech (IIC). The main issues should be organized by one of the traditional methods of organization discussed on pages 350–356.

Part IIC, the listing of how the main issues will be presented in the speech, is the **partitioning step**, as it divides (partitions) the topic. Part IIC may be viewed as the "road map" of the speech because it specifically tells the audience where the "main stops" will take place on the road through the body of the speech. A speaker, for example, whose central idea is that "there are several problems with the use of radiation therapy" might say, "To understand these radiological difficulties, we will look at the effects of radiation therapy, the after-effects of receiving radiation, and the poor quality of radiation facilities in hospitals." The "stops," as the speech progresses, will be at "harmful effects," "after-effects," and "poor quality of the radiation facilities." These segments are arranged by the topic method of arrangement.

As you proceed from segment to segment, you should use transitions, which are statements of what the next segment will be. The *transition* forecasts the coming issue. For example, you could say, "Turning, then, to our first point, let's consider the current state of facilities and equipment that exists today for radiation therapy." You would continue to use transitions for each connection between major segments of the body to help listeners understand and remember.

Except for the first transition, which forecasts only what is going to be presented in the upcoming section, the other transition consists of two parts: a restatement of the previous issue and a forecast of the next one. When moving from the second segment of the body of the speech to the third, you, the speaker, would state, "Yes, there are harmful effects of radiation therapy. Let's now examine the after-effects of receiving radiation."

Once the last issue in a partitioned speech has been discussed, the presentation ends with a conclusion that restates the central idea and the main issues. As in any good conclusion, this summary gives listeners a chance to review the points that have been discussed.

A general outline for the partitioning sequence looks like this:

I. Introduction
   A. Attention material
   B. Orienting material

II. Central Idea
   A. Statement of central idea
   B. Preview of how the central idea will be developed
   C. Listing of issues arranged by the method of issue arrangement
      1. First main issue
      2. Second main issue
      3. Third main issue
      (and so on)

III. Body (Transition: forecast of the first issue)
   A. First main issue
      1. Discussion of first main issue through examples, illustrations, and explanations
      2. Additional discussion of first main issue through examples, illustrations, and explanations (and so on)
      (Transition: restatement of first main issue and forecast of second issue)

B. Second main issue
   1. Discussion of second main issue
   2. Additional discussion of second main issue (and so on)
      (Transition: restatement of second main issue and forecast of third issue)

C. Third main issue
   1. Discussion of third main issue
   2. Additional discussion of third main issue (and so on)

IV. Conclusion
   A. Summary (restatement of issues and central idea)
   B. Clincher

Here is an example of a speech following the partitioning method of organization. Its central idea is "to inform the audience of the alternatives a child advocate intake counselor has by listing and discussing the alternatives available":

I. Introduction
   A. Attention material: Each of us probably makes hundreds of decisions every day. We decide what to eat, what to wear, what television program to watch, what time to go to bed.
   B. Orienting material: In my work as an intake counselor with the Department of Juvenile Services, I must make decisions that can seriously affect a child's life. An intake counselor gets the police report when a juvenile commits a crime, calls in the parents and the child to decide what actions should be taken, and counsels them. An investigation of such work can help you understand some of the procedures that local governments use to combat the problems of juvenile delinquency.

II. Central Idea
   A. Let us consider the alternatives an intake counselor has.
   B. The counselor can select from three major decisions.

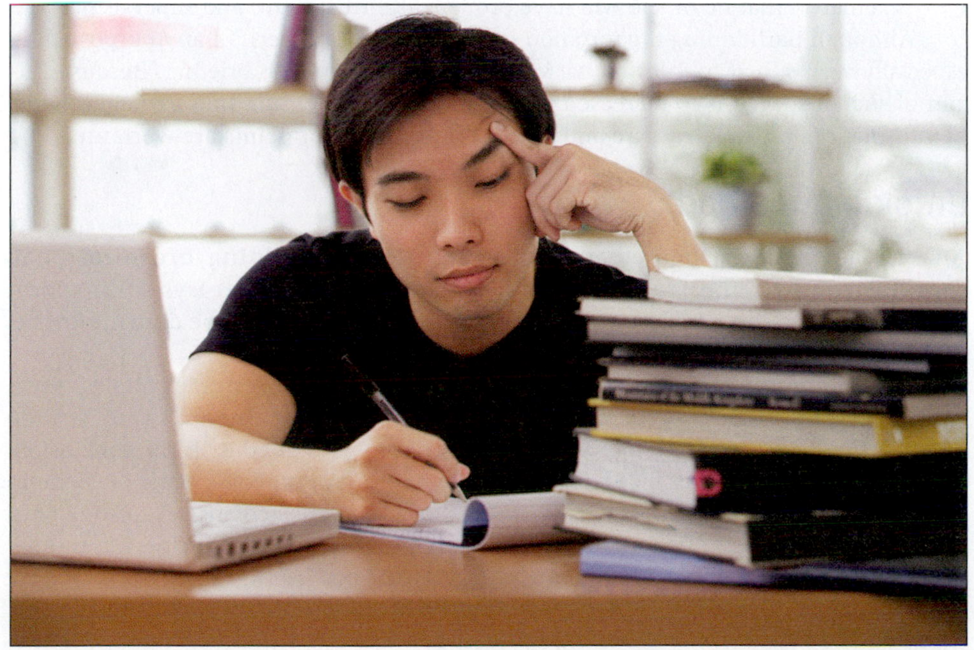

A speaker must make careful decisions about the type of introduction to use, the statement of the central idea, methods for organizing the material in the body of the speech, and various techniques for concluding the presentation.

C. These decisions are to
   1. Send the case to court.
   2. Close the case at intake.
   3. Place the child on informal supervision for forty-five days.

III. Body
(One decision a counselor may make is to send the case to court.)
   A. The law states that you must send the case to court if
      1. The charge is denied.
      2. The juvenile has a prior record.
      3. You notice signs of trouble in the family.
      4. The case is like Felicia's. Felicia...
      (Thus a case may be sent to court. A counselor also may decide to close a case at intake.)
   B. There are several reasons for closing the case at intake.
      1. The child admits guilt.
      2. The incident was a first offense.
      3. The parents are supportive, and the home life is stable.
      4. An example of a case closed at intake was Henrietta's. Henrietta...
      (As a result, a case may be closed at intake. A counselor also may decide to put a juvenile under informal supervision.)
   C. Supervision for forty-five days is warranted if
      1. The child or the family is in need of short-term counseling.
      2. The procedure is not used often.
      3. The court has never ordered this in the past.
      4. The case is like Lamont's. Lamont...
      (Through informal supervision, some children can be helped.)

IV. Conclusion
   A. Summary: The basic decision an intake counselor has is whether to arrange court appearances, stop the action at the beginning, or supervise the client.
   B. Clincher: The goal of the intake process is to provide whatever is best for the child so that he or she will have proper care, treatment, and supervision.

Although partitioning organization can be used for a speech of any purpose, it is especially well suited to informative speaking and informative briefing. Because the aim of such a speech is to increase the listener's comprehension of a particular body of information, a clear structure and repetition of the major points are warranted.

Unfolding Method

Another alternative pattern that can be used is the **unfolding organizational speech structure**. This is an inductive style in which the speaker lays out supporting evidence and then draws a conclusion, leading the listeners to be drawn into the argument.

The *inductive reasoning process* begins with specific instances or examples, then formulates a reasonable generalization or conclusion from them.[15] One test of whether the instances effectively develop the concepts presented is "Is the conclusion reached *expected* and *accepted*.[16] If, for example, you said to someone, "One plus one is two." The person would accept what you said since the expected answer to "one plus one is two." On the other hand, if you said, "One plus one is nine," the person should reject your solution. The expected outcome is "two," not "nine." Since the expected answer is not presented, the answer will not be accepted. Moral: In developing the arguments to prove your various contentions, be sure to use statistics, examples, and other information that will lead audience members to accept your answer because the conclusion you reach is the expected conclusion.

Three major tests can be used to evaluate the examples that are used to reach the conclusions:[17]

1. Are enough cases represented to justify the conclusion? Or are you forming a conclusion based on only one or a few examples?
2. Are the examples typical? That is, do they represent the average members of the population to which the generalizations are applied? Or are they extreme cases that may show what could happen, but not what usually happens?
3. Are the examples from the time under discussion, or are they out of date?

The unfolding format lends itself to persuasive speaking (as will be discussed in Chapter 15). The basic format for the unfolding method, as the title indicates, is to get the audience's attention and provide the necessary orienting material in the introduction, state the central idea, and then present the body of the speech in an order that unfolds the arguments in favor of the proposal one at a time, one building on the other, so the speaker's arguments for the speech build one on the other. For example, a speaker who believes that a particular candidate for office is the best candidate would give a basic reason for his belief (the candidate has shown good character), another factor (she has used that good character to do good deeds), then (her good deeds have resulted in progressive legislature being passed which has helped the community), then (this help for the community is the basis for her seeking higher office which she has proven she is capable of holding).

Here is a sequence for an unfolding format:

I. Introduction
   A. Attention material
   B. Orienting material

II. Statement of Central Idea

III. Body (organized by some method of issue arrangement)
   (Transition)
   A. First issue
      1. Discussion of first issue through examples, illustrations, and explanations
      2. Additional discussion of first issue through examples, illustrations, and explanations (and so on)
      (Transition)
   B. Second issue
      1. Discussion of second issue through examples, illustrations, and explanations
      2. Additional discussion of second issue through examples, illustrations, and explanations (and so on)
      (Transition)
   C. Third issue
      1. Discussion of third issue through examples, illustrations, and explanations
      2. Additional discussion of third issue through examples, illustrations, and explanations (and so on)

IV. Conclusion
   A. Restatement
   B. Clincher

This next outline develops a speech according to the unfolding method of organization. The central idea is "to persuade each member of the audience, by listing and discussing the reasons, that he or she should donate his or her body to science":

I. Introduction
   A. Attention material: Picture a three-year-old girl attached to a kidney dialysis machine once a week for the rest of her life. Picture a little boy whose world is blackness, or a father who is confined to his bed because he has a failing heart.
   B. Orienting material: Such pictures are not very pleasant. But you can do something about them.

II. Statement of Central Idea: You should donate your body to science.

III. Body
   A. Organ banks need organs so that people who need them may function normally.
      1. List of organs that can be donated
      2. The need for speed in transplanting organs
   B. Organ donations have been used both to save lives and to improve the quality of life of the recipients.
      1. Statistics on the number of donors
      2. Statistics on the number of lives saved
      3. Examples of the improved quality of life of recipients
   C. Your body can also be used as an instrument for medical education.
      1. Who can donate and how
      2. The need to eliminate shortages
         (As a result, your entire body can continue to serve a useful purpose.)

IV. Conclusion
   A. Summary
      1. Organs are needed so that others can function normally.
      2. Your body can be used for medical education.
   B. Clincher
      1. I am a benevolent person who believes that everyone is born with a benevolent nature. I know that you and I will help those less fortunate than we are. I am a potential organ and cadaver donor through my will. A donor's card can be obtained through any medical foundation. I cannot overemphasize the need for body and organ donations.
      2. Don't, as the proverb states, wait for George to do it. You do it! Take immediate action to become an organ and cadaver donor.

There are alternative formats that can be used for the unfolding method, but the general idea is the same. For example, if your prior analysis reveals that members of the audience oppose your stand, you should not state the central idea early in the presentation. In this is the case, you present the body of the speech before stating the central idea, thus not "tipping your hand" too early thus giving yourself a chance to build your case before you come to your stand. For example, if you are trying to persuade an audience composed of Republicans to vote for the Democratic candidate you favor, it would be wise to lay a foundation by outlining your candidate's stands that would benefit the listeners. Then propose they vote for her.

In this variation, you present the main points, moving from areas of shared agreement. If you arrange and develop the main issues carefully, establishing your purpose statement just before you reach the conclusion, you may be able to get your desired effect. This outline illustrates this alternative method for using the unfolding format:

I. Introduction
  A. Attention material
  B. Orienting material
  (Transition)
II. Body (organized by some method of issue arrangement)
  A. Discussion of first issue
    1. Examples and illustrations
    2. Examples and illustrations (and so on)
  B. Statement of first issue
  (Transition)
  C. Discussion of second issue
    1. Examples and illustrations
    2. Examples and illustrations (and so on)
    (Transition)
III. Statement of Central Idea
  (Transition)
IV. Conclusion
  A. Restatement
  B. Clincher

Case Method

Another alternative method is the **case method of organizational speech structure** in which the speaker discusses the central idea without breaking it into subpoints. As a result, this format is especially suitable for a single-issue speech. If, for example, your central idea is that "left-handed people are discriminated against," then the body of the speech includes a series of examples of how left-handed people are discriminated against.

Here is the general format for a speech developed by case organization:

I. Introduction
  A. Attention material
  B. Orienting material
  (Transition)
II. Central Idea
  (Transition)
III. Body (organized in a sequence)
  A. Example (a case)
  (Transition)
  B. Example (a case)
  (Transition)
  C. Example (a case, and so on)
  (Transition)
IV. Conclusion
  A. Summary
  B. Clincher

The following outline develops a speech according to the case method of organization. As with the partitioning method, cases or examples may be arranged chronologically, spatially, or by a speaker's own creativity. The central idea is "to inform the audience of some ways in which left-handers are discriminated against from their fingers to their souls (spatial method of development)":

I. Introduction
   A. Attention material: Have you ever pondered the design of a butter knife or the structure of a gravy ladle?
   B. Orienting material: These structural problems are important to all of us who are afflicted with a key social problem: left-handedness.
   (Those of us who are left-handed believe that...)

II. Statement of Central Idea
   A. Left-handers are discriminated against.
   B. Let's look at some examples.

III. Body
   A. Example: Tell a story of the difficulties encountered when using scissors.
   (Transition: Another experience I've had...)
   B. Example: Tell a story of the problems with school desks designed for right-handed people.
   (Transition: This experience points out another one...)
   C. Example: Tell a story of the problems with words such as *gauche* and *south-paw*.
   (Transition: So you see...)

IV. Conclusion
   A. Summary: Left-handers are discriminated against all the way from the design of scissors to the names they are called.
   B. Clincher: If you are left-handed, however, no matter the discrimination, you are in good company: Eleven presidents of the United States have been left-handed!

Transition into the Question-And-Answer Session

If a question-and-answer session is to follow the prepared address, the speaker should incorporate a transition into the conclusion section. The speaker might say, for example, "And so we've seen what I consider to be the effects of our current policy on the national security database. I'd be happy to respond to any questions you may have." If there are going to be restrictions on the question-and-answer session, this would also be the appropriate place to mention them. For instance, you might also say, "I would appreciate it if you would restrict your comments to a specific question rather than express your stand on the issue."

If the question-and-answer transition is used, the outline of the conclusion section of a speech would be:

I. IV. Conclusion
   A. Summary
   B. Clincher
   C. Transition to question-and-answer session

Role of Culture on Speech Structure

It should be recognized that the U.S. American way of structuring speeches is not the way listeners from other cultures are accustomed to attending to presentations. Here are some examples of how culture affects the organization of ideas:

- In some cultures, a *spiral form of explanation* is used. In this mode, a statement is made and then a story or analogy that deals with the statement is presented. It is left to the listener to apply the parallels and draw outcomes related to the original statement. (In other words, the traditional conclusion step is not included in the speech.) This is a method often used in Arabic, Native American, and some Asian cultures.
- Arabic speakers value telling a story or a series of parables and letting the listeners figure out the moral of the narrative. This indirect presentational style, with little structure, often confuses those who are used to a direct format in which a statement is made and evidence is presented to clarify the proposition.
- Arabs use "a completely different persuasive style than that set in Western logic. The Arabic argumentative style depends greatly on parables from the *Koran,* which are based on the concept 'because Islam says so.'"[18] This organizational style often causes Western listeners to disregard the information because it is not based on logic proofs, such as statistics and research findings.
- Because discourse for Navajos is designed to secure order, harmony, and balance, they are interested in dialogue, not a speaker who is expounding a point of view to silent listeners. Public speaking, Navajo style, is interactive, with no prescribed structure.[19] Most Native Americans, representing the communication style of high-context cultures, resort to hints and implicit analogies, rather than direct statements.[20]

Communicating Culturally

Foreign Audience? Differences in Cultural Patterns

- You might think you are putting your audience to sleep in Japan, but don't worry. In Japan it is common to show concentration and attentiveness in public by closing the eyes and nodding the head up and down slightly.—Then again, maybe you really are boring.
- Applause is accepted as a form of approval in most areas of the world. In the United States, applause is sometimes accompanied by whistling. If you hear whistles in many parts of Europe, you better run because it is a signal of disapproval.
- If you were finishing a speaking engagement in Argentina and you waved goodbye, U.S. style, the members of the audience might all turn around and come back to sit down. To them the wave means, "Hey! Come back." In other parts of Latin America and in Europe the same wave means "no."
- Do not expect standing ovations when speaking in public in Australia. It doesn't seem to be part of their culture.
- South of the border people don't like us to refer to ourselves as Americans. We must remember that we are not the only ones. There are North Americans, Central Americans, and South Americans.

Source: "Foreign Audience? Differences in Cultural Patterns" from *Public speaking: International perspective on humor*. Copyright © 2007 by Advanced Public Speaking Institute. Reprinted with permission. www.public-speaking.org

COMMUNICATING in Careers

Considering Organizational Culture

Whenever you speak within an organization, learn as much as you can about its culture before you create your speech—even expectations for introductions can differ in specific settings. Today, for example, was graduation day at my university, and a business leader from the community gave the commencement address. She did not start with a statistic, a visual aid, or any other attention strategy mentioned in this chapter; instead, she first referred to the occasion, congratulated the graduates, and expressed respect for the university—acknowledging both the organization and the cultural event (graduation) before introducing the topic of her speech. It would have seemed abrupt and strange to the graduates and their families on this special occasion if she had launched into her speech immediately.

Source: "Considering Organizational Culture" from *Public speaking: Concepts and skills for a diverse society*, 3rd Edition by C. Jaffe.

REFLECT ON THIS:

1. Where can you find out about a corporation's culture?
2. Why would it have seemed abrupt and strange to the audience if the speaker had launched into her speech immediately?

In speeches given by Africans there is a tendency to use metaphors, parables, and stories to dramatize the emotional impact of a message.

- The overall Russian persuasion style centers on a structure pattern that starts with "an agreement in principle (i.e., the big picture) and then fills in the details. Russian negotiators, consider compromise as a sign of weakness, a retreat from a correct and morally justified position, therefore, they are prepared to wait out their opposition."[21]
- The Chinese tend to present ideas through a variety of indirectly related views. Their pattern is the opening, amplification, preliminary exposition, first argument, second argument, third argument, final argument, and conclusion. The most important part is the amplification, which consists of two or three sentences that express the topic. This is in contrast to the European American tradition of the body being the most important part of the presentation because it amplifies the reason for taking specific actions.
- Japanese speakers can be indirect in what they want the listener to know. The Japanese language forces the listener to construct meaning based on shared knowledge between the listener and the speaker.[22]
- African Americans are a high-context culture in which the group is more important than the individual. Often there is no specific theme or organizational pattern but a stringing together of stories, anecdotes, and biblical quotations in a random order.[23]
- Athabaskans, an oral-based society of native Alaskan speakers, "think it rude to explicitly state the conclusions they want listeners to draw. It is enough for them to simply present a set of facts and let audience members draw their own conclusions."[24]
- "Members of Italian, Slavic, Jewish, and many African cultures have a tendency to use effusive metaphors, parables or stories to dramatize the emotional impact of their message."[25]

In Conclusion

IN CONCLUSION

A public communication message is usually divided into four parts: introduction, central idea, body, and conclusion. Attention material can be personal references, humorous illustrations, references to the occasion or setting, rhetorical questions, action questions, unusual or dramatic devices, quotations related to the theme, or statements of the theme.

Orienting material, which includes historical background, definition of terms, personal history and/or the speaker's tie to the topic, and the topic's importance to the listeners, gives an audience the background necessary to understand the basic material of the speech.

The body of a speech in the Western world normally takes one of six forms: spatial arrangement, time arrangement, topical arrangement, causal arrangement, comparison–contrast arrangement, or problem–solution arrangement. A summary restates the major points of the speech. Clinchers can include personal references, humorous stories, illustrations, rhetorical questions, unusual or dramatic devices, or quotations.

Alternate modes of speech organization are the partitioning, unfolding, or case methods.

It must be remembered, however, that not all audiences will be European American and that cultures and languages differ in the very assumption of how information should be organized, of what is to be or not to be described and expressed. A speaker is wise to take into consideration the general culture of the audience and adapt the speech materials accordingly.

LEARN BY DOING

1. Your instructor asks for a volunteer and gives him or her a card with a drawing on it. Each member of the class has a sheet of paper and a pencil. The volunteer explains to the class how to draw the diagram exactly as it appears on the card. No one is allowed to ask any questions. When the volunteer has finished giving directions, the members of the class compare their drawings with the original. After the activity, the class discusses these questions:
   - **a.** If the volunteer did not do so, would it have helped if he or she had given a general overview of what to draw before beginning to give directions? Discuss this question in relation to your reading about the purpose of an introduction.
   - **b.** Did the instructions have a conclusion? How could a conclusion restating the major points have helped you?
   - **c.** Did any words used in the directions confuse you, causing you to make an error or not be able to follow the instruction? What were they? How did they cause problems?
   - **d.** Was the structure of the directions clear?
   - **e.** Do you think a question-and-answer session following the instructions would have been valuable? Why or why not?
2. Do activity 1 again using a different diagram. This time, a different volunteer builds on the positive things the first volunteer did and makes improvements based on the class discussion. This time,

the activity is followed by a question-and-answer session. Note how many people altered their drawings during the question-and-answer session. Reach some conclusions about the value of question-and-answer sessions.

3. A speaker informs the class about an unusual topic—something about which the audience probably has no knowledge. Sample topics are the language of bees, the Kaballah, the country of Malawi, or organic architecture. Be sure the speech has a clear structure and lasts no more than three minutes.

4. Select a subject about which you are an expert, and present a speech to your classmates in such a way that when you finish, they too have an understanding of the topic. Clearly structure the speech, and take no more than six minutes to deliver it.

5. Prepare a speech of no more than five minutes informing the class about a controversial theory. Sample topics: The Loch Ness monster exists, Rational Emotive Therapy can alter behavior, Alcoholism is an inherited disease. Explain the theory and the various arguments concerning the theory. Do not include your own views in the presentation. Be sure the speech is clearly structured.

6. You are assigned to give a speech about your education (elementary, high school, college). Prepare an introduction for the presentation representing each of these introductory devices:
   a. Personal reference
   b. Humorous story
   c. Rhetorical question
   d. Unusual or dramatic device

KEY TERMS

introduction to a speech 344

orienting material 348

statement of the speech's central idea 348

body of a speech 349

method of issue arrangement for the body of a speech 350

spatial method of issue arrangement 351

time method of issue arrangement 351

topical method of issue arrangement 352

causal method of issue arrangement 353

comparison method of issue organization 353

contrast method of issue arrangement 353

comparison–contrast method of issue arrangement 354

problem-solution method of issue arrangement 354

conclusion of a speech 356

partitioning organizational speech structure 357

partitioning step 358

unfolding organizational speech structure 360

case method of organizational speech structure 363

Public Speaking: The Informative Speech

characteristics and classifications of informative speeches • informative briefings • question-and-answer sessions

CHAPTER 14

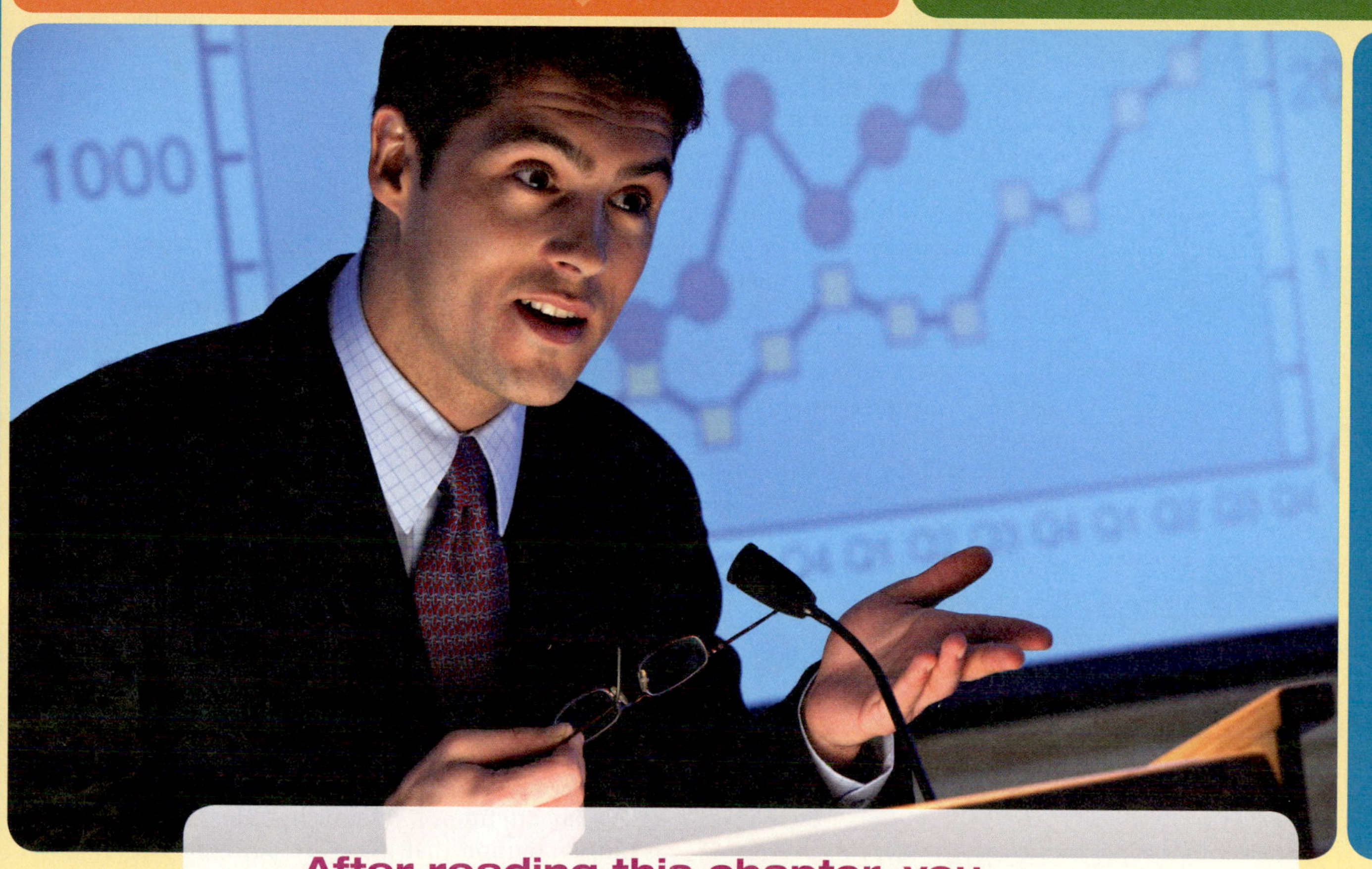

After reading this chapter, you should be able to

- Define informative speaking
- Explain the characteristics of informative speaking
- List and explain the classifications of informative speeches
- List and clarify the types of informative briefings
- Give details on how to manage a question-and-answer session
- Develop a speech of introduction

About 1600 years ago, St. Augustine identified three purposes for speaking publicly: to teach, to please, and to move. In succeeding centuries the purposes were described as: to enlighten the understanding, to please the imagination, to move the passions, and to influence the will. And further along in the evolution of speech theory and instruction, the outcomes were described as: to inform, to entertain, to stimulate through emotion and to convince through reasoning.[1] At present, communication theorists generally agree there are two purposes: to inform and to persuade. Some add to entertain as a classification. For our discussion we will only discuss to inform and to persuade as the entertaining speech follows the same concepts as an informative speech.

Informative speaking has been defined as discourse that imparts new information, secures understanding, or reinforces accumulated information. This idea may appear to be a straightforward concept, but even informative speaking may require the speaker to be persuasive by motivating the audience to listen or perhaps change a point of view through learning new information.

Your authors recognize that although the purposes of informing and persuading "may seem to be completely separate, they often coexist in a single speech—as where a speaker aims to both share new information and also to use that information to influence attitudes and behavior."[2] For example, when you were in high school a college representative may have come to your school to inform you about her campus. Some might say that her underlying purpose was to persuade you to attend to the school she represented. Others may argue it depends on what she said, as to what she expected of you. If she only talked about the school's programs and activities, and did not suggest that you consider going to X College, then, according to this text's concepts, it was informative. However, if she added the appeal for you to consider attending, then it became persuasive.

Socially COMMUNICATING

The Ethics of Informative Speaking

1. Be sure you can ethically defend your choice of a topic.
2. Mention all major positions on a topic when there are differing perspectives.
3. Present all information on a topic that is important for audience understanding.
4. Do not distort information that is necessary for audience understanding.
5. Do sufficient research to speak responsibly on your subject.
6. Do not omit relevant information because it is inconsistent with your perspective.
7. Strive to be as objective as possible.

Source: Osborn, M., Osborn, S., & Osborn, R. (2009) *Public speaking* (8th ed.). Boston: Pearson.

REFLECT ON THIS: Why do you think it is necessary for you to understand the "Ethics of Informative Speaking"?

We also accept that all communication contains elements of persuasion. After all, the audience in the traditional informative speaking format must be persuaded to accept information that the speaker presents. Indeed, even the act of using materials to gain attention is persuasive because the speaker is asking listeners to pay attention to him or her. However, it is our contention that there are distinguishing elements between an informative and a persuasive speech. They center on the structure of the message and the appeals used in the persuasive format. In addition, there are key words that we think trigger persuasion, such as "therefore you should agree that," "I want you to..." "give to," "vote for" and "believe that" are just a few.

Perhaps you have learned about some of the problems in Sudan by hearing actor and social activist George Clooney talk, for example, but the information has influenced your beliefs about Sudan too.

As you study this and the next chapter, you will be introduced to what your authors think are the unique differences between informative and persuasive speeches and to your responsibilities as a preparer, presenter, and listener of each of these types of speeches. Hopefully, after that discussion, you will be able to decide for yourself whether public speaking is singular or dual purposed.

The Role of Informative Speaking

Oral informative presentations, given one-on-one, one-to-group, or via media such as closed circuit television and intranet broadcasts, have become major vehicles for disseminating, managing, and dealing with information.

Informative speaking is common in business, educational, governmental, community, and cultural venues. Clarifying a zoning change that has been enacted, sharing the design specifics for a new high school or a proposed product, giving a classroom lecture on the value of interpersonal communication, appearing before a college scholarship board, or sharing information about upcoming seasonal offerings at the local community theater, are all examples of informative speaking.

Characteristics of Informative Speaking

As in any other type of speaking, the development of an informative presentation depends on audience analysis. Consideration must be given to the listeners' knowledge about the subject, the concepts they know that can function as a foundation to their gaining the information, and the extent to which definitions, understandable analogies, examples, and clarifiers need to be used. A speaker also must determine the appropriate language level, attention devices, and structure of the message that will best fit the recipients. An astute speaker determines the real needs of the listeners by thorough audience analysis and then uses that information to develop the speech.

In an informative presentation, a speaker must always keep the purpose of the presentation in mind. Thus, a clear statement of central idea is essential. Consider these two examples:

- To inform the audience of what the Heimlich maneuver is, how it was developed, and how this technique can prevent people from choking to death.
- At the conclusion of this speech, I want the members of the audience to know what the Heimlich maneuver is and what steps are used to do the maneuver.

In the examples, the subject is the same, but the goal is different. The first statement informs about the maneuver and its value. The second informs about the maneuver and then teaches the steps for performing it. Both are stated in a manner that narrows the subject and indicates specifically what will be included in the speech. Thus, the statement of central idea serves as a fence around the territory to be covered in a presentation and indicates how to "corral" the information. If you do not set up boundaries, you may find yourself discussing many things but not achieving your desired outcome. In addition, you might wander into persuasion and try to convince the audience that the Heimlich maneuver is better than the techniques of back slaps or finger sweeping.

Classifications of Informative Speaking

Informative presentations may be classified as speeches about objects, processes, events, and concepts. In addition, there can be specific types of informative speeches, including informative briefings, team briefings, one-on-one briefings, technical reports, presentations of professional papers, lectures, question-and-answer sessions, and speeches of introduction.

Speeches about Objects

Speeches about objects describe a particular thing in detail. The object may be a person, place, animal, structure, machine, or anything else that can be touched or seen. First the object is identified, and then details concerning some specific attribute of the object are discussed.

Here are some examples of statements of central ideas for informative speeches about an object and each presentation's method of arrangement: "To inform the audience about the development of telephones from the earliest models to the smart phones" (chronological arrangement); and "To inform the audience of the physical similarities and differences between Siamese and Himalayan cats" (comparison–contrast arrangement).

Speeches about Processes

Speeches about processes instruct the audience about how something works, is made, or is done so that they can apply the skills learned. The purpose may be to gain understanding of the process or to be able to do something. This technique, for example, can be used in training workers to operate a piece of equipment or in

Speeches about processes instruct the audience about how something works.

explaining a manufacturing process. Speeches about processes often lend themselves to development according to a chronological method of organization. In this method, the speaker describes the first step of the process, then the second, and so on.

Statements of central idea for informative speeches about processes include: "To inform listeners of the step-by-step process in finding sources in the Ebsco Host databases" (chronological arrangement); and "To demonstrate the process used to fill out the income tax short form" (chronological arrangement).

Speeches about Events

Speeches about events inform the audience about something that has already happened, is happening, or is expected to happen. This type of presentation tends to work well in a chronological, comparison–contrast, or spatial arrangement. Here are some statements of central ideas for informative speeches about events: "To inform the audience of the spread of the AIDS virus in Africa through a statistical examination of the years 1980 to 2012" (chronological arrangement); "To inform the audience of the similarities and differences in the United States and Russian revolutions based on their economic causes" (comparison–contrast arrangement); and "To inform the audience about the major battles fought in the U.S. Civil War by discussing them from the most northern to the most southern conflicts" (spatial arrangement).

One of the approaches of speeches about events is to inform an audience about something that has already happened, such as explaining important incidents that took place during the Civil War.

Speeches about Concepts

Speeches about concepts examine theories, beliefs, ideas, philosophies, or schools of thought. Much of your academic life is spent listening to speeches about concepts. Concept topics include explanations and investigations of business theories, philosophical movements, psychological concepts, and political theories.[3]

Because some of the ideas relating to concepts are abstract, the speaker must be sure to use precise language, define terms, give historical background, avoid undefined slang and jargon, and use clarifying support materials such as audio, visual, and audiovisual aids.

Examples of statements of central ideas for informative speeches about concepts are "To inform the audience about three classical research theories that explain the myth that abused children grow up to be child abusers" (topical arrangement); and "To inform the audience of the similarities and differences between the theories of Evolution and Intelligent Design" (comparison–contrast arrangement).

Informative Briefings

Business, organizational, and technical communicators often gain up-to-date knowledge in their fields as a result of informative briefings. The fundamental objective of an **informative briefing** is to present information to a

COMMUNICATING

in Careers

McDonalds, Hamburgers, and Informative Speaking

McDonald's owner Ray Kroc once asked if anyone in a particular audience knew what business they were in. How would you reply? Probably the same as most do, "Hamburgers."

No, they are not in the hamburger business. They are in the real estate business. They own more prime commercial real estate than just about any body else.

So what is the real meaning of the information you are presenting? List all of the various meanings. Share or weave the most relevant meanings into the body of the talk. Help the audience to see past the hamburgers to the real estate as it were.

Source: Steele, J. (2008). *The informative speech body*. Retrieved from speechmastery.com

REFLECT ON THIS:

1. Did the title of this tidbit of information catch your attention? If so, why?
2. What are the implications for you as an informative speaker?

specialized audience, followed by the exchange of data, ideas, and questions among participants. Organizations, for example, use this technique to explain new or existing organizational policies, procedures, and issues. For instance, a sales manager of an automobile agency may inform her staff about the new models, or a Dean of Students may explain a college's academic policies to a group of entering freshmen.

As with any other speech, preparation for an informative briefing requires careful analysis of the audience to determine what background and definitions will be needed to ensure audience comprehension. If the audience has extensive knowledge, the speaker does not have to cover background material in as much depth as he or she would for uninformed listeners. The automobile agency sales manager does not have to go into detail with her experienced staff about the auto manufacturer and the history of the agency. On the other hand, she would give that background for a meeting of new salespersons. The Dean of Students does not have to explain the layout of the campus or the college's grading policy to upper-level students who will be advising the new freshmen, but must explain both of these factors to new freshmen.

Team Briefings

In a college course or at work, you may find yourself acting as part of a team asked to complete a project. The group may be asked to present a **team briefing** on its findings or recommendations. This is usually a presentation by a series of speakers rather than a single speaker. Team briefings, for example, are used in technology organizations in which design projects or project proposals must be pitched to potential clients or funding agents. In a classroom, teams often are formed to do research or perform an experiment. For example, a group in your communication class, while studying nonverbal communication, may be asked to relate the effect of invasion of territory by one person while carrying on a conversation with another person. The group would do research on territorial invasion, write a hypothesis, design an experiment to prove the hypothesis, carry out the experiment, and then present a team briefing to the class about its findings. Some, or all members of the group speak. Commonly the topic is divided into parts. For example, in the territorial invasion project briefing a different person could be assigned to explain to the audience each aspect of each of the segments of the process.

In order to use group time efficiently, each member should first prepare and rehearse her or his individual briefing. Then, when the team meets, the entire presentation needs be blended together. This planning will entail deciding the format for the program, the speaking order of the presentations, and whether each speaker will have a question-and-answer session or whether there will be an inquiry session for the entire group in which any panel member can answer the audience's probes.

Because a common communication format for team briefings is to have one individual serve as the facilitator, someone will have to be selected, appointed, or elected. The facilitator's role is usually to introduce the presentation and the speakers, make transitions between each of the speakers, conduct the question-and-answer session, and then provide a final summary.

One-on-One Briefings

You may find yourself giving a **one-on-one briefing** to a person or a small group of individuals. Financial analysts, for example, may be called on to brief key decision makers in an informal, conversational presentation. For example, an analyst may present a short summary of the latest projections of the financial status of an organization. Although the presentational climate is usually informal, it still follows the basic rules of effective public speaking regarding audience adaptation, clear structuring, and effective oral and physical presentation. The process is sometimes referred to as a *table-top briefing* because it commonly takes place with the participants seated around a conference table rather than the speaker standing before a group.

The briefer usually makes an opening statement about the topic and then presents a short statement of the findings, which is followed by an extensive question-and-answer session.

Technical Reports

The **technical report** is a statement describing a process, explaining a technique, or discussing new elements to people within a business or industry or to people outside it, such as customers or researchers who may be interested in the topic.

Because the information is often scientific or dependent on knowledge of special terminology, the speaker must do careful audience analysis. If the report is to be

A speaker should know exactly how much time has been allotted for the presentation and plan to stay within that time limit.

given to nontechnical people, all specialized words must be defined, and analogies familiar to the audience should be included to clarify the ideas. This does not mean a speaker has to "water down" the material, but the presenter must give examples and present ideas in a variety of ways to make sure that the audience understands the concepts.

For a more technically oriented audience, a depth of background information would not be necessary. For example, a representative of a medical machinery corporation, in presenting information about a new fMRI (functional magnetic resonance imager) to a group of curious but uninformed psychologists interested in the potential for using the device for brain examinations, was careful to avoid explaining the mechanical theory behind the equipment. Instead, she explained how the results of the brain scans could be read because of the use of the equipment. If she were speaking to a group of MRI salespeople, however, who already had the necessary technical knowledge, she would detail the development of the machinery, the technical aspects of the equipment, how it is operated, and its various uses.

If the group is small, consider using an interactive model of communication in which audience members are encouraged to ask questions so you can adapt your message to ensure they get immediate clarification.

When you structure a technical report that involves a recommendation, it is usually wise to start with a statement of the proposal in which you state exactly what you are suggesting or are going to discuss. After you have stated the idea, explain how you arrived at the conclusions or recommendations. This is the problem–solution or cause and effect method of organization (see pages 354–356).

Professional Papers

Another type of informative speaking that you may encounter is the professional paper. A **professional paper** is a speech in which the presenter briefs his or her audience on some findings that relate to the speaker's or the listeners' area of interest. For example, some colleges stage graduate or undergraduate research conferences for students to present their research findings. Or some students and college professors present their research findings or theories at a professional or academic meeting such as the National Communication Association's yearly convention or an American Psychological Association's regional conference.

Some presenters choose to present their papers word-for-word, while the listeners follow along, which normally doesn't result in a very engaging presentational style. The most effective presenters will speak extemporaneously and, following the presentation, hand out copies for listeners to read at another time. This method avoids having the listeners reading your paper while you are speaking. If the listeners need some specific information as you are speaking, an outline can be distributed before you make your speech, or a PowerPoint handout of the highlights may be used.

Another format for presenting research at these conferences is the poster session. In a **poster session** you prepare a poster, a series of charts, or a PowerPoint program that visually highlights your research or idea. The posters or electronic equipment are usually set up in a room with other charts, displays, and speakers. You will explain your work and answer questions posed by those who have come to look at your findings. For example, if you have ever been to or participated in a science fair or a product sales show, you've been part of a poster session. Most of the presentations will be made one-on-one or to a very small group. Since the audience will be circulating, you must be aware of the time factor and the setting. In general, you will want to prepare a one- or two-minute briefing and be ready to answer questions when they are asked.

Lectures

Probably the most familiar type of informative speaking is the **lecture**, the presentation of material to facilitate learning. Lectures are an integral part of academic life, serving as the main vehicle for presenting information in many subject fields. Lectures also are used in other settings, including speakers for lunch or dinner seminars in corporate headquarters and public lectures by distinguished authorities in museums, arts, religious, or public settings.

A good lecture should be adapted to the intended audience so that the speaker's topic, language, and examples fit the listeners' levels of knowledge and vocabulary. An effective lecture, like any speech, should be clearly organized, with transitions that allow listeners to stay on track and anticipate what is coming next. The speaker should use supporting details to elaborate on each of the points made. A variety of supporting materials (stories, statistics, analogies) should be used.

Humor is also a way of getting and holding attention. Even if you are not a joke teller, you can still make humor work for you. Of course, the funny story or humorous incident should be relevant to the theme and purpose of the speech. The humor should be appropriate. Audience analysis is important here. What might be appropriate at a roast of a retiring football coach would be inappropriate for a speech to the high school football team.

Some techniques for inclusion of humor in a speech include:[4]

- Analogies are a good source of humor. Linking your present situation or problem to something else often provides an opportunity for humor. The link can be either illogical or logical and could even be a personal anecdote.
- Use a funny quote. Quotes can be found online (e.g., amusingquotes.com or allfunnyquotes.com) or in books of quotations (e.g., Klein, A. (2005) *The Wise and Witty Quote Book: More than 2000 Quotes to Enlighten, Encourage, and Enjoy* (New York: Gramercy.) Make sure the quote fits the purpose of the presentation and its topic.

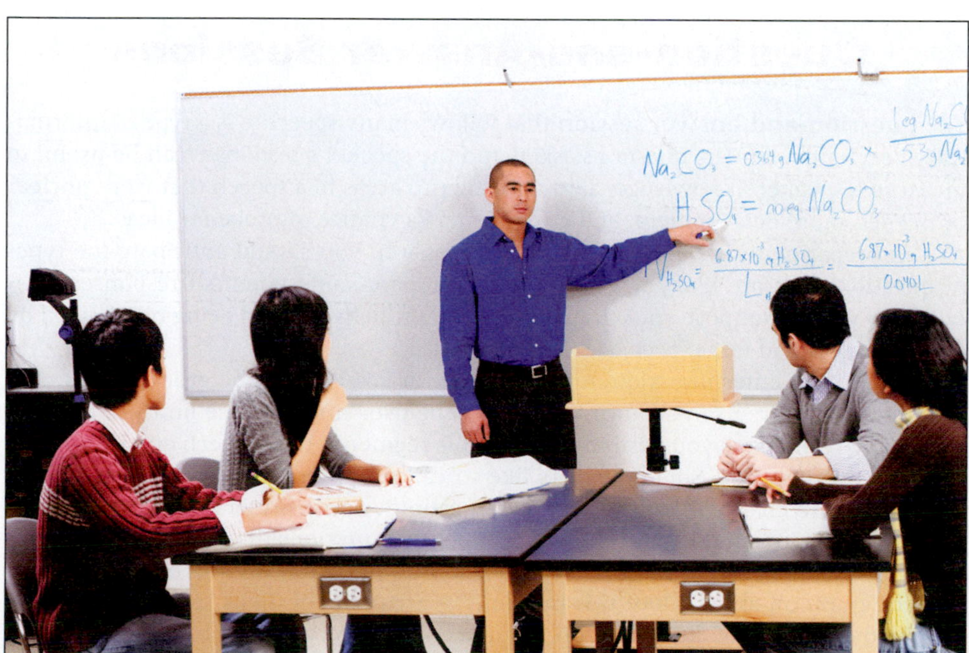

A good lecture should be adapted to the audience so that the speaker's topic, language, and examples fit the listeners' level of knowledge and vocabulary.

- Use an amusing cartoon from newspapers, magazines, or an online search. Show it, read it, or describe it.
- Don't announce when you are about to use humor (e.g., "I'm going to tell you the funniest joke" or "You are going to love this one"). Both of those lines give a forecast that might not be true, and it could turn out to be an embarrassment when no one laughs after your joke or humorous quote. Instead, just unobtrusively insert humor here and there.
- If you are in doubt about the quality or the appropriateness of a joke or quote, leave it out.

Another attention technique is to use questions, which probe for information and invite inquiries during the presentation instead of waiting until the question-and-answer session. Asking questions where the audience can vote for solutions or verbally suggest ideas will gain audience attention. For example, a lecturer, about half-way through his presentation on nonverbal communication, inserted a series of questions regarding masculine and feminine perceived body movement and gesture patterns. The speaker polled the audience to determine their ideas about whether men or women used the described actions. The audience became animated and was curious as to whether they had answered the questions correctly. As the answers were given, many cheered when they were correct.

The timing of a lecture is another key to success. The audience expects a lecturer to stay within the assigned time (such as a class period). You know what happens in a classroom when the end of the time period is near. People pack up mentally and physically. Anticipate that is likely to happen if you are lecturing, and wrap up on time.

We have all sat through good and bad classroom lectures—lectures that held your attention and from which you learned. You probably have also sat through some that put you to sleep. If you are ever asked to present a lecture, recall what kept you engaged when you listened to the good presentations and use those techniques in your own presentation.

Question-and-Answer Sessions

The **question-and-answer session** that follows many speeches is a type of informative speech in itself. The questions asked and the speaker's responses can be useful to measure a speaker's knowledge, alert a speaker to areas in a speech that were unclear or needed more development, and give listeners a chance to probe for ideas.

In preparing for a question-and-answer session, you should anticipate the types of questions you are likely to be asked and prepare some potential responses. This will help you to compose your thoughts and might help to avoid being blind-sided by questions you had not expected.

When you enter into a question-and-answer session, set the ground rules. Ask the program chairperson about the process to be used and the time limit. Tell him or her of any restrictions you wish to place on this segment of the speech and inform the audience of the rules. Some speakers like to call on participants themselves; others prefer that the chairperson entertain the questions. Some presenters want all questions written out beforehand so they can select the questions they will answer.

The most difficult part of many question-and-answer sessions is often to get the first question asked. Once this hurdle is overcome, questions usually flow readily. To overcome the first-question trauma, you may want to have someone in

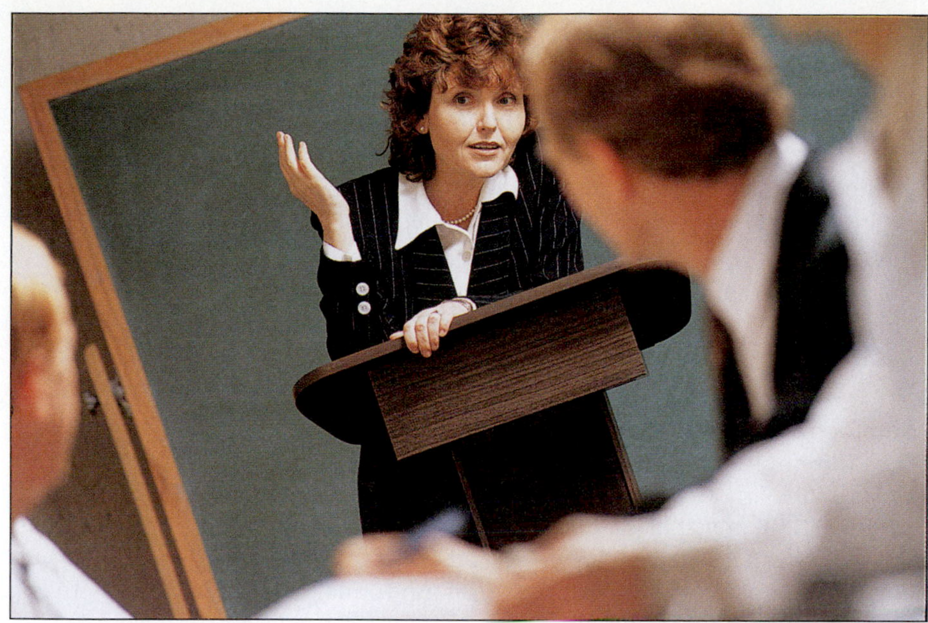

The question-and-answer session is an on-the-spot set of unrehearsed answers.

the audience prepared in advance to ask a question. Another technique is to ask a question yourself. This can be accomplished by stating, "I've often been asked about my attitudes concerning..." and then answering by indicating your views.

Here are some additional suggestions for conducting a question-and-answer session:

- Before you answer a question, restate it so that everyone hears the inquiry. If the question is complicated, simplify it in the restatement.
- Speak to and look at the entire audience rather than only at the questioner.
- Be patient. If you have to repeat material you have already covered, do so briefly.
- If a question goes on and on, prompt the questioner to summarize the question.
- Keep your answers short. Restate the question, give your response, clarify any vocabulary necessary, give an example if appropriate, and then stop.
- Following a response, some speakers ask the questioner whether the answer was satisfactory.
- Back up your responses with examples, statistics, and quotations when appropriate.
- If a question is overly complicated or of interest only to the asker, suggest a discussion with the questioner after the speech or via correspondence.
- If a question is irrelevant, indicate that it is interesting or thought provoking but does not seem appropriate to the presentation. Do not get sidetracked from the purpose of the speech or pulled into a private debate with a questioner.
- If you do not know an answer, say so. You can offer to find out the answer and report back later.
- Limit the discussion to one question per person, and avoid getting caught in a dialogue with a single audience member. Others who have questions will become frustrated, and those who do not will get bored.

- Be willing to be corrected or at least to recognize another's viewpoint. Thank a person for their clarification or acknowledge that more than one point of view is possible (e.g., "That's an interesting idea" or "The idea can be viewed that way"). You may win a battle of words by putting down or insulting a questioner, but you will usually lose the respect of your listeners in the process.
- Know when to end a session. Do not wait until interest has waned or people begin leaving. You can lose the positive effect of a speech by having an overly long question-and-answer session.
- Consider displaying the points using presentation graphics, for example a PowerPoint slide program or a handout. It is helpful for listeners to have the points of the presentation before them so they can be reminded of what you have covered. Alternatively, you can hand out the talking points following your speech.
- Summarize the speech, including the question-and-answer session. Wrap up the entire presentation when you have completed all aspects, perhaps with a closing such as, "Current policy on a national security database just begins to address the many issues that must be considered by security organizations, law enforcement, and policymakers alike. As our interaction together suggests, the impact of these issues is profound. Thank you for being with me today to explore these ideas."

In some instances, a question-and-answer session allows listeners to point out weaknesses in a speaker's arguments or present alternative views. This occurs more frequently after persuasive speeches than after informative presentations. If confronted by a hostile questioner, the speaker has to determine whether to deal with the issue or remind the prober that the purpose of this part of the speech is to ask questions, not give a counter speech or engage in debate. One way to avoid getting into a confrontation is to say to the questioner, "That's an interesting question. I'd be willing to discuss that with you following the presentation" or "Thank you. We've heard my point of view and yours. Let's leave it up to audience to decide which is correct from their perspective."

Speeches of Introduction

The purpose of a **speech of introduction** is to identify the person who will be speaking to the audience and give any other information that may spark listeners' interest in the speaker or the topic. Too often, speeches of introduction are ineffective because the presenter has not carefully prepared remarks appropriate to listeners' needs. When you introduce a speaker, clearly identify who the speaker is by name, title, and the identification he or she wants used. You can talk about where the speaker is from as well as his or her accomplishments and when they were achieved. Establish the credibility of a speaker by highlighting aspects of his or her credentials and background that indicate knowledge or expertise in the subject being discussed.

Remember that listeners have come to hear the speaker, not the person making the introduction, so a speech of introduction should be short and to the point. Here are some suggestions for a speech of introduction:

- Get the information you need from a speaker in advance of the speech so you have time to work on the presentation.
- Be sure you can pronounce a speaker's name as he or she wants it pronounced.
- If possible, ask what background information a speaker wishes to have highlighted.

- Do not over praise a speaker. Indicating that he or she is the best speaker the audience will ever hear, for example, gives the presenter an almost impossible goal.
- Avoid using a statement such as "It is an honor and a privilege" or "This speaker needs no introduction." These are not creative, overused and often sound insincere.
- Set the proper tone for the speech. If, for example, you know that the speech is going to be humorous, try to fit humor into the introduction.

One of your authors was asked to give a speech to an audience of alumni of the communication program of the school at which he taught. He was introduced by one of his former students, who said, "We all know our speaker tonight as an author, entertainment reviewer, theater director, counselor, and a teacher, but to me, his greatest talent is that of an inspirer. My life, and those of countless many of you, has been drastically changed by having him as a professor and friend. He inspired us to 'reach for the highest star and to do the very best you can.' Our speaker, who will share the importance of setting high personal goals, is… ."

The Informative Process in Action

It is helpful to study the process of speech preparation by investigating a model. Figure 14.1 outlines a speech that follows the principles you've learned for developing informative speeches.

Statement of Central Idea: To inform the audience about the importance of the impact of nanotechnology on our future by examining what nanotechnology is and providing individuals with examples of how it can change lives.

Opening material to grasp the listeners' attention	**I. Introduction** A. Attention material: Nanotechnology is so small, if an experiment in the lab were to be hit by a single particle of dust, it would be the equivalent of your car windshield getting hit with a bowling ball at 65 mph. B. Orienting material: With the further development of nanotech, the medical opportunities are endless, which could help cure disease and allow people to live longer healthier lives.
Topic of speech	**II. Central Idea** A. Nanotechnology is currently being developed in all fields, from electronics to medicine. This powerful technology has the ability to truly change the world.
Preview of nanotechnology	B. Let us explore the world of nanotechnology by looking at facilities requirements, size, and medical applications.
First issue (keeping facilities clean)	**III. Body** A. The development of nanotechnology requires extremely clean facilities.

(continued)

FIGURE 14.1 **Informative Process in Action**

Discussion of nanotechnology labs and equipment	1. Any dust or dirt particles will destroy the nanotechnology experiments. a. People working in the facilities must wear specialized suits that cover their bodies. b. They must also wear gloves, goggles, as well as shoe covers to prevent any unwanted debris from entering the lab. 2. Special air filtration systems (hepafiltration) have been installed in nanofabrication labs. a. These systems do not allow any dust or dirt particles to enter the air. b. They are extremely expensive to run, but must remain on at all times to protect the nanotechnology experiments.
Transition	Now that we have an idea about how fragile these nano particles are, let's take a deeper look at their actual size.
Second issue (size of nanotechnology)	A nanometer is one-billionth of a meter. A single strand of hair is 100,000 nanmeters wide!
Discussion of the process of making nanotechnology products	B. The making of nanotechnology parts 1. Nanotechnology parts are made with a process called photolithography, since the parts are too small to see with the human eye. a. Photolithography is three-dimensional. b. Photolithography uses light.
Transition	Understanding how these small parts are made is the first step to seeing how nanotechnology can be made possible in medicine
Third issue (putting nanotech into medicine)	Nanotechnology has the capability in the near future to help people with various diseases, like heart disease.
Discussion of nanorobots	C. As futuristic as it may seem, there is currently talk on developing "nanorobots" to enter the human body and literally eat away the plaque and cholesterol buildup in arteries. 1. Heart disease is the number-one killer in America. Heart attacks occur when arteries become severely or completely blocked. a. The nanorobots would be able to enter the human body through veins. b. They would then be directed to the clogged arteries. c. Last, they would be retrieved back out of the body. 2. These nanorobots have the ability to eliminate clogged arteries and save lives.
Reiteration of main points	**IV. Conclusion** A. Summary 1. In order to make nanotechnology experiments possible, facilities must be extremely clean. 2. A nanometer is one-billionth of a meter. 3. Developments such as the nanorobot have the opportunity to reduce heart disease and save lives.
Restatement of theme to emphasize the importance of the impact of nanotechnology	B. The impossible can be made possible with further developments of nanotechnology.

FIGURE 14.1 (continued)

In Conclusion

IN CONCLUSION

Informative speaking imparts new information, secures understanding, or reinforces accumulated information. Types of informative speaking include presentations about objects, processes, events, and concepts. Informative speeches, when classified by setting or uniqueness, include informative briefings, team briefings, one-on-one briefings, technical reports, presentations of professional papers, lectures, question-and-answer sessions, and speeches of introduction. The challenge for an informative speaker is to get the audience to understand and retain the information presented.

LEARN BY DOING

1. In class, your instructor will match you with a partner. With the assistance of your partner, select a topic for a speech based on audience analysis (your class), setting (your classroom), and purpose (an informative speech of three to five minutes). After both of you have selected your topics, meet with another duo. Each of you will present a short informative speech indicating what topic you have selected and why this subject suits you, the audience, the setting, and the purpose. The speech should have an introduction, statement of central idea, body, and conclusion.
2. Bring to class an object or piece of machinery (e.g., a digital camera, electronic wall stud finder, microscope) that you think members of your class cannot operate or that you have a different approach to operating. Be prepared to teach someone else how to use the equipment. In class, you are placed in a group with four of your classmates. Decide the order in which you will present the material. After this is done, the first speaker gives a two- to four-minute presentation on how the object works. Then the second speaker demonstrates how the object operates. Your success as a speaker is based on whether the person you taught can operate the object.
3. Before a series of speeches is to be given by class members, your instructor assigns you the name of a person in your class whom you will later be introducing. Interview that person and collect all the information you will need to prepare a speech of introduction (topic of the speech, some background information on the speaker, why the subject was chosen, the qualifications of the speaker to present a speech on this topic, and so on). On the day of your partner's speech, introduce her or him.
4. You are going to give a "what-if" speech. On each of three 3 × 5 note cards, indicate something that could go wrong immediately before, during, or after a speech (e.g., you drop your speech outline in a puddle of water just outside your classroom building, or an audience member challenges your statistics during the question-and-answer period). The instructor collects the cards, shuffles them, and hands them out one by one. When you get your card, immediately give a presentation that includes a restatement of the occurrence and a contingency plan for dealing with the situation. (This assignment may take place when a short amount of time remains at the end of any class period.)

5. All students present one-minute speeches in which they state something that bothers them in everyday life. They should tell what the peeve is, why it is a peeve, and what they would like to see done about it, if anything.

6. Use your vocational preference, or an occupation you may be interested in, to investigate some phase of the career and present an informative speech about it. The presentation must include the use of a supplementary aid. Sample speech topics include a future audiologist explains the differences among several brands of hearing aids, a theater major discusses the famous actors who graduated from this college, an aspiring musician demonstrates how music is scored.

7. "The College Speech. Your fellow students and you all have one thing in common: you are students at the same school! Therefore, if you give a speech about your school, you won't have to work hard to make the speech relevant to everybody. Research something interesting that most people don't know about your school. Talk about some famous alumni or some interesting historical trivia. Or talk about an office or service on campus that might be helpful to students, like the Career Center."[5]

KEY TERMS

informative speaking 370
speeches about objects 372
speeches about processes 372
speeches about events 373
speeches about concepts 373
informative briefing 373
team briefing 374
one-on-one briefing 375
technical report 375
professional paper 376
poster session 376
lecture 377
question-and-answer session 378
speech of introduction 380

CHAPTER 15

Public Speaking: The Persuasive Speech

After reading this chapter, you should be able to

- Explain how people are influenced by persuasive messages
- Explain how people are influenced by coercive messages
- Illustrate how speaker credibility, logical arguments, and psychological appeals can affect listeners
- List and explain how speaker credibility, logical arguments, and psychological appeals can be used in the preparation of a persuasive speech
- Analyze a persuasive speech to ascertain its potential effectiveness based on logical arguments and psychological appeals
- Explain the influence of emotion in persuasive speech messages
- Prepare a persuasive speech using credibility, logical arguments, and psychological appeals
- Explain the role of culture on persuasive public speaking

Every day, as a listener, you are bombarded with messages intended to convince you to take some action, accept some belief, or change some point of view. And almost every day, knowingly or unknowingly, you attempt to bring about changes in others. These are all acts of persuasion.

Persuasion is the process of influencing attitudes and behaviors. The route to being a successful persuader is to find the means to answer the question, "What's in it for *you?*" Most people will take actions or adopt beliefs if they can figure out how they can benefit—monetarily, socially, physically, philosophically, or spiritually.

Persuasive Speaking

A **persuasive speech** is intended to influence the opinion or behavior of an audience. Its materials are derived from problems about which people hold differing beliefs and opinions. The persuasive speaker tells listeners what they ought to believe or do.

A persuasive speech may have as its end goal either conviction or actuation.

In a **speech of conviction**, the speaker is attempting to encourage the listener to believe as the speaker does. Topics that fall into this category could include "There is no real danger of nuclear fallout from atomic energy plants," "Global warming is a real threat to the existence of humans," or "I believe that our college should eliminate required courses."

A **speech of actuation** should move the members of the audience to take the desired action that the speaker has proposed—for example, buy the product, sign the petition, go on strike, or adopt the plan presented. Topics that fall into this category could include "Vote for me for President of the University's Student Body" and "Purchase products that are bio-green."

The Process of Persuasion

Much is known about what motivates people to act. Unfortunately, in spite of our knowledge, there are flaws in the system, or no candidate for office would ever lose, no charity would fail to reach its fund-raising goal, and no advertised product would go unsold. This chapter presents theories that attempt to explain the process of persuasion and how—if you are developing a persuasive speech to individuals from the European American culture—you might use those theories to accomplish your goal.

The basic process of persuasion centers on making a claim, then backing up the claim with reasons and emotional appeals that will lead listeners to accept the claim. To do this, you must analyze the audience and develop arguments that will appeal to that particular group.

Several concepts, including the theories of field-related, group, and individual standards, help explain how to figure out what appeal process to use in developing a persuasive argument.

Theory of Field-Related Standards

The *theory of field-related standards* proposes that not all people reach conclusions in the same way and thus may react differently to the same evidence or psychological material. Therefore, in establishing your arguments, you want to include as many appeals as you can to cover the various thought processes of members of your audience.

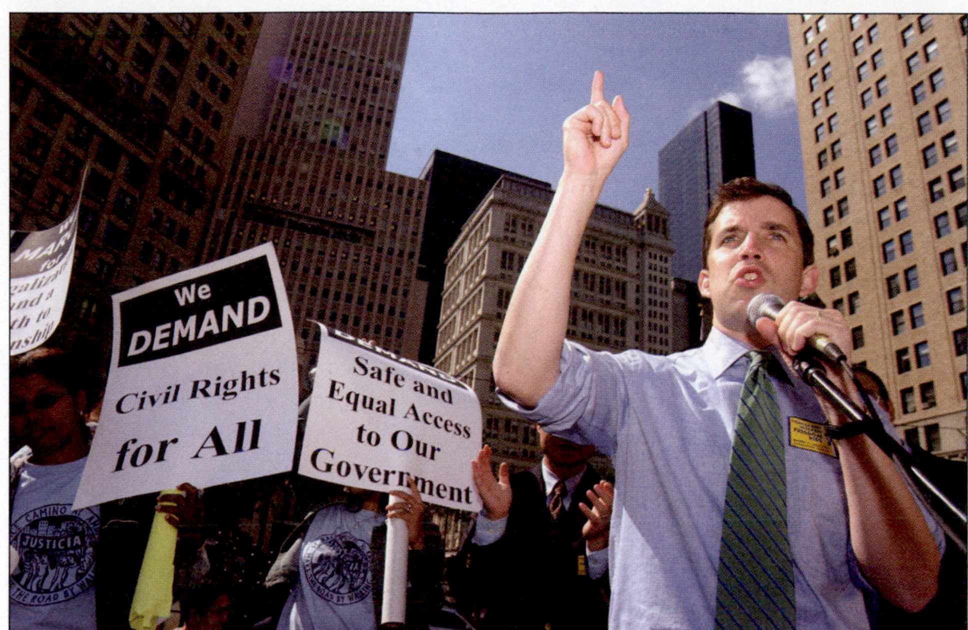

A persuasive speech is intended to influence the opinion or behavior of an audience.

For example, in establishing arguments for why your listeners should vote for a particular candidate, you can list several of the candidate's positions rather than just one and select the positions that most align with the attitudes of those listeners.

It would be foolish for a speaker to believe that an entire audience can be convinced to agree with you. This point was well made when one of your authors served as the public relations director and speech writer for a US congressman. In his first speechwriting assignment, after careful audience analysis your author concluded that he could not find a way to convince every member of the intended audience to vote for the candidate. After indicating this to the future congressman, the writer was told, "Don't worry about trying to get everyone to agree. No matter what I say, about 35 percent will agree with me, and the same percentage will disagree. Try to figure out a way to get to the other 30 percent. They hold the key to the election."[1]

Group-Norm Standards

Group norm standards—the general thinking of a particular group—may be used as a guide for developing your arguments.

If you are speaking to a group of students who commute to school about your idea to solve the campus parking problem, you can assume that they will be interested in your idea, but you may need to talk about benefits for the whole campus in order to convince them to work with you.

If you are speaking to a group of conservative Republicans about your belief favoring gay marriage, you may be able to sway some of the audience by showing that not all conservatives are against same-sex unions by relating that former President George W. Bush's daughter, Barbara Bush, made a video voicing her support for same sex marriage.[2] In addition, that her grandmother, former first lady Barbara Bush told CNN's Larry King, "When couples are committed to each other and love each other, they ought to have the same sort of rights that everyone has."[3] You might also point out that Meghan McCain, daughter of Republican Senator John McCain, and Cindy McCain, the senator's wife, appeared in a video protesting California's Proposition 8, which banned same sex marriage.[4]

Individual Norm Standards

In any group there are those who have power. The theory of *individual norm standards* proposes that being on the side of or getting the backing of the person or persons with power may be a strong tool to influence the group's members to side with your stand. For example, if the elected president of the city council agrees, the rest of the group who elected her are likely to follow her lead. Or, the backing of the most popular member of a sorority may assist you in convincing the members to volunteer at a local food bank.

To be persuasive, you also should develop your arguments to encourage listeners to believe that the solution, plan of action, or cure that you are presenting is the best solution. Two methods you might consider using to accomplish your persuasive goal are critical thinking and comparative-advantage reasoning.

To apply *critical thinking,* you establish criteria and then match the solutions with the criteria. For example, if you are proposing a plan of action for solving a fraternity's financial problems, you can set criteria that include not having to raise members' dues and planning an activity that can raise money quickly, without extensive planning. You may then propose that the organization stage a lottery, establishing how the lottery fulfills the established criteria.

In contrast, when you use *comparative-advantage reasoning,* you begin by stating possible solutions. Then you demonstrate how the proposal is the most *workable* (can solve the problem), *desirable* (does not cause any greater problems), and *practical* (that it can be put into operation). Establish why your particular proposal has more advantages and fewer disadvantages than any other. To achieve the goal of raising funds, for example, in using the comparative-advantage reasoning process, you could propose that a lottery raffle be set up, explain why this is a workable plan by referring to other organizations that have used the process, and present statistics on the amount of money these groups have raised. Then indicate that a drawing for prizes is desirable because it will not cost members a great deal of money and the risk that the organization will lose money is not great. Next, show that the proposal is practical because the tickets can be ready by the next week and the finance committee has worked out a plan for distributing the tickets and handling the money. Finally, you explain why this system is better than raising dues.

Persuasive Strategies

There are varying theories stimulating an audience to take an action or believe as they do. One of these is The *Elaboration Likelihood Model*[5] which theorizes that if the issue being discussed is one that the listener has encountered before, is interested and involved in, and enjoys thinking about, he or she is more likely to engage in paying attention to and maybe processing the persuader's arguments. This attention does not necessarily guarantee that the listener will be persuaded, but at least it gives the speaker the attention of the receiver and, if the arguments are emotionally appealing and logically sound, there is a chance for persuasive results.

The listener also may be persuaded because the message resonates with his or her values or things in which he or she believes. Such factors as change/mobility, equality, individualism, free enterprise, informality, directness, practicality and materialism are important to many U.S. citizens.[6] (See Figure 15.1.) Messages that tap into these values probably have the greatest effect in eliciting change, because listeners can connect with the appeals.

1. Personal Control over the Environment
Many U.S. Americans no longer believe in the power of Fate, and they have come to look at people who do as being backward, primitive, or hopelessly naive.

2. Change
In the American mind, change is seen as an indisputably good condition.

3. Time and Its Control
Time is, for the average American, of utmost importance.

4. Equality/Egalitarianism
Equality is, for Americans, one of their most cherished values.

5. Individualism and Privacy
Each individual is seen as completely unique, totally different from all others.

6. Self-Help Concept
In the United States, a person can take credit only for what he or she has accomplished by himself or herself.

7. Competition and Free Enterprise
Americans believe that competition brings out the best in any individual.

8. Future Orientation
Valuing the future, and the improvements Americans are sure the future will bring, means that they devalue the past and are, to a large extent, unconscious of the present.

9. Action/Work Orientation
Americans routinely plan and schedule an extremely active day. Any relaxation must be limited in time, pre-planned, and aimed at "recreating" their ability to work harder and more productively once the recreation is over. Americans believe leisure activities should assume a relatively small portion of one's total life.

10. Informality
Americans are one of the most informal and casual people in the world. American bosses often urge their employees to call them by their first names. Dress is another area where American informality will be most noticeable.

11. Directness, Openness, and Honesty
Many other countries have developed subtle, sometimes highly ritualistic, ways of informing other people of unpleasant information. Americans, however, have always preferred the direct approach.

12. Practicality and Efficiency
Americans have a reputation of being an extremely realistic, practical, and efficient people.

13. Materialism/Acquisitions
Americans value and give higher priority to obtaining, maintaining, and protecting their material objects than they do in developing and enjoying interpersonal relationships.

FIGURE 15.1
The Values U.S. Americans Live By

Source: Adapted excerpt from *The values Americans live by* by L. Robert Kohls. Copyright © 2006 L. Robert Kohls. Reprinted with permission of L. Robert Kohls Literary Estate.

To be persuaded, listeners also may rely on a strong sense of *social support*. The long-term staying power of messages depends not only on how the appeal resonates with the individual but also on the degree to which the individual perceives that he or she has the support of others, thus enabling the person to feel that "we are all in it together." As you think about an upcoming persuasive speech, consider how you can provide social support to your audience. Some principles that persuaders who

Culturally COMMUNICATING

Australian View of Persuasive Speaking

Public speaking is taught in Australian universities to local students and to students from Asian countries studying in Australia. The advice given to students about public speaking follows U. S. American or Australian texts, which are generally similar in approach. However, the way of speaking advocated takes little account of a multicultural audience, and an implicit assumption appears to be that there is but one way of communicating in public—that given to us by rhetoricians in Greece and Rome who set the "rules" for public speaking centered around *logos* (or reason), *ethos* (or good character), and *pathos* (the evocation of feelings of pity or sympathetic sadness; a play on emotions). However, students of intercultural communication can find that scholars suggest that the rhetorical tradition of Europe and U.S. America reflect not a universal communication style but rather the cultural patterns of logical, rational, and analytic thinking favored in those countries.

Source: Power, M. R., & Galvin, C. (1997). The culture of speeches: Public speaking across cultures. *Culture Mandala: The Bulletin of the Centre for East-West Cultural and Economic Studies, 2*(2), 2.

REFLECT ON THIS:

1. Do you agree that there is no universal communication style?
2. If so, what are the implications for you as a public speaker?

are keying on social support should consider when attempting to get people to respond include:[7]

- *The principle of liking.* People like those who like them, so, if possible, try to find a common bond.
- *The principle of reciprocity.* People will repay in kind, so a potential strategy is to give what it is you want to receive in return.
- *The principle of social proof.* People will follow the lead of those similar to them, so attempt to use the examples of their peers to reinforce your effort.
- *The principle of consistency.* People will make their commitments if they're based on active, voluntary choices.
- *The principle of authority.* People defer to experts, so don't assume that your expertise or that of your sources are self-evident. If you are an expert on a topic, such as you are speaking on the value of knowing life-saving techniques and you have saved someone while servicing as a life guard, you need to let the audience know your background and experiences. If you are using quotations from an expert, use oral footnotes to establish the person's authority. For example, does knowing that this list of suggestions was developed by a Harvard University professor have a positive influence on your being convinced to consider the proposed actions? A poll of students who were given this list to read in class indicated that after finding out the identification of the author's affiliation, they were more open to the recommendations than when it was a list with an unidentified source.
- *The principle of scarcity.* People want more of what they have less of, so indicating how they can get more of the scarce commodity may have a mobilizing effect.

Role of Influence in Persuasion

One of the purposes of the persuasive process is to influence, to get the listener to take some action or believe in a concept. The persuasive process occurs, for instance, when salespersons from different publishing companies present speeches in an attempt to persuade the professors of the basic communication course on your campus to use their textbook for the course. Based on the presentations, the professors may be influenced to buy the publications from a salesperson because of her arguments stressing her book's lower cost, higher resale value, and supplemental online student aids.

Normally, the intended audience has a choice of what actions to take. However, a particular form of influencing takes place when listeners are not given a voluntary choice. For example, a speaker at a union meeting says, "Either we accept the proposal as presented or we go on strike." You might not want to choose either of those options, yet if the vote is set up with only those two, you must choose. This attempt to change behavior relies on force and is known as coercion. *Coercion* takes place when the listener perceives that he or she has no choice but to accept what the speaker proposes. Much political unrest is the result of the coercive control of the populace. The lack of choice in deciding on personal matters and being restricted from freedom of actions was one of the causes of the 1776 United States revolution, the Russian revolution, and the 2010–2011 overthrow of several governments in the Middle East. Though coercion works for a period of time, history shows that often it backfires in the long run as seen in the rising up by populations against coercive political regimes. Be aware of this potential result when you consider using coercion as a persuasive technique.

Word War II German leader Adolf Hitler used fear, hatred, social pressure, and shock to dull his listeners' senses to the point where they performed acts they would not have done if they were objectively evaluating potential consequences.

Another type of attempt to use influence includes presenting *psychological appeals* aimed at emotionally stirring audience members to action. Such factors as fear, hatred, social pressure, and shock can be used to dull listeners' senses to the point where they perform acts they may not consider if they were to step outside the emotion of the situation and objectively evaluate potential consequences. Before and during World War II, German dictator Adolf Hitler used emotional appeals focused on building a "master race" that included killing all those he deemed inferior: Jews, gypsies, homosexuals, and his political enemies. Many people responded to these appeals and participated in the destruction of other human beings as a result.

Persuasion can be accomplished by *repeated exposure to messages*. Seldom does one persuasive message result in any major change of belief on the part of the receiver. As a result, massive amounts of time and money are spent waging persuasive campaigns by systematically and repeatedly exposing listeners to a message with the objective of enhancing retention of its basic persuasive thesis. This is the reason that the electorate is inundated with speeches and other publicity about candidates during political campaigns, and advertisers run ads over and over until they make their impact. Imagine that in your Spanish class you have a series of three brief oral reports to give in Spanish. If you give each report on a different argument related to the same need for improved Mexican American civil rights, then you are exposing your audience to your underlying theme each time you present (repeated exposure).

Do not assume that all persuasion is negative or immoral. Persuasive communication strategies are essentially *amoral*—neither good nor bad. It is only the ways in which the strategies are used, and to what ends, that give communication a dimension of morality. By knowing this, and being equipped to recognize manipulative and coercive methods, you may be able as a listener to protect yourself from being exploited.

Classical Components of the Persuasive Message

The classical Greek philosopher-rhetorician Aristotle described what has become Western culture's system of persuasion as based on three components: speaker credibility (**ethos**), logical arguments (**logos**), and psychological appeals (**pathos**).[8] Although Aristotle developed his rhetorical model more than 2,000 years ago, his theory still characterizes essential components for the development of an effective persuasive message.

Speaker Credibility

Ethos, the reputation, prestige, and authority of a speaker, as perceived by the listeners, all contribute to *speaker credibility*. In most persuasive situations, listeners' acceptance of the speaker as a credible person will make it easier for the speaker to get acceptance of the message.

A person's reputation can help or hinder his or her persuasive ability. For example, in a positive vein, if Stephen Spielberg, multi-Academy Award winning film director, addressed a college audience consisting of cinema majors on the skills they need to be an effective motion picture director, he would have initial credibility, so he would likely get a positive reception and his views would have a good chance of being accepted.

A negatively perceived speaker would have a much more difficult persuasive task. If, as a listener, you dislike, mistrust, or question the honesty of a person, she or he will have a difficult time persuading you to accept her or his beliefs. President George W. Bush encountered increasingly negative approval ratings as the war in Iraq dragged on during the final months of his administration. In May of 2008, for example, USA Today/Gallup reported Bush had a 28 percent approval and 67 percent disapproval rating.[9] Consequently, the White House undertook efforts to position President Bush more aggressively on other important foreign and domestic issues, including the sinking economy and the rising fuel costs, so that his speeches and legislative proposals might receive positive responses from the public and legislators.

A speaker who has a reputation for being knowledgeable about the topic, or is a celebrity, or has a positive personal reputation with the audience comes to speak with pre-acknowledged credibility. Shakira, for example, not only is a popular musician, but because of her life experiences in her Columbian homeland, she has credibility to persuade people to contribute to child welfare causes in South American countries.[10]

The creditable speaker has the three Cs of credibility needed for being persuasive: competence, charisma, and character.

Competence Through Experience *Competence* refers to the wisdom, authority, and knowledge a speaker demonstrates. For an audience to feel that you are competent in the subject area being discussed, you must demonstrate that you know what you are talking about. This ordinarily means including up-to-date information and showing your familiarity with the material. In other words, explain your personal connection. In a speech designed to "persuade the audience members to set up a fundraising site for their favorite charity through FirstGiving,"[11] you will have credibility if you used the website to help you raise $200 through a fundraising page you set up for a cycling competition you entered last year.

Thus, if at all possible, you'll want to connect yourself with the topic. Suppose you are proposing a plan of action concerning safety regulations. If you have had experience on a construction crew and refer to this experience, your listeners will more readily accept your

Positively perceived speakers often find audiences receptive to their messages.

point that the construction industry needs more stringent safety regulations than if you did not have the personal experience. To establish the tie, use statements such as, "It has been my experience that..." and "On the job, I observed that... ."

Competence by Authority Another way to establish credibility is to build on someone else's knowledge. For example, if you aren't an expert on a topic, you can strengthen your position by quoting recognized experts in the field. In this way, listeners draw the conclusion that if experts agree with your stand, then your contention must have merit. This approach is an appropriate device commonly used by students in their public speaking classes when presenting persuasive speeches. In quoting material, establish the qualifications of your sources with such phrases as, "Tom Brady, New England Patriots' All Star quarterback, explained how difficult it is to make the transition from the college football (University of Michigan) to the pros (New England Patriots). He said..."

Charisma Another characteristic of credibility is *charisma.* Words synonymous with charisma are *appealing, concerned, enthusiastic,* and *sincere*. People with charisma are compelling and have the ability to entice others. A charismatic speaker grabs and holds attention. John F. Kennedy and Martin Luther King Jr. were masters at getting masses of people to follow them because of their ability to mesmerize audiences. Oprah Winfrey has that effect on television viewers. Television psychologist Dr. Phil McGraw holds viewers' attention by successfully using humor, knowledge, and a down-home, folksy approach. Then Illinois Senator Barack Obama mesmerized the nation as the keynote speaker at the 2004 Democratic Convention with his youthful, dynamic, sincere, and articulate presentation and continued to impress voters during the 2008 Democratic presidential primary campaign which lead to his election. The *New York Times* characterized the effect as "The Charisma Mandate."[12]

People with charisma such as President John F. Kennedy are compelling, and have the ability to entice others by grabbing and holding their attention.

Some televangelists are capable of getting their followers to give vast amounts of money because of the power of the listeners' unwavering belief in the messenger. The late Pope John Paul II was considered to be an effective and compelling communicator. "He didn't use a dignitary tone but connected to his audience by speaking from his heart, from the gut, soul-to-soul."[13] On the other hand, his successor, Pope Benedict, evokes such comments as, "He's cold."[14] "A hard-liner."[15] "Benedict pales in comparison to his predecessor John Paul II in almost every respect, including looks, vitality, charisma, showmanship, tenure and popular appeal."[16]

Think about a report you heard in one of your classes. The student who acted bored, just trying to get the assignment over with probably had little impact on you. But the speech delivered by a student able to muster high energy and passion probably made a more lasting impression on you. Enthusiasm has a way of being contagious so that listeners feel enticed to become more engaged.

Character Your reputation, honesty, and sensitivity all aid in developing your *character*. People who are assumed to be of high character based on the experiences they have had, the positions they hold, or the comments others have made about them engender trust.

Positively perceived speakers often find audiences receptive to their messages. Speakers who are viewed negatively need to try to alter their listeners' beliefs by emphasizing qualities about themselves that the audience may respond to positively. For example, a former convict, speaking to an audience about the need for altering prison procedures, started his presentation with these comments:

> I am a paroled convict. Knowing this, some of you may immediately say to yourself, "Why should I listen to anything that an ex-jailbird has to say?" It is because I was in prison, and because I know what prison can do to a person, and because I know what negative influences jail can have on a person, that I want to speak to you tonight about the need to change prison procedures.[17]

Sometimes speakers can change the attitudes of audience members who disagree with their views by directly taking on the issues of disagreement and asking listeners to give them a fair chance to be heard. For example, a Democratic candidate speaking before a predominantly Republican audience stated:

> I realize that I am a Democrat and you are Republicans. I also realize that we are both after the same thing: a city in which we can live without fear for our lives, a city in which the services such as trash and snow removal are efficient, and a city in which taxes are held in check. You, the Republicans, and I, the Democrat, do have common goals. I'd appreciate your considering how I propose to help all of us achieve our joint objective to make this city a better place in which to live.[18]

Not only are the components of credibility—competence, charisma, and character—important, but developing a logically constructed speech can be critical to persuading listeners.

Logical Arguments

If it doesn't make sense, the audience is less likely to be swayed. To a Euro American audience, "making sense" generally means being logical (*logos*). The statements and the supporting evidence add up to a reasonable match. Listeners, especially when they are dealing with information about which they know little or are skeptical, look for logical connections in the messages they are receiving.

A college professor summarized the logical argument concept in this way: "Ask whether the recommendation/conclusion is *expected* and, therefore, would be *accepted*." She went on to explain that as a speaker you should ascertain whether the recommendation you are making, the action you are urging the audience members to act on, are the actions that follow the evidence given. For an example, she offered, "If I said 2 parts of hydrogen combined with 1 part of oxygen results in water, you would probably say, "okay, that makes sense." (The answer is expected based on the information given, therefore, acceptable.) On the other hand, "if I said 2 part of hydrogen combined with 1 part of hydrogen results in fire, you would most likely say, "That's ridiculous." Why? "Fire is not the expected answer."[19]

Structure of Logical Arguments

There is no one best way to get everyone to agree with you. However, these qualities of a presentation will provide a good foundation:

- A clear statement of the purpose of the speech so that the audience knows what you are proposing.

COMMUNICATING in Careers

To Help or Not

The bioethicist Peter Singer raised an ethical dilemma on his blog, *The Life You Can Save.*

- First premise: Suffering and death from lack of food, shelter, and medical care are bad.
- Second premise: If it is in your power to prevent something bad from happening, without sacrificing anything nearly as important, it is wrong not to do so.
- Third premise: By donating to aid agencies, you can prevent suffering and death from lack of food, shelter, and medical care, without sacrificing anything nearly as important.
- Conclusion: Therefore if you do not donate to aid agencies, you are doing something wrong.

Source: From "News you can use! From the lab to your life" by Peter Singer, *Psychology Today*, November/December 2009, p. 28.

REFLECT ON THIS: Do you agree or disagree with Singer's conclusion? Why? Why not?

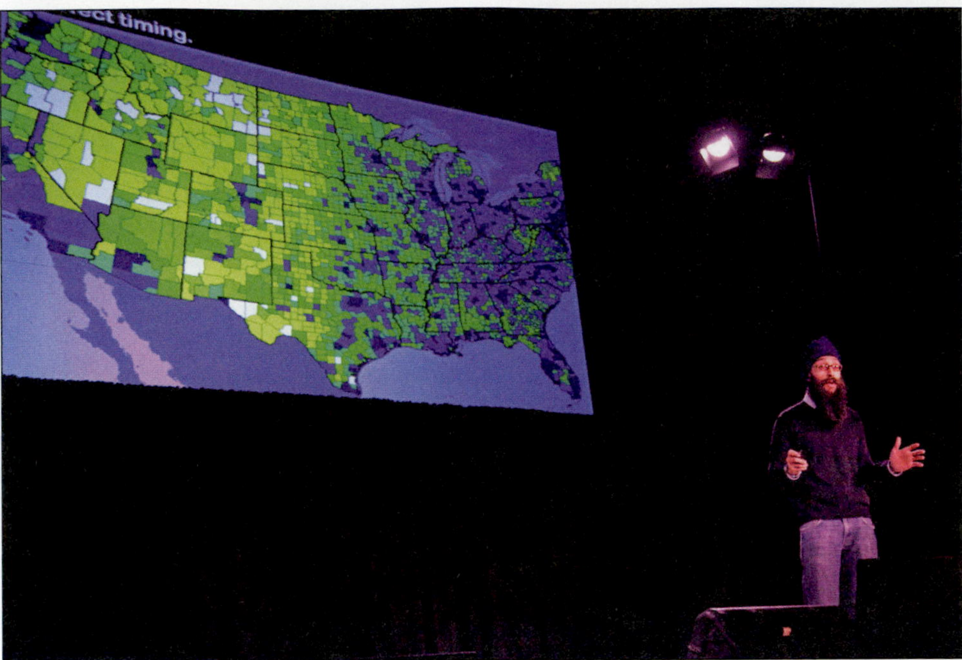

Evidence, such as specific instances, statistics, and data, is perceived to be the most persuasive form of supporting material.

- Good reasons that you believe or want the audience to believe in the proposal.
- Reference to credible sources if you are not a recognized expert on the topic.
- Arguments that follow a clear structure for ease of understanding and that develop the main point(s).
- Absence of false facts, partial information, and biased stands

To lead your listeners to your conclusion, it often is wise to choose an argumentative structure that fits your analysis of what approach is most likely to engage your listeners and lead them to accept your persuasive claim. These persuasive claims—your central idea—are argument propositions.

A *proposition of fact* states the existence of something in the past, present, or future by offering the reasons why the proposition should be believed (e.g., The New England Patriots will win the Super Bowl this year because of their strong defense, outstanding quarterback, and a long history of success in the event.).

A *proposition of value* offers an evaluation of a person, place, or thing. In the proposition of value (e.g., Cleveland, Ohio, is a fine place to live for lovers of the arts because of its vast artistic resources including the Cleveland Orchestra, Cleveland Art Museum, Rock and Roll Hall of Fame, Cleveland Play House, Great Lakes Theatre, and numerous dance and small professional theatre companies). A proposition of value always has a value term (e.g., *good, bad, right, or wrong)*.

A *proposition of policy* is the most commonly used persuasive method. It centers on stating that something should or should not be done (e.g., The United States should disengage from Afghanistan because of the financial expense and number of casualties; it's a war that can't be won).

An *inductive argument* is based on probability: what conclusion is expected or believed from the evidence. The more specific instances you can draw on in an inductive argument, the more probable your conclusion will be. A video clip of actress and social advocate Angelina Jolie talking about the plight of several refugee groups, for example, may prompt the audience to agree with her contention that refugees around

COMMUNICATING in Careers

Cultures and Acceptable Evidence

Reasoning plays an important part in business contexts. Yet, not every culture reasons in the same way.... Cultures differ in what is considered acceptable evidence, reasonable, and persuasive styles (the preferred way to convince others).

European Americans prefer facts as evidence. The myriad detective stories on television suggest this emphasis on facts: the physical aspects of the crime scene, the accounts of people who saw the events, the scientific data from DNA. These facts lead investigators to not only the behavior of individuals involved in the crime, but also their motivation.

For some cultures, facts are not as acceptable. For Muslims, stories or parables, particularly from the Koran, are acceptable as well as powerful forms of evidence. The story is told and the lesson from the story is assumed conclusive. In cultures influenced by Confucianism, metaphor analogies are used for evidence. In African cultures, testimony is not a powerful form of evidence as it is in the U.S. legal system. Some African cultures believe that the word of a witness should be disregarded because if the person speaks up about seeing something, she or he must have an agenda and is therefore not objective.

Source: "Cultures and Acceptable Evidence" from "How do I criticize? Let me count the ways" from *Intercultural communication: A text with readings,* 1st Edition by Pamela J. Cooper, Carolyn Calloway-Thomas, Cheri J. Simonds.

REFLECT ON THIS:

1. Assume you are going to give a speech with the central idea, "To persuade the audience that television mystery shows use facts to lead investigators to identify a perpetrator of a crime." Use a specific case from a TV mystery show to illustrate your point.
2. Using the same show, indicate how the program would have been developed if it had been developed for either a Muslim or an African audience.

the world need relief aid. If you are trying to persuade the audience of the dangers of "global warming," you might start by giving examples of the increase in the number of global droughts, floods, ecological disasters, and ice-cap melting in polar regions. This leads to the probable conclusion that the world is experiencing climate change. The inductive argument moves from the specific to the general. It can take one of two forms: (a) the generalization conclusion or (b) the hypothesis conclusion.

In a *generalization conclusion,* a number of specific instances are examined. From these, you attempt to predict some future occurrence or explain a whole category of instances. Underlying this is the assumption that what holds true for specific instances will hold true for all instances in a given category. Perhaps you've seen Haitian Hip-Hop Artist Wyclef Jean discuss the numerous challenges facing Haiti. His list of personal examples may lead you to the conclusion that donations should be made to a nonpolitical, grassroots group to aid his country.[20] This logic would be a generalization conclusion.

In a *hypothesis conclusion,* a hypothesis is used to explain all the evidence. For the argument to have substance, however, the hypothesis must provide the best explanation for that evidence. For example, in overriding the decision of the Texas Department of Child Protective Services (TDCPS) to remove children from a polygamist group, the Supreme Court ruled that the TDCPS overreached when it swept the children into foster care, knowing little about the religious group; used an ambiguous telephone call of questionable validity; accepted as truth the word of disgruntled former members; and did not learn from a brush with another Texas-based religious sect that led to the fiery death of 21 children at the Branch Dividian compound.[21]

In addition to inductive arguments, persuasive speakers can make use of the *deductive argument,* which is based on logical necessity. Often the reasoning starts from a general statement and leads to a specific instance. If you accept the premise of the deductive argument—the proposition that is the basis of the argument—then you must also accept its conclusion.

One type of deductive argument is the *categorical syllogism,* an argument that contains premises and a conclusion. For instance, in a speech with the central idea of persuading the listeners of what the symptoms are that lead doctors to diagnose chronic fatigue syndrome, a speaker might state:

> *(Premise)* A proven sign of chronic fatigue syndrome is an off-balance immune system.
>
> *(Premise)* A proven sign of chronic fatigue syndrome is a positive diagnosis for human herpes virus 6.
>
> *(Premise)* A proven sign of chronic fatigue syndrome is a positive diagnosis for human B-cell lymphotropic virus.
>
> *(Conclusion)* Therefore, a person diagnosed with an off-balance immune system, human herpes virus 6, and human B-cell lymphotropic virus can be diagnosed as having chronic fatigue syndrome.

As communicated, a syllogism usually takes the form of an *enthymeme,* in which a premise usually is not directly stated. The omitted premise is shared by the communicators and therefore does not need to be verbalized. For example, while speaking to those attending a conference on writing assessment, a speaker might state, "If we can teach our children, from all backgrounds, to write with joy, originality, clarity, and control, then I don't think we have much else to worry about regarding their writing abilities," a conclusion based on the premise shared by his listeners that children should be taught effective writing skills. An important step in analyzing your audience is to determine if the listeners share the unstated premise on which you base your argument. If you believe they do not, then you ought to build that assumption into the argument you spell out for your listeners.

Another type of deductive argument is the *disjunctive argument*—an either-or argument in which true alternatives must be established. For example:

> In a professional baseball game, the Kansas City Royals and the New York Mets played to completion without the game being a tie.
>
> Either the Kansas City Royals won or the New York Mets won.
>
> The New York Mets did not win.
>
> Therefore, the Kansas City Royals won.

Still another form of deductive argument is the *conditional argument,* which sets up an if-then proposition. In this form, there are two conditions, with one necessarily following from the other. The chief executive officer of a major accounting firm proposed that the federal government adopt a new accrual accounting system so that the public and Congress could monitor the federal budget. He could argue, "*If* citizens demand the financial information to which they are clearly entitled, incentives would be created for sound fiscal management—and perhaps for more enlightened political leadership—*then* we could expect to see better-informed decision making (i.e., less fiscal recklessness) and a reduction in the risks caused by the misallocation of capital."

Persuasive Evidence

The persuasive speaker, in Western cultures, not only must structure the persuasive argument but also must support these contentions. What is perceived to be the most persuasive form of supporting material—*evidence*—includes testimony from experts, statistics, and specific instances. If you can offer solid data to support your contentions, they will lend substance to your argument. For example, a speaker who attempts to persuade listeners that the U.S. Food and Drug Administration (FDA) needs more funds to hire inspectors can cite specific instances from the agency's files. Real cases are on record that show that potatoes contaminated with insecticide and ginger ale containing mold were sold to consumers. The speaker also can cite statistics indicating that only 500 FDA inspectors are available to monitor 60,000 food-processing plants in the United States.[22]

When using evidence, verify that the evidence has a factual base. Make sure that your sources are valid and current. Many students look online for their information and assume that if it appears online, it is valid. That assumption is wrong! For example, a student who was speaking about the changing image of gays and lesbians stated that Marcia Cross, an actress on the television show *Desperate Housewives*, was a lesbian. One of the other students challenged the speaker about the validity of the information during the question-and-answer session that followed the speech. The speaker agreed to do further research, including determining whether the information was an *urban legend* (story popularly regarded as true but usually containing a mixture of fact and fiction), and to report back to the class. At the next session she reported that the information was not true. She had searched on Snopes.com (a source for ascertaining whether urban legends are true or false) and showed classmates a clip from the television show, *The View*, which showed co-host Barbara Walters questioning Cross on rumors regarding her sexuality. "I'm not gay," said Cross.[23]

The lesson for public speakers is to be sure to confirm the validity of the information you use, don't always rely on a single entry, and surely don't assume that a blog or online source is accurate.

Socially COMMUNICATING

Factual Claims

Here you argue what exists or does not exist, what's led to a current situation, or what will or will not happen; you assess their validity using terms such as *true* or *false*, *correct* or *incorrect*, *yes* or *no*. The following three types of factual claims are common:

1. **Debatable points** (there is life on other planets; Lee Harvey Oswald acted alone in killing President Kennedy)
2. **Causal relationships** (secondhand smoke leads to lung disease; television violence influences children to commit violent acts)
3. **Predictions** (Dreyfus mutual fund will gain value within six months; global warming will cause massive flooding along both the east and west coasts of the United States within twenty-five years.)

Source: "Factual Claims" from *Public speaking: Concepts and skills for a diverse society*, 3rd Edition by C. Jaffe.

REFLECT ON THIS: Write two debatable points, two causal relationships, and two predictions that could be used for topics of persuasive speeches.

Reasoning Fallacies

Speakers sometimes, intentionally or not, present material that contains logical flaws, **reasoning fallacies**. As a speaker, you should be aware that you might fall prey to these fallacies. Wise listeners should be aware of protecting themselves from accepting fallacious reasoning.

Speakers may reach an unwarranted conclusion from an insufficient number of instances. For example, a speaker may argue that gun control legislation is not necessary because, even though guns were used in the college campus shootings at Virginia Tech and Northern Illinois University, most college campuses are safe. Seems like a logical conclusion? This argument development ignores all other gun uses beyond the college campus, thus limiting the scope and numbers of possible cases in support of the need for gun control.

Be aware that no *analogy* (stating that one idea or action is the same an another action or idea) is ever totally true, as no two cases are ever identical. Speakers use faulty analogies when they assume that the shared elements will continue indefinitely or that all the aspects relevant to the case under consideration are similar. The speaker who argues that the AIDS crisis is analogous to the bubonic plague that ravaged medieval Europe, for example, overlooks the medical advances that make the AIDS crisis very different and that how the diseases are spread is also different.

When a speaker claims, without qualification, that something caused something else, faulty reasoning may have been used. For example, the speaker would argue that the lack of job availability in the United States is the direct result of the number of illegal immigrants in the country. He is ignoring that there is more than one cause and is not taking other factors into consideration.

Sometimes a speaker uses irrelevant arguments to obscure the real issue. This can be done by attacking the personal character of someone related to the issue. For instance, some arguments against the Health Care and Education Reconciliation Act of 2010 called the system *Obamacare,* which was a negative term coined to deride the President. In other words, they chose to belittle the President rather than discuss the relationship of the Act to the nation's health care needs.

Another negative method of reasoning works on passions not related to the issue. For example, when pop singer Britney Spears was accused of "being a bad mother," some music fans insisted she was innocent. Their devotion to her as an entertainer overshadowed the implicating evidence.[24]

Another fallacy device is an attempt to prove that a statement is true because it cannot be disproved. For example, supporters of pit bull terriers argue that they are not dangerous pets because dog bite statistics show the breed to rank ninth in number of bites, after poodles and cocker spaniels. Of course, the number of pit bulls in this country is minuscule in comparison with the number of poodles and cocker spaniels, but this fact was ignored.

The Role of Emotions in Persuasion

Up until this point of the discussion of persuasion, most of the emphasis has been placed on the use of logical approaches to achieve the persuasive goal. However, research indicates that "attempts at persuasion would be more successful when messages were framed with emotional overtones matching the emotional state of the receiver and that these changes would be mediated by emotion-induced biases *(pathos)* involving expectancies attached to arguments contained in the messages."[25]

"In 55 B.C.E., Marcus Tullius Cicero, echoing the sentiments of even earlier rhetoricians (e.g., Aristotle, *On Rhetoric*), admonished the orators of his day to appreciate the power of specific emotions in the art of persuasion. It was through manipulations of emotions such as anger, despair, and hopeful compassion, many classical orators argued, that opinion could be swayed most effectively. A person who gained mastery both in the evocation of emotion and in the emotional framing of argumentation was believed to be among the most successful practitioners of persuasion."

The words of Cicero are as valid today as they were in B.C.E. Research has shown that in spite of the call for making speeches logical, based on the theory of Western logic that encourages using facts and expert opinions to back up contentions, audiences are more swayed by emotional appeals. This is not meant to underplay the value of facts, but to really get action, the appeal to emotions stimulates more. The 2011 elections seem to back this up. Often Tea Party candidates sold themselves on the emotional appeals of fear, unhappiness, use of jingoistic phrases like "death squads," "Speak for Yourself Obama! We ARE a Christian Nation!," "Socialism Is for the Elite—Ask the Slaves Who Live Under Communism & Islam,' "RISE UP—RELOAD—REVOLT," and "They Think We're Stupid"[26] to emotionally stimulate susceptible voters. They were often short on facts, not even exposing how they planned to carry through their purported goals, but long on emotional appeals. The results of the election, in which numerous Tea Party candidates were elected, illustrates, in part, the effect of emotion over logic.

As a research study illustrated, "Appeal to the emotions as sources of leverage in persuasion is a venerable strategy and one that continues to be used by politicians and marketers alike. Candidates, for example, often attempt to raise the ire of their audience against certain policy positions; marketers attempt to evoke disgust among potential customers to help convince them."[27]

Psychological Appeals

With the idea in mind that emotion is a strong motivator in the persuasive process let's look at the value of *psychological appeals,* which enlist listeners' emotions as motivation for accepting your arguments. Just as you must select your arguments and enhance your credibility on the basis of what you know about your listeners, so must you also select psychological appeals on the basis of what you think will stir their emotions. The purpose of incorporating some emotional appeals in your speech is to keep your listeners involved as you spell out your persuasive plan, even

Persuasive speakers who use the survival-of-the-species psychological motivation highlight such factors as the safety of the listener and the listener's family.

though they may not distinguish the emotional from the rational in your presentation.

Appeals to Satisfy Basic Needs

People tend to react according to whether their needs are being met. Several theories attempt to illustrate what needs people have, and persuasive speakers can use these as a guide to organizing emotional appeals to trigger need satisfaction.

One approach to understanding need satisfaction is (Abraham) *Maslow's Hierarchy of Human Needs* (Figure 15.2). Based on this view, a speaker must determine the level of need of a particular group of listeners and then select appeals aimed at that level.[28]

Maslow suggested that all human beings have five levels of needs. His original thinking was that one need had to be satisfied before a person could go onto satisfying the next need. However, newer thinking favors the idea that need levels may all function at the same time.

According to Maslow's theory, the first, most basic level is *physiological needs:* hunger, sleep, sex, and thirst. For example, in order to convince the citizens of Afghanistan to cooperate in helping get rid of the Taliban, members of the U.S. military offer food or indicate that once the insurgents have been destroyed, the United States will build water wells and housing.

The second level of human need, *safety needs,* encompasses security, stability, protection, and/or strength. Organizations that have had to reduce their workforces and lay off employees have found it persuasive to offer seminars on job searches, résumé preparation, and other career skills. Employees concerned about the security of their positions are quick to sign up for such offerings.

The third level consists of *acceptance needs:* the needs for love and belonging. College and university alumni representatives use this need in speeches intended to motivate alumni to contribute to endowment funds for the sake of being part of their alma mater.

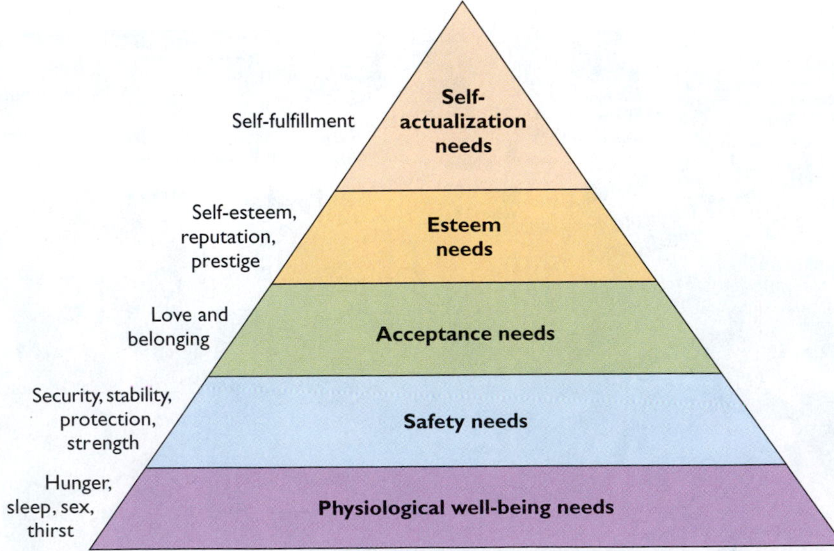

FIGURE 15.2
Maslow's Hierarchy of Needs

Source: From Abraham Maslow, *Motivation and Personality* (New York: HarperCollins Publishers, Inc., 1954).

Esteem needs form the fourth level that Maslow identified. Human needs at this level involve both self-esteem (desire for achievement and mastery) and esteem by others (desire for reputation and prestige). Athletic coaches use appeals to esteem in their pep talks before games to persuade team members to do their best.

Finally, Maslow identified the fifth level in the hierarchy as *self-actualization needs:* desire for self-fulfillment or achieving one's greatest potential as the ultimate level for which people reach. Recruiters attempt to influence potential military personnel with slogans such as "Be the best that you can be."

The *Ethnographic Theory of Human Drives,* another attempt to explain human needs, proposes that survival of the species, pleasure seeking, security, and territoriality must be satisfied.

Persuasive speakers using the *survival-of-the-species* aspect of this theory try to appeal to such factors as the physical and psychological safety of the person and his or her family. A speaker presenting a message "to persuade the audience not to text and drive" may appeal to the audience based on the statistics concerning the life-threatening dangers of operating a vehicle while texting.

Pleasure seeking drives center on the idea that people spend a great deal of their lives seeking happiness. For example, in discussing why a city income tax is needed, a municipal spokesperson might indicate that the funds would be going toward refurbishing the city's recreation facilities.

Security means keeping things on an even keel, in balance, under control. In analyzing an audience, try to figure out their fears about change and uncertainty. For example, in light of the seeming increase in the number of child abductions, when speaking to audiences, police stress ways for parents to feel secure by forming neighborhood watches, being aware of sexual offenders in the neighborhood, walking their children to school, and having children play in large groups.

Humans mark off and defend territory. This is *territoriality.* To activate this appeal, you must ascertain that audience members are concerned about what is already theirs, or you can instill the belief that something will belong to listeners. Homeowners, for example, may give speeches to a planning commission by taking on zoning issues when it appears that a jurisdiction will change laws that might alter the nature of their neighborhoods, thus lowering the value of their home.

You can use multiple appeals in your speech. In a speech "to persuade the audience to protect their credit score," a speaker might appeal to all of these needs:

- Survival—For you to be able to protect the welfare of yourself and your family, you need sound financial resources.
- Pleasure seeking—If you have a good credit rating, you will be able to buy the things you really want.
- Security—A good credit rating will help you avoid financial surprises in your future.
- Territoriality—You want to control your own finances, not have a creditor or bank stepping into your business or contacting your employer about your finances.

Human needs connect with human values and principles that are held in esteem. European American values shape the way persuaders appeal to listeners and establish themes.[29]

Appeals to Motivate Listeners

Research in persuasion (including psychology, communication, marketing, advertising, and public relations) offers us a catalog of different motivational appeals.[30] As a speaker, you should select those appeals that will be most appropriate for your particular listeners and for your persuasive goal. The appeals that you select can then be incorporated into your discussion of your arguments and evidence, especially examples. Being aware of the appeals can assist you in determining which ones will be appropriate for your listeners.[31]

As a speaker, you can select from among these appeals and build them into your presentation:

- *Anger.* Anger can be a strong motivator if listeners are irritated about a particular issue. Outrage over injustice, violence, or discrimination, for example, can motivate people to action. People who are upset about a proposed highway that will displace neighborhoods will respond to appeals to express their anger and disagreement to highway planning commissioners.
- *Fear*. This appeal is used to raise apprehension in a listener. A representative of the food industry speaking to individuals who have had heart attacks could use this approach to discuss no-salt and low-cholesterol products. Although the fear appeal can be powerful, there can be a danger in its use. Be sure to give a solution with the fear because listeners can become frightened if they perceive the situation as hopeless. Long-time smokers, for example, may assume that because of their long history of smoking, there is no sense in quitting because the damage has already been done.
- *Guilt*. People may feel guilty for either doing or not doing something. Some clergy turn to this appeal in sermons. The "greening" of America movement

Outrage over injustice, violence, or discrimination can motivate people to action, as it did during the uprisings in Egypt in January 2011.

taps into citizen guilt for polluting the environment and causing global warming.

- *Happiness*. We seek happiness (pleasure) in life, and persuaders should understand the psychological appeal of this need for satisfaction and well-being.
- *Health*. A strong appeal is the need for good health. A "healthy you" is the bottom line for motivational appeals in advertising, public service messages, and speeches stressing the need to change the nation's physical and psychological health care system.
- *Hero worship*. Referring to a famous person who feels as they do about a subject may be the motivating factor to convince an audience to take a desired action. Following the September 11, 2001, terrorist attacks, speakers who needed a hero image referred to the firefighters and police officers who had lost their lives while trying to save others.
- *Humor*. People enjoy laughing and are often taken off guard when they are enjoying themselves. Humor has also been credited with relieving pain and helping in the development of positive mental health.

COMMUNICATING

The Power of the Internet

Bill Clinton wandered into the University of South Carolina Student Center around midnight and found a single student on a computer. The student said, "give me a minute," and within 10 minutes, a flash crowd of 300 students had arrived to hear the former president give an impromptu speech.

Source: From S. Schifferes, *Internet, key to Obama victories*, BBC News, November 10, 2008, http://news.bbc.co.uk/l/hi/technology/7412045.stm

REFLECT ON THIS:

1. In 2011, the social media was credited with getting flash crowds in Egypt to take a stand for Democracy and overthrow the government. Has the Internet become too powerful a force?
2. How would you go about getting a group of students on your campus together to take a stand regarding a cause about which you felt strongly?

- *Loyalty*. Appeals to commitment—to respect the nation, friends and family, or organizations—can motivate. "It's the American way," is an example of appeals to loyalty to the nation.
- *Nostalgia*. Some people like to look back at "the good old days" and appreciate being reminded of events and people of the past that evoke pleasant memories. A speaker can refer to Fourth of July picnics and how wonderful things were in the good old days.
- *Revulsion*. An appeal to disgust can be effective. A speaker, for instance, can illustrate the effects of water pollution on the Chesapeake Bay by showing listeners some water samples in an attempt to motivate them to support legislation to clean up the bay. As with fear, revulsion can arouse such strong feelings that listeners may tune out the message. For example, antivivisectionists risk overwhelming their listeners with photographs of maimed laboratory animals, so care must be taken in selecting examples.
- *Safety*. Concern for safety ranks high in human needs. Safety is a major issue. Those desiring controls over the sale of natural herbs as medicine stress the issue of safety because there is no national testing of the ingredients in those products.
- *Savings*. Fluctuations of the world economy continue to convince people that they need to save money. Speakers representing financial institutions appeal to individuals to save and to invest their money.

- *Sex*. Sex sells. Sex is a major motivational appeal in the global marketplace and almost inescapable in advertising messages. A controversial but effective advertising campaign for Candies, a perfume product, showed a woman in front of an open medicine cabinet filled with condoms. The attention drawn to the explicit sexual nature of the advertisement caused sales to skyrocket.
- *Sympathy*. By showing photographs of impoverished elderly people, a speaker can compel listeners to give time, money, or other resources. A sympathetic bond, often coupled with guilt, is created with those less fortunate.

Structure of the Persuasive Message

The structure of a persuasive speech should allow the listener to reach the behavioral or mental change the speaker desires.

Problem–Solution Method of Development

A typical method of developing a persuasive message is to use the problem–solution arrangement. The speaker identifies what is wrong and then presents the cure or recommendation for its cure.

A structure of the body of a speech that develops inductively would be:

I. Body
   A. Identify the situation (what is wrong).
   B. Identify the problem (what has to be changed).
   C. List the possible solutions to the problem.
   D. Evaluate the solutions for workability, desirability, practicality.
      1. Workability—Can the proposed solutions solve the problem?
      2. Desirability—Will the proposed solutions cause bigger problems?
      3. Practicality—Can the proposed solutions be put into effect?
   E. Recommendation of the solution that is most workable, desirable, and practical.

When you are listing the possible solutions (section C), two strategies are available: placing the strongest argument first so that it will have the greatest impact on listeners at the outset, or placing the strongest argument last to ensure that listeners retain it.

Another consideration is whether to develop section D—evaluation of solutions—by simply listing the reasons that the solution to be proposed is workable, desirable, and practical, or to investigate both sides of each solution, including the one to be recommended. One potential problem in developing both sides of an argument is that you may raise issues and ideas that your listeners have not previously considered.

An alternative to the illustrated pattern would be to place what is section E—identification of best solution—at the start of the body, thus beginning by revealing the solution and then explaining why this solution was selected. In general, if you feel that the audience is or may be on your side, state your arguments first and allow your listeners to believe along with you for the rest of your presentation (a deductive mode of reasoning). But if you perceive your audience to be hostile to your position, build the background and then present the arguments when you think that your listeners are ready for them (a more inductive line of reasoning).

Monroe's Motivated Sequence

An alternative persuasive structure is the *Monroe's Motivated Sequence*.[32] This plan describes the sequence by which a listener is taken through a five-step persuasive message:

1. The attention step is the first section of the introduction.
2. The need (problem) is developed in the first section of the body of the speech.
3. The second section of the speech body is the satisfaction (plan of action).
4. And the third section of the body is the visualization (benefits of the proposed solution).
5. The final step is your conclusion or action step, in which you challenge the listener to take a specific course of action.

Imagine that you decided to present a motivational speech to your class with the purpose: "To persuade the audience to take steps to improve their learning." The developed speech, using the Monroe Motivated Sequence, would look like this:

Introduction

I. Attention

Gain audience focus. As you would when using any speech structure, begin with a startling statistic, a fascinating projected photograph, or a provocative quotation to grab your audience. Longer attention grabbers include jokes and stories. Audience attention can be very brief, so once you have it, you need to move on quickly. This process should move the audience towards a general curiosity about your speech. If you fail to engage the audience at the start, then you will have your work cut out to recover the situation. If you let your passion come through and you demonstrate caring towards your audience, the motivational process will be much easier.

A. Jana's story demonstrates how each of us can improve our learning.

B. How many of you are learning everything you want to learn in college?

Body

II. Need

Trigger a concern about a problem or a desire that each listener has. When you stimulate a need, you audience will start wondering about a solution.

A. College is expensive.

B. College takes time.

C. College learning can affect your quality of life.

III. Satisfaction

This step is not about creating satisfaction, but proposing a way in which the audience can satisfy the need that you have just stimulated. Solve the problem. Fear appeals do not work unless you can guide your audience to an appropriate response. So, when you arouse your audience to acknowledge a problem, you have to help them figure out how to solve the problem.

A. By doing preparation homework before class and practice homework after class, you will learn more.
B. Attend class every day.
C. Believe in yourself and put forth effort.
D. Seek a sense of community in each class.

IV. Visualization
Now that you have proposed a solution, the next step is to move listeners to see your solution as the right answer for them. Help the audience picture in their minds how they can put the solution in place. This step is what makes the Motivated Sequence uniquely successful because you will help the audince see your proposal as complete and successful. Describe a specific scene where the audience can picture themselves taking the specific action you propose. To motivate the audience, help them to see themselves actually doing what you propose. By staying narrow and focused, this visualization process becomes easier.

A. Picture yourself attending that 8:00 class tomorrow and finding out what is on the next test.
B. Imagine doing the homework before class so you really understand your professor's lecture.
C. Picture yourself crossing the stage at graduation knowing that you have learned what you set out to learn in college.

Conclusion

V. Action
Finally, you need to prompt the listeners into action, implementing the solution that you propose is the right thing to do. Make a direct call for action and include a clincher.

A. Keep up on your assignments and attend class every day.
B. Clincher. Tell a real story of someone who used these methods to improve learning.

Culture and Persuasion[33]

We live in a multicultural world. Many public speeches are presented before heterogeneous audiences whose views of what is a persuasive message vary greatly. These public interactions can take place in a vast number of settings, including a college classroom, business sales meeting, international conference, or a religious setting. In speaking it is imperative that you remember, "because logic has cultural aspects, an understanding of social life requires an understanding of how people think in their own cultural context."[34]

Not all cultures regard western persuasive methods as being valid or even important. If you are speaking to an audience primarily composed of Arabic or Hispanic members, for example, know that their basic method of conveying information is through the use of stories that illustrate the point being made but do not necessarily directly state the conclusion to be reached.

"Thai, Arab, and Chinese discourse all have rhetorical traditions that emphasize the importance of emotion in assessing truthfulness."[35] Speeches in Arabic contain strong emotional assertions, using implied arguments and indirect language.[36] The Chinese tend to make a statement and just keep repeating it without any changes.[37] Thai's tend to use a combination of logical arguments, emotional appeals, plus a stronger appeal to the speaker's ethos.[38] In other words, "trust me because of my high character and here are the emotional triggers and facts."

The native American Lakota speaker uses stories to develop persuasive arguments, but "may not make explicit the link to the conclusion."[39] Likewise, Latin American speakers tend to use descriptions to lead others to a conclusion that is not stated specifically but is reached by use of drama and emotions.[40]

Many individuals in the African American community use *reality communication* in their persuasive speech making. It centers on "tellin' it like it is" with a "cool, steady and persistent toughness that developed over years of overcoming difficulty."[41] This *Asserting Point of View* is described by researchers as assertive by some and aggressive by others because there is tendency for the language and speaking tone to be intense, outspoken, challenging, and forward.[42]

Members of Italian, Slavic, Jewish, and many African cultures have a tendency to use effusive metaphors, parables, or stories to dramatize the emotional impact of a persuasive message.[43]

So, if your audience analysis indicates that you are speaking to an audience of Arabic businesspeople, rather than giving a series of statistics and expert options for proof in a speech, you may want to tell a relevant story or a parable from the *Koran*.

If you were listening to an African American student in your speech class—and she displays an intensity of language and challenges the generally accepted concepts of the Euro American students in class—she should be respected for using the norm pattern of her culture. This does not mean, if you are in opposition to her viewpoint, that you should unquestioningly accept her point of view. As a communicator who understands the differences in cultural speaking style, you should listen open-mindedly, not rejecting her ideas just because they follow a different form of persuasion.

As for your adapting to the style of your audience, if you are to speak outside of your norm culture, you may need to consult an expert in the persuasive cultural patterns of the listeners, and, if it is comfortable and possible for you to do so, adapt to those patterns.

The Persuasive Process in Action

In the U.S. and most European countries, psychological appeals, coupled with a speaker's credibility and well-reasoned and well-supported arguments, provide a sound approach to influencing others to change their beliefs or actions. The sample speech outlined in Figure 15.3 illustrates the interaction of these persuasive elements.

Statement of Central Idea: To persuade the audience that stem-cell research is beneficial by explaining the ethical issues behind stem-cell research, showing how stem cells can be used to test new drugs, as well as how stem cells may be used to treat diseases that can save lives in the near future.

Attention material to involve listeners	**I. Introduction** A. Attention material: Millions of people in the world suffer every single day from devastating diseases, ones for which we have no cure. Stem-cell research creates a promise to better our lives.
Orienting materials to relate topic to listeners and to help establish the speaker's credibility **Topic of speech**	B. Orienting material: Stem cells may one day have the ability to treat diseases such as Parkinson's, Alzheimer's, diabetes, and even cancer. Stem cells can provide a great advantage to our world. However, much more research is needed in order to perfect this method that has the opportunity to treat diseases that besiege people like you and me everyday.
Central point of speech	**II. Central Idea** Although there are some ethical issues that surround stem-cell research, it is essential that we look at the numerous benefits that surround the idea of stem-cell research.
First issue: The "problem" behind stem-cell research	**III. Body** A. Main ethical issue surrounding stem-cell research 1. Embryonic stem-cell studies are controversial because they involve the destruction of human embryos. a. The embryos used are only three to five days past conception, and are known as blastocysts. In fact the cells are so small that they cannot be seen with the human eye. b. The embryo has absolutely no consciousness, no feeling, and no self-awareness.
Second issue: Discussion of how stem cells could be useful in the treatment of Parkinson's disease	2. Those in favor of pro-life feel this is wrong. a. However, with a surplus of created embryos due to in vitro fertilization they could be donated to help the research, since not all of them will be created into life anyway. b. There is also a program called "Store-a-tooth." i. Recent studies have found that there are potent stem cells in baby teeth and wisdom teeth. ii. Instead of throwing baby teeth away, they can be donated for research.
Transition	(Although there seem to be a few ethical concerns about stem-cell research, the pros outweigh the cons, as this science has the potential to cure disease and prolong life.) B. Stem cells for future treatment of disease 1. Parkinson's Disease a. What is it? i. Neurodegenerative disorder that affects over 5 million people over the age of 50 worldwide. ii. PD results from the loss of brain cells called dopaminergic neurons in the area of the brain called the substantia nigra.

FIGURE 15.3 **The Persuasive Process in Action**

iii. Effects of PD are tremors, muscles becoming rigid, and shaking of the limbs uncontrollably.

b. How can stem-cell research help?

i. This research has the ability to take stem cells and grow them into new brain cells.

ii. The next step would be transplanting them into the patients, which would help with the effects of PD.

Transition

(Not only can stem-cell research help patients with Parkinson's disease, but there are also an enormous amount of other benefits that stem-cell research can provide to our world.)

Third issue: Explanation of how stem-cell research can be used to test drugs

C. Stem cells can be used to test new drugs and the new generation of cell tissue.

1. New medicines can be tested for safety on differentiated cells.
2. Cancer cell lines can be used to screen for anti-tumor drugs.
3. Stem cells offer the possibility to be a renewable source of replacement cells. These replacement cells can be used to treat Alzheimer's, spinal cord injuries, stroke, burns, heart disease, and many other diseases.

Reiteration of main points

IV. Conclusion

A. Restate the issues

1. The current debate surrounding stem-cell research is whether the destruction of embryos is ethical, but keep in mind there are many ways to donate stem cells.
2. If stem-cell research were permitted, we would be able to treat diseases that we are unable to treat now.
3. Stem cells can also be used to test new drugs as well as the generation of cell tissues.

Final appeal

B. Clincher

1. Stop and think for a minute about someone you know who has or has had Parkinson's, cancer, Alzheimer's, or diabetes. Think about how hard it was to watch them struggle through these terrible diseases with no hope for a treatment or cure. Now imagine this would never have to happen again. We should all support stem-cell research, so both you and I never have to lose another loved one to disease again.

In Conclusion

IN CONCLUSION

Persuasion is the process by which one party purposefully secures a change of behavior on the part of another party. The basic process of persuasion centers on a speaker making a claim and backing it up in such a way that listeners accept the claim. Successful persuasive strategies center on the use of speaker credibility, logical arguments, and psychological appeals. The most persuasive speaker will combine these persuasive elements to reach the listeners and accomplish their communication goal. Persuasive public speakers organize their speeches by use the problem–solution or Monroe's Motivated Sequence methods.

LEARN BY DOING

1. Prepare a speech on a topic about which you have strong feelings. Propose a change in a current procedure, take a stand on a view concerning the subject, or propose a plan of action. The topic should be one to which your listeners can relate and react so that you can persuade them. An example of a topic for this speech might be "This college should not raise tuition."
2. Select a controversial topic and prepare a speech in which you advocate a particular solution to the problem. Your task is to persuade your listeners to accept your solution. A topic for this speech might be "Euthanasia should be a legal option for terminally ill patients."
3. Prepare a speech analyzing the persuasive strategies used by some groups in advocating a particular cause (e.g., gay rights or Native American rights). Select a number of persuasive messages by spokespersons for the group you choose, and use examples from these messages to illustrate your analysis of the persuasive strategies.
4. Find a speech or letter to the editor that illustrates one or more of the psychological appeals described in this chapter.
5. Make a list of what you perceive to be the differences in preparing persuasive speeches and informative speeches.

KEY TERMS

persuasion 386
persuasive speech 386
speech of conviction 386
speech of actuation 386
ethos 392
logos 392
pathos 392
reasoning fallacies 399

Public Speaking: Presenting the Message

oral and physical factors in speech presentation • use of supplementary aids • manuscript presentation • rehearsing a speech • public speaking anxiety

CHAPTER 16

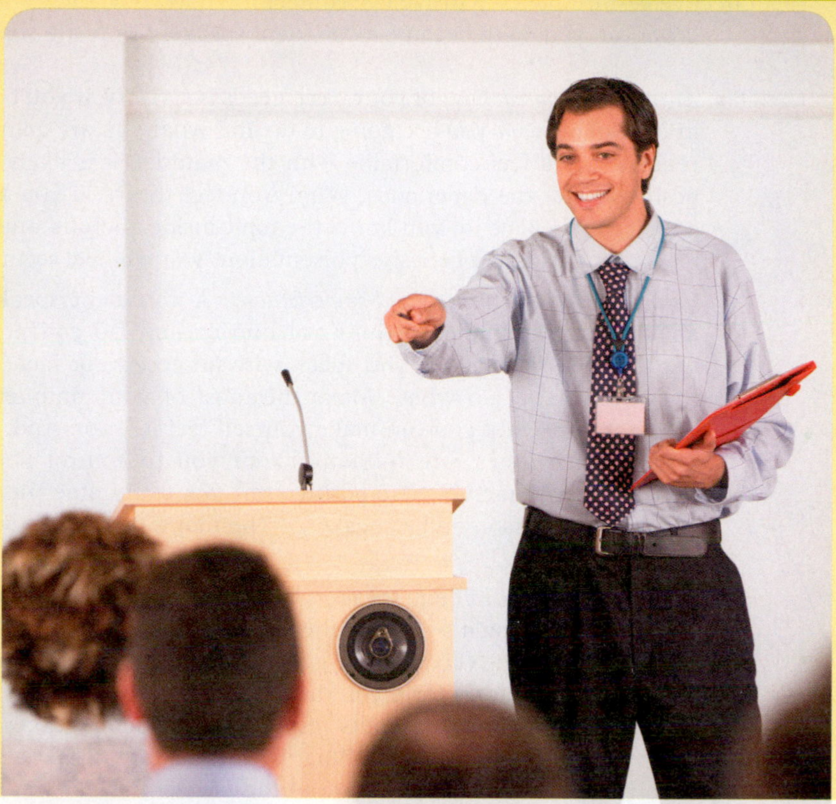

After reading this chapter, you should be able to

- Understand what you can do to speak with confidence
- Identify the oral and physical factors that lead to an effective presentation
- Clarify how to use supplementary aids in a presentation
- Know how to use an outline or manuscript while speaking
- Apply the necessity of rehearsal as a requirement for successful public speaking
- Acknowledge and evaluate the role of culture in public speaking presentations by incorporating adaptations within a speech presentation.
- Explain public speaking anxiety and some ways of dealing with it
- Analyze the role of culture in speech apprehension
- Present an effective public speech

Speaking with Confidence

"Audiences are drawn to a speaker with confidence."[1] In contrast, speakers who act nervous are perceived as less capable than confident ones.[2] But what is confidence and where does it come from? "A confident speaker exudes positive energy that feeds and excites the audience."[3] She exudes confidence because she believes in herself and what she is saying. A confident speaker uses vocal variety, proper pronunciation, effective gestures, and inclusive eye contact.

What can you do to become a confident speaker? Here are some suggestions:[4]

- *Always be prepared.* One of your basic needs is security. If you believe that you are in control of what you are going to do and what you are going to say, and have rehearsed and feel comfortable with the material, it is likely that you will feel positive about the experience. Why? You feel secure. If you are speaking about a topic you believe in, you know the topic inside and out, and you've organized your thoughts into a cohesive presentation, you will feel secure.
- *Embrace your uniqueness and imperfections.* A confident speaker doesn't worry about what the audience thinks of him or her. Do you perceive yourself as too tall? Too skinny? Do you speak with an accent, or have a speech or hearing impairment? So what? Make the most of your uniqueness. Be proud of who you are. Only you can make yourself feel inferior. And, if you allow what you perceive others are thinking about you to control your thoughts, then you victimize yourself. "Use positive self-talk to reframe the way you perceive yourself as a person and a speaker."[5] The major message to yourself should be, "I'm confident."
- *Don't apologize.* Confident speakers are often nervous. However, they don't let the audience know it by rolling their eyes or using the trite "I'm really nervous" or "I really am not very good at giving speeches." Why? Because instead of the audience feeling sorry for them, they feel pity. A confident speaker doesn't want pity; a confident speaker wants respect! A confident speaker appears calm and relaxed, even when nervous. What if you make a mistake, trip over a cord, or drop your note cards? "Take care of the problem as quickly as possible, lighten up the situation with a little humor, and then move on."[6]
- *Understand the role of vocal and physical elements in presenting a public speech.* Speak, don't read; project to the person seated the furthest in the back seat so all can hear you; gesture naturally; be as enthusiastic as you can; be yourself, don't act.

After the speech is prepared, it must be presented to the audience. The delivery has two components: the oral and the physical aspects.

Aspects of Oral and Physical Speech Presentation

Speakers who capture their listeners' attention are likely to share certain qualities: confidence, ease, authority, conviction, credibility, sincerity, warmth, animation, enthusiasm, vitality, intensity, concern, and empathy. They also make effective use of eye contact, conversational tone, and a variety of pitch, pacing, projection, and phrasing.

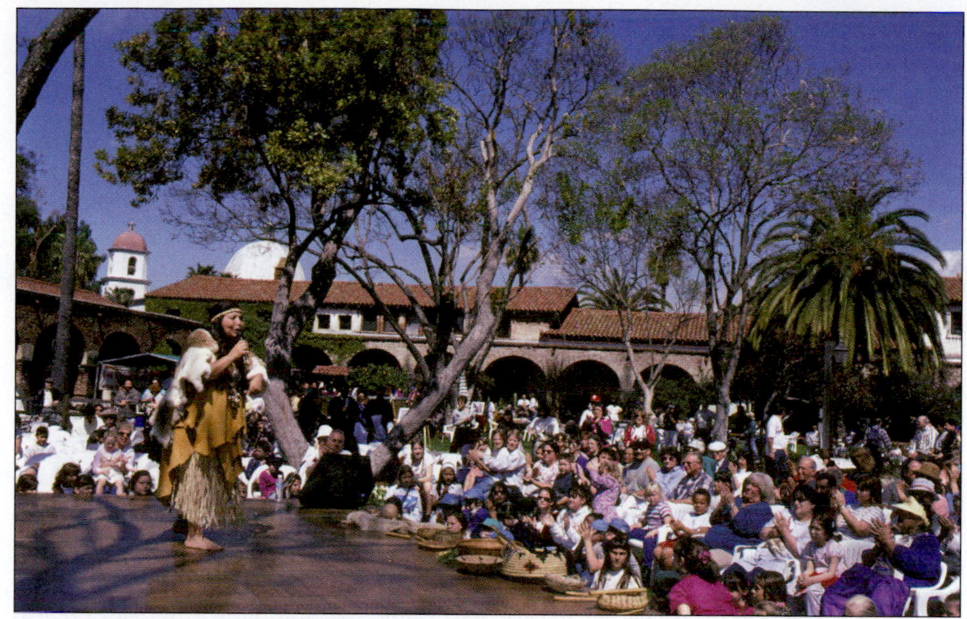

When a speaker is dynamic and enthusiastic, uses effective vocal and physical delivery, and exudes confidence, audience members are likely to listen with more attention.

Vocal Delivery

A speech can be enlivened by effective vocal and physical delivery. Audience members tend to listen with more attention when a speaker is dynamic and enthusiastic.

Vocal Variety A question often asked by novice public speakers is: How fast or slow should I speak? There is no accurate rate, but speaking with vocal variety, speaking in a number of different speeds to match the mood of the ideas you are presenting, is desirable.

"The average speech rate in the mid-Atlantic states is about 120 to 140 words per minute. It is faster in some places such as New York City, and slower in other locales."[7] In general, in preparing a manuscript the normal rate would be the equivalent of one-half to two-thirds of a double-spaced page per minute. Speaking slower than that can lead to listener boredom.

Someone who speaks in a *monotone*—a flat verbal sound resulting from a constant pitch, volume, and rate—will often cause the audience to tune out. On the other hand, speaking so rapidly that the listener can't understand may result in confusion.

Therefore, the goal should be to speak in a manner that will allow you to be easily understood, hold the audience's attention, and allow for clarity of ideas. A factor that can affect how rapidly you speak is your pronunciation. If you can't be understood, no matter how fast or slowly you speak, you will not achieve your speaking goal.

Pronunciation "There are many different and acceptable ways of pronouncing American English, because our language is spoken differently in various parts of the United States."[8] Standard American English—the language generally recognized by linguists as representative of the general population of the United States—spoken in most of the Midwest and West Coast—tends to be the most acceptable of the regional dialects. Though all regional dialogues are acceptable as long as the audience can understand what is being said. Speech becomes substandard if pronunciations cause misunderstandings and set a negative tone for the presentation.[9]

Because you will be evaluated on the basis not only of what you say but also on how you say it, you should be aware of some common pronunciation problems, their causes, and how to correct the sounds:[10]

- *Sloppy or incorrect articulation.* If you say "air" for *error* and "dint" for *didn't*, you are mispronouncing because of lazy use of the articulators (tongue, jaw, teeth). Be conscious of dropping the *g* sound at the end of words ending in *-ing*, such as *going*, *doing*, and *watching*. Also be aware of slurring words together. "Alls-ya-godado" is not an understandable substitute for *all you have to do*.
- *Unaware of correct pronunciation.* Listening and reading vocabularies are far greater than speaking vocabularies. In preparing a speech, look up in a dictionary or a pronunciation guide any word for which the pronunciation is unfamiliar.
- *Vowel distortion.* Some of us have grown up in environments in which words are mispronounced because of vowel substitutions. *Milk* may have been pronounced as "melk," *secretary* may have been "sekatury," and *many* may have been "minny." Being aware of the distortions allows you to begin monitoring your own pronunciations and correcting them, if you so desire, or be inspired to go to a speech therapist for assistance.
- *Pronunciation outside the normal pattern.* Assuming that Standard American English is the norm, certain pronunciations usually are not considered acceptable in the marketplace of business, education, and the professions. *Asked* is not "ax" and *picture* and *pitcher* are not the same word.
- *Those who speak American English as a second language.* Individuals who speak American English as a second language will often carry with them pronunciations from their native language. All languages do not have the same sounds. For example, Japanese does not have an *l* sound (e.g., the *l* in *look*). To the Japanese ear, the word *plastic* may sound like "prastic," so that's the way it will be pronounced. This type of "mispronunciation" is not intentional; rather, it is simply a reaction to the difference in sounds.

Physical Elements

The physical elements of public communication include gestures and eye contact. The way you use visual aids is another physical element.

Gestures **Gestures** incorporate the use of hands, body movements, and facial expressions. Hand gestures can add the extra emphasis to a point in a speech. A good speaker keeps his speech flowing smoothly with both his voice and his hands. When you're passionate about a subject, hand gestures can nonverbally convey the purpose and intent behind the words.[11] Your gestures and movement should be natural and spontaneous, prompted by your ideas and feelings.[12] The more emotional you are, the more dynamic will be your gestures.

Knowing the importance of movement, students in speech classes sometimes ask their instructors to teach them how to gesture. Unfortunately, it is impossible to do so, because gesturing is the result of the speaker's degree of involvement, excitement, dynamism, and personality. Each person uses his or her own characteristic gesture pattern while communicating. Some people use a great number of gestures, whereas others use just a few.

Gestures should be natural. That is why you should not worry about what to do with your hands. Forget them, and they will take care of themselves. Your hands will be active when your body calls for movement. If you are orally dynamic, your body will be too. If you are orally boring, so will be your body. Your gestures, while speaking before an audience, should parallel the gestures you use when speaking in a conversation. You don't ask yourself when speaking to a friend, "What should I do with my hands?" Your hands just do their own thing, move naturally. The more excited you get, probably the more you use your hands. The less dynamic, the less you will exhibit physical, facial, and body movements. Beware to avoid gripping the lectern so tightly that you cannot let go, and do not have your hands jammed inside your pockets and be unable to get them out.

Eye Contact Establishing eye contact—looking into the eyes of your audience as you speak—is another key to effective speaking. Members of an audience will tend to feel involved in the presentation if you look at them. Maintaining eye contact also helps you receive feedback so you can adjust your presentation accordingly. To use **eye contact** effectively, look directly at listeners, not over their heads. Shift your focus so that you are not maintaining contact with just one section of the audience, and be especially careful not to overlook those in the front or back rows.

Using a Script or Outline

Using a script (manuscript or outline) can be difficult because you must look at the audience at the same time that you are trying to present your material with animation and naturalness. You will have to work out some system for following the script in an unobtrusive way so that you also can look at the audience without losing your place. Be careful not to move or flip manuscript pages unnecessarily; this draws attention away from you and toward the manuscript.

Some speakers run the index finger of their hand down the side of the script so that they are continuously pointing to the start of the next printed line or major point they will be presenting. Then when they look up, they can find their place when they return to the script.

One method for establishing eye contact with an audience while following a manuscript in an unobtrusive way is *eye span*. You can train your eyes to glance down, pick out a meaningful phrase or a sentence, and deliver it to the audience. As you reach the end of the phrase, but before you have finished saying it, glance down and grasp the next idea to be spoken.

Avoid a flat-sounding reading style. Instead, read and speak according to the meaning by stressing important words and ideas, and vary your tone of voice so that you are speaking naturally. It is helpful to underline key words and to mark off phrases. Slash marks (*virgules*) can be used to indicate a pause or a stop. Usually, a / is used for a short pause, / / for a longer pause, and / / / for a full stop.

Underscores can be placed beneath a word or a phrase to indicate that it should be stressed. Usually a single underscore indicates a minor stress, and a double signifies a stronger stress; a triple underscore represents the point at which you should increase the volume and the power of your vocal delivery. For example, the word *now* is to be stressed in the sentence: Do it <u>now</u>. Notice that the entire meaning of the sentence changes if the underscoring becomes: Do <u>it</u> now.

Communicating Socially

Start and Finish Your Talk without Notes

Few people can actually memorize an entire speech. Most of us have to rely on some sort of notes or outline. But you should make every attempt to anchor your opening and closing statements firmly in your mind so that you can look directly at your audience while delivering those lines.

Source: American speaker. (2008). Briefings Publishing Groups.

REFLECT ON THIS: Give three reasons why it is a good idea to memorize the opening and closing remarks of a speech.

How about: Do// it now! If you think underscoring and insertion of virgules will help you to present the material in a meaningful way, use them.

It also helps to arrange the script in a manner that keeps you from getting lost. Double- or triple-space the information, number the pages, do not divide sentences by starting them on one page and finishing them on another. Do not write on the backs of the pages. Use a large font size (e.g., 14) so you can easily read the notes.

If you are using standardized sheets of paper, place them on a lectern or place them on a table so that your hands are free. If you plan to move away from the lectern, put that segment of material on a notecard, a clipboard, or an iPad, so you can take it with you.

If you are going to use notecards, write on only one side so you don't get lost, and number each card. It is best to hold the note cards or clipboard with one hand rather than two as it leaves the vacant hand free for gesturing.

Public Speaking Anxiety/ Stage Fright

A major concern brought up in introductory communication courses is: *I get stage fright when I give a speech.*[13] *What can I do about it?* It may be a surprise to you, but professional public speakers and even your communication professor often feel nervous before a speech or before a class. The difference between them and less experienced speakers is that the professionals know that the anxiety will be present, have some techniques for coping with the natural bodily reactions, and don't let the natural reactions of the body control them.

"Public speaking anxiety[14] is also known as *glassophobia* (taken from the Greek *glosa*, meaning tongue, and *phobos*, meaning fear or dread)."[15] Very few speakers escape the dreaded "butterflies." "It is a serious problem for a large number of people and has been found to affect career development as well as academic performance."[16] Research suggests that "the fear of public speaking is the No. 1 rated fear in America."[17]

The number-one fear of Americans is speaking in public.

Do You Have Public Speaking Anxiety?

This instrument is composed of six statements concerning feelings about speaking in public. Indicate the degree to which each statement applies to you by marking whether you (1) strongly agree, (2) agree, (3) are undecided, (4) disagree, or (5) strongly disagree. Work quickly. Record your first impression.

____ a. I have no fear of giving a speech.

____ b. Certain parts of my body feel very tense and rigid while I am giving a speech.

____ c. I feel relaxed while giving a speech.

____ d. My thoughts become confused and jumbled when I am giving a speech.

____ e. I face the prospect of giving a speech with confidence.

____ f. While giving a speech, I get so nervous I forget facts that I really know.

Scoring: Add 18 to your scores from items a, c, and e, and then subtract your score from the total of items b, d, and f. This is your final score.

Interpretation: Scores can range from a low of 6 to a high of 30. If your score is 18 or above, you are like the overwhelming majority of Euro Americans in that you display public speaking apprehension.

Interested in ascertaining your speaking anxiety level? If so, complete the *Do You Have Public Speaking Anxiety?*

Public speaking anxiety has two components: the physiological and the emotional. The physiological centers on a person perceiving that he or she is threatened. The body goes into fight or flight mode. The body gets ready, as our early ancestors did when confronted by wild animals, to flee from getting devoured, or to take a stand and defend ourselves. Often, the result is accelerated heart rate, an increase in blood pressure and irregular breathing patterns. This causes perspiration, uncontrollable shaking, shivers, flushing of the face, dry mouth, fidgeting, stammering or stuttering.[18] Sound familiar?

The emotional aspect of public speaking anxiety is the perceived fear of making a fool of yourself and being humiliated before others, which sabotages the ego and destroys your self confidence.

The good news is that public speaking anxiety is manageable and can be overcome through desire and effective training.

Conquering Public Speaking Anxiety

Here are some principles that might help you both understand public speaking anxiety and work toward conquering it:

- *Speaking in public is not inherently stressful.* "Most of us believe parts of life are inherently stressful. In fact, most of us have been taught to believe that life as a whole is very stressful! To deal with any type of stress effectively, you first must understand that life itself, including public speaking, is *not* inherently stressful. Thousands of human beings have learned to speak in front of groups with little or no stress at all."[19] "If they can conquer the fear of public speaking, so can you!"[20]
- *You don't have to be brilliant, witty or perfect to succeed.* "You can make mistakes, get tongue-tied, or forget whole segments of your talk."[21] "The essence of public speaking is: give your audience something of value."[22] If you have a clear statement of central idea and have developed it effectively, you will succeed.

- *When you speak in public, nothing that bad can happen!* "One thing that adds to the fear of public speaking is the dread people have that something awful, terrible, or publicly humiliating will happen to them."[23] The odds of this happening are remote. In all the years your authors have been teaching public speaking, no student or client has ever died. A few speakers have forgotten what they intended to say, or didn't say exactly what they had intended, but no one has been humiliated because of it unless a speaker imposed the humiliation on himself or herself. No one is perfect. Unless you are totally unprepared, all you can do is the best you can do, and that is not a crime.
- *You don't have to control the behavior of your audience.* "There are certain things you do need to control—your own thoughts, your preparation, arrangements for audiovisual aids, how the room is laid out—but one thing you don't have to control is your audience. They will do whatever they do."[24] This does not mean that you should ignore the audience. Audience analysis and adaptation are important, but thinking you need to change or control other people is a hidden cause of stress in many areas of life.
- *Your audience truly wants you to succeed.* "Most of your listeners are scared of public speaking. They know the risk of embarrassment, humiliation, and failure you take every time you present yourself in public. They feel for you. They will admire your courage."[25] "This means that most audiences are truly forgiving. While a slip of the tongue or a mistake of any kind might seem like a big deal to you, it's not very meaningful or important to your audience. Their judgments and appraisals will usually be much more lenient than yours. It's useful to remind yourself of this point, especially when you think you've performed poorly."[26]

These suggestions for dealing with stress in public speaking may also be helpful:

- *Do not avoid the experience of giving a presentation.* The more you speak, the more comfortable you will get. Although your nervousness may not go away completely, it should let up as you get more experience.
- *Accept that you will experience some nervousness.* All speakers encounter at least a moment of anxiousness as they begin because they are, essentially, facing the unknown.
- *Do not take drugs or alcohol because you think they will relax you.* Although there has been some recent research that shows that in extreme cases such prescription drugs as Paxil or generic drugs such as Bravina[27] can help in containing physically caused anxieties, drugs and alcohol tend to dull your reflexes and increase your chances of forgetting and making a fool of yourself. (Just picture how a person who is drunk or on drugs tends to act.)
- *Use relaxation techniques.* Before beginning a presentation, some speakers find it helpful to take several deep breaths and expel all the air from their lungs. Others like to shake their hands at the wrists to "get out the nervousness." Some people favor grabbing the seat of their chair with both hands, pushing down, holding the position for about five seconds, and repeating this movement about five times. This tightens and then loosens the muscles, which causes a decrease in physical tension.[28]
- *Recognize the anxiety.* Another approach is to think of the experience of getting up before the audience and to feel the anxiety. Let it stay in your mind, imagining that you are going through the experience. Let yourself be as nervous as you can;

COMMUNICATING

in Careers

Public Speaking and Distracting Mannerism Tips

For most people, public speaking is intimidating. The thought of giving a speech or presentation in front of an audience, whether it is comprised of friends or strangers, may be enough to make your knees shake. However, with a little confidence and practice, you can improve your public speaking abilities and become a more effective communicator. There are ways to improve public speaking and avoid distracting mannerisms.

1. Speak Slowly and Clearly
   - When speaking to your audience, avoid running through the speech or presentation material too rapidly. Instead, speak slowly so that the audience has time to comprehend your words. Be sure to enunciate so that your speech is crisp and clear. Remember that nothing is more frustrating to an audience than having to sit through a speech or presentation that is incomprehensible. Taking the time to speak slowly and clearly can mean the difference between a positive or negative reaction to your speech.
2. Avoid Distracting Mannerisms
   - Novice public speakers are often unaware of certain mannerisms that can be distracting to the audience. Behaviors such as shuffling papers, constantly clearing your throat, or using the words "um" or "like" too frequently can shift the audience's focus away from your words. Be conscious of mannerisms or tics you may be prone to when you are nervous or anxious. One way to do this is to have someone listen to you when you practice your speech. This person can then provide feedback as to what you might subconsciously do that is distracting. Alternatively, you can record yourself speaking and listen to the playback. Once you determine whether or not you have any mannerisms or tics you need to manage, you can practice controlling them.
3. Engage the Audience
   - Good public speakers make eye contact with their audience and engage them with the subject matter. Simply reading your speech from a paper or looking down at the floor is dreary and uninspiring. Speaking without modulating your voice can also bore your listeners. Look at your audience and connect with them. When appropriate, use vocal inflections and pauses at certain points in your speech for emphasis. By utilizing these simple techniques, you will keep your audience interested in your subject matter.

Source: "Public Speaking and Distracting Mannerism Tips" by Arielle Bhumitra, JD., from www.ehow.com. Copyright © 2008 by Marina Bhumitra. Reprinted with permission.

psychologically push it as far as you can. Some people report that by imagining the upcoming experience in its worst way, the actual experience becomes much easier.[29]

- *Prepare.* Highly anxious speakers are less likely to spend time preparing and rehearsing their speech.[30] Ironically, this avoidance of getting ready is exactly the opposite of what most research shows aids a person to overcome fear of speaking. It is well documented that preparation and rehearsal develop security, one of your basic needs and a key to effective speech performance.[31]
- *Practice visualization.* We all tend to perform the way we expect to perform, so expectancy restructuring is based on the idea that if you expect to do well, then you will do well. To overcome the fear, prepare a well-structured and well-documented speech so that you have confidence in your material. Then go through the process of *visualization*—seeing yourself in the actual setting in

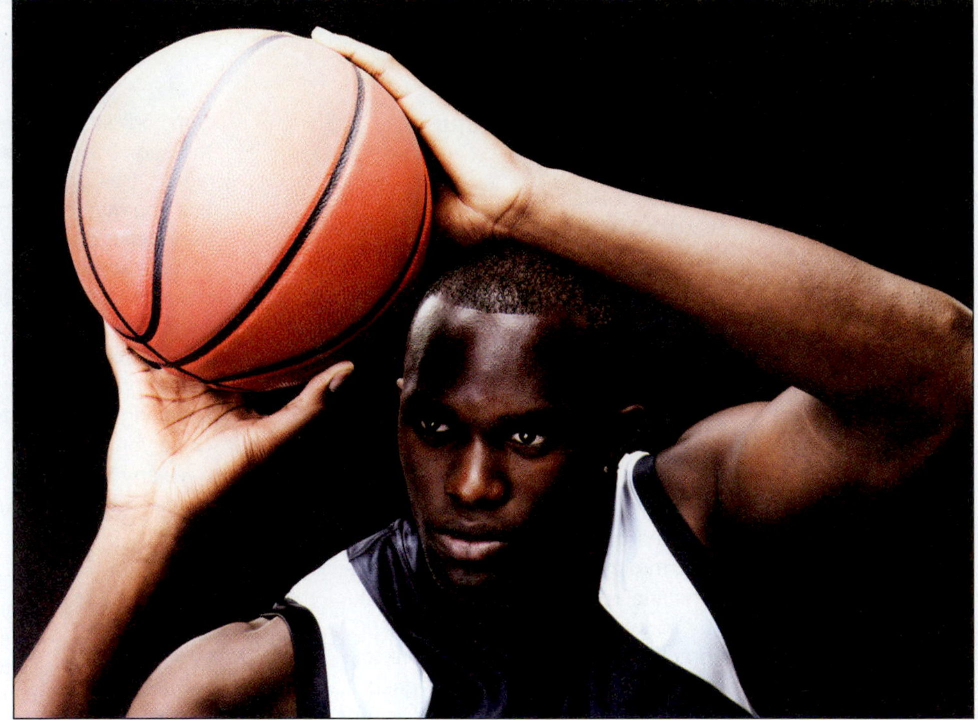

Public speakers, much like athletes, can use positive visualization to raise their level of success.

which you are going to give the speech and making a successful presentation. Picture yourself getting out of your chair, walking to the front of the room, arranging your materials on the lectern, looking at the audience, and giving the speech. As you see yourself presenting the material, look at various people. They are nodding their heads in agreement; they are interested and are listening attentively. Finally, imagine yourself ending the speech, the audience applauding, and returning to your chair, feeling good about yourself. The more you visualize this positive experience, the more your expectation level of success should increase. You will be expecting success, not failure.

- *Think about something else just before your speech*. Distraction can help lower stress.[32] Instead of talking to a classmate about your fears about the upcoming speech, a conversation about last night's ball game may be more helpful.

After following the suggestions just presented, individuals who are still traumatized by the prospect of giving a speech may need mental health support. Some hospitals and health centers have phobia clinics that could be of assistance.[33]

Presenting Visuals in a Speech

Visuals can assist you in making the presentation listenable and in maintaining attention. Keeping in mind that visuals are aids for making your presentation comprehensible and engaging, you can use these guidelines to employ visuals effectively:

- Use the visual aid as an aid, not as a replacement for your oral presentation (i.e., don't just display a projection or chart and expect the audience to read and understand the information). You are the presenter, not the aid.

- Display the visual only at the point when you are speaking about that particular information. Don't expose it before you need it or after you've referred to it.
- Don't block the audience's view by standing between the visual and your listeners.
- Speak to your listeners, not to your visual.
- Know the visual well enough that you don't have to study it while you are speaking.
- Point to the particular place on the aid that you are discussing as you discuss it. (For example, if you are using a map, use a laser pointer to illustrate exactly what country you are discussing.)
- If you use handouts, be sure to integrate them fully into your presentation by passing them out at the point when you are going to refer to the material so that your listeners will not be distracted by reading the material rather than listening to you.

Using YouTube and Computer Downloads

If you are going to use YouTube or any other computer download in your speech consider these presentational suggestions:

- Give a transition from your speech that cues the audience regarding what they are about to see and why it is relevant to your message.
- You may want to turn the sound down before the video starts then adjust to the appropriate volume as it starts. This avoids a blast of sound at the start of the material.
- Avoid trying to talk over the video's sound. Turn the sound off while you talk or wait until the video ends before you continue talking.

Using Presentation Graphics

In Chapter 12 a discussion was presented of how to select and prepare presentation graphics, such as PowerPoint, Prezi, Visual Understanding Environment (VUE), and Apple's Keynote. Now, let's examine some suggestions for their use:

- *Practice thoroughly.* Because of differences in equipment, it is best to practice with the actual equipment that you will use during the presentation. Work with the computer and/or the projector so that you can use the equipment smoothly.
- *Learn how to use your personal digital assistant, the wireless mouse, or remote control so that you can get to the right slide at the precise time in the sequence of your talk when it should appear.* While practicing, remember that listening to a speaker read word for word from a slide that is visible to all is both uncreative and boring.
- *Be patient.* If something goes wrong—and with the use of electronic equipment, it well may—don't panic. Theories differ about whether to try to cover up the error. Some people apologize or make a joke about the technical problem. Others just fix the problem and go on. If the cause of your error is your apparent lack of preparation or familiarity with the equipment, the audience will probably be less forgiving than if the cause is a mechanical glitch or a slip of the finger.
- *Maintain control of the presentation.* The speaker, not the technology, must maintain control. For example, have a neutral colored blank page in your PowerPoint

inserted at a place where you are going to speak without a visual so that the audience isn't looking at the previously used image or distracted by the frame that will be used next.

- *Be prepared for the worst.* Have a contingency plan available in case of equipment failure or a power outage. Ask yourself what you will do if at the start or during the speech, the equipment malfunctions. Many speakers print copies of the necessary graphics for distribution as a hedge against negative possibilities, others present the material as if no visual had been intended. In general, avoid statements such as, "If I had the slide to show, it would illustrate..." or "This point would be clearer if I had the visuals." Statements such as these add nothing to the message development.
- When you get to the room or auditorium where you will make your presentation, check out the facilities.
    (a) If you did not bring your own electronic equipment, make sure any equipment that has been ordered is present and working. Be sure the right software has been loaded.
    (b) Pull down the projection screen.
    (c) Check the lighting to determine the appropriate level for the audience's viewing.
    (d) Check the power connections to be sure that they are operational.
    (e) Check the focus. Walk around the room to make sure that the visuals are readable from all seats in the room.
- *Don't talk to the screen.* Avoid turning (or even occasionally glancing) back at the screen. The projection is there to support, not replace, what you're saying. Maintain your eye contact and interaction with your listeners so they focus on you and your message, not your slides.

Unfortunately, examples abound of speakers who failed to use presentation tools effectively. Consider, for example, Alex's biology instructor. She prepared a PowerPoint presentation for every class meeting in the course, an activity that took many hours of work on her part. Sound like a good idea? Not the way she did it! The slides were a dark background with white lettering, and the projector was so weak that the room had to be totally dark the entire presentation time. The students found it hard to stay awake. And the controls were located at the back of the room, so she stood behind the class. As a result, they couldn't see her, nor could she read feedback on the students' faces. Instead of using bullets, phrases, and outlines, the instructor wrote a paragraph on each slide, which she read aloud. The students felt that if she had intended to read to them, she should have just put the information on a handout, let them read the material themselves, and skipped the class session. The biology instructor's intentions were good, but her lecturing with the overused and poorly developed PowerPoint program was a boring, nonadaptive disaster. Don't be like Alex's biology teacher when you prepare and use an electronic program for your speeches.

Rehearsing the Speech

If possible, start to prepare far enough in advance so that you have sufficient material, the speech is well structured and well organized, and you have a chance to practice it. Some speakers try to convince themselves that they will do better if they just get up and talk, with little or no thought about what they will say. This is a fool's contention. It is usually the excuse of a procrastinator or a person who is not properly aware of his or her responsibility to the audience and self. Yes, some speakers can get up and "wing it," but the normal mortal usually cannot. Rehearsal is a key to effective speech performance.[34] So prepare and practice!

There is no one best way to rehearse. For some people, sitting at a desk and going over the material by mumbling through the outline or notes is the starting point. This will alert you to ideas that do not seem to make sense, words you cannot pronounce, places where you go blank because you need more notes, and areas that need more or fewer examples. Make the changes, and continue to review your notes orally until you are satisfied with the material. You might ask someone to listen to the speech. The person can then give you feedback on your presentation. If you're on a campus or in an organization that has a communication lab or media center, take advantage of that facility and schedule a run-through before a video camera. If the center has a speech tutor/coach who can review your recorded presentation to help you polish the presentation take advantage of the service.

It is well documented that preparation and rehearsal are keys to effective speech performance.

Some speakers take advantage of the Internet when rehearsing speeches. You can record your speech on video, for example, then upload it to YouTube to see what you and others think. You can run your ideas past your friends via e-mail, put your arguments out on your blog to see reactions, or upload your practice speech video to Facebook.com and ask for feedback from friends before your final presentation. Remember, however, if you make the speech public, and something goes wrong, you are opening yourself to be the next YouTube viral joke.

For many speakers, the most important part of rehearsing is to run a positive movie in your head of your speaking experience.[35] "You may not know this, but the brain and body can't tell the difference between something you vividly imagine and reality. When you learn something new, a pathway is created in your brain between neurons. This pathway is your brain's way of remembering. Because the brain can't tell the difference between real and vividly imagined events, even mental practice can help establish new patterns."[36] "So, formulate an indelible stamp on your mind of a mental picture of yourself as succeeding. Hold this picture. Never let it fade."[37] Mohammad Ali, former heavyweight boxing champion, used what he called *future history* in preparing for his fights. "He said he always rehearsed the fight in his head, again and again before he even stepped foot in the ring."[38] His success rate was 17 wins out of 19 fights. He credits his future history practice for his accomplishments. You too can take on and whip the world of public speaking, by using the technique of imaging as part of your rehearsal process.

Stop practicing when you are comfortable with your material and have worked out the problems related to using notes and supplementary aids. You are striving to become as comfortable as you can in what is a stressful situation for almost all of us.

Some people like to go through a visualization practice just before they go to sleep. If you decide to do this, as you lie in bed, see yourself successfully going through your speaking experience, from getting out of your seat, to hearing the applause at the end of the presentation.

Dealing with Difficulties During a Speech

As you proceed through your speech, you can do several things to help make this a positive experience for both you and the audience:

- *Try to be relaxed as you speak.* A psychological theory conceptualizes that how you stand affects your ability to avoid your body's tightening.[39] The tightening often results in shallow breathing, dry mouth, and shaking hands and legs. Using the *triangle stance* can help you stop your body from stiffening. In the triangle stance you place foot A at a slight angle and foot B at about a 45-degree angle, as if it were coming out of the arch of foot A. Keep your feet about six inches apart. Shuffle your feet slightly until you feel comfortable and balanced. Place your weight on foot A. You will feel leg and foot B relax. You may also find that it helps if you slightly extend the hip on the foot-A side of your body. As you proceed through a speech, you can alter your stance by changing the positions of feet A and B, but always remember to put your body weight on the foot that is farther back. It may sound silly and simplistic, but it does work for many people!
- *Look at the people in the audience who are alert during the presentation.* You can find these people by watching for those who nod in agreement or smile at you as you speak. Typically, presenters feel good when they get positive reactions.
- *Take time to get yourself organized at the lectern.* Arrange your notes on the lectern so that page 1 is on the left and the rest are on the right. Halfway through page 2, slide (don't flip) the page over to cover page 1. Continue to do this so that you are not pausing at the end of each page to move it over. Sliding allows you to move pages without calling attention to the act; flipping pages can be distracting as it draws attention to the pages for no reason.
- *Accept that mistakes are going to happen.* Even professional speakers and media announcers fumble words. If you are well prepared, you are more likely to be able to adjust to problems.

The Role of Culture on Speech Presentation

"Culture has a powerful effect on communication. Whether the culture derives from our nationality, race, ethnicity, religion, work environment, peer group, or even gender, we can't ignore its effect on communication."[40]

As in all other parts of this text that deal with generalizations—in this case, cultural generalizations—do not assume that the statements fit every member of the particular group being described. The conclusions reached are based on research findings. You may find, as a member of the group being described, that you do not fit the generalization. The nature of most research is to find norms that describe, recognizing that not every member of the group is being described.

To this point in the chapter we have placed an emphasis on Euro American speakers, not separating out gender or other cultural factors. Because of the multicultural nature of this nation, you will probably be speaking before people of various cultures. In addition, you may be placed in situations where, because of your career or interests, you will speak to people from differing cultures in their home settings. To illustrate the differences, let's examine a few public speaking cultural variations.

Black American public speaking and preaching traditions encourage the speaker to be innovative, novel, and dynamic.

Because African Americans typically come from traditions where storytelling, preaching, gospels, spirituals, dancing, and speaking are all part of the public speaking environment, audiences often expect to be entertained, comforted, and inspired.[41] Listening to Jesse Jackson, or former rapper and Pentecostal minister Joseph Simmons (also known as Rev Run), or some of the other Black spokespersons, is often a unique situation for those not used to African American speechmaking and preaching. "The rhetorical situation demands that the rhetoric be innovative and novel, for unlike the traditional [Euro American] public speaking situation where the speaker talks without interruption to a usually passive audience, a formal Black speaking situation shows how the speaker, the message, and the audience are one."[42] Listeners often shout out in agreement or repeat the message of the speaker for emphasis. This is not being disrespectful; rather, it is showing support for the speaker and the involvement of the members of the audience in the proceedings. In presenting in such an environment, the speaker must learn to be flexible, not get distracted, and appreciate that the response is based on the listener being an active part of your presentation.

The message for those not familiar with African American listeners is that "the language and delivery components are necessary to capture an audience, for many Black audiences are notoriously unresponsive to small voiced, unimaginative and uncreative speakers."[43]

Do not be lulled into a false sense of security when speaking before a Chinese audience. Listeners will often nod their heads up and down as they listen, thus giving Euro Americans the idea that the listeners are agreeing. This is not necessarily so. Chinese people are polite, and nod their heads vertically only to indicate that they are receiving the message. Chinese seem to avoid free expression of personal views and feeling, so don't be concerned if they do not ask questions during the question-and-answer session, even when encouraged to do so.[44] The same is to be said for the Japanese, who will seldom ask questions in public forums. The concept of "saving face" is so ingrained that they will not put speakers on the spot for fear that the speaker will be embarrassed in the eyes of others for not knowing the answer.

"The traditional West African storyteller, called the *griot*, weaves a story with song and dance, and enlivens a tale with all sorts of sound effects."[45] Pops, clicks, and clapping sounds dramatize the presentation, and members of the audience respond like a chorus. If you are speaking before an audience made up of Western Africans, or those who emigrated to the United States from that area, don't be surprised to hear those sounds.

In Arab cultures, the poetic words of speakers are often accented with fiery harangues of sound.[46] This is also true of many Arab American speakers.[47]

Hispanic and other Latino males "favor an elegant, expressive, or intense [verbal and nonverbal] narrative form of public communication."[48] As you listen to speakers from these cultures, much of these patterns of oral and physical presentation will emerge.

Native American speakers, as well as some Asian and Asian American speakers, tend not use direct eye contact, as it is a form of disrespect.[49]

"Differences in feminine and masculine communication patterns also surface in public contexts. Historically, men have dominated the speaking arena. Thus, it's not surprising that the assertive, dominant, confident masculine style is the standard for public speaking."[50]

Women who are effective in public speaking often "manage a fine balance in which they are sufficiently feminine to be perceived as acting appropriately for women and sufficiently masculine to be perceived as acting appropriately."[51] Speakers such as Ann Richards (former Texas governor), Golda Meir (the first woman Prime Minister of Israel), and Margaret Thatcher (former Prime Minister of Great Britain), all fit that mold. Before becoming U.S. Secretary of State, Hillary Rodham Clinton had trouble finding the "right" style, as she sometimes was declared too masculine or at times too feminine in her presentational style.[52]

Sarah Palin, 2008 Republican vice presidential candidate, polarized audiences with her speaking style. As one pundit stated, "I've seriously had enough of the winking, the giant-chinned-smirking, the too-sibilant forks-on-a-chalkboard 's' sounds, the 'nookyooler,' the 'you betchas,' and especially her Romper Room-like penchant for naming and labeling everyone in her audiences: 'Romper bomper stomper boo, tell me, tell me, tell me, do! I see Joe the Plumber, Roscoe the Racist, Zed the Gimp... .'"[53] At the same time, Palin's lack of polished public speaking abilities was what drew certain people to her because they identified with her down-to-earth and "she speaks like me" style.

Cultural differences have been found regarding anxiety as related to public speaking. Research in the United States indicates that public speaking apprehension is highest among Asian Americans and lowest among Jewish Americans.[54]

International research showed that speaking apprehension varied from a low of 31 percent in Israel to a high of 57 percent in Japan and 55 percent in Taiwan.[55] In Mexico, Germany, India, and Newfoundland, speech anxiety was more similar to the U.S. statistic.[56] There is gender difference reported in the United States, because men have typically learned tactics for concealing their apprehension because it is considered a feminine trait.[57] Internationally, the same pattern seems to be the case. For example, in Mexico, males are less likely than females to report public speaking apprehension.[58]

Research shows that "fifty percent of Japanese students would be classified as highly apprehensive about giving speeches."[59] "United States college students show less apprehension than Japanese college students."[60] This is likely the result of the cultural norms in Japan that do not value talkativeness; therefore, the Japanese tend not to be outspoken in contrast to Euro Americans who are encouraged to speak out for their rights.[61]

None of the culturally influenced styles is either correct or incorrect, just different. But knowing that there are different styles can alert you, as a speaker, to be aware that you may not get the same response from one audience as from another because of the difference in presentation and receiving styles. As a listener you can be more effective if you realize that the oral and physical style of the speaker may not parallel to your presentational style, but that should not influence your ability to comprehend the message.

In Conclusion

IN CONCLUSION

In presenting the speech, the vocal elements and the physical elements are important. Competent speakers are confident. Some people have anxiety associated with giving a speech. Techniques are available for lessening the fear. Major ways of coping with speech anxiety include being prepared, rehearsing, and visualizing being successful. Using a script or outline and visual aids requires certain knowledge about the need for presentational techniques. Rehearsing can be an important aspect of speech presentation. Anticipating potential problems that might arise during a speech may help you to deal with them if they occur. Some cultural differences will require that you adapt your speaking and listening style in order to be most effective speaking to representatives of a particular culture.

LEARN BY DOING

1. The class sits in a circle. The instructor throws a ball to someone in the circle and passes an envelope to that person. The person selects a statement from the envelope, takes a minute to prepare, and gives a one- to two-minute presentation on the topic. Before speaking, the first person tosses the ball to someone else, who will be the second speaker. While the first person is speaking, the second person selects a topic and prepares a speech. Each speaker tosses the ball to another speaker until all members of the class have spoken.
2. Some of the most commonly mispronounced words in Standard American speech are *across, acts, actually, all, ambulance, any, asked, because, catch, doing, familiar, fifth, genuine, get, going, horror, hundred, introduce, just, library, next, nuclear, particular, picture, prescription, probably, pumpkin, recognized, sandwich, secretary, Washington, with.* Look up each word in a dictionary or pronunciation guide. During a class session, you will be asked to pronounce these words and use them in sentences.
3. Videotape one of your classroom presentations. Watch the video. Pay attention to your gestures, facial expression, vocal variety, and rate of speed. Did you look comfortable and confident? If you were to give the speech again, what changes would you make in your physical and vocal actions?

KEY TERMS

gestures 416
eye contact 417
public speaking anxiety 419

Appendix

Informative Speech Topics

General Topics

Abuse of the elderly
Abusive relationships
Academic dishonesty ... an epidemic
Academic services on campus
Alcohol abuse on college campuses
Amazon.com
Baidu.com
Black holes
Blogspot.com www.blogspot.com
Bone marrow transplants
Botox
Cell phones—uses and abuses
Christianity, Judaism & Islam ... their common history
Cloning
College rankings—how they are determined
Color blindness
Computer innovations
Controlling relationships—the signs of
Cyber addiction
Date rape
Dyslexia
Earthquakes—their causes
Ebay.com
Emotional intelligence
Extreme sports—the risks and thrills
Facebook.com
First impressions, lasting impressions
Gay historical figures: (e.g., Alexander the Great, Czar Alexander I of Russia, Susan B. Anthony, Stephen Foster, John Meynard Keynes, Harvey Milk)
Gay athletes: Billie Jean King (tennis), John Amaechi (basketball), Billy Bean (baseball), Glenn Burke (baseball), John Curry (skating), Rudy Galindo (skating), Ramona Gatto (kickboxing), David Kopay (football), Greg Louganis (diving), Dave Pallone (baseball umpire)
Genetic modification of crops, animals
Golden spirals in nature
Google.com
Healthy eating
Herbs as medicine
History of ___________ (e.g., the railway locomotive, windshield wiper, the street light, basketball, fireworks)
History of your college
Left-handedness challenges
Life and contributions of ___________ (e.g., Maya Angelou, Julius Caesar, Winston Churchill, Elena Kagan)
Linkedin
Live.com
Making a living will
Money-making ideas
Money-saving ideas
Nanotechnology
NASCAR
Obesity epidemic
Origami in action (show how you can make things out of paper)
Procrastination
Psychological problems (e.g., dual-personalities, alcoholism, anorexia, bulimia)
REM cycle of sleep
Services for people with disabilities
Seven wonders of the world
snopes.com
Stem cells, as a scientific process
Tattoos, a short history of
3-D glasses, how they work
Time management
Twitter.com
Tzedakah, charity, fairness, justice
Video games, their history and evolution
Voodoo
Water (e.g., value of drinking enough, water safety when hiking, purification)
Women in the military
Wordpress.com
Youtube.com

Famous Persons or Their Contributions

Actor (e.g., Halle Berry, James Franco, Natalie Portman, Lucy Liu)
Architect (e.g., I. M. Pei, Frank Owen Gehry)
Artist (e.g., Salvador Dali, Claude Monet, Picasso)
Author (e.g., Amy Tan, Charles Dickens)
Classical musician (e.g., violinist Midori, cellist Yo Yo Ma, opera singer Anna Netrebko)
Technical innovators (e.g., Bill Gates, Steve Jobs)
Fashion designer (e.g., Vera Wang, Anna Sui)
Filmmaker (e.g., Steven Spielberg, Sofia Coppola)
Financial expert (e.g., Warren Buffett, Suze Orman)
Historical figure (e.g., Henry VIII, Joan of Arc, W.E.B. DuBois)
Media/Journalist (e.g., Edward R. Murrow, Bob Woodward)
Military leader (e.g., General Douglas MacArthur)
Performer (e.g., Usher Raymond, Taylor Swift, Queen Latifah, Adam Lambert, Lady Gaga)
International political leader (e.g., Nelson Mandela, Mahatma Gandhi, Golda Meir)
Scientist (e.g., Elizabeth H. Blackburn, Stephen Hawking, Albert Einstein)
Sports great (e.g., Lionel Messi, Michael Jordan, Hank Greenberg, Yao Ming, Johnny Estrada, Bob Feller, Harrison Dillard, Roger Federer, Michael Phelps)

Nature

A day in the life of a Beluga Whale
Cats and lions: How do they compare?
Endangered species preservation (e.g., okapi, elephant, tiger)
Is an owl really wise?
Natural phenomenon (e.g., earthquake, tidal waves)
The cortex: Its importance to you
The secret life of an eel
Why dolphins jump out of the water
Wolves in the living room: How the wolf evolved into the domestic dog

Persuasive Speech Topics

(The topic needs to be restated as a stand—for or against, good or bad—or a belief.)

__________ (fill in the name of a person) is a negative influence on civility in America.
Academic freedom
Airplane travelers should be required to undergo whole-body scanning
Alternative medicine . . . truth or quackery
Animal rights
Body piercings
Business ethics, an oxymoron
Cats can help people live longer
Civility is dead in the United States
Climate change . . . fact or fiction
Closed adoption . . . good or bad
Community volunteering (e.g., a local soup kitchen, school)
Computer password protection
Congressional filibuster regulations stop the democratic process
Creationism versus Evolution
Credit card responsibility
Credit scores
Death penalty
Donate blood at the upcoming campus event
Drugs can reverse the aging process
Drunk driving penalties
E-mail your congressperson or senator about __________
Euthanasia
Facebook privacy
Fat tax on food
Federal government should raise the retirement age
Foreign oil dependence
Free health insurance for all
Free speech on campus
Gambling dangers
George W. Bush: worst president in history
Green campus policies
Hate crimes
Hate speech
Health care
Healthier eating
Heroism in the 21st century
Home schooling
Human cloning . . . good or bad?
Identity theft prevention
Individual steps to take to protect the environment
Internet dating . . . good or bad?
Internet has replaced the newspaper
Judges should be elected
Junk foods should not be sold on campus
Kindness—pass it along today
Lying is necessary to maintain a good relationship
Marriage or civil unions should be federally legalized for all couples
Military family sacrifices
Military pay
Ocean drilling for oil
Obesity is a disease

Online courses are a good choice
Organ donations (e.g., sign your driver's license)
Physician-assisted suicide
Political hotspots (e.g., Pakistan, North Korea)
Polygamy
Racial profiling
Recycling
Religious right
Seat belts, mandatory or not?
Service animals and their importance to people with disabilities
Serving your country... a mandatory requirement
Sponsors of political ads should be identified
Stem cell research
Study abroad... a requirement for all college students
Steroid use
Students should not be taught cursive writing
Talk radio... shared ignorance
Tanning salons should be made illegal
Terrorism... justified?
Textbooks—alternative methods of selling and lending
Texting is a negative social experience
Texting while driving should be made illegal
Traffic photo law enforcement is unjust
Twitter: Its impact on political revolt
Unrest in the Middle East
Uniforms in public schools are needed
Vampires are/aren't real
Violent video games
Volunteering: What can you do about it?
War in Afghanistan or Iraq or Vietnam or Korea
Wild animals should not be used for entertainment purposes

Glossary

accent a nonmainstream pronunciation and intonation used by a person. It may represent a specific region of a country (e.g., southern dialect).

accenting relationship between verbal and nonverbal communication nonverbal behavior intended to accent parts of a verbal message, much as underlining or italicizing emphasizes written language (e.g., pounding on a desk while saying, "I want it done now!").

action chain a behavioral sequence between two or more participating organisms in which there are standard steps for reaching a goal (e.g., meeting and greeting customs).

action questions queries intended to get the audience involved in a speech and to make listeners think and respond.

ad lib speaking a speech in which a speaker has no time to organize ideas.

adaptors movements that accompany boredom, show internal feelings, or regulate a situation (e.g., glancing continually at your watch while waiting for a friend who is late).

adjourning the stage of group operation in which it goes out of existence.

aesthetics the study of communication of a message or mood through color or music.

affect display facial gestures that show emotions and feelings, such as sadness or happiness.

affirmation saying something that inspires positive beliefs and actions (e.g., "I can give a speech without being scared").

agenda the order of business for a meeting or discussion.

aggressive behavior a response to conflict that centers on domination and focuses on the communicator getting his or her own way at all costs.

amoral neither good nor bad.

analytical thinking a system of dissecting events and concepts into pieces that can be linked into chains of statements backed up by facts and/or examples.

analogy a comparison of an unfamiliar concept to a familiar one.

androgyny the possession of both masculine and feminine communication patterns.

anger an emotional response to stimuli; an emotional defense mechanism to relieve the stress of an overly stressful situation; the feeling of being upset with yourself or others (or both).

anxiety the perception of a real or perceived threat or danger that affects your perceptions and your intrapersonal or interpersonal performance; based on negative intrapersonal messages.

APA style a footnoting style developed by the American Psychological Association and commonly used for source identification in social science publications and presentations.

apologizing the act of a person saying he or she is sorry.

appraisal interview sometimes referred to as a performance review, the interviewer helps the interviewee realize the strengths and weaknesses of his or her performance.

appreciative listening takes place when a person engages in enjoyment of or sensory stimulation to a message, such as listening to humorous speakers, comedians, or music videos.

approval seeking behavior seeking out the approval of others, turning over a person's destiny to others because of the lack of ability to make decisions with approval of others.

arbitration a process for deciding disputes in which a third party, who is an expert in a particular field, decides a the conflict will be resolved.

artifactics the study of those things that adorn the body and send messages to others about us as well as our selection of these items (e.g., clothing, makeup, eyeglasses, and jewelry).

asking seeking out information by inquiring.

assertive communication a form of communication within conflict resolution that takes place when a person stands up for his or her rights without attacking others.

assignment of meaning the process of putting the stimulus into some predetermined category.

asynchronous conference participants contribute to an online conference database at different times.

attention the step in listening in which the receiver focuses on a specific stimulus selected from all the stimuli received at any given moment.

attitudes a person's predispositions.

audience analysis assessing the demographic, psychographic, and rhetorographic characteristics of your prospective listeners.

audio aids supplementary aids that allow the listener of a speech to hear what would normally have to be imagined (e.g., records, tape recordings, or duplications of sounds).

audiovisual aid supplementary aids that allow the listener of a speech to see and hear what would normally have to be imagined (e.g., films, videotapes).

autocratic leader a leader who dominates and directs a group according to his or her personal goals and objectives, regardless of how inconsistent these goals are with group members' goals.

avatars virtual conferencing models that allows users to represent themselves.

avoiding stage of relationships the stage in Knapp's Relationship Termination Model that is highlighted by the partners physically separating.

beauty premium an economic theory which indicates that handsome men and good looking women tend to earn more and get hired more easily than unattractive individuals.

behavior pattern recognition training in detecting signs that are outside the normal range of nonverbal behavior.

behavioral interview designed to allow employers to know what skills the applicant may have and how these skills would translate into performance on the job.

beliefs a person's convictions.

being oriented approach to life a striving for life goals that is not based on evaluation of a person's self-worth or self-value, exemplified by Native Americans, Hindus, Buddhists.

Bem Sex-Role Inventory a questionnaire developed that allows an individual to evaluate how he or she perceives himself or herself on a masculine/feminine scale.

Berko 1-3-6 Decision-Making Technique a format for using the nominal group technique that takes place after the specific decision to be made or problem to be solved is agreed on by the group and members are ready to work toward solution.

bipolar questions a form of closed interview question, requiring a yes or no response (e.g., "Would you like to work for this company?").

blended families families created by divorce and remarriage or death and remarriage.

blink rate the pattern by which individuals blink their eyes while communicating. Fast or slow blink rates can indicate nervousness.

body of a speech the segment of the speech that is developed through major points as well as any subpoints needed to discuss the speaker's central idea.

body synchrony the study of posture and the way a person walks and stands as a means of communication.

body language a generally used term to identify nonverbal communication.

bonding stage of relationships the fourth stage in the Knapp Relationship Escalation Model; it centers on a formal, sometimes legal, announcement of the relationship taking place, which includes the use of such terms as *marriage* and *civil union*, or the forming of a business partnership.

brain dominance the pattern by which an individual learns and listens, which reflects whether a person is linear, global, or combined linear and global.

brainstorming consists of generating possible solutions without evaluation of them at the time of their proposal.

bridging a technique used by a listener in which there is a relating of one part of a sender's message to another in order to insure clarity of a sent message.

bullicide cyberbulling which leads to suicide.

bullying verbally or physically attacking someone.

Bushisms words, phrases, pronunciations, and semantic or linguistic errors and gaffes that appeared in the speeches and communication of President George W. Bush.

business casual the relaxed clothing style worn in business and corporate environments.

case method of organizational speech structure a speech organizational mode, which is suitable for a single issue speech, in which the speaker discusses the central idea of the presentation without breaking it into subpoints.

causal method of issue arrangement a method of arrangement for the body of a speech in which the speaker shows how two or more events are connected in such a way that if one occurs, the other will necessarily follow.

categorical syllogism an argument that contains premise(s), which lead to a logical conclusion.

cellular phones/smartphones wireless digital assistants, which not only act as a means of electronically vocal interaction, but may contain cameras and e-mail devices.

centralized decision-making process a method of making decisions, common in Mexico and other Central and South American countries, that centers on the view of authority as being inherent within the individual, not his or her position.

channel the mode by which the communication is conveyed from source to source as it flows one on one or via electronic channels or physical contact.

character a speaker's reputation, honesty, and sensitivity, which engenders trust.

charisma a characteristic of speaker credibility, which is based on the speaker's ability to entice others by being appealing, concerned, enthusiastic, and sincere.

chronemics the study of time as a communication tool.

circular time phenomenon the use of time in which precise time is not of importance; integration of past and future into a peaceful sense of the present.

circumscribing stage of relationships the stage in Knapp's Relationship Termination Model that is highlighted by the diminishment of volume and quality of the intercouple communication.

clarifying and confirming technique a strategy that calls for the listener to ask for additional information or explanation in order to gauge the sender's intent.

clincher to a speech the section of a speech that gives the speaker a chance to reinforce the major ideas presented and then wrap up the presentation with a final message.

closed question interview questions that provide alternatives, narrowing the possibilities for response, and probe for opinions on opposite ends of a continuum.

clusters grouping of nonverbal factors such as gestures, posture, eye contact, clothing styles, and movement together in order to attempt to ascertain the meaning of the message being conveyed.

Code of Ethics for Speakers a credo approved by the National Communication Association, which states specific traits that define an ethical speaker in the European American culture.

coercion centers on a leader offering a selection of choices, all of them undesirable, to the membership, but making the group member or members select one of them for action or compliance.

coercive power influence based on possible negative outcomes that are used as weapons.

cognitive dissonance the imbalance between your values, attitudes, and beliefs.

cognitive language conveys information, generally through denotative words.

cognitive modification teaching a person how to modify his or her negative thinking.

cognitive processing how people process information in relationship to their values, attitudes, and beliefs by comprehending, organizing, and storing ideas.

collectivism individuals from collective societies, like those in Asia and South America, stress loyalty to the group, rather than to the individual.

comfort space bubble the personal space distance within which people feel comfortable.

committee a small group responsible for study, research, and recommendations about an issue whose actions are usually brought back to a larger group for action.

communication a conscious or unconscious, intentional or unintentional process in which feelings and ideas are expressed as verbal and/or nonverbal messages that are sent, received, and comprehended.

communication apprehension speech anxiety; the fear of participating in the communication act. Also identified as shyness, Social Anxiety Disorder, or Social Phobia.

communication ethics the principle that speakers decisions about what to say should be based on moral principles.

communication noise any internal or external interference in the communication process.

communication system a pattern by which people relate to and interact with each other.

comparison method of issue organization a method of arrangement for the body of a speech in which the speaker describes how the two types of entities are alike.

comparison–contrast method of issue arrangement a method of arrangement for the body of a speech in which the speaker shows similarities and differences of the entities being discussed.

comparative-advantage reasoning stating possible solutions and then demonstrating how the proposal is most workable, desirable, and practical.

complementing relationship of verbal and nonverbal communication the supporting of a verbal message with nonverbal actions.

compliance gaining the process of getting others to agree with or otherwise engage with you by using the skills of persuasion.

comprehension listening listening that attempts to recognize and retain the information of a message.

computer-based retrieval system an online search engine, such as Google.com, that allows researchers to compile a bibliography or information relevant to a specific topic.

computer-mediated communication (CMC) intrapersonal or interpersonal style interaction using a digital or computer device.

computerized graphics programs electronic techniques, such as PowerPoint which provides the opportunity to input visuals and audio into a speech.

conclusion of a speech the ending section of a speech; its purpose is to summarize what has been said and/or motivate the listeners to take a prescribed action.

conditional argument a form of deductive argument which sets up an if-then proposition.

conflict any situation in which you perceive that another person with whom you're interdependent is frustrating or might frustrate the satisfaction of some concern, need, want, or desire of yours.

conflict accommodation managing conflict by putting the needs of others ahead of your own, thereby giving in and not asserting your displeasure.

conflict-active societies cultures which accept that conflict is an important part of life and haggling and disagreement are expected.

conflict avoidance not confronting a conflict by sidestepping, postponing, or ignoring a problem, no matter how unpleasant.

conflict-avoidance societies cultures which believe that face-to-face confrontations are to be avoided.

conflict competition a form of conflict resolution, often referred to as *aggression,* whose purpose is to get another person to comply with or accept your point of view, without concern for the other person.

conflict compromise conflict resolution that attempts to satisfy the needs of both parties, but often results in trading some of what you want for some of what the other person wants.

conflict integration a form of conflict resolution where there is concern about both persons' needs. Unlike compromise, both parties realize that they can participate in a win-win resolution and are willing to collaborate.

conflict smoothing over a form of conflict accommodation in which a person seeks to preserve the image that everything is okay.

conflicting relationship between verbal and nonverbal communication a difference of intent between the verbal and nonverbal messages.

Confucian principle of I a theory, part of the Confucian philosophy, that requires that a person be affiliated and identify with a group of people over long periods of time.

congruency the relationship between current and past patterns of behavior, as well as the harmony between verbal and nonverbal communication.

connotative meanings implied or suggested meanings.

connotative words words with implied or suggested meanings.

consensus means "all"; thus, in a consensus decision, every member of the group must agree on a proposal before it can be put into action.

contact cultures those cultures characterized by strong tactile modes of communication (e.g., Latin Americans, Mediterraneans, French, Arabs).

context the physical and the cultural setting where the communication is taking place and the general psychological attitude of those assembled.

contrast method of issue arrangement a method of arrangement for the body of a speech in which the speaker tells the differences between two entities.

conversation an interpersonal interaction between at least two people.

cough meter signs an audience gives a speaker, such as coughing, throat clearing, physical restlessness, that signal that the speaker has lost the audience's attention.

coordination a technique used in speech outlining that identifies each comparable segment of an outline with a similar designator (e.g., I, A, a)

counseling interview an interview format used by mental health professionals, friends, and family members, that is designed to provide guidance and support to the interviewee.

credibility the listener's perception of the speaker's trustworthiness, competence, and dynamism that can lead the listener to accept or reject a message.

critical listening centers on the listener's comprehending and evaluating the message that has been received.

critical thinking establishing criteria and then matching the proposed solutions with the criteria.

criticism the act of judging.

cultural noise communication problems that result from preconceived, unyielding attitudes derived from a group or society about how members of that culture should act or believe.

cultural relativism worldview and standpoint that no culture is superior to any other one, and that any culture deserves to be described, understood, and judged on its own premises.

culture individuals who have a shared system of interpretation; identifiers are the region of a country, religious affiliation, political orientation, socioeconomic status, gender, sexual orientation, age, vocation, avocation, family background, marital status, and parental status.

cutaway a visual aid that allows the listener of a speech to see inside of an object.

cyber addiction a psychological compulsion in which individuals are so involved in Internet usage that they use it to the point of neglecting personal and work responsibilities.

cyber bullying harassment that takes place using an electronic medium.

cyber stalking following and harassing others online.

cybernetic process the process that describes that the human cortex functions much like a computer, receiving, storing, processing, and retrieving information.

Cybernetics the study of the nervous system and the role it plays in the internal control of communication in humans.

decentralized group communication networks all communication in this group communication network pattern flows with no set pattern or control by the leader or any group member.

decode the process of translating the received messages.

deductive argument an argument based on logical necessity that starts from a general statement and leads to a specific instance.

demographics speech listeners' characteristics based on their descriptions and backgrounds; includes such factors as age, gender, religion, ethnicity, education, occupation, and race.

denotative meanings direct, explicit meanings.

denotative words words with direct, explicit meanings of words.

DESC scripting a way of dealing with interpersonal conflicts that centers on the process of **D**escribing, **E**xpressing, **S**pecifying, and stating **C**onsequences

desirability a test of a solution to a problem that centers on whether the suggested solution will cause greater problems.

devil effect a negative evaluation of a person because of the way the person looks, regardless of his or her intelligence or job performance.

dialect a social or regional variation of a language.

differentiating stage of relationships the stage in Knapp's Relationship Termination Model in which one or both of the partners becomes aware of the need to assert independence.

difficult group members group members who create dissent, are self-centered, attack others rather than dealing with the issues, and won't stick to the agenda.

digital media assisted communication using electronic methods.

digital communication communication using electronic methods.

direct aggression an outward expression of dominating or humiliating communication.

direct questions explicit interview questions that require specific.

directions instructions for accomplishing a task, achieving an effect, or getting somewhere.

directive intervention an interview technique used by mental health professionals in which specific activities should be carried on outside the counseling session (e.g., writing a letter to or directly confronting a person who has abused the client).

disjunctive argument an either-or argument in which true alternatives must be established.

discriminative listening listening that attempts to distinguish auditory and visual stimuli.

discussion question the issue or problem with which a group, interview, or discussion will deal.

division a technique used in speech outlining in which each division is fleshed out by adding clarifiers, examples and/or illustrations.

doing oriented approach to life desire to live an achievement oriented life, exemplified by Euro Americans, and Asian Americans.

doublespeak a form of vagueness that is deceptive, evasive, or confusing with the intention of misleading or distorting reality.

dyad two people.

dysfunctional relational system a relationship that has established rules and processes of actions that are not satisfying to one or both of the participants.

e-bbreviations computer shorthand, also referred to as e-lingo.

e-commerce conducting business via the Internet.

Economic Model of Relationships a systematic way to evaluate relationships by applying the concept that people make judgments about interpersonal contacts by comparing relational rewards and costs.

egospeak the art of boosting our own ego by speaking only about what we want to talk about, and not caring at all what the other person is speaking about.

Elaboration Likelihood Model if the issue being discussed is one the listener is interested and involved in, he or she is likely to pay attention to a persuader's arguments.

electronically mediated communication (EMC) communication using electronic devices including cell phones, electronic mail, instant messages, blogs, and social networks.

e-lingo computer shorthand, also referred to as e-bbreviations.

e-mail electronic messages sent via the Internet.

emblems cultural-specific nonverbal acts that have a direct verbal translation or dictionary definition consisting of one or two words.

emotive language employs emotional connotative words to express the feelings, attitudes, and emotions of the speaker (e.g., riveting, gripping).

empathic assertion a statement or statements that recognize the other person's position but that state your own needs. It may follow a simple assertion or be the first step in the assertive process.

empathy the ability to understand another person's problem from the perspective of that person rather than from the listener's perspective.

employment interview an interview that provides a way of entering the job market; changing positions; getting promotions; achieving salary increases; gaining admission for universities, internships, or assistantships, and graduate and professional programs.

employment stress interview designed to determine how an interviewee might function under pressure.

encode the process of creating a message.

enthymeme a syllogism in which a premise is implied, not directly stated.

environmental noise outside interference that prevents the receiver from getting the message.

ethical communicators those who respect the integrity of ideas and concerns from the listeners.

ethical public speaker does not expose the audience to falsehoods or premeditatedly alter the truth or invent or fabricate statistics.

ethics the systematic study of what should be the grounds and principles for acceptable and unacceptable behavior.

ethnocentrism the belief that the views and standards of an individual's own in-group are superior to the views and standards of the out-group.

ethnographers researchers who study cultures.

Ethnographic Theory of Needs a theory developed by ethnographers that proposes that humans are born with four need drives (survival of the species, pleasure seeking, security, and territoriality), which explain why humans communicate and act as they do.

ethos speaker credibility.

Euro Americans people living in the United States who either emigrated or had ancestors who emigrated to the U.S. from the European continent.

evidence supporting material that includes testimony from experts, statistics, and specific instances.

Expectancy Violation Theory the exchange of information that is high in relational content will be perceived either positively or negatively depending on how much the two people like each other.

experimenting stage of relationships the second stage in the Knapp Relationship Escalation Model; it centers on determining whether there is interest in furthering the relationship.

expert a person who, through knowledge or skill in a specific field, gains respect for his or her opinions or expertise.

expert power a person's capacity to influence another person because of the knowledge and skills the person has or is presumed to have.

exposition information included in a speech that gives the necessary background information to listeners so that they can understand the material being presented.

extemporaneous speaking the speaker knows in advance that she or he will be giving a speech, can prepare by doing research and planning the speech.

extended families a cluster of relatives who may also include friends.

eye-accessing cues a neuro-linguistic psychological theory that eye movements aid in accessing inner speech since the eye movements stimulate different parts of the brain.

eye contact looking into the eyes of the audience as a presenter gives a speech.

eye gaze the length of time that people look into each other's eyes while communicating.

eye span a method for establishing eye contact with an audience while reading from a manuscript.

fabrication making up information or guessing at information and presenting it as if it were factual.

face a concept in certain cultures which concerns socially approved self-image and other-image.

Facebook an online social network community (facebook.com).

Facebook addiction chronic obsession with using Facebook.

facebooking a term meaning to connect with someone through Facebook.

FACS (Facial Action Coding System) a process used to collect data about how the face conveys messages.

facework the verbal and nonverbal strategies that are used to maintain, defend, or upgrade a person's own social self-image and attack or defend the social images of others.

facsics the study of how the face communicates.

factual statements comments based on observable phenomena or common acceptance.

fair fighting a pattern of conflict resolution in which the participants work toward an amicable solution to the problem while realizing that the relationship is also important.

false ignoring the decision made in relational conflict to stop talking about a topic of disagreement or pretend nothing is wrong.

family an assemblage of people who have legally been declared a group or who have defined themselves as such.

feedback a verbal and/or a nonverbal reaction or response to the message.

feedback cues the process of asking questions, nodding or head-shaking, smiling or frowning and verbalizations to indicate the receiver is listening and/or comprehending the sender's message.

First Amendment speech the protected right of people in the United States to speak without restrictions—to be free to say what they want within the guidelines of the first amendment of the U. S. Constitution as interpreted by the Supreme Court.

first brain/second brain theory the first brain to develop is the emotional brain (the right lobe), and therefore it triggers first, causing instinctive action; then the second brain, the logical brain, is triggered.

flat world platform a convergence of the personal computer, with fiber-optic cable, with workflow software that enables individuals all over the world to collaborate.

fMRI a functional magnetic resonance imaging machine which scans the brain for functions and reactions to various stimuli.

focus groups a group designed to test reactions to a particular product, process, or service offered by an organization.

follow-up assertion a statement or statements used when the simple or empathic assertion is not successful in getting the desired action. It takes the form of a restatement of the simple or empathic assertion and then a statement of your own position.

forecast a statement that alerts the audience to ideas that are coming.

formal outlining format a rule in speech outlining which dictates that an outline follow a specific format such as topics or sentences.

formal time the division of time into specific referents, such as centuries, years, months, days, hours, and minutes.

forum a question-and-answer session that often follows a symposium, during which the participants field questions from each other as well as from any audience member.

frame of reference a perceptual screen used by receivers to filter message ideas based on their background and culture.

free rein leader/ laissez-faire leader a leader who is non-directive and empowers group members to do their own thing.

freedom of speech the protected right to speak without restrictions—to be free to say what a person wants.

functional relational system a system that is operating to the general satisfaction of the participants.

funnel schedule an interview format in which the questions are sequenced to take the interview from more general to more specific information.

gender one's psychological, social, and interactive characteristics, (man/woman), in contrast to sex, which is one's biological or physical self (male/female).

generalization conclusion a number of specific instances are examined and a prediction of probability is made based on those instances.

gestics the study of the movements of the body, such as gestures, that can give clues about a person's status, mood, cultural affiliations, and self-perception.

gestures the speaker's use of hands, body movements, and facial expressions while speaking; can either substitute for, complement, conflict with, and/or accent verbal communication.

global listeners/learners individuals who tend to prefer a generalized rather than specific description.

GoToMeeting a Web conferencing tool that allows participants to meet online in real time rather than in a conference room.

goal of the speech the purpose of a speech (e.g., to inform or to persuade), which is expressed in terms of its expected outcome.

grammar is the system of rules for combining the components of any language.

green-flag words emotional trigger words that create positive stimulations that trigger emotional responses.

griot the traditional West African storyteller who weaves a story with song and dance.

group a system characterized by interconnectedness of the individuals who make up a collection of individuals, who have a goal and a purpose.

group cohesion the interconnectedness of the members of a group.

group conforming the stage of group operation when the members of the group have worked through the storming stage.

group forming the first phase of group operation with the purpose of group members getting to know each other.

group maintenance focuses on the social dimension of the group in which the central communicative function is to gain and maintain the cohesiveness of the group.

group norm standards the general thinking of a particular group that is used as a guide for developing a speaker's arguments.

group norming the second phase of group operation with the purpose of developing the rules by which the group will operate.

group norms the rules by which the group will operate. These norms can be explicit (written and agreed on, as in a constitution) or implicit (understood but not formalized).

group performing the action stage of group process in which the members start to work toward accomplishing the group's goals.

group setting where a group meets; includes the size, shape, color, temperature, and decor of the room.

group storming the stage of group operation when conflicts erupt.

group task roles focuses on the group accomplishing its goals by initiating ideas, using reasoned thought, being cognizant of time constraints, encouraging other participants.

groupthink the mode of thinking in which people engage when concurrence seeking becomes so dominant in group that it tends to override realistic appraisal of alternative courses of actions.

groupware specially designed software that meeting participants use to perform tasks such as brainstorming and decision making.

gustorics the study of how taste communicates.

halo effect positive evaluation of a person or thing, not because of his or her talents or display of proficiency, but because of such factors as physical appearance.

Halogen eAppraisal an electronic program intended to enhance the appraisal process by aligning employee goals and developing a high-performing workforce.

haptics the study of the use of touch as communication.

hearing a biological activity that involves reception of a message through sensory channels.

hedges powerless language in the form of an inarticulate that adds meaningless words to a statement (e.g., "It's *like* difficult to concentrate").

hesitations powerless language in the form of an inarticulate in which verbal pauses are placed within communication (e.g, "um," "you know").

hidden agenda when individuals work for their own unstated ends rather than for the group's objectives; the result is usually counterproductive.

high-context communication societies emphasizes how the message can be conveyed through indirect language and the nonverbal channels of silence and subtle tone of voice.

high-context cultures cultures in which the information is situated in the communicators themselves and in the communication setting, so fewer words are necessary. In high-context cultures, it is the responsibility of the listener to understand.

holistic thinking the use of storytelling and parables to explain and clarify contentions.

hypothesis conclusion used to explain the evidence presented.

ideal self who you would like to be or think you should be.

identifying language centers on naming persons or things specifically, thus being able to clarify exactly what a person is speaking about.

illustrators kinesic acts accompanying speech that are used to aid in the description of what is being said.

I–Me dichotomy the difference between your self-perceived "me" and your other-perceived "me"; the difference between the way you perceive yourself and others perceive you.

impromptu speaking a speech given with little or no preparation.

inarticulates uttered sounds, words, or phrases that have no meaning or do not help the listener gain a clear understanding of the message, such as the phrase *stuff like that.*

individualism people from individualistic cultures, like the U.S., stress personal loyalty before group loyalty.

inductive argument a statement of probability based on the expected conclusion that should be the result of the presented evidence.

inferences interpretation beyond available information or jumping to conclusions without using all of the information available.

informal time a flexible use of time exemplified by such terms as *soon* or *right away.*

information-gathering interview an interview in which the interviewer sets out to obtain information from a respondent.

informative briefing a classification of informative speaking, which presents information to an audience, followed by an exchange of data, ideas ,and questions by the participants.

informative speaking discourse that imparts new information, secures understanding, or reinforces accumulated information.

in-group the group in a society that has the most influence.

initiation stage of relationships the first stage in the Knapp Relationship Escalation Model; it centers on the exchanging of basic information about the participants.

innate neurological programs automatic nonverbal reactions to stimuli with which people are born.

inner speech silent intrapersonal spoken language used to generate symbolic and conceptual thought while in the process of creating word meanings.

insighting words words or phrases that trigger strong feelings, either positive or negative.

integrating stage of relationships the third stage in the Knapp Relationship Escalation Model; it includes the relationship described by such terms as *best friends, couple, boyfriend–girlfriend/boyfriend–boyfriend/girlfriend–girlfriend, engaged.*

intensifiers powerless language in the form of an inarticulate that adds meaningless stress words within a sentence (e.g., "It's *so awesome* of you to come").

interactional model of communication a schematic that illustrates how the receiver receives and decodes the message, then encodes feedback and sends it back to the source, thus making the process two-directional. The source then decodes the feedback message, encodes a new message that adjusts to the feedback (adaptation).

intercultural communication communication between individuals with whom there is little or no cultural bond (e.g., Japanese citizen with little knowledge of New Zealand and a New Zealander with little knowledge of Japan or its customs who are speaking with each other).

intercultural-intimate conflict any antagonistic friction or disagreement between two partners due, in part, to cultural or ethnic group membership differences.

internal summary a short restatement of what has just been said in the section that you are about to leave before proceeding to the next segment.

Internet a worldwide network of networks which together carry various information and services, such as electronic mail, online chat, and file transfer.

interpersonal communication an interactional process in which two people send and receive messages; forms include face-to-face or mediated conversations, interviews, and small-group discussions.

interpersonal relationships social associations, connections, or affiliations between two or more people which centers around on shared commonalities.

interrogation interview an interview designed to secure information from an interviewee through use of probing techniques.

interview a purposeful conversation between two or more persons that follows a basic question-and-answer format.

interview agenda outlines the procedures that will be followed to achieve the purpose of the interaction.

interviewee the person who is the subject of the interview.

interviewer the person responsible for arranging for and conducting the interview.

intimate space distance in the Euro American culture, a space varying from direct physical contact with another person to a distance of eighteen inches.

intracultural communication interaction between those who have a common cultural bond (e.g., Spaniard to Spaniard, female to female, Catholic to Catholic).

intrapersonal communicator a person internally communicating with himself or herself.

intrapersonal communication communicating with yourself, encompassing such activities as thought processing, personal decision making, listening, and determining self-concept.

introduction to a speech the segment of a speech with the purpose of gaining the listeners' attention and orienting them to the material that will be presented.

inverted funnel schedule an interviewing pattern which identifies a problematic performance and then confronts the barriers need to be overcome to make improvement.

Johari window a graphically represented theory that helps you ascertain your willingness to disclose who you are and allows others to disclose to you.

kinesics the study of communication through the body and its movements.

Knapp's Relationship Escalation Model a communication-based explanation of how relationships develop and continue.

Knapp's Relationship Termination Model describes how, at any stage of the Knapp's Relationship Escalation Model, participants may work toward ending the relationship.

language a system of arbitrary signals—such as sounds, gestures, or symbols—that is used by a nation, people, or distinct community to communicate thoughts and feelings. The system includes rules for combining its components, referred to as grammar.

language distortion the intentional or unintentional distortion of information through ambiguity, vagueness, inferences, or message adjustment.

Language-Explosion Theory humans build language skills from a central core of influence, and then expand the skills through the circles of influence in which a person is involved.

large group a group consisting of more than a dozen persons.

law-enforcement interrogation an interview format de-signed to ascertain whether an interviewee has committed a crime.

leaders those who guide the group.

leadership refers to those who influence others to accomplish goals.

leadership power the ability of a member or members of a group to influence others' opinions and actions.

leading questions interview questions that encourages a specific answer; implies how the interviewee should answer the question.

lecture an informative speech intended to facilitate learning about a particular field.

left hemisphere of the brain responsible for rational, logical, sequential, linear, and abstract thinking.

legal interrogation an interviewing technique used in courts of law to gain evidence.

legitimate power influence that stems from one person's perception that another person has the right to make requests of him or her because of the position that the other person occupies or because of the nature of the relationship.

linear one-dimensional; going in one direction.

linear learners/listeners individuals who tend to take information at face value, and who prefer knowing that the information is useful and can be applied.

linear model of communication a schematic that illustrates the process by which a source encodes a message and sends it to a receiver through one or more sensory channels without a feedback loop. The receiver then receives and decodes the message.

linear time the use of time that centers on punctuality (e.g., present in most of Western Europe, North America, and Japan).

linguist a social scientist who studies the structures of various languages—to provide concepts that describe languages.

Linguistic Relativity Hypothesis theorizes that a person's understanding of the world, and how the person behaves in it, are based on the language a person speaks. Also known as the Sapir-Whorf Hypothesis.

linguistics the study of the sounds, structure, and rules of human language.

listenable speech one that is formatted in a way that when it is received, it is understood by listeners.

listener apprehension the fear of misinterpreting, inadequately processing, and/or not being able to adjust psychologically to messages sent by others.

listening a process that involves reception, attention, perception, the assignment of meaning, and the response to the message presented.

litigation a conflict resolution in which a dispute is settled by presenting evidence to a judge or a jury.

loaded questions a type of leading interview question designed to elicit an emotional response.

logos logical arguments.

lose-lose negotiations a style of negotiation in which neither person is satisfied with the outcome because neither gets what he or she wants.

low-context communication societies emphasis is on the expression of ideas through explicit verbal messages.

low-context cultures cultures in which communicators expect to give and receive a great deal of information. The speaker is responsible for making sure the listener comprehends all.

maintenance dimension of groups the members of a group meeting their interpersonal needs.

majority voting a vote in which the winner must receive more than half of the votes, excluding those who do not vote or who abstain (i.e., do not want to vote).

manuscript speech mode a speech in which the material is written out and delivered word for word from a text.

Maslow's Hierarchy of Human Needs a theory that all human beings have five levels of needs (psychological, safety, acceptance, safety, acceptance, and self-actualization).

material self your possessions and physical surroundings.

media radio, television, the Internet, magazines, newspapers, and films as types of communication.

media interview takes place when an interviewer asks questions of a guest.

mediated meetings electronically held teleconferences, video conferences, and computer or virtual conferences that allow for meetings to be held any place where someone is located.

mediation a conflict resolution process in which a neutral person, who has no vested interest in the outcome, facilitates communication between parties without imposing a solution in order for the participants to understand and resolve their dispute.

Meet-While-Standing Theory a meeting in a setting with no furniture, forcing people to stand while making decisions in a more expedient use of time.

memorable language word selections, which are colorful, rhythmical, and compelling, selected to compel the listener to remember the presentation.

memorized speech mode a speech is written out word for word and then committed to memory.

MERMER a system of brain fingerprinting that records messages emitted by the brain before the body physically reacts in an attempt to establish whether the person is lying.

messages the content of communication.

method of issue arrangement for the body of a speech the structured way the body of a speech is organized.

method of speech development encompasses how you plan to approach the presentation.

mind mapping a method of arranging materials visually rather than in list form. This is a mode often favored by global thinkers/listeners who are stimulated by pictures rather than words.

mirror questions an interview question intended to get a person to reflect on what he or she has said and expand on it. (For example, the interviewer may say, "You've worked for this corporation for years, and you feel you're getting nowhere . . .")

mockup a visual aid that allows the listener of a speech to see the building up or tearing down of an article.

modes of speech presentation impromptu, extemporaneous, manuscript and memorized, the preparation methods and reference aids used in a speech.

monotone speaking in a flat, boring tone as a result of a constant pitch, volume and rate.

Monroe's Motivated Sequence a five-step plan for structuring a persuasive speech (attention, need, satisfaction, visualization, action).

moral-ethical self a person's evaluation of his/her belief system and moral behavior.

movement the study of the movements of the body, such as gestures, which can give clues about a person's status, mood, cultural affiliations and self perception, also termed gestics.

multicultural a society consisting of varied cultural groups (e.g., the United States is a multicultural society due to its population that is composed of people of many nationalities, races, sexual orientations, and genders).

multiculturalism a political and attitudinal movement to ensure cultural freedom.

MySpace an online social network community (e.g., myspace .com).

nationality the nation in which one was born, now resides, or has lived in or studied for enough time to become familiar with the customs of the area.

natural families a married couple with or without children.

negotiation the act of bargaining to reach an agreement with at least two people or groups working on a mutual problem that is intended to satisfy all parties.

neuro-linguistic programming (NLP) a psychological theory that indicates that every movement is an important source of body language.

Nominal Group Technique of Decision Making centers on brainstorming without direct group interaction in the initial stage with the purpose of encouraging idea generation from all individuals, but avoids criticism, destructive conflict, and long-winded speeches.

nonassertive behavior a form of communication that centers on avoiding conflict.

noncontact cultures those cultures characterized by a lack of strong tactile modes of communication (Germans, Japanese, English, North Americans).

nondirective interviewing techniques a counseling interview technique in which the interviewer takes a passive role by leading an interviewee to solve a psychological problem.

nonstandard dialects low-prestige dialects (e.g., dialects other than Standard American English in the United States).

nonstandard English dialects deviations of English that do not conform to the rules of Standard American English (e.g., Spanglish).

nonverbal communication all messages that people exchange beyond the words themselves.

ocalics the study of the eyes as a receiver and conveyer of communication.

olfactics the study of smell as a communicator.

online interview using cyberspace for recruiters to meet with candidates; may take place on instant messaging and may be conducted with or without the use of Web cameras.

one-on-one briefings a classification of informative speech in which a person or small group presents a finding or concept to a single individual.

open-ended questions interview questions that specify only the topic (e.g., "What is your educational background?").

opinion inferences or judgments made by a speaker.

oral footnote an oral reference used in a speech that indicates that the material being presented is a paraphrase or quotation generated by a source other than the speaker.

oral history interview an informative interview as a way for families to preserve their history by questioning members of the family who have stories and customs they can share.

organizational noise communication problems created by the lack of a clear structural order in which the information is presented.

orienting material provides the background necessary to understand the basic material of a speech.

other-perceived Me the person who others perceive you to be. It may be the same as or different from your self-perceived I.

out-group a collectivity with which an individual does not identify or the group or groups in a society who have little or no power (e.g., historically in the U.S.—women, blacks, gays).

outline a step-by-step structure of what a speaker will say arranged by headings and subordinate points in a sequential order.

paralanguage/paravocalics the study of how vocal quality (rate, volume, pitch, pause, and stress) communicates nonverbally to the listening ear.

parallelism expression of ideas in an outline in similar forms, such as the outline all written in nouns or phrases or sentences.

paraphrases someone else's ideas put into your own words.

paraphrasing a concise restatement of what has been presented by the speaker.

parliamentarian a person well versed in the rules of order and meeting management, to assist the group in following the rules.

participants those members of a group who interact to bring about the actions of the group.

partitioning organizational speech structure a deductive format to a speech in which, as the speech proceeds, the presentation is partitioned into a number of points.

partitioning step a device used in a speech that lists how the main issues will be presented in the presentation.

participatory leader/democratic leader a leader who facilitates a group according to the goals of its members and allows them to form their own conclusions.

part-of-the-whole voting voting method that occurs when a specific number or percentage of those who are eligible to vote is required to bring about some action.

passive aggression communication that pretends that there is nothing wrong but, at the same time, derails any attempt to solve a problem that isn't to your liking in a way that doesn't appear to be aggressive.

pathos psychological appeals.

perception a screening process that attempts to analyze what has been input.

perceptions the way a person views the world.

perceptual filter strains the stimuli the listener receives and separates what makes sense from what doesn't.

performance review an appraisal interview in which the interviewer helps the interviewee realize the strengths and weaknesses of his or her on-the-job performance.

personal digital assistant (PDA) an electronic communication device that extends the self through access to other people by primarily interpersonal communication (e.g., phone, video, Facebook).

personal ethical value system the basis for your decision making and your understanding of why you will or will not take a particular stand or action.

Personal Report of Communication Apprehension (PRCA-24) a questionnaire designed to ascertain whether a person has a fear of participating in the communication act.

Personal Report of Intercultural Communication Apprehension (PRICA) a measure whose purpose is to evaluate a person's comfort or discomfort in communicating with individuals from different cultures.

personal space distance in Euro American culture, a space distance varying from eighteen inches to four feet, sometimes called the *comfort space bubble.*

persuasion the process of influencing attitudes and behaviors

persuasive interview an interview with the purpose of changing or reinforcing a person's beliefs or behavior.

persuasive speech a public presentation by a speaker intended to influence the opinion or behavior of the audience.

phatic language the function of the words is to perform a social task (e.g., informal personal greetings).

physical characteristics the study of what height, weight, and skin color communicate about an individual.

physical elements of public communication the gestures and eye contact used by a speaker while presenting a speech.

physical self our physical being.

physiological-impairment noise a physical problem that blocks the effective sending or receiving of a message (e.g., deafness or blindness).

plagiarism occurs when a speaker uses the ideas and words of others as his or her own without giving credit to the originator of the material.

pleasure seeking (as a basic need) reflexive, inborn reactions that people instinctively use for communicating pleasure or lack of pleasure as they exploit their conquests, stress their influences, and reinforce their accomplishments.

pluralism the concept that stresses that individuals can maintain their individual identities and still be part of the larger group.

plurality means "most." In voting, the option receiving the most votes wins.

polygraphs/lie detectors devices used to read the body's reactions by measuring changes in blood pressure, respiration, and/or skin response in order to detect a conflicting relationship in order to attempt to establish whether the person is lying.

positive relationship a relationship that allows freedom of expression and reflects acceptance of the feelings of both people.

poster session an informative speech in which the presenter prepares visuals in the form of charts, posters, or PowerPoint handouts, which are used during the speech to explain a professional paper.

postspeech analysis evaluating the effect of the speech following the presentation through the question-and-answer session, questionnaires, and personal feedback.

power the ability to control what happens—to create things you want to happen and to block things you don't want to happen.

power role the ability to influence another's attainment of goals. Power can center on controlling another person or persons, influencing the efforts of others, and/or accomplishing a goal.

practicality a test of a solution to a problem that centers on whether the suggested solution can be put into practice.

presentation graphics software-prepared visuals that are projected to aid a speaker in illustrating an idea during a speech.

presentation software computer applications used to improve communication through a multimedia approach.

primary group tension the normal jitters and feelings of uneasiness that group members experience when they first congregate.

primary signal system the senses: seeing, hearing, tasting, smelling, and touching.

primary sources of information sources used in a speech to develop clarification or proof that represent the original reports of the observations or research.

prior to the speech analysis audience analysis before the speech is given.

probes interview questions that are used to elicit a detailed response, including his or her point with more direction and depth, such as "Why do you feel that way?"

problem-solution method of issue arrangement a method of arrangement for the body of a speech in which the speaker attempts to identify what is wrong and to determine how to cure it or make a recommendation for its cure.

problem-solving interview the interviewer and interviewee meet to solve a dilemma.

process of the speech analysis observing the audience for feedback during the speech.

procrastinator a person who is habitually tardy, has an aversion for being on time or doing tasks on time.

professional paper a classification of informative speech presented at a convention or meeting of experts in a professional or academic field.

pronunciation the way a word is spoken.

proposal–counterproposal negotiating a method of negotiation in which a plan or solution is presented and then a counter offer is made.

proposition of fact states the existence of something in the past, present, or future by offering the reasons why the proposition should be believed.

proposition of policy a persuasive technique that states that something should or should not be done.

proposition of value offers an evaluation of a person, place, or thing.

proxemics the study of how people use and perceive their social and personal space.

psychographics speech listeners' attitudes and beliefs.

psychological appeals emotional triggers a speaker uses which are aimed at emotionally stirring audience members to take the desired action.

psychological noise communication problems created by emotional issues such as stress, frustration, or irritation.

psychological vulture a person's negative self-thoughts and beliefs. It attacks a person's perceived weaknesses and eats at the person's self-worth.

public communication characterized by a speaker sending a message to an audience.

public meetings a group gathering in which members or interested individuals may attend the sessions (e.g., corporation stockholders' meeting, school board meeting, city council meeting).

public self the you let others know; the you that you have decided to let others see.

public space distance the desired separation between people in public gatherings, approximately 12 to 24 in Euro American settings.

public speaking involves a transaction between a speaker and an audience.

public speaking anxiety the fear of giving speeches, sometimes referred to as *stage fright.*

pupilometrics a theory that indicates that pupils dilate when the eyes are focused on a pleasurable object and contract when focused on an unpleasurable object.

purpose of the speech centers on the speaker's expected outcomes for the presentation.

question-and-answer session a follow-up to the prepared address during which the speaker answers inquiries from the audience.

quotations material written or spoken by a person in the exact words in which it was originally presented.

real self what you think of yourself when you are being most honest about your interests, thoughts, emotions, and needs.

real-time conference all participants take part in a conference at the same time, such as in a web conference when all participants are at their computers at the same time.

reasoning fallacies material presented by speakers which contains logical flaws.

recalibration restructuring a communication or family system which has become dysfunctional.

receiver the recipient of the message.

reception the initial step in the listening process.

red-flag words emotional trigger words that create intrapersonal negative reactions.

referent power influence based on personal loyalty, friendship, affection, and admiration.

reflective nonverbal reactions the display of culturally learned nonverbal behavior (e.g., touching/nontouching patterns, length of eye contact while conversing).

reflexive nonverbal reactions automatic reactions to stimuli based on inborn neurological drives (e.g., eye blinks, facial flushing, facial expressions).

regulators nonverbal acts that maintain and control the back-and-forth nature of speaking and listening between two or more people (e.g., nods of the head, eye movements, and body shifts are all regulators used to encourage or discourage conversation).

relational conflict disagreements in a relationship; recognizable stages are development of tension, false ignoring, resentment, and unforgiveness.

relational fusion a process in relationships in which one partner defines, or attempts to define, reality for the other; one partner, the controller, dictates what is good, right, and acceptable for the other partner.

reliability research that is found to be true each time the experiment or study on which it is based results in the same outcome.

reprimanding interview an interview in which the interviewer helps the interviewee analyze problems caused by the latter so that corrections can be made.

requesting the process of asking, expressing a desire, or soliciting for something.

reward power influence based on a person having the best or only source of desired rewards.

rhetorical language used to influence thoughts and behaviors (e.g., often used in advertisements).

rhetorical questions queries for which no outward response is expected.

rhetorographics the place, time limit, time of day, and emotional climate of a speech.

right hemisphere of the brain responsible for intuitive, spatial, and visual matters.

risky shift phenomenon holds that decisions reached after discussion by a group display more experimentation, are less conservative, and contain more risk than decisions reached by people working alone before any discussion is held.

Robert's Rules of Order a book that lists and organizes the rules of parliamentary procedures by which groups can operate.

rule of 5 × 5 indicates that no PowerPoint slide or chart should use more than five words per line and no more than five lines per slide.

running bibliography a technique for noting footnote sources of the research accumulated to be used in a speech.

sales interview a cultural-specific interview with the purpose of persuading someone to purchase a product or service.

Sapir-Whorf Hypothesis theorizes that a person's understanding of the world, and how the person behaves in it, is based on the language a person speaks. Also known as the *Linguistic Relativity Hypothesis*.

sarcasm a bitter or cutting remark created by words, and often reinforced by nonverbal tone and sometimes the body positions or facial expressions of the speaker.

schema the categorical assignment of meaning that allows for the development of scripts for processing information.

schemata mental representations carried in the brain that are shaped by the language categories and the way brains process information.

second employment interviews provides more detailed information about an employment position and, at the same time, further determines the candidate's fit to the organization and the job.

Second Life a virtual conferencing Internet-based virtual world that enables meeting participants to interact with each other through use of avatars.

secondary group tension the stress and strain that occur within a group later in its development. Frequent causes of this problem are having to make a decision, shortage of time to accomplish the task, differences of opinion, and difficult members.

secondary sources of information sources used in a speech to develop clarification or proof that report, but did not originally generate, the observations or research.

security (as a basic need) reflexive, inborn reactions that cause people to seek equilibrium, balance. When security is absent, people feel a lack of control, get uneasy, and become overly cautious and uncertain.

security interrogation an interview approach intended to screen individuals to ascertain if they are a security risk.

selective communication the ability of humans to choose the symbols that best represent the idea or concept to be expressed.

selective perception allows a listener to narrow attention to specific bits or piece of information.

self-concept your idea or picture of yourself; the accumulation of knowledge about the self, including such dimensions as beliefs regarding personality traits, physical characteristics, abilities, values, goals, and roles.

self-confidence a person's sense of competence and effectiveness

self-credentialing verbal mode a communication style in which emphasis is placed on drawing attention to or boasting about one's accomplishments.

self-declared families a group who has decided to live together as a family, usually without legal recognition.

self-disclosure intentionally letting the other person know who you are by communicating self-revealing information.

self-fulfilled person a person who is not intimidated into a negative self-concept and realizes that there will always be problems, frustrations, and failures in life.

self-humbling verbal mode a communication style in which emphasis is placed on lowering oneself via modest talk, verbal restraints, and the use of self-deprecation.

self-love accepting yourself as a worthy person because you choose to do so.

self-perceived I the image you project; the way you perceive yourself. It is revealed through the words, ideas, actions, clothing, and lifestyle you choose.

self-talk intrapersonally communicating within yourself; an inner dialogue.

semantic noise communication problems created by the meaning of words.

semantics the study of the relationship of language and meaning.

sensorium frames the listener's perceptual filter so that all of the senses are brought to bear so the listener can logically and emotionally respond to information.

sentence outline a speech presentation tool that has complete sentences for all entries and usually has correct punctuation.

sex one's biological or physical self (male/female).

sexual harassment generalized sexist remarks or behavior; inappropriate and offensive sexual advances; solicitation of sexual activity.

shyness the fear of participating in the communication act. Also identified as *communication apprehension, Social Anxiety Disorder*, and *Social Phobia*.

Significant-Other Theory the selection of specific people or groups whose language, ideals, and beliefs we allow to influence us.

signposting speaker stating, during a speech, where the listeners have been, where they are presently, and where they are going.

silent majority those who say nothing during the decision-making process.

simple assertion a statement or statements in which a person states the facts relating to the existence of a problem.

single-parent families a family consisting of one parent with a child or children.

Six-Step Standard Agenda for Decision Making a descriptive procedure for decision-making.

slang words that are related to a specific activity or incident and are immediately understood by members of a particular group.

small group ecology the physical placement of members of small groups in relation to one another; includes placement of chairs and the size and shape of the tables and desks.

small groups a group consisting of three to twelve persons.

small talk an exchange of information between two people that normally is on the surface level, usually centering on biographics (name, occupation, college major, hometown, college attended or attending).

smartphone a digital communication device that has computer and Internet communication capabilities.

smell adaptation occurs when people gradually lose the distinctiveness of a particular smell through repeated contact with it.

smell as a communicator each person has a unique ability to detect, identify, and distinguish smells to varying degrees; the study of smell is olfactics.

smell blindness occurs when people are unable to detect smells.

smell memory the ability to recall previous situations when encountering a particular smell associated with them.

smell overload takes place when an exceptionally large number of odors or one extremely strong odor overpowers the smeller.

Social Exchange Theory a concept which states that people make judgments about interpersonal contacts by comparing relational rewards and costs.

social cognition is the process of sharing perceptions with others from similar groups or cultures.

social loafing when group membership leads people to work less than they would if they were working alone because they think their participation in the group cannot be measured.

social support to be persuaded, the long-term staying power of messages depends not only on how the appeal resonates with the individuals but also on the degree to which the individual perceives that he or she has the support of others.

social networking talking online in such communities as Facebook.com, MySpace.com, and Twitter.com.

social orientation a person's nationality, race, gender, sexual orientation, and religion that are the basis for her or his identity.

social self your interactions with others.

social space distance in Euro American culture, a four- to twelve-foot zone that is used during business transactions and casual social exchanges.

source the originator of the message.

space distances a theory of Edward and Mildred Hall that people desire a certain amount of distance between themselves and others based on their cultural teachings and inborn drives.

Spanglish a dialect of English in which the vocabulary is mostly Spanish, with a smattering of English words and some fractured traditional English syntax.

spatial method of issue arrangement a method of arrangement for the body of a speech in which the speaker sets a point of reference and follows a geographic pattern.

speaker competence the wisdom, authority, and knowledge a speaker demonstrates.

speaker credibility the reputation, prestige, and authority of the speaker as perceived by the listeners, which helps to establish the acceptance of the speaker's ideas.

speaker inventory an examination by a prospective speaker of his or her life experiences and interests that can be useful for selecting a topic for a presentation.

speaking setting encompasses where the speech is given, what the time limit is, when the presentation is made, and the attitude of the audience.

specific instances condensed examples that are used to clarify or prove a point in a speech.

speech-independent gestures bodily movements tied to speech, referred to as emblems.

speech of actuation the speaker attempts to move the member of the audience to take the desired action being proposed.

speech of conviction the speaker attempts to encourage the listener to believe as the speaker believes.

speech of introduction an informative speech with the purpose of introducing a speaker to an audience.

speech to inform a speech with the purpose of imparting new information and securing understanding, or reinforcing information and understandings acquired in the past.

speech outline a clear step-by-step structure of a speech that indicates what will be said and in what order.

speech participants the speaker and the members of the audience.

speech planning outline a brief framework used to think through the process of the speech.

speech presentation outline a framework in which the speaker fleshes out the planning outline with examples and illustrations and writes in internal summaries and forecasts.

speech-related gestures bodily movements directly tied to or that accompany speech; referred to as *illustrators, affect displays, regulators,* and *adaptors.*

speech topic the subject of a speech.

speeches about events a classification of informative speech intended to tell about something that has already happened, is happening, or is expected to happen.

speeches about concepts a classification of informative speech which examines theories, beliefs, ideas, philosophies, or schools of thought.

speeches about objects a classification of informative speech with the purpose of describing a particular thing in details, such as a person, place, animal, or structure.

speeches about processes a classification of informative speech intended to instruct the audience about how something works, is made, or is done.

spiral form of explanation a method of speech structure in which a statement is made and then a story or analogy that deals with the statement is presented, with the responsibility for interpretation left to the listener.

spiritual self what we are thinking and feeling.

stagnating stage of relationships the stage in Knapp's Relationship Termination Model that is highlighted by the individuals starting to avoid discussing the relationship.

Standard American English the language generally recognized by linguists as representative of the general population of the United States (e.g., words and grammatical forms are those of nationally published magazines, such as *Time* and *Newsweek,* and newspapers, such as *USA Today* and the *New York Times*). These words tend to represent the vocabulary of the West, the Midwest, the Midland, and the southern section of New England.

standard dialects high-prestige dialects.

statement of central idea defines the subject and develops the criteria by which to evaluate the material to be included in the speech.

statement of the speech's central idea the segment of a speech intended to keep the speaker on course for developing a purposeful and well-organized speech, while indicating the response the speaker wants from listeners.

statistical surveying methods developed by statisticians for collecting data.

statistics a collection of numerical information arranged as representations, trends, or theories.

stories illustrations which tell of real or fictional happenings used to enhance interest in speeches.

study group established to enable individuals to work together to study and learn with the assistance of others.

study of language examining meaning based on the words used, the way the words are placed together, and the backgrounds and experiences of the communicators.

subordination a technique used in speech outlining in which major and minor headings are organized from general to specific or from abstract to concrete.

substituting relationship of verbal with nonverbal the replacement of verbal communication with nonverbal communication (e.g., shaking the head up and down to indicate "yes").

summary of a speech the first part of a speech's conclusion, it restates the major points.

super leadership guidance in which people are led to lead themselves and thereby release the self-leadership energy within each person.

supplementary speech aids visual, audio, audiovisual, and computerized graphics used during a speech with the intention of facilitating the listeners' understanding.

support group a system that allows people to interact with others who share similar goals or problems whose purpose is to increase people's knowledge of themselves and others, to assist people to clarify the changes they most want to make in their life, and to give people some of the tools necessary to make these changes.

supporting speech material information used by a public speaker that clarifies a point being made in the speech or offers evidence of the validity of presented argument.

survival (as a basic need) reflexive, inborn reactions that we instinctively use to communicate our fear of a possible ending of our existence.

symbol a word or sound that is designated in a language system to represent an image or idea (e.g., *pencil, beautiful*).

symposium a group format in which participants give prepared speeches with no interaction among themselves or with the audience.

syntactical noise communication problems created by grammatical usage.

syntax the customary way of putting words together in a grammatical form, within a particular language.

systematic desensitization people are taught first to recognize tension in their bodies and then how to relax through a step-by-step process.

table-top briefing a form of one-on-one briefing in which the participants are seated around a conference table rather than the presenter standing before a person or group.

tag questions inquiries added onto the end of statements, such as "That movie was terrific, don't you think?" The intent is to get the communicative partner to enter the conversation; powerless language in the form of an inarticulate that asks a question that is not a meaningful part of the statement (e.g., "Put away your toys, *okay?*").

talking points the major ideas to be stressed in a speech, also may refer to bullet points in an abbreviated outline format that serve as a framework for the speech and are used in a rehearsal session and as the notes for the actual presentation.

task dimension of group the members of a group meeting the goal of the group, which may include decision making, informing, appraising and examining, problem solving, and creating interest in staying on track.

taste as a communicator each person has the ability to distinguish and classify tastes in varying degrees; the study of taste is gustorics.

taste adaptation a person getting so used to a taste that he or she cannot taste it when eaten.

taste blindness the inability to taste.

team briefing a classification of information speech in which a series of speakers present the findings or recommendations of a group activity.

technical report a form of informative speech in which a scientific or mechanical process or technique is explained to an audience.

technical time precise time, as in the way some scientists look at how things happen in milliseconds.

techno-babble computer language used for personal communications. Technobabblers interface with each other and debug their relationships.

teleconferencing consists of telephone conference calls and speakerphone meetings.

telephone job interview an employment interview conducted via land or smartphones.

terminating stage of relationships the final stage of Knapp's Relationship Termination Model; it is highlighted by a breakup of the relationship.

territory (as a basic need) physical or perceptual areas that you mark off or possess and within which you feel secure.

testimony a direct quotation (actual statement) or a paraphrase (reworded idea) from an authority that is provided by a speaker to clarify ideas, back up contentions, and reinforce concepts.

texting/text messaging sending of short messages (160 characters or fewer), using the Short Message Service from mobile or smartphones.

Theory of Field-Related Standards since not all people reach conclusions in the same way, arguments must include as many appeals as possible to cover the various thought processes of members of an audience.

Theory of Individual Norm Standards proposes that being on the side of or getting the backing of the person or persons with power may be a strong tool that a speaker can use to influence the group's members.

therapeutic listening the type of listening used in mental health, social work, and counseling that requires a listener to learn when to ask questions, when to stimulate further discussion, and when, if ever, to give advice.

time as a communicator the way people handle and structure their time communicates information about them; also referred to as chronemics.

time method of issue arrangement a method of arrangement for the body of a speech that orders information from a beginning point to an ending one, with all the steps developed in numerical or time sequence.

topic outline a speech presentation tool that has words or phrases for all entries and usually has little or no punctuation after entries.

topic selection the subject about which the speaker selects to speak.

topic of the speech the specific subject of a speech.

topical method of issue arrangement a method of arrangement for the body of a speech in which a speaker explains an idea in terms of its component parts.

touch avoidance the degree to which an individual dislikes being touched.

town meeting a meeting in which a presenter opens the session with a short prepared statement that establishes the framework for the meeting, followed by individuals in the audience engaging in a forum with the speaker.

transactional model of communication a schematic that illustrates how communicators simultaneously process messages.

transformational leadership the role of a leader who takes on the role of changing both the behavior and the outlook of his or her followers.

triangle stance a posture/stance technique used by speakers to aid in relaxing their bodies as they speak.

turnitin.com an online proprietary system that instantly identifies papers containing unoriginal material and acts as a powerful deterrent to stop student plagiarism before it starts.

two-valued reasoning/orientation divides all decisions into a right or wrong/good or bad structure so that there is no flexibility in reaching conclusions.

unfolding organizational speech structure an inductive style of organizing a speech in which the speaker lays out supporting evidence and then draws a conclusion, leading the listeners to be drawn into the argument.

unresolved group storming the situation when a group is unable to resolve its problems and can't move beyond the storming stage.

urban legends myths, often spread on the Internet, which consist of stories thought to be factual by those circulating them. They are not necessarily untrue, but they are often distorted, exaggerated, or sensationalized.

validity in experimentation or observation, the process that is followed that results in correctness.

values what a person perceives to be his/her positive or negative worth, as well as the worth of things and others.

victim a person who is denied the right to decide how to live his or her own life.

victimizer a person or establishment that interferes with another person's right to decide how to live his or her own life.

video conferencing meetings conducted with one-way video and two-way audio as well as fully interactive two-way video and two-way audio.

video interview employment interviewing conducted via video rather than a face-to-face setting.

virgules slash marks inserted into a manuscript that can be used to indicate a pause or a stop.

virtual conferencing takes place when meeting participants are connected to an Internet-based virtual world that enables its users to interact with each other through avatars.

virtual interview an approach to screening job candidates in which computer-generated images (avatars) are used to navigate through an interview site that uses keyboarding or questions and answers or talking.

visual aids supplementary aids, which appeal to the sense of sight, that are used during a speech to facilitate the listeners' understanding.

visualization a technique in which a public speaker sees himself or herself in the actual setting in which he or she is going to give the speech and making a successful presentation.

vocal cues the rate, volume, pitch, pause, and stress of sounds that communicate nonverbally to the listening ear, also referred to as paralanguage.

voting a procedure that takes place when members are given an opportunity to indicate agreement, disagreement, or no opinion on an idea or candidate.

Web conferencing meetings in which participants log on to a central conference database through their personal computer.

western problem-solving sequence a method of solving problems that has four segments: identify the problem, search for solutions, test those solutions, and put a solution into practice.

Wikis Internet sites which offer free information; the best known Wiki is Wikipedia, a widely used online encyclopedia of questionable facts because it allows anyone with an Internet connection to create or alter any entry; a source generally not recommended for use as a primary or secondary source of information.

willingness to communicate a person's willingness to take risks, analyze his or her communication, and make adjustments in order to participate in the communicative act.

win-lose negotiations a style of negotiation that centers on one person getting what he or she wants while the other comes up short.

win-win negotiation a style of negotiation in which the goal is to find a solution that is satisfying to everyone.

work team a small group of workers who function as teams to make and implement decisions about their own work.

workability a test of the solution to a problem that centers on whether the suggested solution will solve or help solve the problem.

working memory capacity the dual-task process made up of both the memory and the attention functions as listeners attempt to process the speaker's message.

World Wide Web a collection of interconnected documents linked by hyperlinks and URLs accessible via the Internet.

yes-response questions a form of leading interview question that is stated in such a way that the respondent is encouraged to agree with the interviewer (e.g., "You would agree with me, wouldn't you, that this company's policies are fair?").

Notes

CHAPTER 1

1. Taylor, J. (2010, November). Rapid change as the constant: The undergraduate communication degree of the near future. *Spectra*, p. 8.
2. Emanuel, R. (2005). The case for fundamentals of oral communication. *Community College Journal of Research and Practice, 29*, 153–162.
3. (Taylor, p. 10).
4. (Taylor, p. 11).
5. Morreale, S., Worley, D., & Hugenberg, B. (2010, October). The basic communication course at two- and four-year U.S. colleges and universities: Study VIII—The 40th Anniversary. *Communication Education, 59*(4), p. 406.
6. Buhl, L. (2007). *6 soft skills that could land you the job*, Yahoo! HotJobs. Retrieved from http://hotjobs.yahoo.com/jobseeker
7. (Morreale, p. 407).
8. (Emanuel, p. 2).
9. (Emanuel, p. 2).
10. Ting-Toomey, S. & Chung, L. C. (2005). *Understanding intercultural communication*. New York: Oxford University Press, p. 2.
11. Friedman, T. L. (2007). *The world is flat: A brief history of the twenty-first century*. New York: Picador/Farrar, Straus and Giroux, pp. 10–11.
12. Based on Berlo, D. K. (1960). *The process of communication*. New York: Holt, Rinehart and Winston.
13. Advertisement, WordPerfect-Macintosh. Ogden, UT: WordPerfect Corporation.
14. Factors that cause communication difficulties are sometimes called *interference*. In this text, these factors are referred to as *noise*.
15. Coventry, K. R., Lynott, D., Cangelosi, A., Monrouxe, L., Joyce, D., & Richardson, D. C. (2010, March). Spatial language, visual attention, and perceptual simulation. *Brain and Language, 112*(3), 202–213. doi 10.1016/j.bandl.2009.06.001
16. Shannon, C. E., & Weaver, W. (1949). *The mathematical theory of communication*. Urbana, Illinois: University of Illinois Press.
17. Berlo, D. K. (1960). *The process of communication*. New York: Holt, Rinehart and Winston.
18. Barnlund, D. C. (2008). A transactional model of communication. In. C. D. Mortensen (Ed.), *Communication theory* (2nd ed.) (pp. 47–57). New Brunswick, New Jersey: Transaction.
19. Bloom, M. (2008, February 2). Personal correspondence regarding the need to acknowledge the sociological theories of media. South Euclid, OH: Notre Dame College.
20. *American time use survey summary*. (2007, June 28). United States Department of Labor news release. Retrieved from www.bls.gov/news.release/atus.nr0.htm2; *Internet world stats, usage and population statistics*. (2007, December 31). Miniwatts Marketing Group. Retrieved from www.internetworldstats.com, p. 1.
21. Internet world stats. (2010, June 20). Miiniwatts Marketing Group, *Usage and population statistics*. Retrieved from www.internetworldstats.com/top20.htm
22. Johnson, D. (2005, April 4). A bloody day on the Rez. *Newsweek*, 3.
23. Justin, N. (2007, April 12). Political moments in radio, TV that defined people and times. *The Cleveland Plain Dealer*, E5, as reprinted from *Minneapolis-St. Paul Star Tribune*.
24. Jelinek, P. (2010, December 22). Obama signs 'don't ask, don't tell' repeal. *Yahoo! News*. Retrieved from http://news.yahoo.com/s/ap/20101222/ap_on_go_pr_wh/us_gays_in_military
25. See Cerf, V. (n.d.). *Ever wondered how the Internet got started?* Retrieved from www.webmastercourse.com/articles/internet/history
26. Madrid, J., & Wiseman, R. (2003). Computer-mediated communication, Social skills, and loneliness. *Conference Papers—International Communication Association*, 1–33. doi:ica_proceeding_11316
27. McGlynn III, J. (2007). *More connections, less connection: An examination of computer-mediated communication as relationship maintenance*. Conference Papers—National Communication Association.
28. Postman, N. (1990, Fall). The antidote to trivialization. *NPQ*, 55.
29. For a discussion on pluralism, see Samovar, L., Porter, R., & McDaniel, E. (2006). *Intercultural communication: A reader*. Belmont, CA: Thomson Higher Education, pp. 156–158. For a more scholarly discussion, see Lili, S. (2008). *On the conception of differences and commonality: Pluralism, dialecticism, paradoxism, and poetic unfinishedness in critical and cultural rhetorical intercultural communication scholarship*. Conference Papers—National Communication Association. Or Ford, J., & Klumpp, J. (1985). Systematic pluralism: An inquiry into the bases of communication research. *Critical Studies in Mass Communication, 2*(4), 408.
30. A treatise on the concept of multiculturalism: Henry, W. A. III. (1993, Fall, special edition). The politics of separation. *Time*, 75. For a meta-analysis of behaviors, see Bradford, L., Allen, M., & Beisser, K. R. (2000). Meta-analysis of intercultural communication competence research. (2000). *World Communication, 29*(1), 28–52. For a contemporary view, see *Culture and multiculturalism*. The Ayn Rand Institute. Retrieved from www.aynrand.org/site/PageServer?pagename=media_topic_multiculturalism&JServSessionIdr007=8j6x3uvd32.app5a, 2008. Or Cardon, P. W. (2008, October). A critique of Hall's Contexting Model: A meta-analysis of literature on intercultural business and technical communication. *Journal of Business & Technical Communication, 22*(4), 399–428.
31. Yen, H. (2009, December 16). White Americans' majority to end by mid-century. *Yahoo! News*. Based on Census Bureau: http://www.census.gov Retrieved from http://buzz.yahoo.com/article/1:y_news:132df6f771ce02d454befbe5b1a62006/White-Americans-majority-to-end-by-mid-century-AP
32. (Yen).
33. Neuliep, J. W., & McCroskey, J. C. (1997). The development of intercultural and interethnic communication apprehension scales. *Communication Research Reports, 14*, 385–398. Bippus, A., & Dorjee, T. (2002). The validity of PRECA as an index interethnic communication apprehension. *Communication Research Reports, 19*(2), 130–137. Ting-Toomey, S. & Chung, L. (2005). *Understanding intercultural communication*. New York: Oxford University Press, p. 234.
34. Archibold, R. (2010, April 23). Arizona enacts stringent law on immigration, *The New York Times*. Retrieved from http://www.nytimes.com/2010/04/24/us/politics/24immig.html
35. (Archibold).
36. (Samovar et al., p. 433).
37. See http://www.semesteratsea.org/
38. A comment included on a student evaluation of the Intercultural Communication course for the Fall/Winter 1999–2000 school year.
39. Sherman, M. (October 2, 2010). *Free speech cases at top of Supreme Court's agenda*. Retrieved from http://www.supremecourt.gov/
40. College speaking 101. (2009, February 27). *Los Angeles Times*. latimes.com
41. Hudson, D. L. Jr. (2005, September 13). *Free speech on public college campuses. Overview*, First Amendment Center. www.firstamendmentcenter.org
42. Lawless, J. (2010, November 23). *Twitter tirades test limits of freedom of speech. Yahoo! News*. Retrieved from http://news.yahoo.com/s/ap/eu_britain_twitter_trouble/print
43. Roth, Z. (2010, November 9). *Can criticizing the boss on Facebook get you fired? Yahoo! News*. Retrieved from http://news.yahoo.com/s/yblog_upshot/20101109/us_yblog_upshot/can-criticizing-the-boss-on-faxebk-get-you-fired/print
44. Franklyn S. Haiman has written extensively on the First Amendment to the Constitution of the United States and the Speech Arts. This quote appeared in Haiman, F. (1993). *Speech arts and the First Amendment*. Carbondale: Southern Illinois University Press, p. 3. An expansion of First Amendment concepts is in Haiman, F. (2008). Articles by Franklyn Haiman. *The American Prospect*. Retrieved from www.prospect.org
45. Haiman, F. (2008). Articles by Franklyn Haiman. *The American Prospect*. Retrieved from www.prospect.org
46. Dershowitz, A. (2008). *Finding Jefferson: A lost letter, a remarkable discovery, and the First Amendment in an age of terrorism*. Retrieved from www.alandershowitz.com
47. (Dershowitz, 2008).
48. Jaschite, S. (1993, August 4). Nominee reflects on "hate speech:" Sees Supreme Court taking up the issue. *Chronicle of Higher Education* A-23. For an international look at

the topic of freedom of speech, see Kierulf, A, & Rønning, H. (Eds.) (2009). *Freedom of Speech abridged? Cultural, legal, and philosophical challenges*. Gothenburg, Sweden: Nordicom, University of Gothenburg.

49. See for example, Slagle, M. (2009). An ethical exploration of free expression and the problem of hate speech. *Journal of Mass Media Ethics, 24*(4), 238–250. doi:10.1080/08900520903320894. Or Reed, C. (2009). The challenge of hate speech online. *Information & Communications Technology Law, 18*(2), 79–82. doi:10.1080/13600830902812202
50. Chang, N. (2001, November). The USA Patriot Act. Center for Constitutional Rights. Also see Finan, C. M. (2007). *From the Palmer Raids to the Patriot Act: A history of the fight for free speech in America*. Boston: Beacon Press.
51. Herman, S. (2003). The USA Patriot Act and the U.S. Department of Justice: Losing our balances? *Jurist Legal Intelligence News*. Retrieved from jurist.law.pitt.edu
52. Johannesen, R. L., Valde, K. S., & Whedbee, K. E. (2007). *Ethics in human communication* (6th ed.). Prospect Heights, IL: Waveland Press.
53. (Johannesen, Valde, & Whedbee, 2007).
54. Sarlin, B. (2010, May 11). Andrew Sullivan's Kagan crusade. *The Daily Beast*. Retrieved from http://www.thedailybeast.com/glogs-and-stories/2010-05-11
55. (Sarlin).
56. Hartman, R. R. (2010, October 28). Tea party founder defends attack on congressman's Muslim faith. *Yahoo! News*. Retrieved from http://news.co/s/yblog-upshot/20101028.
57. (Hartman).
58. Osborn, M., & Osborn, S. (2006). *Public Speaking* (7th ed.). Boston: Houghton Mifflin, p. 19. For a discussion on ethical communication and ethical speakers, see pp. 19–24. For a more specific perspective, see Slagle, M. (2009). An ethical exploration of free expression and the problem of hate speech. *Journal of Mass Media Ethics, 24*(4), 238–250. doi:10.1080/08900520903320894

CHAPTER 2

1. Bernárdez, E. (2010). Language and culture: A review of aspects of cognitive ethnolinguistics. *Review of Cognitive Linguistics, 8*(2), 376–385. doi:10.1075/ml.8.2.07ber
2. Begley, S. (2009, July 9). What's in a word? Language may shape our thoughts. *Newsweek*, p. 31. Based on the research of Lera Boroditsky, psychologist at Stanford University. See Boroditsky, L., & Ramscar, M. (2002). The roles of body and mind in abstract thought. *Psychological Science* (Wiley-Blackwell), *13*(2), 185; or Fausey, C. M., & Boroditsky, L. (2010). Subtle linguistic cues influence perceived blame and financial liability. *Psychonomic Bulletin & Review, 17*(5), 644–650. doi:10.3758/PBR.17.5.644
3. (Begley).
4. Miller, L. (2009, July 9). The misinformants: What 'stealth jihad' doesn't mean. *Newsweek*, p. 16.
5. Definition is based on: Language. (2005). *American Heritage Dictionary of the English Language* (4th ed.). Retrieved from www.ask.com/reference/dictionary/ahdict/46762/language
6. Corballis, M. C. (2002). *From hand to mouth: The origins of language*. Princeton, NJ: Princeton University Press. Also see Gillis, J. (2002, August 15). Gene mutations linked to language development. *Washington Post*, A13.
7. Wilcox, S. (2009). William C. Stokoe and the Gestural Theory of language origins. *Sign Language Studies, 9*(4), 398–409.
8. The social construction of reality concept has its roots in Berger, P. L., & Luckman, T. (1966). *The social construction of reality: A treatise in the sociology of knowledge*. New York: Doubleday. For a contemporary discussion, see Littlejohn, S. W., & Foss, K. A. (2007). Theories of social and cultural reality. *Theories of human communication*. Belmont, CA: Wadsworth.
9. (Corballis, 2002).
10. (Corballis, 2002).
11. (Corballis, 2002).
12. Contreras, R. (2009, July 9). *Frenemy, locavore among new words in Webster's. Yahoo! News*. Based on information from John Morse, president of Merriam-Webvster's Collegiate Dictionary. Retrieved from http://www .Merriam-Webster.com
13. (Contreras).
14. (Contreras).
15. Contreras, R. (2010, December 21). Audacity of 'austerity.' 2010 Word of the Year. *Yahoo! News*. Retrieved from http://news.yahoo.com/s/ap/20101220/ap_on_re_us/us_word_of_the_year
16. Bailey, H. (n.d.). *Sarah Palin coins 'word of the year.' Yahoo! News*, Retrieved from http://news.yahoo.com/s/yblog_theticket/20101115/pl_yblog_theticket/almost-5-million-people-watched-sarah-palins-alaska
17. Heher, A. M. (2007, March 21). *McDonald's seeks to refine "McJobs."* Associated Press. Retrieved from www.oed.com, www .mcdonalds.com
18. (Heher, 2007).
19. (Heher, 2007).
20. Harrison, D. (2010, October 5). Harrison speaking at a news conference organized by the national Geographic Society and reported by Living Tongues Institute for Endangered Languages. Retrieved from http://www .liningtongues.org
21. (Turner, pp. 3–4).
22. Roberts, S. (2010, April 29). Listening to (and saving) the world's languages. *New York Times*. Retrieved from http://www.nytimes.com/2010/04/29. Based on the research of Daniel Kaufman, Graduate Center of the City University of New York.
23. (Roberts).
24. (Roberts).
25. (Roberts).
26. Retrieved from http://www.mountlebanon.org/aramaiclanguage.html
27. (Leonard, 2005).
28. Constitutional topic: Official language. (n.d.) *USConstitution.net*. Retrieved from http://www.usconstitution.net/consttop_lang.html
29. Ohlemacher, S. (2007, September 12). 20 percent of people living in U.S. speak language other than English at home. *The Post and Courier*. Evening Post Publishing Co, as reported by Associate Press. Retrieved from http://www.postandcourier.com/news/2007/sep/12/language15626/
30. The theory was proposed by Wiener, N. (1950). *The human use of human beings*. New York: Da Capo Press, republished in 1988. For a contemporary application, see Armand, L. (2008). Language and the cybernetic mind. *Theory, Culture & Society, 25*(2), 127–152. doi:10.1177/0263276407086794
31. For a more detailed discussion of linguistic theories and their application, see Thompson, N. (2003). *Communication and language: A handbook of theory and practice*. Basingstoke, UK: Palgrave Macmillan.
32. Mead, G. H. (1934). *Mind, self, and society*. Chicago: University of Chicago Press. Republished 1967.
33. A theory developed by American linguists Edward Sapir and Benjamin Whorf. For an updated discussion of the theory, see *Current interpretations of the Sapir-Whorf Hypothesis*. Retrieved from www.geocities.com/CollegePark/4110/whorf.html For scholarly applications, see Tohidian, I. (2009). Examining linguistic relativity hypothesis as one of the main views on the relationship between language and thought. *Journal of Psycholinguistic Research, 38*(1), 65–74. doi:10.1007/s10936-008-9083-1; or Allan, K. (2010). Vantage Theory and linguistic relativity. *Language Sciences, 32*(2), 158–169. doi:10.1016/j.langsci.2009.10.002
34. Farb, P. (1993). *Word play*. New York: Alfred A. Knopf, p. 197.
35. For a discussion of the functions of language, see Warnick, B. & Inch, E. S. (2005). *Critical thinking and communication*. Upper Saddle River, NJ: Prentice-Hall; or Jackson, H., & Stockwell, P. (2011). *Introduction to the nature and functions of language* (2nd ed.). New York: Continuum.
36. For example research in this area, see Jing-Schmidt, Z. (2007). Negativity bias in language: A cognitive-affective model of emotive intensifiers. *Cognitive Linguistics, 18*(3), 417–443. doi:10.1515/COG.2007.023
37. For a discussion of phatic language, see Nordquist, R. (2010). *Phatic communication*. Retrieved from http://grammar.about.com/od/il/g/jargonterm.htm; *What is phatic communication?* (2003–2010). Retrieved from http://www.wisegeek.com/what-is-phatic-communication.htm. For contemporary theory building, see Stenström, A., & Jörgensen, A. (2008). A matter of politeness? A contrastive study of phatic talk in teenage conversation. *Pragmatics, 18*(4), 641–657; also see Kissine, M. (2009, February). Illocutionary forces and what is said. *Mind & Language, 24*(1), 122–138.
38. For a discussion of the controversy over language diversity, see Evans, N., & Levinson, S. C. (2009). The myth of language universals: Language diversity and its importance for cognitive science. *Behavioral & Brain Sciences, 32*(5), 429–448. doi:10.1017/S0140525X0999094X
39. Mader, D. C. (1992, May 3). *The politically correct textbook: Trends in publishers' guidelines for the representation of marginalized groups*. Paper presented at the Eastern Communication Association Convention, Portland, ME; also see Montaner, C. (2008). Journalism, Puritan paranoia, and political correctness. *Journal of Mass Media Ethics, 23*(2), 161–164. doi:10.1080/08900520801909459
40. (Mader, 1992).
41. (Mader, 1992).
42. For a discussion of language distortion, see Koehl, H. (2006, November 24). Psychobabel: A ponerological approach to modern doublespeak and the distortion of language. *Signs of The Times*. Retrieved from www.sott.net/signs/editorials/signs.php. Also see Atwood, K. (2008, March 7). Misleading language: The common currency of "CAM" characterizations. *Science Based Medicine*. Retrieved from www.sciencebasedmedicine.org
43. For a complete discussion of doublespeak, see Lutz, W. (1989). *Doublespeak*. New York: Harper and Row. To see examples of doublespeak, go to www.doublespeak-show.com/ Also see Bosik, M. (2004, Summer). Listening to doublespeak. *Listening Professional, 3*(1), 13–19.
44. Weisberg, J. (2010, Spring). The complete Bushisms. *Bushisms: President George Herbert Walker Bush in his own words*. New York: Workman Publishing Company. For an interesting analysis, see Goldzwig, S. R. (2010, Spring). The anti-intellectual presidency: The decline of presidential rhetoric from George Washington to George W. Bush. *Rhetoric & Public Affairs, 13*(1), 145–148.
45. (about.com: Political Humor).
46. Brown, R. (1959). *Words and things*. New York: Free Press, p. 22.
47. Based on the classic work of Howard Mims. See Mims, H. A. (1979, August 31). On Black English: A language with rules. *Cleveland Plain Dealer*, A21; Camden, C., Mims, H., & Motley, M. T. (1985, Summer). Convergent validity of three communication data collection techniques: An analysis of Black American English grammatical usage. *Western Journal of Speech Communication, 49*(3), 166–176. Also see Van Hofwegen, J., & Wolfram, W. (2010). Coming of age

in African American English: A longitudinal study. *Journal of Sociolinguistics, 14*(4), 427–455. doi:10.1111/j.1467-9841.2010.00452.x
48. (Mims, 1979).
49. Definition is based on Joseph DeVito's classic dictionary dedicated to the exclusive study of communication terms. DeVito, J. A. (1986). *The Communication handbook: A dictionary*. New York: Harper and Row, p. 94.
50. (Mims).
51. Nashville mayor vetoes English-only measure. (2007, February 13). *USA Today*, 4A; Favora, T. (2009, June 25). *American cities debate English-only legislation.* City Mayors Society. Retrieved from http://www.citymayors.com/society/us-english-only.html
52. Dokoupil, T. (2010, May 24 & 31). Why English only will get the ok in Oklahoma. *Newsweek.*
53. Material in this section is based on the work of W. Zelinsky, as discussed in Andersen, P. A., Lustig, M. W., & Andersen, J. F. (1987, June). Regional patterns of communication in the United States: A theoretical perspective. *Communication Monographs, 54*, 128–144. For a listening perspective, see Floccia, C., Butler, J., Goslin, J., & Ellis, L. (2009). Regional and foreign accent processing in English: Can listeners adapt? *Journal of Psycholinguistic Research, 38*(4), 379–412. doi:10.1007/s10936-008-9097-8
54. Mama Grizzly noun pl. –zlies. (2010, October 4). *Newsweek*, p. 30.
55. (Mama Grizzly).
56. Boorstein, M. (2010, August 29). Sharia becomes hot-button term with a malleable meaning, *The[Cleveland] Plain Dealer,* A12.
57. Weintraub, J. (2004, March/April). From AOK to Oz, the historical dictionary of American slang. *Humanities, 25*(2). Retrieved from www.neh.gov/news/humanities/2004-03/slang.html; People, etc. (1977, April 10). *Elyria (Ohio) Chronicle-Telegram Scene*, 2. For an interesting discussion of language, see Preece, S. (2010). Multilingual identities in higher education: Negotiating the "mother tongue", "posh" and "slang." *Language & Education: An International Journal, 24*(1), 21–39. doi: 10.1080/09500780903194036
58. Neumeister, L. (2006, February 12). "Cool" still as cool as ever in slang. *Cleveland Plain Dealer.*
59. For a discussion of technology jargon, see Fandrych, I. M. (2007). Electronic communication and technical terminology: A rapprochement? *Journal of Language & Communication, 1*(1), 147–158.
60. What's in a word? A job, Hood senior's study says. (1991, June 6). *Washington Post,* Md8.
61. Walton, D. (2007, August 26). "Um, pardon me while I figure out what I'm saying." *Cleveland Plain Dealer,* M5.
62. (Walton, 2007).
63. (Walton, 2007).
64. Castro, J. (1988, July 11). Spanglish spoken here. *Time,* 53.
65. Edwards, B. (2003, September 23). *Spanglish, A new American language: Book documents English words with a Spanish twist.* Retrieved from http://www.npr.org/templates/story/story.php?storyid=1438900 Interview by NPR's Bob Edwards with Ilan Stevens, author of Stevens, I. (2004). *Spanglish: The making of a new American language*. New York: Harper.
66. (Edwards).
67. (Castro, 1988) as stated by Carmen Silva-Corvalan, University of Southern California. For related discussion, see Rothman, J., & Rell, A. (2005). A linguistic analysis of Spanglish: Relating language to identity. *Linguistics & the Human Sciences, 1*(3), 515-536. doi:10.1558/lhs.2005.1.3.515. And Chavez, C. (2006). Spanglish in persuasive communications: A study of code-mixing and linguistic preference in advertising (Top Interactive Paper). *Conference Papers—International Communication Association,* 1–27.
68. For an interesting discussion of English language learner variations, see Walsh, S. (2010). Which English? Whose English? An investigation of 'non-native' teachers' beliefs about target varieties. *Language, Culture & Curriculum, 23*(2), 123–137.
69. Sanchez, R. (1998, April 19). After Ebonics controversy, Oakland seeks viable lesson plan. *Washington Post,* A10.
70. Mims, H. A. (2000). Cleveland State University, symposium lecture.
71. Hispanic and Black high school graduation rates very low. (2004, February 26). *ParaPundit.* Civil Society Institute's Results for America (RTFA) Project and Advocates for Children of New York. Retrieved from www.parapundit.com
72. Based on research by Sandra Terrell and Francis Terrell.
73. Reagan's 'tear down this wall' speech turns 20. *USATODAY.com* (2007, June 12). Retrieved from USATODAY.com
74. Adapted from the concepts of Thomas R. Nilsen.
75. Smith, S. (2000, September/October). Words that sting. *Psychology Today, 24.*
76. (Smith, 2000).
77. (Smith, 2000).
78. Smalley, S. (2008, January 17). The power of words. Huffington Post. Retrieved from http://www.huffingtonpost.com/susan-smalley/the-power-of-words_b_81918.html

CHAPTER 3

1. For an in-depth discussion of nonverbal communication, see Burgoon, J., Guerrero, L. K., & Floyd, K. (2010). *Nonverbal communication*. Boston: Pearson.
2. For an extended discussion of universal nonverbal clues, read Darwin's universal faces, in P. Anderson. (Ed.). (2004). *The complete idiot's guide to body language.* New York: Penguin Group, pp. 53–56. Anderson also authored a scholarly text: Anderson, P. (2007). *Nonverbal communication: Forms and functions* (2nd ed.). Longwave, IL: Waveland Press. Interpretation of negative facial expressions appears to be culturally bound, see Jack, R., Blais, C., Scheepers, C., Schyns, P., & Caldara, R. (2009). Cultural confusions show that facial expressions are not universal. *Current Biology, 19*(18), 1543–1548. doi:10.1016/j.cub.2009.07.051
3. Burgoon, J. K., Buller, D. B., & Woodall, W. G. (1996). *Nonverbal communication: The unspoken dialogue* (2nd ed.). New York: McGraw-Hill, p. 1. The book is no longer in print, but is considered a precedent-setting text in the field of nonverbal communication and is still used as a classic reference by some communication instructors. Additional material on the topic maybe found in Burgoon, J., Guerrero, L. K., Floyd, K. (2010). *Nonverbal communication*. Boston: Pearson.
4. (Burgoon, Buller, & Woodall, 1996, p. 136).
5. (Burgoon, Buller, & Woodall, 1996, p. 1).
6. (Burgoon, Buller, & Woodall, 1996, p. 136).
7. (Anderson, Foreword, pp. 1 & 2).
8. McClave, E., Kim, H., Tamer, R., & Mileff, M. (2007). Head movements in the context of speech in Arabic, Bulgarian, Korean, and African-American vernacular English. *Gesture,* 7(3), 343–390.
9. Anderson, p. 55, based on the research of Irenäus Eibl-Eibesfeldt. Eibl-Eibesfeldt, I. (1980). Strategies of social interaction. In R. Plutchik & H. Kellerman. (Eds.). *Emotion: Theory, research and experience*. New York: Academic.
10. Bryner, J. (2009). *Smiles are innate, not learned*. Retrieved from Live Science.com. Referring to the research of David Matsumoto, psychologist, San Francisco State University and reported in *The Journal of Personality and Social Psychology*. (2009, January).
11. (Bryner).
12. (Anderson, p. 55).
13. (Anderson, p. 39).
14. Clifford Wright, C. (1989). *NLP workbook, Introductory level, Books 1 and 2.* Portland, OR: Metamorphous Press. For a description and discussion of neurolinguistic programming, see www.nlpinfo.com/ and http://www.neurolinguisticprogramming.com/ Neurolinguistic programming never had the scientific research base to support its value: Tye, M. (1994). Neurolinguistic programming: Magic or myth? *Journal of Accelerative Learning & Teaching, 19*(3-4), 309–342. Based on positive practitioner anecdotes, however, the theory continues to be applied in medical and other fields; see, for example, Bigley, J., Griffiths, P., Prydderch, A., Romanowski, C., Miles, L., Lidiard, H., et al. (2010). Neurolinguistic programming used to reduce the need for anesthesia in claustrophobic patients undergoing MRI. *British Journal of Radiology, 83*(986), 113–117. doi:10.1259/bjr/14421796
15. (Wright, 1989, p. 4).
16. For a further discussion of thinking and eye movement, see Adler, E. (1998, November 26). Speak to me with thine eyes (and head and arms). *Washington Post,* C5.
17. Doheryt-Sneddon, G. (2006, March). Nonverbal communication. *SPECTRA,* National Communication Association. For the complete report, go to http://insidehighered.com/workplace/2006/01/13tips
18. Tracy, J., & Robins, R. (2008). The nonverbal expression of pride: Evidence for cross-cultural recognition. *Journal of Personality & Social Psychology, 94*(3), 516–530.
19. Hall, E., & Hall, M. (1971, June). The sounds of silence. *Playboy, 18.* Hall, E. T. (1977). *Beyond culture*. Garden City, New York: Doubleday & Company.
20. *World citizens guide.* (2005). Southern Methodist University and Business for Diplomatic Action. Retrieved from traveler@worldcitizensguide.org
21. For an extensive discussion of international gestures, see Axtell, R. E. (2007). *The complete guide to international business and leisure travel.* Hoboken, NJ: John Wiley and Sons. Also see Axtell, R. (1991). *Gestures: The do's and taboos of body language around the world.* New York: John Wiley and Sons, pp. 317–328.
22. (Kachka).
23. Sigmund Freud. *The Columbia Word of Quotations,* entry 23110, Retrieved from www.bartleby.com/66/10/23110.html
24. The primary article that defined and explained expectancy violation theory: Burgoon, J. K. (1978). A communication model of personal space violation: Explication and an initial test. *Human Communication Research, 4*, 129–142. For further explanation, see Canary, D., Cody, M., & Manusov, V. (2008). *Interpersonal communication: A goals-based approach.* Boston: Bedford/St. Martins, p. 130.
25. Lane, D. R. (2001). *Honors: Communication capstone, interpersonal context.* Lexington, KY: University of Kentucky. Retrieved from www.uky.edu/~drlane/capstone/interpersonal/evt.html
26. Masip, J., Garrido, E., & Herrero, C. (2009). Heuristic versus systematic processing of information in detecting deception: Questioning the truth bias. *Psychological Reports, 105*(1), 11–36. doi:10.2466/PR0.105.1.11-36
27. APA. (2008). Website of the American Psychological Association. Retrieved from www.psychologymatters.org/polygraphs.html
28. Lindner, M. (2009, May 13). *How to sniff out a liar*. Retrieved from Forbes.com. Referring to the research done by the American Polygraph Association.
29. (Schmid, 2002).

30. Perina, K. (2002, January–February). Truth serum, brain scans may be foolproof lie detectors. *Psychology Today*, p. 15.
31. Parmar, N. (2004). Deception detection: Brain fingerprinting spots crime and innocence. *Innovation*. PBS documentary series, Episode 8. For further investigation, see Knapp, M. L. (2007). *Lying and deception in human interaction*. Boston: Allyn & Bacon.
32. (Parmar, 2004).
33. No specific identifying channels of nonverbal communication have been universally defined. The names used here are a compilation of those that have appeared in various textbooks on communication.
34. Key, A. P. F., Stone, W., & Williams, S. M. (2009, March/April). What do infants see in faces? ERP evidence of different roles of eyes and mouth for face perception in 9-month-old infants. *Infant & Child Development, 18*(2), 149–162, doi 10.1002/icd.600
35. (Hickson et al., p. 222).
36. Schmidt, K., Bhattacharya, S., & Denlinger, R. (2009). Comparison of deliberate and spontaneous facial movement in smiles and eyebrow raises. *Journal of Nonverbal Behavior, 33*(1), 35–45.
37. A research study conducted by Joe Teece, Boston College neuropsychologist.
38. What to keep an eye on. (2006, January 31). *Cleveland Plain Dealer*, A3. Originally printed in the *Baltimore Sun*.
39. (Hickson et al., p. 155).
40. (Adler, p. C5).
41. (Adler, p. C5).
42. See Church, R., Garber, P., & Rogalski, K. (2007). The role of gesture in memory and social communication. *Gesture*, 7(2), 137–158.
43. (Anderson, pp. 81–82).
44. (Axtell, p. 87).
45. (Anderson, p. 81).
46. (Burgoon, p. 41).
47. Bryner, J. (2010, January 29). *Pondering the future makes us lean forward, literally*. Retrieved from LiveScience, com. Based on the research of Lynden Miles, Louise Nind and Neil Macrae.
48. (Anderson, p. 68).
49. (Anderson, p. 68).
50. Samovar, L., Porter, R., & McDaniel, E. (2006). *Intercultural communication: A reader*. Belmont, CA: Thompson Higher Education, p. 253.
51. For a discussion on gender and touch, see Hickson
et al., p. 78.
52. Graham, J. (2007, November/December). A hands-on approach. *Psychology Today*, p. 24.
53. (Graham, 2007).
54. (Anderson, p. 75).
55. Anderson, L, (n.d.). *Environmental psychology and nonverbal behavior, 3*(2), 89–106. Reprinted with kind permission from Springer Science and Business Media.
56. (Knapp, pp. 273–284).
57. Irvine, M. (2004, September 8). *Employers, schools issue new dress codes*. U.S. National–AP. Retrieved from www.wjla.com/headlines/0904/171582.html
58. Binkley, C. (2008, April 17). Business casual: All business, never casual. *The Wall Street Journal*, D1.
59. Gumbiner, J. (2008). *What's business casual attire?* Retrieved from http://career-advice.monster.com/business-etiquette/Whats-Business-Casual-Attire/home.aspx Also see Kiddie, T. (2009). Recent trends in business casual attire and their effects on student job seekers. *Business Communication Quarterly, 72*(3), 350–354.
60. Pemberton-Sikes. (2007). *What is business casual?* Retrieved from http://www.sideroad.com/Business_Attire/business-casual.html
61. Krakovsky, M. (2003, September/October). Haven't we met? *Psychology Today, 17*.
62. Bennett, J. (2010, July 26). The beauty advantage. *Newsweek*, p. 47.
63. Based on the research of economist Daniel Hamermesh. Retrieved from http://webspace.utexas.edu/hamermes/www/ and referred to in the section on his blog, *My Beauty Papers*.
64. Bennett, based on a survey conducted by *Newsweek*.
65. Black bodies. (1999, April 19). *20/20 ABC-TV*. ABC News Home Videos, #T990419.
66. Olivardia, R., Pope, H. G. Jr., Borowiecki, J. J. III, & Cohane, G. H. (2004, July). Biceps and body image: The relationship between muscularity and self-esteem, depression, and eating disorder symptoms. *Psychology of Men and Masculinity*, 112–120. Abstract available at www.sciencedirect.com/science. For a related discussion regarding female perception, see Coleman, R. (2008). The becoming of bodies. *Feminist Media Studies, 8*(2), 163–179. doi:10.1080/14680770801980547
67. Leathers, D., & Eaves, M. H. (2008). *Successful nonverbal communication, principles and applications*. Boston: Pearson Education, p. 154. The statistics are from a classic study reported in *The eyes have it*. (1973, December 3). *Newsweek*. For an extensive discussion on personal appearance, see Leathers, Chapter 7.
68. (Hickson et al., p. 162).
69. (Hickson et al., p. 162).
70. Mangels, J. (2006, December 20). Society doesn't let short boys stand tall. *Cleveland Plain Dealer*, M4. Based on the writings of Hall, S. S. (2006). *Size matters*. Boston: Houghton Mifflin.
71. (Hickson et al., p. 161).
72. (Burgoon, p. 224, referring to research by Edward Hall).
73. (Burgoon).
74. Anderson, pp. 117–120, based on the research of Edward and Mildred Hall.
75. For an extensive discussion of paralanguage, see Reiman, pp. 187–207.
76. Harms, W. (2006, December 4). Verbal gestures unconsciously used during speech. *Advice for Speech-Language Pathologists & Audiologists*, p. 16.
77. Hughes, S., Farley, S., & Rhodes, B. (2010, September). Vocal and physiological changes in response to the physical attractiveness of conversational partners. *Journal of Nonverbal Behavior 3*(34), 155–167. doi 10.1007/s10919-010-0087-9
78. (Harms).
79. (Harms).
80. Small, M. (2008, June 6). *Sarcasm seen as evolutionary survival skill*. Retrieved from LiveScience.com. Based on the research of neurophysiologist Katherine Rankin.
81. (Knapp, pp. 204–205).
82. Kim, Y. Y. (2006). Intercultural personhood: An integration of eastern and western perspectives. In Samovar, L., Porter, R., & McDaniel, E. (2006). *Intercultural communication: A reader*. Belmont, CA: Thomson Higher Education, p. 411.
83. (Kim, 2006).
84. There are many popular press sources available for people who need to learn cultural expectations for personal or business travel, such as the following: Kernecker, H. (2005). *When in Mexico, do as the Mexicans do: The clued-in guide to Mexican life, language, and culture*. New York: McGraw Hill; Ostrowski, P., & Penner, G. (2009). *It's all Chinese to me: An overview of culture and etiquette in China*. North Clarendon, VT: Tuttle Publishing.
85. For a discussion on culture and chronemics, see Hickson et al., pp. 315–320.
86. The incident reported was at George Washington University. The student's name was omitted by request.
87. (Hickson et al., p. 319).
88. The classic observations regarding procrastination can be found in Ellis, A., & Knaus, W. (1979). *Overcoming procrastination*. New York: AEI Publications, 1979. For help in overcoming procrastination, see Steel, P. (2010). *The procrastination equation: How to stop putting things off and start getting things done*. Boston: Prentice Hall.
89. Kimbrough-Robinson, C. (2007). Procrastination: The death of opportunity. *Quill, 95*(2), 43.
90. Szalavitz, M. (2007). Stand and deliver. In K. Duffy (Ed.). *Personal Growth and Behavior*. (35th annual ed.) . Dubuque, IA: McGraw Hill, pp. 62–63.
91. See, for example: Chen, D., & Dalton, P. (2005). The effect of emotion and personality on olfactory perception. *Chemical Senses, 30*, 345–351; or Retiveau, A. N., Chambers, IV, E., & Milliken, G. A. (2004). Common and specific effects for fine fragrances on the mood of women. *Journal of Sensory Studies, 19*, 373–394.
92. Andrews, L. (2007, November/December). The hidden force of fragrance. *Psychology Today, 57*.
93. (Hickson et al., p. 300).
94. Ilmberger, J., Heuberger, E., Mahrhofer, C., Dessovic, H., Kowarik, D., & Buchbauer, G. (2001). The influences of essential oils on human attention: Alertness. *Chemical Senses, 26*, 239–245.
95. Bosemans, A. (2006). Scents and sensibility: When do (in)congruent ambient scents influence product evaluations? *Journal of Marketing, 70*(3), 32–43.
96. Low, K. E. (2006). Presenting the self, the social body, and the olfactory: Managing smells in everyday life experiences. *Sociological Perspectives, 49*(4), 607–631.
97. Kirk-Smith, M. D. (1994). Culture and olfactory communication. In R. A. Gardner, B. Chiarelli, & F. C. Plooij (Eds.) (pp. 385–406), *Ethological roots of culture*. Netherlands: Kluwer Academic Publishers.
98. Haselton, M. (2009). Olfactory attractiveness: The role of scent cues in attraction and mate choice. *Conference Papers—International Communication Association*.
99. For a discussion of these and other influences of smell as a communicator, see Hickson et al., 299–306.
100. (Andrews, p. 8.).
101. (Andrews, p. 8.).
102. (Andrews, p. 8.).
103. Waskul, D. D., & Vannini, P. (2008). Smell, odor, and somatic work: Sense-making and sensory management. *Social Psychology Quarterly, 71*(1), 53–71.
104. Results from tests run by Muzak Limited Partnership, (n.d.).
105. Music's affects on the human body. (n.d.). Retrieved from http://hs.riverdale.k12.or.us/~dthompso/exhib_03/jasonc/Music's_Affects_on_the_Human_Body.html. Also see Sakamoto, H. (2002, September). Psychocirculatory responses caused by listening to music, and exposure to fluctuation noise or steady noise. *The Journal of Sound and Vibration, 250*(1), 23–29.
106. McCormick, P. (1979, January 12). Rock music can weaken muscles. *Elyria (Ohio) Chronicle-Telegram*, Encore, p. 15; Change, S. C., & Jacquline S. (2005). How, "La la la: The effects of music on muscle strength." California State Science Fair. Retrieved from http://search.yahoo.com/search?p=rock+music+can+effect+muscles&fr=yfp-t-501&toggle=1&cop=mss&ei=UTF-8
107. Tanner, L. (2005, December 26). Physicians take note of music's power to heal. *Cleveland Plain Dealer*, A-2, based on research by Dr. Ary Goldberger of the Harvard Medical School and Abraham Kocheril of the Carle Heart Center in Urbana, IL.
108. (Tanner, 2005).
109. Britt, R. (2005, May 19). Red outfits give athletes advantage. *Live Science, Health SciTech*. Based on research by Russell Hill and Robert Barton, University of Durham. As reported in the May 19, 2005 issue of *Nature*.
110. (Britt, 2005).
111. Goudarzi, S. (2007, March 5). Study: Seeing red lowers test scores. *Live Science, Health*

SciTech. Based on research by Andrew Elliot, University of Rochester.

112. (Goudarzi, 2007).
113. For a discussion of taste/gustoric communication, see Hickson et al., pp. 294–295.
114. For discussion about touch affecting taste see: Krishna, A., & Morrin, M. (2008). Does touch affect taste? The perceptual transfer of product container haptic cues. *Journal of Consumer Research, 34*(6), 807–818.
115. Miller, L. (2004, April 17). Airport security watching behavior patterns. *Cleveland Plain Dealer*, A10.
116. Keller, J. (2010, September). Can body language predict elections? The Atlantic. Retrieved from http?//www.theatlantic.com/politics/print/2010/10/can-body-language-predict-elections/65424/.
117. (Keller).
118. Keller. About Sair de la Motte, founder and CEO of Nonverbal Solutions, Portland, Oregon.

CHAPTER 4

1. Oldsenburg, D. (1987, March 18). Sometimes people only hear what they really want to hear. *Washington Post*. Reprinted in *Cleveland Plain Dealer*, G1. Using materials developed by Montgomery, R. (1984). *Listening made easy*. New York: AMACOM, as used in Berko, R., Aitken, J., & Wolvin, A. (2010). *I Comm: Interpersonal concepts and competencies*. Lanham, MD: Rowman & Littlefield, p. 67.
2. Watkins, K. J. (2007, December 3). *How much time do you spend listening?* Retrieved from www.alumbo.com/article/39652-How-Much-Time-Do-You-Spend-Listening .html
3. (Watkins, 2007).
4. Adams, W., C., & Cox, E. S. (2010). The teaching of listening as an integral part of an oral activity: An examination of public-speaking texts. *The International Journal of Listening, 24*(2), p. 90. doi: 10.1080/10904011003744524
5. (Adams & Cox, 2010).
6. Sobieski, S. (2010, January/February). Side effects, Why left and right matter. *Psychology Today*, p. 49. For an extended discussion on learning styles and a learning styles test, see: *Learning styles explained*. Retrieved from http://www.ldpride.net/learningstyles.MI.htm
7. Janusik, L. A., & Wolvin, A. D. (2009). 24 hours in a day: A listening update to the time studies. *International Journal of Listening, 23*(2), 104–120. doi:10.1080/10904010903014442
8. Weaver, S., & Weaver, I. (2008). Talk to the hand: Listening style preferences and aggressiveness. *Individual Differences Research, 6*(4), 260–268.
9. See Barker, L., & Watson, K. (2001). *Listen up*. New York: St. Martin's Press, Chapter 4.
10. National Institute on Deafness and Other Communication Disorders. (n.d.). *Quick statistics*. Retrieved from www.nidcd.nih.gov/health/statistics/quick.htm
11. (National Institute on Deafness and Other Communication Disorders).
12. Hoover, A., & Krishnamurti, S. (2010). Survey of college students' MP3 listening: Habits, safety issues, attitudes, and education. *American Journal of Audiology, 19*(1), 73–83. doi:10.1044/1059-0889(2010/08-0036
13. (National Institute on Deafness and Other Communication Disorders).
14. Interview with Marcia Warren, CCC-A, licensed audiologist, July 10, 2008.
15. Mobley, P. (2006, December 28). *Listening*. ez@articles. Retrieved from http://ezinearticles.com/? Listening&id=397732 Individual differences in cognition and recall vary greatly, as explained in Sasaki, T. (2009). Individual differences in working memory capacity in recency effects: From the recall process. *Psychological Reports, 104*(2), 545–548. doi:10.2466/PRO.104.2545-548
16. Davidson, J. (2002). *The complete guide to public speaking*. Hoboken, NJ: Wiley.
17. Zanden, B. V. (n.d.). *Preparing an effective presentation*. Retrieved from www.cs.utk.edu/~bvz/presentation.html
18. (Zanden).
19. (Zanden).
20. See Janusik, L. A. (2007, June). Building listening theory: The validation of the conversational listening span. *Communication Studies, 58*, 139–156, for a discussion of the applications of working memory to understanding listening cognition.
21. *Are people speaking faster (and are they being heard)?* (2002, November). Retrieved from http://answers.google.com/answers/threadview?id=112576
22. (Are people speaking faster).
23. Academic Skills Center, Dartmouth College. (2001). Based on the research of Ralph Nichols. Retrieved from www.dartmouth.edu/~acskills/docs/10_bad_listening_habits.doc
24. Humes, L. E., Burk, M. H., Coughlin, M. P., Busey, T. A., & Strauser, L. E. (2007). Auditory speech recognition and visual text recognition in younger and older adults: Similarities and differences between modalities and the effects of presentation rate. *Journal of Speech, Language & Hearing Research, 50*(2), 283–303. doi:10.1044/1092-4388(2007/021) Ward, N., & Nakagawa, S. (2004). Automatic user-adaptive speaking rate selection. *International Journal of Speech Technology*, 7(4), 259–268. Retrieved from EBSCO*host.*
25. Concept developed by Andrew Wolvin and Carolyn G. Coakley.
26. Beard, D. (2009). A broader understanding of the ethics of listening: Philosophy, cultural studies, media studies and the ethical listening subject. *International Journal of Listening, 23*(1), 7–20.
27. Bernstein, E. (2010, November 16). She talks a lot, he listens a little. *The Wall Street Journal*. Retrieved from http:online.wsj.com. Based on the research of Marianne Legato, founder of the Partnership for Gender-Specific Medicine at Columbia University.
28. (Bernstein, 2010).
29. Research findings on gender differences in listening are mixed. Many scholars have found no significant difference due to gender. For an overview, see Fitch- Hauser, M., Powers, W. G., O'Brien, K., & Hanson, S. (2007). Extending the conceptualization of listening fidelity. *International Journal of Listening, 21*(2), 81–91.
30. *Right brain vs. left brain*. (n.d.). Retrieved from http://www.funderstanding.com/v2/educators/right-brain-vs-left-brain
31. (*Right brain vs. left brain*).
32. The science of brain hemisphere is extremely complex. See, for example, Blake, M. (2009). Inferencing processes after right hemisphere brain damage: Maintenance of inferences. *Journal of Speech, Language & Hearing Research, 52*(2), 359–372. The terms *right-brained* or *left-brained* have become an oversimplified (and perhaps misleading), yet convenient and commonly understood way of referring to an individual's processing preferences. For a simplified discussion, see Wagner, K. (2007, August 22). *Right brain vs. left brain*. About.com For a discussion of global and linear brain theory, see Hopper, C. (2003). *Practicing college study skills: Strategies for success* (3rd ed.). Boston: Houghton Mifflin. For an example of a research application, see Greenberg, S., & MacGregor-Hannah, M. (2010). Disruptive effect of holistic bias on processing of other-race faces following face categorization. *Perceptual and Motor Skills, 110*(2), 567–579. doi:10.2466/PMS.110.2.567-579
33. Wendy Richmond builds an interesting case that our visual and linear processing may be influenced by culture. See Richmond, W. (2001, August). Promoting visual thinking. *Communication Arts, 43*(4), p. 186.
34. Based on information from Dr. Paul Torrance and Dr. Bernice McCarthy. (2005). Excell, Inc., P. O. Box 6, Fox River Grove, IL.
35. Hall, E. T., & Hall, M. R. (1989). *Understanding cultural differences*. Yarmouth, ME: Intercultural Press. Also see Hall, E. T. (1993). *An anthropology of everyday life*. Harpswell, ME: Anchor.
36. Franks, P. (2001). *Native Americans and the value of silence/listening*. Paper presented at the International Listening Association convention, Chicago, IL.
37. Rogers, C. R., & Roethlisberger, F. J. (1952, July-August). Barriers and gateways to communication. *Harvard Business Review, 30*, 46–52.
38. Take note: Doodling can help memory. (2009, May 19). Health Today. Retrieved from http://health.yahoo.net/tips/boost-your-memory-with-scribbles
39. (*Take note*, 2009).
40. For information on Logitech io2 Digital Writing System and Livescribe see: http://www.labnol.org/software/organize/compare-logitech-io2-pen-livescribe-smartpen-review/1592/
41. Jones, R. C. (2008). The "why" of class participation: A question worth asking. *College Teaching, 56*(1), 59–63.
42. Rocca, K. A. (2010). Student participation in the college classroom: An extended multidisciplinary literature review. *Communication Education, 59*(2), 185–213. doi:10.1080/03634520903505936
43. Lee, J. (2010). Online support service quality, online learning acceptance, and student satisfaction. *Internet & Higher Education, 13*(4), 277–283. doi:10.1016/j.iheduc.2010.08.002; Paechter, M., & Maier, B. (2010). Online or face-to-face? Students' experiences and preferences in e-learning. *Internet & Higher Education, 13*(4), 292–297. doi:10.1016/j.iheduc.2010.09.004
44. Taxonomy developed by Andrew Wolvin and Carolyn Coakley.
45. Titsworth, B. S. (2004, October). Students' notetaking: The effects of teachers' immediacy and clarity. *Communication Education, 53*(4), 3–5.
46. (Titsworth, 2004).
47. (Titsworth, 2004).
48. (Titsworth, 2004).
49. Barber, A., & Goldberg, A. A. (2000). Principles of confirmation. In K. M. Galvin & P. J. Cooper (Eds.). *Making connections*. Los Angeles: Roxbury, pp. 139–141.
50. Hadwin, A., Kirby, J., & Woodhouse, R. (1999). Individual differences in notetaking, summarization, and learning from lectures. *Alberta Journal of Educational Research, 45*(1), 1–17.
51. In 1975, Lawrence Wheeless differentiated *receiver apprehension* from *communication apprehension*. It was reported in Wheeless, L. W. (1975, September). An investigation of receiver apprehension and social context dimensions of communication apprehension. *Speech Teacher, 24*, p. 263. For additional discussion of listener/receiver apprehension, see Wilcox, A. K. (2002, November). *Receiver apprehension and college students: An examination of remediation via interactive skills training*. Retrieved from Lewiston, Idaho: Lewis-Clark State College. www.lcsc.edu/humanities/Wilcox-paper.htm. Or Bodie, G., & Villaume, W. (2003).

Aspects of receiving information: The relationship between listening preferences, communication apprehension, receiver apprehension, and communicator style. *International Journal of Listening,* 1747–1767.

52. Nichols, M. P. (2009). *The lost art of listening How learning to listen can improve relationships* (2nd ed.). New York: Guilford Family Therapy.
53. Magid, L. (2010, January 31). *PBS documentary questions tech and our future.* News.Cnet.com. Retrieved from http://news.cnet.com/8301-19518_3-10444847-238.html
54. The concept of egospeak was developed by Edward Addeo and Robert Burger and presented in their classic book, Addeo, E., & Burger, R. (1974). *Egospeak.* New York: Bantam Books, p. xiv.
55. Based on Potter, W. J. (2007). *Media literacy.* Thousand Oaks, CA: Sage.

CHAPTER 5

1. The professor was Dr. Gerald Phillips of The Pennsylvania State University. Included among his graduate students were some of the future major researchers and textbook authors of the late twentieth and early twenty-first centuries including James C. McCroskey, Lawrence B. Rosenfeld, Julia T. Wood, Mark Knapp, Steve Lucas, and Roy Berko.
2. Referred to in Berko, R., Aitken, J., & Wolvin, A. (2010). *IComm: Interpersonal concepts and competencies.* Lanham, MD: Rowman & Littlefield, p. v.
3. See http://faculty.buffalostate.edu/smithrd/UAE%20Communication/Unit4.pdf
4. Brownell, J. (2010). *Listening, attitudes, principles and skills.* Boston, MA: Pearson, p. 19.
5. A concept developed by Robert McGarvey. Retrieved from www.mcgarvey.net
6. (McGarvey).
7. Spring, N., & Briggs, W. (2006). The impact of blogging real or imagined? *Communication World, 23*(3), 28–32.
8. Jensen, M. (1984). Memoirs and journals as maps of intrapersonal communication. *Communication Education, 33*(3), 237.
9. Honeycutt, J. M. (2002). *Imagined interactions: Daydreaming about communication.* Cresskill, NJ: Hampton Press.
10. Fry, R., & Prentice-Dunn, S. (2005). Effects of coping information and value affirmation on responses to a perceived health threat. *Health Communication, 17*(2), 133–147. doi:10.1207/s15327027hc1702_2
11. Zagacki, K., Edwards, R., & Honeycutt, J. (1992). The role of mental imagery and emotion in imagined interaction. *Communication Quarterly, 40*(1), 56–68.
12. Vocate, D. R. (1994). *Interpersonal communication: Different voices, different minds.* Hillsdale, NJ: Erlbaum, p. 176. For a discussion of the work of L. S. Vygotsky, see Vocate.
13. (Vocate, 1994).
14. A concept stated in Adler, R. B., Rosenfeld, L. B., & Proctor, R. F. II. (2009). *Interplay: The process of interpersonal communication* (11th ed.). New York: Oxford University Press.
15. Honeycutt, J., Choi, C., & DeBerry, J. (2009). Communication apprehension and imagined interactions. *Communication Research Reports, 26*(3), 228–236. doi:10.1080/08824090903074423
16. Mitra, A. (2008). Using blogs to create cybernetic space. *Convergence: The Journal of Research into New Media Technologies, 14*(4), 457–472. doi:10.1177/1354856508094663
17. Albrechtslund, A. (2010). Gamers telling stories. *Convergence: The Journal of Research into New Media Technologies, 16*(1), 112–124. doi:10.1177/1354856509348773; Young, R. (2007). Story and discourse: A bipartite model of narrative generation in virtual worlds. *Interaction Studies, 8*(2), 177–208.
18. Turkle, S. (2005). *The second self computers and the human spirit.* Twentieth Anniversary edition. Boston: MIT Press.
19. Wei, L. P. (May 24–28, 2007). Self, space, place, and media: A social-embodied cognition review of intra- and /or inter- personal communication in digital-media networked world. Paper accepted to the *57th Annual Conference of the International Communication Association: Creating Communication: Content, Control, Critique* (*ICA '07*), San Francisco, CA, USA.
20. Adapted from items presented in *Tennessee Self-Concept Scale* (1964). Nashville, TN: Counselor Recordings and Tests.
21. *Tennessee Self-Concept Scale.*
22. Janda, L. (1996). *The psychologist's book of self-tests.* New York: Berkley Publishing Group, p. 72.
23. (Janda).
24. (Janda).
25. Gail Dusa, as cited in McGarvey, R. (1990, March). Talk yourself up. *USAir Magazine,* 90.
26. A idea based on the concepts of Sidney Simon.
27. Dave Grant, as noted in McGarvey, p. 93.
28. Bernie Zilbergeld, as noted in McGarvey, p. 94.
29. Festinger, L. (1957). A *theory of cognitive dissonance.* Evanston, IL: Row, Peterson.
30. Raconteurist. (2007, January 24). *Perception and communication, the educational process of a seasoned dame.* Retrieved from http://www.associatedcontent.com/article/132238/perception_and_communication.html?cat=72. Also see Wood, J. T. (2004). *Interpersonal Communication, everyday encounters.* Thousand Oaks, CA: Wadsworth.
31. (Raconteurist).
32. Wahlross, S. (1974). *Family communication.* New York: Macmillan, p. xi.
33. Long Beach City College of Theatre Arts and Speech. (1976). *Communicate* (3rd ed.). Dubuque, IA: Kendall/Hunt.
34. James, W. (1990). *The principles of psychology.* New York: Holt, Rinehart and Winston.
35. Byrne, B. M. (1996). *Measuring self-concept across the lifespan: Methodology and instrumentation for research and practice.* Washington, DC: American Psychological Association.
36. The verb *to be* provides us with our basic label of ourselves. Native Americans and those from some other cultures, such as West Africans, may have difficulty understanding and applying this concept because of linguistic and cultural differences. Most U.S. Americans, however, should find it an understandable concept.
37. Luft, J. A. (1963). *Group process: An introduction to group dynamics.* Palo Alto, CA: National Press, Chapter 3.
38. Based on Rosenfeld, L. (n.d.). *Relational disclosure and feedback,* unpublished paper developed by Lawrence Rosenfeld, Department of Communication, University of North Carolina, Chapel Hill, NC. Final format developed by Lawrence Rosenfeld and Roy Berko.
39. For a discussion of communication and ethnography, see Stuart Sigman, S. (1996). *A matter of time: The case for ethnographics of communication,* unpublished paper presented at the Speech Communication Association Convention, November 23, 1996. See also Goodall, H. L. (1996). Transforming communication studies through ethnographic practices, unpublished paper presented at the SCA Convention, November 23, 1996.
40. The description presented is based on a synthesis of theories about ethnography.
41. http://www.docsports.com/NBA/betting.html (February 25, 2011).
42. McCroskey, J. (2009). Communication apprehension: What have we learned in the last four decades. *Human Communication, 12*(2), 157–171.
43. See, for example, Ayres, J., A. Wilcox, K., & Ayres, D. M. (1995). Receiver apprehension: An explanatory model and accompanying research. *Communication Education* 44, 223–235; Aitken, J. E., & Neer, M. R. (1993). College student question asking: The relationship of classroom communication apprehension and motivation. *Southern Communication Journal,* 59, 73–81; and Richmond, V. P., & McCroskey, J. C. (1997). *Communication: Apprehension, avoidance, and effectiveness,* (5th ed.) Englewood Cliffs, NJ: Prentice-Hall.
44. Azar, B. (1995). Shy people have inaccurate self-concepts. *American Psychological Association Monitor,* 24.
45. (Azar).
46. Keaten, J., & Kelly, L. (2008). "Re: We really need to talk": Affect for communication channels, competence, and fear of negative evaluation. *Communication Quarterly, 56*(4), 407–426. doi:10.1080/01463370802451646
47. McCroskey, J., & Richmond, V. (1980). *The quiet ones: communication apprehension and shyness.* Dubuque, IA: CommComp, Gorsuch Scarisbrick, p. 21. For further investigation, see Teven, J., Richmond, V., McCroskey, J., & McCroskey, L. (2010). Updating relationships between communication traits and communication competence. *Communication Research Reports, 27*(3), 263–270. doi:10.1080/08824096.2010.496331
48. Hendrick, B. (2003, July 27). Biology might be at root of some people's shyness. *Cleveland Plain Dealer,* L5.
49. (Schrof & Schultz, p. 50).
50. Daly et al. In addition, see www.jamesmccroskey.com/
51. Chesebro, J. W., et al. (1992). Communication apprehension and self-perceived communication competence of at-risk students. *Communication Education, 41,* 345–360.
52. For a discussion of the effects of communication apprehension on math, English, reading, and intelligence scores, as well as on grades in general, see Bourhis, J., & Allen, M. (1992). Meta-analysis of the relationship between communication apprehension and cognitive performance. *Communication Education, 41,* 68–76.
53. Based on an unpublished investigation of speech reticence conducted by Doug Pederson, Pennsylvania State University, 1971.
54. (See Daly et al.).
55. (Richmond & McCroskey).
56. (Richmond & McCroskey).
57. (Richmond & McCroskey).
58. The classic study regarding this theory was proposed by Jerome Kagan in 1962 and has been reported on in such articles as: Kagan, J. (2001). Temperamental contributions to affective and behavioral profiles in childhood. In S. G. Hoffmann & P. M. Dibartolo (Eds.), *From social anxiety to social phobia: Multiple perspectives* (pp. 216–234). Needham Heights, MA: Allyn & Bacon and Kagan, J., Reznick, J. S., & Snidman, N. (1987). The physiology and psychology of behavioral inhibition in children. *Child Development,* 58, 1459–1473.
59. (Azar, Shy people.).
60. Results have been documented by Dr. Roy Berko, crisis counselor, while working with communicative apprehensive clients in "Overcoming Shyness and Communication Anxiety" workshops.
61. Casriel, E. (2007, March/April). My friend Joe Raffeto, A desert guide. *Psychology Today,* 70. Based on the work of Bernardo Carducci, Director of Indiana University Southeast's Shyness Research Institute.
62. (Casriel, 2007).
63. (Richmond and McCroskey, pp. 97–101).
64. (Richmond and McCroskey, p. 36).
65. (Richmond and McCroskey, p. 49).
66. (Schrof & Schultz, p. 54).
67. (Schrof & Schultz, p. 54). See also Raghunathan, A. (1999, May 18). Drug firms work on treatment for extreme forms of shyness. *Cleveland Plain Dealer,* 8A. Paxil was the first selective serotonin reuptake inhibitor to win approval by the Food and Drug

Administration for treatment of debilitating shyness. In addition, the drugs Zoloft and Prozac may be of some value.

68. Cooper, P., Calloway-Thomas, C., & Simonds, C. (2007). *Intercultural communication: A text with readings*. Boston: Pearson Education, p. 86.
69. Ting-Toomey, S. & Chung, L. (2005). *Understanding intercultural communication*. New York: Oxford University Press.
70. (Ting-Toomey & Chung, 2005).
71. (Ting-Toomey & Chung, 2005).
72. (Ting-Toomey & Chung, 2005, p. 70).
73. (Ting-Toomey & Chung, 2005, p. 70).
74. (Cooper, Calloway-Thomas, & Simonds, p. 98).
75. (Ting-Toomey and Chung, p. 169).
76. (Ting-Toomey & Chung, 2005, p. 170).
77. (Ting-Toomey & Chung, 2005, p. 170).
78. Chen, G. M., & Starosta, W. J. (1998). *Foundations of intercultural communication*. Boston: Allyn and Bacon, p. 131.
79. Dugas, D., Powers, W., & Sawyer, C. (2007). Extroversion versus similarity: An exploration of factors influencing communication accuracy of social cognitions. *Human Communication, 10*(3), 303–310.

CHAPTER 6

1. Berko, R., Aitken, J., Wolvin, A. (2010). *IComm: Interpersonal concepts and competencies*. Lanham, MD: Rowman & Littlefield, p. v.
2. For recent research trends, see Smith, S. W., & Wilson, S. R. (Eds.). (2009). *New directions in interpersonal communication research*. Thousand Oaks, CA: Sage Publications.
3. Berko, R., Rosenfeld, L., & Samovar, L. (1997). *Connecting: A culture-sensitive approach to interpersonal communication competency*. Ft. Worth: Harcourt Brace, p. 16. For additional information on interpersonal communication; Adler, R. B., Rosenfeld, L. B., & Proctor, R. F. II. (2009). *Interplay: The process of interpersonal communication*. (11th ed.). New York: Oxford University Press; Berko, R. M., Aitken, J. E., & Wolvin, A. D. (2010). *ICOMM: Interpersonal concepts and competencies*. Lanham, MD: Rowman & Littlefield.
4. Bambacas, M., & Patrickson, M. (2008). Interpersonal communication skills that enhance organizational commitment. *Journal of Communication Management, 12*(1), 51–72. doi:10.1108/13632540810854235
5. (Marchant, 1999, p. 303).
6. Kellas, J., Trees, A., Schrodt, P., LeClair-Underberg, C., & Willer, E. (2010). Exploring links between well-being and interactional sense-making in married couples' jointly told stories of stress. *Journal of Family Communication, 10*(3), 174–193. doi:10.1080/15267431.2010.489217
7. For further discussion of the "I," see Hall, C. S., & Lindzey, G. (1957). *Theories of personality*. New York: Wiley, p. 483.
8. Marwell, G., & Schmitt, D. R. (1990). An introduction. In J. Price Dillard (Ed.). *Seeking compliance: The production of interpersonal influence messages*. Scottsdale, AZ: Gorsuch Scarisbrick, pp. 3–5.
9. For a discussion of left brain/right brain theory, see Edwards, B. (1989). *Drawing on the right side of the brain*. Los Angeles: Jeremy Tracher; Pechura, C., & Martin, J. (Eds.), *Mapping the brain and its function*. Washington, DC: Institute of Medicine National Academy Press; and Cutter, R. (1994). *When opposites attract: Right brain/left brain relationships and how to make them work*. New York: Dutton. For contemporary information, see sources in relevant chapter 4 footnote.
10. A belief of Murray Banks, a professional speaker, who speaks extensively on leadership, change, performance, and lifestyle.
11. Adapted from Cuming, P. (1981). Empowerment profile. *The power handbook*. Boston: CB, pp. 2–5.
12. Berko et al., p. 428. Also see Barraclough, R. A., & and Steward, R. A. (1992). Power and control: Social science perspectives. In Richmond, V. P., & McCroskey, J. C. (Eds.). *Power in the classroom*. Hillsdale, NJ: Erlbaum, pp. 1–4; Adapted from Cumming, P. (1981). Empowerment profile. *The power handbook*. Boston: CBI, pp. 2–5.
13. Farley, S. D., Timme, D. R., & Hart, J. W. (2010). On coffee talk and break-room chatter: Perceptions of women who gossip in the workplace. *Journal of Social Psychology, 150*(4), 361–368.
14. Bordon, G. A. (1991). *Cultural orientation: An approach to understanding intercultural communication*. Englewood Cliffs, NJ: Prentice-Hall, p. 116.
15. Servaes, J. (1998, Summer). Cultural identity in East and West. *The Howard Journal of Communication, 1*, 64.
16. Carlyle, T. (n.d.). LandOfWisdom.com. Retrieved from www.landofwisdom.com/category/heart/
17. Kouzes, J. M., & Posner, B. Z. (2008). *Leadership challenge* (4th ed.). San Francisco, CA: Wiley, Chapter 10.
18. For a discussion concerning the differences between male and female communication, see Arliss, L. P., & Borisoff, D. J. (1993). *Women and men communicating: Challenge and changes*. Ft. Worth: Harcourt Brace; Tannen, D. (1990). *You just don't understand*. New York: Morrow; Wood, J. T. (2010). *Gendered lives: Communication, gender, and culture*. Belmont, CA: Wadsworth. For further investigation, see Brannon, L. (2008). *Gender: Psychological perspectives*. Boston: Prentice Hall; Stewart, L., Cooper, P., Stewart, A., & Friedley, S. (2002). *Communication and gender* (4th ed.) Boston: Pearson; Ivy, D. K., & Backlund, P. (2007). *GenderSpeak: Personal effectiveness in gender communication* (4th ed.). Boston: Allyn & Bacon.
19. Tyre, P., Scelfo, J. (2006, July 31). Girls will be girls. *Newsweek*, 46, quoting neuropsychiatrist Louann Brizendine, author of *The female brain*.
20. Moir, A., & Jessel, D. (1991, May 5). Sex and cerebellum: Thinking about the real difference between men and woman. *Washington Post*, K3.
21. (Moir & Jessel, 1991).
22. Arliss, L. P., & Borisoff, D. J. (1993). *Women and men communicating: Challenge and changes*. Ft, Worth: Harcourt Brace, p. 3.
23. (Arliss & Borisoff, p. 9).
24. Mathias, B. (1993, May 3). Male identity crisis. *Washington Post*, C5.
25. Burleson, B., Dindia, K., & Condit, C. (1997). *Gender communication: Different cultural perspectives*. A panel discussion at the National Communication Association Conference, Chicago.
26. Adapted from Bem, S. L. (1974). The measurement of psychological androgyny. *Journal of Consulting and Clinical Psychology, 42*, 155–162. The original inventory developed by Bem contains sixty items—twenty masculine, twenty feminine, and twenty neutral (neither masculine nor feminine exclusively).
27. Heilman, M., Caleo, S., & Halim, M. (2010). Just the thought of it!: Effects of anticipating computer-mediated communication on gender stereotyping. *Journal of Experimental Social Psychology, 46*(4), 672–675. doi:10.1016/j.jesp.2010.02.005
28. What's in a word? A job, hood senior's study says. (1991, June 6). *Washington Post*, MD8.
29. (Tannen, pp. 43–44).
30. Mehl, M., Vazire, S., Ramirez-Esparza, N., Slatcher, R., & Pennebaker, J. (2006, July). Are women really more talkative than men? *Science*, 6. Details on methods and analysis are available on *Science* online.
31. For a discussion on interruptions, see Stewart, Cooper, Stewart, & Friedley, p. 54; Wood, pp. 31, 144.
32. Based on the research of H. G. Whittington, James P. Smith, Leonard Kriegel, Lillian Glass, and Hilary Lips, University of Kansas, Department of Psychology.
33. (Whittington, Smith, Kriegel, Glass, & Lips).
34. (Whittington, Smith, Kriegel, Glass, & Lips).
35. Hertenstein, M., & Keltner, D. (2011). Gender and the communication of emotion via touch. *Sex Roles, 64*(1/2), 70–80. doi:10.1007/s11199-010-9842-y
36. *Third of U.S. teens with phones text 100 times a day*. (2010, April 20). Reuters. Retrieved from http://www.reuters.com/article/idUSTRE63J4EX20100420
37. Colley, A., Todd, Z., White, A., & Turner-Moore, T. (2010). Communication using camera phones among young men and women: Who sends what to whom? *Sex Roles, 63*(5/6), 348–360. doi:10.1007/s11199-010-9805-3
38. Wood, J. T. (2010). *Gendered lives: Communication, gender, and culture*. Belmont, CA: Wadsworth.
39. Fanning, P., & McKay, M. (1993). *Being a man: A guide to the new masculinity*. Oakland, CA: New Harbinger, p. 13.
40. Zinczenko, D. (2007, December 17). Why men don't talk. *Men's Health*. Retrieved from http://health.yahoo.com/experts/menlovesex/73762/why-men-dont-talk; additional material on this subject is discussed in Zinczenko, Z. (2006). *Men, love and sex: The complete user's guide for women*. Tantor Media.
41. (Zinczenko, 2006).
42. (Gray, pp. 11–13).
43. *What is sexual harassment*? (2011). Retrieved from www. sexualharassmentsuport.org
44. (*What is*).
45. (Sexual harassment in the workplace, 2006).
46. (Sexual harassment in the workplace, 2006).
47. (Sexual harassment in the workplace, 2006).
48. (Sexual harassment in the workplace, 2006, p. 134).
49. (Sexual harassment in the workplace, 2006, p. 133).
50. Farkas, K. (2011, January 3). Notre Dame College has improved how it addresses all forms of harassment, including sexual assaults. *The [Cleveland] Plain Dealer*. Retrieved from http://blog.cleveland.com/metro/2011/01
51. (Sexual harassment in the workplace, 2006, p. 13).
52. An increase in male-on-male sexual harassment shows larger truths about abuse in the workplace. (2010, January 12). *Newsweek*. Retrieved from http://www.newsweek.com/2010/01/12/abuse-of-power.html
53. (An increase).
54. Morin, R. (1992). Harassment consensus grows. *Washington Post*, A22.
55. For a support community for anyone who has experienced sexual harassment go to: http://www.sexualharassmentsupport.org/
56. Based on the writings of Rebecca Ray, senior vice president, director of training, American Skandia Corporation.
57. Elias, M. (2004, July 28). Bullying crosses the line into workplace. *USA Today*.
58. (Elias, 2004).
59. (Elias, 2004).
60. (Elias, 2004).
61. (Elias, 2004).
62. Tong, S., Van Der Heide, B., Langwell, L., & Walther, J. (2008). Too much of a good thing? The relationship between number of friends and interpersonal impressions on Facebook. *Journal of Computer-Mediated Communication, 13*(3), 531–549. doi:10.1111/j.1083-6101.2008.00409.x

63. Pulley, B. (2010, December 26). Dating apps grow as Facebook users search for romance. *The [Cleveland] Plain Dealer*, p. A10.
64. Based on a theory of Jon Nussbaum. For further investigation, see Nussbaum, J. F. (2007). Life span communication and quality of life. *Journal of Communication, 57*, 1–7; Pecchioni L., Wright, K. & Nussbaum, J. F. (2005). *Lifespan communication*. Mahwah, NJ: Erlbaum.
65. (Nussbaum).
66. The classic work on Uncertainty Reduction Theory is Berger, C., & Calabrese, R., (1975). Some explorations in initial interaction and beyond: Toward a developmental theory of interpersonal communication. *Human Communication Research, 1*, 99–112.
67. Ting-Toomey, S. & Chung, L. (2005). *Understanding intercultural communication*. New York: Oxford University Press.
68. The information in this section is based on Knapp, M. L., & Vangelisti, A. L. (2008). *Interpersonal communication and human relationships* (6th Ed,). Boston: Allyn & Bacon.
69. Sheeks, M., & Birchmeier, Z. (2007). Shyness, sociability, and the use of computer-mediated communication in relationship development. *CyberPsychology & Behavior, 10*(1), 64–70. doi:10.1089/cpb.2006.9991
70. Original source of Social Exchange Theory: Thibaut, J. W., & Kelley, H. H. (1959). *The social psychology of groups*. New York: John Wiley & Sons. For a discussion of the economic model of relationships, see Berko et al, p. 289.
71. Based on the research of Anthony Brandt.
72. Kelly, L., Keaten, J., Hazel, M., & Williams, J. (2010). Effects of reticence, affect for communication channels, and self-perceived competence on usage of instant messaging. *Communication Research Reports, 27*(2), 131–142. doi:10.1080/08824091003738040
73. The discussion in this section is based on the writings of Lindgren, V. (n.d.). *Recognizing relationship warning signs*. Retrieved from www.lindgrenmt.com/warning.htm
74. Knapp, M. L., & Vangelisti, A. L. (2008). *Interpersonal communication and human relationships* (6th ed.) Boston: Allyn & Bacon.
75. Social Exchange Theory (Thibaut & Kelley) continues to be used in research. For a modern application, see Sutphin, S. (2010). Social exchange theory and the division of household labor in same-sex couples. *Marriage & Family Review, 46*(3), 191–206. doi:10.1080/01494929.2010.490102
76. Thimm, C. (2010). Technically-mediated interpersonal communication. In D. Matsumoto (Ed.). *APA handbook of interpersonal communication* (pp. 57–76). Washington, DC: American Psychological Association.
77. eHarmony.com (2011). Retrieved from http://www.eharmony.com/
78. Pew. (2010). *Teens and mobile phones*. Pew Internet and American Life Project. Retrieved from http://pewinternet.org/Reports/2010/Teens-and-Mobile-Phones/Chapter-2/The-typical-American-teen-who-texts-sends-1500-texts-a-month.aspx
79. Facebook.com. (2011). Retrieved from http://www.facebook.com/press/info.php?statistics
80. Kee, K., Park, N., & Valenzuela, S. (2009). Is there social capital in a social network site?: Facebook use and college students' life satisfaction, trust, and participation. *Journal of Computer-Mediated Communication, 14*(4), 875–901. doi:10.1111/j.1083-6101.2009.01474.x
81. Facebook.com. (2011). Retrieved from http://www.facebook.com/press/info.php?statistics
82. Phulari, S. S., Khamitkar, S. D., Deshmukh, N. K., Bhalchandra, P. U., Lokhande, S. N., & Shinde, A. R. (2010). Understanding formulation of social capital in online social network sites (SNS). *International Journal of Computer Science, 7*(3).
83. Konijn, E. A., Sonja Utz, S., Tanis, M., & Barnes, S. B. (Eds.). (2008). *Mediated interpersonal communication*. Florence, KY: Routledge.
84. For a discussion of computer-mediated communication, see Shedletsky, L. J., & Aitken, J. E. (2004). *Human communication on the Internet*. Boston: Allyn & Bacon/Longman; Shedletsky, L. J., & Aitken, J. E. (Eds.) (2010). *Cases on online discussion and interaction: Experiences and outcomes*. Hershey, PA: IGI Global.
85. Wiredville, U.S.A. (1999, September 20). *Newsweek*, 62.
86. Miller, M. J. (2004, February 17). Do-it-all cell phones. *PC Magazine, 23*, 6.
87. Cooper, C. (2009). Generation Net and the cell phone: The blurring of interpersonal and mass communication. *American Communication Journal, 11*(1), 1–11.
88. Joseph Walther has provided a consistent body of work on this topic, including Walther, J. (1992). Interpersonal effects in computer-mediated interaction. *Communication Research, 19*(1), 52; Walther, J., Van Der Heide, B., Tong, S., Carr, C., & Atkin, C. (2010). Effects of interpersonal goals on inadvertent intrapersonal influence in computer-mediated communication. *Human Communication Research, 36*(3), 323–347. doi:10.1111/j.1468-2958.2010.01378.x.; Wang, Z., Walther, J., & Hancock, J. (2009). Social identification and interpersonal communication in computer-mediated communication: What you do versus who you are in virtual groups. *Human Communication Research, 35*(1), 59–85. doi:10.1111/j.1468-2958.2008.01338.x
89. Fram, A. (2010, November 2). Study: Wireless-only homes 'the new norm.' *The [Cleveland] Plain Dealer*, p. D5, based on a study by the Center for Disease Control and Prevention.
90. Fram, a comment by Stephen Blumber, a senior scientist at the Center for Disease Control and Prevention.
91. Fatal wreck spurs cell phone fight. (2003, January 10). *Pittsburgh Tribune-Review*. Retrieved from www.pittsburghlive.com, based on research by the Center for Cognitive Brain Imagery at Carnegie Mellon University.
92. Dekunle, S. (2010, October 8). *Cell phones: The death of human interaction*. Retrieved from http://www.diamondbackoneline.com/opinion/call-phones-the-death-of-human-interaction
93. (Dekunle).
94. Suggestions synthesized from Nokia. (2003, July 1). *Cell phone courtesy month: Five basic cell phone rules*. Retrieved from www.classbrain.com; *Proper cell phone etiquette*. (n.d.). cellphonecarriers.com; Mark Toft, M. (2004). Cell phone etiquette. Retrieved from www.staples.com; also see Strawbridge, M. (2006). *Netiquette: Internet etiquette in the age of the blog*. Ely, UK: Software Reference Ltd.
95. *Internet world statistics*. (2010, June 30). InternetWorldStats.com. Retrieved from http://www.internetworldstats.com/stats14.htm
96. (*Internet world statistics*).
97. (Slabbeert, 2006).
98. (gotomeeting.com).
99. Sherer, K. (1997). College life on-line: Healthy and unhealthy Internet use. *Journal of College Student Development, 38*(6), 655–665.
100. Silk, A. (2010, January 31). *Think that Facebook addiction is harmless?* Retrieved from http://www.thecowl.com/2.7828/think-that-facebok-addiction-is-harmless
101. Carnes, P. (2004, February 27). *The criteria of problematic online sexual behavior.* Stated in a workshop presented at the Free Clinic of Cleveland.
102. (Carnes, 2004).
103. Payne, W. (2006, November 14). More people say heavy Internet use is disrupting their lives, and medical experts are paying attention. *The Washington Post*, F01.
104. For a discussion of Internet addiction and electronic media usage by college students, which includes a reference to the study regarding the ten percent addiction rate, see: *Internet use and study habits by gender—How students use the computer lab*. Retrieved from http://www.evc-cit.info/psych018/observation_samples/observation2498.pdf
105. Based on information listed on NetAddiction.com, the Center for Internet Addiction Recover, as referenced in Silk.
106. Based on psychiatrist Nathan Andrew Shapira's study on obsessive Internet use, referred to in Shapira, N. A., Lessig, M. C., Goldsmith, T. D., Szabo, S. T., Lazoritz, M., Gold, M. S., & Stein, D. J. (2003). Problematic Internet use: Proposed classification and diagnostic criteria. *Depress Anxiety, 17*(4), 207–216. Adapted from materials presented at a workshop by Carnes, P. (2004, February 27). *The criteria of problematic online sexual behavior*. Cleveland (OH) Free Clinic.
107. Dr. Elias Aboujaoude, director of Stanford's Impulse Control Disorders Clinic, as referenced in Silk.
108. (Carnes, 2004).
109. (Carnes, 2004).
110. Mitchell, A. (2004, January 24). *Bullied by the click of a mouse*. Retrieved from www.globeandmail.com/servlet/story/RTGAM.20040124.wbully0124/BNStory/
111. (Mitchell, 2004).
112. Holladay. J. (2010, Fall). Cyberbullying. *Teaching Tolerance*, p. 43.
113. Vanderberg, E., & DeFalco, B. (2010, September 30). *Outrage, remorse after Rutgers student's death*. Retrieved from http;news.yahoo.com/s/ap/20100930
114. Huffstutter, P. J. (2007, November 23). Fatal cyber-bullying hits home. *Los Angles Times*, as reproduced in *Cleveland Plain Dealer*, A12.
115. Cyberstalking. (n.d.). Your Dictionary.com. Retrieved from http://law.yourdictionary.com/cyberstalking
116. *1999 Report on cyberstalking*. (1999). US Government. Retrieved from www.usdoj.gov/criminal/cybercrime/cyberstalking.htm
117. (*1999 Report on cyberstalking*)
118. Keaten, J., & Kelly, L. (2008). "Re: We really need to talk": Affect for communication channels, competence, and fear of negative evaluation. *Communication Quarterly, 56*(4), 407–426. doi:10.1080/01463370802451646
119. Sklaroff, S. (1999, March 22). E-mail. *U.S. News and World Report*, 54.
120. *How TIME "person of the year" Mark Zuckenberg changed dating*. (2010, December 16). Retrieved from http://www.yourtango.com/202065340
121. (*How TIME*).
122. How TIME, referred to Julie Spira, YourTango Expert and author of *The rules of netiguette: How to mind your manners on the web*.
123. (*How TIME*).
124. Jones, S. (2010, July 29). *Study: Women top men in online social networking. The [Cleveland] Plain Dealer*, C4, based on a study by comScore.Inc.
125. Facebook users average 7 hrs a month in january as digital universe expands. (2010, February 16). NielsenWire. Retrieved from http://blog.nielsen.com/nielsenwire/online_mobile/facebook-users-average-7-hrs-a-month-in-january-as-digital-universe-expands/
126. McDonald, S. N. (2005, July 5). Facebook frenzy. The Associated Press.
127. St Xavier get pokes in, but fails to rattle Tanski. (2007, December 1). *Cleveland Plain Dealer*, D1.
128. Tancer, B. (2007, October 24). My Space v. Facebook: Competing Addictions. *Time*.

Retrieved from www.time.com/time/printout/0,8816,1675244,00.html
129. Lang, K. G. (November 19). Facebook friend turns into Big Brother. *LaCrosse Tribune*. Retrieved from http://lacrosse-tribune.com/news/local/article_0ff40f7a-d4d1-11de-afb3-001cc4c002e0.html
130. Jaschik, S. (2009, November 13). *Furor over anti-gay blog*. Inside Higher Education. Retrieved from http://www.insidehighered.com/news/2009/11/13/purdue
131. Engelking, P. (2010, April 23). *UMD students in trouble for racist Facebook remarks*. CBS Broadcasting Inc. Retrieved from http://wcco.com/local/umd.facebook.racism.2.1653311.html
132. Lyons, D. (2010, May 24 & 31). The high price of Facebook. *Newsweek*, p. 22.
133. Wortham, J., Facebook unveils simplified privacy controls. (2010, May 27). The *[Cleveland] Plain Dealer, C2.*
134. (Lyons).
135. *Facebook, the privacy and productivity challenge*. (n.d.). Sohpos.com. Retrieved from sophos.com
136. Swartz, J. (2007, September 12). Soon million of Facebookers won't be incognito. *USA Today*, 3B.
137. *What you need to know about Facebook*. (n.d.). Office of Career Services, University of Central Missouri, adapted from materials developed by Kathleen Mcabe, Director of Peer Education at Creighton, University.
138. Mulholland, R. (2009, December 12). *Anti-social network aims to be Facebook killer app*. Retrieved from http://news.yahoo.com/s/afp/20091210
139. *Nielson mobile survey*. (2008, September 22. Cnet.com. Retrieved from http://news.cnet.com/8301-1035_3-10048257-94.html
140. Richtel, M. (2009, July 27). Texting raises crash risk 23 times, study finds. *The New York Times*. Based on statistics from CTIA, the cellular phone industry's trade group. Retrieved from http:finance.yahoo.com/insurance/article/107411/texting-raises-crach-risk-23-times,study
141. *Comment section*. (2007, September 07). The online rocket. Retrieved from http://media.www.theonlinerocket.com/media/storage/paper601/news/2007/09/07.Opinion/Ourview.Textmessaging.Service.Should.Be.Used.Properly-2954612.shtml
142. Stanton, J., Associate Professor of Information Sciences, as quoted in Friedman, T. L. (2007). *The world is flat*. New York: Picador/Farrrar, Straus and Giroux, p. 522.
143. Richtel, M. (n.d.). Based on a study by Virginia Tech Transportation Institute.
144. *Arizona may ban vehicular text-messaging*. (2007). United Press International. Retrieved from www.upi.com/NewsTrack/Top_News/2007/08/15/arizona_may_ban_vehicular_textmessaging/2863.
145. (Richtel).
146. (Richtel).
147. *Texting teen falls down open manhole on Staten Island*. (2010, September 7). Retrieved from http://www.myfoxny.com/dpp/news/local_news/nyc/090710
148. Walker, T. (2010, November 24). *Titans Vince Young apologizes to Fisher via text*. Yahooo! Sports. Retrieved from http://sports.yahoo.com/nfl
149. The Techdirt blog. *Techdirt, the insight company for the information age*. Retrieved from www.techdirt.com/articles/20031027/0024253F.shtml
150. *When texting becomes an addiction*. (2010, September 1). CBS Morning Show. Retrieved from http://www.cbsnews.com/stories/2010/09/01/early-show/living/parenting/main6825771.shtml
151. *Pitflls of child text messaging*. (2007, October 5). Info on text messaging. MSN.com. Retrieved from MSN.com
152. (*When texting becomes an addiction*).
153. Belloni, M., & Gardner, E., (2011, January 5). *Courtney Love's tweets lead to court trial*. Retrieved from http://news.yahoo.com/s/nm/us_courtneylove/

CHAPTER 7

1. Kruger, P. (1994, April). How to talk to anyone about anything. *Redbook*, p. 132.
2. Samovar, L., Porter, R., & McDaniel, E. (2006). *Intercultural communication: A reader*. Belmont, CA: Thomson Higher Education, p. 436.
3. For a discussion of cultural personal space, refer to Samovar, pp. 281–286.
4. Coventry, K. R. Lynott, D, Cangelosi, A., Monrouxe, L., Joyce, D., & Richardson, D. C. (2010, March). Spatial language, visual attention, and perceptual simulation. *Brain and language 112*(3), 202–213. Doi 10.1016/j.bandl.2009.06.001
5. Request Definition. (2008). Request, *Webster's New World Telecom Dictionary*. Indianapolis, IN: Wiley Publishing. Retrieved from www.yourdictionary.com/request.
6. Ludden, L. L., & Capozzoli, T. (2000). *Supervisor savvy: How to retain and develop entry-level workers*. Indianapolis, IN: JIST.
7. Goldman, A. (1993). Ethics and cognitive science. *Ethics, 103*, 337–360.
8. Encyclopedia of EQI.org 2010. Retrieved from http://www.eqi.org/empathy.htm
9. Bryner, J. (2010). *Today's college students lack empathy*, LiveSciencc.com. Based on the theories of Edward O'Brien, University of Michigan's Institute for Social Research. Retrieved from http://www.livescience.com/culture/empathy-college-students-generation-me-100528.html
10. (Bryner).
11. (Bryner).
12. (Bryner).
13. (Bryner).
14. (Bryner).
15. (Bryner).
16. (Bryner).
17. (Bryner).
18. Berko, R., Rosenfeld, L., & Samovar, L. (1997). *Connecting: A culture-sensitive approach to interpersonal communication competency*. Ft. Worth: Harcourt Brace, p. 372.
19. For further investigation, see Berko, R. M., Aitken, J. E., & Wolvin, A. D. (2010). *ICOMM: Interpersonal concepts and competencies*. Lanham, MD: Rowman & Littlefield.
20. Fiedler, C. (2010, December). *Defusing conflict*. The Costco Connection, p. 57, based on Medea, A. (2005). *Conflict unraveled: Fixing problems at work and in families*. Chicago, IL: PivotPoint Press.
21. Fiedler, based on Puhn, L. (2010). *Fight less, love more: 5-minute conversations to change your relationship without blowing up or giving in*. New York: Rodale.
22. Donohue, W. A., with Kolt, R. (1992). *Managing interpersonal conflict*. Newbury Park, CA: Sage, p. 2.
23. (Donohue & Kolt, p. 3).
24. (Donohue & Kolt, p. 3).
25. For a further discussion, see DeVito, J. A. (2010). *The interpersonal communication book* (12th ed.) Boston: Allyn & Bacon, Chapter 12.
26. (Donohue & Kolt, pp. 12–17).
27. Lerner, H. G. (2005). *The dance of anger: A woman's guide to changing the patterns of intimate relationships*. New York: Perennial Library.
28. Based on the concepts of Marlene Arthur Penkstaff.
29. A theory of Dr. Susan Forward, media psychologist and author. Retrieved from http://www.susanforward.com/media.htm
30. (Forward).
31. The principles are based on the theories of Sonya Friedman.
32. A crisis counseling concept presented by Roy Berko, May 17, 2008, the Society for the Scientific Study of Sexuality, Cleveland, OH.
33. This is a principle of Gestalt therapy, as explained by Les Wyman, Gestalt Institute, Cleveland, OH.
34. (Fiedler).
35. (Fiedler).
36. "Activity 1," a handout developed by Mary Adams Trujillo and Laurie Miller and distributed at the workshop, "Responding to Conflict around Issues of Difference." National Conference for Community and Justice, Northern Ohio Region, February 19, 1999, Cleveland, OH.
37. (Trujillo).
38. (Trujillo).
39. (Trujillo).
40. Dr. Andrew Slater introduced the concept of assertiveness in the 1940s. It is commented on in Epstein, R. (2002, March/April). Ask Dr. E. *Psychology Today*.
41. Discussion based on shyness-workshop materials prepared by DeMark, P. (n.d.). Lorain County Community College, Elyria, OH.
42. Bower, S., & Bower, G. (1976). *Asserting yourself*. Reading, MA: Addison-Wesley, p. 87.
43. For a discussion on business negotiation, see Cai, D. A., & Drake, L. E. (1998). The business of business negotiation: Intercultural perspectives. *Communication Yearbook, 21*, 153–189.
44. Concepts in this section are based in part on *12 Skills [Negotiation Skills]*. Conflict Resolution Network. Retrieved from www.crnhq.org.
45. (*12 Skills [Negotiation Skills]*).
46. Budish, A. (2005, April 12). What's arbitration? What options do consumers have? *Cleveland Plain Dealer*, C5.
47. (Budish).
48. *Code of Virginia*, Chapter 20.2, Section 8:01-576.4 (July 1993).
49. For information on mediation, see Shailor, J. G. (1994). *Empowerment in dispute mediation: A critical analysis of communication*. Westport, CT: London; Noce, D. J. D. (1993). *Mediation fundamentals: A training manual*. Richmond, VA: Better Business Bureau Foundation of Virginia; Menkel-Meadow, C. J., Love, L. P., & Schneider, A. K. (2008). *Mediation: Practice, policy, and ethics*. New York: Aspen Publishers.
50. For a discussion of culture and conflict, see Samovar, Porter, and McDanile, pp. 141–143 and Ting-Toomey, & Oetzel, J. (2007). Intercultural conflict: A culture-based situational model. In P. Cooper, C. Calloway-Thomas, & C. Simonds, (Eds.), *Intercultural communication: A text with readings*. Boston: Pearson Education, pp. 121–129.
51. Rowland, D. (1985). *Japanese business etiquette*. New York: Warner Books, p. 5; for more information, see Alston, J. P., & Takei, I. (2005). *Japanese business culture and practices: A guide to twenty-first century Japanese business*. Bloomington, IN: iUniverse.
52. Copeland, L., & Griggs, L. (1985). *Going international*. New York: Random House, p. 109; for more information, see Chaney, L. H., & Martin, J. S. (2008). *Global business etiquette*. Westport, CT: Praeger.
53. Mia Doucet, M. (2007, October). Costly western assumptions. *Control Engineering, 54*(10), p. 32.
54. (Berko, Rosenfeld, & Samavor, p. 374).
55. Ting-Toomey, S., & Chung, L. C. (2005). *Understanding intercultural communication*. New York: Oxford University Press, p. 268.
56. (Ting-Toomey & Chung).
57. For a discussion of cross-cultural conflict styles, see Ting-Toomey & Chung, pp. 274–275.
58. (Ting-Toomey & Chung).

59. (Ting-Toomey & Chung).
60. (Ting-Toomey & Chung).
61. (Ting-Toomey & Chung).
62. *When and how to apologize.* (n.d). A pamphlet produced by the University of Nebraska Cooperative Extension and the Nebraska Health and Human Services System.
63. Retrieved from Tesdell, D. R. (1997, February 10). *The top 10 ways to apologize to someone you have hurt or offended.* lifecoach@coachdt.com
64. (Tesdell, 1997).
65. Zander, R. S. (2001, July 29). The power of an apology, *Parade*, p. 8.
66. *Japanese language, expressing apologies.* (n.d.). Retrieved from http://search.about.com/fullsearch.htm?terms=Japanese%20 Language
67. (*Japanese language, expressing apologies*).
68. (*Japanese language, expressing apologies*).
69. (*Japanese language, expressing apologies*).
70. This concept was described in Ting-Toomey, S. (1994). *The challenge of Facework.* Albany: State University of New York Press, p. 185. A search of the current literature in the field of apologies shows no contradictions of these findings.
71. (Ting-Toomey).
72. (Ting-Toomey).

CHAPTER 8

1. Stewart, C., & Cash, W. (2010). *Interviewing: Principles and practices.* Burr Ridge, IL: McGraw-Hill.
2. Glenn, P. (2010). Interviewer laughs: Shared laughter and asymmetries in employment interviews. *Journal of Pragmatics, 42*(6), 1485–1498. doi:10.1016/j.pragma.2010.01.009
3. Thompson, D. (2010, February 9). The scariest employment graph I've seen this year. *The Atlantic.* Retrieved from http://www.theatlantic.com/business/archive/2010/02/the-scariest-employment-graph-ive-seen-this-year/35662/; Headapohl, J. (2011, January 10). *Average length of unemployment in Michigan is 40 weeks.* MLive.com. Retrieved from http://www.mlive.com/jobs/index.ssf/2011/01/average_length_of_unemployment_in_michig.html
4. Job interview 2.0—How technology is transforming the job hunt. (2008, November 21). *Cleveland Jewish News*, p. 35.
5. Job interview 2.0. Quoting Debra Pierce, director of career services at Miami International University of Arts & Design.
6. Personal conversation with human resources director of a major food corporation.
7. Needleman, S. (2009, April 14). The interview that'll bag you a job. *The Wall Street Journal*, Retrieved from http://finance.yahoo.com/career-work/article/106924, as quoting Wendy Alfus Rothman, president of Wenroth Consulting Inc.
8. Needleman. Quoting Kathy Marsico, senior vice president of human resources at PDI Inc.
9. For a resource on questions and job searches, see Hansen, K., & Hansen, R. (2007). *The quintessential guide to job interview preparation.* DeLand, FL: Quintessential Careers Press.
10. Louw, K. J., Derwing, T. M., & Abbott, M. L. (2010). Teaching pragmatics to L2 learners for the workplace: The job interview. *Canadian Modern Language Review, 66*(5), 739–758. doi:10.3138/cmlr.66.5.739
11. Bolles, R. N. (2008). *What color is your parachute?* Berkeley, CA: Ten Speed Press.
12. Personal conversation at a recruitment event.
13. Endicott, F. S. (n.d.). *Making the most of your job interview.* New York: New York Life Insurance Company.
14. Weisul, K. (2010). *The weirdest interview questions of 2010. BNet.* Retrieved from http://www.bnet.com/blog/business-research/the-25-weirdest-interview-questions-of-2010/520
15. Decker, J. (n.d.). *Interviewing.* Retrieved from www.RetirementJobs.com
16. (Decker).
17. McGarvey, R. (1990, May). Tailoring an image. *USAir Magazine*, 76. An additional source is Levinson, J. C., Perry, D. E., & Hardy, D. (2009). *Guerrilla marketing for job hunters 2.0: 1,001 unconventional tips, tricks and tactics for landing your dream job* (2nd ed.). Somerset, NJ: Wiley.
18. (McGarvey, p. 78).
19. Doyle, A. (n.d.). *How to dress for a job interview.* About.com: Job Searching. Retrieved from http://jobsearch.about.com/od/interviewattire/a/interviewdress.htm
20. How to: Dress for a job interview. (2010). *Caterer & Hotelkeeper, 200*(4647), 56.
21. (Doyle).
22. Sinberg, L. (2009, July 22). *What not to wear to work.* Forbes.com. Retrieved from http://www.forbes.com/2009/07/22/office-fashion-sexy-forbes-woman-style-clothes.html
23. (Doyle).
24. (Doyle).
25. *What not to wear to an interview: Top 20 wardrobe malfunctions.* (n.d.). Career Builder. Retrieved from www.careerbuilder.com
26. Personal conversation with General Motors executive.
27. U.S. Department of Labor, Employment and Training Administration. (n.d.). *Merchandising your job talents.* Washington, DC: Government Printing Office, pp. 7–8.
28. Burns, K. (2009, September 28). 15 ways to annoy your job interviewer. *U.S.News.* Based on Burns, K. (2009). *The amazing adventures of working girl real-life career advice you can actually use.* New York: Running Press.
29. *EEO Interview Guidelines*, 29 C.F.R. § 1602 *et seq.*; DC Code § 1-2501 *et seq.*; and DCMR, Title 4, Ch. 5, Employment Guidelines. See The Catholic University of America http://counsel.cua.edu/employment/questions
30. Based, in part on, Moran, P. (2010, September 7). *8 things the employers aren't allowed to ask you.* Financial Edge. Retrieved from http://financialedge.investopedia.com/financial-edge/0910/8-Things-Employers-Arent-Allowed-To-Ask-You.aspx
31. Ron Grant, president of Meridian Resources, Greenville, SC.
32. Brown, C. M. (2010). Ace the phone interview. *Essence (Time Inc.), 41*(1), 84.
33. Doyle, A. *Video job interviews.* About.com. Retrieved from http://jobsearch.about.com/od/jobinterviewtypes/a/videointerv.htm
34. (Job interview 2.0).
35. Job interview 2.0. Quoting Mac Scoleri, director of career services at the Art Institute of New York City.
36. Schlach, K. (n.d.). *Virtual recruiting for real-world jobs.* Retrieved from www.npr.org/templates/story/story.php?storyId=13851345&sc=emaf
37. (Schlach).
38. (Schlach, quoting Polly Pearson, an EMC vice president).
39. (Schlach).
40. Brown, C. M. (2010). Ace the phone interview. *Essence (Time Inc.), 41*(1), 84.
41. Personal conversation with corporate attorney for a utility company.
42. Gioia, J. L., & Catalano, R. M. (2011). Meaningful exit interviews help one bank cut turnover and save. *Global Business & Organizational Excellence, 30*(2), 36–43. doi:10.1002/joe.20367
43. A psychological theory developed by Roy Berko, certified crisis counselor, in teaching clients how to be nondirective in their communication.
44. Brownell, J. (2003, April 1). Applied research in managerial communication: The critical link between knowledge and practice; applying the lessons of managerial communication studies can help managers become more influential and effective in their daily activities. *Cornell Hotel & Restaurant Administration Quarterly, 44.*
45. Retrieved from www.performance-appraisal.com/methods.htm
46. Retrieved from www.halogensoftware.com
47. For a discussion of this issue, see the websites of Amnesty International, www.amnesty.org/en/campaigns/Counter+Terror+with+Justice/issues; and American Civil Liberties Union www.aclu.org/safefree/detention/closeguantanamo.html
48. Waterboarding: Interrogation or torture? (2008,May 23). *CBS News.* Retrieved from www.cbsnews.com/stories/2007/11/01/national/main3441363.shtml.
49. (Bolles).

CHAPTER 9

1. Rothwell, J. D. (2010). *In mixed company* (7th ed.). Boston: Wadsworth Cengage Learning, p. 48.
2. (Rothwell, p. 48).
3. (Rothwell, p. 42).
4. Silva, D., & Sias, P. M. (2010). Connection, restructuring, and buffering: How groups link individuals and organizations. *Journal of Applied Communication Research, 38*(2), 145–166. doi:10.1080/00909881003639510
5. Choi, S., Kim, Y., Sung, Y., & Sohn, D. (2011). Bridging or bonding? *Information, Communication & Society, 14*(1), 107–129. doi:10.1080/13691181003792624
6. Armstrong, R. W., Williams, R. J., & Barrett, J. D. (2004, September). The impact of banality, risky shift and escalating commitment on ethical decision making. *Journal of Business Ethics*, Part 2, *53*(4), 365–370.
7. The term *groupthink* was conceived by Irving Janus, as explained in Janis, I. (1972). *Victims of groupthink.* Boston: Houghton Mifflin, and further discussed in Janis, I. (1983). *Groupthink: Psychological studies of policy decisions and fiascoes.* Boston: Houghton Mifflin. For another discussion of the concept, see Rothwell, pp. 199–206.
8. Broder, D. S. (2004, April 11). Rice reveals missing steps at White House. *[Cleveland] Plain Dealer*, A3.
9. (Broder, 2004).
10. Moorhead, G., Ference, R., & Neck, C. P. (2001). Group decision fiascoes continue: Space shuttle Challenger and a revised groupthink framework. In M. H. Davis (Ed.), *Social Psychology 2001–2002.* Guilford, CT: McGraw-Hill/Dushkin, p. 201.
11. The theory of Bibb Latane, Kipling Williams, and Stephen Harkins.
12. For a discussion of communication in work teams, see: Grice, T. A., Gallois, C., Jones, E., Paulsen, N., & Callan, V. J. (2006). "We do it, but they don't": Multiple categorizations and work team communication. *Journal of Applied Communication Research, 34*(4), 331–348. doi:10.1080/00909880600908591
13. For an examination of work teams, see *Work teams—building effective teamwork.* Retrieved from www.strategosinc.com/team_series.htm
14. For a discussion about and a list of support groups, see http://dailystrength.org/
15. For an example of an online support group, go towww.supportpath.com/
16. Stommel, W., & Koole, T. (2010). The online support group as a community: A micro-analysis of the interaction with a new member. *Discourse Studies, 12*(3), 357–378. doi:10.1177/1461445609358518
17. A concept confirmed by Roy Berko, certified crisis counselor.
18. Study was done by Dr. David Spiegel as reported on CancerandCareers.org (2008). Retrieved fromwww.cancerandcareers.org/women/strength/cancer support_groups

19. Blackshaw, P. (2010). Why you shouldn't forsake the focus group for online discussions. *Advertising Age, 81*(39), 17.
20. For a discussion on the various definitions of a *family*, see Turner, L. H., & West, R. (2006). *Perspectives on family communication* (3rd ed.). Columbus, OH: McGraw-Hill.
21. *Planning and conducting effective public meetings.* (2005, April 2). Ohio State University Extension Fact Sheet. Retrieved from www.ohioline.osu.edu/cd/fact/1555html
22. Tuckman, B. W., & Jensen, M. A. (1977). Stages of small-group development revisited. *Group Organizational Studies, 2*, 419–427.
23. (Rothwell, pp. 65–66).
24. (Rothwell, p. 142).
25. Aakhus, M., & Rumsey, E. (2010). Crafting supportive communication online: A communication design analysis of conflict in an online support group. *Journal of Applied Communication Research, 38*(1), 65–84. doi:10.1080/00909880903483581
26. Group members seem to have a better perception of each other when seen as peers: Myers, S. A., Shimotsu, S., Byrnes, K., Frisby, B. N., Durbin, J., & Loy, B. N. (2010). Assessing the role of peer relationships in the small group communication course. *Communication Teacher, 24*(1), 43–57. doi:10.1080/17404620903468214
27. Hall, W. C. (2008, February 28). Do effective speakers make effective presidents? *USA Today*. Retrieved from http://wyntonhall.com/_do_effective_speakers_make_effective_presidents_70477.htm
28. Robert, H. M. III, & Evans, W. J. (2000). *Robert's rules of order, Newly revised* (10th ed.). Glenview, IL: Scott, Foresman. The source is also available on CD and in an online searchable version: www.robertsrules.com.
29. In parliamentary procedure, the term *consensus* means "unanimous." In nonparliamentary use, the term is often assumed to mean "generally." For voting purposes, it is synonymous with "all." See Robert & Evans, pp. 52–55.
30. (Robert & Evans, pp. 399–400).
31. *Part-of-the-whole voting* is sometimes referred to as *2/3 voting.* For a discussion, see Robert and Evans, pp. 396–397.
32. For an analysis of jury conflict, see: Weingart, L. R., & Todorova, G. (2010). Jury tensions: Applying communication theories and methods to study group dynamics. *Small Group Research, 41*(4), 495–502. doi:10.1177/1046496410369564
33. (Rothwell, p. 195).
34. (Rothwell).
35. (Janis, p. 197).
36. The classic Dewey inductive process was first discussed in Dewey, J. (1910). *How to think.* Boston: D. C. Heath, pp. 68–78.
37. (Janis, p. 219).
38. (Janis, p. 203).
39. For discussions of the Nominal Group Technique for Decision Making, see: http://www.managementskillsadvisor.com/nominal-group-technique.html and http://crs.uvm.edu/citizens/decisions.htm
40. A process refined by Roy Berko from a concept of Eileen Breckenridge.
41. (Rothwell, p. 221).
42. Mayer, M. (1998, Summer). Behaviors leading to more effective decisions in small groups embedded in organizations. *Communication Reports, 11*, 123–132. For an analysis of the value of discussion, see Reimer, T., Reimer, A., & Czienskowski, U. (2010). Decision-making groups attenuate the discussion bias in favor of shared information: A meta-analysis. *Communication Monographs, 77*(1), 121–142. doi:10.1080/03637750903514318
43. For a discussion on group meeting spaces, see Leathers, D., & Eaves, M. H. (2008). *Successful nonverbal communication, principles and applications.* Boston: Pearson Education.
44. (Leathers & Eaves).
45. Knapp, M. L., & Hall, J. A. (2009). *Nonverbal communication in human interaction* (7th ed.). Belmont, CA: Wadsworth.
46. (Leathers).
47. (Leathers).
48. For a discussion of round and rectangular tables, see Knapp & Hall, pp. 177–179.
49. From the research of R. Sommer, as found in Knapp & Hall, pp. 116–118.
50. (Leathers).
51. (Knapp & Hall, p. 168).
52. (Knapp & Hall).
53. Bluedorn, A. C., Turban, D. B., & Love, M. (1999). The effects of stand-up and sit-down meeting formats on meeting outcomes. *Journal of Applied Psychology, 84*(2), 277–285.
54. Engleberg, I., & Wynn, D. (2009). *Working in groups* (5th ed.). Boston: Houghton Mifflin. For a specific application, see Weingart, L., & Todorova, G. (2010). Jury tensions: Applying communication theories and methods to study group dynamics. *Small Group Research, 41*(4), 495–502. doi:10.1177/1046496410369564
55. The 3M Meeting Management Team with Drew, J. (1994). *Mastering meetings: Discovering the hidden potential of effective business meetings.* New York: McGraw-Hill, pp. 114–115.
56. For information regarding Second Life, go to secondlife.com
57. Fehl, L. (1999, March). The world at your fingertips. *Successful meetings*, p. 91.
58. Boudreau, J. (2009, August 16). *Video conferencing makes business travel less of a necessity,* [Cleveland] Plain Dealer, p. D6, referring to a study by Alan Bender, Embry-Riddle Aeronautical University.
59. (Fehl).
60. For an extensive discussion about virtual meetings, see: Stack, L. (2010). *SuperCompetent: The six keys to perform at your productive best.* Hoboken, NJ: John Wiley & Sons.
61. (Zimmerman).
62. Zimmerman, based on the concepts of Bob Preston, chief collaboration officer at Polycom.
63. (Engleberg & Wynn).
64. (3M, p. 115).
65. (3M).
66. (Engleberg & Wynn).
67. (Fulk, p. 75).
68. (3M, p. 116).
69. (3M, p. 123).
70. (GotoMeeting.com).

CHAPTER 10

1. For discussion of group communication, see: Harris, T. E., & Sherblom, J. C. (2010). *Small group and team communication* (5th ed.). Boston: Allyn & Bacon; Engleberg, I. N., & Wynn, D. R. (2009). *Working in groups: Communication principles and strategies* (5th ed.). Boston: Allyn & Bacon.
2. For an extended discussion on culture and its effect on groups, see Rothwell, J. D. (2009). *In mixed company* (7th ed.). Belmont, CA: Wadsworth/Thomson Learning; Ting-Toomey, S., & Chung, L. (2005). *Understanding intercultural communication.* New York: Oxford University Press.
3. Stewart, E. C., Danielian, J., & Foster, R. (2007). Cultural assumptions and values. In P. Cooper, C. Calloway-Thomas, & C. Simonds (Eds.), *Intercultural communication A text with readings.* Boston: Pearson Education.
4. (Rothwell, pp. 13–15).
5. Samovar, L., Porter, R., & McDaniel, E. (2006). *Intercultural communication: A reader.* Belmont, CA: Thomson Higher Education, pp. 24–25.
6. Moriizumi, S., & Takai, J. (2010). The relationships between Japanese interpersonal conflict styles and their language expressions. *Journal of Social Psychology, 150*(5), 520–539. doi:10.1080/00224540903365349
7. For a discussion on cultural decision making, see Ting-Toomey & Chung, pp. 340–341, 344–347.
8. (Ting-Toomey & Chung).
9. For a discussion on Euro American decision making, see Rothwell, chapter 7.
10. For explanations of Japanese communication styles, see Martin, J., & Nakayama, T. (2007). *Intercultural communication in contexts.* New York: McGraw-Hill, p. 54, and Ting-Toomey & Chung, pp. 274–275.
11. (Rothwell, citing the work of P. Wetzel).
12. van Emmerik, I. H., Euwema, M. C., & Wendt, H. H. (2008). Leadership behaviors around the world: The relative importance of gender versus cultural background. *International Journal of Cross Cultural Management, 8*(3), 297–315.
13. For a detailed discussion, see Schnurr, S. (2009). *Leadership discourse at work: Interactions of humour, gender and workplace culture.* Hampshire, UK: Palgrave Macmillan.
14. O'Neill, K. (2009). Leadership and discourse at work: Interactions of humor, gender and workplace culture. *Discourse Studies, 11*(6), 741–742. doi:10.1177/1461445609348425
15. Wood, J. T. (2010). *Gendered lives: Communication, gender, and culture* (10th ed.). Belmont, CA: Thompson High Education, p. 236.
16. (Wood, 2010).
17. (Wood, 2010, p. 237).
18. (Rothwell, p. 21, in D. J. Canary and K. S. House).
19. (Rothwell, p. 258, referred to research by K. Propp).
20. (Rothwell, p. 91, based on the research of A. Kohn).
21. (Rothwell).
22. (Rothwell, p. 254, based on research by L. Stewart and by A. Nicotera and A. Rancer).
23. (Rothwell, p. 132, citing the research of M. M. White).
24. Ideas were originally explained by Stewart, L., Stewart, A., Friedley, S., & Cooper, P. (1990). *Communication between the sexes.* Scottsdale, AZ: Gorsuch Scarisbrick, p. 162, and further expanded on in Stewart, L., Cooper, P. Stewart, A., & Friedley, S. (2003). *Communication between the sexes.* Boston: Pearson Education, pp. 155.
25. (Stewart, Stewart, Friedley, & Cooper).
26. (Rothwell, p. 123).
27. Blumenthal, B. (2009, December 2). *5 behaviors of manipulative people.* Yahoo! Retrieved from http://shine.yahoo.com/channel/life/5-behaviors-of-manipulative-people-549848/
28. A concept developed at the Gestalt Institute of Cleveland during a workshop regarding dealing with difficult people, as reported by Roy Berko, one of the workshop participants.
29. Based on the theories of Dr. Joy Brown, media psychologist.
30. (Blumenthal).
31. (Rothwell, pp. 31–33).
32. For a research-based approach to exemplary student leadership, see Kouzes, J. M., & Posner, B. Z. (2010). *Student Leadership Practices Inventory.* Josey-Bass. Retrieved from http://www.studentlpi.com/
33. French, J. R. P., & Raven, B. J. (1959). The bases of social power. In D. Cartwright (Ed.), *Studies of social power.* Ann Arbor, MI: University of Michigan Press. For an update, see ValueBasedManagement.net (2008, March 25). Retrieved from www.valuebasedmanagement.net/methods_french_raven_bases_social_power.html

34. The idea is based on this classic work: Burns, J. M. (1978). *Leadership.* New York: Harper and Row.
35. *What is transformational leadership?* (2003, February.) Leading Today. Retrieved from www.leadingtoday.org/Onmag/feb03/transform22003.html
36. For a discussion of superleadership, see Kotelnikov, V. (n.d.). Ten3 business e-coach. *What is superleadership?* Retrieved from www.1000ventures.com/business_guide/crosscuttings/leadership_super.html; and Neck, C., & Manz, C. (2006). *Mastering self-leadership: Empowering yourself for personal excellence* (4th ed.). Upper Saddle River, NJ: Prentice-Hall.
37. Based on *Leadership Styles* as found in *Dynamic leadership handbook.* MGA Michael Grinder and Associates. Retrieved from http://www.michaelgrinder.com/ For an additional discussion on perspectives of leadership, see Rothwell, pp. 135–140.
38. Carte, T. A., Chidambaram, L., & Becker, A. (2006, July). Emergent leadership in self-managed virtual teams: A longitudinal study of concentrated and shared leadership behaviors. *Group Decision and Negotiation, 15*(4), 323–343.
39. (Rothwell, p. 131).
40. (Rothwell, p. 131).
41. Medhurst, M. J., in Hall, W. C. (2008, February 28). Do effective speakers make effective presidents? *USA Today.* Retrieved from USAToday.com
42. Hackman, M., & Johnson, C. (n.d.). *Teaching leadership from a communication perspective,* unpublished paper. Department of Communication, University of Colorado, Colorado Springs, CO, p. 6. For an in depth synthesis of communication and leadership research, see Hackman, M. Z., & Johnson, C. E. (2008). *Leadership: A communication perspective.* Prospect Heights IL: Waveland Press, Inc.
43. Based on a concept developed by Patricia Hayes, Indiana University–Bradley.
44. A concept developed by Julie Ann Wambach.
45. Contributed by Isa Engleberg. Used with permission.

CHAPTER 11

1. The study that revealed this is Kendall, K. (1974, Fall). Do real people ever give speeches? *Central States Speech Journal, 25,* 235. Other follow-up studies have affirmed the conclusion.
2. For further investigation, see Hancock, A., Stone, M., Brundage, S., & Zeigler, M. (2010). Public speaking attitudes: Does curriculum make a difference? *Journal of Voice, 24*(3), 302–307. doi:10.1016/j.jvoice.2008.09.00
3. The concept of the listenable speech as discussed by Rubin, D. (1993). Listenability = Oral-Based Discourse + Considerations. In A. E. Wolvin & C. G. Coakley (Eds.), *Perspectives on listening.* Norwood, NJ: Ablex, pp. 261–281. The explanation and recommendations presented in this text are those adapted by Andrew Wolvin and Roy Berko.
4. (Rubin).
5. Doetkott, R., & Motley, M. (2009). *Public speaking delivery styles: Audience preference and recollection.* Conference Paper—National Communication Association.
6. Glenn, E. C., Emmert, P., & Emmert, V. (1995). A scale for measuring listenability: The factors that determine listening ease and difficulty. *International Journal of Listening, 9,* 44–61.
7. The Wolvin Listenability Paradigm, in Wolvin, A. D., Berko, R. M., & Wolvin, D. R. (1999). *The public speaker/The public listener.* Los Angeles: Roxbury, pp. 68–78.
8. Menzel, K., & Carrell, L. (1994, January). The relationship between preparation and performance in public speaking. *Communication Education, 43,* 17.
9. Reeves, J. (2011, January 18). Associated Press. Retrieved from http:new.yahoo.com/s/Alabama_governor_governor_christians
10. Reeves, quoting Bill Nigut, the Anti-Defnamation League Regional Director.
11. (Reeves).
12. Johnson, R. (n.d.). *Alabama governor apologizes for remarks on Christians.* Associated Press. Retrieved from http:new.yahoo.com/s/ap/200110119/ap_on_re_us/us_alabama_governor_christians
13. Goodwin, L. (2010, October 29). *School board member to quit after telling gay kids to kill themselves.* Retrieved from http://news.yahoo.com/s/yblog_upshot/20101029/pl_yblog_upshot/ar-school-board-member-resigns-after-telling-gay-kids-to-die
14. (Goodwin).
15. Associated Press. (2010, December 29). *ESPNews anchor apologizes for using writer's words.* Retrieved from http://abcnews.go.com/Sports/wireStory?id=12504582
16. Gabriel, T. (2010, August 2). As Internet influence has grown, students less aware of plagiarizing. [Cleveland] *Plain Dealer,* A4.
17. Gabriel, based on a survey by Donald L. McCabe, co-founder of the Center for Academic Integrity at Rutgers University.
18. Schulte, B. (2002, October 8). Web of cheating. [Cleveland] *Plain Dealer,* E1.
19. (Schulte).
20. www.Turnitin.com
21. Humpherys, C. (2009, August 11). *Deny, deny, deny: Mistruths and fabrications in professional sports.* Retrieved from http://sportschumpt.net/2009/08/11/deny-deny-deny-mistruths-and-fabrications-in-professional-sports/1108
22. (Humpherys, 2009).
23. (Humpherys, 2009).
24. (Humpherys, 2009).
25. (Humpherys, 2009).
26. (Humpherys, 2009).
27. Higgs, R. (August 21, 2010). Flawed data persist on cap and trade. [Cleveland] *Plain Dealer,* p. B1.
28. For an extended discussion of demographics, see Griffin, pp. 101–103.
29. The Newsroom. (2010, April 20). *Obama clashes with gay rights hecklers in L.A.* Retrieved from http://news.yahoo.com/s/ynews/ynews_ts1697
30. (*Obama clashes*).
31. Arrington, R. (2010). *Networking and public speaking for Internet marketers — learn how to deliver compelling presentations.* Seattle: Amazon.
32. For an extended discussion of speech outlining, see Griffin, pp. 218–224.
33. Based on http://owl.english.purdue.edu/handouts/esl/index.html
34. owl.english.purdue.edu

CHAPTER 12

1. NSF. (2005). *Frequently asked questions regarding: Information and intelligent design.* Arlington, VA: National Science Foundation. NSF 05-551. Retrieved from www.nsf.gov/funding/pgm_summ.jsp?pims_id=13503&org=IIS and Koehler, A. E. C. (2006). *Some thoughts on the meaning of open access for university library technical services, 32*(1), p. 17.
2. To access *Readers' guide to periodical literature,* go through your college databases or www.hwwilson.com/Databases/Readersg.htm#Literature
3. For issues about the pros and cons of using Wikipedia, see Fernando, A. (2010, July/August). Are you still not a Wikipedian? *Communication World, 27*(4), 8–9; Rush, E., & Tracy, S. (2010, August). Wikipedia as public scholarship: Communicating our impact online. *Journal of Applied Communication Research, 38*(3), 309–315.
4. *Popularity of Wikipedia.* (2007, May 1). Retrieved from techxplolrer.com
5. Sack, B. (n.d.). *More accurate Wikipedia warnings.* Retrieved from www.cracked.com
6. For one discussion about contributors, you can listen to National Public Radio broadcast: (December 6). *Wikipedia to require contributors to register.* Retrieved from http://www.npr.org/templates/story/story.php?storyId=5041077
7. Smith, T. (2007, November). *Wikipedia—A reliable source for students—Nay.* Retrieved from www.nuimsu.com/spoke/november-2007/wikipedia-reliable-source-students-nay
8. The catalog can be obtained from ABC News by calling 800-505-6139.
9. Reuters. (2009, June 17). *Internet most popular information source.* New York: Reuters. Retrieved from http://www.reuters.com/article/idUSTRE55G4XA20090617
10. For a discussion of library research, see *Basic library research.* Retrieved from www.dushkin.com/online/study/dgen1.mhtml For computer searches, see Shaw, M. (2007). *Mastering online research.* Cincinnati, OH: F & W Publishing; Doyle, T., & Barr, L. R. (2004). *Research navigator guide.* Boston: Allyn and Bacon.
11. Knowlton, S. R. (1997). How students get lost in Cyberspace. *The New York Times, 50* ((964), 4A, p. 18.
12. Wood, J. (2007). *Gendered lives: Communication, gender, and culture.* Belmont, CA: Thomson Higher Education, p. 153.
13. For an in-depth discussion of styles, see Bourhis, J., Adams, C., Titsworth, S., & Harter, L. (2002). *Style manual for communication studies.* New York: McGraw-Hill.
14. Heath, C., & Heath, D. (2007). *Made to stick.* New York: Random House.
15. Slan, J. (1998). *Using stories and humor.* Boston: Allyn and Bacon, p. 26. This book is strongly recommended by The National Speakers Association and Toastmasters International. For a discussion of humor in speeches, see Osborn, M., & Osborn, S. (2006). *Public speaking* (7th ed.). Boston: Houghton Mifflin, pp. 490–491.
16. Obama, B. (2011, January 12). *Memorial in Arizona.* Video: http://www.youtube.com/watch?v=OEiitkI2WH0; text: http://www.huffingtonpost.com/2011/01/12/Obama-arizona-memorial-sp_n_808335.html
17. Green, M. C., & Brock, T. C. (2005). Persuasiveness of narratives. In T. C. Brock & M. E. Green (Eds.), *Persuasion.* Thousand Oaks, CA: Sage, pp. 117–142.
18. Building and maintaining a diverse and high quality workforce. *(n.d.) U.S. Office of Personnel Management, para 4. Retrieved from* http://www.opm.gov/diversity/diversity-2.htm
19. Huff, D. (1993). *How to lie with statistics.* New York: Norton, pp. 123–142. Although dated, this book still appears to be one of the definitive discussions of how statistics are manipulated. Also see Best, J. (2004). *More damned lies and statistics: How numbers confuse public issues.* Berkeley, CA: University of California Press.
20. For extended discussions of communication research, see Rubin, R., Rubin, A., & Paul M. Haridakis, P. A. (2009). *Communication research: Strategies and sources,* (7th ed.). Belmont, CA: Wadsworth/Thompson Learning.
21. For a discussion of Dr. John Money and the John/Joan case, see: van der Leun, J. (2011, January 25). AOL Health. Retrieved from http://www.aolhealth.com/2011/01/25/the-john-joan-case

22. The classic book on the use of evidence and the role of bias is Newman, R., & Newman, D. (1969). *Evidence*. Boston: Houghton Mifflin. For additional information, see Evidence. (2008). *Handouts and Links*, www.unc.edu/depts/wcweb/handouts/evidence_use.html
23. Deer, B. (n.d.). *Journal: Study linking vaccine to autism was fraud*. Retrieved from http:///news.yahoo.com/s/ap_on_he_me/eu_med_autism_fraud Based the investigative reporting by Brian Deer and printed in the medical journal, *BMJ*. See original article by Deer, *Nailed: Dr. Andrew Wakefield and the MNR-autism fraud*. Retrieved from http://briandeer.com/mmr/lancet-summary.htm
24. (Deer).
25. (Deer).
26. Knowlton, S. R. (1997, November 2). How students get lost in cyberspace. *Washington Post*, 18.
27. (Pino-Marina, 2002).
28. www.snoopes.com
29. Christensen, J. (2005, May 10). Jeff vs. the bloggers. *The Advocate*, 48.
30. Cope, J. (1998, April). Data overload: Separating gold from garbage. *Hemisphere*, 33.
31. There are solid research-based sources that can generate discussion about effective PowerPoints, such as the following: Amare, N. (2006). To slideware or not to slideware: Students' experiences with powerpoint vs. lecture. *Journal of Technical Writing & Communication, 36*(3), 297–308.; Katt, J., Murdock, J., Butler, J., & Pryor, B. (2008). Establishing best practices for the use of powerpoint as a presentation aid. *Human Communication, 11*(2), 193–200; Mackiewicz, J. (2008). Comparing PowerPoint experts' and university students' opinions about PowerPoint presentations. *Journal of Technical Writing & Communication, 38*(2), 149–165. doi:10.2190/TW.38.2.d.; Stoner, M. (2007). PowerPoint in a new key. *Communication Education, 56*(3), 354–381. doi:10.1080/03634520701342052
32. For a discussion of popular presentation software, see *Presentation Magazine*. http://www.presentationmagazine.com/presentation-software-the-top-ten-10-134.htm

CHAPTER 13

1. Maynard, S. K. (1996). Contrastive rhetoric: A case of nominalization in Japanese and English discourse. *Language Sciences, 18*, 944.
2. For many years, speech scholars have examined public speaking strategies used by famous U.S. Americans. For a classic example that discusses the use of organization and logic, see Windes, R. R. (1961). A study of effective and ineffective presidential campaign speaking. *Speech Monographs, 28*(1), 39.
3. Lindeborg, R. A. (1990, September). A quick and easy strategy for organizing a speech. *IEEE Transactions on Professional Communication, 33*, 133–134.
4. The *Communication Teacher* offers ideas about how to organize speeches, including using the mind mapping technique: Paxman, C. G. (2011). Map your way to speech success! Employing mind mapping as a speech preparation technique. *Communication Teacher, 25*(1), 7–11. doi:10.1080/17404622.2010.513994
5. For a discussion of the potential problems of using irony, see Pexman, P. M., Whalen, J. M., & Green, J. J. (2010). Understanding verbal irony: Clues from interpretation of direct and indirect ironic remarks. *Discourse Processes, 47*(3), 237–261. doi:10.1080/01638530902959901
6. Mandel, M. (1996). *Stories for speakers*. New York: Jonathan David.
7. Frost, R. (n.d.). *The road not taken*. For a copy of the poem go to http://poemhunter.com/poem/the-road-not-taken/
8. Feldman, C. (2011, January 18). IRS stops automatically mailing income tax forms. *Kansas City Star*. Retrieved from http://www.kansascity.com/2011/01/18/2593490/irs-stops-automatically-mailing.html
9. Jaffe, C. (2001). *Public speaking: Concepts and skills for a diverse society* (3rd ed.) Belmont, CA: Wadsworth/Thomson Learning, p. 166.
10. (Jaffe, p. 174).
11. Lang, A. (1989, Fall). Effects of chronological presentation of information on processing and memory for broadcast news. *Journal of Broadcasting and Electronic Media, 33*, 441–452.
12. (Jaffe, p. 174).
13. Jorgensen-Earp, C. (n.d.). *Making other arrangements: Alternative patterns of disposition*. Unpublished course handout, Lynchburg, VA: Lynchburg College; as found in C. Jaffe, p. 174.
14. Based on theories of organization proposed and developed by Donald Olson, University of Nebraska.
15. (Jaffe, p. 365).
16. A concept proposed by Fran Bostwick, speech professor, Lorain County Community College, Elyria, Ohio.
17. (Jaffe, p. 366).
18. (Jaffe, p. 366).
19. One of the experts in the field of Native American languages is Gerry Philipsen. For an investigation of his works, see Part IV of Martin, J., Nakayama, T., & Flores, L. (2001). *Readings in intercultural communication: Experiences and contexts*. New York: McGraw-Hill.
20. Ting-Toomey, S., & Chung, L. C. (2005). *Understanding intercultural communication*. New York: Oxford University Press, p. 190.
21. (Ting-Toomey & Chung).
22. Lustig, M. W., & Koester, J. (2006). *Intercultural competence* (5th ed.). Boston: Pearson Allyn and Bacon.
23. For extended discussions on African American communication, see Jackson, R. L. II. (2004). *African American communication & identities: Essential readings*. Thousand Oaks, CA: Sage; and Hecht, M., Jackson, R. L., & Ribeau, S. (2002). *African American communication: Exploring identity and culture* (2nd ed.). Mahwah, NJ: Lawrence Erlbaum Associates.
24. (Jaffe, p. 337).
25. (Ting-Toomey & Chung, p. 190).

CHAPTER 14

1. A series of concepts described by Clella Jaffe in Jaffe, C. (2006). *Public speaking concepts and skills for a diverse society*. Belmont, CA: Wadsworth/Thomson Learning.
2. Zarefsky, D. (2011). *Public speaking strategies for success* (6th ed.). Boston: Allyn & Bacon, p. 16.
3. Read more at Suite101: Great Informative Speech Topics: Informative speaking topic ideas for your public speaking class: http://www.suite101.com/content/great-informative-speech-topics-a15040#ixzz1CZBgQV2p
4. Concept developed by attorney Stephenie Slahor, P.O. Box 2615, Palm Springs, CA.
5. *Great informative speech topics*. Retrieved from Suite101.com. (n.d.). www.suite101.com/content/great-informative-speech-topics-a15040

CHAPTER 15

1. Representative Donald Pease, congressmen, Ohio 13th congressional district from 1976–1992.
2. Bailey, H. (2011, February 1). *Breaking with her father, Barbara Bush voices support for gay marriage*. Retrieved from http:new.yahoo.com/s/yblog_theticket/20110201/ts-yblog
3. (Bailey).
4. (Bailey).
5. The theory was proposed by Petty, R. E., & Cacioppo, J. T. (1986). The Elaboration Likelihood Model of persuasion. In L. Berkowitz (Ed.), *Advances in experimental social psychology*. New York: Academic Press, pp. 123–181. For further investigation, see Polk, J., Young, D., G., & Holbert, R. L. (2009). Humor complexity and political influence: An elaboration likelihood approach to the effects of humor type in The Daily Show with Jon Stewart. *Atlantic Journal of Communication, 17*(4), 202–219. Communication & Mass Media Complete. EBSCO; Westcott-Baker, A. (2010). *The pitfalls and promise of neuroscientific methods: The case of the Elaboration Likelihood Model*. Conference Papers—International Communication Association (2009), 1–31.
6. Adapted from Kohls, R. (2006, January). *The values Americans live by*. Retrieved from www.uri.edu/mind/VALUES2.pdf
7. Cialdini, R. B. (2001, October). Harnessing the science of persuasion. *Harvard Business Review, 79*, 72–79.
8. Aristotle (1932 trans.). *The rhetoric of Aristotle*. Trans. L. Cooper. New York: Appleton-Century-Crofts.
9. (PollingReport.com, May 6, 2008).
10. http://www.alasthemovement.org/default_en.asp
11. Retrieved from *First Giving boasts 13 million online donations for 8000 charities*. http://www.firstgiving.com/content/home
12. Zernike, K. (2008, February, 17). Follow me: The charisma mandate. *New York Times*, WK1.
13. Jones, D. (2005, April 5). Business leaders can learn from Pope. *USA Today*, 3B.
14. A Papal pilgrimage, (2008, April 21). *Newsweek*, p. 14.
15. ("A Papal").
16. (Miller, 2008).
17. Based on a speech given by an inmate of the Grafton Prison Farm, Grafton, OH. Name and setting withheld by request.
18. Congressman Donald Pease, 13th Ohio Congressional District, speaking to the Elyria (OH) Republican Women's Club.
19. Professor Fran Bostwick, Lorain County Community College.
20. See http://www.yele.org/
21. Roberts, M. (2008, June 1). Polygamist raid now a fiasco. Cleveland *Plain Dealer*, A12.
22. US FDA. (2009). Department of Health and Human Services. Retrieved from http://www.fda.gov/AboutFDA/ReportsManualsForms/Reports/BudgetReports/2007FDABudgetSummary/ucm112799.htm
23. AP. (2005, February 9). Marcia Cross denies "coming out." Associated Press. Retrieved from www.msnbc.msn.com/id/6942214. Explaining that the *Desperate Housewives* star said she wasn't a lesbian after *The View* cohost Barbara Walters questioned her on rumors regarding her sexuality. "I'm not," said Cross.
24. *Britney Spears bad mother backlash begins*. (n.d.). Gawker. Retrieved from http://defamer.com/hollywood/britney_spears/britney-spears-bad-mother-backlash-begins-176117.php and www.idontlikeyouinthatway.com/2007/02/britney-spears-is-wonderful-mother.html
25. (*Britney Spears)*.
26. *The 50 most ridiculous Tea Party slogans*. (2009, April 14, 2009). Retrieved from http://www.eyesonobama.com/blog/content/id_51507/title_The-50-Most-Ridiculous-Tea-Party-Slogans/

27. DeSteno, D., Petty, R., Rucker, D., Wegener, D., & Braverman, J. (2004). Discrete emotions and persuasion: The role of emotion-induced expectancies. *Journal of Personality and Social Psychology, 86*(1), p 43.
28. Maslow, A. (1970). *Motivation and personality*. New York: Harper & Row, pp. 35–58. How Maslow's hierarchy is reflected in societal needs is demonstrated in Sirgy, M. J. (1986, July). A quality-of-life theory derived from Maslow's developmental perspective. *American Journal of Economics and Sociology, 45*, 329–342.
29. McElroy, J. H. (1999). *American beliefs*. Chicago: Ivan R. Dee, p. 220.
30. An interesting list of strategies can be found in Chandler, S., & Richardson, S. (2008). *100 ways to motivate others*. Pompton Plains, NJ: Career Press.
31. Discussion adapted from the theories of Gronbeck.
32. Gronbeck, B. E., Ehninger, D., & H. Monroe, A. H. (2009). *Principles and types of speech communication* (17th ed.). Boston: Pearson.
33. For an extended discussion of public speaking, persuasion and culture, see: Lustig, M., & Koester, J. (2010). *Intercultural competence interpersonal communication across cultures* (6th ed.). Boston, MA: Allyn & Bacon, pp 228–235.
34. Hamill, J. (1990). *Ethno-logic: The anthropology of human reasoning*. Urbana: University of Illinois Press, p. 23.
35. Lustig, p. 231.
36. (Lustig).
37. (Lustig).
38. (Lustig).
39. Bliss, A. (2001). Rhetorical structures for multilingual and multicultural students. In X. G. Panella (Ed.), *Contrastive rhetoric revisited and redefined*, Mahwah, NJ: Erlbaum.
40. (Lustig, p. 231).
41. This discussion of African American persuasive techniques is based on ideas originally presented in Hecht, M., Collier, M. J., & Ribeau, S. (1993). *African American communication ethnic identity and cultural interpretation*. Newbury Park, CA: Sage Publications, p. 103 and expanded upon in Hecht, M., Jackson, R., & Ribeau, S. (2008). *African American communication: Exploring identity and culture*. Mahaw, NJ: Lawrence Erlbaum; Wright, K. (2009). *The African American experience: Black history and culture through speeches, letters, editorials, poems, songs, and stories*. New York: Black Dog & Leventhal Publishers.
42. (Hecht et al., p. 104).
43. Ting-Toomey, S., & Chung, L. (2005). *Understanding intercultural communication*. New York: Oxford University Press, p. 190.

CHAPTER 16

1. Braithwaite, L. (2008, April 7). Public speaking—What's confidence and how do I get it? EzineArticles. Retrieved from http://ezinearticles.com
2. Public speakers with high communication apprehension are perceived by others as having less competence. Bodie, G. D. (2010). A racing heart, rattling knees, and ruminative thoughts: Defining, explaining, and treating public speaking anxiety. *Communication Education, 59*(1), 70–105. doi:10.1080/03634520903443849
3. (Braithwaite).
4. Based on the concepts of Braithwaite.
5. (Braithwaite).
6. (Braithwaite).
7. Schwartz, K. (2008, April 9). *Speech rate too fast? Tips to slow down*. Ezine Articles. Retrieved from http://ezinearticles.com/?expert=Katie_Schwartz
8. Hyde, S. W. (2003). *Television and radio announcing* (4th ed.). Boston: Allyn & Bacon, p. 81.
9. For an extended discussion of pronunciation and articulation, see Hahner, J., Sokoloff, M., & Salisch, S. (2001). *Speaking clearly: Improving voice and diction* (6th ed.). Columbus, OH: McGraw-Hill.
10. (Hyde, pp. 83–85).
11. *How to use hand gestures in public speaking*. (2008). eHow careers and work editor. Retrieved from www.ehow.com/how_2274513_use-hand-gestures-public-speaking.html
12. Osborn, M., & Osborn, S. (2007). *Public speaking* (8th ed.). Boston: Allyn & Bacon, p. 361.
13. James C. McCroskey has led our field in research about communication apprehension. A practical classic is Richmond, V. P., & McCroskey, C. (1997). *Communication: Apprehension, avoidance, and effectiveness* (5th ed.). Boston: Allyn & Bacon. For a more scholarly work, see Daly, J. A., McCroskey, J. C., Ayres, J., Tim Hopf, T. & Sonandre, D. M A. (Eds.). (2009). *Avoiding communication: Shyness, reticence, and communication apprehension*. New York: Hampton Press.
14. In communication research, the term "communication apprehension" is used. For an interesting overview of research on communication apprehension, see Bodie, G. D. (2010). A racing heart, rattling knees, and ruminative thoughts: Defining, explaining, and treating public speaking anxiety. *Communication Education, 59*(1), 70–105. doi:10.1080/03634520903443849
15. *What is public speaking anxiety? Is it Curable?* (2009-1010). Retrieved from http://www.bravina.com/public-speaking-anxiety.html
16. Ayres, J., & Hopf, T. (1993). *Coping with Speech Anxiety*. Norwood, NJ: Ablex, p. xi.
17. Psychologist Shirley Impelizari, appearing on *The Early Show*, CBS-TV, July 31, 2002. The original source for identifying public speaking anxiety as the number-one fear was Bruskin/Goldring Research Report, February 1993. This finding was duplicated by a February 2001 Gallup Poll. Retrieved from http://answers.google.com/answers/threadview?id=47686
18. *What is public speaking anxiety? Is it curable?* (2009-1010). Retrieved from http://www.bravina.com/public-speaking-anxiety.html
19. (Orman, p. 1).
20. (Orman, p. 2).
21. (Orman, p. 2).
22. (Orman, p. 2).
23. (Orman, p. 6).
24. (Orman, p. 6).
25. (Orman, p. 7).
26. (Orman, p. 7).
27. http://www.bravina.com
28. Only anecdotal evidence is available to demonstrate that these activities are effective.
29. Discussion based on information given by Les Wyman, Gestalt Institute, Cleveland, OH.
30. Daly, J. A., Vangelisti, A. L., & Weber, D. (1995). Speech anxiety affects how people prepare speeches: A protocol analysis of the preparation processes of speakers. *Communication Monographs, 62*, 383–397.
31. Menzel, K. E., & Carrell, L. J. (2001). The relationship between preparation and performance in public speaking. *Communication Education, 43*, 17–26.
32. Priem, J. S., & Solomon, D. (2009). Comforting apprehensive communicators: The effects of reappraisal and distraction on cortisol levels among students in a public speaking class. *Communication Quarterly, 57*(3), 259–281. doi:10.1080/01463370903107253
33. There are mental health centers that specifically deal with public performance apprehension such as the Public Speaking–Social Anxiety Center of New York. Retrieved from www.speakeeezi.com
34. (Menzel & Carrell, pp. 17–26).
35. Jameson, J. (2008, January 24). *The number one tip for overcoming fear of public speaking—part two—the science bit*. Ezine Articles. Retrieved from http://ezinearticles.com
36. (Jameson).
37. (Jameson).
38. (Jameson).
39. A concept proposed by Dr. Les Wyman, Gestalt Institute, Cleveland.
40. Griffin, C. L. (2008). *Invitation to public speaking* (3rd ed.). Boston: Wadsworth Cengage Learning, p. 7.
41. For an extensive discussion of African American/Black communication, see Ribeau, S., Hecht, M., & Jackson, R. (2002). *African American communication* (2nd ed.). Mahwah, NJ: Lawrence Erlbaum.
42. Cummings, M. S. (n.d.). *Teaching the Black rhetoric course*. An unpublished paper, Educational Resources Information Center, p. 5.
43. (Cummings).
44. For a discussion of Chinese gestures and physical expression, see Neuliep, J. (2003). *Intercultural communication: A contextual approach* (2nd ed.). Boston: Houghton Mifflin, 240, 243, 249.
45. (Griffin, p. 7).
46. (Griffin).
47. (Griffin, p. 8).
48. (Griffin, pp. 7–8).
49. (Griffin).
50. Wood, J. T. (2007). *Gendered lives: Communication, gender, and culture*. Belmont, CA: Thompson Higher Education, p. 133.
51. (Wood, 2007).
52. Schlesinger, R. (2008, April 3). *Hillary's speaking style*. Retrieved from Huffingtonpost.com, www.huffingtonpost.com/robert-schlesinger/hillarys-speaking-style; and, Bruce Newman, B. (2008). *Comparing style apples and oranges*. Faith Writers, Faithwriters.com
53. Cesca, B. (2008, November 8). *The mandatory rejection of Sarah Palin*. Retrieved from www.huffingtonpost.com/bob-cesca/the-mandatory-rejection-o-b-139062.html
54. Henderson, L., & Zimbardo, P. Shyness. (2008). Shyness, *Encyclopedia of mental health*. San Diego, CA: Academic Press, p. 9. Retrieved from www.shyness.com/encyclopedia.html
55. (Henderson & Zimbardo).
56. (Henderson & Zimbardo).
57. (Henderson & Zimbardo).
58. (Henderson & Zimbardo).
59. McDowell, E. E., & Yotsuyanagi, N. (n.d.). *An exploratory study of communication apprehension, willingness to communicate, and sense of humor between college students from the United States and Japan*. An unpublished paper, Educational Resources Information Center, p. 12.
60. (McDowell & Yotsuyanagi).
61. (McDowell & Yotsuyanagi).

Index

INDEX OF ACTIVITIES/QUESTIONNAIRES

Included in this text are activities that will help you become a more aware communicator. In addition, the online website to this text contains additional materials that you may select to do on your own, or may be assigned by your instructor.

KEY TERMS

Note: Definitions of all key terms used in the text, as well as important other terms, may be found in the Glossary of this book. Listed here is an alphabetic list of ideas discussed in the text.

TOPICS

Photo Credits

Chapter 1: Page 1: Juice Images/PhotoLibrary; page 2: Wavebreakmedia Ltd./Shutterstock; page 4: Huntstock/Age Fotostock; page 10: Peter Turnley/Corbis; page 20: David M. Russell/Harpo/© Sony Pictures Television/Courtesy: Everett Collection; page 22: Bob Daemmrich/The Image Works; page 25: Digital Vision/Getty Images **Chapter 2**: Page 34: Supri Suharjoto/Shutterstock; page 38: Geri Engberg/The Image Works; page 47: Robert Kneschke/Shutterstock; page 50: Dieter Klar/Picture-Alliance/DPA/Newscom **Chapter 3:** Page 52: *The Star-Ledger*/Cie Stroud/The Image Works; page 54: Jeremy Richards/Shutterstock; page 58: Bob Daemmrich/The Image Works; page 63 (left): Jim Watson/AFP/Getty Images; (center): Charles Dharapak/AP Photos; (right): Jim Watson/AFP/Getty Images; page 65: Spencer Grant/PhotoEdit; page 69: Eco Images/Getty Images; page 71: Digital Vision/Getty Images; page 73: MBI/Alamy **Chapter 4:** Page 80: Monkey Business Images/Shutterstock; page 86: Glow Images, Inc./SuperStock; page 91: Paula Bronstein/Stone/Getty Images; page 93: Jack Hollingsworth/Photodisc/Thinkstock; page 99: Paul Drinkwater/NBCU Photo Bank/AP Photos **Chapter 5:** Page 106: Patrizia Tilly/Shutterstock; page 112: Juice Images/Alamy; page 116: Sonda Dawes/The Image Works; page 121: Sonda Dawes/The Image Works; page 124: David Young-Wolff/PhotoEdit **Chapter 6:** Page 130: Alexander Raths/Shutterstock; page 135: Don Smetzer/PhotoEdit; page 138: Ronnie Kaufman/Corbis; page 142: Stockbyte/Thinkstock; page 152: Bob Daemmrich/The Image Works; page 155: Blend Images/Getty Images; page 158: Jupiterimages/Photos.com/Thinkstock; page 163: David J. Green/Alamy **Chapter 7:** Page 173: Jetta Productions/Iconica/Getty Images; page 177: Redlink Production/Corbis; page 180: Brand X Pictures/Thinkstock; page 187: Jupiterimages/Liquidlibrary/Thinkstock; page 198: Heiner Heine/Imagebroker/Alamy; page 203: Jeff Greenberg/The Image Works **Chapter 8:** Page 210: Mark Peterson/Redux; page 212: Michael Newman/PhotoEdit; page 215: Jeff Greenberg/The Image Works; page 222: George Doyle/Stockbyte/Thinkstock; page 228: Meg Takamura/Getty Images; page 230: David Kelly Crow/PhotoEdit; page 235: EdBockStock/Shutterstock; page 239: Stockbyte/Thinkstock **Chapter 9:** Page 243: Richard Green/Alamy; page 247: Photodisc; page 248: Getty Images; page 249: Monkey Business Images/Shutterstock; page 259: David Young-Wolff/Getty Images; page 264: Chris Haston/ NBC/Everett Collection; page 267: Comstock/Photolibrary **Chapter 10:** Page 271: Jeff Malet Photography/Newscom; page 273: Jon Burbank/The Image Works; page 276: Bob Mahoney/The Image Works; page 284: Steve Debenport/iStockphoto; page 289: Big Cheese Photo LLC/Alamy **Chapter 11:** Page 293: Hill Street Studios/Blend Images/Corbis; page 294: Ed Bock/Corbis; page 299: Jeff Greenberg/The Image Works; page 301: LHB Photo/Alamy; page 308: Creatas/Thinkstock **Chapter 12:** Page 319: Dmitriy Shironosov/Shutterstock; page 321: Yellow Dog Productions/Getty Images; page 325: Catherine Karnow/CORBIS; page 328: Jewel Samad/AFP/Getty Images/Newscom; page 337: Candybox Photography/Dreamstime **Chapter 13:** Page 343: Chris Rout/Alamy; page 345: Bob Daemmrich/The Image Works; page 346: Eric Isaacs/Wenn/Newscom; page 347: David J. Sams/Getty Images; page 359: Asia Images Group/Getty Images; page 366: David Young-Wolff/PhotoEdit **Chapter 14:** Page 369: Flying Colours Ltd/Digital Vision/Getty Images; page 373: Sarah Hadley/Alamy; page 377: Glow Asia/SuperStock; page 379: Bruce Ayres/Getty Images **Chapter 15:** Page 385: Jim Young/Reuters; page 387: Ramin Talaie/Corbis; page 391: Popperfoto/Getty Images; page 394: Bettmann/Corbis; page 396: Randy Duchaine/Alamy; page 401: Cleve Bryant/PhotoEdit; page 404: Alfred/Sipa/Newscom **Chapter 16:** Page 413: Blend Images/Alamy; page 415: A. Ramey/PhotoEdit; page 422: Yuri Arcurs/Alamy; page 425: David Young-Wolff/PhotoEdit; page 427: Tim Boyle/Getty Images

ANSWERS FOR TWO-VALUED REASONING QUESTIONNAIRE (PAGE 41)

CHAPTER 2

a. T The story states, "When Dale arrived in St. Louis, it was only two days before the wedding."

b. ? There is nothing in the story that says Dale did or didn't get married.

c. ? We are not sure who is the "she" referred to in the story. We are also not sure if Dale is a female or a male.

d. ? There is nothing in the story that says whether or not a travel agent made the reservation, only that "Dale went to a travel agency to arrange some plane reservations."

e. ? The story says that the bride and groom took a trip to Hawaii. We don't know if Dale went to Hawaii. We also don't know if Dale is a male or female.

KEY TO *PERSONAL REPORT OF COMMUNICATION APREHENSION (PRCA-24)* (PAGE 123)

CHAPTER 5

Your total score should range between 24 and 120. If your total score is below 24 or above 120, you have made a mistake in computing. Scores on each of the four contexts (groups, meetings, interpersonal conversations, and public speaking) can range from a low of 6 to a high of 30. Any individual score above 18 indicates some degree of apprehension in that particular communication environment.